Personnel/Human Resource Management

The Irwin Series in Management and The Behavioral Sciences
Consulting Editors   L. L. Cummings and E. Kirby Warren

1989 Fourth Edition

Personnel/Human Resource Management

Herbert G. Heneman III
The University of Wisconsin-Madison

Donald P. Schwab
The University of Wisconsin-Madison

John A. Fossum
The University of Minnesota

Lee D. Dyer
Cornell University

IRWIN

Homewood, IL 60430
Boston, MA 02116

© RICHARD D. IRWIN, INC., 1980, 1983, 1986, and 1989

Sponsoring editor: William R. Bayer
Project editor: Suzanne Ivester
Production manager: Carma W. Fazio
Compositor: Better Graphics, Inc.
Typeface: 10.5/13 Caledonia
Printer: R. R. Donnelley & Sons Company

Library of Congress Cataloging-in-Publication Data

Personnel/human resource management.

Includes index.
1. Personnel management.   I. Heneman, Herbert
Gerhard, 1944–
HF5549.P4514   1989   658.3   88–13661
ISBN 0-256-06929-8

Printed in the United States of America
1 2 3 4 5 6 7 8 9 0 DO 6 5 4 3 2 1 0 9

Preface

This fourth edition of *Personnel/Human Resource Management* contains many features and changes that we believe constitute improvements over the previous editions. The book continues to be built around the Personnel/Human Resource (P/HR) management model. The model, however, has been placed in a broader strategic and administrative context. To this end we have taken the first chapter from the previous edition and split it into two expanded chapters. Chapter 1 introduces and discusses the P/HR model. This is followed by a section labeled "Organization Context." This section identifies six major issues confronting organizations: productivity, product quality, customer service, labor costs, work-force flexibility, and unethical practices. We show how P/HR management can help organizations address each issue. An administrative process model is then presented that illustrates the constant interplay between P/HR management and the administrative process. Linkages back to the P/HR model and the six major issues are also shown.

Chapter 2 ("P/HR Management in Operation") discusses the need for a P/HR department and its typical structure at both corporate and operating levels. P/HR activities are then treated from two perspectives: that of line managers and that of staff managers in the P/HR department. It is shown that while perspectives differ, organizations are moving increasingly toward a shared relationship between line and staff managers. The effectiveness of the P/HR management activities is dealt with from both line and staff management perspectives, with an emphasis on alternative ways for assessing the effectiveness of the P/HR department. These assessment procedures include managerial performance appraisal systems, aggregate outcome and cost data analysis, utility analysis, and constituent opinions. The chapter concludes with a discussion of careers and professional activities in P/HR management.

To make room for these two expanded chapters, we have sought to "streamline" others somewhat. In addition, we have deleted the "Hours of Work" chapter from the third edition. Some of that material has been incorporated into Chapter 12 ("Internal Staffing and Career Management").

Instructor and student reactions to the cases we developed for the third edition have been very positive. Consequently, we have kept these cases intact in this edition. The cases are in the areas of (1) performance assessment, (2) external staffing, (3) employee development, (4) compensation, (5) labor relations, and (6) work design and change. The cases are written to provide students with challenges in both problem identification and problem solution. Extensive analysis of each case is provided in the instructor's manual.

The instructor's manual has been expanded in two ways. First, as noted above, we provide written analysis of the six cases. Second, the number of true-false and multiple choice test items for each chapter has been increased substantially. Other features of the instructor's manual remain as before. Phil Benson (New Mexico State) assumed responsibility for revising the instructor's manual, and we gratefully acknowledge his contributions.

We have completely revised Chapter 8 ("Human Resource Planning"). There is now more of a direct tie-in to business planning and strategy. Also, emphasis is placed on staffing planning as a key way of focusing and integrating P/HR activities and thereby enhancing organizational success.

We have paid close attention, as in previous editions, to references. We have eliminated a high percentage of relatively old references and added a substantial set of new ones. We exercised judgment by providing references to works that we felt were of high quality. Also, we sought references that contained many useful references themselves. In this way, the student can easily "backtrack" and quickly develop a comprehensive list of references for a topic area.

In addition to the major features and changes described above, we have many specific new or expanded topics that we treat. They are:

1. Immigration and its effects.
2. Labor force quality and demographic changes.
3. Tax laws and COBRA.
4. Age discrimination and research.
5. Sexual harassment.
6. Acquired Immune Deficiency Syndrome (AIDS).
7. Empirical research on job analysis.
8. Health care cost containment.
9. Utility of P/HR activities and programs.
10. Private pension plans.

11. Employee welfare plans (EAPs, wellness programs, child care, elder care).
12. EEO laws, regulations, court decisions.
13. Effects of unions on employers and employees.
14. Unions and political involvement.
15. Lie detectors and the Employee Polygraph Protection Act.
16. Health exams (physical, drugs, AIDS, genetic screening).
17. Situational employment interviews.
18. Validity generalization.
19. Uniform Guidelines on Employee Selection Procedures.
20. Health problems (reproduction hazards, video display terminals, smoking, stress).
21. College recruiting.
22. Layoffs and the Worker Adjustment and Retraining Notification Act.
23. High-involvement work systems.
24. Employment-at-will.
25. Strategic issues in development of pay systems.
26. Attendance and turnover.
27. Administration of performance appraisal systems.
28. Alternative work arrangements (temporary help, short-term hires, on-call employees, homework).

These changes made in this edition have come about both because of changes in the P/HR management field and changes in our own way of thinking about the field. Decisions about changes, as well as those things we have chosen to retain, have greatly benefited from the thoughts of others. Specifically, we gratefully acknowledge the inputs of Chris Berger (Purdue), Judy Olian (Maryland), Bruce Wonder (Western Washington), Robert Heneman (Ohio State), Cliff Baker (North Carolina State), Ken Carson (Arizona State), and Michael Mount (Iowa). Excellent clerical and research support was provided by Jo Churey, Pat Dickerson, Christiane Labelle, Therry Wils, Jennifer Byer, Kelly Malowski, Dorothy Peterson, Janet Christopher, Kathy McCord, Jean Trager, Susan Kasper, Maryann Sveum, Molly Casserly, Georgiana Herman, and Mariann Nelson.

Herbert G. Heneman III
Donald P. Schwab
John A. Fossum
Lee D. Dyer

Contents

PART ONE
PERSONNEL/HUMAN RESOURCE MANAGEMENT AND ITS
ENVIRONMENT   **3**

1   **Personnel/Human Resource Management: Model and Organization Context**   **4**
Personnel/Human Resource Management Model: *Personnel/Human Resource Outcomes. Individuals and Jobs. Personnel/Human Resource Activities. External Influences.* Organization Context: *Challenging Issues. Administrative Process.*

2   **P/HR Management in Operation**   **26**
The P/HR Department: *Need for the P/HR Department. Structure of the P/HR Department.* P/HR Activities: Line and Staff Perspectives: *Line Managers' Perspective. P/HR Department Perspective. A Shared Relationship.* P/HR Management Effectiveness: *Line Managers. The P/HR Department. Constituent Opinions.* Jobs and Careers in Personnel/Human Resource Management: *Types of Jobs. Career Opportunities and Preparation. Career Progression. Salaries.* Professional Activities in Personnel/Human Resource Management: *Professional Organizations. Publications.*

3   **External Influences**   **52**
Economic Conditions. Labor Markets: *Defining and Measuring the Labor Force. Trends in the Labor Supply. Immigration. Labor Force Quality. Part- and Full-Time Work. Federal Programs to Reduce Unemployment. Trends in Labor Demand. Implications for P/HR Management Activities.* Labor Unions. Laws and Regulations: *The Legal System. Labor-Management Relations. Wage and Hour Laws. Income Maintenance Programs. Tax Laws. Safety and Health. Immigration Law.* The Special Case of Equal Employment Opportunity: *Title VII of the Civil Rights Act (as Amended). Executive Order 11246 (as Amended). Sexual Harassment. Age Discrimination in Employment Act (ADEA).* Employment and Acquired Immune Deficiency Syndrome (AIDS).

     Appendix: Laws Regulating P/HR Management   **81**

PART TWO
INDIVIDUALS AND JOBS   **91**

4   **Employee Ability and Job Analysis**   **92**
Employee Ability: *Types of Abilities. Differences in Ability. Human Capital and*

Ability. Abilities and Requirements. Job Analysis: *The Rationale for Studying Jobs. Job Requirements. Job Analysis Methods. Sources of Error in Job Analysis. The Choice of an Analytic Method. Uses of Job Analysis by the Line Manager.*

5   **Organizational Rewards and Employee Motivation**   118
Rewards. Measuring Job Rewards: *Job Diagnostic Survey. Minnesota Job Description Questionnaire. Evaluation.* Motivational Processes: *Expectancy Theory.* Influencing Motivation: *Managerial Roles. Motivating Specific Behaviors.*

PART THREE
ASSESSING PERSONNEL/HUMAN RESOURCE MANAGEMENT
OUTCOMES   139

6   **Employee Performance**   140
Performance Measurement Purposes: *Administrative Decisions. Employee Feedback and Development. Evaluation of Policies and Programs.* Current Practices. Performance Measurement Issues: *Identifying Performance Dimensions. Establishing Performance Standards.* Performance Measures: *Performance Appraisal. Measures of Physical Output.* Administrative Challenges: *Error Identification and Reduction Approaches. A Process Perspective. Equal Employment Opportunity.*

7   **Satisfaction, Attendance, and Retention**   168
Job Satisfaction: *What Is Job Satisfaction? Surveying Job Satisfaction.* Attendance and Retention: *Absenteeism. Turnover.*

Case for Part Three   Burton's Incorporated   195

PART FOUR
HUMAN RESOURCE PLANNING   201

8   **Human Resource Planning**   202
Human Resource Planning: *Some Preliminary Issues. The Planning Model. Determining Future Human Resource Requirements. Determining Future Human Resource Availabilities. Conducting External and Internal Environmental Scanning. Reconciling Requirements and Availabilities: Gaps and Objectives. Action Planning. Summary.* Affirmative Action Planning: *Analysis. Action Planning.* Human Resource Information Systems: *The Data Base. System Specifications. Security and Privacy.*

PART FIVE
EXTERNAL STAFFING   245

9   **Recruitment**   246
Recruitment Planning: *Number of Contacts. Types of Contacts.* Strategy Development: *Where to Look. How to Look. When to Look.* Searching: *Source Activation. "Selling".* Screening. Evaluation and Control: *Monitoring. Feedback.* The Special Case of Campus Recruiting: *The Job Seeker's Perspective.*

Appendix: Preparing a Resume   291

10   External Staffing Concepts   300
Validation of Predictors: *Empirical Validation. Predictor-Criterion Relationship. Content Validation.* Decision Making: *Utility of a New Predictor. Establishment of Hiring Standards.* External Staffing: Some Potential Limitations: *Validity Generalization Problems. Validity Ceiling. Predictor Unreliability. Unanticipated Changes.* External Staffing Concepts and Equal Employment Opportunity: *Bona Fide Occupational Qualifications. Testing and the Uniform Guidelines.*

11   External Staffing Processes   330
Selection Predictors: *Tests. Training and Experience Requirements. References and Recommendations. Application Blanks and Resumes. Health Exams. Employment Interview.* Administration of Staffing Systems: *Predictor Usage. Validation. Use of Multiple Predictors. Selection Decisions. Standardization. Equal Employment Opportunity. Applicant Reactions to Staffing.*

Case for Part Five   Fossil Chemical   360

**PART SIX
INTERNAL STAFFING AND DEVELOPMENT**   367

12   Internal Staffing and Career Management   368
Internal Staffing: *Filling Job Vacancies. Eliminating Employee Surpluses. Correcting Behavioral Problems: Employment-at-Will and Discharge. Retirement.* Alternative Staffing Arrangements: *Alternative Work Arrangements: Temporary Help, Short-Term Hires, On-Call Employees, Homework. Alternative Work Schedules: Part Time, Flextime, Compressed Workweek.* Career Management: *Career Planning. Career Development. Career Counseling. An Example of a Career-Management System. Evaluating Career Management.*

13   Employee Development   416
Prevalence and Nature. Employee Development as a Process. Identifying Employee Development Needs: *Does a Performance Discrepancy Exist? Is the Performance Discrepancy Important? Is Employee Development a Potential Solution? Is Employee Development the Preferred Solution? When Does It Not Matter?* Formulating the Employee Development Plan. Designing Training Programs: *Setting Instructional Objectives. Determining Program Content. Selecting Instructional Techniques.* Teaching: *Goal Setting. Material Presentation. Practice. Feedback. Classroom Demeanor.* Evaluating Employee Development Programs: *Evaluating Training Programs. Evaluating the Overall Employee Development Effort.*

Case for Part Six   Arthur C. Kaplan and Company   457

**PART SEVEN
COMPENSATION**   461

14   Pay Level and Pay Structure   462
Developing Job Hierarchies: *The Equity Criterion. Arranging Jobs in a Hierarchy:*

Job Evaluation. Pricing a Job Hierarchy: *Linking Internal and External Criteria. Developing a Pay Structure. Administering and Controlling the Pay Structure.* Consequences of Inequitable Pay Structures: *Behavioral Responses. Comparable Worth.*

15   Pay Systems and Their Consequences   490
Individual and Group Pay Systems: *Conventional Pay Systems. Incentive Pay Systems. Prevalence. Gain-Sharing Plans.* Employee Responses to Pay Systems: *Performance. Attendance. Retention. Satisfaction.* Developing and Administrating Pay Systems: *Strategic and Cultural Perspectives. Implications for Pay Systems.*

16   Benefits   522
The Development of Compensation Benefits: *Employee Attitudes about Benefits. Employer Attitudes about Benefits. Union Perspectives on Benefits. Government Encouragement of Benefit Growth.* Types of Major Benefits: *Payments for Time Not Worked. Insurance Benefits. Retirement Benefits. Income Maintenance. Employee Welfare Programs.* Benefits Administration: *Benefit Objectives and Evaluations. Controlling Benefit Costs. Cafeteria-Style Benefit Plans. Communicating Employee Benefits. Tax Reform Considerations.* Equal Employment Opportunity: *Sex Discrimination. Age Discrimination.*

Case for Part Seven   Consolidated Chicken Products   559

**PART EIGHT
LABOR RELATIONS   565**

17   Labor Unions   566
The Development of Labor Unions: *Historical Roots.* The Changing Economic Environment: *Mechanization. Foreign Competition. Deregulation.* Labor Law: *Railway Labor Act. Norris-LaGuardia Act. Wagner Act. Taft-Hartley Act. Landrum-Griffin Act. Civil Service Reform Act, Title VII. Administrative Bodies.* Union Structures: *The National Union. Local Unions. The AFL-CIO. National Union Mergers. Union Democracy. National Unions and Public Policy.* Major Activities of Unions. The Motivation to Join Unions. Organizing and Repesentation: *Organzing Campaigns.* The Effect of Campaign Tactics. The Effects of Labor Unions: *Effects on Employers. Effects on Employees.*

18   Labor-Management Relations   600
The Environment for Bargaining: *Deregulation. Foreign Competition. Nonunion Entries. Legal Requirements to Bargain. Bargaining Power. Bargaining Structure.* Issues in Bargaining: *Wage Issues in Bargaining. Nonwage Bargaining Issues.* The Negotiating Process: *Preparation for Negotiations. Strategies and Tactics. Costing Contracts. Recent Contract Outcomes and Concessions. Bargaining Impasses. Approving an Agreement. Public Sector Differences.* Contract Administration: *Grievance Procedures. Union and Management Organization for Contract Administration. Types of Grievances. Effects of Grievances on Employers and Employees. Arbitration.* Employee Relations in the Nonunion Organization: *Partially Organized Establishments. Unorganized Establishments. Grievance Procedures.* The Impact of Collective Bargaining on P/HR Activities. Labor-Management Relations and Equal Employment Opportunity: *Promotions and Seniority. Affirmative Action. Fair Representation.*

Case for Part Eight   United Castings   645

PART NINE
WORK ENVIRONMENT   651

19   Work and Workplace Design   652
     Goal Setting: *Prosaic Programs. Management by Objectives.* Job Design: *Approaches to Job Design. Effects of Changes in Job Design.* Participative Work Groups: *Participative Decision Making. Quality Circles. Self-Managing Work Teams.* High-Involvement Work Systems: *Approaches Centering on SMWTs. Approaches Centering on Rewards. Approaches Centering on Labor Relations. Approaches Centering on Start-Ups. Evaluation.*

20   Occupational Safety and Health   686
     Laws and Regulations: *Workers' Compensation Laws. Occupational Safety and Health Act (OSHAct).* Accident Measurement: *Accident Incidence Rate. Accident Costs.* Safety Programs: *The Role of Top Management. The Role of Safety Committees. Identifying Causes of Accidents. Reducing Accidents.* Occupational Health: *Environmental Health Hazards. Employee Stress. Disabled Employees.*

     Case for Part Nine   Benton Incorporated   715

Name Index   719
Subject Index   727

Personnel/Human Resource Management

PART ONE

Personnel/Human Resource Management and Its Environment

1

Personnel/Human Resource Management: Model and Organization Context

Simply stated, work organizations combine raw materials, capital goods, and labor to produce products or services. This combination is apparent when the employer produces, for example, a consumerable good. Anyone who has toured an integrated automobile assembly facility, such as the Ford Rouge manufacturing complex in Dearborn, Michigan, would see it clearly. Iron ore is converted to steel, the steel is stamped and shaped by huge presses, and the formed parts are assembled by line employees into automobiles. Less easy to observe or recognize are activities of human service organizations. A county agency for assisting and counseling teenage runaways combines the same factors, but in different proportions. Here the raw materials are the troubled youngsters, the capital goods are the office and its equipment, and the employees are the intake and case workers, counselors, and support staff.

The labor input is vital to the success of both the Rouge plants and the county youth-assistance agency. Indeed, this is the case for virtually all organizations. Without effective employees, the organization produces its goods and services inefficiently and may even place its very survival at risk. Clearly, organizations need to be concerned about human resources.

Personnel/human resources (P/HR) management addresses this concern through a set of functions or activities that are designed to influence the effectiveness of an organization's employees. These include such things as recruitment, staffing, training and development, and compensation. Most managers engage in these activities daily with prospective employees and their own subordinates. Most larger organizations also have a separate personnel department that assists in administering these activities as organizationwide systems or programs.

This book is built around a model of P/HR management. It shows the specific types of activities undertaken to influence employee effectiveness and suggests a general strategy for achieving this end. The model also shows that these activities are substantially influenced by certain factors external to the organization, such as laws and regulations.

The model is discussed below in some detail and is then used in the beginning of each subsequent chapter to more precisely identify major topical areas of coverage. Its use also will remind the reader of the overall scope of P/HR management activities and objectives.

P/HR concerns exist within any organization. As such, the organization context in which P/HR management exists, and which, in fact, it helps to create, must be identified and described. This is done in two ways in the present chapter. First, examples of major issues confronting organizations (for example, product quality) are suggested. It is shown how each of these issues has a definite P/HR management component, both as part of the problem and as part of the solution. Second, the nature of the general administrative process and its relationship to P/HR management are indicated. The relevance of the P/HR model to the process is shown, and examples of organization practices are provided to highlight the interplay between P/HR management and its organization context.

PERSONNEL/HUMAN RESOURCE MANAGEMENT MODEL

It was previously stated that P/HR management is aimed at influencing the effectiveness of employees in the organization. The managerial activities, external influences, and important outcomes associated with this are contained in the model shown in Figure 1–1.

Major activities are listed in the left-hand portion of the model. From a strategy viewpoint, the activities seek to match the ability and motivation of employees with the requirements and rewards of the job. To the extent that this match is achieved, employee effectiveness will be favorably influenced in terms of a number of outcomes. Examples of these outcomes include employee job performance and attendance, as well as others. Major external influences on P/HR management within the organization are identified at the top of the model. These include economic conditions, laws and regulations, labor unions, and labor markets. All the fundamental components of the model are discussed in more detail below. The discussion begins with the outcomes, since they are the underlying reason for the existence of the activities and the matching process.

Personnel/Human Resource Outcomes

Figure 1–1 indicates several outcomes that P/HR activities attempt to influence. These are attraction of employees to the organization, employee job performance, retention of employees, attendance at work, and job satisfaction. While these are probably the most important outcomes for most organizations, the "other" category acknowledges potentially important outcomes for a particular organization (for example, employee safety).

A critical outcome of concern in P/HR management is the attraction of the necessary numbers and types of employees to the organization. Without them, the organization cannot function.

Once employees are obtained, job performance becomes an important

FIGURE 1–1
Personnel/Human Resource Management Model

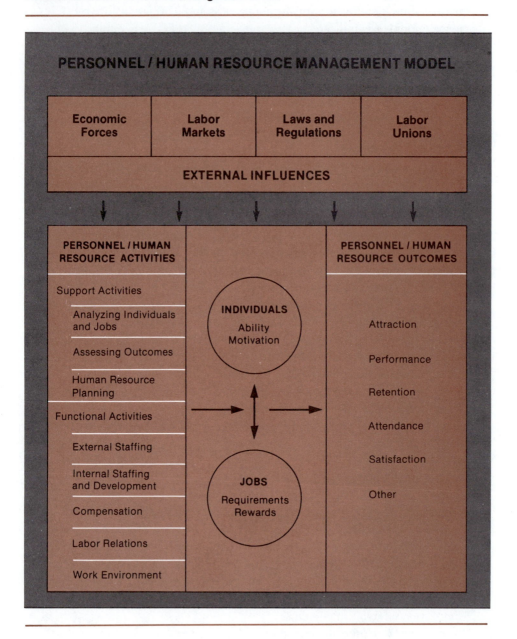

criterion of employee effectiveness. Employees are hired to perform tasks for the organization, and the more proficiently they do so, the greater their contribution to the organization.

Retention of employees and favorable attendance patterns represent forms of employee commitment to the organization, and they facilitate the performance of job tasks without interruption. Both outcomes, therefore, have substantial cost implications for the organization.

Employees agree to join, and continue to work for, an organization as long as their needs are being adequately satisfied. Organizations thus view employee job satisfaction as an important outcome for several reasons. For example, it may be easier to recruit if applicants perceive a high likelihood that their needs will be fulfilled. To an extent, better-satisfied employees may be more willing to remain with the organization, and they may even have more favorable attendance patterns.

Other outcomes may also be important to the organization. One example is that of employee physical and mental well-being. Such factors as accidents and the stresses employees experience on the job are receiving increasing attention and concern by organizations.

Implied in the above discussion of outcomes is a fundamental point. Specifically, whatever the outcomes, they represent dimensions along which human resources (the labor input) contribute to attainment of the efficiency and survival goals of the organization. As such, they may be used as a basis for judging the effectiveness of the organization's P/HR systems and programs. Also, they usually may be used for indicating the directions in which the effectiveness of individual employees should be assessed. If job performance is an important outcome, for example, the organization will need a performance appraisal system. Likewise, a concern for attendance as an outcome will require a system for recording the attendance of employees.

Normally, the organization would like to influence multiple outcomes, since all are related to the attainment of its objectives. Unfortunately, however, this is often difficult because the outcomes are not that closely related to each other (see Chapters 6 and 7). For example, highly satisfied employees do not necessarily perform better than less-satisfied employees.

Hence, undertaking a program to improve employee performance may be effective in doing so but may not have much of an effect on satisfaction one way or the other. P/HR activities thus must be designed for, and targeted toward, the specific outcome(s) the organization wants to influence. Failure to do so can greatly lessen the impact of the activities.

Individuals and Jobs

Falling between activities and outcomes are individuals and the jobs they perform (see Figure 1–1). Individuals have varying abilities to do such things as perform job tasks effectively and attend work regularly. They also have varying motivations to engage in those behaviors. It is primarily the combination of ability and motivation that determines P/HR outcomes.

Ability and motivation do not exist in a vacuum, however. Rather, they exist within the context of the job the employee is performing. Every job has certain requirements. These could be general in nature, such as a requirement that the jobholder be a college graduate. Or they could be highly specific, such as an ability to read technical journals in a foreign language.

Accompanying requirements are certain rewards offered by the job, such as pay, benefits, co-workers, challenge, amount of responsibility, and opportunities for promotion. Each reward has the potential both to influence motivation and to satisfy employee needs. For example, employees paid according to how well they perform may be motivated toward high performance. The additional pay will likely also be satisfying to those high performers who receive it.

Thus, it is the interaction between characteristics of the individual employee and characteristics of the job that influences P/HR outcomes. The abilities and motivations of the employee must be matched with the requirements and rewards of the job. To the extent that this occurs, the outcomes can be affected in ways that contribute to attainment of organizational goals.

Personnel/Human Resource Activities

P/HR activities reflect a management's personnel policies, programs, and procedures. They are designed to influence both indirectly (support activities) and directly (functional activities) the match between individuals and jobs. Major types of activities are shown on the left-hand side of Figure 1–1; they are described next.

Support activities

Support activities are not intended to directly influence the individual-job match. Rather, they serve in a supportive role for, or as an input to, the functional activities. The three major support activities are analyzing individuals and jobs, assessing outcomes, and human resource planning.

Analyzing individuals and jobs.   For effective matching of the individual's ability and motivation with the job's requirements and rewards, individuals must be analyzed to determine their abilities and motivations for various tasks. In addition, jobs must be analyzed to identify the ability requirements necessary for the employee to complete the job's tasks successfully. It is also necessary to identify the rewards associated with the job and how these rewards can be used to motivate employee behaviors and satisfy important employee needs.

Assessing outcomes.   Focusing on outcomes logically suggests that their characteristics be systematically assessed (measured) by the organization. Results of the assessment will indicate how effective employees (or activities) have been in the past. In turn, the results may serve as an input to guide employees or activities in the future.

Consider the case of job performance. Assessing this outcome is usually done through some form of a performance appraisal system. Results of the appraisal tell both the employee and the organization how effectively the job is being performed. Moreover, the results may be used as a way of developing a plan for improvement in those performance areas where deficiencies are noted. Such a plan can then be useful in guiding the employee to higher levels of future performance.

Human resource planning.   Human resource planning involves two major support functions. It first seeks to forecast the numbers and types of employees that will be needed on each job in some future time period. Second, armed with forecasting results, managers may develop plans for coping with the results through a series of coordinated activities.

To illustrate what might be involved, assume that the business plan of a small, but successful, microcomputer company is to double sales in the next five years. Personnel forecasting results estimate that, to do this, the organization will need 25 additional computer programmers in the next two years. Should these programmers come from inside or outside the organization, or both? If from inside, how will they be identified and chosen, and what special training might be necessary? If from outside, where will programmers be recruited, and what types of rewards will be offered to attract them? Human resource planning attempts to raise and then answer such questions.

Functional activities

Functional activities are undertaken to directly affect the individual-job match and thus the P/HR outcomes. Their success in doing this will depend, in part, on the existence and effectiveness of the support activities. Of course, many other factors will also be influential in this regard, as suggested in Figure 1–1. The figure also shows that the major functional activities are external staffing, internal staffing and development, compensation, labor relations, and the work environment.

External staffing. External staffing activities are concerned with bringing new employees into the organization from the outside. Recruitment is the external staffing activity used to generate applicants for job vacancies. Staffing *per se* attempts to identify which applicants are most likely to be effective on the job. To this end, organizations use many selection techniques, such as tests and interviews. They may also undertake studies to determine how valid these techniques are for accurately identifying those applicants most likely to be effective.

Internal staffing and development. Rarely do organizations rely only on external staffing to fulfill employment needs. Many of these needs can only be met through internal staffing and development activities. Internal staffing is concerned with the movement of current employees within and out of the organization. As such, it involves the administration of systems for promotion, transfer, demotion, layoff, discharge, and retirement.

Usually, internal staffing is accompanied by employee training and development activities. These seek to provide employees with the knowledge and skills needed to adapt to current or future jobs. Invariably, this means some form of on- or off-the-job training.

Compensation. Compensation represents a series of potential rewards of vital importance to most employees. Because of this, organizations expend considerable effort in various compensation activities.

Some of these involve establishing wages and salaries for jobs, based on the jobs' contents and on such labor market considerations as the relative availability of new employees for the jobs. At times, employees on the same job will not be paid equally. That is, there will be pay differentials based on such factors as performance or length of service. Use of pay to reward these outcomes requires a number of administrative activities to ensure that pay is being consistently and fairly used as a reward.

Increasingly, employees are receiving indirect compensation through a variety of benefits. Included here are vacations and holidays, pensions, health and life insurance, savings plans, profit sharing, and many legally required benefits, such as social security. Each benefit requires careful design and administration, as does the total benefit package.

Labor relations. Millions of employees in the country are members of labor unions and professional associations. These organizations seek to negotiate terms and conditions of employment with management. Hence, a significant part of labor relations is preparing for and conducting negotiations with the union. These negotiations result in a labor contract that specifies the terms and conditions of employment.

Additional labor relations activities occur after the contract is negotiated. For example, provisions in the contract may be vague, resulting in different interpretations by labor and management. When this occurs, labor and management must meet with each other to resolve their differences through activities that are commonly called "contract administration."

Work environment.   Employees, and their contributions to the organization, are affected by conditions in their work environment. The design of jobs and the subsequent relationships with other jobs are important here. Many organizations are experimenting with job redesign (for instance, adding more tasks and responsibilities) as a way of making the job more compatible with the ability and/or motivation of employees. Another example is organizations' development of "quality circles" (groups of managers and employees) that formally solicit ideas on how to improve product quality and productivity. These sorts of workplace-design programs require care in implementation and usually involve high levels of employee involvement and participation.

Major problems confronting P/HR management are occupational illnesses, injuries, and deaths. To attack these problems, unsafe working conditions and unsafe employee behaviors need to be identified and systematically measured. Safety programs can then be implemented to reduce accidents and illnesses, based on knowledge of their likely causes. Likewise, we are learning that the work environment can be a very stressful place, leading to such health problems as poor physical fitness and drug abuse. P/HR activities must be developed to address such problems.

Interrelationships among activities.   Although major activities were discussed separately above, in practice they are highly interrelated.[1] Suppose, for example, it is decided that as a way of controlling labor costs, the starting salary for newly hired management trainees will not be raised from the previous year. This decision may make it more difficult to attract new trainees, requiring an increase in recruiting efforts. The qualifications of those recruited may also be lower than those of past years' recruits, thus requiring new training and development activities. In the long run, these new trainees may not be as promotable as those previously hired, suggesting that promotion policies may have to be reexamined and possibly changed. In short, a decision made in one activity area frequently affects others.

---

[1] W. C. Byham, "Applying a Systems Approach to Personnel Activities," *Training and Development Journal* 35, no. 12 (1981), pp. 60–65.

External Influences

Figure 1–1 also shows that forces outside the organization affect P/HR management. Of primary importance here are the external influences of economic conditions, labor markets, laws and regulations, and labor unions.

In both private and public organizations, economic conditions influence financial "health." In turn, this will have a major bearing on P/HR policies and programs. Under favorable economic conditions, expansion of existing programs and creation of new programs (for example, offering employees day care for their children) are very likely. With less favorable or deteriorating conditions, contraction or cancellation of some programs may be necessary. Employees may have to forego a scheduled salary increase, for example.

In labor markets, organizations seek employees (demand for labor) and individuals offer their availability to organizations (supply of labor). Labor supply and demand have implications for all activities, but particularly for compensation and external staffing. Moreover, they are generally not subject to organization control, thereby creating potential turbulence and uncertainty for P/HR management.

Virtually all the activities discussed above are subject to laws and regulations at the local, state, and federal levels. Federal laws and regulations, in particular, have become of major importance to P/HR management. Some of these may be traced back to the 1930s; others are of more recent origin. Since 1960, major federal laws have been passed, and regulations issued, in such areas as safety and health, equal pay for equal work, pensions, equal employment opportunity, and affirmative action.

Labor unions, as already noted, seek to bargain with management over the terms and conditions of employment for their members. As a consequence, most P/HR activities are subject to joint decision making when employees are represented by a union. Labor unions also affect the activities less directly through lobbying efforts that seek to influence the types of laws and regulations that are passed.

All in all, it is difficult to overstate the importance of external forces on the conduct of P/HR activities. In fact, their impact is so pervasive that Chapter 3 is devoted exclusively to a more detailed discussion of it.

In summary, human resource outcomes are critical to the success and survival of organizations. The quality of the match between characteristics of individuals (ability and motivation) and jobs (requirements and rewards) determines how favorable the outcomes are. Some P/HR activities influence the match indirectly (support activities), while others have a more direct impact (functional activities). External influences complicate these activities and the matching process. Since the organization has relatively little control over these influences, it must often modify its P/HR activities to meet changing conditions in the external environment.

ORGANIZATION CONTEXT

P/HR management exists within an organization context. It is part and parcel of the organization, and of the organization's administrative processes. P/HR management shapes, and is shaped by, the organization and these processes. This dynamic interplay between P/HR management and its organization context is explored more fully below.

Challenging Issues

One probably does not think of the retailing industry as being in a state of P/HR management turbulence. Yet it is. Illustration 1–1 provides some examples of P/HR issues that are challenging this industry. Note that these issues may be readily interpreted within the context of the P/HR model (Figure 1–1).

At a more general level, organizations face many issues that have P/HR management implications and solutions. These issues include:

- Productivity.
- Product quality.
- Emphasis on service.
- Labor costs.
- Work-force flexibility.
- Unethical practices.

Productivity

Productivity refers to the output of goods/services produced per unit of input. Labor productivity specifically refers to output per hour. Other things being equal, organizations with high productivity are more competitive.

The issue is that there is a productivity "crisis" in which productivity levels and growth rates for many organizations have lagged behind their competitors, both at home and abroad.[2] The effects, at the extreme,

---

[2] A. Neef and J. Thomas, "Trends in Manufacturing Productivity and Labor Costs in the U.S. and Abroad," *Monthly Labor Review* 110, no. 12 (1987), pp. 25–30. T. Rollins and J. R. Bratkovich, "Productivity's People Factor," *Personnel Administrator* 33, no. 2 (1988), pp. 50–57.

ILLUSTRATION 1–1

P/HR Management Issues in Retailing

The shopping list of retailers' human resource issues is long enough to make any department store Santa breathless:

• Perhaps the industry's greatest problem is the declining labor pool. The population of 16 to 24 year olds—those who comprise the largest portion of the sales force—is expected to decrease 25 percent by 1992. In addition, retailers are in stiff competition for entry-level workers with other equally growing service areas such as fast-food restaurants and hotels and motels.

• The quality of service in general has fallen to new depths. *Time* magazine, which devoted a recent cover story to the subject, notes that employees are often overworked in order to keep labor costs, and therefore prices, low.

Jobs have been simplified in order to cut down on errors, yet this has hurt morale and workers' ability to handle problems on their own. And the low pay and lack of advancement in their careers have sapped their motivation, according to the magazine.

Companies are scrambling for philosophies, programs, and policies that will turn around their workers' performance and give them an edge over the equally rude and uncaring staffs of their competitors.

• A department store career doesn't hold the same allure for today's generation of workers as it did for their parents. Many now entering the work force have had much more exposure to the high-growth specialty stores that have sprung up at shopping malls all over America than department stores, which have been called "the fabulous invalids of retailing."

• With the specialty chains' exponential growth, however, has come an endemic set of problems. They have had a difficult time holding onto both entry- and managerial-level workers who cut their retailing teeth at The Gaps and The Limiteds, but are lured away to the bigger stores by higher pay, better benefits, and more opportunity for advancement.

• Many specialty stores have been presented with an additional dilemma arising out of the schizophrenic-like nature of their needs: On one hand, they must attract employees who can relate to their youthful customers and merchandise. Yet their equally young managers must possess the requisite level of sophistication to handle the rigors of burgeoning growth.

• More and more retailers are putting greater numbers of employees on commission in an effort to recruit and retain better qualified people by making sales jobs more lucrative. But at least one analyst warns that broadening the commissioned work force has come to be regarded as a panacea for human resource problems.

Another expert cautions that if companies are going to install programs such as personalized selling, complete with "professional salespersons" whose compensation is largely commission, they had better have developed methods to measure just how productive workers are and be able to demonstrate the advantages of the new system to employees.

Source: S. Vittolino, "Retailers Shop for Solutions," *Human Resource Executive* 2, no. 1 (1988), pp. 28–31.

have been layoffs, plant closings, mergers, and divestitures (selling off) of business units.

The challenge is to increase productivity growth rates in general, including labor productivity. Here is where P/HR management activities can play an important role. Improving existing P/HR activities and undertaking new ones can help more closely match individuals and jobs. One example is the development of productivity gain-sharing programs in which employees receive monetary bonuses for productivity increases (see Chapter 15 for more details). Such programs seek to strengthen the match between employee motivation and job rewards.

Product quality

Competition is increasingly being waged on not only a price dimension, but a quality dimension as well. A visible example here is the automobile industry. Japanese automakers (for instance, Honda) are offering cars that are affordable and superior relative to U.S. automakers. Partly as a consequence, General Motors' share of the U.S. auto market, for example, has dropped dramatically.

In response, U.S. automakers have assigned a high priority to improving product quality. The quality emphasis has been supported by a series of P/HR strategies and activities. Some of these have involved work environment changes in the form of employee quality circles, increased employee participation in decision making, and self-managing work teams (see Chapter 19 for elaboration). New compensation programs, such as profit sharing, are also being implemented. Attempts to improve the labor relations climate are also underway.

Note that these changes affect both the ability requirements of jobs (such as increased communication and social interaction skills) and job rewards (for example, more participation and teamwork). Current employees thus must adapt to such changes, and new employees must be sought whose abilities and needs are compatible with the new job requirements and rewards.

Emphasis on service

More and more organizations are service oriented. Examples include banking, financial planning, health care, retailing, day care, and mail delivery. Changes toward a service emphasis inevitably lead to changes in the nature of jobs, such as making customer service and satisfaction an important component of the job. While this may affect many P/HR activities, assessing P/HR outcomes is vitally affected. For example, organizations may change the performance appraisal system by actually evaluating employees on how well they provide service and satisfaction to the customer. The telephone companies, such as Ameritech and Nynex, are doing precisely this for many employee groups.

Labor costs

Labor costs (i.e., wages, salaries, benefits) are a major component of total costs for organizations. Nationwide, about 65 percent of total cost is in the form of labor costs.[3] Naturally, there is considerable variation around this overall percentage, depending on such factors as type of industry and geographic area.

Controlling labor costs thus becomes a key strategy in the private sector for improving the organization's competitive posture and in the public sector for maintaining taxes at levels acceptable to the public. Labor "cost containment" has thus emerged as an important mechanism for improving organizational effectiveness. Implementation of this mechanism has occurred through numerous P/HR initiatives and activities. Examples include: (1) instituting pay freeze or reduction programs, (2) tying pay more closely to organization success, as in profit sharing, and (3) requiring employees to pay a greater percentage of their benefit costs, especially for health insurance premiums and pensions.

Work-force flexibility

When an organization must respond to changes in its economic/political environment (due to foreign competition or government deregulation, for instance), it must have a flexible work force to assist in the transition. For example, IBM recently underwent a substantial reorganization in response to new competitive pressures. Part of the reorganization involved: (1) reducing its worldwide workforce from 403,000 to 390,000 employees without any layoffs (IBM has a long-standing P/HR policy against layoffs), and (2) redeploying many staff people. These changes were achieved in two years through a combination of special retirement incentive programs and transfer of headquarters staff into more direct assignments such as sales and customer service. The staff moves were accompanied by many P/HR activities (e.g., training) to ensure that employees would be well prepared for their new job requirements and rewards.[4]

---

[3] *Economic Report of the President.* (Washington, D.C.: U.S. Government Printing Office, 1988).

[4] B. J. Gray, "Top 50," *Human Resource Executive* 2, no. 1 (1988), pp. 10–21 +.

Unethical practices

Ethical issues constantly confront organizations. Price gouging, falsification of data, and misleading advertising are but a few of many well-publicized cases. Ethical treatment of one's employees is also emerging as an issue. It involves a variety of problem areas such as confidentiality of information, right to privacy, sexual orientation, sexual harassment, exposure to safety and health hazards, equal employment opportunity, and employee honesty.[5] Formulation of policies by the organization to deal with such issues is in part a matter of responding to external influences in the P/HR model—namely, laws and regulations. Addressing these issues directly can also help create a work environment conducive to a positive impact on P/HR outcomes, particularly satisfaction and retention of employees.

In all of the above issues and examples, it can be seen that P/HR management affects, and is affected by, many broad-based organizational concerns. Interplay such as this is also reflected in the workings of the organization's administrative process.

Administrative Process

Figure 1–2 portrays the relationship between the organization's general administrative process and P/HR management. On the left side of the figure is the administrative process, and on the right is P/HR management. Before discussing specifics of Figure 1–2, note two points. First, external influences play a critical role. Second, the administrative process and P/HR management move in tandem with each other, and there is reciprocal influence between them.[6]

Turning first to the administrative process, organization goals are established (for example, to increase sales 10 percent over the next two years) and strategies for goal pursuit are developed (such as to expand

---

[5] G. Edwards and K. Bennett, "Ethics and HR: Standards in Practice," *Personnel Administrator* 32, no. 12 (1987), pp. 62–66; J. Hoerr, "Privacy," *Business Week*, March 28, 1988, pp. 61–66.

[6] This discussion draws from L. Baird and I. Meshoulam, "Managing Two Fits of Strategic Human Resource Management," *Academy of Management Review* 13 (1988), pp. 116–28; J. E. Butler, G. R. Ferris, and D. Smith Cook, "Exploring Some Critical Dimensions of Strategic Human Resource Management," in *Readings in Personnel and Human Resource Management*, eds. R. S. Schuler, S. A. Youngblood, and V. L. Huber (St. Paul: West Publishing, 1988), pp. 3–13; L. Dyer and G. W. Holder, "Toward a Strategic Perspective of Human Resource Management," in *Human Resource Management: Evolving Roles and Responsibilities*, ed. L. Dyer (Washington D.C.: ASPA/BNA Handbook of Human Resource Management, 1988); W. J. Rothwell and H. C. Kazaras, *Strategic Human Resources Planning and Management* (Englewood Cliffs, N.J.: Prentice-Hall, 1988).

FIGURE 1–2
Administrative Process and P/HR Management

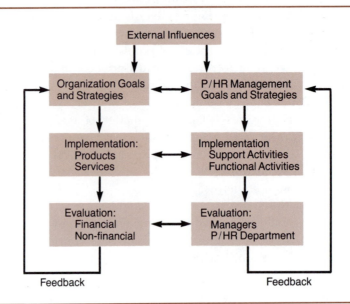

sales territory). Strategy is then implemented throughout the organization, ultimately affecting the types, quantity, and quality of products and services offered. At the end of the cycle, evaluations are made to gauge the effectiveness of the strategies implemented. Evaluation may focus on both financial (e.g., actual increase in sales) and nonfinancial (e.g., customer satisfaction) indicators. Results of the evaluation are then fed back and used in the derivation of new goals and strategies, subject to new external realities.

P/HR management goals and strategies are formulated in conjunction with those of the organization. Returning to the sales example, a goal to increase sales 10 percent may require enhancing employee abilities and motivation to perform. Employee abilities may be improved through hiring more qualified salespeople, as well as through providing additional training for them. Motivation may be enhanced by designing new incentive pay systems for the salespeople, where pay is directly tied to sales performance.

Once strategic choices are made, they are then implemented in the form of specific policies and programs. These policies and programs correspond to the P/HR activities (both support and functional) contained in the P/HR model (Figure 1–1). Implementation will typically be shared between managers and the P/HR department staff. For example, the P/HR department may design and conduct a new training program for salespeople, with input on program content coming from sales managers.

At the end of the cycle, both managers and the P/HR department will be evaluated. Sales managers, for example, may be evaluated during their performance appraisal on how well they succeeded in boosting the actual sales of their subordinates. The P/HR department may be evaluated on more aggregate indicators such as sales force productivity improvement or the cost-effectiveness of the training program that was conducted. Feedback of evaluation results to the next "round" of P/HR goal and strategy formulation occurs, also subject to new and anticipated external influences.

A competitive strategy example

How does the interplay between the administrative process and P/HR management actually work? The following example provides an illustration.

Organization goals and strategies can be classified many different ways. One such classification is based on three different types of competitive strategy.[7] These strategies are:

1. *Innovation*—develop products and services different from one's competitors.
2. *Quality enhancement*—improve the quality of products and services offered.
3. *Cost reduction*—become the lowest-cost producer of a product or service.

These three strategies are best thought of as "pure" types; they could also be used in various combinations. Thus, within an organization, different units (such as product divisions) may use different strategies.

Each competitive strategy has implications for the P/HR activities that are likely to be most appropriate for, and supportive of, the strategy. An example of this possibility, involving the innovative strategy, is provided in Illustration 1–2. It describes Frost, Inc., a small manufacturing company that moved toward greater production automation as an innovative strategy for increasing product flexibility. Accompanying this strategic choice were various P/HR strategies and activities.

---

[7] Based on M. E. Porter, *Competitive Strategy* (New York: The Free Press, 1980); M. E. Porter, *Competitive Advantage* (New York: The Free Press, 1985); R. S. Schuler and S. E. Jackson, "Linking Competitive Strategies With Human Resource Management Practices," *Academy of Management Executive* 1 (1987), pp. 207–19.

ILLUSTRATION 1–2

An Innovative Strategy: One Company's Experience

Frost, Inc. is one company that has made a conscious effort to match competitive strategy with human resource management practices. Located in Grand Rapids, Michigan, Frost is a manufacturer of overhead conveyor trolleys used primarily in the auto industry, with sales of $20 million. Concerned about depending too heavily on one cyclical industry, President Charles D. "Chad" Frost made several attempts to diversify the business, first into manufacturing lawn mower components and later into material-handling systems, such as floor conveyors and hoists. These attempts failed. The engineers didn't know how to design unfamiliar components, production people didn't know how to make them, and salespeople didn't know how to sell them. Chad Frost diagnosed the problem as inflexibility.

Frost decided that automating production was the key to flexibility. Twenty-six old-fashioned screw machines on the factory floor were replaced with 11 numerical-controlled machines paired within 18 industrial robots. Frost decided to design and build an automated storage-and-retrieval inventory control system, which would later be sold as a proprietary product, and to automate completely the front office to reduce indirect labor costs. The new program was formally launched in late 1983.

What at first glance appeared to be a hardware-oriented strategy turned out to be an exercise in human resource management. "If you're going to reap a real benefit in renovating a small to medium-size company, the machinery is just one part, perhaps the easiest part, of the renovation process," says Robert McIntyre, head of Amprotech, Inc., an affiliated consulting company Frost formed early in the automation project to provide an objective, "outside" view. "The hardest part is getting people to change."

Frost was clearly embarking on a strategy of innovation. As it turns out, many of the choices the company made about human resource practices were intended to support the employee role behaviors identified as being crucial to the success of an innovation strategy.

For example, the company immediately set out to increase employee identification with the company by giving each worker 10 shares of the closely held company and by referring to them henceforth as "shareholder-employees." The share ownership, which employees can increase by making additional purchases through a 401(d) plan, are also intended to give

SUMMARY

P/HR management is concerned with enhancing the contributions of employees toward the effectiveness of the organization. The P/HR management model shows that these contributions are gauged in terms of specific P/HR outcomes, especially the attraction, performance, retention, attendance, and satisfaction of employees. Influencing employees on these outcomes requires matching job requirements and rewards with individual ability and motivation. To implement this matching process, numerous P/HR activities are undertaken by the organization's P/HR department as well as by individual managers. Support activities indirectly affect the individual-job matching process; they include analyzing

ILLUSTRATION 1–2 (concluded)

employees a long-term focus, which is another behavior important for an innovation strategy to succeed. Additional long-term incentives consist of a standard corporate profit-sharing plan and a discretionary profit-sharing plan administered by Chad Frost.

Frost's compensation package was also restructured to strike a balance between results (productivity) and process (manufacturing). In Frost's case, the latter is a significant consideration, since the production process is at the heart of the company's innovation strategy. Frost instituted a quarterly bonus that is based on companywide productivity, and established a "celebration fund" that managers can tap at their discretion to reward significant employee contributions. The bonuses serve to foster other needed employee role behaviors. By making the quarterly bonus dependent on companywide productivity, the company is encouraging cooperative, interdependent behavior. The "celebration fund", meanwhile, can be used to reward and reinforce innovative behavior.

Frost encourages cooperative behavior in a number of other ways as well. Most offices (including Chad Frost's) lack doors, which is intended to foster openness of communication. Most executive perks have been eliminated, and all employees have access to the company's mainframe computer (with the exception of payroll information) by way of more than 40 terminals scattered around the front office and factory floor.

In our view, a vital component of any innovation strategy is getting employees to broaden their skills, assume more responsibilities, and take risks. Frost encourages employees to learn new skills by paying for extensive training programs, both at the company and at local colleges. It even goes further, identifying the development of additional skills as a prerequisite for advancement. This is partly out of necessity, since Frost has compressed its 11 previous levels of hierarchy into four. Because this has made it harder to reward employees through traditional methods of promotion, employees are challenged to advance by adding skills, assuming more responsibilities, and taking risks.

Source: R. S. Schuler and S. E. Jackson, "Linking Competitive Strategies with Human Resource Management Practices," *Academy of Management Executive* 1 (1987), pp. 213–14.

individuals and jobs, assessing outcomes, and human resource planning. Functional activities are intended to have a direct impact on the matching process; the specific activities are external staffing, internal staffing and development, compensation, labor relations, and the work environment. All P/HR activities are strongly dependent on a series of external influences. The model identifies these influences as economic conditions, labor markets, laws and regulations, and labor unions.

P/HR management is not isolated from the broader organization context. One way to recognize and understand this is to identify examples of critical issues confronting organizations. Such issues currently include productivity, product quality, emphasis on service, labor costs, workforce flexibility, and unethical practices. Examination of these issues

suggests that P/HR management, as exemplified by the P/HR management model, plays an important role in creating the issue and in contributing to its resolution.

The broader organization context for P/HR management also involves
administrative processes. Here, the organization sets goals and derives
strategies for attaining them. These strategies are then implemented.
Finally, the effectiveness of the strategies and their implementation is
evaluated. P/HR management unfolds, and is conducted in, a similar
manner. But there is a dynamic interplay that occurs between the
administrative process and P/HR management. Thus intertwined, each
shapes—and is shaped by—the other. Ultimately, both are linked together by being subject to a variety of common external influences.

2

P/HR Management in Operation

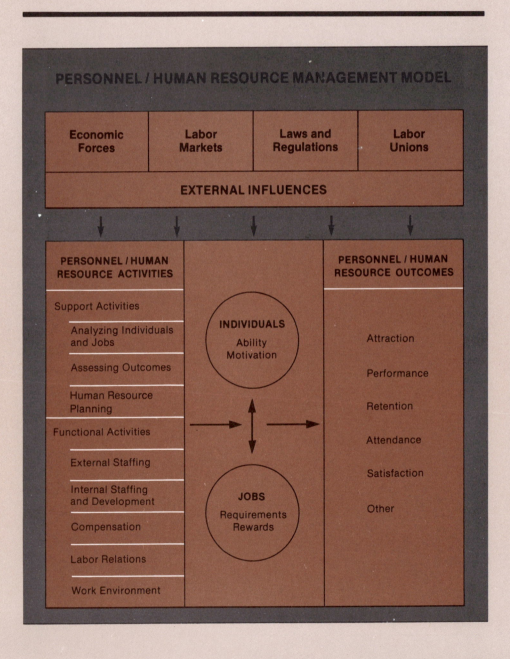

PERSONNEL / HUMAN RESOURCE MANAGEMENT MODEL

Economic Forces	Labor Markets	Laws and Regulations	Labor Unions

EXTERNAL INFLUENCES

PERSONNEL / HUMAN RESOURCE ACTIVITIES

Support Activities

  Analyzing Individuals and Jobs

  Assessing Outcomes

  Human Resource Planning

Functional Activities

  External Staffing

  Internal Staffing and Development

  Compensation

  Labor Relations

  Work Environment

INDIVIDUALS
Ability
Motivation

JOBS
Requirements
Rewards

PERSONNEL / HUMAN RESOURCE OUTCOMES

Attraction

Performance

Retention

Attendance

Satisfaction

Other

After reading this chapter you should be able to speak to the questions posed in each of the following personnel/human resource incidents:

1. The Bruce Park Press is a small publishing company with about 100 employees and annual sales of $8 million. Sales have been flat for several years, due to a limited set of "titles" and the fact that none of these titles has been well received in the marketplace. As president, you have decided on an aggressive plan to increase sales by obtaining many new titles and more reputable authors, developing a national sales force, and greatly expanding direct mail advertising. Your goal is to have sales of $25 million and an accompanying work force of 250 employees within seven years. As you develop your strategy, you must decide whether or not to create a separate P/HR department to administer P/HR activities. What factors would you consider in making this decision?

2. You are staff specialist in the corporate personnel department of a large retailing company with many stores located throughout the southwestern United States. Managers, such as store and department managers, have a tradition of independence in wanting to "run their own shop," without interference from staff departments such as personnel. The new senior vice president for personnel comes from the ranks of these managers. In her new job, however, she is beginning to sense that such unrestrained independence by managers may be causing some problems. At lunch one day, she asks you to suggest what types of problems might arise, and what types of specific roles might be defined for the personnel department in order to address these problems. What would you respond?

3. The Collins Cosmetics Company develops, manufactures, and distributes cosmetics and cosmetic accessories such as illuminating mirrors. Products are targeted to the "mature man and woman" market, which has been greatly expanding in numbers and sales. Unfortunately, the company has not shared in this growth and indeed is experiencing declining sales and market share. The founder and president, M.A. Collins, is a former cosmetologist who has always paid most of her attention to the "product," rather than the "people," side of the business. She finally decides that at least part of the company's problems might be "people" ones, and decides to investigate how effective the P/HR department is, and has been, in administering various P/HR activities. She asks you, her personal assistant, to prepare a written report that suggests some ways the department's effectiveness might be judged. To whom in the company might you talk about this, and what sorts of suggestions would you make to the president?

The previous chapter examined the general nature of P/HR management through the P/HR management model. Placing the model within the broad organization context, it was then shown how P/HR management fits into the general administrative processes of an organization. The present chapter shows how P/HR management works in actual operation within the organization. It thus "brings to life" the nature of P/HR management as it can and does occur.

To do this, several issues are dealt with. The first issue is the existence of a P/HR department that has responsibility for administering the numerous activities shown in the P/HR model. Here, reasons for the existence of such a department are identified, along with an indication of the structure of a typical P/HR department.

P/HR activities are conducted both by individual (line) managers throughout the organization and by specialized (staff) managers within the P/HR department. The second issue is how line and staff managers approach these tasks, and some possible differences between these two types of managers in terms of their perspectives about the activities. It is shown that, while there are differences, line and staff managers ultimately must work together, treating the P/HR activities as a shared responsibility.

Assessing the effectiveness of P/HR activities is the third issue addressed. Effectiveness questions are examined for both individual managers and the P/HR department. Particular emphasis is placed on the P/HR department and the multiple ways its effectiveness may be judged.

Finally, P/HR management as a profession is described. Specific types of jobs, salaries, and career patterns are described, along with the types of professional activities in which individuals in the P/HR field typically engage.

THE P/HR DEPARTMENT

Almost all organizations have an identifiable P/HR function, and this function directs the types of activities shown in the P/HR model (refer back to Figure 1–1). In a small organization, say under 200 employees, the total function may be performed by a single person such as the owner or general manager. Moreover, many times managing the P/HR function will be only a part of that person's job duties. Increasingly, though, small organizations are placing greater emphasis on the P/HR function.[1] Accompanying this is a trend toward having (1) a person with full-time

---

[1] M. I. Finney, "HRM in Small Business: No Small Task," *Personnel Administrator* 32, no. 11 (1987), 36–44.

P/HR responsibilities, and (2) a formal P/HR department in even small organizations.

As organization size increases, so does the likelihood of finding the P/HR function housed within one or more formal departments. Various titles are used for these departments: "Personnel," "Industrial Relations (IR)," "Human Resources (HR)," "Personnel/Human Resources," and "Employee Relations (ER)." These titles may be, and are, used interchangeably.

Increases in organization size also increase the likelihood of there being not one but multiple P/HR departments within the organization. A company with a corporate headquarters and two manufacturing plants, for example, may have a P/HR department at the *corporate* level and two more departments at the *operating* (for instance, plant, division, business unit) level.

With this general background, two specific topics will be examined. First, what explains the existence of a P/HR department? Second, what does the structure of the department look like, and how does it fit into the organization's overall context and structure?

Need for the P/HR Department

Management creates a P/HR department. The interesting issue is why this happens. Several factors appear to contribute to this phenomenon, both currently and historically.[2]

Importance of human resources

Organizations are increasingly recognizing that the labor input—their human resource—is vital to their success. As one chief executive officer of a company said:

> Human resources is a function that has only been given attention within the last few years. . . . The most important asset we have is our people and none of us is working up to our potential. This (human resources) is the area that's trying to develop that potential and get more out of our employees. If we're going to be competitive with the Japanese and others we're going to have to tap this potential.[3]

---

[2] This discussion draws from E. A. Burack and E. L. Miller, "A Model for Personnel Practices and People," *Personnel Administrator* 24, no. 1 (1979), pp. 50–56; M. A. Frohman, "Human Resource Management and the Bottom Line: Evidence of the Connection," *Human Resource Management* 23 (1984), pp. 315–34; M. Van Glinow, M. J. Driver, K. Brousseau, and J. B. Prince, "The Design of a Career Oriented Human Resource System," *Academy of Management Review* 8 (1983); pp. 23–32. V. V. Murray and D. E. Dimick, "Contextual Influence on Personnel Policies and Programs: An Explanatory Model," *Academy of Management Review* 3 (1978), pp. 750–61.

[3] R. Foltz, K. Rosenberg, and J. Foehrenbach, "Senior Management Views the Human Resource Function," *Personnel Administrator* 27, no. 9 (1982), pp. 37–54.

Survey data are consistent with this opinion. Chief executive officers from over 200 companies throughout the country were asked to indicate the degree of P/HR department involvement they expected in several activities. Results for 1982 and 1987, and projections for 1992, are shown in Figure 2–1. Inspection of these data clearly shows that P/HR department involvement in the activities has grown, and that involvement is expected to increase even more by 1992.

Complexity of managers' jobs

Managers' jobs have become more complex and demanding. Often managers are faced with P/HR problems that go beyond their expertise or require more time than they can devote to them. When this happens, P/HR specialists are needed, and a personnel department is established.

External influences

The passage of employment laws and regulations creates an immediate need for individuals who can interpret them and develop programs that will ensure compliance. It is not by chance that equal employment opportunity and occupational safety and health have become major activities. Both are a direct result of the passage of two federal laws— Title VII of the Civil Rights Act in 1964 and the Occupational Safety and Health Act in 1970.

In addition, unions and labor market influences have played a prominent role in contributing to the development of the personnel function. The increasing diversity of the labor force, in terms of gender, race, and age, has created the need for frequent reassessment of activities in order to cope with this change—from recruitment practices to promotion systems to benefits—to ensure equal opportunites and compliance with legislation.

Need for consistency

Exclusive reliance on the judgment of line managers in P/HR decisions often leads to inconsistent treatment of employees. For example, some line managers may give raises to favored subordinates, while others may grant pay raises according to their subordinates' performance. Over time, these inconsistencies result in feelings of inequity and dissatisfaction as subordinates become aware of differential treatment.

Laws and regulations set standards to which organizations must consistently adhere. The requirement that some employees be paid one and one-half times their hourly pay rate for each hour worked in excess of 40

FIGURE 2-1

CEO Opinions About P/HR Department Involvement

	Year		
Involvement in	1982	1987	1992
Planning activities			
Developing HR strategies	4.9	6.0	6.2
Monitoring staffing levels	5.1	5.7	5.9
Organization planning	4.6	5.4	5.9
Staffing activities			
Recruiting professional/technical talent	2.5	6.1	6.1
Executive recruiting	4.5	5.3	5.3
EEO/affirmative action	6.0	5.7	5.7
Outplacement	3.2	3.7	3.9
Training and Development Activities			
Career planning and development	3.9	4.4	5.1
Management succession planning	3.9	4.5	5.3
	4.4	5.3	5.8
Technical training	4.2	4.3	4.8
Performance and compensation activities			
Performance appraisal	5.3	6.0	6.1
Merit pay	5.4	5.9	6.0
Incentive pay	3.9	5.3	5.8
Productivity improvement	3.9	4.7	5.3

Note: 1 = slightly involved; 7 = heavily involved.

Source: J. W. Walker and G. Moorhead, "CEOs: What They Want from HRM," *Personnel Administrator* 32, no. 12 (1987), pp. 50–59.

hours per week cannot be ignored by line managers; it is a legal standard, and failure to comply with it can result in penalties to the organization.

Unions represent employees by negotiating contracts that regulate wages, hours, and other employment conditions. Labor relations specialists are concerned with uniformly implementing the contract as negotiated, and avoiding possible precedent-setting commitments by uniformed line managers.

In short, consistency of treatment of employees is a basic necessity in organizations. One reason the personnel department exists is to ensure that this occurs, primarily through the development (with line management) of uniform P/HR policies and procedures that are to be followed by all managers.

Structure of the P/HR Department

P/HR departments exist in a multitude of forms. The exact form will depend on such factors as organization goals and strategy, structure, and size. Consequently, there is no one generic type of P/HR department structure.

A "feel" for structure, however, may be gotten from examining the organization chart of a fictitious retailing organization (refer to Figure 2–2). The company has both a corporate level and an operating level, including the P/HR function. For simplicity's sake, only relevant portions of the total organization structure are shown.

At the corporate level the company is divided into five functional areas (stores, operations, marketing, personnel, and finance). Each of these areas is headed by a senior vice president, who reports to the president and chief executive officer.

The corporate personnel department is divided into major P/HR activity areas (planning, employment, compensation, training and development, and labor relations). Each activity is headed by a vice president who reports to the senior vice president. Each vice president, in turn, has numerous people reporting to him or her. While job titles for these people are not shown, examples in the employment area might include recruiter, employment interviewer, test administrator, and researcher. Usually the vice presidents and their subordinates would be referred to as *specialists* since they have a specialized set of job duties within a single P/HR activity.

Moving to the operating level, it can be seen that the company has a number of stores. Each store is headed by a store manager, and one of the people reporting to him or her is the personnel manager. How many employees report to the personnel manager, and their job duties, will depend greatly on the size of the store. Usually, the personnel manager and his or her subordinates will be referred to as *generalists* because their job duties encompass many different P/HR activities. However, there may also be some specialists in the stores' personnel departments.

As noted, there are many different types of P/HR departments. Each, and its structure, is tailor-made to the specific characteristics of the organization. The example provided in Figure 2–2, however, is not all that unusual, and it does convey a sense of this important function and how it relates to management and the rest of the organization. Keeping this in mind, an examination of two somewhat differing perspectives on the delivery of P/HR activities—those of individual managers and those of members of the P/HR department—will follow.

P/HR ACTIVITIES: LINE AND STAFF PERSPECTIVES

P/HR activities pervade organizations, large and small, public and private. These activities are conducted by managers of two types—line and staff. *Line managers* are those with direct responsibility in the

FIGURE 2-2

Ficticious Organization Structure: Retailing Organization

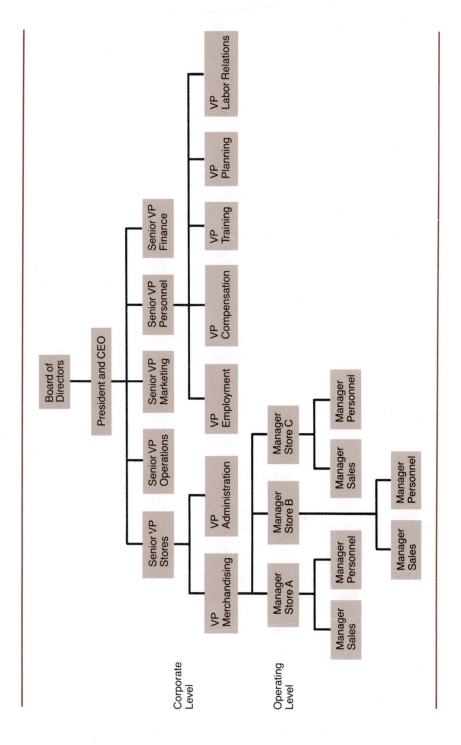

administrative process (refer back to Figure 1–2) for establishing goals and strategies and/or for implementing them. Examples of line manager job titles include:

President
Chief executive officer
School district superintendent
Merchandise manager
Sales manager
Supervisor
Head nurse
Hospital administrator

Staff managers are primarily concerned with providing line managers specialized assistance (such as data analysis, record keeping) and with maintaining coordination and control mechanisms (e.g., financial). Managerial employees in the P/HR department are typically considered staff managers. Other examples of staff managers include:

Accounting manager
Advertising manager
Data processing manager
Payroll manager
Legal services manager
Quality control supervisor

As stated, both line and staff managers are involved in P/HR activities. Because of their differing roles in the administrative process, however, line and staff managers have differing perspectives on how to best manage human resources.

Line Managers' Perspective

Most line managers have subordinates for whom they are responsible, and they daily make P/HR decisions in the supervision of these subordinates. These decisions involve such diverse areas as work assignments, performance appraisal and feedback, training and development, pay raises, discipline, promotions, and staffing.

Some important forces help shape these decisions. First, there is a desire for considerable individual discretion in decision making. Line managers feel that if they are responsible (accountable) for their subordinates, they should have corresponding authority to manage them. Relative to the P/HR model, this translates into line managers wanting primary responsibility for the individual-job matching process and the P/HR activities that will affect it.

Second, line managers are subject to short-term pressures, and they may not fully understand long-run organization goals and strategies. There are thus pressures on the line manager to "produce now"; how this is done may conflict with other long-run goals. Pressures on managers of coal miners to increase miners' productivity, for example, may conflict with long-run goals to improve safety and develop a better relationship with the union.

Third, the above forces may combine to create "I'll go it alone" feelings by line managers. Often this attitude appears in the form of a lack of concern for other managers and their jobs (that is, lack of team-work), and in a resistance to influences and controls from staff managers. A classic P/HR illustration of such resistance is for line managers to want to award merit pay increases to their subordinates as they see fit, without regard for the organization's overall merit pay policies and guidelines (which are normally administered by the P/HR department).

P/HR Department Perspective

Employees in the P/HR department are considered staff employees. They and the department exist to serve line management. Indeed, it is line management that creates the P/HR department in the first place. Within this overall framework, there are three more specific roles or perspectives for the P/HR department: service, advisory, and control.

Certain P/HR activities are performed as *direct services* to line man-agement. For example, the various employment laws and regulations impose a myriad of record-keeping requirements on the organization. The personnel department, rather than individual line managers, is normally responsible for keeping records.

In its *advisory capacity*, the personnel department lends its expertise by providing advice to line management on the conduct of P/HR ac-tivities. This advice comes in several different forms. In part, it can serve as an input into overall organizational planning (for example, advice on the probable availability of qualified individuals in an area where the organization is considering building a new plant). Or it might pertain to broad P/HR policies, such as the stance of the organization toward having its employees represented by a labor union.

The advice could also focus on the desirability or feasibility of a new program, such as an organization-sponsored day-care center for its em-ployees. Finally, line managers also rely on P/HR advice in handling problems with individual employees.

Control relationships go beyond the advisory and service roles be-cause the personnel department directly influences line management decision making. Usually this control is necessary to get consistency of treatment. Consider a policy (created in response to a legal requirement) not to discriminate on the basis of sex in hiring decisions. In an advisory capacity, the personnel department would refer qualified applicants to a line manager, who would then make the final hiring decision. In a control capacity, however, the personnel department would require the line manager's hiring decision to receive final clearance from the personnel department.

A Shared Relationship

Discussion so far suggests some potential for tension and conflict between line managers and the P/HR department, especially in the case of the department's advisory and control roles. Consider the advisory role. Here the department may initiate giving advice to line management without line management requesting or wanting the advice. This may create resentment among line managers in the form of thinking the P/HR department has "gone too far." Or, even if the advice is requested by line management, the quality of the advice then given may be poor. In turn, this may cause line management to distrust the P/HR department, and to question the department's ability to effectively contribute to organization goals and strategies.

The P/HR department's control role directly impinges on line managers' discretion and authority. This obviously may lead to resentment by line managers. It may also cause line managers to ignore or bypass such control.

There is thus an almost inevitable strain or tension between line management and the P/HR department perspectives. Despite this, there is also an increasing recognition that the management of the organization's human resources must be a shared responsibility between line management and the P/HR department.

The following study illustrates this point.[4] Thirty-five people, representing eight "constituencies" from four organizations, took part in the study. The constituencies were (1) line managers, (2) professional employees, (3) hourly employees, (4) union stewards or officers, (5) operating unit heads, (6) corporate human resource executives, (7) operating level human resource managers, and (8) academic human resource experts. These people were asked to respond to the following question for each of 122 P/HR activities: "To what extent should each of the following activities be performed by a field (that is, operating-level) personnel

---

[4] A. S. Tsui, "Defining the Activities and Effectiveness of the Human Resource Department: A Multiple Constituency Approach," *Human Resource Management* 26 (1987), pp. 35–69; A. S. Tsui and G. T. Milkovich, "Personnel Department Activities: Constituency Perspectives and Preferences," *Personnel Psychology* 40 (1987), pp. 519–38.

department?" Each activity was rated "definitely yes," "not sure or maybe," or "definitely not."

Results of the study were as follows: Seventeen of the activities received a "definitely yes" from all 35 respondents. These activities are shown in Figure 2–3. As can be seen, the activities are diverse and involve a mixture of service, advisory, and control roles for the P/HR department. Of the remaining activities, 84 received a "definitely yes" from at least 50 percent of the constituencies. Finally, it was also found that the results depended somewhat on which constituency type was doing the rating, as well as the organization the person was from.

Thus, it is clear that the various types of people (including line

FIGURE 2–3

Seventeen Most Important Human Resource Department Activities (result of a Delphi study)

1. Provide advice and counsel to management on individual employee problem identification and solution (e.g., deal with adverse or difficult personnel situations such as absenteeism).
2. Communicate to management the philosophy, legal implications, and strategy relating to employee relations.
3. Provide advice and counsel to management on employee relations problems.
4. Ensure consistent and equitable treatment of all employees.
5. Administer grievance procedure according to policy (e.g., identify and analyze problems, review deviations and exceptions, resolve problems).
6. Provide advice and counsel to management on staffing policy and related problems.
7. Coordinate the hiring procedure (e.g., establish starting salaries, send offer letters, follow up to obtain acceptance, administer medical questionnaires).
8. Communicate compensation/benefits programs to management (e.g., interpret/explain compensation policies and procedures, inform management of legal implications of compensation practices).
9. Process enrollments and communicate benefits program to employees.
10. Resolve benefits administration problems.
11. Process benefits claims (e.g., health, workers' compensation, pension, unusual or unique claims).
12. Assist management in resolving salary problems involving individual employees (e.g., salary equity issues).
13. Maintain employee and organization files (e.g., keep files orderly and systematic).
14. Ensure compliance with federal and state fair employment practices.
15. Communicate sexual harassment policy and other communications of general EEO philosophy and objectives.
16. Consult with management on the practical implications of corporate human resource programs.
17. Keep up with HR programs developed at the corporate or central personnel departments.

Source: A. S. Tsui, "Defining the Activities and Effectiveness of the Human Resource Department: A Multiple Constituency Approach," *Human Resource Management* 26 (1987), pp. 35–69.

managers) served by the P/HR department feel that the department has a definite important role to play in conducting a diverse set of activities. This, coupled with the previously discussed evidence on increased involvement of the P/HR department in many employment activities, indicates that a shared relationship between line management and the P/HR department will increasingly be the desired norm.

P/HR MANAGEMENT EFFECTIVENESS

The conduct of P/HR activities ultimately leads to questions about the effectiveness of these activities. This was previously identified as the evaluation issue in our discussion of the administrative process (refer back to Figure 1–2). Here we will expand on this issue, examining it from both line management and P/HR department perspectives.

Line Managers

From a line manager's viewpoint, the P/HR model suggests that P/HR activities done by the manager are intended to influence the match between each subordinate and his or her job. The model also suggests that the manager's effectiveness in achieving the match can be determined by gauging the "standing" of each subordinate on the P/HR outcomes. Stated differently, the individual manager's P/HR management effectiveness is determined by assessing how well he or she attracts and retains subordinates, and maximizes their job performance, attendance, and satisfaction.

Making such assessments normally will occur through the organization's managerial performance appraisal system as follows. Ideally, influencing the outcomes of subordinates would first be defined as a standard job requirement for the manager. Then, the manager's handling of this requirement would be assessed periodically. Results of the assessment would then be given to the manager, and would influence reward (e.g., merit pay raise) decisions for the manager. Such feedback and rewards can be useful in motivating effective management of human resources. Much more will be said about these notions in our discussion of "Assessing Outcomes" (Chapters 6 and 7).

The P/HR Department

The P/HR model suggests that the effectiveness of the P/HR department ultimately can be determined by judging how well the department also does in achieving the matching process. However, this must now be done at an aggregate level, the level at which the department is functioning to serve line management. Such levels could be corporate, operating, or both. All of this will depend on the structure of the organization and the placement of the P/HR department(s) within it.

Various approaches to the assessment of effectiveness at the aggregate level are possible. These include (1) managerial performance appraisal systems, (2) aggregate outcome data, (3) aggregate cost data, (4) utility analysis, and (5) constituent opinions. Each is discussed below.

Managerial performance appraisal systems

Assessing an individual manager's performance vis-à-vis his or her subordinates' outcomes requires some type of formal managerial performance appraisal system. Such systems are normally administered by the P/HR department. Thus, one way to assess the effectiveness of the department would be to determine if it is providing an effective appraisal system to management. Characteristics of such a system will be identified in Chapter 6, ("Employee Performance").

Aggregate outcome data

Results of outcome assessments of individual employees can be fed into the P/HR department. There they can be aggregated and analyzed. Consider the example of aggregate data in Figure 2–4.

Data are reported for four outcomes: job satisfaction questionnaire scores, attendance (unexcused absence rate), performance ratings (total

FIGURE 2–4
Ficticious Aggregate P/HR Outcome Data

	Average		
P/HR Outcome	This Year	Last Year	Two Years Ago
Job satisfaction			
Pay	10.2	11.1	11.9
Promotion	12.1	13.0	13.7
Co-workers	11.9	12.7	13.9
Work itself	11.5	14.0	14.5
Supervision	10.6	11.8	12.6
Attendance			
Unexcused absence rate	2.7%	1.9%	2.1%
Performance			
Total rating score	26.3	25.8	25.9
Retention			
Voluntary turnover rate	15.1%	13.9%	13.1%

score), and retention (voluntary turnover rate). All of the data are in the form of overall averages for the division of a company. The P/HR department for the division compiles the data on an annual basis. Results are shown for the current year and the two previous years. With these data, two basic issues involving effectiveness of the P/HR department can be addressed: *outcome levels* and *outcome trends.*

Outcome levels.   This issue involves judging whether the organization's current outcome levels are acceptable and consistent with its goals and strategies. For example, in this year's unexcused absence rate acceptable? Judgments here might be influenced by such factors as knowledge of unexcused absence rates in other companies and costs (for example, of sick pay). Is the rate consistent with organization goals and strategies? Here one might consider factors such as productivity improvement and cost-containment goals.

If the outcome levels are found to be less than desired, then this becomes at least in part a judgment that the P/HR department is lacking in effectiveness. Such feedback and conclusions can be helpful to top management as it charts new goals and strategies for the organization. It can also be useful to the P/HR department. For example, the P/HR department may evaluate, and recommend improvement in, the organization's attendance control activities in order to better serve management.

Outcome trends.   This is simply a judgment about whether the outcome levels are moving in the desired directions over time. Examination of the satisfaction and voluntary turnover data in Figure 2–4, for example, indicates general downward trends in all job satisfaction areas, and a slight upward trend in voluntary turnover. Are these desirable trends? Answers to this question ultimately must be couched in terms of goals and strategies. Once again, these judgments will imply other judgments about the effectiveness of the P/HR department (in this case, its activities designed to influence satisfaction and retention). In short, outcome trend data also provide useful information to both line management and the P/HR department.

Aggregate cost data

P/HR activities obviously are not cost-free. Thus, costs associated with their occurrence need to be compiled and analyzed.[5] Here, both *cost analysis* and *budget allocation analysis* are useful.

Cost analysis.   This involves keeping detailed records of the costs

---

[5] W. F. Cascio, *Costing Human Resources: The Financial Impact of Behavior in Organizations,* 2d ed. (Boston: Kent, 1987).

FIGURE 2–5
Examples of Cost Analysis Indexes

Job analysis
  Task questionnaire administration
  Job description update per employee

Recruitment
  Total costs per recruit
  Travel costs—recruiters
  Administrative costs

Staffing
  Total selection costs per new hire
  Testing costs per new hire
  Interviewing costs per new hire

Compensation
  Total benefit costs
  Total salary costs
  Overtime pay costs
  Salary and benefit costs per employee

Safety and health
  Health insurance premiums per employee
  Disability insurance premiums per employee
  Workers' compensation—total costs
  Lost-time injury costs per employee

incurred for a specific activity or program, such as a particular training program. Often it is useful to compute these costs on a per employee basis. Examples of measurement indexes for cost analysis are shown in Figure 2–5.

Budget allocation analysis.   Involved in this analysis is an examination of how the total P/HR department budget is allocated to the major P/HR activities. It typically is done by calculating the percentage allocation of the budget to each activity. Figure 2–6 shows an example of this.

FIGURE 2–6
Example of Budget Allocation Analysis

P/HR Activity	Percent of P/HR Department Budget
Job Analysis	5%
Planning	10
Assessing Outcomes	10
External Staffing	35
Internal Staffing	8
Development	12
Compensation	15
Labor Relations	3
Work Environment	2

Judgments about the data in cost and budget allocation analysis involve the same two issues as those in aggregate outcome data. Specifically, (1) are the levels acceptable and consistent with organization goals and strategies? and (2) are the trends in the desired directions? Answers to these questions will help management and the P/HR department, just as with aggregate outcome data.

Utility analysis

Utility analysis seeks to estimate both the costs and benefits of a P/HR activity in economic terms.[6] The intent is to provide management information that can be used to answer the age-old question "Is it worth it." Examples of programs and areas that might be likely candidates for utility analysis include:

- Use of a new selection device in hiring.
- Implementation of a new training program.
- Relocation program for transferred employees.
- Provision of a day-care facility for employees.
- Implementation of no smoking policy.
- An early retirement program.

A recent utility analysis example may help clarify its general nature.[7] A company wanted to know "Is it worth it" to use various types of selection procedures for hiring management trainees over the next 10 years. Answering the question involved simultaneous consideration of many factors, as well as some assumptions (we will ignore these factors and assumptions for now, and return to them in Chapter 10—External Staffing Concepts). Taking these into account, the payoff to the selection program in typical, best, and worst case scenarios was simulated. Results of the simulation are shown in Figure 2–7 for five different scenarios. Displayed are the cumulative net present values of dollar gain or loss over the 10-year period for hiring *one* management trainee each year with the selection procedure.

As can be seen, the typical scenario yielded a dollar gain of $890 in the first year, and the payoff accumulated to $27,613 by the 10th year. By

---

[6] For a review of the literature see J. W. Boudreau, "Utility Analysis for Human Resource Management Decisions," in *Handbook of Industrial and Organizational Psychology*, ed. M. D. Dunnette (Chicago: Rand McNally, in press); J. W. Boudreau and C. J. Berger, "Decision-Theoretic Utility Analysis Applied to External Employee Movement," *Journal of Applied Psychology* 70 (1985), pp. 581–612; W. F. Cascio, *Costing Human Resources*.

[7] J. R. Terborg and J. S. Russell, "The Economic Impact of Valid Employee Selection Practices for Entry-Level Mangement under Typical, Best, and Worst Case Scenarios," in *Readings in Personnel and Human Resource Management*, eds. R. S. Schuler, S. A. Youngblood and V. L. Huber (St. Paul: West Publishing, 1988), pp. 530–41.

FIGURE 2–7

Dollar Utilities Associated with Hiring One Person per Year for 10 Years Under Typical, Best, and Worst Case Scenarios

	Cumulative Net Present Value of Dollar Gain or Loss				
Time Line	*Typical*	*Best # 1*	*Best # 2*	*Worst # 1*	*Worst # 2*
Year 1	890	4,618	2,169	< 248>	< 42>
Year 2	2,554	13,473	6,500	< 453>	71
Year 3	4,809	26,131	12,871	< 620>	274
Year 4	7,507	42,190	21,134	< 751	523
Year 5	10,525	59,770	31,128	< 852>	792
Year 6	13,768	77,821	45,522	< 927>	1,070
Year 7	17,154	95,843	55,023	< 978>	1,350
Year 8	20,622	113,535	68,378	<1,010>	1,627
Year 9	24,121	130,759	82,367	<1,026>	1,898
Year 10	27,613	147,399	96,756	<1,028>	2,161

Source: J. R. Terborg and J. S. Russell, "The Economic Impact of Valid Employee Selection Practices for Entry-Level Management under Typical, Best and Worst Case Scenarios," in *Readings in Personnel and Human Resource Management,* eds. R. S. Schuler, S. A. Youngblood, and V. L. Huber (St. Paul: West Publishing 1988), pp. 530–41.

contrast, results for the two best case scenarios showed payoffs of $147,399 and $96,756 by the 10th year. One worst case scenario showed a cumulative *loss* of $1,028, while the other showed only a slight gain of $2,161. The gains and losses, remember, are for only *one* trainee hired per year. One could adjust these figures for the number of trainees assumed hired each year to estimate the *total* likely utility of the selection procedures. Armed with such utility information, management could then make a more informed decision about whether it would be "worth it" to use the selection program.

Utility analysis is a potentially useful way of evaluating the effectiveness of the P/HR department from the standpoint of payoffs occurring as a result of its current, or anticipated, activities. Utility analysis, though, is still in its infancy. It involves making numerous "guesstimates." These usually include program costs, economic value of such program benefits as an increase in job performance, how big the impact of the program will be on employees, and how many employees will be affected by the program. Bearing this cautionary note in mind, specific examples of utility analysis applications will be given throughout the remainder of this book.

Constituent Opinions

Some people argue that the effectiveness of the P/HR department is ultimately a matter of the reputation it establishes with the people it

FIGURE 2–8

Examples of Client Interview Questions about the Effectiveness of the P/HR Department

1. What kinds of changes have you observed in the evolution of the personnel department over these last three years?
2. Do you think greater effort should be made to obtain employee input regarding fringe benefit needs or desires?
3. How adequate are human resource planning activities in the company?
4. Is the personnel department supplying you with acceptable job candidates?
5. To what extent do supervisors and managers receive timely and acceptable advice about the labor contract with the union?

Source: Large public utility company.

serves (clients or constituents). These people include employees, line managers, staff managers, union leaders, and possibly even government officials. Such a viewpoint suggests it would be valuable to assess constituents' opinions about the effectiveness of the P/HR department.

One mechanism that has long been used to gather such information is the *client interview.*[8] Using a set of predetermined questions, one or more members of the P/HR department, or outside consultants, will conduct the interviews. Examples of such questions, taken from a large utility company, are found in Figure 2–8. Responses to the questions are analyzed and typically a report is then prepared for top management. The report will contain both positive and negative evaluation information, along with recommendations for change.

Another approach is to begin by first surveying the constituents to determine what they view as meaningful criteria for evaluating P/HR department effectiveness. After the constituents have identified and reasonably agreed upon these criteria, they can then proceed to actually evaluate the department, using interviews and/or questionnaires. In this way, the constituents not only evaluate the department, but also participate in developing the criteria on which they will base their evaluations.

One recent study took this approach.[9] Five general evaluation criteria or dimensions were found to be meaningful to the surveyed constituents. Moreover, there were more specific criteria identified within each dimension. All these criteria, contained in Figure 2–9, were then used as the basis for the actual evaluation of P/HR department effectiveness.

---

[8] W. R. Mahler, "Auditing PAIR," in *ASPA Handbook of Personnel and Industrial Relations*, eds. D. Yoder and H. G. Heneman, Jr. (Washington, D.C.: Bureau of National Affairs, 1979), pp. 2-91–2-108.

[9] Tusi, "Defining the Activities and Effectiveness of the Human Resource Department"; see also L. R. Gomez-Mejia, "Dimensions and Correlates of the Personnel Audit as an Organizational Assessment Tool," *Personnel Psychology* 38 (1985), pp. 293–308.

FIGURE 2-9   Criteria for Evaluating the Effectiveness of Human Resource Departments (evaluation criteria)

I. Responsiveness

1. Quickness and effectiveness of responses
2. Employees' trust and confidence
3. Level of cooperation from HR department
4. Degree of objectivity and neutrality
5. Average response time to employee inquiries
6. Degree of uniformity and fairness
7. Average time it takes to resolve disputes
8. Number of personnel files lost or misplaced
9. Employees' opinion of HR department's effectiveness
10. Degree to which HR department is open and available
11. Degree of mutual respect and teamwork with line managers
12. Legal conformity of pay plans and benefit programs
13. Degree of involvement in employee grievances
14. Quality of service provided
15. Accuracy of benefit enrollment data
16. Results of personnel audits
17. This HR department compared to others

II. Managing Cost and Negative Performance

1. Voluntary vs. involuntary turnover rate
2. No. of complaints from job applicants
3. No. of equal pay complaints
4. Rate of voluntary controllable turnover.
5. No. of terminations due to poor performance
6. Staffing cost per employee
7. Acceptance per offer ratio
8. Ratio of HR department headcount to population served
9. No. of applicants to each open position
10. No. of grievances filed and resolved
11. No. of complaints that go outside company
12. Percentage of employees received performance appraisal
13. Percentage of employees with development plans

III. Proactivity and Innovativeness

1. Innovation of personnel policies to enhance employee morale and company allegiance
2. Frequency of line management consultation with HR department
3. Presence of a "standout" accomplishment or result
4. Having a strategy to support line management business plans
5. Effectiveness in developing a positive company image among employees
6. Performance against goals
7. Evaluation by corporate HR
8. Effectiveness in dealing with poor performing employees
9. Satisfaction of clients—managers and employees
10. Quality of information and advice to top management
11. Time lapse between establishment of policies at HR and practice in field units
12. Number of programs initiated by the HR department directed toward enhancing the effective utilization of the "people" resource

IV. Training and Development

1. No. of training programs held per year
2. Percentage of employees who participated in training
3. Training course effectiveness ratings
4. No. of hours training per employee

V. Affirmative Action Accomplishments

1. Minority promotion rate
2. Percentage of minority in applicant pool
3. Minority turnover rate
4. Affirmative Action goal attainment

Source: A. S. Tsui, "Defining the Activities and Effectiveness of the Personnel Department: A Multiple Constituency Approach," *Human Resource Management* 26 (1987), pp. 35–69.

JOBS AND CAREERS IN PERSONNEL/HUMAN RESOURCE MANAGEMENT

Types of Jobs

Just as the structures of personnel departments vary considerably among organizations, so do the types of P/HR jobs within these departments. There are four basic types of jobs, however: support, professional/technical, operating personnel manager, and executives.[10]

Support jobs are primarily clerical in nature, involving typists, clerks, and receptionists. Most characteristic of such jobs is a concern with gathering data and maintaining records. Individuals in these jobs typically have a high school or technical school background.

Professional/technical jobs are specialist jobs within a functional activity area, such as compensation, external staffing, and labor relations. Occupants of these jobs frequently have multiple levels of skill and responsibility. For example, in the area of individual development, a training program coordinator for first-level supervisors might be an entry-level job. At the top of this functional activity, one might be a manager of management development, responsible for all training and development activities.

The operating personnel manager is typically a generalist who administers and coordinates programs across all relevant functional activities. The operating personnel manager is required to "fight fires" as they occur and apply organizational policies and knowledge about human behavior to deal with specific incidents. With the increased knowledge now available about individual and group behavior in organizations, the operating personnel manager can often act as a consultant to line managers in helping solve their personnel problems.

The top level consists of P/HR executives. They help link the personnel function with other staff and line functions at the top level of management. They allocate resources to the various functional personnel activity areas. The top personnel executive also has input into the goals and directions of the organization, advising other top managers about the opportunities and constraints facing them in the utilization of personnel and participating with them in establishing the goals and strategies of the organization.

---

[10] D. Yoder and H. G. Heneman, Jr., "PAIR Jobs, Qualifications, and Careers," in *ASPA Handbook of Personnel and Industrial Relations,* eds. D. Yoder and H. G. Heneman, Jr. (Washington, D.C.: Bureau of National Affairs, 1979), pp. 8-19–8-49.

In private organizations, the executive usually is a vice president who has either progressed through P/HR jobs or a combination of line and P/HR positions. In public organizations, the executive may be appointed to the position by the governor or mayor, rather than being a civil servant who has risen to the top job through promotion.

Career Opportunities and Preparation

Career opportunities have been, and are projected to continue to be, promising. The field has witnessed considerable employment expansion, and that is likely to continue. The Department of Labor conservatively estimates there will be a 33 percent employment growth for P/HR specialists by 1995 and a 44 percent growth for employment interviewers.

Preparing oneself to participate in this growth on a career basis will likely require careful educational planning, particularly in choice of college major and specific coursework. P/HR executives of the country's 300 largest companies, for example, report a strong preference for entry-level P/HR employees who majored in business administration, with somewhat less of a preference for social science majors. Majors in science, humanities, and education were decidedly less preferred. For coursework, these same executives expressed a strong preference for courses in specific P/HR functional areas.[11] In order, the top choices were:

1. Personnel management.
2. Employee selection.
3. Compensation administration.
4. Equal employment/affirmative action.
5. Managerial principles and practices.
6. Training and development.
7. Labor relations.

Career Progression

Since there are multiple P/HR management jobs, they involve multiple levels of authority and responsibility. Therefore, it is increasingly possible to pursue P/HR management jobs from the standpoint of a long-term career commitment.

---

[11] T. J. Bergmann and M. J. Close, "Preparing for Entry Level Human Resource Management Positions," *Personnel Administrator* 24, no. 4 (1984), pp. 95–100.

How might a person progress in a P/HR career? Entry into the field typically occurs in one of two ways. One way is to assume an entry-level professional/technical job on completion of a bachelor's or master's degree. As previously noted, this would be a specialist job in a particular function.

The other method of entry is indirect. Here, the first job is in line management, usually as a first-level supervisor, and may be coupled with participation in a general management training program. After gaining some line management experience, a transfer to an entry-level professional/technical or operating personnel manager job occurs.

Some organzations prefer the latter method of entry. It "seasons" the person and provides experiences in, and knowledge of, the day-to-day operation of the organization. In fact, an organization may not hire individuals into P/HR management jobs unless they have such line management experience.

After the entry-level job, a P/HR management career may unfold in a variety of ways, depending on the nature and size of the organization.[12] One career path could involve advancement within a functional area, thereby maintaining an orientation as a personnel specialist. Another path could be movement to an operating personnel manager job. Also possible is movement from one functional area to another, such as from compensation to labor relations.

These career movements are often accompanied by movements between corporate and operating levels of the organization. For many organizations, geographic movement accompanies career movement. Finally, advancement of the career may necessitate changing organizations as well.

Salaries

Salaries for P/HR managers are comparable to those of other staff department managers, and salary increases for P/HR managers have at least kept pace with increases received by other managers.[13] Results of a nationwide survey of 1987 salaries for various types of P/HR managers are shown in Figure 2–10. As can be seen, average salaries ranged from

---

[12] F. Louchheim and V. Lord, "Who Is Taking Care of Your Career?" *Personnel Administrator* 33, no. 4 (1988), pp. 46–51; J. M. Williams, "Managing Your Career Climb," *Personnel Administrator* 33, no. 4 (1988), pp. 38–42.

[13] K. Ropp, "HR Management for All Its Worth," *Personnel Administrator* 32, no. 9 (1987), pp. 34–43.

FIGURE 2–10

Salaries in P/HR Management Jobs (average income by title)

	Average Salary
Top HR Management Executive	$86,800
Top Corporate Personnel Executive	68,900
Human Resource Manager	43,000
Labor Industrial Relations Executive	73,100
Division or Regional HR Executive	59,800
Top Corporate Security Manager	47,600
Top Employee Relations Executive	54,100
EEO Manager	45,700
Employment and Recruiting Manager	40,900
Recruiter	24,900
Employee Training Manager	40,200
Management Development Manager	45,900
Top Comp & Benefits Executive	59,100
Branch Personnel Manager	38,900
Personnel Assistant	18,900

Source: K. Ropp, "HR Management for All Its Worth," *Personnel Administrator* 32, no. 9 (1987), pp. 34–43.

under $20,000 for a personnel assistant to over $86,000 for the top P/HR executive. It should be emphasized that these are only *average* figures for each job title. The survey also found considerable variability around the averages. This variability was due to such factors as size of employer, geographic location, and educational requirements.

PROFESSIONAL ACTIVITIES IN PERSONNEL/HUMAN RESOURCE MANAGEMENT

Professional Organizations

There are a variety of professional organizations for P/HR professionals. Most cities have a personnel association that includes management and professional specialists from many local employers. Nationally, the American Society for Personnel Administration (ASPA) includes personnel executives, managers, and specialists at many levels in many different sized organizations. Compensation specialists may join the American Compensation Association. Professionals in human resource planning and forecasting may belong to the Human Resource Planning Society. Industrial and labor relations managers and specialists often join local chapters of the Industrial Relations Research Association.

Publications

As described below, there are several different types of professional publications available on a periodic basis. Most P/HR professionals will keep up with several.

Current events

For day-to-day events that have an impact on P/HR management activities and outcomes, the *Daily Labor Report*, published by the Bureau of National Affairs, is probably the most complete publication available. Reporting services, which are updated as events occur, are available from several publishers including the Bureau of National Affairs, Commerce Clearing House, and Prentice-Hall. These usually address several specialized functional areas, such as compensation, fair employment practices, labor relations, and pensions and benefits. Reporting services also offer reports of government agency and court decisions, such as *Fair Employment Practice Cases*, *Labor Relations Reference Manual*, and *Wage and Hour Cases* published by the Bureau of National Affairs.

General journals

Several journals are published for the general practitioner. Many of the articles describe new developments in functional activities at the generalist level. These include *Personnel*, *Personnel Journal*, *Personnel Administrator*, *Public Personnel Management*, *Human Resource Management*, *Organizational Dynamics*, *Harvard Business Review*, and *Academy of Management Executive*.

Academic journals

Academic journals likely to contain important research findings for P/HR professionals include *Academy of Management Journal*, *Academy of Management Review*, *Human Relations*, *Industrial Relations*, *Industrial and Labor Relations Review*, *Journal of Applied Psychology*, *Journal of Labor Research*, *Organizational Behavior and Human Decision Processes*, *Personnel Psychology*, and others.

Specialist journals

Journals exist for several distinct fields. For example, *Training and Development* is the journal of the American Society of Training Directors. *Compensation and Benefits Review* contains articles of interest to compensation and benefit professionals. The Human Resource Planning Society publishes *Human Resource Planning.* Labor relations professionals usually keep up with the *Arbitration Journal.* The government publishes many series and its own labor market and industrial relations journal, *Monthly Labor Review.* Professionals need to read several of these to be aware of new developments in both the environment and practice of P/HR.

SUMMARY

The existence of P/HR activities creates the need for a P/HR department to administer them, both alone and in conjunction with line managers. A typical P/HR department is organized according to the major activities, and in larger organizations there may be separate departments at the corporate and operating levels. While line and staff managers in the P/HR department may have differing perspectives on the conduct of P/HR activities, they increasingly recognize that theirs is a shared relationship. To this end, evaluating the effectiveness of the activities is important, and there are multiple methods for doing this.

Employment possibilities in P/HR jobs are good and projected to increase. Careful career preparation will be necessary, however, both for obtaining entry-level jobs and progressing in one's P/HR career. Salaries for these jobs are quite reasonable. Continued professional growth is enhanced through participation in P/HR organizations and in reading professional journals.

DISCUSSION QUESTIONS

1. Why is consistency of treatment of employees so important in an organization, and in what ways can the P/HR department help bring this about?

2. What factors might account for the fact that the P/HR department has increased in importance, and is projected to increase even more?

3. What types of skills are likely to be necessary for a P/HR department specialist to be effective in an advisory role with line managers?

4. What sorts of problems might arise in judging the effectiveness of the P/HR department solely in terms of aggregate outcome data?

5. What types of liberal arts courses might prove useful in developing a fuller understanding of P/HR management and in preparing for a career in the field?

3

External Influences

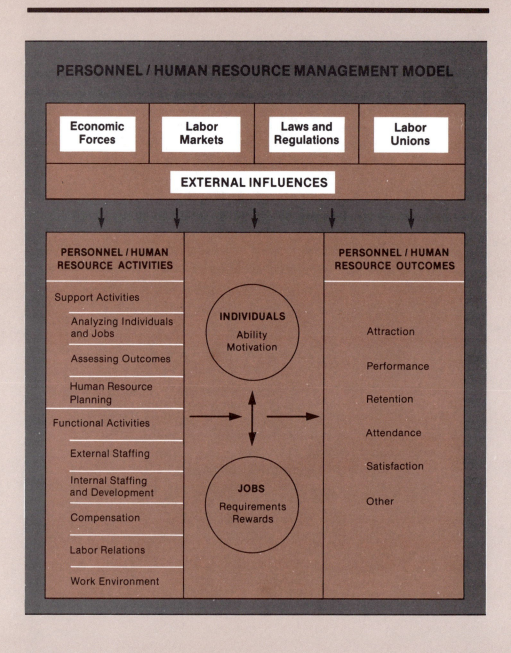

PERSONNEL / HUMAN RESOURCE MANAGEMENT MODEL

Economic Forces	Labor Markets	Laws and Regulations	Labor Unions

EXTERNAL INFLUENCES

PERSONNEL / HUMAN RESOURCE ACTIVITIES

Support Activities

Analyzing Individuals and Jobs

Assessing Outcomes

Human Resource Planning

Functional Activities

External Staffing

Internal Staffing and Development

Compensation

Labor Relations

Work Environment

INDIVIDUALS
Ability
Motivation

JOBS
Requirements
Rewards

PERSONNEL / HUMAN RESOURCE OUTCOMES

Attraction

Performance

Retention

Attendance

Satisfaction

Other

After reading this chapter you should be able to speak to the questions posed in each of the following personnel/human resource incidents:

1. You are a personnel planner for a large heavy-equipment manufacturer. The company's hourly production employees are represented by the United Auto Workers. The most recent collective bargaining agreement includes a provision entitling 30-year employees to retire with full pension benefits. You are also aware that Congress recently amended the Age Discrimination in Employment Act to forbid companies generally to require an employee to retire. What is the likely impact of these two provisions on the makeup of your firm's work force five years in the future? Will the retirement benefit effect outweigh the Age Discrimination Act change?

2. You are a personnel planner concerned with projecting future employment trends for your organization. The organization has a task force concerned with hours of work, promotion ladders, and compensation policies. As an adviser to the task force, you have been asked to provide an overview of the nature and probable impacts of changing characteristics in the labor force. Where should you turn to find out what these changes are likely to be?

3. You are a member of a manufacturing task force considering a government contract for your plant. If you get the contract, it will constitute about 30 percent of your plant's business for the next five years. Are there any special employment laws or regulations for doing business with the government? Do they affect all employees or just those working on government contracts? Are there any cost impacts related to accepting this project?

External influences refer to employment rules and environments within which the organization operates. The general model portrays the basic effect of the external influences on P/HR management. Overall, P/HR activities have to be adapted to affect outcomes at desired levels in the face of changes in external influences. External influences are described in this chapter; succeeding chapters elaborate on these effects.

More specifically, this chapter focuses on three of the major external influences shown in the overall model—economic conditions, labor markets, and laws and regulations and their effects on P/HR activities and ultimately on outcomes. Labor unions, the fourth external influence, are introduced in this chapter and covered in detail in Chapters 17 and 18.

Over time, labor markets change with respect to the distribution of the population by age, sex, education, training, and interest in employment. These changes influence individual behavior and attitudes that, in turn, require adaptation in various P/HR activities. Laws and regulations generally serve to constrain the practice of P/HR management.

ECONOMIC CONDITIONS

General economic and business conditions have widespread effects on P/HR management. The level of economic activity, and whether it is increasing or decreasing, will influence the numbers and types of employees demanded by an organization. As a contrast, compare what has happened in the high-tech sector with what has happened in the mining sector. Employment expansion and job creation has occurred in the former, and contraction and work-force reduction has been the order of the day in the latter.

The 1980s have witnessed some of the widest variations in economic conditions within a short period of time that the United States has seen this century. At the beginning of the decade, inflation was running about 10 percent and unemployment was increasing. During the decade, inflation was reduced at times to less than 2 percent, while recently returning to the 4 to 5 percent range. Unemployment dropped to the 5 percent range. While most of the decade was preoccupied with the disappearance of manufacturing jobs, the first half of 1988 saw virtually all of the new jobs created in manufacturing.

In the same decade, short-term interest rates began near 15 percent, dropped to the 5 to 6 percent range in the middle of the decade, and rose to the 9 percent range in 1988. As business activity increases and capacity limits are being stretched, new investment is considered. But as business activity improves, the demand for money increases, interest rates rise to attract money for investment, and as a result, investment in new plant and equipment becomes more expensive.

Near the beginning of the decade, the value of the dollar relative to other currencies rose rapidly, partly as a result of declining inflation that increased the confidence of foreign investors. The dollar's value also increased because of the high interest rates that were offered relative to other currencies, making the real rate of return substantially higher. Consider, for example, a situation in which the British pound would be worth $2 in exchange. If the interest rate for U.S. debt averaged about 12 percent while interest was 6 percent on British debt, and if borrowers had equal expectations about inflation rates for both currencies, they would prefer to purchase American debt as long as the price of the dollar was below the price of the pound. At the same time, however, goods and services purchased from abroad would decrease in price relative to U.S. goods. Consider, for example, that an automobile buyer was looking for a German luxury car. Assume that the value of the deutschmark against the dollar declined from 75 cents to 50 cents. Assume also that a Cadillac cost $15,000 and a Mercedes cost $30,000. As the relative values of the two currencies changed, the Mercedes price could be reduced to $20,000 and the same profit made, or the price could be reduced to $25,000 and 25 percent more profit could be made. Thus, with the U.S. dollar high, the trade balance became increasingly unfavorable to the United States, and jobs involved in manufacturing goods declined markedly. Late in the 1980s, the value of the dollar fell with the decline in interest rates, exports began to rise, and the price of imports began to rise.

All of these economic changes have had major effects on the labor market. The price of labor (pay and benefits) will influence the types of jobs created in ability requirements and rewards. In response to high labor costs, many jobs are being simplified and mechanized to attract less high-priced talent (for example, checkout clerks in a grocery store). The price of labor will also have a bearing on where jobs are created and located. As suggested in Chapter 1, economic conditions play a role in determining which P/HR activities are desirable and affordable. An organization experiencing financial losses, for example, is unlikely to implement so costly a new benefit, as a dental plan for employees. Indeed, such an organization may ask employees to take actual pay and benefit cuts to lower labor costs. Concessions like these have occurred in such industries as air travel, trucking, and meat packing.

In summary, other things being equal, increases in the value of the dollar will decrease employment in goods-producing industries; higher interest rates are associated with decreasing employment; and decreasing inflation relative to other currencies influences both international trade and interest rates.

LABOR MARKETS

The term *labor market* refers to the myriad of changing influences and activities involving labor demand and supply, which themselves greatly depend on economic conditions. From the organization's standpoint, the numbers and types of employees needed during a given period reflect the relative *demand for labor*. From the individual's standpoint, a part-time job as a cafeteria helper or a 30-year progression from a personnel assistant position to vice president of P/HR are both instances of *supplying labor*.

Defining and Measuring the Labor Force

The U.S. Department of Labor's Bureau of Labor Statistics (BLS) collects and publishes labor market data. State and local agencies, employer organizations, and private reporting services also collect and publish labor market data.[1] Before any data can be interpreted by a user, the basic terms to describe the data must be defined. Figure 3–1 contains definitions of labor market terms, such as *unemployment, participation rate*, and *accessions*.

Data sources

The BLS publishes much of its labor force information from the data gathered in the Current Population Survey (CPS). It uses the definitions shown in Figure 3–1. The unemployment figures do not include so-called *discouraged workers* who may have given up trying to find jobs, nor does it reflect *underemployment*. For example, any for-pay work during the reporting week qualifies a person as being employed, even though that person would have worked more hours if the opportunity had existed. Nor are data available to determine whether jobs held were consistent with the abilities and training of those surveyed.

---

[1] U.S. Department of Labor, Bureau of Labor Statistics, *BLS Handbook of Methods*, Bulletin 1910 (Washington, D.C.: U.S. Government Printing Office, 1976). This publication provides information on the many statistical series published by the BLS, their bases and interpretation.

FIGURE 3–1

Labor Force Definitions of the Bureau of Labor Statistics

Term	Definition
Labor force	All noninstitutionalized individuals over the age of 16 who are working or looking for work.
Employed	Any work for pay during the reporting week as an employee, independent professional, or self-employed person, or 15 or more hours of work as an unpaid family worker. Persons who are temporarily sick, on strike, experiencing bad weather, or on vacation are considered employed.
Unemployed	Not now employed but looking for work (at some point within the last four weeks), including: waiting for recall from layoff or due to report to work in next 30 days. Unemployed persons can be job losers (layoffs), leavers (voluntary quits), reentrants (out of the labor force for over two weeks but now looking for work), and new entrants (persons looking for a job for the first time).
Labor force participation rate	The number of persons in the labor force divided by the total number of noninstitutionalized individuals over the age of 16.
Unemployment rate	Proportion of the labor force that is unemployed.
Separations	Persons leaving employment due to quits, layoffs, retirements, discharges, deaths, or induction into military service.
Accessions	Persons added to payrolls as new hires or recalls from layoffs.

Source: Adapted from U.S. Department of Labor, Bureau of Labor Statistics, *BLS Handbook of Methods*, Bulletin 1910 (Washington, D.C.: U.S. Government Printing Office, 1976).

Other data

A variety of additional data is available to assist organizations and individuals in planning and employment decision making. For compensation analysts and location planners, BLS area wage surveys and state and local labor force projections are available, giving wage and labor supply data by occupation for specific geographical area. For individuals, counselors, and organizations involved in career planning, occupational outlook information is available projecting future job demands.

The analysis of these employment information sources can help the personnel planner to identify trends and patterns in the labor supply that may require reactions in the future.

Trends in the Labor Supply

Slightly more than 65 percent of people over 16 are labor-force participants. This is expected to increase to almost 68 percent by the year

2000.[2] Many factors influence the labor-force participation behavior of individuals. Some of these are demographic factors, while others derive from economic and social changes.

Changes in the makeup of the population

The labor force participation rate depends to some extent on the demographic makeup of the population at any given time. The history of past labor force behavior tells planners and policymakers that the participation rate for men is higher than for women and that people between the ages of 25 and 54 participate at higher rates than those younger and older. Thus, significant changes in the birthrate over periods of time mean that participation rates may change over time.[3]

Subgroup participation rate changes

Recently there have been some marked changes in the labor-force participation of women. Women are more likely to remain in the labor force during childbearing years (and less likely to have as many children), and they are reentering the labor force in larger proportions than in the past. Some of the recent increase in labor-force participation rates is due to these changes in behavior. In 1986, women made up 44 percent of the labor force with projections that this will increase to 47 percent by the year 2000. Participation rates of women with children is over 55 percent, rising to almost 75 percent for mothers of teenagers.[4] Racial minorities will increase at rates about two to four times faster than those of whites. The most rapidly growing subgroup will be Hispanics, increasing almost 75 percent between 1986 and 2000.[5] The rates for men have declined slightly, but this decline has been more than offset by the increased participation of women, so the total labor-force participation rate is expanding.

There is a greater willingness among older workers, both male and female, to retire early. Before 1978, employers could require employees to retire at age 65. However, mandatory retirement was banned in 1985 for most occupations. This change could lead to an increase in participa-

[2] H. N. Fullerton, Jr., "Labor Force Projections: 1986 to 2000," *Monthly Labor Review* 109 (September 1987), pp. 19–29.

[3] R. E. Kutscher, "Overview and Implications of the Projections to 2000," *Monthly Labor Review* 109 (September 1987), pp. 3–9.

[4] S. E. Shank, "Women and the Labor Market: The Link Grows Stronger," *Monthly Labor Review* 110 (March 1988), pp. 3–8.

[5] Fullerton, "Labor Force Projections."

tion among persons over 65. On the other hand, the increased amounts set aside for pensions and legislated pension security provisions, together with union-negotiated early retirement plans, probably will support a continued decline in participation rates for persons over 55 if they do not perceive that future inflation will erode expected benefit levels below desired standards of living. Early evidence shows that participation rates for both men and women over 55 have continued their moderate declines since 1978.[6]

As a result of the decline in birthrates during the 1960s and 1970s, the U.S. labor force is increasingly aging. The combined effects of increased participation by women and the greater likelihood of high participation rates for men between 18 and 44 and both men and women between 45 and 64 mean that by the year 2000, participation rates will probably have increased by 3 percentage points.[7] Older employees are presently more likely to be in agriculture, retail sales, and service industries. They are more likely to be involved in sales, service, and managerial occupations, and less likely to be in professional-technical, clerical, craft, and operative positions.[8]

Age and sex changes in the composition of the labor force have probably increased unemployment by about 0.8 percent since 1957.[9] Although older persons are less likely to be unemployed than those who are younger, their durations of unemployment are substantially longer if they lose their jobs.[10] To the extent that older employees are in declining occupations or industries, unemployment will be an increasing problem for them.

Immigration

Immigration, both legal and illegal, has been a continuing issue in the U.S. labor supply. The wave of immigrants who came to the United States in the 1800s fueled a growing labor supply that enabled the United States to become an increasingly competitive international trader. Many of these immigrants came from countries with troubled economic situations or class systems that made advancement difficult.

Over the last two decades, increasing numbers of Hispanic immi-

---

[6] M. H. Morrison, "The Aging of the U.S. Population: Human Resource Implications," *Monthly Labor Review* 106, no. 5 (1983), pp. 13–19.

[7] Fullerton, "Labor Force Projections."

[8] Morrison, "The Aging of the U.S. Population."

[9] P. O. Flaim, "The Effect of Demographic Changes on the Nation's Jobless Rate," *Monthly Labor Review* 102, no. 3 (1979), pp. 13–23.

[10] Morrison, "Aging of the U.S. Population," p. 17.

grants have crossed the border looking for the same opportunities. Most of these people entered illegally and many have remained. Recent immigration law has offered amnesty and legal status for many who have resided continuously in the United States for extended periods.

Relatively little evidence is available about the impact that recent immigrants have had on the labor supply and the economy. However, there is evidence that the length of time that an immigrant has been in the United States and the degree of unionization in the industries in which illegal immigrants are employed positively influence the wage rates they earn. Employers have seldom hired illegal immigrants for jobs requiring substantial on-the-job training since the investment would be lost if the individual were to be apprehended and deported.[11] Enforcement of immigration laws primarily benefits legal residents in similar populations, but may not necessarily benefit low-skill workers in general. Restrictions on immigration would be expected to reduce national income since there would be an inadequate supply of individuals for available jobs at particular skill levels and wage rates.[12]

Labor Force Quality

Substantial increases in the educational level of the work force have occurred during the last two decades. For example, the proportion of the labor force who were college graduates or had some college education doubled while the proportion of persons with less than four years of high school declined from 41 percent to 15 percent. This increased educational quality is also associated with changes in the makeup of the unemployed. For example, over the period between 1967 and 1987, unemployment of individuals who had not graduated from high school increased from 4.3 to 11.1 percent while college graduates increased from 0.8 to 2.3 percent. During this same period, the unemployment rate for all individuals aged 25 to 64 increased from 3.0 to 5.7 percent. Jobs held by persons without high school diplomas were increasingly vulnerable to takeover by more highly educated individuals. This trend, however, should decline as the number of entrants to the labor force decreases during the remainder of the century.[13]

---

[11] B. R. Chiswick, "Illegal Aliens: A Preliminary Report on the Employer-Employee Survey," *American Economic Review* 76 (May 1986), pp. 253–57.

[12] W. J. Ethier, "Illegal Immigration: The Host-Country Problem," *American Economic Review* 76 (1986), 56–71.

[13] W. J. Howe, "Education and Demographics: How Do They Affect Unemployment Rates?" *Monthly Labor Review* 110 (1988), pp. 3–9.

Part- and Full-Time Work

Part-time work (defined by the BLS as 35 or fewer hours per week) has increased during the 1980s. Recent evidence shows that the majority of persons who work part time do so voluntarily. Larger proportions of individuals who work part time (both voluntarily and involuntarily) are women. Younger and older persons are more likely to have part-time schedules, but there are no differences between majorities and minorities.[14] Employees of temporary help agencies often work part time and are more frequently women, young, and black. They are most frequently employed as industrial helpers and clericals, groups that require little on-the-job training by employers.[15]

Federal Programs to Reduce Unemployment

After several years of government programs to reduce unemployment, which were primarily aimed at increasing labor demand in local areas, Congress enacted the Job Training Partnership Act (JTPA) to influence labor supply behavior. The JTPA provides grants to states for use in designated occupational areas in local communities. No public service employment is authorized by the legislation, and at least 70 percent of expenditures must go for training activities. Training programs generally last two years and are designed by private industry councils in designated service areas. States have responsibilities for overseeing funded projects.[16]

Trends in Labor Demand

The demand for labor is derived from the demands of consumers for the products and services labor produces. As consumer tastes change and as new products become available, the volume of demand for particular occupations changes. For example, when oil prices surged in the early

---

[14] T. J. Nardone, "Part-time Workers: Who Are They?" *Monthly Labor Review* 109 (February 1986), pp. 13–19.

[15] W. J. Howe, "Temporary Help Workers: Who They Are, What Jobs They Hold," *Monthly Labor Review* 109 (November 1986), pp. 45–47.

[16] R. Guttman, "Job Training Partnership Act: New Help for the Unemployed," *Monthly Labor Review* 106, no. 3 (1983), pp. 3–10. For early evidence on its implementation and results, see H. A. Hunt, K. Rupp, and Associates, "The Implementation of Title IIa of JTPA in the States and Service Delivery Areas: The New Partnership and Program Directions"; R. Cook, W. M. Turnage, and Associates, "The Title III Dislocated Worker Program"; and C. A. Haulman, F. A. Raffs, and B. Rungeling,, "Florida's JTPA Experience: Preliminary Observations," *Proceedings of the Industrial Relations Research Association* 37 (1984), pp. 85–106.

1970s, there was a great increase in demand for petroleum engineers to identify profitable areas for oil exploration. Other changes in labor demand occur as the result of changes in costs for other factors of production and the introduction of new production technologies. For example, as robots become increasingly versatile and productive or as their prices fall, the demand for assembly employees at present wages will fall. Employees may also find that different sets of skills are necessary, so the demands for certain types of training among potential employees may increase or decline.

Changing job requirements have an impact on the demand for employees by geographical area, industry, and occupation. Figures 3–2 and 3–3 present some occupational and industrial trends projected to occur between now and the year 2000. Trends are apparent that signal an increase in employment in nonmanufacturing industries with major net gains for wholesale trade, finance, and services.[17] In almost all of these industries, the demand for managers, technicians, salesworkers, and service workers will increase while the need for laborers, clericals, and precision production workers will increase far more slowly.[18] Many of the changes for individual employers will come as new plants are constructed and choices can be made about substituting machines for labor. An example of this approach is the increased use of robots for welding, painting, and other assembly operations in automobile manufacturing. This has occurred because robot prices have declined relative to wages and because health and safety regulations may require lower exposure rates to hazards and toxic materials than employers can economically meet.

Implications for P/HR Management Activities

Major trends in labor supply and demand concern P/HR professionals because they signal both unique opportunities and potential problems. Methods that can be used to meet these opportunities and overcome the problems are detailed in many of the later chapters. An assessment of the overall impact of recent changes is necessary here to point toward activities that can help.

Where unemployment was a societal problem during much of the

---

[17] For additional details, see V. A. Personick, "Industry Output and Employment through the End of the Century," *Monthly Labor Review* 109 (September 1987), pp. 30–45; and N. C. Saunders, "Economic Projections to the Year 2000," *Monthly Labor Review* 109 (September 1987), pp. 10–18.

[18] G. T. Silvestri and J. M. Likasiewicz, "A Look at Occupational Employment Trends to the Year 2000," *Monthly Labor Review* 109 (September 1987), pp. 46–63.

FIGURE 3-2

Employment by Broad Occupational Group, 1986 and Projected to 2000 Moderate Alternative, and Percent Change in Employment for Selected Periods (numbers in thousands)

Occupation	1986		Projected, 2000		Percent Change			
	Number	Percent	Number	Percent	1972–79	1979–86	1972–86	1986–2000
Total employment	111,623	100.0	133,030	100.0	20.3	10.9	33.4	19.2
Executive, administrative, and managerial workers	10,583	9.5	13,616	10.2	34.9	28.7	73.7	28.7
Professional workers	13,538	12.1	17,192	12.9	29.8	21.4	57.5	27.0
Technicians and related support workers	3,726	3.3	5,151	3.9	39.9	24.7	74.5	38.2
Salesworkers	12,606	11.3	16,334	12.3	24.3	24.4	54.6	29.6
Administrative support workers, including clerical	19,851	17.8	22,109	16.6	23.5	9.5	35.2	11.4
Private household workers	981	.9	955	.7	−23.0	−11.5	−31.9	−2.7
Service workers, except private household workers	16,555	14.8	21,962	16.5	25.7	16.0	45.9	32.7
Precision production, craft, and repair workers	13,924	12.5	15,590	11.7	21.7	6.5	29.6	12.0
Operators, fabricators, and laborers	16,300	14.6	16,724	12.6	8.7	−9.2	−1.3	2.6
Farming, forestry, and fishing workers	3,556	3.2	3,393	2.6	−5.1	−5.6	−10.4	−4.6

Source: G. T. Silvestri and J. M. Lukasiewicz, "A Look at Occupational Employment Trends for the Year 2000," *Monthly Labor Review* 110 (September 1987), p. 47.

FIGURE 3–3

Employment by Major Sector, 1972, 1979, 1986, and Projected to 2000

Employment (in thousands)

Sector	1972	1979	1986	Projected, 2000			Change, 1986–2000		
				Low	Moderate	High	Low	Moderate	High
Total	84,549	101,353	111,623	126,432	133,030	137,533	4,809	21,407	25,910
Nonfarm wage and salary	73,514	89,481	99,044	113,554	119,156	123,013	4,510	20,112	23,969
Goods producing	23,668	26,463	24,681	23,148	24,678	25,906	−1,533	−3	1,225
Mining	628	958	783	672	724	779	−111	−59	−4
Construction	3,889	4,463	4,904	5,643	5,794	6,077	739	890	1,173
Manufacturing	19,151	21,042	18,994	16,833	18,160	19,050	−2,161	−834	56
Durable	11,050	12,762	11,244	9,654	10,731	11,193	−1,590	−513	−51
Nondurable	8,101	8,280	7,750	7,179	7,429	7,857	−571	−321	107
Service producing	49,846	63,018	74,363	90,406	94,478	97,107	16,043	20,115	22,744
Transportation and public utilities	4,541	5,135	5,244	5,410	5,719	5,903	166	475	659
Wholesale trade	4,113	5,204	5,735	7,015	7,266	7,361	1,280	1,531	1,626
Retail trade	11,835	14,989	17,845	21,795	22,702	23,079	3,950	4,857	5,234
Finance, insurance, and real estate	3,907	4,975	6,297	7,508	7,917	8,159	1,211	1,620	1,862
Services	12,117	16,768	22,531	30,778	32,545	33,708	8,247	10,014	11,177
Government	13,333	15,947	16,711	17,900	18,329	18,897	1,189	1,618	2,186
Agriculture	3,523	3,401	3,252	2,784	2,917	3,009	−478	−335	−253
Private households	1,693	1,326	1,241	1,122	1,215	1,234	−119	−26	−7
Nonfarm self-employed and unpaid family workers	5,819	7,145	8,086	8,972	9,742	10,277	886	1,656	2,191

FIGURE 3-3 *(concluded)*

Sector	Average Annual Rate of Change (in percent)					Percent Distribution of Wage and Salary Employment					
				1986–2000					Projected, 2000		
	1972–79	1979–86	Low	Moderate	High	1972	1979	1986	Low	Moderate	High
Total	2.6	1.4	0.9	1.3	1.5	—	—	—	—	—	—
Nonfarm wage and salary	2.8	1.5	1.0	1.3	1.6	100.0	100.0	100.0	100.0	100.0	100.0
Goods-producing	1.6	−1.0	− .5	.0	.3	32.2	29.6	24.9	20.4	20.7	21.1
Mining	6.2	−2.8	−1.1	− .6	.0	.9	1.1	.8	.6	.6	.6
Construction	2.0	1.4	1.0	1.2	1.5	5.3	5.0	5.0	5.0	4.9	4.9
Manufacturing	1.4	−1.4	− .9	− .3	.0	26.1	23.5	19.2	14.8	15.2	15.5
Durable	2.1	−1.8	−1.1	− .3	.0	15.0	14.3	11.4	8.5	9.0	9.1
Nondurable	.3	.9	− .5	− .3	.1	11.0	9.3	7.8	6.3	6.2	6.4
Service producing	3.4	2.4	1.4	1.7	1.9	67.8	70.4	75.1	79.6	79.3	78.9
Transportation and public utilities	1.8	.3	.2	.6	.8	6.2	5.7	5.3	4.8	4.8	4.8
Wholesale trade	3.4	1.4	1.4	1.7	1.8	5.6	5.8	5.8	6.2	6.1	6.0
Retail trade	3.4	2.5	1.4	1.7	1.9	16.1	16.8	18.0	19.2	19.1	18.8
Finance insurance and real estate	3.5	3.4	1.3	1.7	1.9	5.3	5.6	6.4	6.6	6.6	6.6
Services	4.8	4.3	2.3	2.7	2.9	16.5	18.7	22.7	27.1	27.3	27.4
Government	2.6	.7	.5	.7	.9	18.1	17.8	16.9	15.8	15.4	15.4
Agriculture	− .5	− .6	−1.1	− .8	− .6	—	—	—	—	—	—
Private households	−3.4	− .9	− .7	− .1	.0	—	—	—	—	—	—
Nonfarm self-employed and unpaid family workers	3.0	1.8	.8	1.3	1.7	—	—	—	—	—	—

Source: V. A. Personick, "Industry Output and Employment Through the End of the Century," *Monthly Labor Review* 110 (September 1987), p. 32.

1980s, the lowered birthrate that began in the late 1960s is now being reflected in fewer younger persons entering the work force. Employers will be increasingly concerned with attracting and retaining employees during the remainder of the century. The changing occupational patterns match well the more extensive educational preparation of the work force, but there may be potential problems with long-service workers and changing occupational opportunities.

There will be a continuing problem, however, in the management of so-called baby boomers as they move through the organization. First, there may be relatively few promotional opportunities since many workers are available for a given position. Second, these workers may block promotional opportunities for more recent hires. Retention, then, may be a problem for these new hires.

The greatest pressures from this surge and decline in new labor force entrants will probably be in the staffing, training, and development areas, and in the design and administration of reward systems to motivate improved performance and skill development. Organizations should experience a better-quality work force from a better-educated labor supply, but may have more difficulty motivating employees during periods when jobs are relatively plentiful.

The increasing proportion of women who are participating in the labor force creates opportunities in personnel selection. As growing numbers of individuals do participate, employers will need increasingly to attend to child-care alternatives, flexible scheduling, and parental leave periods.

Major changes are taking place in the creation and dissolution of particular jobs.[19] This will mean that employers must attend more carefully to the selection, training and development, and compensation of employees in the future to provide opportunities and rewards for acquiring the skills that new occupations will require.[20]

These opportunities and problems indicate why P/HR managers must continuously monitor the labor market to recognize and anticipate situations that affect the demand for and supply of labor. Likely changes will influence the types of activities used. The P/HR manager must also be aware of the interests of labor unions and the legal constraints that govern the boundaries of personnel policies. Illustration 3–1 points out

---

[19] R. W. Rumberger, "The Changing Skill Requirements of Jobs in the U.S. Economy," *Industrial and Labor Relations Review* 34 (1981), pp. 578–90.

[20] J. A. Fossum, R. D. Arvey, C. A. Paradise, and N. E. Robbins, "Modeling the Skills Obsolescence Process: A Psychological and Economic Integration," *Academy of Management Review* 11 (1986), pp. 362–74.

ILLUSTRATION 3–1

Tomorrow's Jobs: Plentiful, But . . .

America's wondrous job-creation juggernaut rolls on and on, seemingly immune to trade deficits and stock market crashes, indifferent to whatever Democratic or Republican administration tries to take credit for it. The Bureau of Labor Statistics reports the U.S. economy has produced 31 million new jobs since 1972. It will add another 21 million by the end of the century.

This exuberant growth continues to astound Europeans, whose own job engine stalled long ago. Unemployment over the past four years has steadily declined in the United States to 5.6 percent, and steadily worsened in Europe to the present near-record 12 percent. And when American workers lose their jobs, they experience the world's shortest periods of unemployment—less than seven weeks for most versus six months in Europe and over three months in Japan.

But all is not joy in the new job market. One problem: a growing mismatch between the emerging jobs, which will call for increasingly higher levels of skill, and the people available to fill them. The number of workers entering the U.S. labor market has fallen to its lowest level in four decades. The newcomers will increasingly be women, disadvantaged minority workers, and non-English-speaking immigrants—more new immigrant labor than at any time since the end of World War I. The doddering public education system is leaving many of the new entrants ill-prepared.

Tomorrow's jobs are also bound to tax the resilience of the people holding them. The labor market will be a place of churning dislocation, of companies coming and going, jobs changing and being redefined, as the United States copes with rapid technological change and an ever more competitive global economy. The old career-long marriage between employer and employee is giving way to a series of one-night stands.

This is the downside of the powerful force that is producing the jobs in the first place—the "creative destruction" of capitalism, as Joseph A. Schumpeter called it. Flexibility is the oil that lubricates the job engine, allowing existing companies to abandon obsolete enterprises and new companies to meet new demands. The Europeans who heap scorn on America's "hire and fire" mindset have shackled their own economies with rigid labor laws and laid regulatory mine fields for the small businesses that generate new jobs. U.S. companies, by contrast, have been able to shift resources and workers nimbly as the competitive environment changes. Aspiring entrepreneurs face few hurdles to starting businesses, and if they fail, as most do, the lash of ignominy falls lightly.

The good news is that plenty of new jobs will be created tomorrow just where they are being created today: in small startup businesses. Entrepreneurs, those innovators *par excellence,* have been the midwives of job development, birthing new enterprises at the prodigious rate of 1.3 million each year. *Inc.* magazine reports that the number of employees in the 500 fastest-growing privately held companies jumped fivefold to over 500,000 in the past five years. David L. Birch, a consultant and author of the recent book *Job Creation in America,* calculates that roughly half a million expanding companies account for 95 percent of the new jobs since 1982.

Source: Louis R. Richman, "Tomorrow's Jobs: Plentiful, But . . . ," *Fortune,* April 11, 1988, pp. 42–56.

the opportunities and pitfalls facing employers and employees in the future.

LABOR UNIONS

Employees organized unions to exert their collective power vis-à-vis employers. In this way they can influence their levels of compensation, working conditions, job rights, and the like. Unionization means that many P/HR activities that involve organized employees are jointly determined by management and the union. The activities are then carried on by management, subject to monitoring by the union.

Like other organizations, unions have growth and survival goals. This means they must attend to the desires of their members and accomplish outcomes for them that they would be unable to achieve without the union. It is likely that unions will maintain an adversarial relationship with employers to continually attempt to achieve more and to be seen by their members as working hard. This is reasonable since unionization typically results from employee dissatisfaction with an employer's policies and because the union has prevailed in the face of substantial employer opposition. More will be said about the role of labor unions in Chapters 17 and 18.

Both labor and management are governed by laws and regulations that specify what types of activities are permissible and how collective bargaining will be conducted in the United States. These will be covered next.

LAWS AND REGULATIONS

Laws and regulations prescribe the types of practices that are either required or prohibited and the possible consequence of failing to abide by the requirements. Many laws and regulations follow economic or social changes that have affected the nation. In some instances, the laws apply to large segments of society; in others, they protect identified subgroups.

Several of the major U.S. employment laws directly stem from the economic conditions that prevailed during most of the 1930s. These laws generally have several purposes: (1) expanding employment, (2) compensating workers at levels that allow them to maintain at least a minimum standard of living, (3) providing income maintenance during periods of job loss, disability, or retirement, and (4) promoting employees' abilities to bargain collectively. In the 1960s, the emphasis shifted toward equal employment opportunity. The underlying legal system will be examined first, followed by comprehensive summaries of major employment laws and regulations in the United States.

The Legal System

Laws and regulations are passed by Congress and the legislatures of the 50 states. Many of these laws are implemented and enforced by administrative agencies. While federal laws establish the minimums to which employers must adhere, state laws can have more comprehensive requirements or regulations in areas federal laws may not address. For example, states may have minimum wage laws that apply to employees not covered under the Fair Labor Standards Act, or establish minimum wage rates at levels higher than those in the federal legislation.

Federal and state agencies involved in employment issues have a number of responsibilities. First, they write rules and procedures interpreting the legislation for employers and employees. After these rules have been promulgated, the agencies may inspect employers' activities to determine whether they conform to the regulations. Agencies may also investigate employees' complaints that laws and regulations are being violated. Some agencies are empowered to issue orders to employers to cease unlawful activities or order corrective procedures.

Informal methods are also available for settling allegations of violations. For example, both the National Labor Relations Board and the Equal Employment Opportunity Commission seek to settle disputes between complainants and employers when an alleged violation occurs. Complaints may be dismissed by such administrative agencies if mutually agreeable solutions, consistent with the laws, are reached.

Where employers (or unions) believe that administrative decisions are incorrect under the applicable laws, they may appeal these decisions. In the case of the National Labor Relations Board, all cases are first heard by an administrative law judge (ALJ). The ALJ renders a decision that is reviewed by board members, approved, disapproved, or modified. Then an order is issued. Under other laws, the agency may be required to go to a federal court to obtain a judgment against an employer. Here the court hears evidence of an alleged violation and renders a judgment. If the law was violated, the employer is required to make restitution to affected employees. Where the court finds no violation, the employer is permitted to continue the practice.

Where either agencies or employers feel that federal courts have incorrectly interpreted the law in reaching a decision, they may appeal to higher levels of the federal court system. Ultimately, some cases are appealed to the Supreme Court. These decisions help to clarify the intent and coverage of the law for all employers.

Labor-Management Relations

One branch of employment law in the United States regulates labor-management relations. Until the 1920s and early 1930s, this area was relatively unregulated, and the mood of the public was generally counter to the philosophy and tactics of the labor movement. But with the advent of the Great Depression, Congress passed laws to promote collective bargaining and balance the power of labor and management. Later, as the scales of power tipped toward unions and as certain groups within labor and management were found to be abusing their trust, Congress amended and passed new laws to restore the balance and to control the behavior of union and management officials.

Significant labor legislation began with the passage of the Railway Labor Act in 1926. This law enabled rail workers to be represented by unions in negotiations with employers (collective bargaining). The representation and bargaining rights accorded to rail workers were extended to most private-sector employees in 1935 with the passage of the Wagner Act.

To maintain the relative balance in bargaining power between employers and unions and to guarantee rights of individual union members, the Taft-Hartley Act was passed in 1947 and the Landrum-Griffin Act was signed into law in 1959. Chapter 17 contains more detail on the history and development of labor law.

The basic provisions, coverage, and administrative agencies involved with each major federal labor law are presented in Figure A3–1 in the appendix to this chapter. It should be noted that, in the public sector, federal employees are covered by Title VII of the Civil Service Reform Act of 1978 and that state and local employees are covered by the laws or court rulings in their 50 states.

Wage and Hour Laws

Most of the federal wage and hour laws were enacted in the 1930s. This was not the first activity in this area, however; in 1840 President Martin Van Buren's executive order limited the workday for employees on federal projects to 10 hours. Protective legislation limiting hours for women and children was passed by many states in the early 1900s.

Wage and hour laws generally are designed to require employers to pay not less than a minimum or a prevailing wage rate for covered employees. They also establish maximum numbers of hours covered employees can work before they are entitled to an overtime pay premium. The major federal wage and hour laws are either written to affect broad classes of employees in a large number of industries or to influence practices within a given industrial area. These laws apply to both non-federal public- and private-sector employers. A broad overview is contained in Figure A3–2 in the appendix.

Income Maintenance Programs

Income maintenance legislation was enacted during the 1930s to provide employees with income security during periods of retirement, disability, or employment and to provide benefits to family members in case of covered employees' deaths. The legislation generally requires employers (and sometimes employees) to pay a payroll tax to a governmental agency that, in turn, disburses benefits to eligible recipients. Figure A3–3 in the appendix provides a summary of the major legislation in this area. This area will be covered in substantial detail in Chapter 16.

Tax Laws

The Internal Revenue Code has both direct and indirect effects on P/HR management. The direct effects are related to requirements that organizations not discriminate in benefit programs between persons at different levels of the organization if they wish to deduct them as business expenses. The indirect effects are related to differential expensing of human and physical assets. When employers get incentives under the tax code for investing in equipment rather than employment, overall decreases in employment occur.

There have been substantial changes in tax laws as they apply to employment since the passage of the Tax Reform Act of 1986. Among other things, the marginal tax rates for both corporations and employees were decreased. This means that the costs of compensation (and other expenses) are higher to most organizations since they can deduct less, while the value of a given pay increase is greater to employees since—with lower marginal rates—employees have more spendable income.

The act also increases the need of employers to ensure that they do not discriminate between employee groups in the provision of benefits. The tax reform law defines two major groups of employees for tax purposes: highly compensated employees (HCEs) and nonhighly compensated employees (NHCEs). HCEs include anyone who (1) owns 5 percent or more of the company, (2) earns more than $75,000 per year, (3) earns more than $50,000 and is in the top 20 percent of all employees, or (4) is an officer of the company making more than $45,000. NHCEs are all others.

To gain favorable tax treatment for benefit plans, employers must ensure that at least 50 percent of all employees eligible to participate are

NHCEs; that at least 90 percent of NHCEs are eligible and will receive at least 50 percent of the benefits available to HCEs. Finally, the plan must not discriminate in the favor of HCEs.[21]

Safety and Health

Originally, safety and health legislation was enacted to protect coal miners. Comprehensive national legislation aimed at protecting employees in all industries was enacted in 1970. Mine safety acts were consolidated and strengthened in 1977. Basically, these acts require employers to remove hazards and correct environmental conditions likely to contribute to accidents or poor health. The operation of the acts and employer responses are covered in detail in Chapter 20. Figure A3–4 in the appendix summarizes the major provisions of the present acts.

Immigration Law

The Immigration Reform and Control Act took effect in 1987. Its major provisions prohibit employers from knowingly hiring an alien who is not authorized to work in the United States. Employers, however, are forbidden to discriminate on the basis of national origin and to thereby reduce job opportunities for persons who belong to ethnic groups with high illegal immigration rates.[22]

Employers are required to check the legal status of all employees hired after November 6, 1986. Employers must fill out an I-9 form for each new hire and have these forms available for inspection by the Immigration and Naturalization Service (INS). Employers are now penalized if they have failed to ascertain the legal status of their workers.[23]

THE SPECIAL CASE OF EQUAL EMPLOYMENT OPPORTUNITY

The summaries of major laws and regulations in Figures A3–1 through A3–4 show that, with few exceptions, each touches on a limited aspect of P/HR management (such as compensation). Because of this, many of

---

[21] B. T. Beam, Jr., and J. J. McFadden, *Employee Benefits*, 2d ed. (Homewood, Ill.: Richard D. Irwin, 1988), pp. 72–74.

[22] *Daily Labor Report*, October 7, 1987, pp. AA–1.

[23] See M. E. Recio, "Reform Breeds Its Own Crisis," *Business Week*, March 30, 1987, pp. 26–27.

these laws and regulations are discussed in more detail in appropriate chapters later in the text.

Equal Employment Opportunity (EEO) laws and regulations are a different matter. They are much more diverse in effect because they prohibit discrimination in virtually all P/HR activities. Thus, an explanation of their major provisions is most appropriate at this point. Treatment of their specific provisions, and their implications for P/HR management, is included in appropriate chapters. Figure A3–5 in the appendix summarizes EEO laws and regulations.

The two major sources of regulations governing EEO and P/HR management practices are Title VII of the Civil Rights Act of 1964 (as amended) and Executive Order 11246 (as amended).

Title VII of the Civil Rights Act (as Amended)

Basic provisions and coverage

Originally passed in 1964, Title VII was amended by the Equal Employment Opportunity Act of 1972. The act prohibits discrimination in all terms and conditions of employment on the basis of race, color, national origin, religion, and sex. This act applies to private employers with more than 15 employees, unions, employment agencies, state and local governments, and educational institutions. Thus, coverage under Title VII is very broad.

Lawful practices

While Title VII's focus is on defining unlawful (discriminatory) practices, it also states three lawful practices.

Discrimination based on national origin, religion, and sex (but not race or color) is permitted if it can be shown that the characteristic is a *bona fide (genuine) occupational qualification* (BFOQ) necessary for the operation of the business. A men's fashion designer, for example, might reasonably argue that having only men as models in a fashion show is a bona fide occupational qualification.

A second provision is that it is permissible to use professionally developed tests for making hiring and promotion decisions. However, the tests must not be designed, intended, or used to discriminate.

Finally, differential treatment of employees in their terms and conditions of employment is permissible with the use of bona fide seniority and merit systems in which employees are selected for, say, promotions based either on their length of service (seniority) or their performance (merit). This provision applies in particular to compensation, promotion, transfer, and layoffs. The systems must not have been designed with a discriminatory intent, however.

Enforcement and remedies

Responsibility for enforcement of Title VII lies with the Equal Employment Opportunity Commission (EEOC), an independent federal agency. Charges of discrimination may be filed with the EEOC by an individual who feels discrimination has occurred. Or the EEOC may file charges of discrimination, and the charges may be very broad, encompassing more than a single individual (for example, all women in the organization's work force). The EEOC may also defer to a state anti-discrimination agency whose practices it has approved.

The party charging discrimination (that is, the plaintiff) must present evidence of reasonable cause to assume that discrimination has occurred. Often this involves the use of statistical data, such as differences in hiring rates for men and women or a comparison of the percentage of minorities on a particular job relative to their availability in the labor market.[24] If reasonable cause is shown, the burden of proof then shifts to the party being charged with discrimination (that is, the defendant). At this point, the defendant must present evidence that the employment practice in question is justified based on business necessity or job relatedness.

In this whole process, the EEQC must first attempt to conciliate the charge with the employer, thus obtaining voluntary (out-of-court) compliance with Title VII. If informal attempts do not succeed, the EEOC may file formal charges in federal court.

When the court finds an organization guilty of discrimination, Title VII provides for the use of certain remedies. These include reinstatement of previous employees, back-pay awards (up to two years *before* the filing of the charge), payment of attorneys' fees, and an order to develop a specific affirmative action plan (AAP). AAPs are systematic attempts to enhance employment opportunities for women, minorities, the handicapped, and other groups who have had great difficulty in either obtaining employment or being employed at levels equal to their qualifications.

---

[24] See R. D. Arvey, *Fairness in Selecting Employees* (Reading, MA: Addison-Wesley Publishing, 1979), pp. 47–57; W. H. Holley, Jr., and H. S. Feild, "Using Statistics in Employment Discrimination Cases," *Employee Relations Law Journal* 4 (1978), pp. 43–58; F. S. Hills, "Job Relatedness vs. Adverse Impact in Personnel Decision Making," *Personnel Journal* 59 (1980), pp. 211–29; and J. Ledvinka, *Federal Regulation of Personnel and Human Resource Management*, 2d ed. (Boston: Kent, 1989), pp. 89–116.

Title VII does *not* require AAPs. However, it permits AAPs under three sets of circumstances. First, the organization may simply adopt its own without any reasonable cause being shown. Second, as part of a voluntary settlement with the EEOC, the organization may agree to implement an AAP. Finally, courts may impose an AAP on an organization found guilty of discrimination. (AAPs are treated in more detail in Chapter 8.)

Evidence indicates that organizations that establish affirmative action goals and timetables for underused groups hire more members of those groups than organizations that do not. Moreover, the more ambitious the goals, the greater the numbers hired.[25]

Guidelines

Less direct enforcement of Title VII by the EEOC is achieved by issuing various written guidelines. These guidelines spell out the EEOC's interpretation of the meaning of Title VII and of legally permissible employment practices. Technically, these *guidelines* are just what the term implies—guides to action. However, many people continue to argue that in reality the guidelines become used as rigid rules and standards for assessing employer compliance with Title VII.

The most important guidelines are the 1978 Uniform Guidelines on Employee Selection Procedures.[26] These guidelines apply to the operation of both external and internal staffing systems. They require the organization to determine if there is *adverse impact* in selection by comparing the hiring rates for various groups (for example, men and women). If the rates are sufficiently different to warrant the conclusion that adverse impact is occurring, the guidelines then specify what actions the employer must take. These steps include eliminating the adverse impact or justifying the staffing system as job related through the conduct of what are known as validation studies. (These are described in Chapter 10.)

Many other guidelines have been issued by the EEOC. These include guidelines dealing with (1) national origin discrimination, (2) sex discrimination, (3) religious discrimination, (4) pregnancy, and (5) sexual

---

[25] J. S. Leonard, "What Promises Are Worth: The Impact of Affirmative Action Goals," *Journal of Human Resources* 20 (1985), pp. 3–20; and J. S. Leonard, "The Impact of Affirmative Action on Employment," *Journal of Labor Economics* 2 (1984), pp. 439–63.

[26] "Uniform Guidelines on Employee Selection Procedures," *Federal Register* 43 (1978), pp. 38, 290–315.

harassment.[27] Because it administers the Age Discrimination in Employment Act, the EEOC has also issued guidelines in this area.[28]

Executive Order 11246 (as Amended)

An executive order (EO) is issued by the president, without approval by Congress, but it has the weight of law. To further attack problems of employment discrimination, EO 11246 was issued in 1967 and has been subsequently amended. It prohibits most federal contractors from employment discrimination on the basis of race, color, national origin, religion, and sex. It also requires large employers covered by the executive order to develop and implement written AAPs for women and minorities. These plans are necessary even though there may be no evidence of discriminatory practices by the employer.

Enforcement

Wide powers were granted the secretary of labor in administering and enforcing the EO. Accordingly, the Office of Federal Contract Compliance Programs (OFCCP) in the Department of Labor was created and given responsibility for the order's day-to-day administration and enforcement. In turn, the OFCCP has issued several regulations and guidelines.

Compliance with the EO and attendant regulations is monitored by the OFCCP through periodic compliance reviews of employers. Findings of noncompliance may result in various penalties, such as cancellation of contracts and disqualification from bidding on future contracts.

Sexual Harassment

Perhaps the area of Title VII Civil Rights enforcement that has received the most attention recently is sexual harassment. The EEOC has issued guidelines requiring that employers prevent situations in which employees are coerced into sexual affairs as a condition of continued employment, pay increase, promotions, and the like. Recently, the Supreme Court decided in *Vinson* v. *Meritor Savings* that the employer also has a responsibility to ensure a working environment that is free of sexual intimidation or hostility.

---

[27] See *Fair Employment Practices Manual* (Washington, D.C.: Bureau of National Affairs, continually updated); and R. G. Schaeffer, *Nondiscrimination in Employment—and Beyond* (New York: The Conference Board, 1980).

[28] For a discussion, see P. S. Greenlaw and J. P. Kohl, "Age Discrimination in Employment Guidelines," *Personnel Journal* 61 (1982), pp. 224–28.

Evidence suggests that women label sexual behaviors and innuendoes at work as harassment more frequently than men. However, in jobs where there is a substantial balance between the proportions of men and women, there is both a greater tolerance for what might pass as harassment in another situation and lower incidents of harassment complaints.[29]

It is not clear at this time what an employer's liability would be for sexual harassment. However, several precautions should lessen the likelihood of potential problems. These include a broadly publicized straightforward policy prohibiting harassment, a grievance procedure that does not require going through one's immediate supervisor, and supervisory training to avoid supervisors' using harassment.[30]

Age Discrimination in Employment Act (ADEA)

Employers are forbidden by ADEA to make employment decisions based on age for persons over 40. There is no upper age limit. Employees may not be mandatorily retired unless they are in bona fide executive positions or are tenured faculty members.

Additionally, employers may no longer prohibit employees from participating in noncontributory pension programs after age 65 and must continue to allow employees to participate in group health insurance plans even after they become eligible for medicare. They must also allow their insurance carriers to be the primary provider for claims.

EMPLOYMENT AND ACQUIRED IMMUNE DEFICIENCY SYNDROME (AIDS)

As the 1980s continue, almost all large firms and many medium and smaller firms have experienced one or more cases of AIDS in their work forces. At this point, however, few organizations have formulated specific policies to govern how AIDS cases will be handled. Of those that do have policies, most cover issues related to leaves of absence and shifts to part-time employment. Some companies provide education, counseling, and the like for employees and work groups where a stricken employee

---

[29] A. M. Konrad and B. A. Gutek, "Impact of Work Experiences on Attitudes toward Sexual Harassment," *Administrative Science Quarterly* 31 (1986), pp. 422–38.

[30] For varying interpretations of court decisions on sexual harassment, see V. E. Hauck and T. G. Pearce, "*Vinson:* Sexual Harassment and Employer Response," *Labor Law Journal* 38 (1987), pp. 770–75; C. F. Cohen, "Legal Dilemmas in Sexual Harassment Cases," *Labor Law Journal* 38 (1987), pp. 681–88; and S. Oglebay and S. E. Kobak, "Predicting Employer Liability for Sexual Harassment," *Employee Relations Law Journal* 12 (1987), pp. 412–23.

works. Many companies have long- and short-run disability programs that include AIDS, along with other diseases and disabilities.

Companies are also concerned with the costs of AIDS. With the exception of a few isolated health care organizations, employers are not testing for AIDS among applicants or present employees.[31] Refusing to hire or firing an employee with AIDS would probably be a violation of the Vocational Rehabilitation Act of 1973 and–depending on where the firm is located–could violate state laws that prohibit discrimination where the disability does not affect the ability to do the specific work required.[32]

Increasing AIDS rates have an adverse impact on premiums for employer group health and life insurance plans. Treatment of an AIDS case has averaged about $150,000, but in San Francisco, this has been decreased to between $25,000 and $47,000, about 50 percent to two thirds the cost of a moderately severe heart problem or cancer.[33]

SUMMARY

Economic conditions create the business in which jobs are created and lost, and in which P/HR activities take place. Other major external influences that have an impact on P/HR management are labor markets and laws and regulations. Firms with organized employees also are influenced by unions. Participants in labor markets are those persons who are working (employed) or looking for work (unemployed). Data on past and present characteristics of labor markets are gathered and published by the Bureau of Labor Statistics in the Department of Labor. Current trends in the labor force indicate that the participation rate for women has increased dramatically over the last several years. This change, combined with the entry of a large number of persons generated by the post-World War II baby boom, has created a relatively large supply of potential employees. This supply, however, will decrease as lower birthrate groups enter the labor supply in the 1990s and beyond.

The federal government regulates and constrains many P/HR prac-

---

[31] For arguments and responses related to whether to test, see D. W. Myers and P. S. Myers, "Arguments Involving AIDS Testing in the Workplace," *Labor Law Journal* 38 (1987), pp. 582–90.

[32] W. J. Kandel, "AIDS in the Work Place," *Employee Relations Law Journal* 11 (1986), pp. 678–90.

[33] For an overview of employer responses, see "Companies Found Not Adding AIDS Policies; Task Force to Draw up Guidelines," *Employee Relations Weekly*, November 2, 1987, p. 1371.

tices. Where labor unions exist, laws govern the conduct of collective bargaining. Employers must adhere to certain rules regarding pay, including minimum wage levels, premiums for overtime, and non-discrimination in wage setting. Legislation mandates participation in plans to ensure steady income levels for employees who are disabled, retired, or unemployed. Rules have been established to require certain environmental arrangements to increase the health and safety of employees. Perhaps the most pervasive rules exist in the area of equal employment opportunity. Employers must take steps to eliminate discrimination on the basis of race, sex, religion, color, national origin, and age. Where evidence of possible discrimination exists, affirmative action may have to be taken to provide opportunities for groups of people to whom they have been denied.

DISCUSSION QUESTIONS

1. Should the BLS measures of the labor force pay more attention to the questions of underemployment and the identification of discouraged workers?

2. What major impacts will the "baby bust" have on staffing organizations in the future, the changing demand for industrial output, and the social security system over the next 40 years?

3. Are the decreasing unemployment levels seen during the last few years reflective of demographic changes in the labor force or problems in the economy in creating jobs?

4. Are affirmative action plans justified because of past discrimination by organizations, or is it unfair to currently give women and minorities preferential treatment?

APPENDIX

LAWS REGULATING P/HR MANAGEMENT

FIGURE A3–1
Federal Labor Law

Law	Coverage	Major Provisions	Federal Agencies
Railway Labor Act	Nonmanagerial rail and airline employees and employers in private sector.	Employees may choose bargaining representative for collective bargaining, no yellow-dog contracts, dispute settlement procedures including mediation, arbitration, and emergency boards.	National Mediation Board, National Board of Adjustment.
Norris-LaGuardia Act	All private sector employers and labor organizations.	Outlaws injunctions for nonviolent union activities. Outlaws yellow-dog contracts.	
Labor-Management Relations Act (originally passed as Wagner Act, amended by Taft-Hartley Act and Landrum-Griffin Act)	Nonmanagerial employees in nonagricultural private sector not covered by Railway Labor Act, postal workers.	Employees may choose bargaining representative for collective bargaining. Both labor and management must bargain in good faith. Unfair labor practices include discrimination for union activities, secondary boycotts, refusal to bargain. National emergency dispute procedures.	National Labor Relations Board, Federal Mediation and Conciliation Service.

FIGURE A3–1 *(concluded)*

Law	Coverage	Major Provisions	Federal Agencies
Landrum-Griffin Act	All private sector employers and labor organizations.	Specification and guarantee of individual rights of union members. Prohibits certain management and union conduct. Requires union financial disclosures.	U.S. Department of Labor.
Civil Service Reform Act, Title VII	All nonuniformed, nonmanagerial federal service employees and agencies.	Employees may choose bargaining representative for collective bargaining. Bargaining rights on noneconomic and nonstaffing issues. Requires arbitration of unresolved grievances.	Federal Labor Relations Authority.

Source: J. A. Fossum, *Labor Relations: Development, Structure, Process,* 4th ed. (Homewood, Ill: BPI/Irwin, 1989), p. 57.

FIGURE A3-2
Federal Wage and Hour Laws

Law	Coverage	Major Provisions	Federal Agencies
Fair Labor Standards Act (FLSA)	Private and nonfederal public-sector employers involved in interstate commerce with two or more employees and having annual revenues greater than $362,500. Exemptions from overtime provisions for managers, supervisors, and executives; outside salespersons and professional workers.	For covered employees, a minimum wage of at least $3.35 per hour; time and one half pay for over 40 hours per week; and restrictions on employment by occupation or industry for persons under 18.	Wage and Hour Division of the Employment Standards Administration, U.S. Department of Labor.
Walsh-Healy Act	Federal contractors manufacturing or supplying goods to the federal government with a value of over $10,000 annually.	Employers must pay wages not less than those prevailing in the area for the type of employment used. Overtime at time and one half for over 8 hours per day and/or 40 hours per week.	Same as FLSA.
Davis-Bacon Act	Federal contractors involved in construction projects with a value in excess of $2,000.	Same as Walsh-Healy.	Comptroller General and Wage and Hour Division.
Service Contracts Act	Federal contractors involved in providing services to the federal government with a value in excess of $2,500.	Same as Walsh-Healy for wages. Blacklisting of deficient contractors.	Same as Davis-Bacon.

FIGURE A3–3
Income Maintenance Laws

Law	Coverage	Funding	Benefits	Agencies
Social Security Act	Retirees, dependent survivors, disabled persons who are insured by payroll taxes on their past earnings or earnings of heads of households. Railroad workers are excluded.	Payroll tax of 7.51 percent on first $45,000 of earnings by *both* employer and employee in 1988. Base earnings from 1984 on equal the ratio of the average covered wages in year minus 2 divided by the average in year minus 3 times the year minus one base.	Retirement payments after age 65, or at reduced rates after 62, to worker and spouse. Survivor's benefits to widow over 60, or widow with dependent children under 18, and dependent children under 18. Disability benefits to totally disabled workers and their children. Health insurance for persons over 65 (medicare). All benefits are automatically adjusted whenever the consumer price index increases by more than 3 percent in a calendar year.	Social Security Administration.

FIGURE A3–3 *(continued)*

Law	Coverage	Funding	Benefits	Agencies
Federal Unemployment Tax Act	All employees except some state and local government, domestics and farm workers, railroad workers, some not-for-profit employers.	Payroll tax of at least 6.2 percent of first $7,000 of earnings paid by employer (except employee also taxed in Alabama, Alaska, California, Pennsylvania, Puerto Rico, and New Jersey). States may raise the percentage and base figures through legislation. Employer contributions may be reduced to not less than 0.8 percent if state experience ratings for them are low.	Generally benefits are available to persons for some specified minimum period who have lost their jobs through no fault of their own. Most states exclude strikers. Benefits average somewhat less than 50 percent of average weekly earnings in the state and are available for up to 26 weeks. During periods of high unemployment, benefits may be extended up to 52 weeks.	U.S. Bureau of Employment Security, U.S. Training & Employment Service, the 50 state employment security commissions.
Workers' Compensation (state laws)	In most states, employees of nonagricultural private-sector firms are entitled to benefits for work-related accidents and illnesses leading to temporary or permanent disabilities.	Depending on the state law, employers may have one or more of the following options: a payroll-based payment to a state insurance system, insurance through a private carrier, or self-insurance, insurance rates depend on the riskiness of the occupation and the experience rating of the insured.	Generally, benefits are around two thirds of an employee's weekly wage and continue for the term of the disability. Other payments are made for medical care and rehabilitative services. Survivor benefits are available if an accident is fatal.	Various state commissions.

FIGURE A3–3 *(concluded)*

Law	Coverage	Funding	Benefits	Agencies
Employee Retirement Income Security Act	All private sector employees over 21 whose employers have a noncontributory retirement plan benefit.	Employer contributions for retirement benefits (voluntary or negotiated fringe benefits).	Under a variety of formulas provides for vesting (ownership) of retirement benefits after a certain length of service even if tenure later ceases. Accrued pension benefits have tax-free portability if employee with vested benefits changes jobs. Employers must fund plans on an actuarially sound basis. Pension trustees must make prudent investments. Vested benefits may be insured by employer through Pension Benefit Guaranty Corporation.	Department of Labor, Internal Revenue Service, Pension Benefit Guaranty Corporation.

Source: U.S. Department of Labor, Employment Standards Administration, *State Workmen's Compensation Laws: A Comparison of Major Provisions with Recommended Standards*, Bulletin 212 (Washington, D.C.: U.S. Government Printing Office, 1971); National Commission of State Workmen's Compensation Laws, *Report* (Washington, D.C.: U.S. Government Printing Office, 1972); *Labor Relations Reporter* (Washington, D.C.: Bureau of National Affairs, updated as necessary); F. R. Marshall, A. M. Cartter, and A. G. King, *Labor Economics: Wages, Employment, and Trade Unionism*, 3d ed. (Homewood, Ill.: Richard D. Irwin, 1976), pp. 473–87, 502–6; *BNA Pension Reporter* (Washington, D.C.: Bureau of National Affairs, September 16, 1974), pp. C6–C20.

FIGURE A3-4
Safety and Health Legislation

Law	Coverage	Major Provisions	Federal Agencies
Occupational Safety and Health Act (OSHA)	Private-sector employers except domestic service employers. Excludes employers covered by Federal Mine Safety Act.	Employers have a general duty to provide working conditions that will not harm their employees. So that employees may know specific standards of care they must use regulations and guidelines are published by the Department of Labor. Agents inspect workplaces with appropriate authorization and may issue citations calling for corrections and penalties. If an employer disputes a citation, a review commission determines its appropriateness. Enforcement authority may be given to states after they have passed laws consistent with OSHA.	Occupational Safety and Health Administration, National Institute for Occupational Safety and Health, Occupational Safety and Health Review Commission.
Federal Mine Safety Act	Employees in underground and surface mining operations.	Establishes procedures for identifying and eliminating exposure to toxic and other harmful materials and for inspecting mines. Mandates health and safety training. Provides benefits for pneumoconiosis (black lung disease).	Mine Safety and Health Administration, Federal Mine Safety and Health Review Commission.

FIGURE A3–5
Equal Employment Opportunity Legislation and Orders

Law or Order	Coverage	Major Provisions	Federal Agencies
Civil Rights Act of 1964, Title VII (as amended)	Private-sector employers with 15 or more employees, state and local governments, federal service workers; unions; employment agencies.	Discrimination in employment decisions prohibited on the basis of race, sex, religion, color, and national origin.	Equal Employment Opportunity Commission (EEOC).
Age Discrimination in Employment Act (as amended)	Persons over age 40 (except between 40 and 65 for bona fide executives).	Prohibits discrimination in employment decisions or mandatory retirement.	EEOC.
Executive Order 11246 (as amended)	Federal contractors and subcontractors.	Contractors underutilizing minorities and women must specify goals and timetables to affirmatively recruit, select, train, and promote individuals from underutilized groups.	Office of Federal Contract Compliance Programs (OFCCP).
Vocational Rehabilitation Act of 1973	Federal contractors and subcontractors.	Contractors must develop AA programs to employ handicapped persons.	OFCCP.
Veterans Readjustment Act of 1974	Federal contractors and subcontractors.	Contractors must develop AA programs to employ Vietnam era veterans. Job openings must be listed with state employment services which will give veterans priority on referrals.	OFCCP.
Equal Pay Act of 1963	Most employers.	Men and women must be paid equal pay for jobs requiring equal skill, effort, responsibility, and working conditions.	EEOC.

PART TWO

Individuals and Jobs

4

Employee Ability and Job Analysis

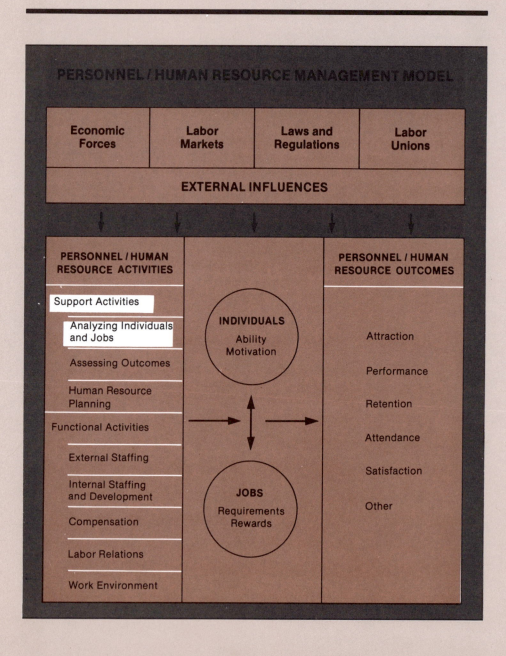

PERSONNEL / HUMAN RESOURCE MANAGEMENT MODEL

Economic Forces	Labor Markets	Laws and Regulations	Labor Unions

EXTERNAL INFLUENCES

PERSONNEL / HUMAN RESOURCE ACTIVITIES

Support Activities

Analyzing Individuals and Jobs

Assessing Outcomes

Human Resource Planning

Functional Activities

External Staffing

Internal Staffing and Development

Compensation

Labor Relations

Work Environment

INDIVIDUALS

Ability
Motivation

JOBS

Requirements
Rewards

PERSONNEL / HUMAN RESOURCE OUTCOMES

Attraction

Performance

Retention

Attendance

Satisfaction

Other

After reading this chapter you should be able to speak to the questions posed in each of the following personnel/human resource incidents:

1.   As the recruiter for the data processing department of the Washburn Bank, NT&SA, a large commercial bank, you have come to the conclusion that it is time to revise the job descriptions for systems analysts. The positions have changed significantly over the past years, and it is necessary to reevaluate them for compensation purposes. What factors should be considered in revising the job descriptions? Is a new approach advisable? How might you justify the time and expense to your superiors?

2.   Your organization, Long Lake Live Bait Company, has decided that it is time for it to have written job descriptions and specifications. The company began in the president's boathouse 15 years ago by selling worms and minnows. Since then it has branched out into worm farming and gathering, minnow seining and marketing, leech harvesting and marketing, and has recently moved into walleye pike farming to supply restaurants around the nation. In the past, when the company was small, all employees knew what their basic responsibilities and requirements were. But now, with several different operations and almost 200 employees, questions are beginning to occur about what is necessary to perform in each of the jobs. How should the company go about gathering job information? What has to be considered when a particular job analysis technique is being evaluated?

3.   You are the chair of a task force responsible for choosing an external consultant to provide a job analysis method for your organization. Your company would like the results of the approach to have utility for staffing, training, and compensation purposes. Avery Associates recommends an observation/interview approach that will yield both job descriptions and specifications for all job families. Human Resource Information Services recommends a person-oriented checklist developed on a national sample of employees that will be given to all employees to develop job specifications. Industrial/Organizational Psychology Counselors, Inc. proposes to develop task statements describing present jobs and then use a statistical technique to cluster them into occupational groupings and use the groupings as a direct method for obtaining job descriptions. What criteria should the task force use to evaluate the proposals? Which consultant seems to be the closest to offering a package to meet your needs? What additional analyses or modifications would you need to meet your requirements?

FIGURE 4-1

The Correspondence between Individual and Job Characteristics

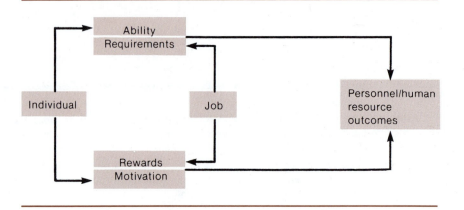

The P/HR activities addressed in this book are aimed primarily at influencing employee behaviors and attitudes such as joining an organization, performing, attending work, remaining with the organization, and achieving job satisfaction. As the general model shows, two characteristics of jobs and two characteristics of people are especially important in this regard.[1]

Major job characteristics include *requirements* and *rewards*. Job requirements refer to the knowledge and skills (resulting from ability and experience) necessary to perform the job. Job rewards are potentially attractive or unattractive consequences of working. They include aspects of the work itself, the social environment (including supervision and co-workers), and the results of P/HR policies and practices as they apply to areas such as pay, discipline, and promotion.

The two critical employee characteristics are the *ability* to engage in specific behaviors—that is, the individual's current capabilities—and *motivation*—that is, the individual's willingness to engage in the specific behaviors.

Ability and motivation combine with job requirements and rewards to influence the performance of specific behaviors leading to P/HR outcomes, as shown in Figure 4-1. The correspondence or overlap between the ability of the individual and the requirements of the job largely

---

[1] The model presented here is based in part on R. V. Dawis, L. H. Lofquist, and D. J. Weiss, "A Theory of Work Adjustment: A Revision," *Minnesota Studies in Vocational Rehabilitation* 23 (Minneapolis: Industrial Relations Center, University of Minnesota, 1968), It departs from the theory of work adjustment most significantly regarding the role of motivation in understanding P/HR outcomes.

determines whether the individual is capable of performing as the organization expects. The correspondence between the individual's motivation and the rewards of the job, alternatively, substantially influences whether the individual is willing to behave as the organization desires.

The distinctions between individual ability and motivation and job requirements and rewards are essential to understanding how P/HR can aid in enhancing desired outcome behavior. In this chapter, the discussion focuses on employee ability and job requirements. The next chapter will focus on employee motivation and job rewards. Taken together, these two chapters serve as a basis for understanding how P/HR activities operate to influence P/HR outcomes.

EMPLOYEE ABILITY

As indicated, ability refers to the individual's capability to engage in a specific behavior. Areas of concern to P/HR management include the individual's ability to join, to attend work, and to remain with the organization. The major focus on ability by organizations has been in predicting future job performance and in shaping the ability to perform in a changing job environment through training and development activities.

While individual differences were recognized by early Greek philosophers, their systematic definition and measurement originated in the late 1800s shortly after Darwin's work kindled interests in variation, inheritance, and evolution.[2] Ability measurement as we know it today was begun by Alfred Binet, a French psychologist, who published the first model mental ability test in 1905.[3] Early tests were aimed at measuring students' scholastic abilities. During World War I, psychologists developed mental measures for adults that were helpful in placing soldiers in military jobs. The measures spread rapidly to industry following the war, and their usage has increased in specificity and sophistication since these applied beginnings.

The identification and measurement of human abilities have proven difficult. While a comparison of theories about the nature of human abilities may yield contradictions,[4] these unsettled issues have not prevented the development of a useful set of measures for use in applied settings that assist in evaluating the performance levels of employees.

---

[2] A review of the history of ability measurement can be found in L. J. Cronbach, *Essentials of Psychological Testing*, 4th ed. (New York: Harper & Row, 1984), pp. 191–205.

[3] Ibid.

[4] L. E. Tyler, *Individual Differences: Abilities and Motivational Directions* (Englewood Cliffs, N.J.: Prentice-Hall, 1974), pp. 67–87.

Specific abilities in individuals are important to organizations because jobs require certain behaviors for successful performance. Job requirements can thus be thought of as *ability requirements* from an employee-characteristic standpoint. To match individuals to jobs—or to improve their abilities to perform—specific, job-related abilities must be defined and measured. Much work has been done on creating taxonomies of human abilities.[5] The next section examines major types of abilities.

Types of Abilities

In Chapter 11, examples of specific ability measures are discussed in conjunction with their use for selection of employees. Therefore, only the general nature of the abilities measured by those tests will be discussed in this section.

Intellectual abilities

Because early efforts to measure ability focused on school success, psychologists quite naturally concentrated on *intellectual* abilities, and Binet's test was such a measure. Despite the apparent success in measuring intelligence, a number of difficult questions remained. One pertained to the meaning or definition of intelligence. Many early investigators viewed intelligence as representing an individual's *inherent* capacity to learn. While such a view makes sense conceptually, it clearly does not reflect what intelligence tests measure. At best, measures reflect the individual's *current* capacity—whatever has been learned from whatever source. Thus, current definitions tend to emphasize that intelligence represents the individual's ability to solve problems that society regards as important.[6] Such a definition acknowledges the possibility that the definition itself may change as the values of society change.[7]

A related problem has to do with the organization of intelligence, its specificity or generality. One approach viewed intelligence as a global characteristic. A person's performance on one intellectual dimension was assumed to be predictive of (highly related to) his or her performance on any other dimension. Another approach assumed that intelligence in-

[5] See E. A. Fleishman and M. K. Quaintance, *Taxonomies of Human Performance* (New York: Academic Press, 1984), pp. 306–53.

[6] C. T. Fischer, "Intelligence Defined as Effectiveness of Approaches," *Journal of Consulting and Clinical Psychology* 33 (1969), pp. 668–74.

[7] D. Weschsler, "Intelligence Defined and Undefined: A Relativistic Appraisal," *American Psychologist* 30 (1975), pp. 135–39.

FIGURE 4-2
Intellectual Abilities

Verbal comprehension: To understand the meaning of words and their relations to each other; to comprehend readily and accurately what is read.

Word fluency: To be fluent in naming or making words, such as making smaller words from the letters in a large one or playing anagrams.

Number aptitude: To be speedy and accurate in making simple arithmetic calculations.

Inductive reasoning: To be able to discover a rule or principle and apply it to the solution of a problem, such as determining what is to come next in a series of numbers or words.

Memory: To have a good rote memory for paired words, lists of numbers, and so forth.

Perceptual speed: To perceive visual details quickly and accurately.

Spatial aptitude: To perceive fixed geometric relations among figures accurately and to be able to visualize their manipulation in space.

Source: Adapted from M. D. Dunnette, *Personnel Selection and Placement* (Belmont, Calif.: Wadsworth, 1966), pp. 47–49. Copyright © 1966 by Wadsworth, Inc. Adapted by permission of the publisher, Brooks/Cole Publishing Company, Monterey, California.

volves many separate (independent) abilities. The theoretical debate has now largely subsided with the growing recognition of truth in both views. People appear to have both general (all dimensions tend to be somewhat related) and specific (people differ in their patterns of abilities) intelligences.[8] These special intellectual abilities are often assumed to fall into the major categories shown in Figure 4–2.

Psychomotor abilities

A second class of abilities that affects work performance has to do with physical capabilities controlled by cognitive processes. These are often referred to as "psychomotor abilities." One classification identifying 11 different categories of physical abilities is shown in Figure 4–3. Research has also shown that there is little relationship among the level of these abilities that a given individual possesses.[9]

Differences in Ability

Individual differences

Individuals differ substantially in the abilities they bring to the work environment. One type, *interindividual differences*, refers to differences

---

[8] Tyler, *Individual Differences*, pp. 82–83.

[9] E. J. McCormick and J. Tiffin, *Industrial Psychology*, 6th ed. (Englewood Cliffs, N.J.: Prentice-Hall, 1974), pp. 147–48.

FIGURE 4–3
Psychomotor Abilities

1. Control precision, involving tasks requiring finely controlled muscular adjustments, such as moving a lever to a precise setting.
2. Multilimb coordination, involving the ability to coordinate the movements of a number of limbs simultaneously, such as packing a box with both hands.
3. Response of orientation, involving the ability to make correct and accurate movements in relation to a stimulus under highly speeded conditions, such as reaching out and flicking a switch when a warning horn sounds.
4. Reaction time, involving the speed of a person's response when a stimulus appears, such as pressing a key in response to a bell.
5. Speed of arm movement, involving the speed of gross arm movements where accuracy is not required, such as gathering trash or debris and throwing it into a large pile.
6. Rate control, involving the ability to make continuous motor adjustments relative to a moving target changing in speed and direction, such as holding a rod on a moving rotor.
7. Manual dexterity, involving skillful arm and hand movements in handling rather large objects under speeded conditions, such as placing blocks rapidly into a form board.
8. Finger dexterity, involving skillful manipulations of small objects (such as nuts and bolts) with the fingers.
9. Arm-hand steadiness, involving the ability to make precise arm-hand positioning movements that do not require strength or speed, such as threading a needle.
10. Wrist-finger speed, involving rapid tapping movements with the wrist and fingers, such as transmitting a continuous signal with a telegraphic key.
11. Aiming, involving an extremely narrow ability defined by a test in which the examinee places dots in circles as rapidly as possible.

Source: M. D. Dunnette, *Personnel Selection and Placement* (Belmont, Calif.: Wadsworth, 1966), pp. 52–53. Copyright © 1966 by Wadsworth, Inc. Reprinted by permission of the publisher, Brooks/Cole Publishing Company, Monterey, California.

between people. Such differences are shown by the vertical variation in ability scores across persons A through F in Figure 4–4. A second type refers to differences in the patterns of abilities within persons and is called *intraindividual differences*. The latter are illustrated in Figure 4–4

FIGURE 4–4
Illustration of Inter- and Intraindividual Differences in Ability

Person	Ability Scores			
	Verbal Comprehension	Word Fluency	Number Aptitude	Inductive Reasoning
A	89	102	95	93
B	125	110	103	98
C	93	85	95	91
D	101	98	120	112
E	117	125	98	96
F	99	102	87	100

by horizontal ability-score differences across the four abilities for each person.

Both types of individual differences are pervasive and have significant implications for P/HR management. To the extent that abilities are related to success in performing jobs (the evidence is summarized in Chapter 11), interindividual differences mean that some individuals can perform any given job better than other individuals. Moreover, because not all jobs have identical ability requirements, intraindividual differences suggest that no employee is equally suited to perform all jobs. As a result, it is important for the organization to be able to measure individual abilities and job ability requirements so that employees can be placed in the type of work they have the best chance of performing acceptably.

Group differences

A substantial amount of evidence exists to show that, on the average, there are ability differences between groups. Depending on the ability measured, differences have been observed between men and women, various ethnic, racial, and socioeconomic groups, and persons of different ages.[10] Occasionally, controversy arises over such differences, especially regarding the extent to which the differences are seen as depending on immutable characteristics (genetic, hereditary, sex, or age differences) or situations (socioeconomic or environmental).[11]

For purposes of P/HR management, several factors about group differences should be kept in mind. First, group differences are seldom good predictors of the abilities possessed by any given individual in that group. That is, individual differences *within* a group are generally more important than differences *between* groups. This is illustrated for two hypothetical groups in Figure 4–5; despite group A's superiority, a substantial percentage of individuals in group B (as shown by the shaded area) exceed the average ability in group A. Second, EEO laws and regulations forbid the use of group membership as a basis for P/HR decisions.

Human Capital and Ability

Ability can also be thought of from an economic perspective. Using this approach, ability represents characteristics embodied in an individ-

---

[10] J. B. Miner and M. G. Miner, *Personnel and Industrial Relations: A Managerial Approach*, 4th ed. (New York: Macmillan, 1985), pp. 78–82.

[11] L. J. Cronbach, "Five Decades of Public Controversy over Mental Testing," *American Psychologist* 30 (1975), pp. 1–14.

FIGURE 4–5
Illustration of Group Differences

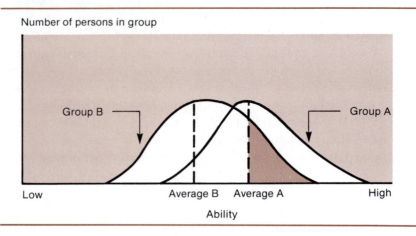

ual that enable the person to generate income. Usually this means that individuals seek to acquire abilities through education, training, and development activities.[12]

The abilities individuals seek to acquire would be those that offered the greatest return in valued rewards, given their perceived aptitudes for acquiring them, and the costs (training costs and foregone income) necessary. Thus, there is a motivational component involved in decisions to acquire, develop, or maintain abilities. One might also expect that economic returns for developing new abilities could potentially decline either with age or the time that an individual expected to remain on a particular job.[13]

Human capital is often divided into two different categories: *general* and *specific*. General human capital (GHC) consists of abilities that are of relatively equal value to many employers. For example, the ability to program in PASCAL would be valuable to many organizations that hire computer programmers. Specific human capital (SHC) involves abilities that are of value primarily to one's present employer, such as the knowledge of rules and procedures. Both require effort to acquire. Individuals can be expected to make their own investments to acquire GHC since an employer would be at substantial risk if the employee

---

[12] See R. Ehrenberg and R. Smith, *Modern Labor Economics*, 3d ed. (Glenview, Ill.: Scott, Foresman, 1988).

[13] For an extended discussion of the economic, motivational, aptitude, and individual variables associated with choices to acquire, maintain, or allow skills to erode, see J. A. Fossum, R. D. Arvey, C. A. Paradise, and N. E. Robbins, "Modeling the Skills Obsolescence Process: A Psychological/Economic Integration," *Academy of Management Review* 11 (1986), pp. 362–74.

learned a new skill on company time and at company expense and then quit. On the other hand, the organization usually needs to induce employees to acquire SHC because time spent learning SHC skills instead of GHC skills lowers returns in the labor market. Thus, such incentives as higher pay and promotions may be necessary to encourage employees to acquire SHC.

Abilities and Requirements

P/HR managers are understandably concerned that employees be able to perform their assigned tasks. A general aim is to obtain a good fit between employee abilities and the requirements of the job to which they are assigned. This may be achieved in several ways. First, it may be accomplished through the staffing process (see Chapters 9, 10, and 11) by choosing job applicants whose abilities best fit the job requirements. Among existing employees, the individual ability-requirements match may be enhanced by altering requirements to fit the individual through promotions and transfers (see Chapter 12) and task redesign (see Chapter 19).

Individual abilities are also changeable. Thus, an alternative P/HR strategy involves changing the abilities of employees through training programs (see Chapter 13) and reordering rewards associated with job requirements to encourage the acquisition of higher ability levels or different abilities (Chapters 14 and 15). To influence performance through staffing and training activities, it is necessary for the organization to gather information about its jobs. The rest of this chapter deals with this need.

JOB ANALYSIS

The Rationale for Studying Jobs

A *job* is a collection of tasks that can be performed by a single employee that contributes to the production of some product or service provided by the organization. Each job has certain ability requirements (as well as certain rewards) associated with it.[14]

All individuals who work within a particular job in an organization do not necessarily perform all of the tasks of the job or spend the same amount of time on the task. For example, a hospital may have a job titled "intensive care unit nurse." The job would require close monitoring of

---

[14] Dawis et al., "Theory of Work Adjustment."

critically ill patients and the ability to make quick and correct judgments. At a given time, however, one nurse may be closely monitoring and caring for an individual recovering from a heart attack, another may be caring for an accident victim, and a third may be assisting a patient with severe breathing problems. Some of the skills required by the current configuration of each of these assignments is not required by the others. When there is sufficient demand for a specific set of skills, or when the individual is incapable of performing the full set in the time available, the job needs to be further specified. The intensive care unit nurse job might be subdivided into the following jobs: intensive cardiac care nurse, intensive trauma care nurse, and intensive respiratory care nurse.

Jobs are a collection of tasks. Relatively similar jobs within an organization make up a *job family*. For example, if the previous nursing situation were extended to include emergency room nurses, surgical nurses, and hospice nurses, they might make up a job family called "special care nurses." In turn, special care nurses, ward nurses, nursing supervisors, visiting nurses, and others would comprise the nursing *occupation*. At a level below the job, each unique subset of tasks that is performed by a particular individual is a *position*.[15] *Job analysis* is the process used to gather information about jobs in order to identify the ability requirements necessary for a job or the knowledge, skills, and abilities currently possessed by jobholders.

A knowledge of job requirements is useful for most P/HR activities; specific applications are presented in the chapters that follow. For the moment, two examples will suffice. First, staffing activities clearly require that job requirements be known and specified. If they are not, the organization will have difficulty selecting from among the applicants those most likely to be effective on the job. Second, establishing wages or salaries for jobs depends in part on knowing the relative ability requirements of these jobs. Higher pay levels usually are provided for jobs with higher ability requirements since the aptitudes necessary to learn the jobs are more sparsely distributed in the population and/or more time and effort is necessary to acquire them.

The P/HR model shows that laws and regulations have an impact on job analysis, especially in the case of equal employment opportunity (EEO). Most EEO cases involve charges that P/HR activities are discriminatory because decisions are made that are not job related; that is, something other than the job and its requirements (for example, the person's sex) served as the basis for a particular decision or type of

---

[15] For an expanded treatment of the definition and study of jobs, see K. Pearlman, "Job Families: A Review and Discussion of Their Implications for Personnel Selection," *Psychological Bulletin* 87 (1980), pp. 1–28.

treatment. To rebut charges, one must be able to demonstrate the job relatedness of the activity in question.[16] Job analysis is a necessary step in being able to do this.

Given the importance of job analysis to most P/HR activities, responsibility for it is logically housed with the personnel department. Line managers are also involved, however. When jobs are to be changed, or departments reorganized, or when an individual's abilities have grown over time within a current job classification, the line manager recognizes the necessity for studying the job to determine what P/HR functional and support activities will be necessary to assist in dealing with the situation.

Job Requirements

Job analysis can focus on the tasks and behaviors needed to produce an output or service or on the knowledge and skills (that is, ability) believed necessary to carry out the job tasks and behaviors. The former is known as a "task-oriented" approach, and the latter is referred to as a "person-oriented" approach. Examples of task- and person-oriented attributes are given in Figure 4–6.[17]

Knowledge and skill requirements can be inferred from a description of tasks and behaviors. But a description of knowledge and skill requirements does not permit an inference about tasks and behaviors. For example, if a job involves a task such as packing materials to precise customer specifications, it can be inferred that knowledge of packing procedures and physical packing skills are probably necessary to complete the task adequately. Conversely, if these knowledge and ability requirements were the only things known, it would be difficult to infer the specific packing task involved.

Job Analysis Methods

The basic output of any job analysis is a *job description* and/or a *job specification*. A job description details the tasks and behaviors associated with performance of the job. A job specification states the employee characteristics (knowledge and skill) inferred to be necessary for per-

---

[16] D. E. Thompson and T. A. Thompson, "Court Standards for Job Analysis in Test Validation," *Personnel Psychology* 35 (1982), pp. 865–74.

[17] For an extension of this discussion of the differences in the approach and application of person- and task-oriented job analysis procedures, see E. J. McCormick, "Job Information: Its Development and Applications," in *ASPA Handbook of Personnel and Industrial Relations*, eds. D. Yoder and H. G. Heneman, Jr. (Washington, D.C.: Bureau of National Affairs, 1979), pp. 4-35–4-83; and M. D. Dunnette, L. M. Hough, and R. L. Rosse, "Task and Job Taxonomies as a Basis for Identifying Labor Supply Sources and Evaluating Employment Qualifications," *Human Resource Planning* 2, no. 1 (1979), pp. 37–51.

FIGURE 4–6

Examples of Task- and Person-Oriented Job Attributes

Task-Oriented Attributes

Works with a minimum of supervision.
Sets up files and records.
Reads diagrams, schematics.
Uses tact, persuasion, or persistence to obtain somewhat personal information from persons.
Allocates costs, payments, cash, and so forth to appropriate persons or departments.
Writes instructional, procedural, or training materials.

Person-Oriented Attributes

Knowledge of optimum ordering quantities of raw materials.
Knowledge of vendor realiability for delivery.
Understanding of raw stock coding system.
Knowledge of customer packing requirements.
Understanding of procedures needed to maintain constant inventory.
Working knowledge of one or more fields of engineering (such as electrical, mechanical, chemical).

Source: Adapted from M. D. Dunnette, "Task and Job Taxonomies as a Basis for Evaluating Employment Qualifications" (Paper presented at the Conference on Affirmative Action Planning Concepts, New York State School of Industrial and Labor Relations, Cornell University, Ithaca, N.Y., November 1977), Exhibits 2 and 3.

formance. Consequently, a job description is a natural result of a task-oriented job analysis approach, while a job specification follows directly from a person-oriented approach. A job specification can also result from a task-oriented job analysis if the analyst goes on to infer knowledge and skill requirements. Illustration 4–1 gives an example of a simple job description.

A relatively large number of techniques is available for job analysis. They vary substantially in their complexity and in their ability to deal with a broad range of jobs. In this section, several techniques are described, together with examples of their use.[18]

---

[18] Particularly valuable sources of information on job analysis definitions and methods are U.S. Department of Labor, Manpower Administration, *Handbook for Analyzing Jobs* (Washington, D.C.: U.S. Government Printing Office, 1972); E. J. McCormick, "Job Information"; E. J. McCormick, "Job and Task Analysis," in *Handbook of Industrial and Organizational Psychology*, ed. M. D. Dunnette (Skokie, Ill.: Rand McNally, 1976), pp. 651–96; S. E. Bemis, A. H. Belenky, and D. A. Soder, *Job Analysis* (Washington, D.C.: Bureau of National Affairs, 1983); E. J. McCormick, *Job Analysis: Methods and Applications* (New York: AMACOM, 1979); E. L. Levine, *Everything You Always Wanted to Know about Job Analysis* (Tampa, Fla.: Mariner, 1983); R. A. Ash, E. L. Levine, and F. Sistrunk, "The Role of Job and Job-Based Methods in Personnel and Human Resource Management," *Research in Personnel and Human Resources Management*, eds. K. M. Rowland and G. R. Ferris (Greenwich, Conn.: JAI Press, 1983), pp. 45–84; and J. V. Ghorpade, *Job Analysis: A Handbook for the Human Resource Director* (Englewood Cliffs, N.J.: Prentice-Hall, 1988).

ILLUSTRATION 4–1
Example of a Job Description

Job Description for Plant Sales Manager

To direct the activities of the plant sales force in promoting and obtaining profitable sales of company's products.

I. SUPERVISORY

1. Interviews and assesses qualifications of applicants for job in the department in order to select person for the job using applicants' resumes, job description, and company personnel policies and procedures manual.

2. Evaluates qualifications and availability of staff in relation to requirements of specific project in order to assign work to staff using project calendar and personnel files as necessary.

3. Role-plays sales presentation demonstrating product and answering questions in order to provide on-the-job training to sales personnel using promotional materials.

4. Reads production reports and project files and/or observes sales presentations and compares actual achievement to preestablished objectives in order to evaluate employees' performances using records, files, and performance appraisal forms.

II. SALES

5. Meets with potential customers, explaining benefits and cost of product in order to make a sale using sample products, promotional material, and order forms.

6. Meets with potential customers in order to obtain information regarding their interests/needs concerning company product using marketing questionnaire.

7. Assesses market conditions as they relate to specific products to develop marketing strategy and plan specific sales program using company planning objectives, economic forecast, and past sales reports.

III. PLANNING

8. Evaluates market conditions in relation to specific product in order to develop plant sales goals for the coming year using company market research and financial reports and trade and journal publications.

9. Discusses sales goals with plant general manager in order to jointly agree on goals for the coming year using company market research and financial reports and trade and journal publications.

10. Reviews quarterly sales objectives in order to assess actual progress/performance and identify problems using monthly sales and financial reports and annual goals.

IV. FINANCE

11. Evaluates credit applications in order to approve/disapprove request for credit using corporate procedures and criteria.

12. Reviews accounts receivable identifying past due accounts in order to ensure collections of delinquent accounts using accounts receivable printout and corporate policies and procedures regarding delinquent accounts.

Source: S. E. Bemis, A. H. Belenky, and D. A. Soder, *Job Analysis* (Washington, D.C.: Bureau of National Affairs, 1983), p. 93.

Observations

With observationally based job analysis techniques, information is gathered through direct intensive study of employees by trained job analysts. Information is collected on sequences of observed behavior. This approach is most often used for the analysis of jobs that consist largely of repeated manual operations over a relatively short time cycle. For example, it would be appropriate for analyzing the jobs of many production or skilled trades employees. These occupations deal more often with objects than with abstract reasoning where the immediate effects of behaviors are more readily apparent. While observational analysis has been used, on occasion, to describe managers' jobs, relatively long periods of time are required to sample the full range of behaviors, and the effect of these behaviors on later results can, in most cases, only be inferred.[19]

Interviewing

This method relies on position holders (and/or supervisors or subordinates) to provide information about behaviors or personal characteristics. The interviewers ask similar questions about all jobs studied. Frequently, the analyst will contact several jobholders to increase the scope and reliability of the interviews. An analyst may use increasing redundancy of information as a rule of thumb to determine when enough jobholders have been interviewed to obtain an adequate sampling of the domain of the job. Often a few position holders will be interviewed by two analysts as another reliability check.

The U.S. Training and Employment Service has combined the observation and interview methods into a hybrid approach for the analysis of jobs. Illustration 4–2 is an example of how they prepare for job analysis and what some of the results of the analysis include.

Critical incidents

The critical incidents technique requires heavy involvement by supervisors and is explicitly task oriented. Supervisors keep records of jobholders' behaviors that have contributed to particularly successful or

---

[19] See H. Mintzberg, *The Nature of Managerial Work* (New York: Harper & Row, 1973); and M. W. McCall, Jr., A. M. Morrison, and R. L. Hannan, *Studies of Managerial Work: Results and Methods*, Technical Report #9 (Greensboro, N.C.: Center for Creative Leadership, no date).

ILLUSTRATION 4–2

The U.S.T.E.S. Approach to Job Analysis

In this approach, the worker is studied in relation to five major variables: (1) worker functions (what is done), (2) methods and techniques (how it is done), (3) machines, tools, equipment, and work aids used (what assistance is necessary), (4) materials, products, subject matter, or services produced (what is accomplished), and (5) employee knowledge, skill, and ability requirements.

To prepare, the job analyst must become familiar with the jobs, technology, characteristics, and jargon of the organization being studied. The analyst must also be prepared to demonstrate how the study will benefit the organization and individuals in jobs to be studied.

The analyst gathers job information through a combination of observation and interview because (1) it allows the analyst to observe an actual sample of employee behavior to see specifically what is done and (2) it enables the analyst to verify, define, amplify, or place in perspective what has been observed by interviewing the worker regarding the job. The technique enables the analyst to determine whether an observed cycle of activities forms the basis for the job or whether the sequence can be altered at the discretion of the worker.

When the observation-interview has been completed and the analyst is sure that the job is understood, a job analysis schedule is prepared. Among other things, it contains both a detailed job description and job specification.

unsuccessful job performance. This method is useful where job cycle times are relatively long and/or when the behaviors of the jobholders have major effects on organizational goal accomplishment.

Supervisors need to see the necessity of their involvement and the importance of the results to gain the motivation necessary to make this technique effective.

Work sampling

With this technique, a small proportion of the behaviors required of any given jobholder is recorded. Two types of sampling may be done: cross-sectional and longitudinal. In a cross-sectional approach, the recording of the job activities of several jobholders at the same time may yield a picture of the overall job. For example, the observation of one day's behavior for each of 30 personnel managers may give a good picture of what the total job encompasses. If few persons are in a given job, the analyst may observe their behaviors at separate time periods. For example, the personnel manager may be observed for 1 day each of 30 random days out of a year to build a description of the job.

Questionnaires and checklists

Questionnaires and checklists differ somewhat in the degree to which they are structured. Questionnaires rely on jobholders to provide most of the narrative description of the tasks, skills, knowledge, and abilities their positions require. They receive some direction about the areas to be addressed, but they generally determine what factors are to be included.

Checklists, on the other hand, already contain the characteristics likely to be encountered in the jobs being analyzed. Checklists require respondents to indicate whether they perform the listed behavior or use the listed abilities. They also are often asked how frequently a task is performed or how important it is to overall performance in their positions.

Of the two, checklists are a more recent innovation. Before the mid-1960s, there was insufficient computing power available to properly use the data that could be generated by a checklist. Typically, a checklist includes 200 or more items that the individual respondent must examine. After many jobholders have responded, highly related behaviors (for example, if a person performs one behavior, s/he is also likely to perform another) are clustered using statistical methods to form factors representing common underlying dimensions of tasks or personal characteristics. Three of the more carefully researched checklist approaches are the Position Analysis Questionnaire (PAQ), the Management Position Description Questionnaire (MPDQ), and the Comprehensive Occupational Data Analysis Program (CODAP).

Position analysis questionnaire.   The PAQ contains job elements within six major dimensions (shown in Figure 4–7).[20] It is designed to be applicable across a broad range of jobs without modification. This, combined with the substantial amount of research performed on the PAQ, allows for comparisons against a growing data base. On the other hand, its sheer bulk, stemming from the large number of items necessary to cover a variety of jobs across many organizations, can lead to resistance in use by raters, particularly if the job analysis requires jobholders to describe their own jobs.

Management position description questionnaire (MPDQ).   This checklist contains task-oriented items with the following characteristics: (1) they are responded to differently by different functions within and across companies; (2) they are responded to differently across management

---

[20] E. J. McCormick, P. R. Jeanneret, and R. C. Mecham, "A Study of Job Characteristics and Job Dimensions as Based on the Position Analysis Questionnaire (PAQ), *Journal of Applied Psychology* 56 (1972), pp. 347–68.

FIGURE 4–7

Position Analysis Questionnaire Job Dimensions

1. Information input:
   a. Sources of job information.
   b. Discrimination and perceptual activities.
2. Mediation processes:
   a. Decision making and reasoning.
   b. Information processing.
   c. Use of stored information.
3. Work output:
   a. Use of physical devices.
   b. Integrative manual activities.
   c. General body activities.
   d. Manipulation/coordination activities.
4. Interpersonal activities:
   a. Communications.
   b. Interpersonal relationships.
   c. Personal contact.
   d. Supervision and coordination.
5. Work situation and job context:
   a. Physical working conditions.
   b. Psychological and sociological aspects.
6. Miscellaneous aspects:
   a. Work schedule, method of pay, apparel.
   b. Job demands.
   c. Responsibility.

Source: Adapted from E. J. McCormick, P. R. Jeanneret, and R. C. Mecham, "A Study of Job Characteristics and Job Dimensions as Based on the Position Analysis Questionnaire (PAQ)," *Journal of Applied Psychology* 56 (1972), p. 349. Copyright 1972 by the American Psychological Association. Reprinted by permission.

levels; and (3) they have relevance for more than one function and company. The format for collecting job information and the methods used to synthesize the data are similar to those used with the PAQ.

The responses of a given manager can be aggregated into a job description with the dimension titles used as major subdivisions within which the items are distributed (see Figure 4–8). Abilities necessary to perform the job can be inferred from the analysis. The MPDQ is useful for selecting managerial employees, identifying and constructing logical career progressions, diagnosing training needs for employees slated to move to new jobs, and rating jobs for pay purposes.[21]

---

[21] For an extended discussion of this procedure, see W. W. Tornow and P. R. Pinto, "The Development of a Managerial Job Taxonomy: A System for Describing, Classifying, and Evaluating Executive Positions," *Journal of Applied Psychology* 61 (1976), pp. 410–18; and L. R. Gomez-Mejia, R. C. Page, and W. W. Tornow, "Development and Implementation of a Computerized Job Evaluation System," *Personnel Administrator* 24, no. 2 (1979), pp. 46–52.

FIGURE 4–8
Descriptive Factors in the MPDQ

Product, marketing, and financial strategy planning.
Coordination of other organizational units and personnel.
Internal business control.
Products and services responsibility.
Public and customer relations.
Advanced consulting.
Autonomy of action.
Approval of financial commitments.
Staff service.
Supervision.
Complexity and stress.
Advanced financial responsibility.

Source: Adapted from W. W. Tornow and P. R. Pinto, "The Development of a Managerial Job Taxonomy:
A System for Describing, Classifying, and Evaluating Executive Positions," *Journal of Applied Psychology*
61 (1976), pp. 410–18. Copyright 1976 by the American Psychological Association. Reprinted by permission.

Comprehensive occupational data analysis program (CODAP).
CODAP was developed by the air force to cluster and describe jobs with
large numbers of incumbents. The procedure requires the development
of task statements that describe work procedures. Frequently, 300 to 500
task statements are developed to analyze and describe the work. Position
holders in the job complete a checklist to indicate the relative amount of
time they spend on each described activity compared to others. To
obtain sufficient responses for the subsequent statistical analysis, 3,000
or more jobholders are necessary. The responses are clustered into
occupational groupings that require similar activities and the same relative work-time distribution. When the checklist begins to identify jobs
that are seen as being essentially similar, no more clustering is done and
the obtained jobs are described. The procedure offers the opportunity to
describe jobs as they are currently practiced and to identify sub-
specialities within occupations. It requires substantial development time
to construct the task statements and large numbers of jobholders to
obtain stable results.[22]

Job analysis methods vary substantially in their construction and their
applicability for certain uses. For example, critical incidents analyses are
judged as more effective for performance appraisal construction than

---

[22] R. E. Christal and J. J. Weissmuller, "New Comprehensive Data Analysis Programs
(CODAP) for Analyzing Task Factor Information," *JSAS Catalog of Selected Documents in
Psychology* 7 (1977), pp. 24–25 (ms. no. 1444).

other techniques, but far below the PAQ for job classification. When practical concerns are judged, the PAQ, for example, is seen as cheaper and more reliable than critical incidents, while larger sample sizes are judged to be necessary for the PAQ than for critical incidents.[23]

Sources of Error in Job Analysis

There are several major sources of error in a job analysis. Among these are inadequate sampling of tasks, response sets by observers or jobholders, changes in the job environment, and changes in employee behavior. These errors can occur in both traditional qualitative approach (such as observation-interview) and quantitative methods that use checklists.

Inadequate sampling

With traditional methods, inadequate sampling may occur because the analyst did not observe or elicit the entire domain of tasks involved. Under a comprehensive system like the PAQ that is applied to a variety of jobs, exhaustive research must first be done to identify a relevant domain of tasks or traits. Unless this is accomplished, the measure will fail to describe or specify important job components. Another sampling problem occurs if people inadequately report what they do or the time they spend on job activities.

If employees provide the information to job analysts or participate by completing checklists or questionnaires, a question may be raised about the relative reliability of the information provided. A study of mental health workers found that employees differed substantially in the care with which they responded to questionnaires, with some checking that they performed duties that it would be impossible for them to do. The study also found that some jobs required relatively larger numbers of respondents than others to achieve reliable results. A minimum of three or more job incumbents appears necessary.[24]

Evidence shows that the job performance of incumbents (high or low) is unrelated to the adequacy with which they describe the domain of a job. Using a sample of high- and low-performing police officers, re-

---

[23] E. L. Levine, R. A. Ash, H. Hall, and F. Sistrunk, "Evaluation of Job Analysis Methods by Experienced Job Analysts," *Academy of Management Journal* 26 (1983), pp. 339–47.

[24] S. B. Green and T. Stutzman, "An Evaluation of Methods to Select Respondents to Structured Job-Analysis Questionnaires," *Personnel Psychology* 39 (1986), pp. 543–64.

searchers found that the generation and application of job measurement scales for a youth officer job were similar in construction and measurement quality.[25]

Response sets

A response set occurs when one consistently answers questions in a predictable or distorted manner. For example, if managers were asked, "How much time do you spend on task A?" and were given the possible answers, "a great deal, quite a lot, some, not very much, or never," some might answer "quite a lot" if they spent two hours per day, while others might respond "some" for the same amount of time.

The response set may depend not only on the person's interpretation of the qualitative labels of the scales, but also on a belief about what the user intends to do with the information. Verification of data is perhaps easier using the qualitative method, although job analysts have also been found to have response sets that have led them to underestimate abilities necessary for job performance.[26]

Analyst inexperience

With the availability of carefully developed job analytic checklists, some preliminary research suggested that the experience level of job analysts was not critical in developing reliable and accurate analyses.[27] However, the necessary generality of checklists leads to many task or ability statements that do not apply to a given job. Reliabilities may thus be inflated because so many items are answered with the statement "Does not apply."[28] Reduced information made available to inexperienced analysts results in reduced reliability and does not correlate with the judgments of expert raters who are familiar with the jobs in question.[29] Thus P/HR managers must be very careful about the training

[25] P. R. Conley and P. R. Sackett, "Effects of Using High- versus Low-Performing Job Incumbents as Sources of Job-Analysis Information," *Journal of Applied Psychology* 72 (1987), pp. 434–37.

[26] N. H. Trattner, S. A. Fine, and J. F. Kubis, "A Comparison of Worker Requirement Ratings by Reading Job Descriptions and by Direct Observation," *Personnel Psychology* 8 (1955), pp. 183–94.

[27] See, for example, A. P. Jones, D. S. Main, M. C. Butler, and L. A. Johnson, "Narrative Job Descriptions as Potential Sources of Job Analysis Ratings," *Personnel Psychology* 35 (1982), pp. 813–28.

[28] R. J. Harvey, "Monte Carlo Baselines for Interrater Reliability Correlations Using the Position Analysis Questionnaire," *Personnel Psychology* 39 (1986), pp. 345–57.

[29] L. Friedman and R. J. Harvey, "Can Raters with Reduced Job Descriptive Information Provide Accurate Position Analysis Questionnaire (PAQ) Ratings?" *Personnel Psychology* 39 (1986), pp. 779–89.

of job analysts, and they must verify that the results of analysis are both reliable and valid.

Job environment changes

These changes are related to the introduction of new processes, particularly where person-machine interactions occur. Assembly operations may change from a manual approach, where the person completes the assembly using tools, to one where the person becomes a machine tender or process monitor. The previously developed descriptions and specifications are no longer applicable to a job with the same title.

Employee behavior changes

These may be affected by the point in the employee's career at which the observation took place. Unless the individual was fully trained, the analysis would reflect behaviors that were still developing.

The Choice of an Analytic Method

The answer to the question "What analysis method should be used?" requires that three questions be asked: (1) "What is the purpose of doing the analysis?" (2) What type of information is needed?" and (3) "How much general information do we now have?"

Purpose of the analysis

As previously noted, several P/HR activities require information inputs from job analysis. The specific activity affected will partially determine which method to use. For example, the results of job analysis are important for constructing internal promotion paths.[30] If this were the major reason for performing the analysis, the development of a checklist would allow the identification of jobs with successively more demanding requirements. The evaluation of the relative level of jobs to help establish salary structures would also require that information from many jobs be gathered simultaneously. On the other hand, preliminary investigations for the design of a training program for a clerical job would not require information from other job areas, and an observation-interview procedure would be more appropriate.

---

[30] F. Krzystofiak, J. M. Newman, and G. Anderson, "A Quantified Approach to Measurement of Job Content: Procedures and Payoffs," *Personnel Psychology* 31 (1979), pp. 341–57.

Types of information needed

The answer to this question indicates whether a task- or person-oriented approach is more appropriate. Earlier it was suggested that person-oriented information could be inferred from task-oriented results, but not the opposite. Thus, if the results of the analysis are to be used to develop a training program that replicates a given job, a task-oriented approach is preferable. If the analysis is to be used for recruiting or compensation, a person-oriented approach is preferred since the desired outcome is a job specification.

Since job information can be gathered by an analyst or provided by a jobholder, a source choice must be made. If the purpose is to provide job-description information, either or both sources would be appropriate. But if a job specification is desired and this specification will have an impact on later personnel decisions, a neutral analyst should gather the information. This cautionary note suggests that most person-oriented approaches, information should be gathered by analysts and not from jobholders.

General information currently available

If there are checklists available that meet the organization's task- or person-oriented analysis needs, these provide a quick, reasonably reliable method for obtaining job data. If they are not available, the time and cost associated with their development are high. There is some evidence that judgments of persons familiar with the jobs are equal in accuracy to quantitative methods,[31] particularly for employee selection purposes.[32] However, if involvement of employees is seen as necessary for implementing changes resulting from job analysis, quantitative techniques requiring their input may be appropriate.

If little information is available, observation-interview approaches are more efficient for diagnosing training requirements and for assisting in the choice of selection techniques (for example, tests) for staffing decisions. If all jobs in a given cluster or organization are to be examined to construct selection or compensation programs, checklists probably offer a better approach, even though the initial start-up costs are high. Over the long run, these costs can be recouped by shifting efforts in analysis from the analyst to the jobholder.

---

[31] P. R. Sackett, E. T. Cornelius III, and T. J. Carron, "A Comparison of Global Judgment vs. Task Oriented Approaches to Job Classification," *Personnel Psychology* 34 (1981), pp.791–804.

[32] E. T. Cornelius III, F. L. Schmidt, and T. J. Carron, "Job Classification Approaches and the Implementation of Validity Generalization Results," *Personnel Psychology* 37 (1984), pp. 247–60.

Uses of Job Analysis by the Line Manager

It is unlikely and unnecessary that the line manager be an expert at job analysis, particularly with regard to how jobs are presently constituted within the organization. The line manager is likely to have employees within the unit that have the same job titles as other employees in the organization. The manager is probably disinterested in how closely the particular job duties of a position-holder are to the overall description, but would be interested in what duties should be expected given a particular rate of pay.

Where the line manager may best be able to put job analysis to work is in a better construction of "what if?" scenarios. For example, what tasks would be performed and what knowledge, skills, and abilities would be necessary if the new equipment proposed by the office equipment vendor's sales representative were installed? The price and projected productivity seemed attractive, but what would the costs of training and development or hiring and transferring employees come to? What would happen if the responsibilities of the department were reorganized among the personnel presently assigned? Would their jobs change and require changes in compensation? Would individuals be able to perform the reconfigured jobs given their skills and/or the time available to perform them? How much learning time might result given the changes? All answers to these questions would benefit from an analysis of the proposed job structure. The results could be combined with tactical choices detailed in subsequent chapters on staffing, training and development, compensation, and work design.

SUMMARY

P/HR management is typically responsible for helping general management obtain, retain, and foster an effective work force. As the model presented in this chapter points out, the match between employee ability and job requirements is essential for helping to achieve these outcomes. Job requirements are typically such that both *intellectual* and *psychomotor* abilities are necessary for successful work performance. Thus, the task for P/HR management is to obtain a satisfactory fit between the abilities possessed by the individual and the requirements of the job. Because of ability differences between and within people, this matching process requires the effective use of a variety of P/HR activities such as selection, training, job design, and transfer and promotion policies.

The two major classes of methods for measuring job requirements are task-and person-oriented analyses. Task-oriented analysis yields job descriptions while person-oriented analysis produces job specifications. A variety of methods such as observation-interview, critical incidents, work sampling, questionnaires, and checklists have been used within both of these broad types. Job analysis data are used to develop performance measures, choose employee selection instruments, develop training programs, identify compensation requirements, and design work.

DISCUSSION QUESTIONS

1. As an employer, what options would you have for making sure that your employees' abilities were properly matched with the job requirements of your organization?

2. When might a person-oriented approach to job analysis be more appropriate than a task-oriented approach?

3. What are some pros and cons of using a checklist like the PAQ?

4. When choosing a job analysis method, what alternatives might you consider to reduce errors from inadequate sampling?

5. For what purposes might an observational job analysis approach be used to study management jobs?

5

Organizational Rewards and Employee Motivation

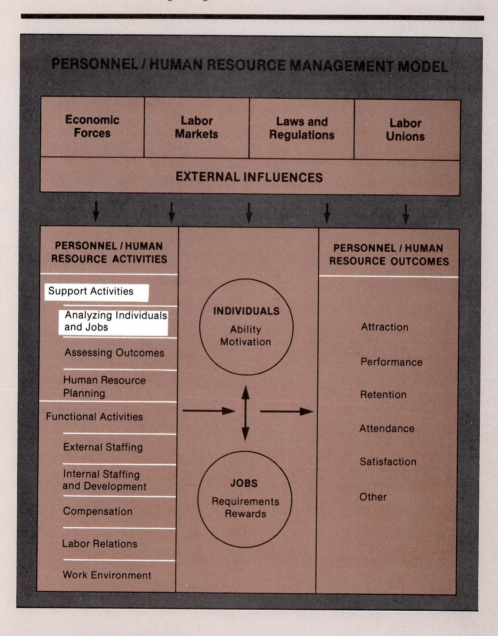

PERSONNEL / HUMAN RESOURCE MANAGEMENT MODEL

Economic Forces	Labor Markets	Laws and Regulations	Labor Unions

EXTERNAL INFLUENCES

PERSONNEL / HUMAN RESOURCE ACTIVITIES

Support Activities

Analyzing Individuals and Jobs

Assessing Outcomes

Human Resource Planning

Functional Activities

External Staffing

Internal Staffing and Development

Compensation

Labor Relations

Work Environment

INDIVIDUALS
Ability
Motivation

JOBS
Requirements
Rewards

PERSONNEL / HUMAN RESOURCE OUTCOMES

Attraction

Performance

Retention

Attendance

Satisfaction

Other

After reading this chapter, you should be able to speak to the questions posed in each of the following personnel/human resource incidents:

1. Your boss has just returned from a management seminar focusing on "The Modern Employee." She is concerned that the organization is not adapting its jobs to the types of rewards that the seminar leader said younger employees were stressing. Now she has asked you to get her some information about the employees in your organization and the rewards they may value. What are the potential rewards? Where can you turn for a method to gather information about them?

2. Your organization is in the process of building another plant in a distant city. Employees in this plant will produce a brand new product. The majority of production jobs for this project have few skill requirements. However, the production process is such that employee motivation appears to be very important. If employees work hard, production will be much greater than if they perform at the level typical of employees in the current plants. The president is very concerned about this and has asked you to recommend personnel/human resource policies that will encourage employee motivation. For the moment, anyway, the president is willing to consider substantial changes in existing personnel/human resource policies if it will help motivate employees in the new plant. What types of policies would you consider recommending? What sorts of constraints, if any, might prevent you from implementing such policies?

3. You have recently been promoted to a first-level managerial position in a state agency. The six employees now reporting to you have all been with the state a long time. They know how to perform their jobs and require little supervision from you along those lines. However, they take a lot of time away from work. Coffee breaks usually exceed the 10 minutes allotted, and they often return from lunch up to 20 minutes late. What sorts of actions might you contemplate to improve these employees' work habits?

FIGURE 5-1

The Correspondence between Individual and Job Characteristics

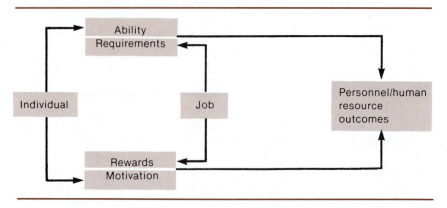

Managers have long recognized the significance of employee abilities and the ability requirements of jobs for achieving P/HR outcomes, especially high employee performance. In the case of both, moreover, management has available well-established measurement procedures. At the same time, managers also understand that employee ability alone is insufficient to achieve satisfactory P/HR outcomes. Not only must employees have the ability to achieve outcomes, but they must also be willing to expend effort to achieve them (see Figure 5-1). Willingness to work toward outcomes has to do with employee *motivation*.

Two questions are at issue. One has to do with what energizes employees in the work environment. What is it about individuals or their work environments that stimulates them to action? This question is referred to as one of *content* since it focuses on an individual's needs or the rewards that may serve to satisfy these needs. The first section of this chapter deals with individual needs and organizational rewards.

The second question is one of motivational *process*. It asks how individuals translate their effort (motivation) to a specific behavior such as high performance. Although essential to understanding behavior, the process question has only recently been addressed in work environments. The second section of this chapter deals with this issue.[1]

The final section combines motivational content and process and addresses administrative issues centering on organizational rewards. It focuses on how managers can use knowledge of motivation to favorably influence P/HR outcomes.

---

[1] The distinction between motivational content and process was first made by J. P. Campbell, M. D. Dunnette, E. E. Lawler III, and K. E. Weick, Jr., *Managerial Behavior, Performance, and Effectiveness* (New York: McGraw-Hill, 1970), pp. 340–58.

REWARDS

What employees find motivating in the work environment has been studied from two different perspectives.[2] Historically, the issue has been approached from the point of view of the individual so that motivational content was often defined in terms of the *needs* experienced by the individual. Some needs, such as hunger, are physiologically based. It is often assumed, however, that psychological needs, such as the desire to excel, are more important in most work environments.[3]

A second approach focuses on rewards individuals seek from work. The pay one receives from work is an obvious reward for most persons; so also may be working with pleasant colleagues. However, preferences for rewards vary widely among individuals depending on the environment to which they have been exposed, especially during their formative years.[4] These differences highlight the importance of studying rewards on an individualized basis. For example, an organization may find that some of its employees value promotional opportunities greatly, others may be indifferent, and still others may find the prospect of promotion aversive.

There are, nevertheless, broad classes of rewards that employees often find motivating. It is inappropriate to suggest that all employees will find a particular reward attractive, but it is legitimate to say that these rewards will generally be influential. They fall into three general groups.[5]

1.   *Work itself.* The type of work one does can be a powerful source of both positive and negative rewards. For example, work may be physically demanding, dangerous, and/or mentally challenging. All represent work outcomes that some employees may find attractive, others unattractive. Since the nature of work is often determined by technological

---

[2] L. L. Cummings and D. P. Schwab, *Performance in Organizations: Determinants and Appraisal* (Glenview, Ill.: Scott, Foresman, 1973), pp. 22–23.

[3] A. H. Maslow, *Motivation and Personality* (New York: Harper & Row, 1954). Maslow's perspective on needs has clearly been the most popular in organizational behavior. Despite its popularity, however, the perspective has received little support. See C. C. Pinder, *Work Motivation: Theory Issues, and Applications* (Dallas: Scott, Foresman, 1984), pp. 55–56. Regarding the two-factor theory, see E. A. Locke, "The Nature and Causes of Job Satisfaction," in *Handbook of Industrial and Organizational Psychology*, ed. M. D. Dunnette (Skokie, Ill.: Rand McNally, 1976), pp. 1,297–1,349.

[4] J. P. Campbell and R. D. Pritchard, "Motivation Theory in Industrial Organizational Psychology," in *Handbook*, ed. Dunnette, pp. 63–130. See also, R. V. Dawis, L. H. Lofquist, and D. J. Weiss, "A Theory of Work Adjustment: A Revision," *Minnesota Studies in Vocational Rehabilitation* 23, (Minneapolis: Industrial Relations Center, University of Minnesota, 1968), p. 64.

[5] These categories are adopted from D. P. Schwab, "Motivation in Organizations," in *Encyclopedia of Professional Management*, 2d ed., eds. L. R. Bittel and J. E. Ramsey (New York: McGraw-Hill, 1985), pp. 584–91.

FIGURE 5-2

Median Rank-Order Valences as Reported by Applicants to the Minnesota Gas Company

	Rank Order	
Consequences	Males	Females
Security	2.5	4.9
Advancement	3.3	5.3
Type of work	3.3	1.5
Company	4.5	4.6
Pay	5.6	6.0
Co-workers	6.0	5.2
Supervisor	6.3	5.3
Benefits	6.8	8.0
Hours	7.6	6.9
Working conditions	7.9	6.5

Lower rank means the outcome is more valent.

Source: C. E. Jurgensen, "Job Preferences (What Makes a Job Good or Bad?)," *Journal of Applied Psychology* 63 (1978), pp. 269-70. Copyright 1968 by the American Psychological Association, Reprinted/adapted by permission of the publisher and author.

considerations, it is important to match employee preferences for work outcomes with the types of jobs they will perform. This matching process can be aided by effective recruiting (Chapter 9), and external (Chapters 10 and 11) and internal staffing (Chapter 12).

2. *P/HR policies and practices.* Management policies regarding employees and the way these policies are administered serve as another source of rewards—again, both positive and negative. For most employees pay is very important. Pay has been found to serve as a motivator in a wide variety of settings (see Chapter 15).[6] Direct assessments have also found pay to be a valued reward across many occupational groups.[7] Other rewards partially within the control of P/HR activities are advancement, work scheduling, and job security. Figure 5-2 shows the median rank order of attractiveness for various rewards as reported by nearly 60,000 men and women who applied for employment with the Minneapolis Gas Company over a 30-year period.[8]

3. *Social environment.* A distinguishing characteristic of work is the fact that it is ordinarily performed in a social environment. Employees

---

[6] E. E. Lawler III, *Pay and Organizational Effectiveness: A Psychological View* (New York: McGraw-Hill, 1971), pp. 117-39, 193-201.

[7] Lawler, *Organizational Effectiveness*, pp. 37-59.

[8] C. E. Jurgensen, "Job Preferences (What Makes a Job Good or Bad?)" *Journal of Applied Psychology* 63 (1978), pp. 267-76.

usually interact with managers and with co-workers. Managers can provide such positive rewards as praise and recognition and such negative rewards as discipline. Co-workers are also a significant part of the social environment and can also provide rewards that are viewed positively (for example, approval) and negatively (for instance, social ostracism).

MEASURING JOB REWARDS

It has been noted that a variety of rewards can be potentially motivating to employees. Moreover, the significance of individual differences has been emphasized. It is not surprising, therefore, that the measurement of what is rewarding to employees is important to managers interested in motivating their employees. The responsibility for such measurement generally falls on the P/HR function.

Rewards can be measured from two perspectives. First, employees can be asked to express their satisfaction with organizational rewards or to indicate the degree to which certain rewards are present or absent in their jobs. The second perspective examines the tasks that are included in the job and from these *infers* the rewards the job offers. This approach requires analysis by nonjobholders (for example, managers). An example of each approach is described below.

Job Diagnostic Survey

The Job Diagnostic Survey (JDS) is designed to measure aspects of the work itself, as viewed by employees.[9] Underlying the survey is a theory suggesting that P/HR outcomes are affected by psychological states of the employee. These, in turn, are said to result from the presence or absence of certain core job dimensions that are contained in the work itself. (This theory is discussed further in Chapter 19.)

The five core job dimensions are defined as follows:

1. *Skill variety.* The degree to which a job requires a variety of different activities in carrying out work that involves the employee's use of a number of different skills and talents.
2. *Task identity.* The degree to which the job requires completion of a "whole" and identifiable piece of work—that is, doing a job from beginning to end with a visible outcome.
3. *Task significance.* The degree to which the job has a substantial impact on the lives or work of other people—whether in the immediate organization or in the external environment.

---

[9] J. R. Hackman and G. R. Oldham, "Development of the Job Diagnostic Survey," *Journal of Applied Psychology* 60 (1975), pp. 159–70.

4. *Autonomy*. The degree to which the job provides substantial freedom, independence, and discretion to the employee in scheduling the work and in determining the procedures to be used in carrying it out.

5. *Feedback from the job itself*. The degree to which carrying out the work activities required by the job results in the employee obtaining direct and clear information about the effectiveness of his or her performance.

There has been a substantial amount of research conducted on the JDS.[10] This research suggests that the specific dimensions of the JDS do not capture variability in jobs precisely as the developers hoped they would. Thus, it might be better to use the total score as a measure of aggregate job scope. On the positive side, employees and their supervisors tend to agree with each other on job scope when using the JDS.

Minnesota Job Description Questionnaire

The Minnesota Job Description Questionnaire (MJDQ) illustrates the second approach to measuring job rewards. It is completed by managers of the jobholders in a given job and asks them to rank the degree to which 21 rewards are present in the job.[11] Figure 5–3 shows the rewards included in the MJDQ.

Patterns of rewards have been identified for a large number of occupations. The work adjustment research has labeled these *occupational reinforcer patterns*. These patterns, in turn, have been clustered according to similarities to form broader occupational groups. By examining these groupings, analysts can infer the presence or absence of major rewards.[12] Figure 5–4 gives an example of a job cluster. In this cluster, opportunities for creativity, ability utilization, social service, responsibility, and variety are prevalent; autonomy and achievement are also available. However, there are not good opportunities for technical aspects of

---

[10] For a good review of this research, see R. J. Aldag, S. H. Barr, and A. P. Brief, "Measurement of Perceived Task Characteristics," *Psychological Bulletin* 90 (1981), pp. 415–31.

[11] See, especially, Dawis et al., "A Theory of Work Adjustment"; D. J. Weiss, R. V. Dawis, L. H. Lofquist, and G. W. England, "Instrumentation for the Theory of Work Adjustment," *Minnesota Studies in Vocational Rehabilitation: 21* (Minneapolis: Industrial Relations Center, University of Minnesota, 1966); F. H. Borgen, D. J. Weiss, H. E. A. Tinsley, R. V. Dawis, and L. H. Lofquist, "The Measurement of Occupational Reinforcer Patterns," *Minnesota Studies in Vocational Rehabilitation: XXV* (Minneapolis: Industrial Relations Center, University of Minnesota, 1968); L. H. Lofquist and R. V. Dawis, *Adjustment to Work* (New York: Appleton-Century-Crofts, 1970).

[12] Borgen et al., "Measurement of Patterns," pp. 45–55.

FIGURE 5–3

Questions from the MJDQ

Scale	MJDQ Statement: Workers on the job . . .
1. Ability utilization	1. make use of their individual abilities.
2. Achievement	2. get a feeling of accomplishment.
3. Activity	3. are busy all the time.
4. Advancement	4. have opportunities for advancement.
5. Authority	5. tell other workers what to do.
6. Company policies and practices	6. have a company which administers its policies fairly.
7. Compensation	7. are paid well in comparison with other workers.
8. Co-workers	8. have co-workers who are easy to make friends with.
9. Creativity	9. try out their own ideas.
10. Independence	10. do their work alone.
11. Moral values	11. do work without feeling that it is morally wrong.
12. Recognition	12. receive recognition for the work they do.
13. Responsibility	13. make decisions on their own.
14. Security	14. have steady employment.
15. Social service	15. have work where they do things for other people.
16. Social status	16. have the position of "somebody" in the community.
17. Supervision-human relations	17. have bosses who back up their employees (with top management).
18. Supervision-technical	18. have bosses who train their employees well.
19. Variety	19. have something different to do every day.
20. Working conditions	20. have good working conditions.
21. Autonomy	21. plan their work with little supervision.

Source: F. H. Borgen, D. J. Weiss, H. E. A.Tinsley, R. V. Dawis, and L. H. Lofquist, "The Measurement of Occupational Reinforcer Patterns," *Minnesota Studies in Vocational Rehabilitation: XXV* (Minneapolis: Industrial Relations Center, University of Minnesota, 1968), p. 12.

supervision, human relations aspects of supervision, compensation, company policies, security, or working conditions.

Evaluation

The JDS and MJDQ represent two ways of measuring rewards in the work environment. The identification of rewards inherent in a job may increase managers' ability to use rewards to motivate. The next section discusses in greater detail just how managers may do this.

MOTIVATIONAL PROCESSES

Up to this point the discussion has focused only on the question of the rewards that employees find potentially motivating. Motivational *process*, the topic of this section, links rewards to specific behaviors. For

FIGURE 5–4

A Cluster of Occupations and Their Associated Rewards (cluster: service occupations, social-educational)

	Scales with Large Differences between This Cluster and Other Jobs	
Occupations	*High*	*Low*
Caseworker	Creativity	Supervision-technical
Counselor, school	Ability utilization	Compensation
Counselor, vocational rehabilitation	Social service	Supervision-human relations
Instructor, vocational school	Responsibility	Company policies
Librarian	Variety	Security
Occupational therapist	Autonomy	Working conditions
Physical therapist	Achievement	
Teacher, elementary school		
Teacher, secondary school		

Source: Adapted from F. H. Borgen, D. J. Weiss, H. E. A. Tinsley, R. V. Dawis, and L. H. Lofquist, "The Measurement of Occupational Reinforcer Patterns," *Minnesota Studies in Vocational Rehabilitation: XXV* (Minneapolis: Industrial Relations Center, University of Minnesota, 1968), p. 50.

example, under what conditions will pay motivate employees to be high performers? How does managerial recognition serve to reduce employee absenteeism? These are the types of motivational process questions that have long perplexed managers.

There are now a number of explanations of how employee behavior is directed to specific outcomes.[13] Reinforcement theory, most commonly associated with B. F. Skinner,[14] seeks to explain behavior by examining the environment (particularly the reward systems) surrounding the individual. Indeed, in its strictest form, reinforcement theory tries to explain behavior without any consideration of a person's internal states (for example, thinking); it is thus called *acognitive*.

Other process theories are called *cognitive* since they assume people consciously direct their behavior in a way that will lead to satisfaction. One, equity theory, is both a content and process theory since it states that the major motivator of behavior in a work environment is people's perceptions of equity or fairness.[15] Individuals are hypothesized to decide whether they are fairly or unfairly treated by comparing what they bring to a work situation (e.g., skill) and what they receive (e.g., pay) with what others bring and receive. If, following this comparison, they

---

[13] A detailed review of these explanations can be found in Pinder, *Work Motivation*.

[14] B. F. Skinner, *Science and Human Behavior* (New York: Macmillan, 1953).

[15] J. S. Adams, "Toward an Understanding of Inequity," *Journal of Abnormal Psychology* 67 (1963), pp. 422–36.

feel unfairly treated, they will be motivated to change something to reestablish equity.

Another cognitive theoretical perspective, called *goal setting*, has been formulated largely by E. A. Locke.[16] This theory emphasizes the role of conscious goals in motivating behavior (see Chapter 19). If accepted by the employee, behavioral goals that are clear, specific, and especially, difficult, lead to higher levels of the behavior.

Yet another cognitive process model is called *expectancy theory*.[17] It hypothesizes that individuals are motivated toward a behavior when they (1) believe they can engage in the behavior, (2) believe consequences will follow from the behavior, and (3) value those consequences.

Expectancy Theory

Each of these theories has received some support in the many investigations of them, and each has its own advocates.[18] In this section, expectancy theory is described at greater length. It will be used as the basic motivation model throughout this book for three reasons. First, at least as much as any other process orientation, expectancy theory has been supported by research findings. This support applies not just for predicting employee performance levels, but also for predicting initial job choice.[19]

Second, expectancy theory is a general theory, inclusive enough to subsume relevant portions of other theories within its framework. For example, the major behavioral predictions of reinforcement theory are essentially similar to expectancy theory predictions.[20] Finally, and significantly, expectancy theory can be helpful in suggesting ways managers can enhance employee motivation through appropriate P/HR activities (as shown in the discussion below).

Expectancy theory assumes that employees or job seekers try to maximize their *expected* satisfaction in any situation. However, because of uncertainties in the environment the individual can only *seek* to

---

[16] E. A. Locke and G. P. Latham, *Goal Setting: A Motivational Technique That Works* (Englewood Cliffs, N.J.: Prentice-Hall, 1984), p. 52.

[17] V. H. Vroom, *Work and Motivation* (New York: John Wiley & Sons, 1964).

[18] See, again, Pinder, *Work Motivation*.

[19] See D. P. Schwab, J. D. Olian-Gottlieb, and H. G. Heneman III, "Between Subject Expectancy Theory Research: A Statistical Review of Studies Predicting Effort and Performance," *Psychological Bulletin* 86 (1979), pp. 139–47; D. P. Schwab, S. L. Rynes, and R. J. Aldag, "Theories and Research on Job Search and Choice," in *Research in Personnel and Human Resources Management*, vol. 5, eds. K. M. Rowland and G. R. Ferris (Greenwich, Conn.: JAI Press, 1987), pp. 129–66.

[20] T. R. Mitchell, "Motivation: New Directions for Theory Research and Practice," *Academy of Management Review* 7 (1982), p. 85.

maximize satisfaction. For example, an employee may believe that high performance will result in a promotion, something that would be satisfying. However, after performing well, the employee may nevertheless not be promoted because management decided to reward someone with longer service with the organization. In addition, those things that the employee expects to find satisfying may not turn out to be so. If promoted, an employee might find that moving to a higher job level was not as satisfying as previously thought. Thus, the expectancy model does not say that people will actually maximize satisfaction, only that they will try to maximize it.

Expectancy: Effort-behavior perceptions

According to the theory, motivation to engage in a specific behavior depends on three perceptions (beliefs) of the individual. One of these, *expectancy*, refers to the individual's perceptions (beliefs) about his/her ability to engage in a particular behavior. Examples of expectancy perceptions include (1) beliefs that job applicants would have regarding the possibility of attaining a job if they applied, and (2) beliefs employees would have about the possibility of being high performers if they tried. In short, expectancy represents the employee's estimate of the likelihood (subjective probability) that a behavior can be achieved, given some level of effort. The theory predicts, other things being equal, that the stronger the expectancy perception (the more confident the individual is about successfully engaging in the behavior), the higher the motivation toward that behavior.

Instrumentality: Behavior-reward perceptions

Instrumentality refers to employee perceptions of the consequences (or results) of a behavior. For example, an employee might ask: "If I perform well, will I receive a salary increase?" "If I attend work every day this week, will my manager compliment me?" A job seeker might ask, "If I quit this job, will I have to move to another city?" Thus, instrumentality represents the employee's subjective estimate of the likelihood that a reward (e.g., pay increase) will follow *if* a behavior (e.g., high performance) is achieved. Note that there may be a unique instrumentality perception for each potential reward. An employee who is confident that high performance will lead to a salary increase (high instrumentality for receiving a raise), for example, may also be confident that the supervisor will not offer praise in any event (low instrumentality for verbal recognition).

Valence

How desirable does the individual find the potential rewards? Are they positive, negative, or neutral? Measurements of the desirability of rewards are called "valence perceptions." The theory makes no a priori predictions about the desirability of specific rewards beyond stating that each may be uniquely valent to various individuals. An employee, for example, may find a salary increase highly valent, may be indifferent to peer group approval, and may find a promotion negatively valent. Thus, in testing or using expectancy theory, it is important to have valence measures for the types of rewards discussed earlier in this chapter.

The overall expectancy model

In general, perceptions of expectancy, instrumentality, and valence combine to influence motivation as shown in Figure 5–5. An employee is expected to be motivated to engage in a behavior (such as high performance) if s/he (1) feels capable of successfully achieving the behavior (high expectancy), (2) believes that the behavior will lead to rewards (high instrumentalities), and (3) finds the rewards attractive (positive valence).

INFLUENCING MOTIVATION

Managerial Roles

Expectancy model concepts can be helpful in suggesting how managers, both line and P/HR, might establish policies and practices to enhance employee motivation. Of the three concepts, managers probably have the least influence on the valences employees attach to various work rewards. Such preferences are fairly well established by the time

FIGURE 5–5
Employee Motivational Process

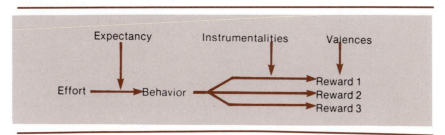

one becomes an employee. On the other hand, there is a good reason to believe that managers can successfully influence employees' expectancy and instrumentality perceptions.

Influencing expectancy perceptions

Since expectancy refers to beliefs about how effort is linked to behavior, attention must be given to the employee's actual ability to perform the task at hand. Thus, the issues considered here parallel the discussion of employee ability in Chapter 4. As noted there, P/HR practices can influence ability in several ways. First, given a task to perform, expectancy perceptions can be improved through selection or training procedures. Selection procedures can be useful in hiring employees whose abilities match the requirements of the job (see Chapters 10 and 11). Training, alternatively, can improve skills of existing employees, thus increasing expectancy perceptions (see Chapter 13). A strategy involving line management practice can take employees' abilities as givens and change the tasks to be performed (see Chapter 4). Such an approach is being increasingly employed by organizations as a method to improve productivity (see Chapter 19). Similarly, the match between task requirements and individual abilities may be improved through the judicious use of transfer and promotion policies (see Chapter 12).

The strategies identified above all attempt to increase expectancy perceptions by improving the correspondence between task requirements and the abilities of individuals. Such strategies presume that employees know what tasks they are to work on and at what levels they are to perform. Surprisingly, such an assumption may often be unwarranted. Line managers would do well to ensure that employees have a clear understanding of what is expected on the job. Goal-setting theory predicts that performance improves if specific, clear, and difficult goals are established.[21] In the context of the expectancy model, such goal setting probably strengthens expectancy perceptions.[22]

---

[21] Support for these assertions is reported by A. J. Mento, R. P. Steel and R. J. Karren, "A Meta-Analytic Study of the Effects of Goal Setting on Task Performance: 1966–1984," *Organizational Behavior and Human Decision Processes* 39 (1987), pp. 52–83. See also Chapter 19.

[22] The reader may reason that difficult goals would lead to lower expectancy perceptions than easy goals, an apparent contradiction between expectancy and goal-setting theories. However, the evidence suggests that when goal difficulty is held constant, those with higher expectancy levels perform at higher levels. See H. Garland, "Relation of Effort-Performance Expectancy to Performance in Goal-Setting Experiments," *Journal of Applied Psychology* 69 (1984), pp. 79–84.

Influencing instrumentality perceptions

Where expectancy perceptions depend largely on ability, instrumentality depends on what will likely happen as a result of the behavior. As such, the critical issue in improving instrumentality is the relationship managers establish linking desired behaviors to rewards. Managers need to make rewards *contingent* on the desired behavior. This means not only that those who engage in the behavior should be rewarded, but that those who do not should not obtain the reward.

It is important to establish the contingency with policy and practice. For example, suppose an organization wants to reward and motivate high performance with a merit pay system (see Chapter 14). Policies and support systems would be needed to establish, among other things: (1) how pay increases are to be related to performance, and (2) how performance is to be measured. Line managers would also be called on to actually assess the performance of employees and to make recommendations about the size of their pay increases. Successful implementation of a program aimed at increasing instrumentality perceptions for valent rewards thus requires an integrated effort of both P/HR and line management.

An alternative to rewarding desired behavior is *punishing* undesired behavior. Research on punishment, however, suggests that its impact on behavior is less predictable than the contingent use of positive rewards.[23] Punishment only communicates what not to do; it does not indicate what should be done. Moreover, unless criticism implied by punishment is positive, the employee being punished may generalize the unpleasant experience to the manager who provides it.[24]

Line managers should not expect to be able to make all consequences that employees find positively valent contingent on desired behavior. First, there are constraints imposed by outside institutions and regulations. For example, the organization may have an agreement with a union to make promotions contingent on length of service. In that case, management could not make promotion contingent on high performance because of the prior agreement. Government regulation, such as the Fair Labor Standards Act, keep organizations from making pay completely contingent on performance among employees covered by minimum wage provisions.

---

[23] Pinder, *Work Motivation*, pp. 202–4.

[24] R. A. Baron, "Negative Effects of Destructive Criticism: Impact on Conflict, Self-Efficacy and Task Performance," *Journal of Applied Psychology* 73 (1988), pp. 199–207.

A second constraint occurs because others in the organization besides managers also control rewards. Especially significant in this context are the rewards administered by co-workers. Co-workers generally influence employees through common group membership.[25] Each employee is typically assigned to a *formal* work group. *Informal* groups, which often do not correspond to formal groups, are also common. Both formal and informal groups develop *norms* (expectations about appropriate behavior) for members.

With respect to the model used here, groups and group norms perform several functions. For one thing, groups are a potent source of reward since approval is often a positive valent consequence for members. The more *cohesive* (experiencing a sense of solidarity) the group, the stronger the motivational impact. Cohesive groups are characterized by a great deal of communication and interaction; thus the group reaction will be felt strongly by the individual. Cohesiveness ensures that the instrumentality between the members' behavior and the group's approval or disapproval will be high.

It is at this point that the compatibility of group with managerial goals becomes especially relevant. If goals are similar, one would expect cohesiveness to lead to higher performance because group rewards would reinforce managerial policies. Alternatively, if group and managerial goals conflict, group cohesiveness would lead to lower productivity because the group would reward alternative behaviors. Both conditions are found in practice.[26]

Groups may also reinterpret instrumentalities that managers try to establish through P/HR policies and procedures. Often the instrumentalities as communicated by the group are more accurate and influential than those specified in organizational policy. This phenomenon has been carefully documented in the case of financial reward systems. To illustrate, a machine shop had a stated policy of paying drill press operators for each unit produced so that in theory the more one produced, the more pay one received.[27] Yet, employees seldom produced beyond a certain amount, even though they had to waste several hours a day to hold their production down. Investigation revealed that employees believed that higher production would result in changes in production standards so that more effort would have to be expended to earn the same amount. In short, the drill press operators believed (had instrumentality perceptions) that high production beyond a certain point

[25] For an overview of groups and group behavior, see E. P. Hollander, *Principles and Methods of Social Psychology*, 3d ed. (New York: Oxford University Press, 1976), pp. 376–425.

[26] M. E. Shaw, "An Overview of Small Group Behavior," in *Contemporary Topics in Social Psychology* (Morristown, N.J.: General Learning Press, 1976), pp. 335–68.

[27] W. F. Whyte, *Money and Motivation* (New York: Harper & Row, 1955), pp. 20–27.

would actually lead to a reduction in pay and/or harder work. These instrumentality perceptions were carefully and forcefully communicated by the informal group.

Motivating Specific Behaviors

Managers are likely to have their greatest motivational impact on employees to the extent that they positively influence expectancy or instrumentality perceptions. Four kinds of employee behavior are of special interest: applications for jobs, work attendance, job performance, and remaining with the organization. Each of these will be discussed briefly below and more fully in subsequent chapters.

Attracting new employees

In the case of job applications, expectancy refers to beliefs about the probability of getting a job if the individual applies. Instrumentalities refer to the linkages between accepting a job and the potential consequences associated with that job. Both depend heavily on the recruiting procedures used by the organization (see Chapter 9).

The expectancy model has been used in a number of situations to assess the predictability of applicants' career and job choices.[28] An investigation of applicants to public accounting firms is illustrative.[29] It found that the higher the job seekers' expectancies that they would be offered a job by a particular accounting firm, the higher the probability that they interviewed for employment at that firm. Moreover, applicants were more likely to accept offers at organizations they believed were instrumental in obtaining valued consequences. Thus, in both cases, job-seeking behaviors conformed to the predictions of the expectancy model.

There is an important distinction between job-choice behavior and behaviors that go on once one is in the organization. Specifically, job seekers are typically not likely to know much about the organization before they join it. That is, their instrumentality perceptions for many consequences will be nonexistent (they will have no idea whether the job will provide certain consequences), or their instrumentality perceptions

[28] For a review, see Schwab et al., "Theories and Research on Job Search and Choice."

[29] E. E. Lawler III, W. J. Kuleck, Jr., J. G. Rhode, and J. E. Sorensen, "Job Choice and Post Decision Dissonance," *Organizational Behavior and Human Performance* 13 (1975), pp. 133–45. A study of blue-collar job seekers found much the same thing. Nearly a third of the reasons given for not applying at a specific organization were personal, including beliefs that they would not be offered a job (that is low expectancy). H. L. Sheppard and A. H. Belitsky, *The Job Hunt: Job-Seeking Behavior of Unemployed Workers in a Local Economy* (Baltimore: Johns Hopkins University Press, 1966), pp. 41–42.

may be highly inaccurate.[30] These perceptions may thus be easily manipulated by organizations that attempt to make job opportunities appear
better than they really are. As will be shown in Chapter 9, however, such
attempts to influence job seekers may lead to reduced satisfaction and
higher subsequent turnover among employees so recruited.

Motivating performance

The expectancy model has been investigated most frequently in the
context of motivating employee performance.[31] These investigations
have found fairly consistently that more highly motivated employees,
according to the model, are also higher performers. For example, a life
insurance company used the expectancy model to asssess the dollar
volume of sales and the percentage of sales quotas achieved by its
salespeople.[32] The higher-performing salespeople had higher expectancy
perceptions (believed their effort would more likely lead to sales success)
and higher instrumentality perceptions.

The implications of such findings for managers are apparent. An
organization can enhance employee motivation, and hence performance,
if it can enhance expectancy and instrumentality perceptions. As indicated, such P/HR activities as selection and training can improve the
former; policies and managerial practices aimed at making rewards contingent on performance can increase the latter.

Motivating attendance and length of service

Length of service, or its opposite (turnover), can also be explained
within an expectancy framework. When considering whether to leave an
organization, the employee would likely consider the ease of leaving
(expectancy), which would depend largely on the available alternatives,
such as other job opportunities. In addition, the employee would probably consider the instrumentality of leaving for valued consequences (the
desirability of leaving). This model and the model pertaining to absenteeism are elaborated in Chapter 7.

Although the expectancy model has not been explicitly used as a way
of predicting and controlling employee attendance and length of service

---

[30] Job seekers' lack of knowledge about characteristics of job opportunities has been well
documented in studies of labor markets. For a review, see H. S. Parnes, *Research on Labor
Mobility* (New York: Social Science Research Council, 1954), pp. 165–69.

[31] For reviews, see T. R. Mitchell, "Expectancy-Value Models in Organizational Psychology," in *Expectancy, Incentive, and Action*, ed. N. Feather (Hillsdale, N.J.: Erlbaum and
Associates, 1980); Schwab et al., "Between Subject Expectancy Theory Research."

[32] R. L. Oliver, "Expectancy Theory Predictions of Salesmen's Performance, *Journal of
Marketing Research*" (1974), pp. 243–53.

to the extent that it has been used with employee performance, its applicability to these issues seems equally clear. In the case of attendance, expectancy refers to the employee's perceived ability to attend. Instrumentality, alternatively, refers to the consequences associated with attending. One study of this sort was performed on unionized production employees at General Motors.[33] Absenteeism (lack of attendance) was found to be more strongly related to the positive consequences of not attending (such as break from routine) than to the negative consequences of not attending (such as loss of wages). These findings suggest that General Motors was not making a link between absenteeism and the negative consequences contingent.

SUMMARY

P/HR management is typically responsible for helping line management obtain, retain, and foster an effective work force. As the model developed in this and the previous chapter points out, both employee ability and motivation are essential for achieving these outcomes. This chapter stressed that motivating employees involves two general issues. One is the identification of valued rewards that may serve to stimulate employees to action. While many such rewards are potentially influential, differences among employees in their preferences make *universal* lists risky. Management is better advised to find out about employee preferences for rewards through systematic measurement efforts.

A second important motivational component has to do with employee perceptions about linkages. As noted, two such perceptions, expectancy and instrumentality, are critical. Expectancy perceptions (linking effort to a behavior) can often be influenced by the same P/HR activities that influence abilities. Instrumentality perceptions (linking the desired behavior to rewards) are strongest when rewards depend on accomplishment of the desired behavior. P/HR policies that foster this dependency encourage motivation.

DISCUSSION QUESTIONS

1. Identify the distinction between content theories of motivation and process theories of motivation. Why is each inadequate for understanding motivation without the other?

2. Of the various sorts of rewards that individuals find attractive, which might a manager have the most control over for motivating employees, and which the least?

---

[33] L. G. Morgan and J. B. Herman, "Perceived Consequences of Absenteeism," *Journal of Applied Psychology* 61 (1976), pp. 738–42.

3. Why do managers have little influence over which rewards employees find valent?

4. How can employees' expectancies be strengthened to enhance performance?

5. Using expectancy theory, explain how co-workers can affect an employee's performance either favorably or adversely.

6. How can organizations use expectancy theory to achieve such desired personnel/ human resource outcomes as attraction, attendance, and retention?

PART THREE

Assessing Personnel/ Human Resource Management Outcomes

6

Employee Performance

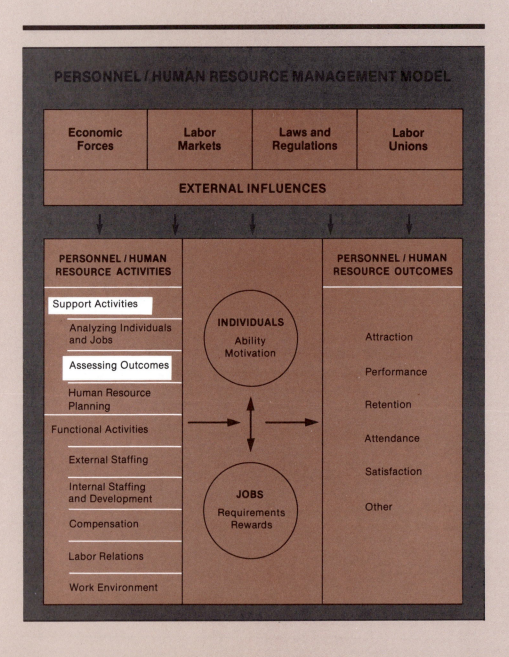

After reading this chapter, you should be able to speak to the questions posed in each of the following personnel/human resource incidents:

1. The hospital you work for has an extensive performance appraisal system for nearly all employees. Separate appraisal forms exist for office, maintenance, and technical employees. Unfortunately, there seem to be many problems with the system. Not all appraisals are completed yearly as they should be, many employee interviews (which are supposed to be completed by the supervisor shortly after the appraisal) are not conducted, and there have been many complaints about the accuracy of the results. As personnel/human resource manager for the hospital, what steps might you contemplate to improve this situation?

2. A consulting firm employs a substantial number of professionals with advanced degrees. The work is structured so that these employees typically work in fairly small groups of four to six with a project manager. At present, performance appraisals are done by the manager at the conclusion of a project (usually between 6 and 14 months). The results are used primarily to determine merit salary increases. Recently it has been suggested that the professionals also provide peer appraisals to go along with manager's appraisal. How do you react to this recommendation? What information, if any, could the professionals provide not already available from the manager? Are there any disadvantages to peer appraisal?

3. You have just been hired by a rapidly growing certified public accounting organization. Because of the growth, the senior partners are contemplating the implementation of several formal personnel/human resource activities. Among these is a proposal to install a formal performance appraisal system. You have been asked to identify the purposes such a system might serve. In addition, you have been asked to recommend a set of purposes that would best serve this organization and to identify likely pitfalls to be avoided. What set of purposes would you identify? What constraints would you want to bring to management's attention?

Managers often believe that the most significant P/HR outcome involves the contributions employees make to the organization's goal attainment. These contributions are called *employee performance*, meaning how effectively employees carry out their job responsibilities. High-performing employees successfully meet their responsibilities and thereby make a contribution to the goals of the organization.

Employee performance is important in the P/HR model because it serves as a crucial outcome variable in evaluating P/HR management. However, before performance can be used for managerial decisions, it must first be *measured*, and that is why assessing outcomes is a human resource activity in the model.

Organizations use many methods to measure employee performance; several are discussed in greater detail later. However, the most frequently used method is called *performance appraisal*, and it is given the greatest attention here. Performance appraisal requires observation and then evaluation of an employee's work by someone, usually the employee's manager. The results of the appraisal are generally recorded on some sort of form, often written in short phrases describing work results or critical employee behaviors. Typically, at least a portion of the appraisal form asks the manager to record assessments in a scaled format, such as a numerical scale ranging from one (unsatisfactory) to seven (satisfactory). Direct numerical comparisons between employees can then be made.

The next section presents a discussion of three common performance appraisal purposes. The following section describes performance measurement practices in organizations. Section three deals with issues to be considered whenever an organization intends to measure employee performance. This is followed by a description of several types of commonly used measurement procedures. The final section is a discussion of administrative challenges in performance measurement.

PERFORMANCE MEASUREMENT PURPOSES

Measures of performance are used by both line and P/HR managers for a variety of specific purposes. In general, however, line management uses them to influence employee performance through administrative decisions and employee feedback. P/HR management usually is also involved in these activities, but uses performance measures additionally to evaluate its own policies and practices.

Administrative Decisions

Traditionally, organizations have used performance assessments primarily to make administrative decisions about employees. Questions pertaining to promoting an employee, choosing employees for layoff or transfer, and making salary increase recommendations are examples of such administrative decisions. Managers responsible for such decisions need to obtain and use measures of employee performance.

Using performance assessments for administrative purposes helps place employees in positions where their abilities can be best used and can be helpful in assigning employees to appropriate future positions. In addition, administrative decisions linked to performance have a strong motivational potential, as discussed in Chapter 5. High performance is encouraged by rewarding the highest performers with such things as salary increases and promotional opportunities. In the terminology of expectancy theory, such actions strengthen employees' instrumentality perceptions between high performance and attractive rewards.

Employee Feedback and Development

Another purpose of performance assessment is to let employees know where they stand relative to performance objectives and organization expectations.[1] Here the manager uses the results of the performance assessment to provide feedback to the employee. In part, this feedback is designed to satisfy what some managers believe are subordinates' rights to know where they stand with the organization.[2] In part, feedback helps employees realize their potential to be high-performers (the self-developmental objective). Feedback encourages self-development through both instrumentality and expectancy perceptions.

By providing concrete evidence of performance levels, feedback can strengthen employee instrumentality perceptions for certain types of rewards. Thus, for example, a high-performing employee will frequently experience feelings of achievement and accomplishment and will associate good performance with these rewards in the future.

Expectancy perceptions (the link between effort and performance) can also be influenced. Accurate feedback can provide information about the

---

[1] J. P. Campbell, M. D. Dunnette, E. E. Lawler III, and K. E. Weick, Jr., *Managerial Behavior, Performance and Effectiveness* (New York: McGraw-Hill, 1970), p. 65.

[2] M. G. Haynes, "Developing an Appraisal Program," *Personnel Journal* 57 (1978), pp. 66–67.

job activities performed well and about activities that need to be performed better. If employees use information about the latter to focus their energies and efforts, feedback can strengthen their expectancy perceptions.

Evaluation of Policies and Programs

Another important use of performance assessments is to evaluate policies and programs implemented to influence work behavior. Consider as an illustration a managerial program developed to redesign the jobs performed by a group of employees. An evaluation of that program might involve a comparison of employee performance before jobs were changed with performance following the change. Or a comparison might be made between performance in the department where the change had been implemented and that of a similar department where the task redesign program had not been introduced. In any event, measures of performance are necessary to determine whether the change had the desired effect.

There are two P/HR activities where performance assessments are especially important for evaluation purposes. One is employee selection, discussed in Chapter 10. Here the problem is to determine whether the procedures organizations use to screen applicants (tests, interviews, and so forth) result in better hiring decisions than if these screening procedures are not used.[3] The second is employee training, a topic discussed in Chapter 13. Here the evaluation program involves deciding whether those trained become more effective performers than those not trained.[4]

CURRENT PRACTICES

A survey by the Bureau of National Affairs found that a majority of organizations use performance appraisals. Figure 6–1 shows that performance appraisals are more likely to be used among office employees than production employees. Such not-for-profit organizations as governmental units and hospitals are almost as likely to use performance appraisals for office employees as are profit-seeking organizations. They are more likely to use them for production employees.

---

[3] G. P. Latham and K. N. Wexley, *Increasing Productivity Through Performance Appraisal* (Reading, Mass.: Addison-Wesley Publishing, 1980), pp. 3–4.

[4] K. N. Wexley and G. P. Latham, *Developing and Training Human Resources in Organizations* (Glenview, Ill.: Scott, Foresman, 1981), pp. 78–100.

FIGURE 6–1

Performance Appraisal Usage in Organizations (percent of organizations)

| | Type of Employee | |
Type of Organization	Office	Production
Manufacturing	87%	56%
Nonmanufacturing	90	69
Not-for-profit	86	76
Less than 1,000 employees	88	62
More than 1,000 employees	88	65
All organizations	88	63

Source: Adapted from Bureau of National Affairs, "Performance Appraisals Programs," *Personnel Policies Forum* 135 (1983).

Evidence from several other surveys tends to confirm the fact that performance appraisals are used widely in both the private and public sectors of the economy.[5] In large organizations several different kinds of appraisal systems may be in operation for different groups of employees.

The Bureau of National Affairs survey also asked respondents to indicate what performance appraisals were used for in their organization. Results are shown in Figure 6–2. Among both office and production employees, performance appraisals are most frequently used for salary increase and promotion decisions, illustrations of administrative uses of

FIGURE 6–2

Uses of Performance Appraisal in Organizations (percent of organizations with appraisal)

| Performance Appraisal Used for: | Type of Employee | |
	Office	Production
Salary decisions	86%	79%
Promotion decisions	79	75
Identifying training needs	71	70
Human resources planning	37	31
Developing skills inventories	20	21
Layoff decisions	16	17

Source: Adapted from Bureau of National Affairs,"Performance Appraisal Programs," *Personnel Policies Forum* 135 (1983).

---

[5] C. Peck, *Pay and Performance*, Research Bulletin, no. 155 (New York: The Conference Board, 1984), pp. 17–22; C. J. Fombrun and R. L. Land, "Strategic Issues in Performance Appraisal: Theory and Practice," *Personnel* 60, no. 6 (1983), pp. 23–31.

performance appraisal. In addition, some organizations use appraisal results as an input to the development and maintenance of employee information systems and for human resources planning. Both of these are clearly P/HR responsibilities.

While the results of performance appraisals are used for a variety of purposes, general management typically does not develop the appraisal procedures, nor does it often assume full responsibility for collecting and analyzing the information necessary to make the appraisal results helpful. Personnel specialists are likely to be involved in the development of a performance appraisal system and in the evaluation of appraisal results.

PERFORMANCE MEASUREMENT ISSUES

To be effective, performance measures should aid management in meeting two requirements. First, the measurement system must identify in what ways there can be positive employee contribution to the organization. This component is referred to as *identifying the dimensions of performance*. Second, the system should help establish *standards of contributions* for each performance dimension identified in the first step. That is, a procedure should help managers differentiate between employees who are performing well and those who are performing poorly on each dimension that is important to job success.

Identifying Performance Dimensions

Virtually any job requires employees to conduct a variety of activities; some are essential, others less so. Job performance is usually *multidimensional*. Further, since jobs differ, activities necessary to make effective contributions differ across jobs.

Figure 6–3 illustrates these issues by showing six dimensions of performance and their applicability to three jobs: executive secretary, typing-pool secretary, and filing clerk. The first four dimensions are specific to the different jobs. For example, only the executive secretary must take dictation and coordinate the superior's activities. Figure 6–3 also indicates that the last two dimensions are common to all three jobs. These more general dimensions represent activities that are important in all three jobs.

An employee's performance on these various dimensions is at least partially independent. For example, an executive secretary may take dictation and type well but be uncooperative with co-workers. Thus, a good measure will get at all important performance dimensions in the

FIGURE 6–3
Dimensionality of Job Performance

Dimensions	Executive Secretary	Typing-Pool Secretary	Filing Clerk
Dictation	x		
Coordination of superior's activities	x		
Copy machine operation		x	
Typing	x	x	
Filing	x	x	x
Cooperation with co-workers	x	x	x

jobs to be included in the system. Failure to do so will mean that the employee's overall contribution to the goals of the organization will not be properly captured.

There are two general ways to approach important job activities. One views performance in terms of the *results* of the job while the other focuses on *employee behaviors* that lead to those results. An example of the former would be the number of sales achieved by an employee; of the latter, the closing techniques used to obtain the sales.

Both approaches are appropriate for defining job performance. Results are often the focus in systems used primarily for such administrative decisions as salary increases. On the other hand, the employee feedback and development objective calls for an emphasis on the employee behaviors that led to the result. Thus, organizational performance measurement systems often combine results and behavioral dimensions.[6]

In short, a procedure is required that (1) permits identification of the multidimensional aspects of performance, (2) identifies either performance results, the behaviors that lead to those results, or both, and (3) identifies dimensions on each job, or at least each job family within the organization.

The P/HR activity that comes closest to satisfying these requirements is *job analysis* (as discussed in Chapter 4.)[7] As that chapter indicated, job analysis represents systematic procedures to study jobs. Use of these systematic procedures helps avoid two common performance measure-

---

[6] D. R. Ilgen and J. L. Favers, "Limits in Generalization from Psychological Research to Performance Appraisal Process," *Academy of Management Review* 10 (1985), 311–21, points out that it is difficult with many jobs to accurately separate employee behaviors from the results of those behaviors. Thus, a measurement procedure that combines the two probably makes the manager's appraisal task easier to perform.

[7] Latham and Wexley, *Increasing Productivity*, pp. 48–51.

ment difficulties: *deficiency* and *contamination*.[8] Deficiency occurs if dimensions that are actually important to job success are not included in the measure of performance. Alternatively, if dimensions extraneous to job success are included in the performance measure, contamination results.

Determining the factors that constitute contamination and deficiency obviously depends on what is important for success on specific jobs. Given the information in Figure 6–3, contamination would occur if a filing clerk was assessed on copy machine operation. However, failure to assess a typing-pool secretary on copy machine operation illustrates measurement deficiency. Also illustrative of deficiency would be failure to assess employees in any of the three jobs on the general dimensions of filing and cooperation with co-workers.

Job analysis as the basis for identifying performance dimensions is not recommended solely because it results in better measurement. Its use is also important if the performance assessment procedure is challenged in equal employment opportunity litigation. Indeed, one review found that in all EEO cases where the organization had based its performance assessment system on job analysis, the defendant (employer) won, while it did so less than 25 percent of the time when job analysis was not used.[9]

Establishing Performance Standards

The second issue to be addressed in the development of performance measures has to do with determining whether a particular employee's behavior or work outcomes constitute good, bad, or neutral performance. This issue involves a question of performance *standards*. Generally speaking, the procedure used to establish standards is highly specific to the type of performance measure. Thus, its discussion is deferred to the next section, which deals with measures.

One generalization can be made, however, and that is the importance of establishing standards before the work is performed. The significance of this dictum has empirical as well as legal foundations. As noted in Chapter 5 (see also Chapter 19), research shows that clear, specific, and

---

[8] B. F. Nagle, "Criterion Development," *Personnel Psychology* 6 (1953), pp. 271–89.

[9] H. S. Feild and W. H. Holley, "The Relationship of Performance Appraisal System Characteristics to Verdicts in Selected Employment Discrimination Cases," *Academy of Management Journal* 25 (1982), pp. 392–406. See also L. S. Kleiman and R. H. Foley, "The Implications of Professional and Legal Guidelines for Court Decisions Involving Criterion-Related Validity: A Review and Analysis," *Personnel Psychology* 38 (1985), pp. 803–33.

difficult goals (standards) often lead to higher performance. From a legal perspective, the specification of standards before the work is performed is the only way of requiring that standards be met.[10]

PERFORMANCE MEASURES

As noted, performance appraisal instruments are by far the most widely used form of performance measurement and are discussed first. Other forms of performance measures are also used on occasion, and they are discussed at the end of this section. Such measures usually focus on physical output, either the amount produced or the amount sold.

Performance Appraisal

For reasons to be discussed below, a plethora of appraisal procedures has been developed over the years. Many of these have received little attention by organizations or were abandoned long ago. The present section discusses only those that are widely used by organizations or extensively researched. These can be conveniently categorized according to whether the standards of performance are established comparatively or absolutely.

Comparative procedures

Comparative procedures are based on the *relative* standing among employees. They allow for such statements as: Employee A is a better employee on dimension X than employee B; both are better performers than employee C. There are several ways that comparative performance appraisal procedures can be conducted: straight and alternation ranking, paired comparison, and forced distribution. Since only straight ranking and forced distribution appear to be used, only they are discussed here.[11]

Straight ranking.   This is a simple appraisal procedure involving a comparison of appraisees. The manager is typically asked to consider all subordinates and to identify the best performer, next best, and so on

---

[10] W. F. Cascio, "Scientific, Legal, and Operational Imperatives of Workable Performance Appraisal Systems," *Public Personnel Management* 11 (1982), pp. 367–75.

[11] Peck, *Pay and Performance*, p. 18. For an overview of comparative procedures, see S. J. Carroll and C. D. Schneier, *Performance Appraisal and Review System* (Glenview, Ill.: Scott, Foresman, 1982), pp. 124–26.

FIGURE 6–4
Forced Distribution at General Motors

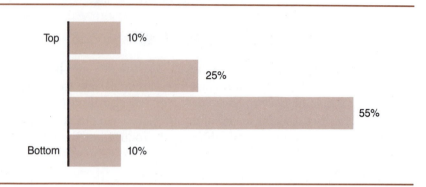

Source: Based on "GM's New Compensation Plan Reflects General Trend Tying Pay to Performance," *The Wall Street Journal,* January 26, 1988.

through all subordinates to the poorest. The procedure is a natural one since ranking people on an informal basis is done frequently.

Forced distribution.   Here, the appraiser assigns employees to a small number of categories, typically three to seven. The distribution is *forced* in that the manager is required to put a certain percentage of employees into each category. It is *comparative* because it is the relative standing of employees that determines the categories in which they are placed.

Figure 6–4, for example, shows a four-category forced distribution that General Motors recently installed to assess performance of over 100,000 white-collar employees.[12] It requires GM office managers to place 10 percent of employees in the top category, 25 percent in the next category, and so forth. If it is reasonable to assume that employee performance is distributed roughly as the categories prescribe, the procedure may be appropriate when performance levels can realistically be divided into only a few categories and/or if the manager cannot make accurate distinctions between each and every employee. The last can occur because there are no observable differences in performance or because the manager lacks knowledge about the small differences in performance levels that exist among employees.

---

[12] J. M. Schliesinger, "GM's New Compensation Plan Reflects General Trend Tying Pay to Performance," *The Wall Street Journal,* January 26, 1988.

Absolute standards

The second major approach to standard-setting in appraisal involves specifying absolute standards of performance. For example, a quality dimension on a job where employees produce a component for a physical product might specify categories of the number of rejects generated ranging from "almost never" to "half or more." The evaluator's task is to assess each employee's performance against these written performance levels. Such procedures are regarded as *absolute* because one's evaluation depends on the written (absolute) standards, not on how one does relative to others in the work group.

When one's performance assessment does not depend on the performance of others, intergroup comparisons are facilitated. In theory, this allows management to determine whether one group is superior to another, whereas comparative procedures cannot do this. As will be shown later, however, absolute standards procedures often fail to realize this potential advantage.

A variety of procedures using absolute standards has been developed. These differ from each other in the way they identify performance dimensions and/or the way they specify the absolute standards for each dimension. The diversity of approaches is illustrated by describing three procedures below.[13] First, the traditional *trait-rating scale* is used frequently, especially among production employees, and has been researched extensively, usually in comparison with some other rating procedure.[14] Behaviorally anchored rating scales, the second, have been researched extensively,[15] but the extent of their use by organizations is in question.[16] The third, management by objectives, is both widely used, largely among managers, and researched.

Traditional trait-rating scale.   Such scales usually have the following characteristics:

1.   Several performance dimensions are identified, usually not based on job analysis.

---

[13] Carroll and Schneier, *Performance Appraisal*, pp. 102–24.

[14] Fombrun and Land, "Strategic Issues in Performance Appraisal."

[15] L. D. Dyer and D. P. Schwab, "Personnel/Human Resource Management Research," in *Industrial Relations Research in the 1970's: Review and Appraisal*, eds. T. A. Kochan, D. J. B. Mitchell, and L. D. Dyer (Madison, Wis.: Industrial Relations Research Association, 1982), pp. 197–220.

[16] In the survey by Fombrun and Land ("Strategic Issues in Performance Appraisal"), the behaviorally anchored rating scale was reported to be used frequently. However, in the Conference Board (Peck, *Pay and Performance*) and BNA (*Performance Appraisal Programs*) surveys, BARS were not reported to be used at all.

FIGURE 6–5

Example of a Traditional Rating Scale

Rating Scale (check one level of performance for each standard)				
	1	*2*	*3*	*4*
Dimensions:	*Unsatisfactory: Needs to Improve Substantially*	*Questionable: Needs Some Improvement*	*Satisfactory: Meets Normal Expectations*	*Outstanding: Substantially Exceeds Normal Performance*
Quality of work				
Quantity of work				
Initiative in work				
Promotability to next level				

2. The dimensions are presumed to be equally applicable to a wide variety of jobs and, hence, are general dimensions. Thus, one performance appraisal form may be used throughout the organization or at least for all employees in major job groupings, such as among all clerical jobs.

3. Absolute standards are also developed judgmentally to represent different levels of performance. These levels constitute the rating scale points on the scales. Moreover, the same standards are typically applied to all dimensions. A typical rating scale format is shown in Figure 6–5.

Behaviorally anchored rating scale.   A very different absolute performance measure is called a "behaviorally anchored rating scale" and is done on a job-by-job basis.[17] Such scales result from steps designed to identify (1) multiple performance dimensions and (2) unambiguous standards representing good and poor performance levels on each dimension.

Figure 6–6 shows nine performance dimensions that were identified using this method on a sales manager job in a retail department store. In addition, Figure 6–7 shows the rating scale and accompanying performance standard statements (called "critical incidents") for the dimension

---

[17] This procedure was originally developed by P. C. Smith and L. M. Kendall, "Retranslation of Expectations: An Approach to the Construction of Unambiguous Anchors for Rating Scales," *Journal of Applied Psychology* 47 (1963), pp. 249–55.

FIGURE 6-6

Multiple Dimensions of a Retail Sales Manager's Job

Dimension
1. Supervising sales personnel.
2. Handling customer complaints.
3. Meeting day-to-day deadlines.
4. Ordering merchandise.
5. Developing special promotions.
6. Assessing sales trends.
7. Using company systems and administrative operations.
8. Communicating with higher management.
9. Diagnosing and alleviating special problems.

Source: Adapted from J. P. Campbell, M. D. Dunnette, R. D. Arvey, and L. V. Hellervik, "The Development and Evaluation of Behaviorally Based Rating Scales," *Journal of Applied Psychology* 57 (1973), pp. 15–22. Copyright 1973 by the American Psychological Association. Reprinted/adapted by permission of the publisher and author.

called "supervising sales personnel." Statements near the top of the scale, for example,

> Could be expected to conduct full day's sales clinic with two new sales personnel and thereby develop them into top salespeople in the department.

represent high performance on this dimension, whereas statements at the other end of the scale such as,

> Could be expected to make promises to an individual about his/her salary being based on department sales even when s/he knew such a practice was against company policy,

represent poor performance. Scale points and statements in between these extremes show other levels of performance that might be observed when a manager is supervising sales personnel.

The steps in developing a behaviorally anchored rating scale are both time consuming and rigorous. For example, the identification of performance dimensions is done through job analysis. Further, the performance standard statements are tested and retested to ensure that managers unambiguously agree on the levels of performance they represent.

Behaviorally anchored rating scales differ from traditional rating scales by more concretely specifying the levels of performance on each dimension. Compare, for example, the rating scale in Figure 6–5 with the critical incidents in Figure 6–7. The more specific standards of the latter are designed to minimize rating errors that occur in traditional rating

FIGURE 6-7

Example of a Behaviorally Anchored Rating Scale Dimension

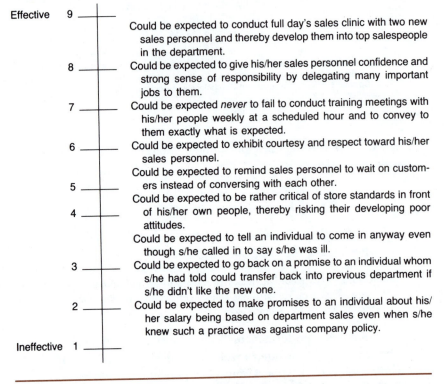

SUPERVISING SALES PERSONNEL

Gives sales personnel a clear idea of their job duties and responsibilities; exercises tact and consideration in working with subordinates; handles work scheduling efficiently and equitably; supplements formal training with his/her own "coaching"; keeps informed of what the salespeople are doing on the job; and follows company policy in agreements with subordinates.

Effective 9	Could be expected to conduct full day's sales clinic with two new sales personnel and thereby develop them into top salespeople in the department.
8	Could be expected to give his/her sales personnel confidence and strong sense of responsibility by delegating many important jobs to them.
7	Could be expected *never* to fail to conduct training meetings with his/her people weekly at a scheduled hour and to convey to them exactly what is expected.
6	Could be expected to exhibit courtesy and respect toward his/her sales personnel.
5	Could be expected to remind sales personnel to wait on customers instead of conversing with each other.
4	Could be expected to be rather critical of store standards in front of his/her own people, thereby risking their developing poor attitudes.
	Could be expected to tell an individual to come in anyway even though s/he called in to say s/he was ill.
3	Could be expected to go back on a promise to an individual whom s/he had told could transfer back into previous department if s/he didn't like the new one.
2	Could be expected to make promises to an individual about his/her salary being based on department sales even when s/he knew such a practice was against company policy.
Ineffective 1	

Source: Adapted from J. P. Campbell, M. D. Dunnette, R. D. Arvey, and L. V. Hellervik, "The Development and Evaluation of Behaviorally Based Rating Scales," *Journal of Applied Psychology* 57 (1973), pp. 15–22. Copyright 1973 by the American Psychological Association. Reprinted/adapted by permission of the publisher and author.

scales. Unfortunately, as discussed below, this particular difference between behaviorally anchored and traditional scales has not been as promising as hoped.[18]

---

[18] See Dyer and Schwab, "Personnel/Human Resource Management Research."

Management by objectives.   A third procedure using absolute standards is management by objectives.[19] The appraisal portion of management by objectives involves two steps. First, a set of performance *objectives* is established for the employee to implement during some future time period, such as the next 6 to 12 months. These objectives may deal with virtually any aspect of performance. A manager, for example, may have objectives set regarding a cost-reduction program, subordinate developmental activities, or the reduction of union grievances.

Setting objectives in this way is similar to job anlaysis. The objectives specified are analogous to performance dimensions in traditional and behaviorally anchored rating scales. However, in management by objectives the goals are established for *individuals*, not *jobs*. In effect, each individual is thought to have a potentially unique job. Two salespersons, for example, may be assigned different objectives even though their jobs involve the same overall activities. In this sense, management by objectives is even more specific than behaviorally anchored rating scales.

The second appraisal step is management by objectives involves rating the employee's performance at the end of the specified period. Here the focus is on how well the employee met the goals established in the preceding step.

Evaluation

Organizations using performance appraisal are likely to use a procedure involving absolute standards.[20] This is somewhat surprising because comparative procedures are often a useful way to sort out differences in employee performance. Further, research suggests that comparative rankings tend to be more closely related to direct measures of productivity (see below) than performance measures using absolute standards.[21] Finally, they are relatively easy to develop, and managers can easily understand the evaluation process.

Two difficulties with comparative procedures mitigate against greater use. First, they do not necessarily reveal whether an employee's per-

---

[19] Much has been written about management by objectives. Two of the better discussions can be found in R. W. Hollman, "Applying MBO Research to Practice," *Human Resource Management* 15 (1976), pp. 28–36; and in S. J. Carroll and H. L. Tosi, *Management by Objectives: Application and Research* (New York: Macmillan, 1976).

[20] Peck, (*Pay and Performance*, p. 18), for example, reported that less than 15 percent of firms in our industry reported using comparative procedures in performance appraisal systems linked to merit systems.

[21] R. L. Heneman, "The Relationship between Supervisory Ratings and Results-Oriented Measures of Performance: A Meta-Analysis," *Personnel Psychology* 39 (1986), 811–16.

formance is acceptable or unacceptable because one's standing depends partly on the general performance level of the group. This issue does not create difficulties if the group is large and if it can be assumed that the average performance level across groups is roughly equal. Unfortunately, these conditions often do not hold in work situations. Employee groups assigned to a single manager are often small, and average performance levels can differ substantially between groups. Thus, an employee who is appraised as a high-performer in one group may not be contributing as much as a member of another work group who receives only an average ranking.

Second, comparative procedures are problematic when used to provide feedback to employees. They only tell the employee if the performance evaluation is above or below others; they do not tell how one might improve. Moreover, comparative feedback may encourage intragroup competition, which is undesirable if work output depends on coordinated group effort.

Turning to measures using absolute standards, traditional trait-rating scales both define the dimensions of performance and specify performance levels in a loose, nonsystematic fashion. Consequently, they usually fail to capture the specific task components of various jobs and probably lead to both contamination and deficiency. Their use is thus not recommended.

Behaviorally anchored rating scales represent an intermediate form of appraisal in terms of generality. They are typically designed to cover only single jobs. A desirable feature of behaviorally anchored rating scales is the fact that they are based on job analysis. The likelihood of contamination and deficiency is thus substantially reduced. The anchoring of the numerical values on the final rating instrument also represents a sophisticated attempt to establish standards of performance.

The most individualized appraisal system is management by objectives. Each employee's job is analyzed, and each employee has, in effect, unique performance standards to work toward. Specificity is desirable if it can be assumed that the goals established are equally difficult for all employees. If not, employees who have had relatively easy goals set may be overrewarded compared to employees who have been given more difficult goals.[22]

---

[22] J. S. Kane and K. A. Freeman, "MBO and Performance Appraisal: A Mixture That's not a Solution, Part 1," *Personnel* 63, no. 12 (1986), pp. 26–36.

Measures of Physical Output

Production measures

Measures of the amount of output produced are sometimes used to assess performance contribution when employees produce an identifiable physical product. Some jobs in manufacturing are suitable for this sort of performance assessment. Such systems in manufacturing go back at least to the 1880s.[23]

Jobs for which measures of physical output are applicable need to satisfy several important requirements. First, the output must be produced on a repetitive basis to determine whether output levels increase or decrease with time or differ between employees. Also, unless the individual or work group is primarily responsible for the amount of output produced, it makes little sense to measure individual employee contributions in terms of units produced. Jobs in integrated production facilities where the pace of the work is largely determined by mechanical processes are thus not well suited to this form of performance assessment, even though such processes may yield an identifiable physical product.[24]

Sales measures

Closely akin to systems designed to measure physical output are systems aimed at assessing sales performance. Instead of producing outputs, organizations employ salespersons to sell their products and services to other organizations and individuals. For these employees, it is often useful to assess contributions by measuring the sales generated.

Many of the issues applicable to the measurement of production pertain also to the measurement of sales. Individual accountability for performance is as necessary for sales as it is for production. This requirement is becoming increasingly difficult to satisfy since the efforts of sales personnel are increasingly integrated with the activities of advertising and market research functions.[25]

---

[23] Procedures to measure productivity and establish production standards are discussed in L. A. Greenberg, *A Practical Guide to Productivity Management* (Washington, D.C.: Bureau of National Affairs, 1973).

[24] T. H. Patton, Sr., *Pay: Employee Compensation and Incentive Plans* (New York: Free Press, 1977), p. 440.

[25] Carroll and Schneier, *Performance Appraisal*, pp. 62–72.

Evaluation

Measures of production and sales apply only to employees in a limited number of jobs. Such measures require that an identifiable product or service be produced or sold. Naturally, many important organizational functions do not involve these activities. Moreover, measures that rely exclusively on output are likely to be inadequate even in the production and sales functions. For example, successful production usually involves activities such as cooperation with fellow employees and adequate maintenance of equipment. Successful sales typically involve behaviors aimed at achieving longer-run goals than the maximization of current sales volume. In such cases, productivity or sales measures alone would be deficient (as defined earlier).

Such difficulties do not keep management from trying to develop quantitative measures of employee performance. The latest efforts of this

---

ILLUSTRATION 6–1

Performance Monitoring with the Computer

The low cost and portability of microcomputers has encouraged employers to use them increasingly as a way of measuring aspects of employee performance. Leprino Foods Co., for example, a business with some 160 trucks on the road, installed a computer device in each to monitor their speed. The company estimated that drivers routinely drove about 10 miles above the speed limit resulting in reduced fuel efficiency and increased maintenance costs. Coupled with the introduction of the computers, the firm established a policy of increasing penalties for exceeding 65 miles per hour (the driver is fired if it happens three times) and a bonus of three cents per mile for every trip made without breaking 60.

A year following the introduction of the computers saw a 25 percent decline in fuel costs and a 20 percent decline in maintenance costs. Accident insurance premiums also declined $50,000. The quarter of a million dollars spent on computers saved three quarters of a million in the first year alone.

The use of computers to monitor performance is a logical, although somewhat frightening, extension of traditional methods designed to measure physical output. They are likely to be deficient, as discussed earlier, and likely to create some problems between employees and their managers.

For example, computer monitoring is employed in the word-processing unit of an Oregon state agency. Management used computer software to keep track of the time the employee was at the machine, the number of pages typed, and the keystrokes per minute. One enterprising employee was fired when it was discovered that she was calling up other employees' documents and destroying pages in order to reduce their productivity relative to her own. She also enhanced her own productivity by, among other things, typing short pages so that her page count looked good.

Source: M. W. Miller, "Productivity Spies: Computers Keep Eye on Workers and See If They Perform Well," *The Wall Street Journal*, June 3, 1985, pp. 1 and 15.

sort typically involve the computer. Office work of all sorts can increasingly be quantified and recorded electronically. A classic example involves word processing where the same computer used to do the typing can be programmed to monitor typing performance. Illustration 6–1 provides another example and illustrates some problems associated with such measurement.

ADMINISTRATIVE CHALLENGES

Up to this point, the emphasis has been on describing performance measure uses and measurement procedures, especially involving performance appraisal. The P/HR function is typically responsible for the development of such instruments, as noted previously.

Line managers are usually responsible for conducting the appraisals once the instrumentation is developed. Unfortunately, the results of their efforts often prove problematic. The greatest difficulty stems from the fact that individuals must conduct performance appraisals, and individuals are prone to many errors of judgment. Consider the task confronting the manager who must do the appraisal.[26] S/he must:

- Select the information to be obtained about the employees to be evaluated.
- Observe the employees and collect the needed information.
- Organize and store the information, often over a fairly long period of time (as much as a year to 18 months).
- Combine and integrate the information in what ultimately becomes the performance appraisal.

Clearly, there are many opportunities for the manager to misjudge the performance of employees. For example, the highest-performing employees may not receive the highest evaluations. As a consequence, human resource management is often called on to help improve the results of appraisals.

Error Identification and Reduction Approaches

Persons interested in improving performance appraisal outcomes usually focus on the types of errors that can creep into appraisal results. Figure 6–8 names and defines a number of such errors that have been

---

[26] For a more detailed discussion of errors and review of studies investigating such errors, see Ibid., pp. 38–42; W. F. Cascio, *Applied Psychology in Personnel Management*, 2d ed. (Reston, Va.: Reston Publishing, 1982), pp. 316–19.

FIGURE 6–8
Common Appraisal Errors

Unreliability	Inconsistency in the evaluations of a group of employees by two or more appraisers.
Leniency	Tendency to overevaluate performance of all employees appraised.
Central tendency	Tendency to erroneously evaluate all employees appraised as average or near average.
Recency	Tendency to take only performance occurring just before evaluation into account.
Halo	Tendency to erroneously evaluate an employee as similar on all dimensions of performance, at a high, medium, or low level.

investigated at length.[27] Until recently, one of two approaches has been used to eliminate such errors.

Attempts to develop appraisal instruments that will help reduce rating errors have been the most common. The behaviorally anchored rating scale is but one such attempt. However, evidence does not indicate that the use of behaviorally anchored scales or other alternative measuring instruments reduces the amount of errors relative to traditional graphic rating scales.[28] The instrumentation approach has simply not been very fruitful.

Another approach has sought to reduce errors by training managers in avoiding common rating errors. While promising in the abstract, training designed to reduce rating errors has not been too successful.[29] Part of the difficulty stems from the fact that much of the training research has been hindered by some serious flaws that go beyond the scope of this text. As a consequence, while it is clear that such training can change the evaluations that managers generate, it is not yet clear that managers have been successful in obtaining more accurate appraisals.

A Process Perspective

Disappointment with the lack of success from efforts at improved instrumentation and training to reduce errors has led to a reexamination

---

[27] F. J. Landy and S. L. Farr, "Performance Rating," *Psychological Bulletin* 87 (1980), pp. 72–107.

[28] For a review of this research, see Dyer and Schwab, "Personnel/Human Resource Management Research."

[29] D. E. Smith, "Training Programs for Performance Appraisal: A Review," *Academy of Management Review* 11 (1986), pp. 22–40.

of performance appraisal and ways in which it might be improved. A broader perspective of performance appraisal is emerging, one that focuses on the entire appraisal process.[30] In this view, the manager is seen as acting in an organizational environment that is instrumental in influencing the types of appraisal results obtained. The environment can be helpful, it can improve the rating results, or it can be harmful.

One way to think about this broader approach for improving appraisal results is to recognize that performance appraisal is a managerial behavior and is thus modifiable by changes in ability and/or motivation. Managers observe their employees, they evaluate what they have observed, and they record their evaluations. If their ability and/or motivation to engage in these activities can be improved, the results of the appraisal process should be improved.

Ability to appraise

The ability to appraise involves several components. One certainly is the knowledge that the manager has of the actual performance dimensions. Another is knowledge of the performance of the employee to be evaluated. A manager is expected to have this sort of knowledge, but that does not necessarily have to be true. For example, the manager may have too many subordinates, or the subordinates may be geographically dispersed (as is often the case in sales). In such cases, knowledge of performance may be difficult to obtain. Or, in some instances, the dimensions of the jobs themselves may be so numerous that the manager has difficulty observing performance. This is sometimes true of professional jobs. In such situations, it may be necessary to provide the manager with assistance (for example, peer appraisals) to provide information on job performance.[31]

Knowledge of performance standards is another ability requirement of valid appraisals. As noted earlier, standards obtained from the appraisal instrument alone do not provide managers with sufficient information to perform an acceptable job of appraising. Top management must clearly specify what standards of performance are to be adhered to. Recent

---

[30] For an expression of this broader perspective, see D. R. Ilgen and J. M. Feldman, "Performance Appraisal: A Process Focus," in *Research in Organizational Behavior*, eds. B. M. Staw and L. L. Cummings (1983), pp. 141–97.

[31] A recent summary of studies indicates that the relationship between manager and peer appraisals is usually quite high. See M. M. Harris and J. Schaubroeck, "A Meta-Analysis of Self-Supervisor, Self-Peer, and Peer Supervisor Ratings," *Personnel Psychology* 41 (1988), pp. 43–62.

research suggests that training can be quite useful for this purpose and thus can help improve appraisal accuracy.[32]

Motivation to appraise

Managers are generally responsible for many tasks—performance appraisal is only one of them. Managers will not be motivated to evaluate effectively unless performance appraisal is recognized as an important dimension of their job, a dimension that if performed well will be rewarded. In short, effective performance appraisal systems require administration such that the manager's instrumentality perceptions—accurate performance appraisal results lead to valent rewards—are positive.

Experience suggests that rewards and punishments often depend primarily on other managerial task dimensions (for example, cost reduction, sales increases). Indeed, the organization may punish accurate appraisals through informal norms about what results are expected. Frequently, lenient results are the expected norm. A manager who provides accurate appraisals in such a climate may actually be punished for doing so.

Evidence suggests that the purpose of the appraisal influences motivation to evaluate and hence the results obtained.[33] Specifically, when appraisal results are used for administrative decisions (for example, salary increases), ratings tend to be higher and less variable than when used in a developmental or coaching context. Thus, ambiguity among managers about performance appraisal uses could lead to inconsistency in appraisal results.

These issues are only illustrative of the types of contextual features of performance appraisal systems that can impact on managerial motivation and hence performance appraisal results.[34] But they do clearly suggest that improvements in evaluation outcomes depend on more than managerial ability alone. Organizations must additionally examine the en-

[32] Smith, "Training Programs for Performance Appraisal." For research, see E. D. Pulakos, "A Comparison of Rater Training Programs: Error Training and Accuracy Training," *Journal of Applied Psychology* 69 (1984), pp. 581–88; and E. D. Pulakos, "The Development of Training Programs to Increase Accuracy with Different Rating Tasks," *Organizational Behavior and Human Decision Processes* 38 (1986), 76–91.

[33] See, for example, S. Zedeck and W. F. Cascio, "Performance Appraisal Decisions as a Function of Rater Training and Purpose of the Appraisal," *Journal of Applied Psychology* 67 (1982), pp. 752–58.

[34] For an elaboration on other contextual factors, see Ilgen and Feldman, "Performance Appraisal."

vironment in which performance appraisal is conducted, modifying it where appropriate, to enhance managerial motivation to provide accurate appraisal results.

Summary

In reflecting on things that influence managers' ability and motivation, it seems clear that P/HR must consider the entire performance appraisal process to achieve accurate results. Policies linking performance appraisal outcomes to other personnel systems (such as merit plans), policies and practices regarding the bases of managerial reward systems,

---

ILLUSTRATION 6–2

Process Approach to Performance Appraisal at Control Data

A performance appraisal system recently implemented at Control Data Corporation (CDC) provides a good illustration of a process perspective to performance appraisal. Their system has four major parts.

1. *Job-related instrumentation.* Working from job analyses of all jobs to be covered by the system, CDC first identified 13 job families consisting of positions having many common characteristics and requiring many common job behaviors. Instruments were developed with the active participation of those who would use the system.

2. *Appraisal model.* This model was developed as a blueprint of the appraisal process specifying how *(a)* work objectives are to be set, *(b)* employees are to be appraised, *(c)* the appraisal instruments are to be completed, *(d)* managers are to conduct developmental appraisal discussions with employees, *(e)* the appraisal information is to be used to determine salary recommendations, and *(f)* the manager is to communicate that salary information to employees.

3. *Support system.* The human resources staff provides support to managers by providing extensive training in the system.

4. *Monitoring and tracking system.* The human resources staff also surveys managerial and employee reactions to the appraisal systems and tracks managers to see that they are following established system procedures. As a part of this process, managers are given feedback on how their evaluations and salary recommendations conform to norms in other departments of CDC.

Notice how this system puts the appraisal instrument, and even the appraiser, into a broader systems context. Explicit efforts are made to improve managerial ability through extensive training. However, in addition, motivation is considered through explicit policies regarding appraisal objectives to be accomplished and, especially, through monitoring and feedback. It is not a panacea, of course, but a good start in trying to bring a process approach to bear in this difficult area of P/HR.

Source: L. R. Gomez-Mejia, R. C. Page, and W. W. Tornow, "Improving the Effectiveness of Performance Appraisal," *Personnel Administrator* 30, no. 1 (1985), pp. 74–82.

and systems monitoring performance appraisal practices all can affect the way managers conduct appraisals. Illustration 6–2 describes one organization's attempt to take this comprehensive approach.

Equal Employment Opportunity

If a measurement system reflects discrimination on the basis of age, sex, or other similar factors, the subsequent actions based on the results may have an adverse impact on employees. For example, if older employees systematically receive lower performance appraisals than younger employees, but there are no *true* performance differences between younger and older employees, the older employees may be adversely affected in subsequent salary raises, promotions, and participation in formal developmental activities. In this instance, bias against older employees crept into assessments of their performance, which in turn led to biased treatment of the older employees.

Much research has been performed on potential bias in performance ratings. This research does not necessarily show that discrimination is involved since actual performance levels were not controlled. It is nevertheless suggestive of discrimination in the case of race since performance appraisal ratings are more adversely affected by minority status than are measures of physical output.[35] In the case of age, the evidence is somewhat more mixed.[36] Nevertheless, there has been a dramatic increase in the number of cases filed charging age discrimination by employers during the 1980s.[37]

Recall that Title VII of the Civil Rights Act explicitly permits the use of a bona fide merit (performance appraisal) system as a basis for guiding subsequent managerial actions (see Chapter 3). If the organization is going to use performance appraisal in this way, it therefore must be sure that the performance appraisal system meets these standards.

As might be expected, there have been numerous court cases involving challenges to performance appraisal systems and decisions about

---

[35] For a review, see J. K. Ford, K. Kraiger, and S. L. Schechtman, "Study of Race Effects in Objective Indexes and Subjective Evaluations of Performance: A Meta-Analysis of Performance Criteria," *Psychological Bulletin* 99 (1986), pp. 330–37.

[36] One review found performance ratings to be more negatively related to age than physical productivity measures. See D. A. Woldman and B. J. Avolio, "A Meta-Analysis of Age Differences in Job Performance," *Journal of Applied Psychology* 71 (1986), pp. 33–38. However, a more recent and broader review found no age-performance relationship and no differences between productivity measures and performance ratings. See B. M. McEvoy and W. F. Cascio, "Cumulative Evidence of the Relationship between Employee Age and Job Performance," *Journal of Applied Psychology* (in press). Research is ambiguous regarding whether sex is related to performance ratings.

[37] S. P. Freedberg, "Forced Exits? Companies Confront Wave of Age-Discrimination Suits," *The Wall Street Journal*, October 13, 1987, p. 37.

employees based on appraisal results. Various people have studied these cases to determine whether certain characteristics of appraisal systems tend to make them more legally defensible.[38] Based on one such review, the following prescriptive recommendations were made for designing and administering a legally defensible performance appraisal system.[39]

1. Conduct a job analysis to ascertain characteristics necessary for successful job performance.

2. Incorporate these characteristics into a rating instrument. Although the professional literature recommends rating instruments that are tied to specific job behaviors (i.e., BARS), the courts routinely accept less sophisticated approaches such as simple graphic rating scales and trait ratings. Regardless of method, written definitive standards should be provided to all raters.

3. Train supervisors to use the rating instrument properly. This involves instructions on how to apply performance appraisal standards when making judgments. The uniform application of standards is extremely important. In 6 of 10 cases decided against the organization, the plaintiffs were able to show that subjective standards had been applied unevenly to minority and majority employees.

4. As demonstrated in several cases, formal appeal mechanisms and review of ratings by upper-level personnel is desirable.

5. The organization should document evaluations and reasons for the termination decision. This information may prove decisive in court. Credibility is enhanced with documented performance appraisal ratings and instances of poor performance.

6. Provide some form of performance counseling or corrective guidance to assist poor performers in improving their performance. As seen in several cases, the courts look favorably on this practice.

It is clear that developmental procedures associated with behaviorally anchored rating scales and management by objectives are more likely to be legally defensible than a traditional trait-rating scale. However, there is one source of potential controversy. If performance appraisal results

---

[38] W. F. Cascio and H. J. Bernardin, "Implications of Performance Appraisal Litigation for Personnel Decisions," *Personnel Psychology* 34 (1981), pp. 211–26; Feild and Holley, "The Relationship of Performance Appraisal System Characteristics," pp. 392–406; W. L. Dandel and P. J. Langer, "Performance Evaluation and EEO," *Employee Relations Law Journal* 6 (1980), pp. 294–303; C. R. Klasson, D. E. Thompson, and G. L. Luber, "How Defensible Is Your Performance Appraisal System?" *Personnel Administrator* 25, no. 12 (1980), pp. 77–83; L. S. Kleiman and R. L. Durham, "Performance Appraisal Promotion and the Courts: A Critical Review," *Personnel Psychology* 34 (1981), pp. 103–22; and M. H. Schuster and C. S. Miller, "Performance Appraisal and the Age Discrimination in Employment Act," *Personnel Administrator* 29, no. 3 (1984), pp. 48–58.

[39] G. V. Barrett and M. C. Kernan, "Performance Appraisal and Terminations: A Review of Court Decisions since *Brito* v. *Zia* with Implications for Personnel Practices," *Personnel Psychology* 40 (1987), pp. 489–503.

have implications across individuals, such as competition for a promotion, some authorities argue that all employees would have to be evaluated using the same instrument. This might not be the case if behaviorally anchored ratings were used on different jobs or management by objectives was used even on the same job.[40]

SUMMARY

Because of its importance as a P/HR outcome, performance measurement is important to organizations. These measures are used (1) to make decisions about employees (such as promotions), (2) as a way to provide feedback to employees, and (3) as an input to evaluating the effect of various other P/HR activities.

A majority of organizations, public and private, attempt to measure employee performance. In some cases, they focus on physical output, either the amount produced or sold. Most measures, however, are performance appraisals where the manager observes and then evaluates an employee's performance.

In developing a performance measure, two issues are critical. The first pertains to the identification of performance dimensions (that is, the work behaviors or outcomes necessary to accomplish the job objectives). Job analysis is essential in this process. The second involves the establishment of performance standards for each dimension. In this last step, judgments are made about whether an employee is performing well or poorly.

Accuracy of performance measurement is an overwhelmingly significant issue. Its achievement requires a substantial organizational commitment. The commitment must be evidenced in the development of appraisal instruments, the training and motivation of managers, and the evaluation of appraisal results. In these areas, the expertise of the P/HR function is vital. Top-management commitment is also necessary in the day-to-day administration of the system. Here, line managers are responsible for actually conducting the appraisals. Such commitment can be beneficial to the organization through improvements in employee performance as a result of a well-developed and implemented system. Appropriate administrative decisions about employees, self-development, and improved management practices as a result of program eval-

---

[40] M. R. Edwards, M. Wolfe, and J. R. Sproull, "Improving Comparability in Performance Appraisal," *Business Horizons* 34, no. 5 (1983), pp. 75–83. For an opposing view, see R. Gruner, "Employment Discrimination in Management by Objectives Systems," *Labor Law Journal* (1983), pp. 364–70.

uations are all potential outcomes of valid appraisal systems. These benefits will be achieved, however, only if the organization is willing to make decisions based on the results obtained from the appraisal process.

DISCUSSION QUESTIONS

1. What do the terms *contamination* and *deficiency* refer to in appraisal? How can the problems they create be reduced?

2. How is job analysis useful in performance appraisal?

3. Under what circumstances is it appropriate to assess performance by measuring results (for example, physical output, sales)?

4. In what ways are behaviorally anchored rating scales superior to traditional rating scales? Are there any relative disadvantages to using a BARS?

5. How can appraisal errors be minimized?

6. From an equal employment opportunity perspective, what would be some desirable characteristics of a performance appraisal system?

Satisfaction, Attendance, and Retention

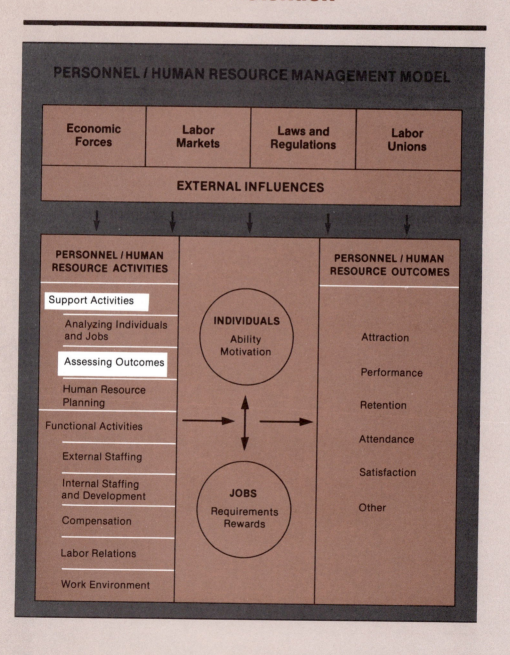

PERSONNEL / HUMAN RESOURCE MANAGEMENT MODEL

Economic Forces	Labor Markets	Laws and Regulations	Labor Unions

EXTERNAL INFLUENCES

PERSONNEL / HUMAN RESOURCE ACTIVITIES

Support Activities

Analyzing Individuals and Jobs

Assessing Outcomes

Human Resource Planning

Functional Activities

External Staffing

Internal Staffing and Development

Compensation

Labor Relations

Work Environment

INDIVIDUALS
Ability
Motivation

JOBS
Requirements
Rewards

PERSONNEL / HUMAN RESOURCE OUTCOMES

Attraction

Performance

Retention

Attendance

Satisfaction

Other

After reading this chapter, you should be able to speak to the questions posed in each of the following personnel/human resource incidents:

1. The grapevine has it that employees in several departments in the hosital you work for are highly dissatisfied. Your immediate supervisor has asked you to look into the problem. What would you recommend as a way of finding out whether satisfaction is too low? How would you go about getting the information you need to answer this question? Would you require anything of management before you recommend collecting such information? What would you recommend doing with the satisfaction information if it is collected?

2. A co-worker of yours has done a report claiming that if everyone in your division maintained a perfect attendance record, current production levels could be maintained with 15 percent fewer employees. The production manager has obtained a copy of this report and is highly interested in its implications for cost reductions. Is perfect attendance a realistic goal? If not, how would you decide what level of attendance is realistically obtainable? Are there any activities that management might undertake to increase employee attendance?

3. The city personnel/human resource department for which you work has, within the last year, begun a substantial program of hiring city maintenance employees. Surprisingly, many of the newly hired employees have already quit. Indeed, so many have quit that the city council has asked for an explanation. The personnel/human resource manager has dumped the problem in your lap. Are the quits really a problem? How do you decide? if you decide that the quits present a problem, what can management to do keep a greater percentage of the new employees on the job?

Employee performance, as discussed in the previous chapter, is one significant P/HR outcome. Many of the activities described in this book are aimed directly or indirectly at improving employee performance. There are, however, other important P/HR outcomes as well.

The present chapter considers three of these that are of concern to both management and employees, namely, employee satisfaction, attendance, and retention (length of service).

The issues to be considered here are similar to the issues discussed in the last chapter. P/HR management plays a similar role regarding satisfaction, attendance, and retention as it does regarding employee performance. Line management looks to the P/HR function for guidance in developing measures of each. It also expects help in collecting employee information on satisfaction, attendance, and retention. Finally, line management looks to P/HR management for assistance in developing and implementing control policies to improve these outcomes or to help maintain them if adequate.

Satisfaction is discussed in the following section. Included is a definition of satisfaction and a description of how management can survey and enhance employee satisfaction. The second section deals with attendance and retention. Emphasis is placed on ways to assess these P/HR outcomes and on ways for management to improve them.

JOB SATISFACTION

For better or worse, employees spend many of their waking hours at work. In addition to working on assigned tasks, they typically interact with other persons (supervisors, fellow employees), and are exposed to organizational policies and practices. All these, in turn, influence employee feelings about their jobs and organizations that employ them. These feelings are often called *job attitudes*.

A variety of attitudes relating to employment has been measured and studied. Examples include (1) job involvement (preoccupation with one's work), (2) organizational commitment (loyalty to one's employer), and (3) job satisfaction. Only satisfaction is discussed here because it has the longest history of both theory and measurement.[1]

---

[1] Evidence suggests that measures of these different attitudes assess somewhat different employee feelings. See, for example, P. B. Brooke, Jr., D. W. Russell, and J. L. Price, "Discriminant Validation of Measures of Job Satisfaction, Job Involvement and Organizational Commitment," *Journal of Applied Psychology* 73 (1988), pp. 139–45. Nevertheless, different employment attitudes often relate to employee behaviors in about the same way. See, for example, D. P. Schwab, "Construct Validity in Organizational Behavior," in *Research in Organizational Behavior*, vol. 2, eds. B. M. Staw and L. L. Cummings (Greenwich, Conn.: JAI Press, 1980), pp. 3–43.

Managers are concerned about job satisfaction for two main reasons. First, they often believe that job satisfaction influences such employee behaviors as attendance and length of service. It is commonly assumed that positive satisfaction leads to positive behaviors. Second, managers seek favorable satisfaction in its own right. In this context, managements view employees as a group to satisfy, much as they attempt to satisfy other groups such as customers, clients, and investors. Positive job satisfaction provides evidence that management is doing all right by its employees.

What Is Job Satisfaction?

The most commonly accepted definition views job satisfaction as depending on an evaluation the employee makes of the job and the environment surrounding the job.[2] This evaluation depends on two components: (1) what the employee actually experiences at work *what is* and (2) what values or desires for rewards the employee brings to the workplace *what should be*. Satisfaction is high when what is corresponds to what should be. Dissatisfaction occurs when the employee believes that these two components do not correspond.

Satisfaction facets

Employees experience satisfaction with many different components or facets of their work environment. Three in particular deserve mention: (1) organizational policies and practices (for example, compensation, promotions, and job security), (2) the people one works with, including supervisors and co-workers, and (3) the work itself.

Bear in mind that satisfaction with any single facet may not be highly related to satisfaction with any other facet. As a hypothetical example, Figure 7–1 shows employee A as satisfied with fellow employees but dissatisfied with the work and P/HR policies. Such independence is significant when management attempts to influence the satisfaction of its work force. To be effective, policies aimed at improving satisfaction require correct identification of those job characteristics that employees believe need improvement. This, in turn, requires that assessments of satisfaction measure each facet separately.

---

[2] An excellent discussion of the meaning of satisfaction is provided by E. A. Locke, "What Is Job Satisfaction?" *Organizational Behavior and Human Performance* 4 (1969), pp. 309–36. See also, E. A. Locke, "The Nature and Causes of Job Satisfaction," in *Handbook of Industrial and Organizational Psychology*, in ed. M. D. Dunnette (Chicago: Rand McNally, 1976), pp. 1,297–1,349.

FIGURE 7-1
Satisfaction with Alternative Job Facets

	Employee	
Facet	A	B
Co-workers	High	Low
Organizational policies	Low	High
Work itself	Low	Low

Individual differences

Individual employees, even though they have the same type of job, are likely to have different levels of satisfaction or dissatisfaction (compare employees A and B in Figure 7-1). To some extent this occurs because employees are likely to experience somewhat different treatment by the organization and coemployees. A supervisor may prefer one employee to another and hence treat the two somewhat differently. Also, promotion opportunities differ among employees because of variation in job performance or seniority.

In addition, however, satisfaction on similar jobs may vary because employee desires and values differ. A large nationwide oil company, for example, found that satisfaction among managers, professional, and technical employees varied depending on characteristics of the community in which the employees lived, even though the type of work and company policies were roughly comparable across communities.[3] It found that satisfaction with pay was generally higher among employees living in lower-cost communities, probably because their income expectations were not as high as those of employees living in more affluent areas.[4]

Again, the implication for company policy is clear. To obtain an accurate picture of employee satisfaction, management must get infor-

---

[3] G. F. Dreher, "Salary Satisfaction and Community Costs," *Industrial Relations* 19 (1980), pp. 340–44. These findings were confirmed on a nationally representative sample of American workers. See R. P. Vecchio, "Individual Differences as a Moderator of the Job Quality-Job Satisfaction Relationship: Evidence from a National Sample," *Organizational Behavior and Human Performance* 26 (1980), pp. 305–35.

[4] A somewhat controversial third reason for expecting individual differences in job satisfaction has also been suggested, namely, that employees are predisposed to be satisfied or dissatisfied before they enter a job. See, for example, B. M. Staw and J. Ross, "Stability in the Midst of Change: A Dispositional Approach to Job Attitudes," *Journal of Applied Psychology,* 70 (1985), pp. 469–80. However, more recent research casts doubt on this interpretation. See B. Gerhart, "How Important Are Dispositional Factors as Determinants of Job Satisfaction? Implications for Job Design and Other Personnel Programs," *Journal of Applied Psychology* 72 (1987), pp. 366–73.

mation from a representative sample of all employees. To focus on only a few, or a haphazardly chosen group of employees may give a misleading view of the feelings of the entire work force.

Surveying Job Satisfaction

Before management can develop policies and practices to increase employee satisfaction, or maintain existing levels if they are found to be acceptable, information must be obtained from the organization's work force. Management can informally acquire some insights into satisfaction levels based on impressions obtained from employees. Unfortunately, information gathered in this way may be misleading. Employees understandably are often reluctant to tell supervisors negative things about their jobs. Moreover, such information will almost certainly be obtained from a nonrepresentative sample of all employees.

An accurate assessment of employee satisfaction ordinarily requires a more formal procedure. *Satisfaction surveys* are often conducted to get systematic information from employees.[5] Such surveys are not as prevalent as assessments of performance, but studies of organizational practice indicate they are conducted frequently. The National Industrial Conference Board, for example, found that 71 percent of large organizations conducted employee attitude surveys.[6] In more than 90 percent of these organizations, the P/HR function was responsible for the survey process.

Satisfaction surveys can provide information on how employees feel about their jobs and the organization. However, surveys are not completely neutral information-gathering devices. Employee expectations may be raised simply because employees are asked to participate in the survey process. Failure to follow up on the survey with appropriate managerial action may result in lower employee satisfaction than existed before. Thus, satisfaction surveys should not even be conducted unless management is ready to make changes in policies and practices as called for by the survey's results.

Assuming management is prepared to make changes, a satisfaction survey involves (1) choice of a satisfaction measure, (2) administration of the measure, (3) analysis of results and feedback, followed by (4) administrative action. Each of these is discussed below.

---

[5] A more complete discussion of satisfaction surveys can be found in R. B. Dunham and F. J. Smith, *Organizational Surveys* (Glenview, Ill.: Scott, Foresman, 1979).

[6] A. R. Janger, *The Personnel Function: Changing Objectives and Organization*, National Industrial Conference Board, Report No. 712, 1976, p. 38.

Satisfaction measures

Satisfaction is usually measured with paper-and-pencil questionnaires completed by employees. Many early satisfaction questionnaires attempted to measure only overall satisfaction.[7] More recently, with the increased knowledge of satisfaction facets, measures have been designed to assess satisfaction along a variety of dimensions. An organization preparing for a survey is well advised to include measures of facets, as well as overall satisfaction, because they provide somewhat different information for managers.[8]

There are several good reasons for using a satisfaction measure that has already been developed rather than tailoring an instrument specifically for the organization in which it is going to be used. First, satisfaction questionnaire construction is a difficult and time-consuming activity.

The second reason is not quite so obvious and has to do with the nature of satisfaction itself. Unlike the measurement of, say, length or weight, satisfaction has no obvious zero point. It is very difficult, in the abstract, to say at what point satisfaction becomes dissatisfaction, or vice versa. Moreover, it is difficult to identify a level of satisfaction that is acceptable in some abstract fashion. As a consequence, it is highly desirable to be able to compare current employee satisfaction levels with some standard or norm.[9]

One such norm can be obtained from one's own employees by assessing satisfaction at more than one time. If the same measuring instrument is used each time, it is possible to find out if satisfaction is increasing or decreasing over time. Another norm can be obtained from satisfaction levels that have been observed among employees in other organizations. These comparisons are possible, however, only if the satisfaction measure has been widely used and information on other employees has been recorded and made available. The satisfaction measures described below have such comparative data available for users.

Although it is desirable to use standardized measures for the reasons given above, the organization may also wish to obtain specific information not available from the satisfaction questionnaire. Specifically developed items can be included in the total survey instrument in those situations. It is especially helpful to provide employees ample oppor-

---

[7] See, as an example of an overall satisfaction measure, A. H. Brayfield and H. F. Rothe, "An Index of Job Satisfaction," *Journal of Applied Psychology* 35 (1951), pp. 307–11.

[8] V. Scarpello and J. P. Campbell, "Job Satisfaction: Are all the Parts There?" *Personnel Psychology* 36 (1983), pp. 577–600.

[9] L. A. Mischkind, "Is Employee Morale Hidden behind Statistics?" *Personnel Journal* 65, no. 2 (1986), pp. 74–79.

FIGURE 7–2
Promotional Opportunity Items for the JDI

Good opportunity for advancement
Opportunity somewhat limited
Promotion on ability
Dead-end job
Good chance for promotion
Unfair promotion policy
Infrequent promotions
Regular promotions
Fairly good chance for promotion

Source: P. C. Smith, L. M. Kendall, and C. L. Hulin, *The Job Descriptive Index,* Department of Psychology, Bowling Green State University, Bowling Green, Ohio 43404. Copyright 1975, Patricia C. Smith.

tunity to write in additional comments about their job feelings. Such information may identify important employee concerns not assessed by the standardized measure.

Job descriptive index.   One widely used standardized measure of satisfaction is called the Job Descriptive Index (JDI).[10] The JDI measures satisfaction with five job facets: (1) work itself, (2) supervision, (3) pay, (4) promotion opportunity, and (5) co-workers. Items for the promotion opportunity facet are shown in Figure 7–2. Employees indicate their satisfaction with each item by simply responding "yes" (if the item describes the facet), "no" (if the item does not describe the facet), or "?" (if the employee cannot decide). The more *yes* responses to such positive items as "good chance for promotion," and *no* responses to such negative items as "dead-end job," the greater the satisfaction.

The Job Descriptive Index is easy to use, and it does not require a high level of reading ability to complete. It can be very useful when management wants information about employee satisfaction with broad facets of work. Comparative satisfaction information is available on a nationwide sample of employees.

Minnesota satisfaction questionnaire.   A more detailed set of facets is measured in the Minnesota Satisfaction Questionnaire.[11] It measures 20 satisfaction facets as shown in Figure 7–3. Each facet is measured by five

---

[10] The development procedures and comparative satisfaction information are contained in P. C. Smith, L. M. Kendall, and C. L. Hulin, *The Measurement of Satisfaction in Work and Retirement* (Chicago: Rand McNally, 1969).

[11] The MSQ is described and comparative data are provided in D. J. Weiss, R. V. Dawis, G. W. England, and L. H. Lofquist, *Manual for the Minnesota Satisfaction Questionnaire* (Minneapolis: Minnesota Studies in Vocational Rehabilitation, Bulletin 45, 1967), p. 22.

FIGURE 7–3
Satisfaction Facets of the MSQ

Ability utilization	Moral values
Achievement	Recognition
Activity	Responsibility
Advancement	Security
Authority	Social service
Company policies and practices	Social status
Compensation	Supervision—human relations
Co-workers	Supervision—technical
Creativity	Variety
Independence	Working conditions

Source: D. J. Weiss, R. V. Dawis, G. W. England, and L. H. Lofquist, *Manual for the Minnesota Satisfaction Questionnaire* (Minneapolis: Minnesota Studies in Vocational Rehabilitation, Bulletin 45, 1967), p. 22. Reprinted with permission of D. J. Weiss et al.

items (items for the advancement facet are shown in Figure 7–4). Employees indicate their feelings about each item on a five-point scale ranging from "very dissatisfied" to "very satisfied."

The Minnesota Satisfaction Questionnaire is also easy to use and, despite its imposing length, does not take long to complete. Organizations interested in more detailed satisfaction information from their employees, especially about facets of work itself, might do well to consider this questionnaire. Comparative satisfaction information is also available for employees in a variety of occupations.

Satisfaction survey administration

Administration of a satisfaction survey must be planned and conducted carefully because there are several biases that can influence the results. As already mentioned, one problem occurs if the sample of

FIGURE 7–4
Advancement Items from the MSQ

The opportunities for advancement on this job.
The chances of getting ahead on this job.
The way promotions are given out on this job.
The chances for advancement on this job.
My chances for advancement.

Source: D. J. Weiss, R. V. Dawis, G. W. England, and L. H. Lofquist, *Manual for the Minnesota Satisfaction Questionnaire* (Minneapolis: Minnesota Studies in Vocational Rehabilitation, Bulletin 45, 1967), p. 22. Reprinted with permission of D. J. Weiss et al.

surveyed employees does not represent the total group to be considered. For example, satisfaction varies systematically with age. Older employees are usually more satisfied than younger employees.[12] A sample that does not adequately represent all age levels in the organization will thus provide an erroneous view. Management often includes all employees in the survey to overcome this type of bias. Such a strategy also avoids the employee resentment that might result if only a portion of the work force participates.

A more subtle bias, having to do with the accuracy of the responses provided by the employees surveyed, can also occur. First, bias is likely if employees are not motivated to answer the questionnaire seriously. To overcome this problem, management should have a specific purpose for conducting the survey and communicate that purpose in the survey instructions. To illustrate, a large national marketing organization found that salespeople were more likely to feel that satisfaction surveys were desirable if they believed management acted on the results.[13] Such a finding again suggests that management should not conduct a satisfaction survey without making a specific commitment to follow up on the results.

A second source of bias occurs when employees are afraid to give honest responses. They may believe their responses will somehow be used against them. If, for example, employees think a supervisor is unsatisfactory, reporting such information may lead to supervisory retaliation.

Overcoming these potential employee biases requires careful planning and administration. The integrity of the survey may be enhanced if it is administered and analyzed by an outside group such as university researchers. In any event, anonymity should be assured and strictly enforced.[14]

Analysis and feedback

Analysis of satisfaction survey information typically involves two issues. Usually management wants to know how satisfaction varies among different groups of employees. This is often accomplished by calculating the average satisfaction on each facet measured for groups in different parts of the organization (such as departments), different job levels, and perhaps employees with different characteristics—such as age, sex, and

---

[12] S. R. Rhodes, "Age-Related Differences in Work Attitudes and Behavior: A Review and Conceptual Analysis," *Psychological Bulletin* 93 (1983), pp. 328–67.

[13] W. Penzer, "Employee Attitudes toward Attitude Surveys," *Personnel* 50, no. 3 (1973), pp. 60–64.

[14] Most firms provide anonymity. See M. LoBosco, "Employee Attitude Surveys," *Personnel* 63, no. 4 (1986), pp. 64–68.

time with the organization. Choice of appropriate groups partly depends on managerial estimates about where differences in satisfaction might exist. Average satisfaction among different groups can then be compared. Comparisons can also be made with employees working in other organizations if a standardized measure with such information is used. About the only constraint is to ensure that the number of employees in any group does not become so small that the responses become unreliable or that individual responses can be identified. [15]

In some cases, the organization may also want to see if satisfaction is related to other behaviors, such as employee attendance or length of service. For example, satisfaction levels across departments could be compared to turnover levels across departments.

If the results of the survey are going to be beneficial, they must be communicated to the managers responsible for the changes suggested. The P/HR department is likely to be involved in providing such feedback. In communicating to managers, it is appropriate to focus on the positive steps that can be taken for future improvement, rather than to concentrate on the problems that caused difficulties in the past. For this reason, it is often wise to start the feedback with top management who will be responsible for establishing policy on the actions taken to improve employment conditions. Starting with top management serves the additional purpose of showing others in the organization that the survey results will be taken seriously.

There are also good reasons to give feedback to the employees who participated in the survey. Feedback will likely have a positive impact on employee attitudes toward the survey process. A large data processing firm, for example, found that employees who received feedback (compared to those who did not) were most likely to (1) believe management was doing something about the survey results, and (2) be satisfied with the feedback procedure. [16] Incidentally, this organization also found that the most favorable employee responses occurred when the feedback was provided to small groups rather than in written form or in plantwide meetings.

Obtaining employee suggestions for improving employment conditions is another reason to provide employees with survey feedback. To illustrate, a plastics division of a paper company accomplished this by

---

[15] For more on survey analysis, see R. C. Ernest and L. B. Baen, "Analysis of Attitude Survey Results: Getting the Most from the Data," *Personnel Administrator* 30, no. 5 (1985), pp. 71–80.

[16] S. W. Alper and S. M. Klein, "Feedback Following Opinion Surveys," *Personnel Administration* 33, no. 6 (1970), pp. 54–56.

establishing a formal task force made up of employees from all levels of the organization.[17] The task force studied the results, made suggestions for change, and developed procedures for implementing the changes. Management concluded that the task force was helpful in getting active employee support for the survey (easing problems of administration) and making useful recommendations for improvements.

Administrative action

The specific actions that management takes following a satisfaction survey, or course, depends on the results. There are, however, several general possibilities to keep in mind.[18]

First, the adequacy of present policy guidelines can be obtained by studying current issues and their impact as revealed by the survey. In addition, new organizations often do not have a well-developed policy manual and typically feel that they can do without it. The attitude survey can indicate whether the organization has matured to the point that some statement of policy might allow for more autonomous action by the managers in the field or by different parts of the organization.

Second, handling supervisory problems is one of the most important aspects of work and yet one of the most difficult. The attitude survey can provide *feedback* on how the workers view the present cadre of supervisors. Only turnover and absenteeism give clearer evidence of supervisory problems than that provided by the satisfaction survey, and these indicators are by nature negative, usually obtained when a problem has reached a worrisome proportion.

Third, the workers' views on the extent to which they are being challenged by their jobs and the tasks required, the opportunities for achievement and growth, and the possibilities for promotion can be tapped by surveys. Misperceptions can be observed and corrected. Budding discontent can be nipped and energies channeled into more constructive efforts.

Fourth, the perception of pay has to be considered one of the more important issues related to the work situation. Pay, as the most universal reinforcer in the organization, is perhaps the most important indication to employees of their importance to the organization. The attitude

---

[17] E. D. Howe, "Opinion Surveys: Taking the Task Force Approach," *Personnel* 51, no. 5 (1974), pp. 16–23.

[18] R. V. Dawis and W. Weitzel, "Worker Attitudes and Expectations," in *ASPA Handbook of Personnel and Industrial Relations, Part 6: Motivation and Commitment*, eds. D. Yoder and H. G. Heneman, Jr. (Washington, D.C.: Bureau of National Affairs, 1979), pp. 23–49.

survey can uncover the feelings about this important issue and can aid the organization in learning how to handle communication and issues related to pay more acceptably.

Often the results of the survey might suggest a fairly substantial change such as a management or supervisory training program or a change in P/HR policy. In those cases, it is desirable to conduct a follow-up survey (after implementation of the change) to determine whether the change has had the desired effect. Illustration 7–1 describes how one organization changed its P/HR policies based on an initial satisfaction survey and how it then monitored those changes with a follow-up survey.

ILLUSTRATION 7–1
Using Satisfaction Surveys to Reduce Voluntary Turnover

A large international manufacturing firm was confronted with an unusually high turnover rate among its home office clerical staff located in Montreal. While other organizations located in the same labor market experienced voluntary turnover rates in the neighborhood of 20 percent per year, this firm consistently had turnover of about 30 percent. At that rate the manufacturer calculated the cost to be about $130,000 per year.

The manufacturer conducted a satisfaction survey of its 350 clerical workers using the Job Descriptive Index (JDI). Five months following the survey, 26 clerical employees had quit. To assess the relationship between satisfaction and voluntary turnover, the average satisfaction of 52 control employees who remained with the organization were compared to these 26 former employees. The controls were matched with the terminators on age, education level, job level, mother tongue, and marital status. The results of this comparison are shown below. Terminators reported lower satisfaction on all JDI facets, especially promotions.

Comparison of Terminators and Nonterminators

JDI Facet	Average Satisfaction Scores	
	Terminators	Nonterminators
Work itself	28.69	35.83
Pay	15.15	15.17
Promotions	9.35	17.16
Co-workers	37.40	41.44
Supervision	38.15	41.66

For both terminators and controls, satisfaction with salary and promotions was unusually low. Employees were unhappy with the administration of their pay and with the fact that they felt they were in "dead-end" jobs. As a result of these findings, the manufacturer changed its personnel/human resource policies regarding both pay and promotions. One year after these changes, voluntary turnover among clerical employees dropped to 18 percent, and two years later it dropped to 12 percent. During the same period, voluntary turnover among clerical employees in the manufacturer's labor market remained about 20 percent.

ILLUSTRATION 7–1 *(concluded)*

Another survey was conducted two years after the initial one to assess any changes of the policies on satisfaction. The average results of this survey are compared with the average for all employees in the first survey below. Note that there was an increase in satisfaction among all facets. However, satisfaction with pay and promotions, in particular, increased dramatically.

Comparison of Initial with Follow-Up Survey

JDI Facet	Average Satisfaction Scores	
	Initial Survey	Follow-up Survey
Work itself	35.33	36.11
Pay	15.01	32.83
Promotions	10.78	24.58
Co-workers	41.53	43.49
Supervision	40.85	43.23

This is an excellent illustration of how satisfaction surveys can be used to improve personnel/human resource practices. Especially noteworthy is the follow-up to see if the policy changes had the desired effect. It is also noteworthy that the firm compared its turnover with other organizations in the same labor market. Without such a comparison, it could not be determined if the reduced turnover was due to the policy changes or due to changes in market conditions that might have reduced turnover in all organizations.

Source: C. L. Hulin, "Job Satisfaction and Turnover in a Female Clerical Population," *Journal of Applied Psychology* 50 (1966); and C. L. Hulin, "Effects of Changes in Job-Satisfaction Levels on Employee Turnover," *Journal of Applied Psychology* 52 (1968). Copyright 1966, 1968 by the American Psychological Association. Reprinted/adapted by permission of the publisher and author.

ATTENDANCE AND RETENTION

Organizations often confront a serious problem of keeping their labor forces working. This problem manifests itself in two ways. The first occurs when employees temporarily stay away from work, referred to as "absenteeism." The second is when employees leave permanently, called "turnover." Relative to the outcomes in the P/HR model, absenteeism and turnover are the opposite of attendance and retention, respectively.

At the outset, it is necessary to distinguish between two types of absenteeism and turnover: *voluntary* and *involuntary*. In the case of absenteeism, voluntary refers to unscheduled absences by the employee. Not reporting to work on Friday to lengthen one's weekend illustrates voluntary absenteeism. Involuntary absenteeism, such as a health related absence, is outside the employee's control. Voluntary turnover refers to terminations initiated by employees. Leaving one's current employer for a higher-paying job is one example. Involuntary turnover, alternatively, is initiated by the employer. Major examples include *layoffs* (when the organization no longer needs the employee) and *dismissals* (when the employee is discharged for incompetence, rule violations, and so forth).

These distinctions are important because the causes of voluntary—as opposed to involuntary—absenteeism and turnover differ. Voluntary absenteeism and turnover are often thought to be influenced by P/HR policies and practices that influence employee satisfaction. Involuntary absenteeism, alternatively, is often outside the control of the employee and the employer. Involuntary turnover often depends on the quality of the initial selection decisions (when employees who cannot perform the jobs for which they were hired must be dismissed) and product scheduling and consumer demand patterns (when employees must be laid off). Whether the problem stems from voluntary or involuntary absenteeism or turnover must, therefore, be correctly identified before implementing control policies.

Absenteeism

Magnitude of the problem

Accurate absenteeism figures are difficult to obtain because not all organizations keep them. Moreover, among those that do, not all calculate absenteeism in the same way. Fortunately, the Bureau of National Affairs has implemented a continuing survey to obtain consistent information from a large sample of public and private organizations.[19] The bureau first conducted a survey and found that the formula most frequently used by organizations that maintain absenteeism statistics is:

$$\frac{\text{Number of employee days lost through job absence during the month}}{(\text{Average number of employees}) \times (\text{Number of workdays})} \times 100$$

To obtain comparable data from all organizations, the bureau asked (1) that absences of less than a day (tardiness) not be included and (2) that long-term absences be counted only through the first four days. Thus, the figures reported by the bureau systematically understate the total

[19] M. G. Miner, "Job Absence and Turnover: A New Source of Data," *Monthly Labor Review* 100, no. 10 (1977), pp. 24–31. The data are reported quarterly in the BNA's *Bulletin to Management*.

FIGURE 7–5

Median Monthly Job Absence Rates: Fourth Quarter, 1988

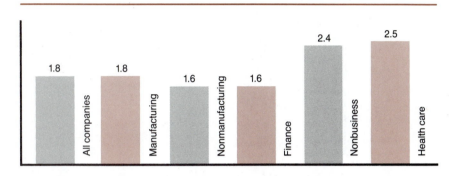

Source: Bureau of National Affairs, *Bulletin to Management,* March 10, 1988, p. 76.

absenteeism problem. Nevertheless, they provide consistent estimates from a wide variety of organizations and hence offer useful comparative information.

Information on average monthly absence rates by type of employer is given in Figure 7–5. Note that there are substantial variations ranging from a low of 1.6 percent in finance and nonmanufacturing in general to 2.5 percent in health care organizations. Individual variation in absenteeism is, of course, much greater.[20]

Measuring absenteeism

Because there is comparable information available, the absenteeism measure recommended by the Bureau of National Affairs (as reported above) is a useful measure. Basically, it provides an estimate of the total time lost due to absenteeism (underestimated as discussed above). It does not, however, distinguish between voluntary and involuntary absenteeism.

Unfortunately, it is difficult to successfully differentiate between these two forms of absenteeism because of problems in acquiring accurate information. Indeed, obtaining reliable absenteeism information, however it is broken down, has proven elusive.[21] Probably the best indicator

---

[20] See, for example, M. Fichman, "Motivational Consequences of Absences and Attendance: Proportional Hazard Estimation of a Dynamic Motivational Model," *Journal of Applied Psychology Monograph* 73 (1988), pp. 119–34.

[21] R. D. Hackett and R. M. Guion, "A Reevaluation of the Absenteeism-Job Satisfaction Relationship," *Organizational Behavior and Human Decision Processes* 35 (1985), pp. 340–81.

FIGURE 7-6
A Model of Employee Attendance

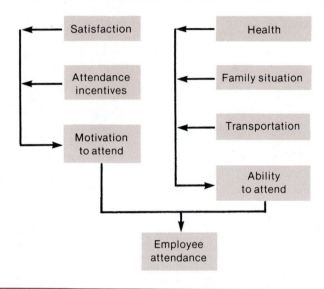

Source: R. M. Steers and S. R. Rhodes, "Major Influences on Employee Attendance: A Process Model," *Journal of Applied Psychology* 63 (1978), p. 393. Copyright 1978 by the American Psychological Association. Reprinted/adapted by permission of the publisher and author.

is *absenteeism frequency*, defined as the number of absences regardless of duration. While this information shares the unreliability difficulties of other measures, it is a better indicator of voluntary absenteeism.[22]

Controlling absenteeism

Many factors influence whether employees attend work on any particular day. Some of the major factors are shown in Figure 7–6. The two most immediate causes are the employee's *ability to attend* and *motivation to attend*. Ability corresponds closely to involuntary absenteeism. Major reasons employees may not be able to attend include personal illness, family problems that keep employees from the job, and difficulties with personal or public transportation. Although involuntary absenteeism of this sort can be predicted to some extent (and hence controlled) through the selection process, factors influencing ability to attend are not easily changed by management actions.

[22] Ibid.

The major opportunity to control absenteeism comes through the employee's motivation to attend. Managers often try to influence motivation through direct policies and practices regarding attendance. Most common are policies against voluntary absenteeism, frequently combined with penalties (including termination as the ultimate penalty) for offenders.[23] These policies, however, appear to be generally ineffective.

More promising results come from organizations that have experimented with the use of positive rewards for good attendance, such as cash bonuses, recognition, or time off with pay. Although not always successful, such policies often reduce absenteeism.[24] For example, Maid Bess Corporation, a manufacturer of clothing, tried a variety of reward programs for attendance in four different plants.[25] Most successful was a program that provided managerial recognition to employees who had no more than one day of absenteeism each quarter. In addition, employees with no more than two days for the year received custom-designed jewelry.

In this plant, absenteeism declined over one third, from 7.56 percent in the prior two years to 4.77 percent during the experimental year. The decrease resulted in dramatic cost savings for Maid Bess. Direct labor costs among the plants 400 employees fell by over $58,000 against a cost of about $10,000 for the program.

Another approach, so-called no-fault absenteeism, recognizes the inherent difficulties in distinguishing between voluntary and involuntary absenteeism.[26] Organizations using this approach recognize that some absenteeism is inevitable and permit a certain amount each year without penalty (perhaps three to five occurrences). They make no attempt to determine whether the absenteeism was voluntary or involuntary. Claimed advantages include (1) reduced supervisory time trying to determine whether an absence was "legitimate," (2) placing responsibility for attendance squarely on employees, and (3) improved attendance. The last advantage, however, needs further documentation and empirical support.

---

[23] D. Scott and S. Markham, "Absenteeism Control Methods: A Survey of Practices and Results," *Personnel Administrator* 27, no. 6 (1982), pp. 73–86.

[24] Three successful examples are described by A. Halcrow, "Incentive! How Three Companies Cut Costs," *Personnel Journal* 65, no. 2 (1986), pp. 12–13.

[25] K. D. Scott, S. E. Markham, and R. W. Robers, "Rewarding Good Attendance: A Comparative Study of Positive Ways to Reduce Absenteeism," *Personnel Administrator* 30, no. 8 (1985), pp.72–83.

[26] For descriptions and examples, see F. E. Kuzmits, "Is Your Organization Ready for No-Fault Absenteeism?" *Personnel Administrator* 29, no. 12 (1984), pp. 119–27; D. Olson and R. Bangs, "No-Fault Attendance Control: A Real World Application," *Personnel Administrator* 29, no. 6 (1984), pp. 53–56.

Some organizations are also taking a second look at traditional *paid sick leave policies*. Increasingly, managers believe that sick leave plans that provide payment for a fixed number of days' leave each year actually encourage absenteeism. Employees see sick leaves as a benefit to be used whether needed or not. Recommendations to reduce the use of such plans (that is, improve attendance) typically involve some positive rewards if sick days are accumulated rather than taken.

A study conducted in a nonprofit hospital illustrates this approach.[27] It provided time-off awards for employees who used fewer than their allotted hours of annual sick leave. Attendance was higher during the three years the program was in effect than the year before and after the study. In addition, attendance improved in the study group relative to a comparison group not in the program. Using utility analysis, the hospital found it made nearly 12 percent yearly on its investment in the program.

In summary, attendance is contingent on many factors. Some of these are outside the control of the individual and hence are essentially outside management's ability to influence. Others, however, appear to be at least partially within the organization's control. Positive rewards for good attendance, perhaps combined with negative sanctions for absenteeism, can lead to improved attendance.

Turnover

Magnitude of the problem

The Bureau of National Affairs also includes a measure of turnover as a part of its regular survey.[28] Again, an initial study found that most organizations calculated turnover as:

$$\frac{\text{Number of separations during month}}{\text{Average number of employees on payroll during month}} \times 100$$

To obtain comparability, the bureau survey asks organizations to include all permanent separations—except that persons laid off are to be excluded from the calculations entirely. Thus, although the measure includes mostly voluntary turnover (quits), it also includes some involuntary turnover (dismissals).

Figure 7–7 shows the median monthly turnover rate by type of employer for the fourth quarter of 1988. There is, as in the case of

---

[27] D. L. Schlotzhauer and J. G. Rosse, "A Five-Year Study of a Positive Incentive Absence Control Program," *Personnel Psychology* 38 (1985), pp. 575–85.

[28] Miner, "Job Absence."

FIGURE 7-7

Median Monthly Turnover Rates: Fourth Quarter, 1988

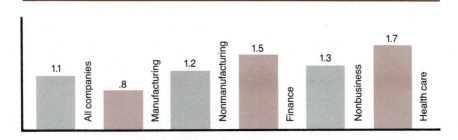

Source: Bureau of National Affairs. *Bulletin to Management.* March 10, 1988, p. 77.

absenteeism, considerable variation. Manufacturing firms had the lowest turnover, and health care organizations had the highest. Variation between organizations within an industry is even greater. For example, among manufacturing firms in December 1988, the survey found that turnover ranged from less than 1 percent to nearly 10 percent.[29]

Turnover, especially voluntary, is often viewed as undesirable, although this is not always true. From the individual's perspective, turnover is a major way to improve employment opportunities. When such mobility results in improved income and/or satisfaction, society and the individual are both benefited. Employee-initiated turnover may also have positive benefits for the organization if poor performers are the ones most likely to leave.

A recent review of many prior studies found that poor performers were more likely to leave voluntarily—and especially involuntarily—than good performers.[30] This would be expected if good performers are rewarded by the organization and/or if poor performers are encouraged to leave.

A related perspective is to consider the desirability of turnover in costs to the organization. Costs of turnover include direct separation costs (e.g., exit interviews), replacement costs (e.g., recruiting), and training costs.[31] However, there are also costs of trying to retain employ-

---

[29] Bureau of National Affairs, *Bulletin to Management*, March 10, 1988.

[30] G. M. McEvoy and W. F. Cascio, "Do Good or Poor Performers Leave? A Meta-Analysis of the Relationship between Performance and Turnover," *Academy of Management Journal* 30 (1987), pp. 744–62.

[31] For a good discussion of costs associated with turnover, see W. F. Cascio, *Costing Human Resources: The Financial Impact of Behavior in Organizations* 2d ed. (Boston: Kent, 1987), Chapter 2.

FIGURE 7–8
Optimal Organizational Turnover

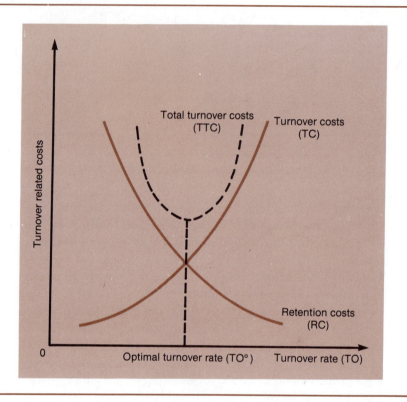

Source: M. A. Abelson and B. D. Baysinger, "Optimal and Dysfunctional Turnover: Toward an Organizational Level Model," *Academy of Management Review* 9 (1984), p. 333.

ees, such as increased salaries that might be used. Figure 7–8 shows that these two types of costs go in opposite directions across different levels of turnover. The figure thus suggests that some positive level of turnover is usually in the best interest of the organization.

Measuring turnover

Again, measuring turnover as recommended by the Bureau of National Affairs makes sense because of the comparative information available from their survey. In addition, however, an organization may wish to distinguish between voluntary turnover, as evidenced through quits, and involuntary terminations initiated by the organization. This is a distinction not made in the bureau's survey, but is important when efforts are made to control turnover.

It would also be desirable to obtain more detailed reasons for voluntary terminations. For example, was the termination due to poor supervision or inadequate wages? Unfortunately, attempts to obtain more detailed breakdowns on the reasons for voluntary terminations, through *exit interviews*, have not been very successful because employees are apparently reluctant, or perhaps unable, to give consistent reasons for terminating jobs.[32] As a result, management probably must be content with differentiating only between voluntary and involuntary turnover. More detailed information on probable causes of turnover may have to be obtained from satisfaction surveys.

Controlling turnover

Managerial activities necessary to control involuntary turnover are very different from activities required to control voluntary turnover. Moreover, activities differ depending on the type of involuntary turnover. For example, if management finds itself dismissing a large number of employees, it might look to several factors. If the terminations are due to rule infractions, an examination of the policies that lead to terminations might be in order. Perhaps the policies are unreasonably harsh, or perhaps supervisors are unduly zealous in applying the rules. Excessive involuntary terminations because of performance inadequacies, alternatively should lead management to examine its selection (see Chapters 10 and 11) or training (see Chapter 13) procedures.

Involuntary terminations because of layoffs present a different set of problems for management to consider. Basically, layoffs occur because of an imbalance between the productive capabilities of the work force and the organization's product or service production needs. Wide swings in production requirements due to rapid changes in the economic climate are largely outside the control of the organization so that layoffs are sometimes unavoidable. With proper planning, however, more moderate or predictable variation can often be achieved without layoffs (see Chapter 12).

Voluntary turnover presents yet another set of issues for management to consider. As in the case of absenteeism, it is caused by many factors.

---

[32] J. L. Zarandona and M. A. Camnso, "A Study of Exit Interviews: Does the Last Word Count?" *Personnel* 62, no. 3 (1985), pp. 47–48.

FIGURE 7-9

A Model of Voluntary Employee Turnover

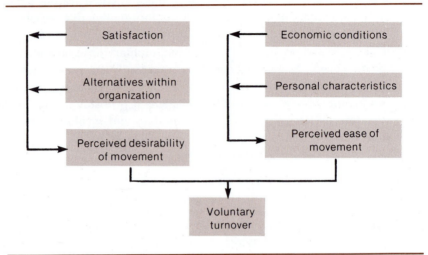

Source: Modified from J. G. March and H. A. Simon, *Organizations* (New York: John Wiley & Sons, 1958), pp. 90–106. Copyright © 1958 John Wiley & Sons, Inc. Reprinted by permission.

Major influences, as specified in one widely accepted model and shown in Figure 7-9, are employees' perceptions of the *ease of movement* and the *desirability of movement*.[33] Ease of movement depends largely on the personal characteristics of the employees and on economic conditions. For example, employees with the best work qualifications are likely to find it easier to leave and find alternative employment opportunities. Also, young employees are much more likely to terminate voluntarily than older employees.[34] Economic conditions as reflected by unemployment levels are negatively related to voluntary turnover as predicted by the model.[35]

Figure 7-9 also shows that voluntary turnover is influenced by employee perceptions of the desirability of leaving, which depends partly

[33] J. G. March and H. A. Simon, *Organizations* (New York: John Wiley & Sons, 1958), pp. 90–106. Other similar models have been proposed by W. H. Mobley, R. W. Griffeth, H. H. Hand, and B. M. Leglino, "Review and Conceptual Analysis of the Employee Turnover Process," *Psychological Bulletin* 86 (1979), pp. 493–522; J. L. Price, *The Study of Turnover* (Ames: Iowa State University Press, 1977).

[34] J. L. Cotton and J. M. Tuttle, "Employee Turnover: A Meta-Analysis and Review with Implications for Research," *Academy of Management Review* 11 (1986), pp. 55–70.

[35] For a review, see C. L. Hulin, M. Roznowski, and D. Hachiya, "Alternative Opportunities and Withdrawal Decisions: Empirical and Theoretical Discrepancies and an Integration," *retical Discrepancies and an Integration*," *Psychological Bulletin* 97 (1985), pp. 233–50.

on what opportunities for other work are seen within the existing organization. Employees may want to leave their current jobs but stay with the organization if other jobs are available through transfer or promotion. To some extent, these opportunities are within the control of management and hence can be used to influence turnover.

A major factor that influences desirability to leave is employee satisfaction. The greater the satisfaction, the lower the probability of leaving.[36] This relationship is especially strong when economic conditions in the external labor market are favorable.[37]

SUMMARY

In subsequent chapters, major P/HR activities are described. These activities are aimed largely at improving the outcomes described in this and the previous chapter. In the present chapter, employee satisfaction, attendance, and length of service were discussed. Attempts to improve these attitudes and behaviors require that they first be measured. Many measures are available, especially for satisfaction, and it is highly desirable that any measure chosen also be used in other organizations so that comparative information can be obtained.

The personnel department is typically responsible for obtaining and retaining information on employee satisfaction, attendance, and retention. It is also often called on to help improve these attitudes and behaviors. As discussed, such improvement depends on correctly identifying the causes of any problems. In the case of attendance and length of service, for example, whether the problem stems from voluntary or involuntary reasons influences the choice of remedial activities. There are also many reasons why employees may be satisfied or dissatisfied. Improved satisfaction can only be achieved if the factors causing dissatisfaction are identified and addressed by appropriate P/HR activities.

DISCUSSION QUESTIONS

1. In what ways can the personnel/human resource function serve line management with respect to assessing the outcomes of satisfaction, attendance, and retention?

---

[36] R. P. Steel and N. K. Ovalle, Jr., "A Review and Meta-Analysis of Research on the Relationship between Behavioral Intentions and Employee Turnover," *Journal of Applied Psychology* 69 (1984), pp. 673–86; Cotton and Tuttle, "Employee Turnover."

[37] J. M. Carsten and P. E. Spector, "Unemployment, Job Satisfaction, and Employee Turnover: A Meta-Analytic Test of the Muchinsky Model," *Journal of Applied Psychology* 72 (1987), pp. 374–81.

2. Why might job satisfaction differ from individual to individual in the same work setting?

3. What are the advantages of using a standardized questionnaire for measuring satisfaction? Are there any disadvantages?

4. What useful information could management acquire as a result of conducting a satisfaction survey?

5. What factors might explain the moderate relationship between satisfaction and attendance?

6. Is turnover always undesirable? When might turnover be beneficial?

Case for Part Three

BURTON'S INCORPORATED

Introduction

At the end of fiscal year 1982, sales at Burton's, Incorporated, a clothing retailer, are down 19 percent and profits are off 21 percent. Although the entire retailing industry has been hit hard by the general economic recession, this drop at Burton's is unexpectedly severe and unprecedented. In fact, according to Burton's executive vice president, Peter Baldwin, if dramatic measures are not taken, the company may not survive the downturn. Times are so tough that Burton's has recently been forced to let go one third of its management staff and put an indefinite freeze on all hiring and promotions.

Company Background

Burton's, Inc., based in Cincinnati, Ohio, is one of three wholly owned subsidiaries of Cincinnati—Burton's, a retailing conglomerate. The company consists of 20 medium-sized stores located throughout Ohio, Indiana, and Kentucky. Burton's also maintains two distribution centers and an administrative headquarters in Cincinnati. The total employment is approximately 2,400 people: 15 executives; 40 staff specialists; 215 first-line sales managers; 150 administrative personnel; 1,800 salespeople and 240 distribution workers. Burton's major customers are primarily middle and upper-middle class families that purchase sportwear, dresswear, and fashion accessories.

In business since the late 1800s, Burton's has developed a fine reputation in the midwestern communities where it has located, and until recently, has enjoyed steady growth in sales and profits. Except for the distribution workers, the company is not presently unionized. However, it is no secret that Burton's management has been trying very hard recently to keep current labor organizing activities to a minimum. Especially in these dire times, management views unionism as a threat to the company's resurgence. In this regard, the personnel office has been called on to conduct a program audit of various personnel practices underway at Burton's. The purpose of this audit is to assess the impact of personnel policies and practices on P/HR outcomes (e.g., employee performance, satisfaction, absenteeism, turnover). The corollary objective of this audit is to identify specific problem areas where policy adjustments may be necessary. The final report to the executive staff will include the personnel department's evaluation of current problems and recommendations for implementing changes in P/HR practices.

Personnel History

Over the past 10 years, Burton's has made several changes to implement the best personnel practices possible. Partially, this has been to circumvent any unionization efforts, but primarily it is an indication of Burton's long-standing belief that their success as a retailing firm depends on the competencies and efforts of each employee.

This commitment to personnel is demonstrated by the fact that in 1978 the company spent $600,000 on a computerized human resource information system (HRIS) developed with the help of Control Data Corporation. The HRIS has successfully automated most employment records (e.g., job titles, salary information, sales levels, attendance, demographics, etc.). Also, Burton's maintains an ongoing training program to help salespeople improve their retail selling skills (RSS) and customer service. The average annual cost of this program is roughly $17,000. To further ensure high ability levels in their work force, the company sets selection standards far above those of their competitors. Whereas other retail companies typically hire unexperienced high school students, Burton's generally requires some retailing or sales experience before considering an applicant for employment. While this policy increases overall labor costs, Burton's management feels confident that the added expense is well justified.

By far the most problematic and volatile personnel issues at Burton's have been regarding promotions and salary increases. Because the company promotes from within, and grants raises on a companywide basis, comparisons generally have to be made across employees in different jobs and departments. To combat arguments of subjectivity and bias pertaining to these decisions, Burton's links these rewards to objective measures of performance.

Specifically, rather than using subjective managerial evaluations of employee performance, ongoing accounts of sales results are maintained for each employee through use of the HRIS. Based on this information, each department manager assigns each employee to one of five categories.

1. Superior/top 10 percent.
2. Very good/next 20 percent.
3. Good/middle 40 percent.
4. Fair/lower 20 percent.
5. Poor/lowest 10 percent.

Administrative decisions are then made across departments using these standardized distributions. Additionally, to provide constant feedback to each employee concerning his or her relative performance, data are updated and posted daily. It is hoped that this feedback is motivating to employees, and in this way there are no surprises when the time comes for semiannual performance appraisal interviews. It is interesting to note that since these changes have been made in the performance appraisal system, there has not been one formal complaint registered regarding salary or promotion decisions. However, sales managers themselves have mentioned occasionally that they do not feel as comfortable now that they are required to assign employees to the "fair" and "poor" categories.

P/HR Outcomes

Despite the concerted efforts of Burton's management to create a top-rate system of human resource management, there are several troubling personnel issues facing the company that management fears may be contributing to declining sales. Although the favorite excuse for depressed sales is the poor economy, external conditions alone cannot totally account for the decline in performance. Several other indicators imply that some of the problem is simultaneously internal to the organization—symptomatic of poor P/HR practices.

For example, there have been recent complaints that employees have not been as patient or courteous to customers as they should be. This was best summarized by one manager who conceded, "My people are beating up the clientele to make a sale—the very opposite of what the RSS program trains them to do." This lack of customer service is frustrating to management since the RSS training has proven effective in the past. Additionally, there seems to be a great deal of competition *within* departments that is hurting a team effort. Although intergroup rivalries *between* departments has always been viewed as normal and healthy, the lack of intragroup cohesiveness is seen as a problem.

Additionally, Burton's has been plagued with increases in lost and damaged merchandise. Management attributes this to the fact that storage rooms are disorganized and unkempt. This is in sharp contrast to the selling floors, which have remained fairly well in order and uncluttered. Nevertheless, material costs have been increasing at an alarming rate.

Regarding labor costs, there are some perplexing patterns. Specifically, absenteeism has increased by 23 percent, meaning that five people have to be hired to do the work formerly accomplished by four. Employee turnover, however, has actually decreased from 17 percent to just under 9 percent, thereby decreasing labor costs overall. Unfortunately, a large percentage (43 percent) of those leaving the company are very good to superior employees. Management views these trends as dysfunctional and intolerable in the long run.

Perhaps the most surprising outcome of the entire personnel audit is the fact that employee satisfaction, measured as an overall global factor, has not decreased noticeably in the past few years. Although there are differences across individual departments on this global measure, satisfaction in general has remained quite stable in the company as a whole (no measure of job facet satisfaction is taken). Despite the results of this general survey, management is certain that morale has diminished in the company, but cannot determine why this trend fails to surface on the company's measure of employee satisfaction.

Questions

1. What are the pros and cons of Burton's performance appraisal system? Do you think it identifies the best employees? Do you think it helps develop employees to perform the best they can? Can declining sales be linked directly and/or indirectly to the appraisal system?

2. What changes would you recommend in the appraisal system?

3. Why do you suppose no one has complained about the appraisal system?

4. Do you think the daily performance feedback is motivating to employees or not? Why?

5. List some of the potential negative consequences of the performance appraisal system at Burton's.

6. How can you account for the fact that absenteeism has increased at Burton's while turnover has decreased, yet the measure of overall satisfaction has remained relatively stable?

7. Why are morale problems not showing up on the global satisfaction measure?

PART FOUR

Human Resource Planning

8

Human Resource Planning

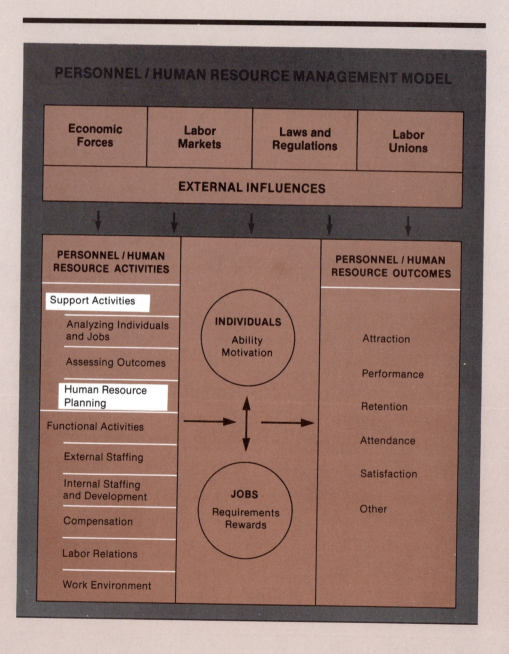

PERSONNEL / HUMAN RESOURCE MANAGEMENT MODEL

Economic Forces	Labor Markets	Laws and Regulations	Labor Unions

EXTERNAL INFLUENCES

PERSONNEL / HUMAN RESOURCE ACTIVITIES

Support Activities

Analyzing Individuals and Jobs

Assessing Outcomes

Human Resource Planning

Functional Activities

External Staffing

Internal Staffing and Development

Compensation

Labor Relations

Work Environment

INDIVIDUALS
Ability
Motivation

JOBS
Requirements
Rewards

PERSONNEL / HUMAN RESOURCE OUTCOMES

Attraction

Performance

Retention

Attendance

Satisfaction

Other

After reading this chapter, you should be able to speak to the questions posed in each of the following personnel/human resource incidents.

1. You are the plant manager at the XYZ Corporation. You have been "requested" by the Corporate P/HR Department to submit an estimate of the numbers and types of people you will need to staff your plant next year. How would you go about making this estimate? What factors would you consider? What types of information would you try to obtain before proceeding with this task? Where would you get it? How would you use it? What things do you think would affect the quality (that is, accuracy) of the estimates you make?

2. You are still a plant manager at the XYZ Corporation. The Corporate P/HR Department has now asked that you provide an assessment of the extent to which you will be able to meet your estimated needs (see 1 above) with existing employees. How would you go about making this assessment? What factors would you consider? What information would you use? Where would you get it? How would you use it? What things do you think would affect the quality (that is, accuracy) of the estimates you make?

3. Suppose the estimates you made in 1 and 2 showed that you expect to be short 3 department heads and 4 supervisors and to have a surplus of about 50 production employees. How would you go about action planning to deal with these imbalances? What factors would you consider? What information would you use? Where would you get it? How would you use it? What action plans do you think you would recommend (after making whatever assumptions you think necessary)?

4. You are the director of affirmative action for your company. You are just completing a "negotiating" session with a compliance officer from OFCCP. She is insisting that you set goals for the employment of women in upper-level management jobs and top-level executive positions at a level you suspect may be unattainable within the five-year time frame being discussed. You have asked for more time to assess the goals and timetable before being locked into them. How would you go about deciding whether the compliance officer's goals are attainable within five years and thus whether they should be agreed to by the firm?

This chapter focuses on human resource planning with attention also being given to two closely related topics: affirmative action planning and human resource information systems.

Human resource planning (HRP) is the process used by organizations to (1) analyze business plans to establish future human resource requirements, (2) estimate future human resource availabilities, (3) reconcile requirements and availabilities, and (4) formulate action plans that will, if properly implemented, contribute to the achievement of business plans and thus to future organizational success. Affirmative action planning (AAP) is a special application of HRP focusing on women and members of minority groups. Its purposes are to (1) determine how the organization stands with respect to the utilization of these protected classes; (2) establish realistic goals and timetables for improving utilization, where necessary; and (3) outline specific programs for meeting established goals and timetables. Human resource information systems (HRISs) use computers to capture, code, store, manipulate, and retrieve the data needed to carry out HRP, AAP, and many other P/HR management activities.

HRP, AAP, and HRISs are considered support activities in the P/HR model. Unlike the functional activities, they are not designed to alter individuals or jobs or to improve the match between individuals and jobs. Rather, they are undertaken to ensure that anticipated business developments and environmental trends are taken into account when the various functional activities are designed and implemented, and to ensure that these functional activities are consistent with one another.

HUMAN RESOURCE PLANNING

For several years, a large supplier of medical products to physicians and hospitals had been working on the development of a new instrument to analyze blood gasses. Finally, it became clear that a major breakthrough was near. With eager anticipation, the company's top managers began to think about bringing the product to market. They verified the market potential. Plans were made to obtain the manufacturing facilities and machinery that would be needed to produce enough instruments to meet the anticipated demand. Distribution channels were mapped out. The managers planned pricing, marketing, and sales strategies that they hoped would generate desired levels of profits. And they contracted with banks to obtain the financing that would be necessary until the product began to generate a positive cash flow. What, then, was left?

The people. Management had yet to think about the people it would take to produce, market, sell, and distribute the product and to provide ancillary support services. How many people would it take? What types? Would the company be able to afford this many people? To what extent could the needed talent be obtained from other units of the company on a timely basis? To what extent would it be necessary to go outside for certain skills? Would these skills be available in the external labor market when needed? What action steps would be necessary to tap the appropriate internal and external sources of talent? Would those brought in come with the requisite skills and abilities, or would some type of training and development be necessary? What steps would have to be taken to ensure that the new personnel would be properly motivated and reasonably satisfied with their jobs?

Providing answers to these types of questions is what HRP is all about. Historically, organizations have been quite good at developing business (i.e., manufacturing, marketing, distribution, and, especially, financial) plans, but, surprisingly, a bit lax about bringing in the human resource component. As an increasing number of business plans foundered on the shoals of talent shortages (or surpluses) and on skill and motivational inadequacies, however, this situation began to change. Recent studies show that about 80 percent of middle-sized and larger companies now do some form of HRP on a regular basis.[1]

Of course, these planning processes vary in comprehensiveness and in the sophistication of the techniques used.[2] In the foregoing case, for example, the medical products company might look just a few months ahead and focus on only a few employee groups (for example, managers, engineers, and salespersons) and be content to do ballpark estimates of its personnel needs and rough plans for recruiting and training the needed talent. Or it might look ahead several years, focus on the entire organization, and attempt to establish not only quite precise estimates of all its personnel needs, but also a complete and coherent package consisting of all the functional P/HR activities noted in the overall model.

Some Preliminary Issues

In other words, organizations cannot simply rush into HRP without thinking through some very important issues. One involves the comprehensiveness of planning; another, planning horizons; a third, coverage; and a fourth, the roles that will be played by line managers and staff planners.

---

[1] J. Craft, "Human Resource Planning," in *Human Resource Management: Evolving Roles and Responsibilities, ASPA/BNA Handbook of Human Resource Management,* vol. 1, ed. L. Dyer (Washington, D.C.: Bureau of National Affairs, 1988).

[2] L. Dyer, "Strategic Human Resource Management and Planning" in *Research in Personnel and Human Resource Management,* ed. K. M. Rowland and G. R. Ferris (Greenwich, Conn: JAI Press, 1985); and S. N. Nkomo, "The Theory and Practice of Human Resource Planning: The Gap Remains," *The Personnel Administrator* 31 (August 1986), pp. 71–84.

Comprehensiveness of planning

Often HRP takes place as an integral part of an organization's annual business planning process; understandably, this is referred to as *plan-based HRP*. This is a logical approach since many organizations do business planning and these plans almost always have human resource implications. And it is always a good idea to have a close linkage between business plans and human resource plans.[3]

Not all important business developments are captured in formal business plans, however, particularly if they occur rapidly or unexpectedly. At one of IBM's high-tech manufacturing facilities, for example, it became clear that costs had gotten out of hand and that major steps were needed to correct the situation. It was clear that many of these steps would involve personnel moves. To deal with this situation it was necessary for IBM (which is very good at plan-based HRP) to undertake a special planning effort to make sure that the personnel moves were done systematically and without undue disruption.[4] This type of planning is referred to as *project-based HRP*.

In addition, many companies choose to do HRP for critical groups of employees on a regular basis, but outside the formal business planning cycle. An example is Ontario Hydro, which has one such process for its top executives and another for its nuclear power plant operators.[5] The first is common practice; the last is made necessary by the long lead times required to develop such employees. The company must anticipate its needs and begin planning recruitment and development up to seven years in advance of the time fully trained operators will actually be required on the job. Planning focused on a single employee group is referred to as *population-based HRP*.

It is unusual for organizations to begin doing plan-, project- and population-based HRP all at once. But experience shows that over time as companies become comfortable with one type of HRP, they often add another and, finally, a third. For example, a firm might begin with

---

[3] Craft, "Human Resource Planning"; R. S. Shuler and S. E. Jackson, "Linking Competitive Strategies with Human Resource Management Practices," *Academy of Management Executive* 1 (1987), pp. 207–19; D. Ulrich, "Strategic Human Resource Planning: Why and How?" *Human Resource Planning* 10, no. 1 (1987), pp. 37–56; and L. Dyer, "Linking Human Resource and Business Strategies," *Human Resource Planning* 7, no. 2 (1984), pp. 79–84.

[4] L. Greenhalgh, R. B. McKersie, and R. Gilkey, "Rebalancing the Work Force at IBM: A Case Study of Redeployment and Revitalization," MIT Sloan School of Management Working Paper No. 1718–85, October 1985.

[5] J. Rush and L. Borne, "Human Resource Planning at Ontario Hydro," in *Human Resource Planning: A Case Study Reference Guide to the Tested Practices of Five Major U.S. and Canadian Companies*, ed. L. Dyer (New York: Random House, 1986).

population-based HRP that focuses on, and thus involves, its top executives. Once the executives are in tune with this form of HRP, the company might add systematic planning for selected projects (for example, the start-up of a new facility) and, ultimately, a human resource component into its regular business planning process.

Organizations that have adopted all three approaches are said to have comprehensive approaches to HRP.[6]

Planning horizons

Since planning involves a look into the future, one important question always is: How far into the future? Again, practices vary.

For plan-based HRP the planning horizons would be the same as those of the relevant business planning processes. In most organizations, this is between three and five years for what is usually called "strategic planning" and between one and three years for so-called operational planning.[7] Planning horizons for project-based HRP vary depending on the nature of the projects involved. Solving a temporary shortage of, say, salespeople might involve a planning horizon of only a few months, while planning for the start up of a new facility might involve a lead time of two, three, or even more years. Population-based HRP focusing on top executives usually looks out only one or two years, while Ontario Hydro's planning horizon for nuclear power plant operators is about seven years.

Coverage

By definition, project- and population-based HRP focus on selected organizational units and/or employee groups. When it comes to plan-based HRP, however, a decision must be made. In most corporations, such planning covers all organizational units (with the possible exception of start-up or entrepreneurial businesses that are exempt from normal corporate procedures). The real difference comes with respect to employee groups.

A common practice is to include only managerial and professional employees on the grounds that they are the most difficult and expensive

---

[6] L. Dyer, "A New View of Human Resource Planning" in *Human Resource Planning: Tested Practices*, ed. L. Dyer. For an example, see L. Dyer and R. A. Shafer, "Formulating Human Resource Strategies in a Professional Service Firm," in *Strategic Human Resource Planning Applications*, ed. R. Niehaus (New York: Plenum Press, 1987), pp. 29–42.

[7] L. Dyer and N. O. Heyer, "Human Resource Planning at IBM," in *Human Resource Planning: Tested Practices*, ed. L. Dyer.

to attract and retain and that they require longer lead times to develop. This is the practice at Corning Glass Works, for example, and at Merck.[8] Some companies, however, especially those with no-layoff policies, include all employee groups.[9]

When HRP involves large numbers of employees, the usual practice is to segment the employee group(s) of interest into job categories. Sometimes job titles can be used, but often there are too many such titles to permit systematic planning. Corning Glass Works, for example, found that its 3,800 managerial and professional employees had 565 different job titles. To reduce these to a workable number, a planning task force first lumped them into the major functions: engineering, manufacturing, sales, purchasing, personnel, and other (including such jobs as lawyers and pilots). Then it placed jobs within functions according to specialties and pay levels, compressing pay levels wherever movements between them were generally automatic. Within engineering, for example, there were electrical, electronic, mechanical, and process engineers, each with two major levels. And there were two types of engineering management, each also with two levels. Eventually, all 565 job titles were grouped into 54 job categories that the task force found both meaningful and manageable.[10]

Roles of line managers and staff planners

Most organizations take the position that line managers are ultimately responsible for the completion and quality of HRP. But the usual practice is to have one or more staff specialists located in the P/HR department to assist with the process.

Initially, a staff specialist takes the lead in proposing which type(s) of HRP will be undertaken and when, and in making suggestions with respect to planning horizons and coverage. Final decisions, however, are usually the prerogative of line management. Once an approach has been decided on, task forces consisting of both line managers and staff specialists (like the one noted above at Corning Glass Works) are often assembled to design appropriate planning processes and do other preliminary work.

Once the processes are in place, the staff typically assumes responsibility for collecting, manipulating, and presenting the necessary data to

---

[8] L. Dyer, R. A. Shafer, and P. J. Regan, "Human Resource Planning at Corning Glass Works," and G. Milkovich and J. D. Phillips, "Human Resource Planning at Merck," both in *Human Resource Planning: Tested Practices*, ed. L. Dyer.

[9] Dyer and Heyer, "IBM."

[10] Dyer, Shafer, and Regan, "Corning Glass Works."

line managers and for laying out alternative action plans. Action planning is usually a joint venture between line and staff, particularly after HRP has been in place for a while and the staff has earned the respect and trust of line managers.

THE PLANNING MODEL

Irrespective of planning type, horizons, or coverage, the heart of most HRP applications is a staffing planning model similar to the one shown in Figure 8–1. This model consists of five phases:[11]

1. Determining future human resource requirements.
2. Determining future human resource availabilities.
3. Conducting external and internal environmental scanning.
4. Reconciling requirements and availabilities, that is, identifying anticipated gaps (surpluses or shortages) between the two and setting objectives.
5. Developing action plans to close the anticipated gaps.

Determining Future Human Resource Requirements

Virtually all HRP begins by determining future human resource requirements, that is, by estimating as closely as possible how many employees the organizational unit of interest will need in each job category by the end of the planning period to do the work that will have to be done.

As Figure 8–1 shows (in the left-hand column), the logical place to begin this process is with an organization's business plans. These plans usually indicate major sales, production, and financial goals. This information tells the human resource planner whether volumes will be going up, staying about the same, or going down. Business plans also tell how management intends to compete in each relevant product line. In some businesses, for example, management may be planning to "buy" the market with low prices, while in others it may be planning to "skim" the market with innovative and/or particularly high-quality products sold at premium prices.[12] In the former case, management will be interested in

---

[11] J. Walker, *Human Resource Planning* (New York: McGraw-Hill, 1980) and L. Dyer, "Human Resource Planning," in *Personnel Management,* ed. K. M. Rowland and G. R. Ferris (Boston: Allyn & Bacon, 1982), pp. 52–77.

[12] For more on business strategies, see Chapter 1 of this text; M. E. Porter, *Competitive Strategy* (New York: The Free Press, 1980); and M. E. Porter, *Competitive Advantage* (New York: The Free Press, 1985). See also, L. Dyer, "Bringing Human Resources into the Strategy Formulation Process," *Human Resource Management* 22 (Fall 1983), pp. 257–73.

FIGURE 8–1
The Staffing Planning Process

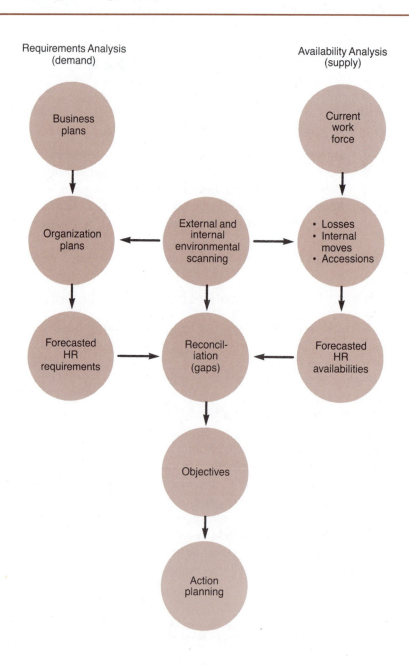

maximizing employee productivity and minimizing head counts (and thus labor costs); in the latter, it might be much more concerned with maximizing employee flexibility and adaptability even at the expense of having a few extra people around. Also, the employees probably would have to be more skilled.

In addition to volumes and strategies, business plans usually reveal whether or not there will be any changes in the basic technologies the organization uses to make, market, and distribute its products or services. Such changes typically are introduced as a means of increasing employee productivity and thus, (other things being equal) reducing future human resource requirements. They also usually alter the skill requirements of jobs, and thus the nature of the job categories that are being planned for.

When establishing future human resource requirements, it is also important to know, as Figure 8–1 also shows, whether management has any plans to restructure or reorganize the business. Such plans, in and of themselves, may lead to the addition or, more likely, elimination of some jobs or job categories, or significant changes in the number of employees needed in certain job categories. For example, when business conditions became particularly competitive during the 1980s, many U.S. corporations made plans to restructure their corporate headquarters. Generally, these plans called for the elimination of one, two, or even three layers of management and significant reductions in the size of some staff groups.

Figure 8–2 is a simplified example of what is involved in establishing future human resource requirements. Several factors can be noted here.

FIGURE 8–2

Establishing Future Human Resource Requirements

	Current Year	Two Years out
Output (Units)	10,000,000	11,000,000
Productivity (output per employee)	10,000	10,837
Human resource requirements:		
• Sales 114	160	120
• Sales 113	210	180
• Sales 112	290	320
• Sales 111	340	395
• Total	1,000	1,015

First, the planning horizon is two years and the forecast is limited to sales employees, lumped into four job categories. Second, the forecast calls for output to increase 10 percent over the two years (from 10 to 11 million units). Third, there is an anticipated productivity improvement of 8.37 percent (from 10,000 to 10,837 units per sales employee). Fourth, total human resource requirements are projected to edge up only 1½ percent (from 1,000 to 1,015) because the 10 percent increase in output is almost offset by the 8.37 percent improvement in productivity ($10,000,000/10,000 = 1,000; 11,000,000/10,837 = 1,015$). Fifth, the sales unit will be restructured a bit; the forecast calls for the head count in the top two sales jobs to decrease both in absolute numbers and as a percent of total employment, while the opposite occurs in the bottom two sales jobs. (This is probably the result of a decision to try to do more work with those who are lower paid, thereby saving on labor costs.)

Clearly, it is no easy matter to translate business and organizational plans into estimates of human resource requirements, particularly in large, rapidly changing organizations that employ thousands of employees in many different job categories. Long planning horizons complicate the task even further. Basically, planners can go at it in one of two ways: statistically and judgmentally.

Statistical techniques

Statistical techniques are useful, but only under a limited set of circumstances for a couple of reasons.[13] First, all such techniques are designed simply to project the past forward; thus, they have limited applicability in organizations whose immediate past and/or forecasted future are characterized by significant alterations in products or services, technologies, or organizational structures. Obviously, this includes a lot of organizations in this day and age. Second, statistical techniques are predicated on the discovery of a systematic historical relationship between a so-called leading indicator (for example, sales or production volumes) and human resource head counts; often, no such relationship can be found.

Nonetheless, statistical techniques do have some useful applications in industry and government. One is in the computer industry, where the large companies use computerized algorithms to determine the number of repair people they will need in the future. The leading indicator is

---

[13] For summary discussions of statistical techniques used to estimate future human resource requirements, see A. O. Manzini and J. D. Gridley, *Integrating Human Resource and Strategic Business Planning* (New York: AMACOM, 1986), pp. 118–50; J. Walker, *Human Resource Planning;* and L. Dyer, "Human Resource Planning."

placed equipment, by type and age. These companies have historical records that show the amount of repair time required by various models of computers year by year. Their business plans then tell them how many of these models will be in place over the planning period. Using the algorithms, it is possible, then, to estimate how much repair time will be involved over the planning period and, in turn, to use this information to estimate the number of repair people that will be required in various job categories. It is even possible to program in various productivity improvement targets and do "what if" analyses to determine how much could be saved in head counts and labor costs if the various targets were met.

Of course, this particular approach does not help in the case of brand-new equipment since there is no experience base from which to work. Here it is necessary, as it usually is, to temper statistical estimates with a dose of human judgment.

Judgmental techniques

This brings us to the second way to establish future human resource requirements: managerial judgment (with or without prior statistical modeling).[14] Sometimes the top managers of a corporation, business, or function simply rely on their knowledge of business and organizational plans to make their best guesses about—or to dictate—what future head counts will be; this is called a "top-down approach." More commonly, perhaps, lower-level managers make initial estimates for their units (for example, a department, plant, or office) and these then are refined and consolidated through a series of reviews at successively higher management levels, known as the "bottom-up approach." Sometimes managers are given checklists of factors to be considered or questions to be asked, various decision aids, or productivity targets to guide their thinking in these matters.

Irrespective of the methods and tools used, it is clear that the process of establishing future human resource requirements provides a number of essential pieces to the HRP puzzle (refer again to Figure 8-2). It immediately tells whether the number of employees in various units and job categories will be going up or down, and by how much. It also tells if productivity has to be increased, or labor costs decreased, and by what amounts. These amounts then become objectives around which action

---

14 J. Fiorito, T. H. Stone, and C. R. Greer, "Factors Affecting Choice of Human Resource Forecasting Techniques," *Human Resource Planning* 8, no. 1 (1985), pp. 1–18; and G. T. Milkovich, L. Dyer, and T. A. Mahoney, "HRM Planning," in *Human Resource Management in the 1980s*, ed. S. J. Carroll and R. S. Schuler (Washington, D.C.: Bureau of National Affairs, 1983), pp. 1–29.

planning can occur. But, most important, the established future human resource requirements serve as standards or targets against which to judge the adequacy of anticipated future human resource availabilities.

Determining Future Human Resource Availabilities

The task here is to estimate the numbers and types of employees that will be available in various job categories at the end of the planning period.

Figure 8–1 (right-hand column) shows the basic process, while Figure 8–3 provides a concrete example. It all begins with an inventory of the employees expected to be in the various job categories (obviously the same ones for which human resource requirements were established) at the start of the planning period (say, January 1 of next year). From these figures are subtracted anticipated losses during the planning period due to retirements, voluntary turnover, and other reasons (involuntary turnover, transfers to other units, and leaves of absence). Then it is necessary to make internal adjustments (plus and minus) across job categories to account for anticipated promotions and demotions. Finally, additions are made to reflect likely accessions through transfers in from other units, returns from leaves of absence, and (sometimes) recruitment. The result of these manipulations is an estimate of future human resource availabilities at the end of the planning period (say, December 31 of next year).

From where do these numbers come? The beginning inventory is extracted from the HRIS (to be discussed later in this chapter). In addition to the raw numbers shown in Figure 8–3, a beginning inventory may also include information about each employee, including name, current job title, length of service with the company and on current job, performance rating, promotability rating, potential rating, salary, location, previous jobs, retirement status, race, and sex (the last two are used for AAP, also discussed later in this chapter). The estimates of the human resource flows (that is, losses and internal moves) can be derived statistically using historical data or judgmentally using the more personal data noted just above.

Statistical techniques

Statistical techniques require extensive analyses of past patterns of employee flows, which are then used to project future flows.[15] As before,

---

[15] For summary discussions of statistical techniques used to estimate future human resource availabilities, see Manzini and Gridley, *Integrating,* pp. 213–32; J. Walker, *Human Resource Planning;* and L. Dyer, "Human Resource Planning."

FIGURE 8-3

A Forecast of Future Human Resource Availabilities

Job Category	(1) Beginning Inventory	(2) Retire-ments	(3) Losses Quits	(4) Others	(5) Internal Moves Promotions out/in	(6) Demotions out/in	(7) Gains Transfers in	(8) Others	(9) Anticipated Internal Supply
1	136	4	0	11	0/13	0/0	3	0	137
2	255	2	18	0	13/26	0/0	3	0	251
3	291	1	29	0	26/39	0/0	8	0	282
4	357	0	36	0	39/0	0/0	0	0	282
	1039								952

they are most useful in stable organizations where past patterns of flows are likely to continue relatively unchanged. Further, they require fairly large numbers of people to work well, the guideline being a minimum of 30 in any given job category. So again, their use is somewhat limited. Because statistical analyses and projections of flows and availabilities require extensive manipulation of large amounts of data, they are often computerized.[16]

A key component of most statistical techniques is a *transition* or *Markov matrix,* which is used to model movements of employees within or across organizational units. A simple matrix is shown in Figure 8–4. The probabilities in part A of that figure represent average rates of historical movements between and out of the three job categories during a particular period of time (for example, last year or the mean of the last three years). To learn how to read the matrix, consider the middle managers. Reading across the row from left to right, the data show that historically an average of 10 percent of these managers have been promoted to top management each year, while 80 percent of them have stayed in middle management, 5 percent have been demoted to lower management, and 5 percent have left the unit of interest. Similar analyses can be done concerning the flows of top- and lower-level managers.

In more complex organizations these descriptive data might be of intrinsic interest to managers as a means of understanding how their units function. Such matrixes are mainly derived, however, to facilitate the forecasting of human resource availabilities. This process is shown in part B of Figure 8–4. It requires only that the beginning staffing levels be multiplied by the appropriate probabilities from part A and that the resulting figures be summed down the columns. In this case, the anticipated human resource availabilities across the three job categories are 100, 190, and 490.

Other statistical techniques used to establish future human resource availabilities include renewal and goal programming models.[17]

Judgmental techniques

In addition to the various statistical techniques, there are three judgmental approaches to establishing future human resource availabilities

---

[16] For an example, see N. O. Heyer, "Managing Human Resources in a High-Technology Enterprise," in *Human Resource Policy Analysis: Organizational Applications,* ed. R. Niehaus (New York: Praeger Publishers, 1985), pp. 45–61.

[17] G. Miller, "A Methodology for Forecasting Human Resource Needs against Internal and External Labor Markets," *Human Resource Planning* 3, no. 4 (1980), 189–200.

FIGURE 8–4
Transition Matrixes

		M_1	M_2	M_3	Exit
A:					
Top Management (M_1)		.80	.00	.00	.20
Middle Management (M_2)		.10	.80	.05	.05
Lower Management (M_3)		.00	.05	.80	.15
	Beginning Staffing Levels	M_1	M_2	M_3	Exit
B:					
Top Management (M_1)	100	80	0	0	20
Middle Management (M_2)	200	20	160	10	10
Lower Management (M_3)	600	0	30	480	90
Forecasted Availabilities		100	190	490	

that enjoy widespread acceptance: *executive reviews, succession planning,* and *vacancy analysis.* In this context, the main difference between statistical and judgmental techniques is that the former treat employees as numbers and forecast their movements based on probabilities. The latter treat them as individuals and forecast their movements person by person.

Executive reviews.   These focus on small and unique groups of employees, most commonly top executives and other managers and professionals judged to have the potential to be top executives some day (thus, executive reviews are a form of population-based HRP).[18] The actual reviews are carried out through a series of meetings at which the top executives in a given unit consider anticipated human resource requirements and then thoroughly discuss each person under review to determine which are likely to be, or should be, promoted, reassigned, developed for future assignments, or drummed out of the organization. Determinations are made based on judgments about performance, promotability, and potential taking into account the long-term career interests of the employees being considered. The results of the process are first, a clear indication of where the organization can expect to have shortages or surpluses of these unique employees and second, career and development plans for these individuals.

---

[18] For more on executive reviews, see the case studies of Corning Glass Works and IBM reported in *Human Resource Planning: Tested Practices,* ed. L. Dyer.

Succession planning.   This procedure is often an adjunct to executive reviews.[19] It helps to identify backup candidates who are, or soon will be, qualified to replace current executives or upper-level managers. Succession planning results are typically summarized on charts such as the one shown in Figure 8–5. These greatly facilitate the planning of likely retirements, terminations, promotions, and transfers within and across organizational units. They also show which managers are in need of further development to become ready to fill job(s) for which they are (or might be) considered as replacements.

Vacancy analysis.   Judgments are made about likely employee flows on an individual basis (as is the case with executive reviews and succession planning), but because larger numbers of employees are usually involved, the results are summarized statistically.[20] Furthermore, reconciliation between anticipated human resource requirements and availabilities is expressly built into the process. As shown in Figure 8–6, the first step is to subtract from the beginning inventory in each job category all anticipated losses; this yields what is called the "effective labor supply" (that is, current employees who are expected to be in the organization at the end of the planning period). These figures are then matched against the previously determined human resource requirements (labeled "Forecasted DL" in Figure 8–6) to derive preliminary estimates of likely shortages or surpluses. These are then analyzed to determine if they can be eliminated through internal moves (promotions or transfers of those in the effective supply), or if employees will have to be brought in from outside the unit or the company, transferred out to other units of the company, or laid off. The idea is to fill every likely shortage and eliminate every likely surplus, thereby creating a balance between anticipated human resource requirements and availabilities.

Conducting External and Internal Environmental Scanning

A number of external influences affect the conduct of P/HR management. As noted in the P/HR model, these include economic forces, labor markets, laws and regulations, and labor unions. Accordingly, these factors are also grist for the HRP mill.

---

[19] For more on succession planning, see D. F. Parker, J. A. Fossum, J. H. Blakslee, and A. J. Rucci, "Human Resource Planning at American Hospital Supply," in *Human Resource Planning: Tested Practices*, ed. L. Dyer, as well as the case studies of Merck and Ontario Hydro reported in the same volume. See also D. W. Rhodes and J. Walker, "Management Succession and Development Planning," *Human Resource Planning* 8, no. 4 (1985), and A. K. Deegan, *Succession Planning: Key to Corporate Excellence* (New York: John Wiley & Sons, 1986).

[20] See the case study on Corning Glass Works reported in *Human Resource Planning: Tested Practices*, ed. L. Dyer.

FIGURE 8–5
Employee Replacement Chart

Organizational unit	Date	Page Of

Position

Incumbent	Age	Yrs.
	Empl.	Yrs.
Promotable to	When	Yrs./mos.
Replacement no. 1	Age	Yrs.
	Empl.	Yrs.
Present position	Promotable	Yrs./mos.
Replacement no. 2	Age	Yrs.
	Empl.	Yrs.
Present position	Promotable	Yrs./mos.

Position

Incumbent	Age	Yrs.
	Empl.	Yrs.
Promotable to	When	Yrs./mos.
Replacement no. 1	Age	Yrs.
	Empl.	Yrs.
Present position	Promotable	Yrs./mos.
Replacement no. 2	Age	Yrs.
	Empl.	Yrs.
Present position	Promotable	Yrs./mos.

Position

Incumbent	Age	Yrs.
	Empl.	Yrs.
Promotable to	When	Yrs./mos.
Replacement no. 1	Age	Yrs.
	Empl.	Yrs.
Present position	Promotable	Yrs./mos.
Replacement no. 2	Age	Yrs.
	Empl.	Yrs.
Present position	Promotable	Yrs./mos.

Position

Incumbent	Age	Yrs.
	Empl.	Yrs.
Promotable to	When	Yrs./mos.
Replacement no. 1	Age	Yrs.
	Empl.	Yrs.
Present position	Promotable	Yrs./mos.
Replacement no. 2	Age	Yrs.
	Empl.	Yrs.
Present position	Promotable	Yrs./mos.

Position

Incumbent	Age	Yrs.
	Empl.	Yrs.
Promotable to	When	Yrs./mos.
Replacement no. 1	Age	Yrs.
	Empl.	Yrs.
Present position	Promotable	Yrs./mos.
Replacement no. 2	Age	Yrs.
	Empl.	Yrs.
Present position	Promotable	Yrs./mos.

Position

Incumbent	Age	Yrs.
	Empl.	Yrs.
Promotable to	When	Yrs./mos.
Replacement no. 1	Age	Yrs.
	Empl.	Yrs.
Present position	Promotable	Yrs./mos.
Replacement no. 2	Age	Yrs.
	Empl.	Yrs.
Present position	Promotable	Yrs./mos.

Source: G. T. Milkovich and T. A. Mahoney, "Human Resource Planning and PAIR Policy," In D. Yoder and H. G. Heneman, Jr., eds., *Planning and Auditing PAIR* (Washington D.C.: Bureau of National Affairs, 1976).

FIGURE 8-6
Vacancy Analysis

Position Category	People Count Jan. 1st	Retire.	Term.	Misc.	Quits	Transfers Out of Division	Effective Supply (SL)	Fore-casted DL	(Vacancies) or Surpluses	In Unit In/Out	In Division Across Units In/Out	Remaining Vacancies or Surpluses	Transfers into Division	Recruit-ment	Other
111	30		2		2		26	31	(5)	3		(8)		8	
112	12					4	8	12	(4)	3		(1)		1	
121	17		2			1	14	17	(3)	4		(7)		7	
122	7		2				5	8	(3)	3					
131	7		1			1	5	7	(2)						
132	6						6	6	—			(2)		2	
141	8					1	7	10	(3)	1					
142	15					2	13	13	—			(2)		2	
151	1					1	0	1	(1)		1				
152	3					1	2	2	—						
171	4					1	3	4	(1)		1				
172	7						7	7	—						

Column group headings: *Anticipated Losses To The Company (Historically - 10%)* spans Retire., Term., Misc., Quits. *Movements w/in Division* spans In Unit In/Out and In Division Across Units In/Out. *Accessions* spans Transfers into Division, Recruit-ment, and Other.

Source: L. Dyer, R. A. Shafer, and P. J. Regan, Jr., "Human Resource Planning at Corning Glass Works: A Field Study," *Human Resource Planning* 5, no. 3 (1982), pp. 115–84.

Environmental scanning is the term applied to the process of tracking trends and developments in the outside world, documenting their implications for the management of human resources, and ensuring that these implications receive attention in the HRP process.[21] Many corporations—AT&T, IBM, Honeywell—maintain fairly elaborate networks of line managers, technical specialists, and human resource specialists who monitor large numbers of publications, broadcast media, futurist think tanks, and conferences for relevant data. Periodically, these data are assembled and trend reports are prepared and made available to those responsible for HRP (as well as for other P/HR activities). These reports usually include a summary of the major environmental trends and their implications for human resource management. Illustration 8–1 shows an excerpt from a trend report prepared at Honeywell.

Of the various areas monitored through environmental scanning, the labor market is most directly relevant to staffing planning. For a start-up firm in genetic engineering, for example, the future availability of geneticists, biologists, and other types of scientists and engineers is an important strategic contingency. If tight labor markets for these skills are expected, the firm must plan to put considerable time and money into attracting and retaining the needed talent (for example, by raising salaries or developing day-care centers and related programs to enhance its attractiveness to female scientists and engineers) or into developing alternative means of accomplishing its key research and development work (for instance, by using technicians wherever possible, thus reducing the need for scientists and engineers).

Clearly, then, a firm grasp of impending developments in the outside world is very helpful to human resource planners. It puts them in an excellent position to influence the nature of business plans (and thus the nature of future human resource requirements) and to ensure that planned P/HR activities are both realistic and supportive of these business plans.

Also important, however, is a firm grasp of an organization's internal environment. Thus, planners must be out and about in their organizations taking advantage of opportunities to learn what is going on. Informal discussions with key managers can help, as can employee attitude surveys (see Chapter 7), special surveys, and the monitoring of key indexes such as employee performance, absenteeism, turnover, and accident rates. Of special interest is the identification of nagging person-

---

[21] L. P. Schrenk, "Environmental Scanning," in *Human Resource Management: Evolving Roles and Responsibilities*, ed. L. Dyer. See also Milkovich, Dyer, and Mahoney, "HRM Planning."

ILLUSTRATION 8–1

Excerpt from A Trend Report

Women have been entering the labor force at a faster rate than men. Projections show the growth rate of women in the labor force to be twice that of men. This will intensify the significance of concerns such as career development, flexible benefits, working hours, and relocation of two-worker families.

Female Participation Rate and Females as a Percentage of the Total Labor Force 1970–1990

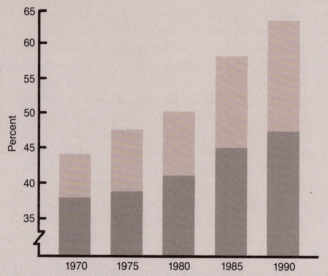

Source: L. P. Schrenk, "Environmental Scanning," in *Human Resource Management: Evolving Roles and Responsibilities, ASPA/BNA Handbook of Human Resource Management,* vol. 1, ed. L. Dyer (Washington, D.C.: Bureau of National Affairs, 1988).

nel problems, as well as prevailing managerial attitudes concerning human resources.[22]

Nagging personnel problems refer to recurring difficulties that threaten to interfere with the attainment of future business plans or other important organizational goals. High turnover in a sales organization, for example, is likely to threaten the viability of a business plan that calls for increased sales quotas or the rapid introduction of several new products.

The values and attitudes of managers, especially top managers, toward human resources are also important to HRP. Trouble brews when these

---

[22] Ibid.

are inconsistent with the exigencies of a firm's business plans. Recently, for example, a mid-sized accounting firm formulated a business plan calling for very rapid growth through aggressive marketing and selected acquisitions of smaller firms. Unfortunately, it appeared that the firm's management talent was inadequate to the task of operating a larger, more complex organization. To make matters worse, there was a prevailing attitude among the top management against investing much money in management development and against bringing in talent from outside the firm. Although difficult, it was necessary for the outside consultant assisting with the planning process to confront management with this dilemma and encourage a change in either the business strategy or their attitudes. Eventually the desire for growth prevailed and the top managers worked with the consultant to develop plans for intensive management training, as well as selective recruiting of management talent. Because the lower-level line managers and personnel specialists with whom the consultant was initially working were fully aware of both the requirements of the business plan and the prevailing talent base and attitudes among the firm's top managers, a potential disaster was averted.

Reconciling Requirements and Availabilities: Gaps and Objectives

Once acquired, information concerning future human resource requirements and availabilities, as well as external and internal environmental conditions, must be brought together to identify potential gaps and the reasons for them, and to decide on appropriate planning objectives (refer back to Figure 8–1).

Reconciliation

The reconciliation process is best examined by means of an example. Figure 8–7 shows a reconciliation chart for the hypothetical organization introduced in Figure 8–3 (the requirements are assumed; the availabilities are from Figure 8–3).

Consider job category 1, for which a shortage of three employees is anticipated. For all intents and purposes this can be ignored since the HRP process is generally too imprecise to warrant concern over such a small variance.

Turning to job category 2, there is a predicted surplus of 50 employees, a potentially serious problem. What is the cause of this surplus? A comparison of the anticipated human resource requirements shown in Figure 8–7 (200) with the beginning inventory shown in Figure 8–3 (255)

FIGURE 8–7

Reconciliation: Matching Human Resource Requirements with Human Resource Availabilities

Job Category	HR Requirements	HR Availabilities	Gap
1	140	137	− 3 (shortage)
2	200	251	+51 (surplus)
3	300	282	−18 (shortage)
4	375	282	−93 (shortage)

suggests immediately that the source is a 20 percent decrease in the usual staffing level. Further investigation might show this to be the result of the automation of certain tasks formerly done manually. This fact must be documented as part of the reconciliation process.

To what can the anticipated shortages in job categories 3 and 4 be attributed? Growth plays a small part, since the forecasted requirements (300 and 375) are slightly higher than the beginning inventory figures in these job categories (291 and 357). Quits are also a factor since they constitute about 10 percent of inventory in both job categories (again, this is determined from Figure 8–3). It would be worthwhile to compare these quit rates with those of others in the industry—here is a role for environmental scanning or competitor analysis[23]—to see where the organization stands. Predicted promotions are also 10 percent or more in both job categories, but the skillful analyst would recognize that these promotion rates probably will not materialize given the anticipated surplus of employees in job category 2. If this promotion blockage results in lower promotion rates than those experienced in previous years, other problems may materialize (for example, even higher than usual quit rates). These facts should also be noted.

In brief, in the reconciliation process, gaps between anticipated human resource requirements and availabilities are identified and the reasons for these clarified. Even the relatively simple reconciliation shown in Figure 8–7 suggests that the organization will have to deal with both employee shortages and surpluses, as well as with reducing labor costs through automation (in job category 2), promotion blockages, and possible increases in voluntary turnover rates.

Larger, more complex organizations that rely on Markov analyses to estimate future human resource availabilities can also use their computer models to do reconciliations. The process is known as simulation or

---

[23] R. Gould, "Gaining a Competitive Edge through Human Resource Strategies," *Human Resource Planning* 9, no. 1 (1986), pp. 31–38.

"what if" analysis.[24] Here analysts systematically alter selected probabilities of movement (see part A of Figure 8–4) and use the computer models to calculate the effects on expected human resource availabilities. The idea is first to generate several solutions that bring availabilities in line with requirements and then to settle on the one that seems most efficient and feasible. Note that this process is the statistical equivalent of vacancy analysis, which was described earlier. (To better understand how simulation works, interested students can generate one or two possible reconciliations manually using the data provided in Figures 8–3 and 8–7.)

Objectives

Objectives derive from the reconciliation process. They are statements of what managers intend to accomplish during the planning period. Once derived, they provide direction for the action planning process, as well as standards against which accomplishments can later be judged.

As the preceding discussion suggests, objectives emanating from staffing planning usually evolve around controlling head count, controlling labor costs and improving productivity (derived from forecasting future human resource requirements), and eliminating potential employee shortages or surpluses by altering employee flows (derived through comparisons of anticipated availabilities and requirements). Examples of specific objectives are shown in the left-hand column of Figure 8–8.

Certain issues can give rise to multiple objectives. For example, staffing planning at a rapidly growing high-technology company might indicate a potential shortage of skilled technicians that cannot be met from within. The company's environmental scan of the relevant labor markets, however, might well turn up the fact that such talent is extremely scarce and that experienced technicians are virtually impossible to find. Under the circumstances, the company might establish as one objective the elimination of the anticipated shortage through outside hiring, and then add a second objective: the elimination of the anticipated skill deficiencies of the new hires during their first six months on the job.

To cite another example, an auto parts manufacturer's business plan might call for the production of increasingly higher quality parts at reduced prices in response to pressures from its customers. Its staffing planning would probably result in objectives calling for increased pro-

---

[24] L. Dyer and G. W. Holder, "A Strategic Perspective of Human Resource Management," in *Human Resource Management: Evolving Roles and Responsibilities*, ed. L. Dyer.

FIGURE 8–8
Personnel Planning Objectives and Possible Activities

Objectives	Possible Activities
A 10 percent increase in output per employee among staff engineers by December 31.	1. Technological change, with corresponding changes in selection, training, transfer or termination, and compensation plans. 2. Organizational change, with corresponding changes in selection, training, transfer or termination, and compensation plans. 3. Increase employees' ability to perform through better selection or training programs. 4. Increase employees' motivation to perform through improved supervision, job enrichment, wage incentives, or discipline.
Eliminate the equivalent of 50 employees from job category 2 by December 31 (see Figure 8–7).	1. Lay off (or fire) 50 employees, perhaps with outplacement services. 2. Promote, transfer, or demote 50 employees, with training as necessary. 3. Institute a special program encouraging early retirement through adjustments in the pension plan. 4. Let attrition eliminate as many employees as it will and cut the hours or pay of the remaining employees.
Add the equivalent of 90 employees to job category 4 by December 31 (see Figure 8–7).	1. Recruit 90 new employees. 2. Recruit, say, 50 new employees and obtain the rest through internal promotions or transfers (with, perhaps, recruitment needed to fill these vacancies). 3. Hire, say, 75 new employees and make up the difference through scheduled overtime or increases in productivity. 4. Subcontract the work and add no new employees.
Develop ready replacements for a minimum of 90 percent of all managerial jobs by December 31.	1. Begin replacement planning. 2. Institute formal training programs. 3. Institute on-the-job development activities (coaching, job rotation, special task forces). 4. Fire inadequate employees and hire better qualified replacements.

ductivity and a reduced number of employees to lower labor costs, as well as more attention to quality among all employees. Recognizing the pressure this would create on employees, however, the firm might also make it an objective to maintain high levels of job satisfaction (to help control absenteeism and turnover) despite the increasingly difficult circumstances.

Action Planning

With objectives in place, the action planning phase of HRP begins (see Figure 8–1). Here is where planners decide how the chosen objectives will be pursued; that is, decide on a human resource strategy that indicates which of the functional activities will be emphasized and what the major policies will be.[25] Basically, action planning is a choice process involving decision making that is partly analytical and partly political. In theory, although not always in practice, the process can be thought of as involving three interrelated steps: generating alternative courses of action, assessing these alternatives, and choosing among them.[26]

Generating alternative activities

The task at this point is to develop for each objective possible courses of action that might be pursued. The guiding philosophy is comprehensiveness; the challenge is to develop as many alternative or complementary activities as possible for each objective. It is a critical process because the ultimate choice(s) can be no better than the best of the alternatives turned up. Figure 8–8 shows for each of the four objectives listed a number of courses of action that might be followed. Figure 8–9 shows sets of both long- and short-term alternatives that GTE Corporation considers possible courses of action to deal with anticipated employee shortages and surpluses. At GTE, calculations have been made of the costs associated with each alternative, and computer models have been developed to facilitate the choice of alternatives by managers anywhere in the corporation.

How are these alternatives generated? They can only come from cause and effect models developed by decision makers. Return to Figure 8–8

---

[25] For more on this approach, see G. T. Milkovich and T. A. Mahoney, "Human Resource Planning and PAIR Policy," in *Planning and Auditing PAIR*, ed. D. Yoder and H. G. Heneman, Jr. (Washington, D.C.: Bureau of National Affairs, 1976), pp. 24–26; Milkovich, Dyer, and Mahoney, "HRM Planning"; and Dyer, "Human Resource Planning."

[26] For an excellent discussion of decision making in this context, see J. W. Boudreau, "Utility Analysis," in *Human Resource Management: Evolving Roles and Responsibilities*, ed. L. Dyer. See also Ulrich, "Strategic HRP."

FIGURE 8–9
Staffing Alternatives to Deal with Employee Shortages and Surpluses

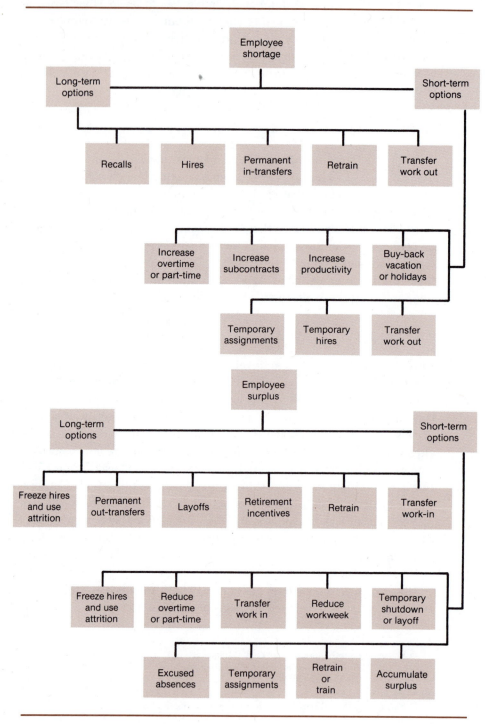

Source: Compliments of Dan Ward, GTE Corporation.

and consider the objective of increasing the productivity of the staff engineering group by 10 percent. Clearly, the decision makers who generated the alternatives shown thought that technology, organization structure, employee ability, and employee motivation were the key variables affecting the productivity of engineers. As a consequence, the activities they recommended are intended to affect these variables.

Assessing alternative activities

A preferred activity is one offering the highest likelihood of attaining the objective of interest within the time limit established at the least cost (or at least at a tolerable cost) with the fewest negative side effects. Thus, each alternative generated must be assessed in terms of various criteria relating to its probability of success and its relative benefits and costs.[27]

This is a difficult task. Individual decision makers face a number of handicaps in carrying it out, the most serious of which is what theorists have called "bounded rationality"—that is, the limited capacity of the human mind to be aware of and consider all of the information relevant to a particular decision. A number of devices has been developed to help overcome the problems associated with bounded rationality, some focusing on the decision-making process *per se* and others on the information used in the process.

A relatively simple device is to use *group decision making* in an attempt to broaden the available knowledge base (at the obvious risk of introducing additional, typically political criteria). Others that have been used in strategy formulation include dialectical inquiry and the devil's advocate approach.[28] The first involves two or more groups, one of which assesses alternatives and makes a recommendation, while the others challenge the assessment (including the assumptions that went into it) and the recommendation and make a formal counterproposal. The groups may then debate to a synthesis, or simply present their positions to a third party (such as a top-level manager) who decides. The devil's advocate approach proceeds in much the same way except that the challenging groups do not make formal counterproposals. Both approaches encourage conflict and thus increase the likelihood that all of the information relevant to a decision is taken into account.

---

[27] For a debate on the relative merits of dialectical inquiry and the devil's advocate approach, see R. A. Cosier, "Dialectical Inquiry in Strategic Planning: A Case of Premature Acceptance?" *Academy of Management Review* 6 (1981), pp. 643–48; I. I. Mitroff and R. O. Mason, "The Metaphysics of Policy and Planning: A Reply to Cosier," *Academy of Management Review* 6 (1981), pp. 649–51; and R. A. Cosier, "Further Thoughts on Dialectical Inquiry: A Rejoinder to Mitroff and Mason, *Academy of Management Review* 6 (1981), pp. 653–54.

[28] Boudreau, "Utility Analysis."

Another way to aid decision makers is to provide them with as much data as possible pertaining to the issue at hand. The data are generated through various types of research projects or activity evaluations, including, in some cases, formal cost-benefit analyses.[29] Also useful are various heuristic devices, such as the one shown in Illustration 8–2, which was

---

ILLUSTRATION 8–2

Program Assessment at Xerox Corporation

General purpose:

To provide a rank ordering of personnel programs to aid in deciding upon priorities.

Procedure:

1. Define and describe the personnel programs (under the system described in this chapter, only programs surviving the screening process would be included here).
2. Separate out for priority treatment those programs that are legally required.
3. Evaluate the remaining programs in terms of:*
   a. Cost effectiveness, that is, the expected benefits and costs. Wherever possible, expected benefits are to be identified through pilot projects, available literature, and so forth. Where this is not possible, target benefits are used.
   b. Technical feasibility, given current or obtainable knowledge and personnel.
   c. Ease of implementation. This is an attempt to document the likelihood of nonacceptance by line management.
4. Rate and rank programs using the following chart. Summary ratings are stated in terms of very desirable, moderately desirable, marginally desirable, not worthwhile, and rankings are made using these categories. Note that the system is structured so that a high rating on one dimension (for example, cost effectiveness) is not conclusive, but that a low rating on one dimension can be.

Step 1. Evaluate feasibility and economic benefitis/ risks. Using predefined standards, separately evaluate each program's technical feasibility, ease of implementation, and net economic benefits. The Service Force Job Enrichment Program was evaluated as follows:

Technical feasibility—High
Ease of implementation—Low
Net economic benefits—High

Step 2. Compare technical feasibility with ease of implementation.

---

[29] Dyer and Holder, "Strategic Perspective."

ILLUSTRATION 8–2 (concluded)

1. The "high" technical feasibility evaluation is matched against "low" ease of implementation, yielding a rating of marginally desirable.

Technical Feasibility	Ease of Implementation		
	High	Medium	Low
High	Very desirable	Very desirable	Marginally desirable
Medium	Very desirable	Moderately desirable	Marginally desirable
Low	Marginally desirable	Marginally desirable	Not worthwhile

Step 3. Compare Step 2 evaluation with net economic benefits

2. Results of the previous evaluation are compared to "high" net economic benefits.

3. To determine overall feasibility category of "marginally desirable."

Step 2 Evaluation	Net Economic Benefits		
	High	Medium	Low
Very desirable	Very desirable	Moderately desirable	Marginally desirable
Moderately desirable	Very desirable	Moderately desirable	Marginally desirable
Marginally desirable	Marginally desirable	Marginally desirable	Not worthwhile

* A fourth factor, economic risk of not acting, is also included. In the context of this chapter, however, given goal acceptance, nonaction is not a feasible alternative.

Source: L. Cheek, "Cost Effectiveness Comes to the Personnel Function," *Harvard Business Review* 51, no. 3 (1973), pp. 96–105. Copyright © 1973 by the President and Fellows of Harvard College; all rights reserved.

developed at Xerox Corporation. Such heuristics help to ensure that all decision makers use the same criteria to judge alternatives and that these criteria are consistently applied across alternatives.

Choosing among activities

Responsibility for scrutinizing the proposed package of alternatives and making final decisions rests with top management. Inconsistencies and overlaps must be ferreted out, and the activities must be seen as feasible in terms of the budget and people likely to be available to implement them.

ILLUSTRATION 8–3

Excerpts from Merck and Company's Human Resource Strategy, 1984–1988

Priority 6

Develop new and more effective ways to accommodate employee participation in joint problem-solving areas and in appropriate policy/practice development.

Opinion surveys, face-to-face-meetings, focus groups, quality circle groups, and labor-management committees have added channels for employees to express their concerns and suggestions. These are just the start of many avenues which will be explored to improve participation and two-way communications between employees and supervisors.

There continues to be room for and need for expanding and improving employee participation. This will be achieved through improved two-way communication between employees and supervisors. Managers and supervisors need to fully understand and to put into practice the belief that the commitment of people is better assured when they are involved in the decision-making process.

Summary of Action Plans:

- Application of "focus group" techniques to develop or revise policies and procedures (successfully tested in 1980 with the Performance Appraisal Program and the Salary Administration Program).
- Continue to measure the effectiveness of management policies, practices, and programs.

Priority 10

Develop innovative approaches to organization design, job design and scheduling, and advanced office systems to improve productivity.

Strengthen our capabilities for more effective organization planning to ensure capability of supporting business plans and objectives. It is critical that skills be broadened in long-term organization planning and in the redesign of jobs and work.

Attract talented professionals who want more flexibility in the workplace.

We will continue our investigation into advanced office systems and the expansion of office automation, which have significant human implications. There is a need to coordinate a stronger planning effort—on a corporatewide basis—between the three elements that are essential to make advanced office systems work effectively. These three elements include the technical (MIS), the physical office design (Engineering), and the behavioral (Human Resources). Given that Merck is office-worker intensive and will become more so in the future, this planning effort has significant implications for the Company's productivity efforts.

Summary of Action Plans:

- Continue to develop skills for effective organization planning and implementation of Advanced Office Systems.
- Expand flexible working hours and test new scheduling and work pattern approaches.
- Continue to improve consulting skills of H. R. professionals.

Source: G. T. Milkovich and J. D. Phillips, "Human Resource Planning at Merck & Co." in *Human Resource Planning: A Case Study Reference Guide to the Tested Practices of Five Major U.S. and Canadian Companies*, ed. L. Dyer (New York: Random House, 1986).

Collectively, the choices made form a human resource strategy.[30] This strategy establishes the human resource objectives that the organization has chosen to pursue and the means that will be used to pursue them. Further, it normally guides the allocation of resources (people and money) to various P/HR management activities.

Illustration 8–3 is an excerpt from a human resource strategy developed at Merck. It contains two of the firm's strategic priorities and a summary of the related action plans for each.

Once formulated, of course, a human resource strategy must be implemented. To a large extent this is what the remaining chapters of this book are all about. Based on the overall human resource strategy, plans for all the functional activities (recruitment, selection, internal staffing, employee development, and so on) are put together. At this point, many firms prepare detailed action plans that show specific objectives, planned action steps, targeted completion dates, and the names of those responsible for seeing that the action steps are carried out.

Summary

If organizations are to avoid always having to run hard to catch up, they must plan. HRP is the process used to do people planning. Although it takes many forms, HRP is basically designed to anticipate likely future events in and around an organization and assess their likely human resource implications and outcomes in the absence of concerted action, and then, when the prognostication is not good, to design concerted actions that will alter events to bring about more favorable P/HR and organizational outcomes. In practice, HRP comes in three varieties: plan-, project-, and population-based. Organizations that use all three are said to have a comprehensive approach to HRP.

Each of the three varieties may be somewhat different from one organization to the next. The most important variations occur with respect to planning horizons, organizational units and employee groups covered, and the roles played by line managers and planning professionals. Irrespective of these variations, however, most applications are based on a basic staffing planning model that has five phases: (1) determining future human resource requirements, (2) determining future human resource availabilities, (3) conducting external and internal environmental scanning, (4) reconciling future human resource requirements and availabilities and setting objectives, and (5) developing action plans.

---

[30] J. Ledvinka, *Federal Regulation of Personnel and Human Resource Management* (Boston: Kent Publishing, 1982), Chapter 6.

The outcome of HRP is a human resource strategy that establishes an organization's major goals or objectives and indicates the ways in which these goals or objectives will be pursued; that is, which P/HR activities will receive priority and what the major policies will be in each area.

AFFIRMATIVE ACTION PLANNING

The concepts of affirmative action were discussed in Chapter 3. Many employers, and particularly government contractors, continue to prepare affirmative action plans annually. Affirmative action planning (AAP) consists of three steps: (1) Conducting a utilization analysis, (2) establishing goals and timetables, and (3) planning action steps.[31] Interestingly, these involve a straightforward application of many of the concepts and principles applied in HRP. Revised Order No. 4 provides federal contractors with specific requirements for their AA plans and programs. The order is administered by the Office of Federal Contract Compliance Programs (OFCCP).

Analysis

The analysis phase of AAP incorporates both a *utilization analysis* and the process of establishing *goals and timetables*.

Utilization analysis

A utilization analysis is used to determine whether, and to what extent, women and minorities are underrepresented in various job categories. (The standard job categories are officials and managers, professionals, technicians, sales workers, office and clerical, craft workers, operatives, laborers, and service workers.) Two pieces of information are required. The first is a calculation of the proportion of women and minorities currently employed in the relevant job categories. The second is a determination of the proportion of qualified women and minorities in the labor market available to be employed in these job categories. Underutilization exists where there is an imbalance between the two proportions. In job categories where underutilization exists, it is necessary to set goals and timetables for its alleviation.

---

[31] Ledvinka, *Federal Regulation.*

ILLUSTRATION 8–4

Computation of Availability Rates for the Job Group "Professional 4" in Division B in Facility X

Source	Percent of Openings Filled from Source	Minority Representation in Source	Availability
Internal			
Professional 3	63.9%	23.52%	.1503
Technical 2	7.7	7.20	.0056
Technical 4	12.4	3.93	.0048
Office/Clerical 5	8.9	4.03	.0036
Transfers-in	1.2	13.52	.0016
External			
hires	5.9	7.60	.0045
	100.0%		.1704
			or
			17.04%

Note: all data in this table are fictitious.

Source: L. Dyer and N. O. Heyer, "Human Resource Planning at IBM," in *Human Resource Planning: A Case Study Reference Guide to the Tested Practices of Five Major U.S. and Canadian Companies*, ed. L. Dyer (New York: Random House, 1986).

Goals and timetables

Long-term goals are usually set equal to established availabilities. And the sizes of the gaps between current employment rates and availability usually determine the length of the timetables, and hence the magnitude of the annual goals that are set.

Establishing realistic timetables and annual goals is no easy matter.[32] It requires accurate estimates of the vacancies (or opportunities) that will occur in various job categories during the planning period. This, in turn, requires high-quality forecasts of future human resource requirements and availabilities that can be obtained only from effective HRP.

The most realistic goals and timetables probably are found in those companies that combine sophisticated availability analyses with computer simulations that model anticipated vacancies (or opportunities).[33] Illustration 8–4 shows how one such company, IBM, combines historical flow and representation data to determine availability for various job

---

[32] For a general discussion of the relationship between HRP and AAP, see J. Ledvinka, "Technical Implications of Equal Employment Law for Manpower Planning," *Personnel Psychology* 28 (1975), pp. 299–322; and G. T. Milkovich and F. Krzystofiak, "Simulation and Affirmative Action Planning," *Human Resource Planning* 2 (1979), pp. 71–80.

[33] See the IBM case in *Human Resource Planning: Tested Practices*, ed. L. Dyer.

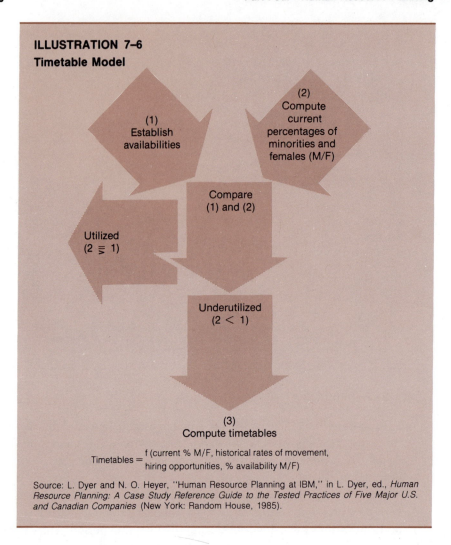

ILLUSTRATION 7–6
Timetable Model

(1) Establish availabilities

(2) Compute current percentages of minorities and females (M/F)

Compare (1) and (2)

Utilized (2 $\geqq$ 1)

Underutilized (2 < 1)

(3) Compute timetables

$$\text{Timetables} = \frac{\text{f (current \% M/F, historical rates of movement,}}{\text{hiring opportunities, \% availability M/F)}}$$

Source: L. Dyer and N. O. Heyer, "Human Resource Planning at IBM," in L. Dyer, ed., *Human Resource Planning: A Case Study Reference Guide to the Tested Practices of Five Major U.S. and Canadian Companies* (New York: Random House, 1985).

categories.[34] Illustration 8–5 shows how the availability data are then used in a goal-programming model to determine an appropriate timetable. In its calculations, the model simultaneously considers (1) the present utilization rate in the job category of interest, (2) growth, (3) historical patterns of losses from the job category, and (4) the percentage of vacancies (or opportunities) that will be allocated to women and minorities (which is set equal to their availabilities).

---

[34] T. Johnson, "Affirmative Action as a Title VII Remedy: Recent U.S. Supreme Court Decisions, Racial Quotas and Preferences," *Labor Law Journal*, September 1987, pp. 574–81.

Availability analyses are run for both women and minorities for each major job category in the company. Further, the results of these calculations are always reviewed and tempered by the responsible managers in various company locations. This demonstrates the magnitude of commitment and expense required for a large company to establish affirmative action goals and timetables.

Action Planning

Establishing goals and timetables is only the beginning. Every bit as important is the process of developing action plans to ensure that the goals and timetables are realized.

The OFCCP, through Revised Order 4, provides employers with a wide range of alternative programs, nearly all of which are used by affirmative action employers. These include:

- Reviewing all aspects of P/HR management for evidence of discrimination.
- Communicating equal employment opportunity and affirmative action (EEO/AA) policies widely both within and outside the company.
- Providing career counseling for minorities and women to heighten their awareness of and aspirations toward higher-level positions.
- Providing special training for supervisors who are responsible for decisions about hiring, firing, promotions, and pay increases to increase their awareness of the law and company policies, and of their own personal biases.

All of the above can be helpful in increasing employment opportunities for women and minorities, particularly when focused on job categories showing persistent underutilization. A more direct but infinitely more controversial approach is the use of preferential treatment in hiring, promotion, and retention decisions. One example would be a plan that requires blacks and whites to be hired or promoted in a fixed ratio (say, 2:1) until such time as utilization is reached. Another plan might require the proportion of minorities and females in a work force to be the same following a layoff as it was before, even if many in these groups have less seniority than their white male counterparts.

No one disputes the potential effectiveness of such plans in attaining utilization. The question is whether the gains of this approach are worth the costs incurred by better-qualified or more senior white males. On this question, government policymakers, enforcement agencies, and the courts have shown a tendency to disagree. In general, however, it now appears that preferential treatment for women and minorities is sanctioned in those cases where it has been ordered by a court to remedy Title VII violations or where it has been voluntarily adopted by an employer as an integral part of a bona fide affirmative action plan. The exception pertains to layoffs. Here the courts have generally held that seniority takes precedence over affirmative action considerations.[35]

HUMAN RESOURCE INFORMATION SYSTEMS

HRP and AAP, as well as many other aspects of P/HR activities (such as staffing, development, compensation, labor relations), create nearly insatiable demands for information. Meeting these demands requires systematic approaches to the gathering, processing, and reporting of data and information—in other words, HRISs.[36]

All organizations have personnel records of some sort, but HRISs are more than this. They are systems specifically designed to capture discrete pieces of data (facts) about people and jobs and to translate these data into usable forms of information. Some HRISs are implemented using an organization's large mainframe or minicomputer (which also contains many other data bases). Increasingly, however, microcomputers, such as IBM PCs or Apple IIEs, that are dedicated exclusively to P/HR management, are used.[37]

The Data Base

As a number of observers point out, there is no end to the data that might go into HRISs. One expert has recommended including 17 major categories containing 148 pieces of data.[38] Some of these are:

1. Personal data: name, payroll number, social security number, date of birth, minority group classification, sex.
2. Recruitment/selection data: Date of first contact, source of contact, date of interview, interviewer(s), date offered employment,

---

[35] A. Walker, *HRIS Development* (New York: Van Nostrand Reinhold, 1982).

[36] R. Nardoni, "Piecing Together a Micro-Based HRIS," *Personnel Journal*, February 1985, pp. 38–43. See also the three-part series on the use of microcomputers in personnel by R. Frantzreb in *The HR Planning Newsletter* 5, nos. 4, 6, and 7 (1985).

[37] G. A. Bassett, "PAIR Record and Information Systems," in *Planning PAIR*, eds. Yoder, Heneman; and Walker, *HRIS Development*, pp. 24–31.

[38] S. H. Simon, "The HRIS: What Capabilities Must It Have?" *Personnel* 60, no. 5 (1983), pp. 36–55.

test scores, interviewer ratings, number of applicants for same job.

3. Work experience data: Jobs held before joining company, jobs held since joining company, specific skills.

4. Compensation data: Salary history, current salary, date due for next salary review.

5. Performance appraisal/promotability data: PA history, current PA rating, promotability rating, date due for next review, career preferences.

6. Attitude/morale data: Absence record, grievances filed.

7. Benefit plan data: Eligibility, participation levels, vacation records.

8. Health/safety/accident data: Exposures to hazardous material, accident records, medical visits, workers' compensation claims.

Designers of HRISs are often tempted to include as much data as possible "just in case." This temptation is to be avoided since data capturing, coding, and storage are expensive. The best general guideline is to distinguish between data that decision makers and outside agencies must have and data that they might find it nice to have, and then exclude the latter.

System Specifications

Figure 8–10 depicts the three major functional components of any HRIS: input, throughput, and output.[39]

FIGURE 8–10
Functional Components of an HRIS

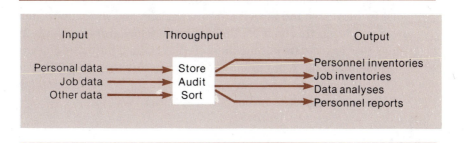

---

[39] For summaries of some of the options, see M. Magnus and D. J. Thomsen, "Microcomputer Software Guide," *Personnel Journal*, February 1986, pp. 49–72; and M. Magnus, "Microcomputer Software Guide: Part II," *Personnel Journal*, April 1986, pp. 53–68.

The input function

The input function establishes responsibilities for collecting relevant data and entering them into the HRIS on an ongoing basis. Data collection is usually done in one of two ways. The first is by tying the system into relevant data sources—particularly personnel forms and records—in such a way that any time a transaction occurs (for example, someone is hired, promoted, or granted a pay increase) the pertinent paperwork flows to the HRIS as well as to payroll and other relevant places. A variant of this is to hold employees responsible for informing HRIS specialists of certain changes (such as moving to a new address) and for periodically updating parts of their records. The second approach to data collection is to network the HRIS with other, perhaps more critical, information systems—most typically payroll—in such a way that data changes in one are automatically made in the other.

The challenge is to ensure that all required data are in the HRIS in the proper form and that they are up to date. Most modern HRISs have what is known as on-line input, which allows an HRIS operator to do data entry on a regular and ongoing basis and provides for immediate data update.

Throughput function

The throughput function is responsible for the actual updating, as well as the storage and maintenance, of the data in the HRIS. Here software design is key. Newer systems are configured in such a way that a single data entry will result in automatic updating across all relevant data bases. And these systems are large and flexible enough to accommodate all data needs and to ensure that there is the capacity to carry out all necessary data manipulations.

To support on-line input, throughput functions operate on real time. That is, they have the capacity to sort, update, and store inputs immediately and to do this on a continuous basis. They also have built-in edit codes that reject data not meeting predetermined format requirements.

Modeling of the types discussed earlier in this chapter (Markov analysis, simulations, goal-programming models for AAP) are examples of relatively sophisticated throughput capacities.

Output function

HRISs are only as good as the outputs they produce. The key is to ensure that the stored data can be manipulated in such a way as to produce the information that users need in a timely fashion and in a usable format. Most HRISs are programmed to produce output in both standardized and ad hoc forms. The former consist of recurring reports, wherein the format stays the same and only the data change from time to time. The latter consist of specialized reports that are unique, or required only infrequently, and that may require special programming to produce. Illustration 8–4 is an example of a specialized report.

Many vendors now produce and sell software packages for use on PCs that are capable of performing virtually any of the more common P/HR applications.

Most HRISs are designed to be interactive. That is, they permit operators to see potential output on their computer monitors as it is being manipulated and to make instant alterations as desired. Only after the data and format are satisfactory is the resulting report printed in "hard copy."

Security and Privacy

Data security is a major problem with HRISs. The beauty of such systems is the access they allow to data about employees and jobs. However, access is a two-edged sword. With increasingly large numbers of people using on-line, real-time, interactive systems, issues of data security arise. Companies go to great lengths to assign and keep current special identification codes that limit users both with respect to the types of data they can see and the nature of the manipulations they can perform. Especially critical to accuracy is the need to restrict the number of people who are able to perform data entry and updates.

The essence of a related problem, privacy, was captured by E. B. deVito in *The Wall Street Journal* a few years ago.[40]

> With machines far and wide
> Growing ever astuter,
> My life's nothing more
> Than an open computer.

Concerns such as this led the federal government to pass the Privacy Act of 1974, which set out stringent requirements for the handling of personnel data about federal employees. Several states have also passed legislation holding private employers responsible for the accuracy of their personnel records and granting employees the right periodically to inspect and, if necessary, correct these records.

---

[40] As quoted in D. W. Ewing, "Due Process: Will Business Default?" *Harvard Business Review*, November–December 1982, p. 115.

In the face of these requirements, and increasing computerization, a growing number of companies have adopted employee privacy programs.[41] Most are designed to: (1) restrict the types of employee data that can be kept to only those that are clearly job related, (2) provide for the periodic purging of outdated data, (3) provide a mechanism for promptly responding to employee inquiries about the data and for resolving disputes over data accuracy, (4) regularly provide printouts for employees containing much of the data the company keeps on them to permit instant correction, if necessary, and (5) assure employees that personal information will be released outside the company only with their approval, except to verify employment or to comply with legitimate legal investigations.

The need to administer these guidelines, and HRISs more generally, has given rise in many P/HR departments to a new activity: the Human Resource Information Center.[42] This new specialization, along with increasing use of HRIS data and systems in the traditional areas of P/HR management, puts great pressure on today's personnel practitioners to become increasingly facile with computers and related data base management techniques.

SUMMARY

HRP is the process used by organizations to: (1) analyze anticipated events in their external and internal environments and assess their attendant human resource implications and (2) formulate action plans that will—if properly implemented—contribute to future organizational success through improved human resource management.

In HRP, analysis is used to gather as much information as possible (or feasible) about future conditions in the business and the external and internal environments surrounding the business, to identify and reconcile gaps between anticipated human resource requirements and availabilities, and to establish objectives. Then, in action planning, this information is used to develop an integrated package of P/HR activities (i.e., a human resource strategy) that will provide the organization with a full complement of capable, committed, and satisfied employees.

AAP is, in many ways, analogous to HRP, except that it concentrates on women and minorities. Here analysis involves carrying out a utilization analysis and establishing goals and timetables. Action planning is

---

[41] D. Harris, "A Matter of Privacy: Managing Personal Data in Company Computers," *Personnel*, February 1987, pp. 34–43.

[42] A. Walker, *HRIS Development*, pp. 166–69.

where affirmative action steps are put together to improve the utilization of women and minorities in various job categories.

As HRP, AAP, and other P/HR management activities become increasingly sophisticated, they require more and better information about people and jobs. This is where HRISs come in. In recent years great strides have been made in harnessing the potential of computers to the effective accumulation, manipulation, and reporting of data and information of value to effective P/HR management.

DISCUSSION QUESTIONS

1. Why might a company decide *not* to do HRP?

2. Why is it that one company includes only its top executives, their replacements, and high potentials in its HRP, while another of comparable size includes all employees?

3. Why is it that one company has a five-year planning horizon for HRP while another of comparable size has only a one-year planning horizon?

4. Is it necessary when doing HRP always to make an estimate of future human resource requirements? Can you think of a situation where this would be unnecessary? Explain.

5. Define productivity. What role does it play in HRP?

6. An experienced P/HR professional once suggested that it is OK to use statistical techniques to estimate future human resource requirements, but not OK to use them to estimate future human resource availabilities because they are "bloodless." Do you agree or disagree? Why?

7. The chapter suggests that vacancy analysis and computer simulations used to do reconciliations are two sides of the same coin. Discuss.

8. Why might human resource planners care about top managers' values and attitudes about employees and about P/HR management?

9. What results did you get when (as the chapter suggested) you "generated one or two possible reconciliations manually using the data shown in Figures 8–3 and 8–7?

10. Some P/HR planning specialists suggest that line managers ought to be kept out of the action planning phase of HRP because they don't know enugh about P/HR management and thus tend to make the process inefficient and the results less sophisticated than they otherwise would be. Do you agree or disagree? Why? What are the implications of your answer for the practice of HRP?

11. Is it possible to do effective AAP without doing effective HRP? Explain.

12. Identify the major activities that occur during HRP and AAP. Show how each one could be facilitated with a well-designed and up-to-date HRIS.

PART FIVE

External Staffing

9

Recruitment

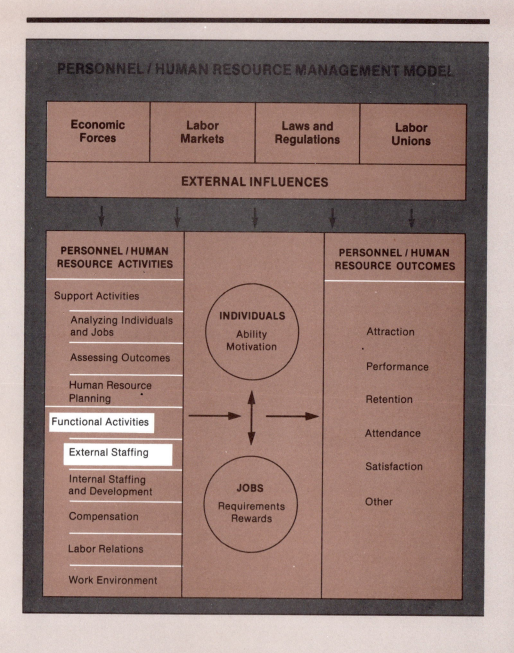

PERSONNEL / HUMAN RESOURCE MANAGEMENT MODEL

Economic Forces	Labor Markets	Laws and Regulations	Labor Unions

EXTERNAL INFLUENCES

PERSONNEL / HUMAN RESOURCE ACTIVITIES

Support Activities

- Analyzing Individuals and Jobs
- Assessing Outcomes
- Human Resource Planning

Functional Activities

- External Staffing
- Internal Staffing and Development
- Compensation
- Labor Relations
- Work Environment

INDIVIDUALS
Ability
Motivation

JOBS
Requirements
Rewards

PERSONNEL / HUMAN RESOURCE OUTCOMES

Attraction

Performance

Retention

Attendance

Satisfaction

Other

After reading this chapter, you should be able to speak to the questions posed in each of the following personnel/human resource incidents.

1. You are the personnel manager of the local hospital. The hospital's chief administrator died last month. With your help, the board of directors has screened the hospital staff for a replacement but has turned up no suitable candidates, so they have decided to recruit on the outside. One member of the board wants to advertise the position in the *New York Times* and *The Wall Street Journal.* Another wants to contact some private employment agencies. A third wants to engage an executive search firm. They ask for your opinion. What information would you like to have before deciding what to do? How would you use this information?

2. You are a graduate of Purdue University now working as a project manager in the engineering division of an aerospace company. The recruiting department of your company has asked you to assume joint responsibility for generating at least six new engineers from P.U. next year. This year the company recruited at P.U., made eight offers, but got no takers. In addition, a professor told you that the top students did not even consider going to the interview as they had been invited directly to competitor companies earlier in the year. There is a concern that several recruiting seasons may go by before the company can catch up and yet it wants to avoid a poorly designed and implemented campus recruitment program. There is a meeting tomorrow of the recruiting department and several line managers who have agreed to help. You have been asked to bring to that meeting a tentative strategy for meeting the goal of six hires, as well as a list of things you want the recruiting department to do. What will be your strategy? What will be on your list of things the recruiting department should do to update its program to compete with other first-line companies and avoid the crisis as the market continues to tighten?

3. You are on a task force of the city council of a major U.S. city. The task force's objective is to review the city's recruiting program and, if possible, to make recommendations for reducing expenditures. The city's personnel manager has agreed to cooperate with the task force and asks what information you'd like to have to get started. What would you tell her?

In this and the next two chapters, the subject is *external staffing*, the general term given to the process of filling job vacancies from outside the organization. External staffing has two components: recruitment, which is the subject of this chapter, and selection, which is covered in Chapters 10 and 11.

Recruitment is the process of seeking out and attempting to attract individuals in external labor markets who are capable of and interested in filling available job vacancies.[1] Recruitment is an intermediate activity whose primary function is to serve as a link between human resource planning (HRP) on the one hand and selection on the other. HRP, and especially staffing planning (see Chapter 8), identifies the job vacancies to be filled from outside the organization. It then is the task of recruitment to generate and, if necessary, pare down the pool of candidates from which new employees are subsequently selected. Recruitment has some direct effect on P/HR outcomes; there is evidence (reviewed later) showing that various approaches differ in the frequency with which they turn up high-quality applicants who eventually become successful employees. Of course, selection is important too, since it is relied on to actually choose candidates who have the ability and motivation to become productive and satisfied employees.

P/HR managers rightly regard recruitment as a significant activity.[2] The failure to generate an adequate number of reasonably qualified job candidates can be costly in many ways. It can greatly complicate the selection process, for example, and lead in extreme cases to the lowering of hiring standards. Lower-quality hires mean extra expenditures for employee development and supervision to attain satisfactory levels of performance and attendance and to avoid unwanted turnover. Furthermore, when recruitment fails to meet organizational needs for talent, a typical response is to raise entry-level pay levels. However, this can distort traditional wage and salary relationships in the organization, resulting in costly readjustments (see Chapter 14). Thus, the effectiveness of the recruitment process can play a major role in determining the resources that must be expended on other P/HR activities, and their ultimate success.

Given its key role and external visibility, it is not surprising to find that a number of external factors influence recruitment. Equal employment opportunity and affirmative action (EEO/AA) laws and regulations

---

[1] Sometimes the term *recruitment* is applied to all searches for job candidates, whether they are conducted inside or outside an organization. In this book, however, the term is applied only to searches that take place outside. Means used to generate (and select) job candidates from within an organization are discussed in Chapter 12.

[2] American Society for Personnel Administration, *The Personnel Executive's Job* (Englewood Cliffs, N.J.: Prentice-Hall, 1979).

are major influences, and their role is discussed throughout this chapter. Labor organizations typically play only a minor role, since their activities in this area are severely constrained by the Labor-Management Relations Act (see Chapter 3). Labor markets, on the other hand, are the arenas in which recruitment takes place, and all recruitment activities must be tailored to fit the general availability of people with needed skills and abilities.

Tight labor markets (those characterized by low unemployment rates) put job seekers at an advantage and complicate the recruitment process; loose labor markets have the opposite effect and complicate the job search process. For instance, demographic changes are creating a tightening of the labor market in many occupations. Labor-intensive industries are already being affected as there is a shift toward a service economy that often requires a better-educated workforce. For example, in the past just about anyone who could read and add could process insurance claims, but now employees need to make tough decisions based on more complex information and use computer technology on a regular basis. Even in manufacturing, a better education may be sought to help solve productivity problems (e.g., Motorola requires its blue-collar employees to perform mathematical analyses as part of its quality improvement program). There is also concern among employers about the quality of the U.S. educational system causing frequent mismatches between applicants' skills and job requirements, even at the managerial level. Collectively, these changes are likely to bring more aggressive recruitment on the part of employers.[3]

Recruitment is one human resource activity that typically requires relatively little action by top or line management (except when it occurs at upper organizational levels). Top management establishes general policies concerning such matters as hiring standards, acceptable and unacceptable sources of applicants (rare, for example, is the organization that does not recruit at its president's alma mater), starting salaries, and the organization's EEO/AA posture. The impetus to begin recruiting generally comes from line management through the staffing/planning process and, more specifically, through the issuance of employee requisitions (that is, specific authorizations to hire).

However, in many organizations, line managers play no further role in the actual recruitment process. In others, they may play an active part in the recruitment of managerial and professional employees, usually by making recruiting trips to various college campuses once or twice a year. Except in small organizations, however, it is uncommon to find line

---

[3] "Help Wanted. America Faces an Era of Worker Scarcity that May Last to the Year 2000," *Business Week*, August 10, 1987, pp. 48–53.

FIGURE 9–1

The Recruitment Process

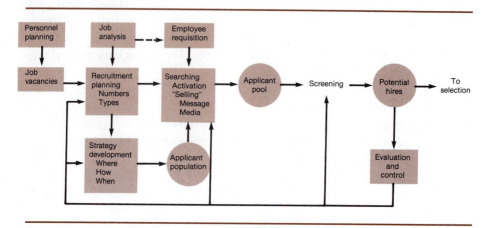

managers heavily involved in the recruitment of technical, clerical, or blue-collar employees.

Thus, the personnel department usually assumes major responsibility for recruitment.[4] It recommends policy to top management, develops strategies and procedures, sometimes shares authority for issuing employee requisitions, lobbies for the involvement of line management where deemed appropriate, sends recruiters into the field where necessary, and maintains the capability to process and screen applications and applicants. It also monitors the entire process for effectiveness, efficiency, and EEO/AA compliance and makes improvements as necessary.

Figure 9–1 shows that the recruitment process consists of five interrelated stages that serve as the organizing theme for the majority of this chapter: (1) planning, (2) strategy development, (3) searching, (4) screening, and (5) evaluation and control. The ideal recruitment program is one that attracts an appropriate number of qualified applicants who will survive the screening process and accept positions with the organization when offered. Recruitment programs can miss the ideal in many ways: (1) by failing to attract an adequate applicant pool, (2) by failing to attract a high-quality applicant pool, (3) by under- or overselling the organization, or (4) by inadequately screening applicants before they enter the selection process. Thus, to approach the ideal, individuals responsible for the recruitment process must know how many and what types of employees are needed, where and how to look for individuals with the appropriate

---

[4] A. R. Janger, *The Personnel Function: Changing Objectives and Organization* (New York: The Conference Board, 1977), pp. 37–40.

qualifications and interests, what inducements to use (and avoid) for various types of applicant groups, how to distinguish applicants who are unqualified from those who have a reasonable chance of succeeding, and how to evaluate their work.

RECRUITMENT PLANNING

Recruitment planning, as shown in Figure 9–1, involves the translation of likely job vacancies and information about the nature of these jobs into a set of objectives or targets that specify the numbers and types of potential applicants to be contacted.

Number of Contacts

Organizations nearly always plan to attract more applicants than they will hire. Some of those contacted will be uninterested, unqualified, or both. Each time a recruitment program is contemplated, therefore, one task is to estimate the number of applicants necessary to fill all vacancies with qualified people.

Precision is impossible, but useful estimates can be made using yield ratios (YRs), which express the relationship of applicant inputs to outputs at various decision points.[5] For example, assume that an organization attempting to recruit salespeople ran a series of newspaper advertisements. The ads generated resumes from 2,000 applicants, of which 200 were judged to be potentially qualified (YR = 10:1). Of these 200, 40 accepted an invitation to be interviewed (YR = 5:1). Of these 40, 30 were actually qualified and offered jobs (YR = 4:3), and of these 30, 20 accepted (YR = 3:2).

In this case, the overall YR is 100:1. Thus, other things being equal, a requirement of 30 hires during a specified period would mean a recruitment target of 3,000. Of course, other things may not be equal. An attempt may be made to improve the YRs. For example, the ads may be reworded to more clearly state hiring requirements, thus eliminating many of the resumes from unqualified applicants. A different recruitment source (for example, employment agencies) may be tried. Outside the employer's control, the state of the labor market may change. A tighter labor market, for example, usually decreases the relative number of applicants and acceptances since job seekers have more alternatives available to them.

---

[5] R. H. Hawk, *The Recruitment Function* (New York: American Management Association, 1967), pp. 27–29.

In other words, in estimating the number of contacts that must be made, YRs can be helpful, but they must be used with care. Furthermore, no YRs will be available for employee groups being recruited for the first time or for recruiting sources and methods that have not yet been tried. In these instances, recruiters must rely on their counterparts in other organizations for help or make their best guesses.

Given the judgment involved in setting numerical targets for recruitment, it is advisable to monitor actual against predicted YRs. This permits periodic adjustments to avoid inadequate applicant flows or excessive recruitment expenditures.

Types of Contacts

To a greater or lesser degree, all recruitment activities can be focused in terms of types of people contacted. For this reason, it is useful to specify the requirements of the jobs to be filled (in knowledge, skills, abilities, and so forth) during the planning stage of recruitment. (These must be delineated later anyway so that applicants can be screened.)

Readers will recall from Chapter 4 that job requirements are determined through job analysis and stated in the form of job specifications. When clear job specifications do not exist, two contrasting tendencies are common.[6] One is to state requirements only vaguely ("Get me an engineer with some sales experience"); the other is to state them too narrowly ("Get me an Ivy Leager who had an A average in electrical engineering, who was captain of her debating team, president of her sorority, and who has spent the last four years selling computers to small businesses in the Midwest"). The price of vague or unnecessarily confining job specifications is likely to be a poorly focused recruiting effort that takes longer and is more expensive than it has to be and that yields applicants of varying quality. This, in turn, puts pressure on the screening and selection processes to weed out the unqualified.[7]

From this point on, it is essential that planners and recruiters recognize that they are involved in a ritual of mutual decision making. While they are making decisions about where, how, and when to look, what to do to attract applicants, and which applicants to accept and reject, their quarry are making decisions of their own. As Figure 9–2 suggests, some

---

[6] For a more complete discussion of these points, see P. V. Wernimont, "Recruitment Policies and Practices," in ASPA *Handbook of Personnel and Industrial Relations*, ed. D. Yoder and H. G. Heneman, Jr. (Washington, D.C.: The Bureau of National Affairs, 1979), p. 92.

[7] J. W. Boudreau and S. L. Rynes, "Role of Recruitment in Staffing Utility Analysis," *Journal of Applied Psychology* 70 (1985), pp. 354–66.

FIGURE 9–2
The Two Faces of Searching and Screening

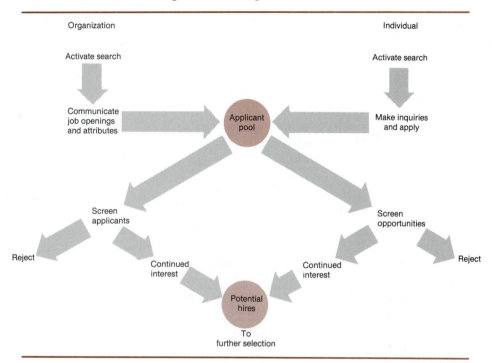

Source: Adopted from D. P. Schwab, "Recruiting and Organizational Participation," in *Personnel Management,* eds. K. M. Rowland and G. R. Ferris (Boston: Allyn Bacon, 1982), p. 105.

are looking for work, and some aren't (even if they know of job openings). Only some of those who are looking for work will respond to a given employer's inducements and apply for a particular job. Only some of those who apply will decide to stay with the process through to the end (given the opportunity).[8]

To do their jobs, planners and recruiters need to know what factors affect these decisions and how. The more they know, the better their own decisions can be. Thus, when considering the remaining stages of the recruitment process, considerable attention needs to be given to the findings from the job search research.[9]

---

[8] D. P. Schwab, "Recruiting and Organizational Participation" in *Personnel Management,* eds. K. M. Rowland and G. R. Ferris (Boston: Allyn & Bacon, 1982), pp. 103–28.

[9] D. P. Schwab, S. L. Rynes, and R. J. Aldag, "Theories and Research on Job Search and Choice," in *Research in Personnel and Human Resources Management,* vol. 5, eds. K. M. Rowland and G. R. Ferris (Greenwich, Conn.: JAI Press, 1987), pp. 129–166. Later in this chapter, some of these findings will be used to draw implications for job seekers as well.

STRATEGY DEVELOPMENT

Once it is known how many of what types of recruits are required, serious consideration can be given to the matters of (1) where to look, (2) how to look, and (3) when to carry out certain activities (refer to Figure 9–1).

Where to Look

To reduce costs, organizations geographically restrict their recruiting efforts to those labor markets most likely to produce results. But where are these? Organizations tend to seek managerial and professional employees nationally or regionally, technical employees regionally or locally, and clerical and blue-collar employees locally.

Job search research seems to support these tendencies. One study, for example, revealed that about one fourth of the managers and professionals looking for work traveled more than 100 miles to do so, whereas only 7 percent of the craft workers, 2 percent of the clerical workers, and 4 percent of the laborers traveled this far. In fact, among the latter three groups, only 13, 33, and 28 percent, respectively, traveled more than 25 miles during their job searches.[10] Other studies of clerical and blue-collar job seekers have substantiated their relative lack of geographical mobility.[11]

The job-seeking behavior of potential applicants is not the only factor dictating recruiting areas. Organizational location plays a part. An organization in, say, Montello, Wisconsin, may not be able to confine its search for managerial or professional employees to the local labor market, but a similar organization in New York City could. Still another consideration is the state of the labor market. Local shortages of certain types of blue-collar workers, for example, sometimes cause organizations to conduct regional recruiting campaigns for these employees (and, on occasion, even to pay their relocation costs, a routine practice at managerial and professional levels).

In the final analysis, organizations recruit where experience and circumstances dictate likely success. Recognizing this, many adopt an incremental strategy in which initial efforts are concentrated in regional or local labor markets and expanded only if these efforts fail to achieve the desired results.

---

[10] See *Jobseeking Methods Used by American Workers*, Bulletin 1886 (Washington, D.C.: Bureau of Labor Statistics, U.S. Department of Labor, 1975), p. 52.

[11] For a review of this research, see H. S. Parnes, "Labor Force and Labor Markets," in *A Review of Industrial Relations Research*, vol. 1, ed. R. L. Ginsburg et al. (Madison, Wis.: Industrial Relations Research Association, 1970), pp. 33–66.

How to Look

In any given recruitment program, choices among candidate sources and search methods must be made. There is sometimes confusion between sources and methods. Sources refer to the labor market segment where qualified applicants are located, while methods are the specific means by which potential employees are attracted to an organization.[12] Examples of sources are high schools and vocational schools, colleges and universities, competitors and other firms, and the unemployed. The major methods include direct applications, employee referrals, advertising, college recruiting, private and public employment agencies and executive search firms, computerized search services, and miscellaneous methods.

Direct applications: write-ins and walk-ins

For many organizations, a major source of applicants of all types (except high-ranking executives) is job seekers who make direct application by mailing in resumes or showing up at the office door or plant gate.

Direct applications provide a backlog of potential employees that can be quickly tapped when job vacancies occur. This particular source of recruits can be virtually cost free. Some organizations find that they obtain all the candidates they need through direct applications, especially at the clerical and blue-collar levels. Most, however, probably find that they cannot or do not wish to rely on this source exclusively.

Employee referrals

Similar to (and indeed often indistinguishable from) direct applications are applicants who are referred by current employees. Often these applicants turn up as a matter of course; in times of short supply, however, employers sometimes offer cash bonuses for each new recruit brought in. Lockheed Missiles and Space Corporation, for example, ran a program in which employees referring candidates who were eventually hired received gifts and became eligible for weekly drawings of $1,000 and a grand prize drawing of $7,500. During the program, there were 3,173 referrals, 1,889 applications, 390 offers made, and 356 acceptances. Total prize money paid was $34,500, or $96.91 per hire—not much considering that three fourths of the hires were clerical, technical, professional, and managerial employees.

---

[12] R. W. Mondy, M. Noe, and R. E. Edwards, "Successful Recruitment: Matching Sources and Methods," *Personnel* 64 (September 1987), pp. 42–46.

Employee referrals are quick, relatively inexpensive, and quite popular with job seekers. Despite these advantages, many organizations shun them. Some are concerned about the possible negative effects of nepotism, inbreeding, and cliques. Others fear that employees will become upset if the applicants they refer are not hired. This method also has some possible negative EEO/AA consequences since referrals tend to be similar to present employees, a problem if existing employees are mostly white males.

Advertising

Advertising includes everything from simple classified ads placed in the help-wanted section of a local newspaper to special appeals made on the radio or even TV (see Illustration 9–1). Job seekers tend to respond to advertisements and many, particularly at the clerical, sales, and managerial levels, find their jobs in this way.

ILLUSTRATION 9–1

VideoSearch's Use of Television for Recruitment

Television. Although television is not a new medium, some people are experimenting with it and trying to make it a more effective recruitment advertising medium.

"Meet Your Next Employer" is a one-half hour television program, airing at 10 P.M. Sunday nights in the Los Angeles area.

The program consists of a series of interviews with senior management from major Fortune 500 companies discussing their employment needs.

It's the brainchild of Richard Katz, founder of VideoSearch, the Santa Ana, California-based firm producing the program.

VideoSearch buys the time from the television station and in turns sells interview time to corporate recruiters. "In Los Angeles, the cost runs approximately $700–$1,000 per minute and you need five minutes for an interview spot," explains Katz.

Companies can buy as little as 30 seconds for a spot recruitment advertisement, however. Some companies send prerecorded videotapes for these short spots.

A toll-free telephone number, valid for a month for each company, allows viewers to call in and apply for the job.

Katz attracts viewers to the program through print advertising in *TV Guide,* the newspaper television guides, and the *Los Angeles Times* classified ad section under appropriate job categories.

Merrill Lynch, Best Products Companies, GTE, and Xerox are among those who have used the service, Katz says. They hired people in sales, as consultants and as retail managers.

Source: M. Meyers, "Is Your Recruitment All It Can Be?" *Personnel Journal* 66 (February 1987), p. 56.

Employment advertising (other than the classified variety) is a specialized skill usually requiring the use of experts to advise on media selection and, especially, design and layout.[13] In clever hands, it can be an effective recruiting tool. But it tends to be relatively slow in producing results since several months may be required to plan, design, and implement an effective campaign. The cost, however, may be less than might be expected since many advertising agencies collect their fees in the form of discounts from the media with which ads are placed. In effect, then, the agencies' services cost the employer nothing above that which would be paid for placing the ad anyway.

College recruiting

College recruiting is probably the method most familiar to readers of this book. Similar efforts, however, take place each year at many high schools, trade and vocational schools, and junior colleges. Because of its special interest and specialized nature, a section is devoted exclusively to college recruiting later in this chapter.

Private employment agencies

Recruiting through private employment agencies tends to focus on clerical employees and lower- and middle-level managers. Private employment agencies offer advantages. First, they can be turned on and off relatively quickly, since they usually have a backlog of clients. Second, some also can do an effective job of screening applicants so that the organization sees only those who are basically qualified.

However, many employers complain that good private employment agencies are difficult to find, and good working relationships with these take many years to build. Furthermore, private employment agencies tend to be expensive, usually claiming as a fee 20 to 25 percent or even more of the first year's salary. Typically, agency fees are paid by the employer, although they sometimes are absorbed by job seekers, particularly for clerical jobs.[14]

---

[13] For discussions of the technical issues involved here, see B. Martin, "Recruitment Adventures," *Personnel Journal* (August 1987), pp. 46–63.

[14] American Management Association, *Hiring Costs and Strategies: The AMA Report* (New York: AMACOM, 1986).

Federal training and employment service

The U.S. Training and Employment Service (USTES) is an amalgam of more than 2,400 state-run (but federally funded) employment agencies. Many job seekers report using the USTES. Indeed, it must be used by all persons who collect unemployment compensation. Relatively few job seekers report obtaining jobs through the USTES, however. Many employers tend to shy away from it, complaining that its referrals are often not interested in accepting employment and are of low quality. Despite the complaints, the USTES can be a rapid means of obtaining job applicants at no cost. Furthermore, employers who work closely with the service find that it can do an excellent job of testing and screening job seekers, especially at the blue-collar level. The service has pioneered in the use of computers to match applicants to jobs rapidly and effectively in both local and regional labor markets.

Executive search firms

Many organizations prefer to fill top- and upper-middle management jobs from within. When outside recruiting is relied on, probably the two most frequently used methods are employee referrals (the "old-boy" and the developing "old-girl" networks) and executive search firms. Executive search firms, as the name suggests, concentrate on recruiting top- and upper-middle managers only. They work closely with employers, usually spending many hours clarifying position specifications and seeking out candidates who fit these specifications precisely. Often these candidates are persons who are employed rather than unemployed, leading to the widespread usage of the term *head-hunting* to describe this type of work.

Executive search firms are expensive. Fees vary, but an average figure for a single search is about 33 percent of the first year's salary, plus expenses. Thus, each time around, a user can expect to pay $25,000 to $75,000 or more. Organizations that must go outside for top-level talent, however, usually have few realistic alternatives.

Computerized search services

Recruitment is yet another P/HR management activity that is being altered by the computer revolution. The use of computers by the USTES has already been mentioned. In addition, a number of private firms have sprung up to take advantage of the new technology. Some employers are beginning to get in on the act.

Originally, use was confined primarily to high-technology companies that recruited large numbers of regular computer users—for example, scientists, engineers, and programmers.[15] Other types of companies are now following high-technology firms and the use of computerized services is expanding, often in tandem with other methods such as job fairs. On-line job hunting involves three situations: (1) the "position wanted ad," which solicits resumes from candidates and invites employers to search the files (this is a passive method); (2) the "on-line classifieds" where the job hunter searches lists of jobs directly from employers or newspapers, trade journals, and so on; and (3) the "two-way street" where both the employers and the job seekers are looking for each other.[16] In some cases, companies pay to register their jobs (through use charges or annual fees); in others, job seekers pay to put their electronic resumes on file; and in still others, both parties contribute to the cost. Responsibility for putting interested employers and job seekers physically in touch with one another rests with the vendor providing the service.

A few companies are proceeding without an intermediary.[17] Mitre Corporation, for example, lists job openings on a computer and then advertises the fact in local newspapers, inviting potentially interested engineers to dial in and "shop" electronically. The company finds that costs per hire with the system run considerably below the $5,500 the company typically spends using more conventional methods. An irritant, however, is the "electronic graffiti" the system generates.

Miscellaneous methods

In addition to the usual candidate sources and search methods, organizations rely on a variety of more specialized approaches to attract employees. Space limitations prohibit a full discussion, but some of these approaches include the use of direct-mail "marketing," special events, professional societies and trade unions, contract recruiting, and temporary help agencies.

In *direct-mail marketing*, companies identify and purchase appropriate mailing lists from magazines, professional associations, trade groups, and the like. Those on the list are then sent specially prepared packets

[15] G. Glickstein and D. C. Z. Ramer, "The Alternative Market Place," *Personnel Administrator* 33 (February 1988), pp. 100–4.

[16] K. Lane, "The Perfect Match—Finding an Employer or an Employee Online," *HR/PC*, vol. 3.1 (November 16–December 31, 1987), pp. 1–5.

[17] W. M. Bulkeley, "Some Concerns Are Recruiting by Computer," *The Wall Street Journal*, February 9, 1983, p. 33.

containing letters and company brochures and are invited to express their interest by phone or return mail.[18]

Special-events recruiting often takes the form of job fairs. Here, an agency arranges to have recruiters from several organizations together in one place at one time and then advertises the event widely, hoping to attract a large number of job seekers for the employers to interview.

Organizations requiring applicants with specialized skills or training sometimes turn to the *professional societies or trade unions* to which these individuals belong. College faculty, for example, have long been recruited through facilities set up at the annual meetings of such professional groups as the Academy of Management and the American Psychological Association.

Contract recruitment is yet another approach that is becoming popular in some circles. A contract recruiter is a consultant who accepts a temporary assignment (typically three to six months) in a company, becoming an integral part of the human resource staff. This gives the company a highly focused recruiting capability, the flexibility to respond to peaks and valleys in employment, and an immediate addition of a personnel professional without incurring the costs or risk of a permanent hire.[19]

Still another method of recruitment is *temporary help agencies*. Recruits from temporary help agencies remain on the agencies' payrolls, and the employer in a sense borrows them for a fee. This avoids the necessity of processing temporary employees onto payrolls and of enrolling them in various benefit programs. It also offers flexibility in times of business downturns, since these temporary employees can be cut back relatively quickly and easily. Sometimes companies lease their employees. This is an alternative to recruitment in that the employees are located (as well as paid) by the firm doing the leasing.[20]

Employer practices

In reality, of course, organizations usually use a number of sources and search methods simultaneously, with the number and types varying depending on the nature of the jobs involved and conditions in the relevant labor markets. Surveys tend to show remarkably consistent practices across firms, namely, a heavy reliance on traditional and pri-

---

[18] R. Sledleckl, "Creating a Direct Mail Recruitment Program," *Personnel Journal*, April 1983, pp. 304–7.

[19] For more details on this approach, see J. Lord, "Contract Recruiting: Coming of Age," *Personnel Administrator* 32 (November 1987), pp. 49–53.

[20] P. C. Driskell, "Recruitment: A Manager's Checklist for Labor Leasing," *Personnel Journal* 65 (October 1986), pp. 108–12.

ILLUSTRATION 9–2

Matching Sources and Methods: How the Colonel Recruits

To solve a 40 percent turnover rate among its restaurant managers in the central Florida area, Kentucky Fried Chicken used a new recruitment strategy that involved:

1. Stressing the benefits of the jobs when advertising, down-playing the company logo, and using employee testimonials.
2. Increasing employee referrals through contests.
3. Developing a new college recruitment program by sponsoring open houses in colleges.
4. Recruiting outside previously established geographic boundaries (e.g., North versus South).
5. Targeting at nontraditional labor market segments: military retirees, displaced homemakers, older employees, the handicapped, and so on.
6. Using special events in areas with high concentration of people (e.g., job fairs at community shopping malls).

As a result of this new approach to recruitment, combined with a retention program, the 40 percent turnover rate dropped to 3 percent. The matching between sources and methods proved to be successful.

Sources: Adapted from R. W. Mondy, R. M. Noe, and R. E. Edwards, "Successful Recruitment: Matching Sources and Methods," *Personnel* 64 (September 1987), p. 46; and "How the Colonel Recruits," *Human Resource Executive* 1, no. 3 (1987), p. 28.

---

marily low-cost options (except when using executive search firms to fill high-level executive jobs). Recent studies involving managerial jobs, for example, indicate a marked preference for the use of direct applications, employee referrals, and newspaper advertising, less usage of college recruiting and private employment agencies, and relatively rare use of such special methods as job fairs, conventions, open houses, and the like.[21] More intensive studies shed light on the practices of particular firms. Illustration 9–2 describes the recruitment strategy put together by Kentucky Fried Chcken to reduce a significant turnover problem among the managers of its restaurants in central Florida.

Choosing among sources and methods

When deciding on the best combination of sources and search methods, the task is to determine which of the many alternatives is most likely to yield the desired number and types of potential candidates within a reasonable period of time at a reasonable cost. For help, personnel professionals can turn to the published research, as well as evaluations of their own previous efforts.

---

[21] P. L. Brocklyn, "Employer Recruitment Practices," *Personnel* 65 (May 1988), pp. 63–65; and American Management Association, *Hiring Costs and Strategies*.

FIGURE 9–3

Data on Recruitment Sources and Methods

Sources and Methods	Blue-Collar			Clerical		
	Used by Job Seekers*	Used by Employers†	Effectiveness Rating (Employers)‡	Used by Job Seekers*	Used by Employers†	Effectiveness Rating (Employers)‡
Direct applications	41%	92%	37%	25%	87%	24%
Employee referrals	32	94	5	23	92	20
Advertising	9	88	31	15	68	39
Educational institutions	n/a	61	3	n/a	66	2
Private employment agencies	1	11	2	15	44	10
USTES	6	72	6	7	63	5
Executive search firms	n/a	2	0	n/a	1	0
Other	11§	8–57	7	15§	1–55	0

* = Percent obtaining job through each method.

† = Percent using each method. Figures total more than 100 percent because of multiple usage.

‡ = Percent rating each method as most effective for this occupational group. Some total more than 100 percent because of multiple responses or less than 100 percent because of non-responses.

§ = Includes educational institutions.

Sources: The data on job seekers are from C. Rosenfeld, "Job Seeking Methods Used by American Workers," *Monthly Labor Review* 98 (1975), pp. 39–42; the other data are from Bureau of National Affairs, *Recruiting Policies and Practices* (Washington, D.C.: Bureau of National Affairs, 1979).

The relevant published research includes that which examines the sources and methods used by job seekers to find jobs and by other employers to find candidates, as well as that which attempts to relate means of recruitment with later job or EEO/AA success. Some of the former research is summarized in Figure 9–3. Not surprisingly, it shows that direct applications and employee referrals are frequently used to obtain jobs among all employee groups.[22] Despite their popularity, employers seem to underestimate the significance of these informal sources, especially among sales, professional and technical, and managerial employees. Among all employee groups, job seekers report advertis-

---

[22] See also H. J. Holzer, "Hiring Procedures in the Firm: Their Economic Determinants and Outcomes," in *Human Resources and the Performance of the Firm*, eds. M. M. Kleiner, R. N. Block, M. Roomkin, and S. W. Salsburg (Madison, Wis.: Industrial Relations Research Association, 1987), pp. 243–74.

	Sales			Professional–Technical			Managerial	
Used by Job Seekers*	Used by Employers†	Effectiveness Rating (Employers)‡	Used by Job Seekers*	Used by Employers†	Effectiveness Rating (Employers)‡	Used by Job Seekers†	Used by Employers†	Effectiveness Rating (Employers)‡
43%	46%	5%	31%	46%	7%	24%	40%	2%
24	74	17	20	68	7	25	65	7
17	75	33	9	89	43	17	82	44
n/a	48	8	n/a	74	15	n/a	50	2
4	63	23	6	71	25	11	75	27
2	34	0	2	41	1	3	27	1
n/a	2	2	n/a	31	5	n/a	54	17
10§	0–43	3	32§	3–75	3	20§	0–57	5

ing to be the third most productive source of jobs; employers tend to estimate its value much higher.

Educational institutions, interestingly, seem to be a major source of jobs only among professional and technical employees and lower-level managers; employers appear to be well aware of these relatively narrow applications. Clerical and managerial job seekers are the only groups that rely heavily on private employment agencies; employers, however, tend to give this source a high rating among sales and professional and technical employees as well. Executive search firms are a factor only at the highest managerial levels, and employers tend to give them relatively high marks.

Usage and judged effectiveness are not the only, or necessarily the best, criteria to be considered by employers in choosing sources and search methods. It is also helpful to have solid data on the quality of recruits turned up through the various approaches. Employers can and do generate these data themselves (as discussed later in this chapter). Some are also published. A common theme has been to relate recruiting sources with employee retention, and the results of these studies are summarized in Figure 9–4. They generally show that informal sources— particularly direct applications and employee referrals—yield more stable employees than formal ones (such as advertising and private employ-

FIGURE 9–4

One-Year Survival Rates as a Function of Recruiting Method

Source	Method*			
	Employee Referrals	Gate Applications	Want Ads	Private Agencies
Decker and Cornelius (1979):				
Bank employees	69%	57%	67%	52%
Insurance agents	70	64	57	62
Abstract service	96	90	79	94
Gannon (1971):				
Bank employees	74	71	61	61
Reid (1972)†:				
Engineering & metal trades	39	25	16	—
Ullman (1966):				
Clerical, Company 1	25	—	12	—
Clerical, Company 2	72	—	26	38

* Some studies reported results from additional methods not included here.

† Value for gate applications was referred to in the study as "notice/off-chance."

Source: D. P. Schwab, "Recruiting and Organizational Participation," in *Personnel Management,* eds. K. Rowland and G. Ferris (Boston: Allyn & Bacon, 1982), p. 113.

ment agencies). One study suggests, however, that this may not be true among blacks; here it was employment agencies that yielded those who were least likely to quit.[23]

Other studies have examined the relationship between sources and search methods and other important personnel outcomes—performance, attendance, and (in one case) satisfaction.[24] They show, once again, that sources and search methods do make a difference, but the pattern of variations within studies across outcomes and across studies is mixed. Thus, unfortunately, the findings provide little guidance for organizational decision makers.

This, of course, complicates an issue only beginning to be addressed by recruitment researchers—the matter of costs and benefits (that is, utility).[25] However, since it has been established that in any given

---

[23] Schwab et al., "Theories and Research"; M. S. Taylor and D. W. Schmidt, "A Process-Oriented Investigation of Recruitment Source Effectiveness," *Personnel Psychology* 36 (1983), pp. 343–54; and D. F. Caldwell and W. A. Spwey, "The Relationship between Recruiting Source and Employee Success: An Analysis by Race," *Personnel Psychology* 36 (1983), pp. 67–72.

[24] P. G. Swaroff, L. A. Barclay, and A. R. Bass, "Recruiting Sources: Another Look," *Journal of Applied Psychology* 70 (1985), pp. 18–20. J. A. Breaugh, "Relationships between Recruiting Source and Employee Performance, Absenteeism, and Work Attitudes," *Academy of Management Journal* 24 (1981), pp. 142–47; and Taylor and Schmidt, "Process Oriented."

[25] American Management Association, *Hiring Costs and Strategies;* Boudreau and Rynes, "Role of Recruitment."

setting some recruitment sources and methods are likely to yield better recruits than others, the task for researchers (and employers) is to determine whether, in a particular instance, the dollar payoffs from having these better recruits exceed the costs incurred in attracting them. To cite just one possibility, if a very expensive recruiting method yields recruits who are only slightly more productive than those unearthed by a much less expensive method, an employer might conclude that on balance it is economically wise to use the cheaper approach. (More will be said about this later in the chapter.)

Economics is not all; there also is the matter of EEO/AA. Various sources and search methods can be looked at in terms of the numbers and qualifications of women and minorities they generate. Direct applications (especially walk-ins) and employee referrals may be particularly problematic in this respect, especially in organizations located in primarily white neighborhoods and those employing mostly white males. Private employment agencies may also be problematic, since minorities have been found to use them less than white workers do (although as noted earlier, black employees recruited in this way tend to stay). Sources and methods yielding relatively few women or minority candidates may not be illegal *per se*. Yet exclusive reliance on them could be illegal, and would certainly do little to advance the cause of affirmative action.

A key component in the implementation of affirmative action may be to adopt candidate sources and search methods not previously used. Suggestions along these lines include colleges and universities with predominantly women and minority enrollments, women and minority organizations (for example, the National Organization for Women and the Urban League), community agencies, and job fairs designed especially to attract women or minorities. Another possibility is the USTES, which has a special responsibility in the placement of minorities.

In sum, choosing among sources and search methods to fashion an overall approach is a complex task requiring knowledge about the search patterns of potential employees; the effectiveness of various methods in turning up employees who will stay, perform, and be satisfied; the value of these benefits vis-à-vis the costs of the various search methods; and the possible EEO/AA implications. Since no particular set of search methods is likely to prove superior on all these criteria, the final choice nearly always involves trade-offs (along with some experimentation).[26]

---

[26] Boudreau and Rynes, "Role of Recruitment."

When to Look

In addition to specifying the numbers and types of job vacancies to be filled, HRP usually provides at least some rough idea of when these vacancies will occur. Thus, in addition to where and how to look, an effective recruiting strategy also attempts to lay out the timing of events.

Especially useful in this respect are time-lapse data (TLD), which show the average time that elapses between major decision points in the recruitment process.[27] Consider again the organization mentioned earlier whose task it was to recruit 30 experienced salespeople in a given period. Yield ratio (YR) analysis showed that 3,000 potential applicants would have to be contacted during this period. But when should these contacts occur?

Suppose an analysis of TLD shows that in the past it typically has taken 10 days for an advertisement to begin producing resumes, 4 days for invitations to interview to be issued, 7 days to arrange for interviews, 4 days for the organization to make up its mind, 10 days for the applicants offered jobs to make up their minds, and 21 more days for those accepting offers to report for work. This suggests that vacancies must be advertised almost two months before they are expected to occur.

Combining the TLD with the YRs developed earlier, the organization can produce a planning chart, such as the one shown in Figure 9–5. The chart shows the numbers that must be met and events that must occur by June 1 or earlier. By inference, it helps to schedule the work activities of recruiting personnel and line managers. It also is useful as a control device. If, for example, by April 1 the organization has not received more than 2,000 resumes, sent 200 invitations, conducted 40 interviews, extended 30 offers, received 20 acceptances, and processed 10 new hires, adjustments in the recruiting plan or strategy should be contemplated. Adjustments might involve changes in the numbers or types of recruits sought, the geographic areas being tapped, or even the sources and methods being used.

SEARCHING

Once a recruiting plan and strategy are worked out, the search process can begin. As Figure 9–1 shows, this stage of the overall recruitment process involves at least two subareas: source activation and selling.

---

[27] Hawk, *Recruitment Function*, pp. 29–33.

FIGURE 9–5
Recruitment Planning Chart for Salespeople

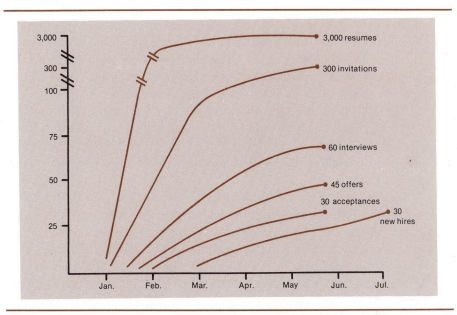

Source Activation

Typically, sources and search methods are activated by the issuance of an employee requisition (as shown in Figure 9–1). This means that no actual recruiting takes place until line managers have verified that an actual job opening exists or will exist.

If the organzation has planned well and done a good job of developing its sources and search methods, activation soon results in a flood of applications and/or resumes. At this point, the recruitment process can become a logistical and administrative nightmare.[28]

Applicants must be screened. Those who pass the screening have to be contacted and lined up for on-site interviews. Applicants from out of town must be transported, housed, fed, and entertained. Managers have to be lined up to entertain and conduct interviews. Unsuccessful appli-

---

[28] For a great discussion of this nightmare, see Hawk, *Recruitment Function*, pp. 46–120.

cants must be sent letters of regret; those chosen must be sent formal offers of employment. The latter must be followed up periodically to assure them of the organization's continued interest. Candidate acceptances and rejections of offers must be processed. Arrangements must be made for those who accept offers to begin work and to be processed onto the payroll. Those who reject offers may be followed up to determine why. Sources and methods must be turned off when the flow of applicants becomes overwhelming or when all positions are filled.

Through all of this, records must be kept. At any given time, the recruiting office must be able to give managers a status report on their openings. Candidates, too, may inquire about where they stand. Furthermore, sufficient information must be kept to allow periodic evaluation of the process.

Clearly, the potential for errors is great. So, too, are the potential costs of errors. Research has shown, for example, that desirable applicants can be lost when an organization fails to make an immediate postinterview follow-up or to maintain contact with candidates over time.[29] Also, delays between the initial contact and a final decision can cause applicants to drop out of the process. Losing candidates in this manner has been found to be particularly likely among black applicants.[30]

For these reasons, then, organizations are well advised to establish procedures to handle the flow of applicants and paperwork well before the actual activation of application flows begins.

Not surprisingly, these administrative procedures are prime considerations for computerization. To help out, especially with college recruiting, many companies have purchased or developed so-called applicant tracking systems. Illustration 9–3 describes the use of one such system at NCR Corporation.

"Selling"

A second issue to be addressed in the searching process concerns the matter of communications. Here organizations walk a tightrope. On the one hand, they want to do whatever they can to attract desirable applicants. On the other hand, they must resist the temptation to oversell their virtues.

[29] J. M. Ivancevich and J. H. Donnelly, "Job Offer Acceptance Behavior and Reinforcement," *Journal of Applied Psychology* 55 (1971), pp. 119–22.

[30] R. D. Arvey, M. E. Gordon, D. P. Massengill, and S. J. Mussio, "Differential Dropout Rates of Minority and Majority Job Candidates Due to 'Time Lags' between Selection Procedures," *Personnel Psychology* 28 (1975), pp. 175–80.

ILLUSTRATION 9–3
NCR's Applicant Tracking System

The Situation:

NCR does its university and college recruiting on a decentralized basis. But, with nearly 1,000 recruiting visits each year to over 200 schools to interview over 10,000 students for roughly 1,500 jobs (not to mention the 10,000 or so write-ins the company receives), there is a need for centralized administration and control. Enter the computer.

The System:

The NCR's particular system operates on a Mentor minicomputer located at the corporation's World Headquarters in Dayton, Ohio. It contains two types of data—on schools and on applicants—all of which can be easily accessed by any of NCR's 35 U.S. facilities. Assume, for example, that the facility in Ithaca, New York, is contemplating a recruiting visit to the Engineering School at the University of Wisconsin-Madison. At the touch of a button, the recruiter in Ithaca can receive a report showing a variety of information about the Engineering School (e.g., its rated quality), NCR's prime contact there, who (if anyone) from NCR has recently recruited there, the amount of money or equipment NCR has donated to the school, the name of the nearest airport and directions to the school from the airport, and preferred hotels in Madison.

As contacts are made with applicants (on campus or through write-ins), electronic mini-resumes are created showing their names, addresses, schools, degrees, majors, GPAs, and so forth. As recruits are interviewed and brought in for site visits, this information is added, along with the ratings they received from the interviewers. Any location in need of talent can scrutinize this information at any time. Also, status reports can be generated as needed when applicants inquire as to where they stand. The system also generates several other reports; one, for example, is the "home state summary report" showing the names, qualifications, and status of applicants preferring to locate in a particular geographic region. Another is a cost-of-hire report by school and for each new hire.

The system also produces personalized (albeit standardized) correspondence automatically as needed. One example is the offer letter, which contains information about the position being offered, its location, the supervisor, the salary, and any response requirements.

The Results:

The system is relatively new, but the results so far show that it has made the process more efficient, improved relations with schools and applicants, and saved money by reducing the number of college visits and streamlining paperwork.

Source: J. E. Lubbock, "A Look at Centralized College Recruiting," *Personnel Administrator,* April 1983.

To effectively "sell" the organization, it is necessary to have models of the factors that influence job seekers to apply for a job and ultimately to join an organization. Unfortunately, the theory and research in this area leave much to be desired.[31] It does appear that in general job seekers make their choices based on very little information about the variety of job opportunities that may be available or about the nature of the organizations and jobs they do know about. Yet it appears that organizational and job attributes, however imperfectly understood, are the factors given greatest weight when actual application and employment decisions are made.[32] Obviously, then, there is a role for recruiting in spreading the word about organizational opportunities and rewards. Other evidence suggests that at least some job seekers are also influenced in their decision making by the tone of their contacts with organizations, and particularly with recruiters. Thus, in selling the organization, attention must be paid to both the message and the media through which the message is delivered.

Message

Expectancy theory suggests that, other things equal, applicants are motivated to apply for and continue to pursue those jobs they believe offer a package of rewards that are valent (see Chapter 5). The question remains, what attributes are most attractive to various types of applicants in the job search context? Of more direct relevance, what message should the organization be delivering in its recruitment literature and in its contacts with applicants?

Unfortunately, clear answers to these questions are lacking.[33] Not surprisingly, job attributes have been found to be major determinants of the decisions to apply for, pursue, and accept jobs.[34] There is some, albeit only suggestive, evidence to show that a few attributes—particularly pay and nature of work offered—are important to the decisions of many types of job seekers. In addition, geographic location and promotional opportunities appear to be important among managerial and professional job seekers, as does degree of job security among many blue-collar applicants. Nature of benefits offered, working conditions, hours,

---

[31] Schwab et al., "Theories and Research"; and Schwab, "Recruiting."

[32] M. S. Taylor and T. J. Bergmann, "Organizational Recruitment Activities and Applicants' Reactions at Different Stages of the Recruitment Process," *Personnel Psychology* 40 (1987), pp. 261–85; S. L. Rynes and H. Miller, "Recruiter and Job Influences on Candidates for Employment," *Journal of Applied Psychology* 68 (1983), pp. 147–54; and G. N. Powell, "Effects of Job Attributes and Recruiting Practices on Applicant Decisions: A Comparison," *Personnel Psychology* 37 (1984), pp. 721–32.

[33] Schwab, "Recruiting"; and S. L. Rynes, H. G. Heneman III, and D. P. Schwab, "Individual Reactions to Organizational Recruiting: A Review," *Personnel Psychology* 33 (1980), pp. 529–42.

[34] Taylor and Bermann, "Organizational Recruitment Activities"; Rynes and Miller, "Recruiter and Job Influences"; and Powell, "Effects of Job Attributes and Recruiter Practices."

and nature of supervision and co-workers appear to be relatively unim-
portant considerations for many. Clearly, there are many exceptions to
these generalizations, and preferences may well change as job seekers
consider trade-offs among attributes in different combinations or packages.[35]

Lacking any more than this to go on, recruiters, not irrationally, tend
to use a "shotgun" approach to communicate attributes to management
and professional job seekers. That is, they attempt to cover all attributes
thoroughly (at least early in the process when little is known about the
individuals involved). For other (and particularly blue-collar) job
seekers, the tendency is to focus primarily on pay and the nature of the
work.

Another, perhaps more consistently applied tendency, is to sugarcoat
the message. This practice has led to considerable controversy. Well-
publicized studies have suggested that employers might do better to
abandon sugarcoating in favor of what have come to be known as realistic
job previews (RJPs).[36] It is argued that RJPs enable job seekers to make
better decisions by reducing perceived coercion and by encouraging
informed self-selection in the job choice process and that they help new
employees cope better with initial job stresses by adjusting their a priori
expectations. Better decisions and better coping, it is further argued,
result in higher levels of job satisfaction among new recruits and reduced
turnover during the crucial first few months of employment.

These assertions have frequently been tested, and the results have
been moderately favorable. Most studies have shown a modest but
significant difference in turnover between employees recruited with and
without RJPs, particularly when relatively complex jobs are involved.[37]
In addition, it has been shown that to some extent RJPs lower initial job
expectations while increasing self-selection, early organizational commitment, job satisfaction, and performance.[38]

What, then, is a message maker to do? Certainly more could be done
to learn which attributes most affect job searchers' decisions to apply for,
pursue, and accept jobs and, based on the findings, to target more
effectively the content of recruiting messages. Further, both ethics and

---

[35] Schwab, "Recruiting."

[36] J. P. Wanous, *Organizational Entry* (Reading, Mass.: Addison-Wesley Publishing, 1980),
pp. 21–84.

[37] G. M. McEvoy and W. F. Cascio, "Strategies for Reducing Employee Turnover: A Meta-
Analysis," *Journal of Applied Psychology* 70 (1985), pp. 342–53; J. A. Breaugh, "Realistic Job
Previews: A Critical Appraisal and Future Research Directions," *Academy of Management
Review* 8 (1983), pp. 612–19.

[38] S. L. Premack and J. P. Wanous, "A Meta-Analysis of Realistic Job Preview Experiment," *Journal of Applied Psychology* 70, no. 4, (1985), pp. 706–19.

evidence favor an absolute commitment to honesty in all recruiting materials and applicant contacts. In some circumstances, it may be desirable to go further and prepare informational booklets, short films, or work samples that give a balanced picture of what certain jobs entail. The last may be particularly useful in situations where job seekers can afford to be selective and where they are thought to have unrealistic expectations about the situations they are getting into (for example, where jobs are unique or unusually complex). Given the expense involved, these "innoculations" might best be given after applicants have been screened and perhaps even after an offer has been made.[39]

Media

The effectiveness of any recruiting message depends in part on the credibility of the media, that is, the agents or contacts through which it is delivered. Credibility is ascribed based on trust, perceived expertise, and personal liking. It is unfortunate for recruiting purposes that the more extensive media—particularly advertising and employment agency representatives—tend also to be those with the lowest credibility. The more intensive ones—friends and relatives and other personal contacts—tend to be more favorably regarded.[40] An investigation of four intensive media—a friend, a recruiter, a job incumbent, and a knowledgeable professor—found that friends and job incumbents were most trusted, were seen as having the greatest expertise, and (along with the professor) were most liked as a recruiting source. Not surprisingly, then, the college seniors who served as subjects were least likely to accept an offer when recruiters had been their primary information source.[41]

The credibility of recruiters, especially college recruiters, has been the subject of considerable research.[42] The findings suggest that credibility is enhanced when recruiters are neither too young nor too old (30 to 55 is apparently best), of stature in their organizations, and verbally fluent. Also preferred are recruiters who take a personal interest in job seekers and who are thoughtful, pleasant, and enthusiastic. It helps, too, if they are prepared for interviews by knowing the company and the job and by being familiar with the candidates' resumes. Moderately struc-

---

[39] Breaugh, "Realistic Job Previews."

[40] Schwab, "Recruiting."

[41] C. D. Fisher, D. R. Ilgen, and W. D. Hoyer, "Source Credibility, Information Favorability, and Job Offer Acceptance," *Academy of Management Journal* 22 (1979), pp. 94–103.

[42] Rynes et al., "Individual Reactions"; and B. Z. Posner, "Comparing Recruiter, Student, and Faculty Perceptions of Important Applicant and Job Characteristics," *Personnel Psychology* 34 (1981), pp. 329–39.

tured interviews, and ones in which interviewers provide both positive and negative information, are preferred. Highly personal, hostile, or threatening questions create negative feelings.[43]

Thus, there is a need for companies to choose carefully the media on which they rely for advertising purposes and the employment agencies and search firms they use. Also, it is clear that in many cases a better job could be done of selecting and training the recruiters that organizations send to campuses and job fairs. One study at a business school, for example, found that less than 60 percent of the visiting recruiters had received any training for the task.[44] Yet, the skills can be taught (see Chapter 13).

Only so much can be accomplished through media development, however. It is very important that the media have messages worth delivering. Two studies compared the relative effects of message and media (recruiters) on job search behavior. Media were found to affect job seekers' perceptions of whether a job would be offered, but it was the message that mainly determined how vigorously various jobs were pursued and whether they were accepted or rejected when offered.[45]

SCREENING

As suggested above and in Figure 9–1, the screening of applicants can be regarded as an integral part of the recruitment process (although many prefer to think of it as the first step in the selection process). The purpose of screening is to remove from the recruitment process at an early stage those applicants who are obviously unqualified for available jobs. Effective screening can save a great deal of time and money. Care must be exercised, however, to ensure that potentially good employees are not lost and that women and minorities receive full and fair consideration and are not rejected in disproportionate numbers without justification (see Chapter 3).

In screening, clear job specifications are invaluable. It is both good practice and a legal necessity that applicants' qualifications be judged based on the knowledge, skills, abilities, and interests required to do the job.

Usually, applicants for managerial and professional positions are screened by a personnel recruiter, although a committee consisting of

---

[43] Data on positive versus negative information are from Fisher et al., "Source Credibility."

[44] Posner, "Comparing Recruiter"; see also S. L. Rynes and J. W. Boudreau, "College Recruiting in Large Organizations: Practice, Evaluation, and Research Applications," *Personnel Psychology* 39 (1986), pp. 729–57.

[45] Rynes and Miller, "Recruiter and Job Influences"; and Powell, "Effects of Job Attributes and Recruiter Practices."

line managers and personnel specialists sometimes is established for this purpose. Applicants for lower-level jobs may be screened by a receptionist or a personnel clerk. In any case, it is important that those who do the screening are carefully trained.

The techniques used to screen applicants vary, depending on the candidate sources and recruiting methods used. Interviews and application blanks may be used to screen walk-ins. Campus recruiters and agency representatives use interviews and resumes. Resumes alone must be relied on when applicants mail them in "cold" or when they respond this way to advertisements. Sometimes, if applicants are not immediately rejected, reference checks are made at this point. Since interviews, application blanks, resumes, and reference checks are used similarly in both screening and selection, more will be said about them in Chapters 10 and 11.

EVALUATION AND CONTROL

Recruitment evaluation and control has two important aspects: monitoring and feedback.

Monitoring

Monitoring involves the tracking of various indicators of performance on an ongoing basis. Extensive lists of such indicators have been developed. In general, however, the more useful ones seem to fall in four categories: quantity, quality, efficiency and utility, and EEO/AA results. Other indicators may also be useful in specific situations.

Quantity

One obvious measure of recruitment effectiveness is whether all job vacancies are filled. Thus, a crude but critical indicator is the rate of new hires in comparison with recruiting and staffing plans.

Quality

To determine quality, recruiting specialists rely on both short- and long-term indicators. In the short run, they make subjective estimates of applicant qualifications (vis-á-vis job specifications), and they keep a careful watch on the percentage of applicants referred to managers who are and are not offered jobs. In the longer run, they track the retention (or turnover) rates and job performance of the applicants who are offered and accept jobs.

Efficiency and utility analysis

Although it is essential for recruiters to supply an organization with an adequate number of qualified people, it also is important to know how efficiently this is being done. As suggested earlier, one method that can be used to track efficiency is to compare results against the planning chart constructed from YRs and TLD (see Figure 9–5). This helps to determine whether events are running on schedule and whether various outcomes are occurring as expected.

Of course, an important indicator of efficiency is cost. Recruiting costs can be apportioned and analyzed in many ways. An especially useful indicator of efficiency is a calculation of average cost per employee hired. Even better is a calculation of whether and to what extent the costs incurred in recruitment are outweighed by the economic benefits accruing to the firm though easier and improved selection, better employee retention, and higher levels of performance and output; that is, a utility analysis.

ILLUSTRATION 9–4

Cost Savings Associated with a RJP

1. The employer first calculates the mean (e.g., .50) and standard deviation (e.g., .50) of the present survival rate for new employees—here bank tellers—over some time period, usually one year. (The survival rate, of course, is the obverse of the turnover rate.)
2. The expected increase in the survival rate of tellers if a RJP is used is then obtained by multiplying the present standard deviation by .12. (This number is the mean size effect found in a meta-analysis, using a sample of 6,000 recruits. It is considered a reasonable estimate of the expected increase in the survival rate for many jobs.) Here: $.5 \times .12 = .06$ and then adding this figure to the current survival rate: $.06 + .50 = .56$.
3. This increase (from .50 to .56) is then translated into a percentage (12%). In the absence of a RJP, a 12 percent increase in replacement costs would be expected.
4. The employer identifies replacement costs for the job in question, for example, $2,800 for the bank teller job.
5. Replacement costs are multiplied by the number of hires needed to retain 100 tellers at the original survival rate with and without a RJP: $200 \times \$2,800 = \$560,000$ without a RJP and $179 \times \$2,800 = \$501,200$ with a RJP. (Notice that with a survival rate of .50 it is necessary to recruit 200 tellers, but with a survival rate of .57 it is necessary to recruit only 179.)
6. The difference shows the returns expected as a result of using a RJP: $560,000 - \$501,200 = \$58,800$.
7. To complete a utility analysis it would be necessary to calculate the returns over more years and compare these with the costs of the RJP.

Source: Steven L. Premack and John P. Wanous, "A Meta-Analysis of Realistic Job Preview Experiments," Journal of Applied Psychology 70, no. 4 (1985), pp. 706–19.

By way of demonstration, Illustration 9–4 shows one way to calculate the initial cost savings associated with the use of an RJP in the recruitment of bank tellers. The savings shown ($58,800) are sizable, and would be even larger in situations where historical turnover rates and replacement costs were higher than those used in the illustration or where the effects of RJPs on turnover rates turned out to be stronger than the average found by previous research.[46] Initial cost savings, however, are not the only relevant issue. To do a full-blown utility analysis it would be necessary to calculate these savings for future years as well as to compare the total to the amount invested in the design and administration of the RJP. This would yield an estimate of the actual return on the investment.

This type of analysis has been done (using hypothetical but realistic data) to compare the relative returns to two commonly used search methods: advertising and a private employment agency.[47] Both methods produced substantial returns. The private employment agency, although more expensive to use, actually produced higher returns because the applicants it generated were prescreened and thus easier and cheaper to select and much more productive on the job. In any given situation, actual dollar returns depend on the number of recruits involved, the accuracy of the firm's selection process, and the nature of the jobs in question. Still, two conclusions are inescapable. First, firms could do a far better job than they do in evaluating the efficiency and utility of their recruitment processes. And second, if they did, the results would provide a strong financial incentive to clean up the generally sad state of these processes in many organizations.[48]

EEO/AA results

The task here is to break down quantity, quality, and efficiency indicators by race, sex, and age. Such breakdowns help to determine, for example, (1) the extent to which a particular candidate source and search method is contributing to the attainment of AA goals and timetables; (2) whether recruiting is generating disproportionate percentages of women, minorities, or older workers who do not succeed on the job; and (3) the relative cost of each woman, minority member, or older worker hired.

---

[46] Premack and Wanous, "A Meta-Analysis."

[47] Boudreau and Rynes, "Role of Recruitment."

[48] Rynes and Boudreau, "College Recruiting."

Such data help to improve EEO/AA efforts in the long run. They also facilitate the preparation of various governmental reports (as well as the preparation of a defense against charges of discrimination should that become necessary).

Other indicators

Overall measures of quantity, quality, efficiency and utility, and EEO/AA results are useful for evaluation and control purposes. Often, however, more specific comparisons among various candidate sources and search methods, geographic regions (where applicable), and individual recruiters are even more useful. As noted earlier, for example, research may show that certain approaches yield significantly better applicants and thus longer tenure, better attending, and better performing employees or significantly more and better women and minorities.[49] Further, although it is axiomatic that some recruiters are better than others, to prove it requires systematic data on the quantity, quality, efficiency, and EEO/AA results accrued by each one.

In yet another vein it is often useful to supplement statistical indicators with more qualitative information from the recruits themselves. A common approach is to ask recruits who receive but do not accept job offers to give their reasons. Questionnaire data may show that poor YRs are due to the message or media used or to some other aspect of the recruiting process. If so, these can be changed. It may be found, however, that the poor YRs can be attributed to a relatively low salary level, a weak benefits package, poor career opportunities, or poorly structured jobs. If that is the case, such weaknesses must be brought to the attention of the human resource people who have responsibility for these activities.

Feedback

Evaluation data provide relatively hard measures of the performance of a recruiting unit or even of individual recruiters. When used with care, and in combination with other measures, they are helpful in making administrative decisions involving budget allocations for the recruiting unit and promotions, pay increases, and the like for recruiting personnel.

---

[49] Schwab, "Recruiting"; Breaugh, "Relationships"; and Taylor and Schmidt, "Process-Oriented."

Evaluation data can also be used to make adjustments in the recruitment process as it is being carried out. Equally as important, however, is ensuring that the data are used to make improvements in recruiting plans and strategies and in search and screening techniques in the next round.

THE SPECIAL CASE OF CAMPUS RECRUITING

Most organizations of any size recruit entry-level managerial and professional personnel on a more or less regular basis. A ready-made source of such recruits is the nation's colleges and universities. Of course, not all entry-level professionals and managers are recruited from campuses, as Figure 9–3 suggests. One study of 72 employers showed that 51 percent of such hires were made directly from campuses (as opposed to 15 percent through write-ins, 14 percent from advertising, 11 percent through employment agencies, and 7 percent from employee referrals).[50] This proportion seems to be relatively stable over time. Another study reported in 1986 found that approximately 50 percent of all managers and professionals with less than three years of work experience were hired through campus recruiting.[51]

Although campus recruiting activities seemed to stabilize in the mid-1980s,[52] they are predicted to intensify during the late 1980s and into the 1990s. The demand for college graduates is expected to be strong even as the demographic trends discussed earlier (see chapter 3), reduce the supply.[53]

To college students, the most visible aspects of this activity will be the hassles of interviews, the thrills of job offers, and the agonies of rejections. Many may not appreciate the considerable effort and resources that are expended by many organizations before, during, and after these events.

Figure 9–6 shows a model of the college recruiting process and Illustration 9–5 shows a set of guidelines for successful campus recruiting. Note that the process pretty much parallels the one described in Figure 9–1. It begins well in advance of actual campus visits, and often includes extensive prerecruiting activities to heighten the organization's

[50] T. L. Dennis and D. P. Gustafson, "College Campuses versus Employment Agencies as Sources of Manpower," *Personnel Journal* 52 (1973), pp. 720–24.

[51] V. R. Lindquist and F. S. Endicott, *Trends in the Employment of College and University Graduates in Business and Industry*, 40th Annual Report (Evanston, Ill.: Northwestern University, 1986).

[52] Lindquist and Endicott, *Trends in the Employment.*

[53] K. H. Hammonds, "Help Wanted," *Business Week*, August 10, 1987, pp. 48–53.

FIGURE 9–6
The College Recruiting Process

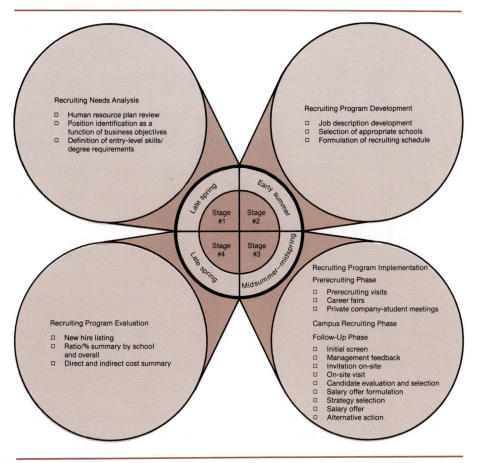

Source: D. L. Chicci and C. L. Knapp, "College Recruitment from Start to Finish," *Personnel Journal* 59, no. 8 (1980), p. 657. Copyright August 1980. Reprinted with the permission of *Personnel Journal,* Costa Mesa, Calif.; all rights reserved.

visibility on campus and to increase the number of students who choose to interview.

Professional recruiters do much, but certainly not all, of the actual interviewing on campus. One study showed that 85 percent of the interviews conducted by 230 well-known companies was done by personnel professionals, compared with 76 percent by company staff or mid-management personnel, 33 percent by senior executives, and 6 percent by a third party under contract. The fact that these numbers total more than 100 percent indicates that many companies often send more than

ILLUSTRATION 9–5

Ten Suggestions to Make the Most of Campus Recruiting

1. Do some homework on the colleges and universities you plan to visit.
2. Send your good people to campus to interview.
3. Provide students with job descriptions and other pertinent information before going to campus to interview.
4. Try to meet with students informally before interviewing.
5. After interviewing, if possible, invite prospective candidates to visit a local facility or branch office.
6. Let interviewees know what will happen next, and follow up with them promptly.
7. Develop coop plans or internships with colleges and universities where you plan to recruit.
8. Develop strong relationships between your company and the colleges and universities you find valuable.
9. Start a program of alumni feedback to colleges and universities.
10. Appear on campus regularly.

Source: J. A. Bellizzi, "Ten Suggestions to Make the Most of College Recruiting," *Personnel Journal*, October 1984, pp. 60–62.

one representative to a campus and that many times the combination consists of P/HR specialists and line managers.[54]

Initial campus interviews usually last 30 minutes, which is not much time for recruiters to make judgments about recruits and for recruits to sell themselves and decide their degree of interest in the company and job. Recruits who do well in the interviews can expect to be invited for a company-paid visit to the facility where they would be working to be assessed further (e.g., through testing and more interviews—see Chapter 10) and for an opportunity to learn more about the company and the job. After the visit, the personnel department assembles all available information on each candidate, and a decision is made about whether to extend an offer and, if so, at what salary.

In making salary offers, companies rely heavily on information about what other companies are paying. This information is gleaned from college placement offices and from published sources.[55] Figure 9–7 shows a standard form of the type many organizations use to determine salary offers. Note that different disciplines receive different base salaries and that companies may pay extra for high GPAs, past work experience,

---

[54] Lindquist and Endicott, *Trends in the Employment.*
[55] As published, for example, in the Lindquist-Endicott report referred to in earlier footnotes.

FIGURE 9–7
Electronics Company's College Recruiting Salary Worksheet

Starting Salary Worksheet

Name of Candidate _____ University _____ Date _____

Degree _____ Undergraduate Overall Average _____

Source Campus ___ Co-op ___ Other ___ Average in Major _____

Undergraduate

I. Base Monthly Figures

Hardware: EE; ME;		Engineering Technology	2,400	
CE; AE; Physics	3,000	Accounting; Business		
Software: Computer		Administration	2,300	
Science, Math	2,600	Liberal Arts; Human-		
Industrial Engineering	2,500	ities; Soc. Science	2,000	_____

II. Scholastic Average in Major (Based on 4.0 System)
   Monthly allowance:

3.5 or better	$330 _____	
3.0 to 3.49	165 _____	
2.5 to 2.99	85 _____	_____

III. Experience
    Monthly allowance:

Related military or	Up to 6 months	$100 _____
Industrial (including	6 to 9 months	130 _____
Co-op)	9 months to 1 year	180 _____ _____

IV. Personal Allowance
    Monthly allowance:
    Technical competence, understanding of field,   Up to $165
    caliber of institution, maturity, and other allow-
    ances not considered above.
                                                                    _____
                                                     Total $ _____

Graduate

V. MS or MA Degrees
   Add to allowance as explained in Section E of
   instructions. Not to exceed $7,000 _____   _____
                                                     Total $ _____

Facility _____ Date _____ Signature _____ Date _____

Signature _____
           Employment Representative

Note: this worksheet has been designed to yield rates which we expect to be competitive. Variations from the allowances set forth above may be made for unusual situations. In such event, agreement should be reached between employment and salary administration personnel, with unresolved differences of opinion to be settled by the industrial relations manager.

Salary information for disciplines not listed above may be obtained from college relations.

Source: Adapted (with adjustments for inflation) from E. C. Miller, "College Recruiting Pay Practices," *Compensation Review* 11, no. 1 (1979), p. 39.

and apparent diligence in one's field. Often, salary offers are negotiable within some range.

Once an offer is extended, a cat-and-mouse game frequently ensues. Companies attempt to lock up preferred candidates early, and candidates fortunate enough to expect several offers attempt to delay making commitments until all options are in and have been properly mulled over.

When the games are over, professional recruiters may take time to evaluate the results, gleaning whatever information will be helpful in improving their performance in subsequent seasons.[56] A recent survey of college recruiting among Fortune 1,000 corporations suggests, however, that most do not take much time, nor do they use very sophisticated data.[57] The most frequently cited measure of success (used by 71 percent of the respondents) was the number of offers accepted. Others often used included cost per hire (50 percent), advertising costs (40 percent), and expenses broken down by school visited (25 percent). In contrast, only 7 percent of the respondents tracked or compared the relative performance levels of employees recruited from various schools.

There is some indication that cost pressures are forcing firms to become more selective in deciding what campus to visit.[58] Thus, the more progressive companies are working to develop long-term relationships with just a few schools, rather than being involved only in short-term recruiting at many. They are trying, through internships and other means, to identify high-potential students early in their college careers and to have them locked up well before graduation.[59] Some firms, such as Mutual of New York and Standard Oil, are even active at the high school level.[60]

On-campus activities used by companies to foster long-term relationships include developing better ties with professors, encouraging company executives to visit classes, working with and supporting various student organizations, and modifying recruitment material to improve their pitches.[61]

---

[56] For a description of an entire campus recruitment program and its results, see T. Bergmann and M. S. Taylor, "College Recruitment: What Attracts Students to Organizations?" *Personnel*, May–June 1984, pp. 34–46.

[57] Rynes and Boudreau, "College Recruiting."

[58] Lindquist and Endicott, *Trends in the Employment.*

[59] M. Hanigan, "Campus Recruiters Upgrade Their Pitch," *Personnel Administrator* 32 (November 1987), p. 56.

[60] Margaret Magnus, "Is Your Recruitment All It Can Be?" *Personnel Journal* 66 (February 1987), pp. 54–63.

[61] Hanigan, "Campus Recruiters Upgrade Their Pitch."

The Job Seekers's Perspective[62]

Experiences vary, but on average only about one half to two thirds of all university and college seniors and departing graduate students attain jobs through on-campus recruiting. Following are some factors that appear to facilitate job search success on and off campus. For more specific guidelines on preparing a resume, see the appendix to this chapter.

Job seeking on campus

Most universities and colleges and many professional schools maintain career centers that serve as major contact points for employers. A major purpose of these centers is to provide a meeting place for job seekers and employers with jobs to fill; but they often take a broader view, also providing students with career counseling, advice on job search strategies, assistance with resume preparation, and training on how to interview. They also serve as a source of information about potential employers (including many that will not be visiting campus) and about alumni contacts who work for these employers.

Most, however, stress the point that it is not their responsibility to find jobs for students. Ultimately, this is the responsibility of each individual—the only one who can make the decisions that must be made during the process and who will have to live with the consequences of these decisions.

The key to successful on-campus recruiting (assuming the job seeker has at least some relevant abilities and motivation) is the interview. As problematic as it is (see Chapter 11), that 30-minute period can make or break a job seeker. One key to a successful interview is preparation by:

- Researching the organization thoroughly.
- Writing a complete and attractive resume. (Relevant guidelines and some examples are shown in the appendix to this chapter.)
- Studying one's own resume to anticipate questions and preparing answers.
- Uncovering the most often asked questions ("What do you expect to be doing in five years?") and preparing answers.
- Engaging in introspection to discover one's own strengths and

---

[62] This section is based on material provided by Kay Gilcher, former director of the Office of Career Service, New York State School of Industrial and Labor Relations, Cornell University and on the *Student Placement Manual* prepared by her office.

weaknesses and working through ways to emphasize the former and deemphasize the latter.
- Preparing several questions to ask interviewers when given the opportunity.
- Rehearsing.

Another key to a successful on-campus interview lies in the job seeker's demeanor during the process. Extrapolating from studies of why applicants are rejected (other than for poor qualifications), it appears that job seekers can help themselves considerably by:

- Dressing neatly in proper business attire.
- Answering all questions in a straightforward manner, neither rambling nor answering in monosyllables.
- Stressing their qualifications, but without conceit or arrogance.
- Being poised.
- Being prepared to ask knowledgeable questions about the company and the job, both to impress the interviewer and to attain the information that is needed to make an intelligent job choice.
- Being enthusiastic, but not overly effusive.

Successfully traversing the on-campus interview usually means an invitation to visit the potential work site and the opportunity to engage in several more interviews and, perhaps, to take various kinds of employment tests (again, see Chapter 11). Typically, these interviews and tests are relatively job specific, since they are designed to assess an applicant's technical knowledge and expertise, as well as the more subjective elements of maturity and organizational fit.

For job seekers with the right stuff—and stamina—the on-site visit is followed by the all-important job offer, and the opportunity to engage in the cat-and-mouse game described earlier. Acceptance or rejection, of course, depends on one's evaluation of the opportunity offered vis-á-vis any alternatives that may be anticipated or at hand.

Job seeking off campus

Among all but the most confident and casual job seekers, it is common to conduct a broad search to locate or make opportunities with the many employers that do not come to campus. Such a process is begun by using all available reference materials, help-wanted advertisements, and personal contacts to maximize one's exposure. It continues by doggedly following every possible lead and persistently conducting a selling campaign worthy of the finest advertising agency. The process requires all of the skills needed in on-campus recruiting, plus a good deal more.

Illustration 9–6 shows a set of appropriate guidelines compiled by an experienced observer of many successful and unsuccessful job search campaigns.

ILLUSTRATION 9–6

What to Do When You're Looking for a Job

Whether you are out of work or just looking for a better paying opportunity, there is no such thing as a foolproof way to get hired. You can, however, boost your chances if you are willing to work hard at aggressively promoting yourself. Here are some guidelines.

Get your foot in the door. In contacting a prospective boss for the first time, your sole objective is to get an interview. If you expect to get hired before the employer has "seen the merchandise," you are in for a heavy disappointment.

The only reason for sending in a resume or application letter is therefore to motivate an employer to meet with you. And that means you shouldn't say anything in a letter or resume that has even the slightest chance of keeping you off his already overcrowded interview schedule. If you think the boss wants an MBA and you didn't even go to college, don't mention your education. Show that you are good at what you do and that you meet whichever criteria you know about, but if you don't meet a given requirement, don't give evidence that shows you to fall short.

Does this mean that you should lie? No, it only means that you shouldn't volunteer information that might be considered in a negative light. Such information can be deadly prior to an interview, but may not hurt at all when divulged *after* you have had a chance to make a good impression in person.

Don't apply for a job unless you can make a case for doing it well. If you can make such a case, whet the employer's appetite for wanting to meet you: be specific, focus on how good you are, and don't say anything that might be viewed as a negative. Most important, ask for an interview; you can't get a hit unless you first get up to bat.

Apply in quantity. Oil people know that to get a gusher, they may have to drill a lot of holes. As a job seeker, you must operate the same way. To get a good offer for a good job, you must be prepared to apply—one at a time—to an army of potential employers.

Aside from going after every advertised job appropriate to your field, make yourself known to recruiters and employment agencies. Apply to every employer whose needs you could make a strong case for meeting.

If you are sending fewer than several dozen applications every week, you're not trying hard enough. For if you don't make the contacts, someone else will.

Tailor your sales pitch to the reader. With the exception of companies looking for a trainee or a corporate president, few employers will be interested in a well-rounded jack-of-all-trades. Usually, prospective bosses will be impressed only if your skills, achievements, educational background, and experience are first rate and directly applicable to the specific job they want done as well as to their specific business. They don't care about anything else. When you include, in a resume or letter, information that is not pertinent, you waste space that you could otherwise use to focus on job-related strengths. You also waste the reader's time, an accomplishment that never makes a good impression.

ILLUSTRATION 9–6 *(concluded)*

So tailor your application as closely as possible to the known or probable requirements of the job you seek. That may be difficult when you are sending out hundreds of applications. At the least, segregate your targets into groups having similar interests, and pursue each group on a tailored basis. Even with individualized cover letters, however, a resume covering your entire career isn't tailored to anything and may point up negatives rather than focusing on your strengths. You'll do a lot better if you throw away your resume and use a series of well-written letters, each of which is customized to highlighting your strengths relative to a specific set of hiring requirements, and whenever possible, personally addressed to whomever you would report if hired.

Don't promise to deliver more than the employer requires. If employers want more, they'll ask for it. Should you offer too much or your claims be too extravagant, you may be viewed as either a dreamer or someone prone to incur significant risks in pursuit of unrealistic goals. Similarly, if you look too good on paper, the reader may erroneously conclude that your salary requirements are too high or that you would be unlikely to be satisfied with the job for long.

They may be right. Perhaps the job is not a good one for you. But why prejudge? Don't oversell, get your foot in the door and decide for yourself.

Ask questions before and give answers. When you get a telephone or in-person interview, don't make the mistake of allowing yourself to just sit there and be interrogated. Take control of the interview by asking questions. Find out what the employer wants. Then use the answers as clues about which of your skills, experiences, and accomplishments to emphasize.

Before the interviewer starts grilling you, ask him to describe what has to be done on the job you are discussing. When you hear something that coincides with one of your strengths, pounce on it and talk about your abilities in that area. Then, probe for details about on-the-job challenges you might encounter. Again, you'll get answers that will clue you in on what to talk about.

When a question comes your way, answer it directly and honestly, but always in a way that puts you in the best light. Answer only the question that has been asked of you; don't ramble on, don't go off to another subject, and don't volunteer negatives. If you don't understand a question, request a clarification. Similarly, should a question seem too general, ask for it to be restated in a more specific manner.

In asking and answering questions, don't hog the conversation and don't be argumentative. Give the impression that you are an intelligent, competent professional who can get the job done and who is genuinely interested in finding out about it.

Keep at it. The foregoing requires an enormous amount of effort, and you may not strike a gusher overnight. If your goals are realistic, however, don't let up. Jobs invariably go to those who do the best job of creatively "selling" their services to employers, and proper implementation of these steps can provide the edge that motivates an employer to interview and hire *you* rather than someone else.

Source: R. M. Hochheiser, "What to Do When You're Looking for a Job," *The Wall Street Journal*, January 17, 1983, p. 14.

SUMMARY

Recruitment is the human resource activity that links human resource planning, and especially staffing planning, with selection. Its purpose is to locate and attract to the organization an adequate number of qualified people. To the extent that this is successfully done, the various P/HR outcomes are enhanced without putting undue pressure on such other activities as selection, employee development, and compensation.

Except in small organizations and in high places, recruitment is primarily carried out by the personnel department. In any given situation, the effort may be minimal or extensive—depending on requirements, labor market conditions, and available resources. In virtually all cases, however, some thought must be given to each of the five stages in the recruitment process: (1) planning, (2) strategy development, (3) searching, (4) screening, and (5) evaluation and control.

In planning, recruiting objectives are established based on likely job vacancies as identified through the staffing planning process. These objectives are stated in terms of the numbers and types of potential candidates to be contacted. Once recruiting objectives are set, a strategy for fulfilling them is worked out. Ordinarily, the recruitment strategy addresses three main issues: (1) the labor market(s) in which search will be conducted, (2) candidate sources and search methods that will be emphasized, and (3) the timing of events.

On completion of the recruitment strategy, attention is turned to the actual search process. Sources and search methods are activated, and an attempt is made to sell, but not oversell, the job and the organization to potential and actual applicants. As the process proceeds, job seekers who are attracted to the organization and apply for employment are screened. Some are rejected as unqualified for the job(s) in question; the rest are passed on to the selection process.

From time to time, the recruitment process is evaluated to determine its overall contribution to the organization, as well as to assess the efficacy of the various candidate sources and search methods used.

Throughout, the process is monitored to ensure compliance with EEO and age discrimination laws and regulations. Where applicable, extra steps are taken to help generate adequate numbers of qualified women and minorities to comply with affirmative action plans.

The product of the recruitment process is a pool of applicants, all of whom have been screened and have expressed an interest in the job(s) involved. It then becomes necessary for the organization to differentiate among these applicants and select the one(s) most likely to be successful. How this is done is the subject of the next two chapters.

DISCUSSION QUESTIONS

1. To what extent and in what ways do various external influences affect organizations' recruitment policies and practices?

2. Why is it useful to think of job search and recruitment as "two sides of the same street"?

3. An organization may spend many thousands of dollars and much managerial time to recruit an experienced plant manager or experienced physicist to work on a new space shuttle, but hardly any money or time to recruit a secretary or someone to load and unload freight cars. Does this simply reflect a bias against relatively low-level work and employees or are there some rational, and possibly even justifiable, reasons for this type of behavior?

4. Notwithstanding the research on RJPs, many companies do a real sales job on potential employees during the recruitment process and make no apologies for it. As a recruiter would you be more inclined to use an RJP or a sales job? Why? As a job seeker would you rather be subjected to an RJP or a sales job? Why?

5. What is the best way for organizations to determine how well their recruitment efforts are working?

6. Given all that is known about the evaluation of recruitment processes, why is it that so many organizations do a terrible job of it?

7. Analyze the checklist in Sample C of the Appendix to this chapter. Can you make improvements on it based on the material covered in the chapter?

Appendix*

PREPARING A RESUME

A resume is the first, and sometimes the only, glimpse a prospective employer has of a job applicant. As such, it should present the image of a professional, organized, competent person. It should be uncluttered, balanced, grammatical, accurate, and readable.

What a Resume Does

The purpose of a resume is to motivate potential employers to interview you. This will be possible if you pay attention to the following elements:

1. Written communication. Your resume is both a vehicle of communication and a demonstration of how you communicate, so both what you say and how you say it are important.
2. Ability to produce. The results you have produced are your personal "bottom line." For instance, past jobs held, courses taken, degree earned, and dates are necessary information.
3. Clear demonstration. What really sets you apart is how clearly you can demonstrate what you have produced. Get to the heart of things. Cite short examples, and put numbers around results if you can. Numbers impress potential employers.
4. Area of concern. You may be the subject of the resume, but the employer is its target. A resume is a directed communication to a particular audience that has specific needs. Speak the language of the field you seek to enter. If you don't know that language, learn it. Read trade journals and other publications in your field.

* Sources: *Student Placement Manual* prepared by the Office of Career Services, New York State School of Industrial and Labor Relations, Cornell University, undated. Lee A. Iacocca. "The Plymouth Guide to Building a Resume" *Business Week Careers* 5, no. 6 (October–November 1987), Special Advertising Section.

What a Resume Contains

Beyond this, the resume should reflect the individual who prepared it. It should stress that individual's job objective, strengths, skills, and accomplishments.

Most resumes include the following information:

1. Identification—name, address, and phone number.
2. Career or job objective.
3. Educational background.
4. Work experience.
5. Activities or community involvement.
6. Interests and/or hobbies.
7. Publications.
8. A reference statement.

Some resumes also include:

1. An experience summary statement.
2. A statement of special qualifications and skills.
3. A statement outlining achievements or accomplishments.

Job or career objective

This is the first item to appear on the resume following the candidate's name and address. For many people, this is the most difficult section of the resume to write because they haven't thought through their past training and experiences to determine where their skills lie and what they enjoy doing.

The important thing is that the job or career objective be specific enough to say something substantive about the job seeker. Such a statement as "A position in personnel or in labor relations" errs by being so broad that it says nothing worthwhile. It does nothing more than define a very broad and general occupational field. A good objective tells the reader whether the resume writer prefers working with data, people, or things and gives examples of the specific activities he or she would like to perform. It may also define the type of organization in which the individual would like to work.

Example: An entry-level position in personnel management with particular interest in recruitment, staffing, affirmative action, and human resources planning.

Example: A position in the research department of a national trade union utilizing skills in statistical analysis and computer systems.

Educational background

Important facts that may be included in this section are schools attended (beyond high school), degrees received, date of graduation, major and minor areas of study, course highlights, academic honors or achievements, special training, study abroad, relevant seminars and symposiums, and professional licenses. This information should be presented in reverse chronological order.

When selecting what information to include, think in terms of job objective. List those courses that provide training or knowledge needed to do the job being sought. Unless the cumulative GPA or class rank is quite high, do not include this information. Likewise, if you made the dean's list first semester sophomore year, but not since, you may not be saying anything very positive by mentioning it.

Work experience

Work experience can be full time, part time, summer, volunteer, educational practicum, or connected with a college or community activity. It can be organized in one or two basic ways that produce very different looking resumes.

The chronological format.   The first, and easiest way, is to organize work experience according to *time*. The entries are presented in reverse chronological order. If you have had a strong continuing work history directly related to the career direction you now wish to pursue, the chronological format is appropriate. See Sample A.

Sample A

EDWARD ALLEN SMITH

New York City Address

315-30th Avenue
Bayside, N.Y. 11470
(212) 659-6745

Washington Address

222 North Freedom Road
Washington, D.C. 20005
(202) 623-6320

JOB OBJECTIVE

To become a Labor Relations Specialist.

QUALIFICATIONS

- Planned and supervised projects.
- Learned personnel management functions through work experiences.
- Prepared budgeting, accounting, and financial reports.
- Performed well under pressure situations.

Sample A *(concluded)*

EDUCATION

1987   Cornell University, Ithaca, New York

    B.S., Industrial and Labor Relations
      Course highlights: Personnel Management, Collective Bargaining,
      Current Issues in Industrial Relations, Labor Law, Labor Union
      Administration, Union Organizing, Financial Accounting.

1982   SUNY Stony Brook, New York

    College degree. Concentration: Economics.
    Earned 75 percent of college expenses.

WORK EXPERIENCE

June 1986–   Treasurer, Sigma Alpha Epsilon Fraternity, Cornell Uni-
present   versity.

- Prepared and supervised $150,000 annual budget for fraternity housing, dining, and social accounts. Reported regularly to the University Bursar, Office of Residence Life, and the Sigma Alpha Epsilon Regional and National Offices.
- Raised funds for the Hillcrest Preservation Fund in 1986 and 1987.

Summer 1985–   Assistant Coordinator, Pepsi Cola—New York City Tri-
present   athlon, New York, New York

- Assisted coordinator in planning and organizing annual triathlete competition.
- Supervised six support employees.
- Obtained municipal permits and the cooperation of municipal and federal agencies.

Summers   Lifeguard, New York City Department of Parks, Recrea-
1981–1984   tional and Cultural Affairs, Rockaway Beach, New York

- Ensured beach safety in popular urban recreation area.
- Trained and supervised new personnel.
- Assisted Lifeguard Borough Coordinator with facilities inspection and various administrative functions.

ACTIVITIES AND AFFILIATION

Sigma Alpha Epsilon Fraternity; Secretary, Society for Arbitration and Neutral Education; Intramural football, basketball, and softball; Masters Swimming; Varsity Swim Team, SUNY Stony Brook; Hall Representative, Dormitory Council, SUNY Stony Brook.

REFERENCES

Available upon request.

The functional format.   The second approach is to organize experience according to *skills possessed.* This format is appropriate when you have had a variety of jobs or assignments not directly related to your career target, but that included relevant functions or responsibilities (for example, supervised eight people, managed a budget). This is a particularly good format for those who, for example, have developed skills through activities rather than in regular work situations (such as, developed a recruitment brochure for a hospital), who have had unrelated previous work experience (for example, worked in a cafeteria during three summers), or who are trying to change from one type of organization to another (for example, worked only with social service agencies, but are now looking for a position with a corporation). The functional paragraphs are presented in order of importance to your future goal rather than chronologically, and they are headlined by type of function performed. Any accomplishment associated with the function is listed in the paragraph. See Sample B.

Sample B

Pamela G. Strausser

R.D. #1
Cortland, N.Y. 13045
(607) 849-6373

Position desired in the administration of personnel programs, utilizing knowledge of personnel-related issues and eight years experience in operations, personnel and employee relations, planning and development, and finance.

OPERATIONS	• Revamped corporate structure and operational/management systems to meet financial crisis. • As Chief Executive Officer, handled daily operations, including financial management and reporting, inventory control, purchasing, administration of organizational policy and procedures. • Directly responsible for 14 different line operations. Liaison with Board of Directors.
PERSONNEL AND EMPLOYEE RELATIONS	• Designed and implemented organizational procedures/employee handbook for three organizations. • Scheduled work, handled grievances, hired and fired for up to 80 employees. • Designed and administered training programs.
PLANNING AND DEVELOPMENT	• Successfully prevented layoffs through design and development of program to expand revenue base. • Was hired to design and implement personnel, control, and reporting systems for 14 departments, following state and federal investigation of fraud. • Developed rural transit system to service three-county area.
FINANCE	• Responsible for all budgeting and financial management (including legal ramifications), for three organizations and four divisions with budgets exceeding $2.5 million.

Sample B *(concluded)*

PUBLIC RELATIONS	• Wrote newspaper columns and press releases, gave radio interviews, and organized advertising campaigns. • Lobbied at local, state, and federal levels and responded diplomatically to outside political pressure.
EMPLOYMENT HISTORY	MAXWELL SCHOOL, Syracuse University, Syracuse, N.Y. 1985–Present
	Administrative Assistant CAPCO, INC., Cortland, N.Y., 1983–1985
	Executive Director Deputy Director Director of Transportation SOLARGEN ELECTRIC MOTOR CAR CORPORATION Cortland, N.Y., 1982–1983
	Assistant General Manager TURN ABOUT COUNSELING CENTER Seaford, Delaware, 1980–1982
	Program Director SENATOR JACOB JAVITS Washington, D.C., 1979–1980
	Other; Chief Clerk for Congressional Committee Manager, Sports Store
EDUCATION	CORNELL UNIVERSITY, School of Industrial and Labor Relations, MS expected 1988 HARVARD UNIVERSITY, Department of Slavic Languages and Literature, BA 1979
INTERESTS	Member of Harvard/Radcliffe Regional Interview Team, various offices in community organizations involved in economic development, very involved in running, tennis, and athletics. I teach dance, write, and dabble woefully at the piano.

Activities or community involvement

This may be treated as a separate section if this information is not included under work experience. Included are those activities that are relevant to the job search, particularly those showing leadership ability, organizational skills, a service orientation, ability to use computerized information systems, and so on.

Interests and hobbies

This section is optional. Inclusion of selected interests and hobbies may add a human dimension and provide an ice-breaking starting point in an interview. Avoid listing interests. Instead, present them in such a way as to convey action and commitment. For example: design and sew clothing, long-distance hiking and backpacking, marathon running.

Publications

Cite the title and name of publication (or publisher) of any articles or books written. It may be appropriate to include this information elsewhere—in the work experience section, for example, if the writing was done within the context of a particular job, or in the educational section if it came directly out of course work.

Reference statement

The final line of most resumes reads "References will be furnished upon request" or "References are available upon request." Never list the names of references on a resume unless permission has been given to do so. Even with permission, it is advisable to leave specific names off for two reasons. First, to help control the number of times a particular reference will be contacted—and eliminate the casual inquiry. Second, to encourage the employer to get the names of references, which provides an opportunity to reaffirm interest in the organization and to follow the progress of the application.

Experience summary statement

This statement is normally found after the job objective and is factual in nature. It serves several purposes, perhaps the most important of which is making sense out of the work history and other experience.

Example: Over seven years of personnel and labor relations experience in manufacturing operations, including union and nonunion facilities at both the plant and division level. Assignments included chief spokesperson in labor negotiations, development of recruiting and outplacement programs, wage and salary control systems, human resource planning, and affirmative action programs.

Statement of special qualifications

This is found after the job objective and focuses on personal qualifications that relate directly to the type of position being sought.

Example: Ability to organize effectively and handle detail, skilled in public speaking, exceptional writing talent, work well under pressure, relate easily to people at all levels within an organization.

Statements outlining achievements and/or accomplishments

Achievements and accomplishments can arise out of interests and hobbies, volunteer work, extracurricular activities, and educational background as well as performance on the job, and can be valuable additions to the resume of someone with little formal work experience. These statements may appear collectively following the job objective or may be incorporated into the resume at the appropriate points.

Example: Financed 100 percent of undergraduate education costs through part-time and summer jobs.
Raised $3,000 for ILR Founders Fund.
'Increased membership in the Society for the Advancement of Neutrals' Education by 300 percent.
Maintained a 3.2 cumulative average while working 20 hours a week.

Statements of achievement and accomplishments should appear throughout the resume whether or not they are emphasized at the beginning.

Whatever its form, the resume should convey strengths, skills, and interests. It should do so as economically as possible. For most undergraduates, this means limiting the resume to one page; for more experienced people, the one-page limit may not be reasonable. If it does go on to a second page, make certain that the fat is trimmed and that the additional space is used wisely.

Finally, it is always a good idea to proofread the resume and correct errors. Sample C provides an example of a checklist used for such a purpose.

Sample C

Monica A. Thomas
18 Nautical Lane
Gloucester, Mass. 01930
(617) 281-0000 (1)

<u>OBJECTIVE</u>   (2)

To apply management experience and French language skills in a corporation overseas.

Sample C *(concluded)*

<u>EDUCATION</u>

1987	B.A., Management, GEORGIA STATE UNIVERSITY
1986	Semester, GSU-London, England
1985–86	8 Credit hours, FORTRAN/Small Business Training-Computer Science (3)

<u>EXPERIENCE</u>

5/83–Present
(summers and
holidays)

FLOWERS BY JOANN, Rockport, Mass.
<u>Sales Assistant</u>

(4)   Sold floral arrangements at $800 to $1,200 (5) volume per month, in person and by telephone and computer. Managed all details of operation including bookkeeping, inventory, and floral design.

(6) 1986
(summer)

CITRONELLA'S TAVERNA, London, England
<u>Waitress</u>

Learned to work effectively with an international clientele.

(7)   Cited by manager for outstanding efficiency and courtesy.

1985
(summer)

THE CLAM SHELL, Salem, Mass.
<u>Hostess</u>

(8)   Established a mood of welcome and enthusiasm.

(9)   Overall patronage increased 35% from June 1 to August 31st.

Successfully managed 6 waitresses and 3 busboys.

<u>ACTIVITIES</u>

American Marketing Association—Member Student Marketing Association

Things to Notice

1. Phone number essential.
2. Job objective targets work direction.
3. High school eliminated. Didn't enhance recent history.
4. Use action words.
5. Numbers impress the reader.
6. Writing the year, not just months and year, is more substantive.
7. Any awards or honors should be cited.
8. More actual details of real results.
9. OK to claim partial credit for overall success.

10

External Staffing Concepts

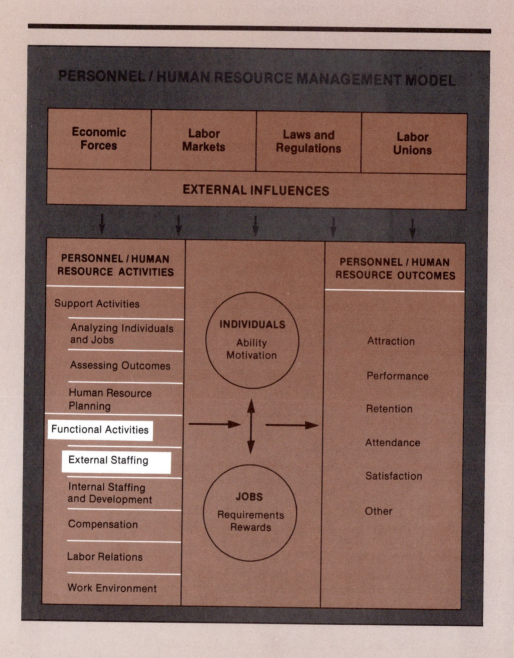

PERSONNEL / HUMAN RESOURCE MANAGEMENT MODEL

Economic Forces	Labor Markets	Laws and Regulations	Labor Unions

EXTERNAL INFLUENCES

PERSONNEL / HUMAN RESOURCE ACTIVITIES

Support Activities

Analyzing Individuals and Jobs

Assessing Outcomes

Human Resource Planning

Functional Activities

External Staffing

Internal Staffing and Development

Compensation

Labor Relations

Work Environment

INDIVIDUALS
Ability
Motivation

JOBS
Requirements
Rewards

PERSONNEL / HUMAN RESOURCE OUTCOMES

Attraction

Performance

Retention

Attendance

Satisfaction

Other

After reading this chapter, you should be able to speak to the questions posed in each of the following personnel/human resource incidents:

1. A heavy construction equipment manufacturer has its corporate headquarters in a large southern city with numerous plants located throughout the country. Each year it hires between 40 and 50 college graduates to serve as management trainees. The training program lasts nine months. Although it involves some classroom training, most of the time is spent on the job working as an assistant to a first-level supervisor.

 The company is experiencing difficulties with the program. A high percentage of the trainees leave the company before completing the program, and the job performance of those who do complete the program is often marginal. The company believes the problem is that the staffing process used to obtain the trainees is invalid. Assume you are a staffing specialist in the company's personnel/human resource department. How would you investigate the validity of the staffing process for management trainees? What factors would you consider before conducting the validation study?

2. A federal correctional facility is very careful in its selection of people to be guards. After completing an application blank, taking a battery of tests, and having a physical exam, each applicant receives an intensive two-hour interview. At the end of the interview, all the information about the applicant is translated by the interviewer into an overall rating of the applicant's fitness for the job. The rating can range from 0–100 points. To be hired, an applicant must receive a rating of 95 or better. Is this hiring standard too high? What factors would you consider in deciding this?

3. You are the personnel manager of a savings and loan institution. Due to high employee turnover coupled with institutional growth, a substantial number of new employees are hired each year. You have been "tracking" applicants as they go through the various selection procedures and have discovered that the hiring (selection) rates for men are higher than they are for women. Moreover, this is the case for virtually all jobs. Is this cause for concern? If so, what options do you have in order to deal with the problem?

In the previous chapter, recruitment was identified as the beginning of the process of obtaining new employees from outside the organization. Recruitment activities generate applicants for jobs. Selection decisions (accept or reject) must then be made about applicants, and that is the topic of this and the next chapter.

Organizations use a wide variety of selection instruments and procedures to assist in making selection decisions, including tests, application blanks, interviews, and training and experience requirements. Collectively, these are known as *predictors*. They will be treated extensively in the next chapter. The present chapter explores the basic concepts involved in the use of predictors for making selection decisions.

Underlying the use of predictors is a definite strategy for influencing P/HR outcomes. That strategy is to predict which applicants are most likely to be effective employees. Thus, predictors are used to assess applicants' ability and motivation relative to the requirements and rewards of the job.

Implementation of this strategy requires that the organization first investigate the validity of predictors. This is accomplished through the conduct of validation studies. The results of a validation study indicate the degree to which a predictor improves the identification of applicants likely to be effective employees.

Following a validation study, certain decisions must be made about a predictor: whether to use it for selecting applicants and, if so, what hiring standards to establish for the predictor. Both of these issues are discussed below.

External staffing, as a strategy for influencing P/HR outcomes, has some potential limitations associated with it. These are identified, as are their implications, for other P/HR activities.

Equal employment opportunity laws and regulations exert substantial influences on external staffing activities and are directly relevant to the concepts developed in this chapter. When external staffing has an adverse impact on a protected applicant group (such as women or minorities), the organization must either eliminate its occurrence or provide evidence that the higher rejection rate for this group is not the result of unfair discrimination. Government regulations and court decisions both suggest the types of evidence necessary.

External staffing concepts require expertise to understand and implement them in an organization. Because of this, the P/HR department is involved in external staffing activities. The department shows line management the desirability of conducting validation studies, and if approval is obtained, the department carries them out. The P/HR department provides the organization with advice on whether to use predictors and on hiring standards. Moreover, the department exerts direct control over line management to ensure that the organization's external staffing activities comply with equal employment opportunity laws and regulations.

VALIDATION OF PREDICTORS

A *valid* predictor is one that yields an assessment of applicants that is in fact predictive of their effectiveness as employees on the job. The validity of a predictor cannot be assumed but must be investigated scientifically in carefully conducted validation studies.

Validation refers to the procedures used for gathering validity evidence about a predictor. The outcome of a validation study indicates the degree to which the predictor is related to a P/HR outcome. Such information may then be used to decide whether to use the predictor for selecting future job applicants. Ideally, validation of a predictor precedes its actual use in selecting applicants. In practice, organizations often use predictors before they are formally validated. Such a practice is possibly dangerous in that the organization may end up unknowingly using predictors with little or no validity.

Two major types of validation studies are possible—*empirical* and *content*. Empirical validation is the more rigorous and complex of the two. It involves examining the relationship between scores on predictors and measures of job success.

For example, the Massachusetts Mutual Life Insurance Company conducted such a study among its life insurance agents.[1] Five predictors were used in the study—age, aptitude test scores, college background, ratings of relationships with people, and length of service and performance on previous job(s). Through a special scoring procedure, information on these predictors was combined to yield a score of one to five. This overall score was then related to two measures of job success—length of service and sales volume. Definite relationships were obtained. For those with a predictor score of five, 57 percent remained on the job for three years and had average sales of $1.5 million by the end of the third year. By contrast, for those with a score of two, only 21 percent stayed on the job for three years, and they averaged less than $0.7 million in sales by the end of their third year.

Content validation is less rigorous and complex than empirical validation because no measure of job success is used in the study. Rather, the content of a predictor is examined, and a judgment is then made about its relationship to the content of the job. The items in a test of skills in the

---

[1] "Spotting a Winner in Insurance," *Business Week*, February 12, 1979, p. 122.

use of a word processor, for example, may be compared with the duties of a word processor operator. In this judgmental process, note that actual scores on the test are not being statistically related to scores on a measure of job success.

Thus, content validation typically yields less substantial evidence about the validity of a predictor than does empirical validation. However, in some circumstances empirical validation is not possible and content validation becomes a viable alternative. A detailed discussion of both validation types, with further examples, is presented below.

Empirical Validation

Figure 10–1 shows the components and their usual sequencing in empirical validation. The process begins with job analysis. Job analysis results then feed into criterion (job success) and predictor measures. Scores on the predictor and the criterion are then obtained from a sample of people and, finally, the relationship between the predictor and criterion scores is systematically examined.[2]

Job analysis

Many uses of job analysis were noted in Chapter 4. In the context of empirical validation, job analysis is used for two major purposes: to identify and define desired P/HR outcomes, and to infer the specific abilities and motivations likely to be related to these outcomes.

The first purpose involves organizational value judgments about what P/HR outcomes are important. Ultimately, these judgments should be based on consideration of overall organizational goals and strategy.[3] Frequently, this will lead to job performance as an outcome, since it is through their performance that employees most directly contribute to organization goal attainment.

Job analysis then involves identifying and defining job performance dimensions. For example, the job of management trainee in a retailing organization might have these performance dimensions: supervising salespeople, developing product knowledge, planning work, and budgeting. In another example, a job analysis of the job of entry-level social worker identified and defined six performance dimensions: problem

---

[2] For more detailed treatments of empirical validation see R. D. Gatewood and H. S. Feild, *Human Resource Selection* (Hinsdale, Ill.: Dryden Press, 1987); B. Schneider and N. Schmitt, *Staffing Organizations*, 2d ed. (Glenview, Ill.: Scott, Foresman, 1986).

[3] J. D. Olian and S. L. Rynes, "Organizational Staffing: Integrating Practice with Strategy," *Industrial Relations* 23 (1984), pp. 170–83.

FIGURE 10–1
Empirical Validation

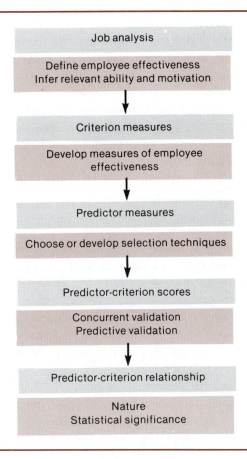

solving, contacts with clients, contacts with staff members, record keeping, planning, and job knowledge.[4]

Job analysis need not be restricted to considering only performance, however. Other outcomes should be considered as potentially important, particularly satisfaction, length of service, and attendance. Based on a careful consideration of these possible outcomes, the organization may define many outcomes as important for a given job.

Whatever outcomes are chosen and defined, the second purpose of job analysis is to infer the abilities and motivations associated with them.

---

[4] H. G. Heneman III, D. P. Schwab, D. L. Huett, and J. J. Ford, "Interviewer Validity as a Function of Interview Structure, Biographical Data, and Interviewee Order," *Journal of Applied Psychology* 60 (1975), pp. 748–53.

Practically, this means forming "guesstimates" about ability and motivation characteristics of job applicants that may be predictive of their effectiveness on the outcomes. For the job of social worker, effectiveness on the previously noted problem-solving dimension might be influenced by applicants' general mental abilities. On the contacts-with-clients dimension, applicants' interpersonal skills might be predictive of effectiveness.

Similar processes are involved in attempting to infer characteristics that might be related to other outcomes. If length of service is a component of effectiveness, for example, it is necessary to ask what specific ability and motivation characteristics are likely to be associated with being a high length-of-service employee (see Chapter 7 for a review of the evidence on this point).

Criterion measures

Once job analysis has identified the outcomes or criteria effectiveness, ways to measure the criteria will be needed (see Chapters 6 and 7). Logically enough, these are referred to as "criterion measures." In the case of job performance, criterion measures are needed for each of the performance dimensions. Sometimes the organization will already have these available as part of its performance appraisal system. Dimensions for which criterion measures are not readily available must have criterion measures developed for them.

It is crucial in this step that criterion measures be obtained or developed for all criteria of effectiveness. After all, job analysis identified them as important criteria, so they must be measured. Failure to do so means that predictors will not be validated against important components of the job.

Predictor measures

Here the issue is determining how to assess the various ability and motivation characteristics identified in job analysis. The whole range of possible predictors needs to be considered at this point. As a general rule, multiple predictors are likely to emerge as possibilities. This is because there will be numerous characteristics to be measured, and some if not all of these may best be measured by different types of predictors. In the social worker job described above, general mental ability may be most appropriately measured by a written test, and interpersonal skills might best be gauged by an interview or work sample. Most of the time, therefore, a reliance on a single predictor is both unlikely and unwise.

Predictor and criterion scores

To perform the validation study, scores on both predictor and criterion measures must be obtained from job applicants or employees. There are two different approaches or designs for doing this: *Concurrent* and *predictive* validation.[5]

Concurrent validation.   In concurrent validation, both predictor and criterion scores are obtained from employees currently on the job for which the validation study is being conducted. This is shown diagrammatically in Figure 10–2.

Concurrent validation has some definite appeals. Administratively, it is convenient and can often be done quickly. Moreover, results of the validation study will be available soon after the predictor and criterion scores have been gathered.

Unfortunately, some potentially serious problems can arise with concurrent validation. One problem is that if the predictor is a test, current employees may not be as motivated as job applicants to do well on the test. Yet it is for future job applicants that the test will be used (assuming results of the validation study are favorable).

In a related vein, current employees may not be that similar to, or representative of, future job applicants. Current employees may differ from future applicants in educational background, age, types of needs, and so forth. Hence, it is not certain that the results of the validation study will generalize to future job applicants. Also, some unsatisfactory employees will have been terminated and some high-performers promoted, leading to a restricted range for observed criterion scores.

FIGURE 10–2
Concurrent Validation Design

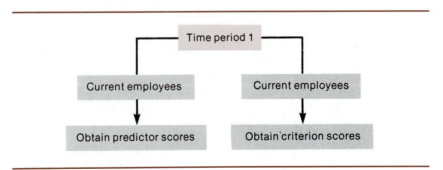

---

[5] For a review of these designs, and spin-offs from them, see M. Sussmann and D. U. Robertson, "The Validity of Validity: An Analysis of Validation Study Designs," *Journal of Applied Psychology* 71 (1986), pp. 461–68.

Finally, current employees' predictor scores may be influenced by the amount of experience and/or success they have had on their current job. For example, scores by mechanics on a test of knowledge of mechanical principles might in part be a reflection of how long they have been on the job, as well as how well they have performed it. This is undesirable because the predictor must be predictive of, rather than the result of, employee effectiveness.

Predictive validation.   Figure 10–3 shows the essential features of predictive validation. Predictor scores are obtained from a sample of job *applicants*, not current employees. Selection decisions are then made about these applicants; how well they score on the predictor in question must *not* be taken into account in the selection decisions. Doing so would amount to assuming the predictor is valid in the first place. Those who were hired will have criterion scores obtained for them. If the criterion is a measure of job performance, it is desirable to wait until employees have had ample time to learn the job before gathering the criterion scores.

Predictive validation overcomes the potential limitations of concurrent validation, since predictor scores are obtained from applicants. Applicants will be motivated to do well on the predictor; they are more likely to be representative of future applicants. And job experience/success cannot influence scores on the predictor, since the scores were obtained before they were on the job.

Predictive validation is not without potential disadvantages, however. It is neither administratively convenient nor quick. Moreover, results are not immediately available, since some time must elapse before criterion scores can be obtained. In general, however, these disadvantages do not outweigh the strengths of predictive validation, making predictive preferable to concurrent validation.

FIGURE 10–3
Predictive Validation Design

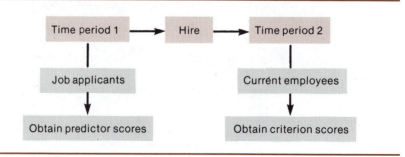

Predictor-Criterion Relationship

Once predictor and criterion scores are available, the next step is to examine the relationship between them. Regardless of whether the study is predictive or concurrent, there are two major issues of concern here: The *strength* and the *statistical significance* of the relationship.

Strength of the relationship.   A useful way to examine how the scores are related is to construct a scatter diagram. Figure 10–4 shows three different relationships in scatter diagram form. The Xs in each scatter diagram represent individual predictor and criterion scores for the people in the sample.

Example A in Figure 10–4 suggests little relationship between predictor and criterion scores. A modest relationship is shown in example B; there is some tendency for criterion scores to increase as predictor scores increase. In example C, a reasonably strong predictor-criterion relationship exists. As should be obvious, the stronger the relationship, the more valid the predictor.

Another way to examine the relationship is to compute a *correlation coefficient*,[6] which is a statistical indicator of the relationship between predictor and criterion scores. In validation studies, it is also called the "validity coefficient."

The symbol for the correlation is r. Numerically, r values can range from $r = -1.0$ to $r = +1.0$. The larger the value of r, the stronger the relationship. When an r value is shown without a plus or minus sign alongside it, the value is assumed to be positive.

Naturally, the value of r bears a close resemblance to the scatter diagram. As a demonstration of this, Figure 10–4 shows approximate r values for each of the scatter diagrams. In example A, a very small r is indicated ($r = .10$). The r in example B is moderate ($r = .35$), and the r in example C is reasonably strong ($r = .60$).

Statistical significance of the relationship.   Once the correlation has been computed, its statistical significance must be determined. Basically, this involves deciding whether the correlation obtained in the study's sample can be generalized to future job applicants. This is analogous to deciding whether the correlation is due to a true, or to a chance, relationship.

As a general rule of thumb, to be statistically significant, a correlation should have a probability of less than 0.05 (5 times out of 100) of occurring by a chance alone before it is concluded that the correlation

---

[6] Formulas for calculating the correlation coefficient are given in any elementary statistics book. In addition, the staffing books cited in footnote 2 also contain the formulas and "how to" examples.

FIGURE 10–4

Scatter Diagrams and Corresponding Correlations

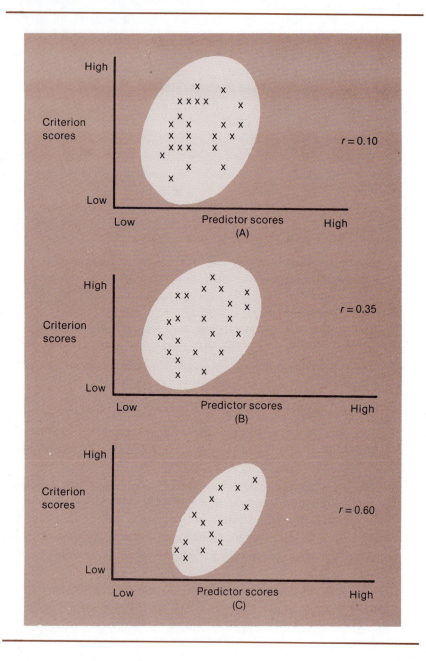

reflects a true relationship in the population of applicants.[7] The decision on statistical significance is a critical one. If it is concluded that the correlation reflects a true relationship (that is, it is statistically significant), the predictor can be used for selecting future job applicants. On the other hand, if the conclusion is that the correlation may be due to chance, the predictor should not be used for selecting future applicants.

An illustration.   Description of an actual empirical validation study for the job of maintenance mechanic is provided in Illustration 10–1. The study involved predicting effectiveness on three performance dimensions, using as predictors three standardized ability tests and a specially constructed work sample. The study follows the same set of empirical validation steps given in Figure 10–1.

Content Validation

Content validation differs from empirical validation in one important respect: There is no criterion measure in content validation. Thus, predictor scores cannot be correlated with criterion scores as a way of gathering evidence about a predictor's validity. Rather, a judgment is made about what the *probable* correlation between the predictor and criterion would be.[8]

When is content validation appropriate? One circumstance is when there are too few people available to form a sample for purposes of empirical validation. While there are differences of opinion on what the minimum necessary sample size is for empirical validation,[9] an absolute minimum is 30 individuals who all perform the same job.

The other major circumstance where content validation is appropriate occurs when criterion measures are not available for use, making empirical validation logically impossible. This is most likely in the case of performance measures.

Figure 10–5 shows that the two basic steps for performing a content validation study are making a job analysis and then choosing or developing a content-valid predictor. These steps are described below. Compar-

---

[7] For elaboration and formulas, consult an elementary statistics book.

[8] Detailed discussions of content validation are contained in A. Anastasis, *Psychological Testing*, 6th ed. (New York: Macmillan, 1988); Gatewood and Feild, *Human Resource Selection*; S. S. Musio and M. K. Smith, *Content Validity: A Procedural Manual* (Chicago: International Personnel Management Association, approximately 1976).

[9] For an overview of the issue and a demonstration that very large sample sizes may be necessary for empirical validation, see F. L. Schmidt, J. E. Hunter, and V. W. Urry, "Statistical Power in Criterion-Related Validation Studies," *Journal of Applied Psychology* 61 (1976), pp. 473–85.

ILLUSTRATION 10–1

Job Analysis.   The job was that of maintenance mechanic. Both foremen and mechanics participated in the job analysis. They identified two crucial dimensions of job performance: use of tools and accuracy of work.

Criterion Measures.   The criterion measures were the foremen's evaluations of mechanics on use of tools, accuracy of work, and overall mechanical ability. The evaluations were made using a paired comparison technique.

Predictor Measures.   The first three predictors were standardized, commercially available paper and pencil tests. The fourth predictor was a four-hour work sample that was specially developed for the job. In the work sample, people performed four tasks: installing pulleys and belts, disassembling and repairing a gearbox, installing and aligning a motor, and pressing a bushing into a sprocket and reaming it to fit a shaft. Performance on these work samples was evaluated by a test administrator, using a carefully developed checklist evaluation form. The form yielded a total work sample score for each person.

Predictor and Criterion Scores.   Predictor and criterion scores were obtained for a sample of 34 currently employed maintenance mechanics. Thus, a noncurrent validation design was used.

Predictor-Criterion Relationship.   Correlations between scores on the predictors and the three criterion measures were computed. The results are shown in the table below. As can be seen, only the work sample correlated significantly with the criterion.

Correlations between Predictor and Criterion Variables

Variable	Use of Tools	Accuracy of Work	Overall Mechanical Ability
Work sample*	.66‡	.42†	.46‡
Test of mechanical comprehension (Form AA)	.08	−.04	−.21
Wonderlic Personnel Test (Form D)	−.23	−.19	−.32
Short employment tests:			
Verbal	−.24	−.02	−.04
Numerical	.07	−.13	−.10
Clerical aptitude	−.03	−.19	−.09

* Performance on the work sample measure and mechanic work experience at this company were insignificantly correlated at −.27.

† $p < .05$

‡ $p < .01$

Source: J. E. Campion, "Work Sampling for Personnel Selection," *Journal of Applied Psychology* 56 (1972), pp. 40–44. Copyright 1972 by the American Psychological Association. Reprinted/adapted by permission of the publisher and author.

FIGURE 10-5
Content Validation

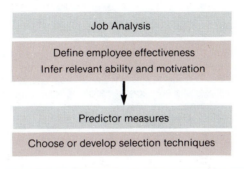

ing the steps in content validation with the steps in empirical validation (see Figure 10–1) shows that the steps in content validation are also a part of empirical validation. Because of this, content validation may be thought of as a subset of empirical validation.

Job analysis

As with empirical validation, content validation begins with job analysis, and the purposes of the job analysis are the same as in empirical validation. Those purposes are to identify and define the components of employee effectiveness and to identify the specific abilities and motivations likely to be associated with such effectiveness. The first purpose thus serves to define the content of the job, and the second purpose serves to identify what the content of the predictor(s) should be.

Predictor measures

Flowing directly from the second purpose of job analysis is identification of the predictor measure or measures. This often involves developing a new predictor that is tailor-made to the specific job and situation.

As an example, job analysis frequently reveals certain types of knowledge that employees must have to adequately perform the job, and this knowledge cannot be efficiently obtained through experience on the job or through a training program. Once the precise nature of the knowledge

ILLUSTRATION 10–2

Job Analysis.   The job was that of apprentice in the mechanical and electrical trades. A thorough job analysis indicated 31 mathematical operations used by apprentices in performance of their job duties.

Predictor Measure.   A commercially available test appeared to sample 19 of the 31 mathematical operations (a separate test was developed for the other 12 operations). To make content validity judgments with regard to the 19 operations, a content validity panel was formed. The panel was composed of craft supervisors, craftspeople, apprentices, classroom instructors of apprentices, and apprenticeship program coordinators. Each member of the panel evaluated each of the 54 items on the test. The evaluation required the individual to indicate:

> Is the skill (or knowledge) measured by this item
> — essential
> — useful but it can be learned on the job
> — not necessary
> to the performance of the job?

The amount of agreement among the panel members was determined for each item. Significant agreement was found for 53 of the 54 test items. The new test was composed of the items considered "essential" by a significant number of panel members.

Source: C. H. Lawshe, "A Quantified Approach to Content Validity," *Personnel Psychology* 28 (1975), pp. 563–75.

is identified, a written test can be constructed for subsequent use in selecting applicants.[10]

In other instances, an existing predictor (usually a test) may be examined and judged to have an acceptable content. If so, it might then be used intact for selection purposes.

Finally, an existing predictor may be modified to develop a content-valid test. An example of this approach is given in Illustration 10–2. Taking an existing knowledge test, a panel of experts made judgments about the content validity of the test, item by item, for the job of apprentice. Only those items that the panel members reliably agreed on as being content valid were then used in constructing a new form of the test for selecting future apprentices.

It should be emphasized that content validation procedures can be applied to *any* type of predictor, or combination of predictors. This is illustrated in a recent content validation study for selecting police emer-

---

[10] An example of this, for the job of construction superintendent, is given in D. D. Robinson, "Content-Oriented Personnel Selection in a Small Business Setting," *Personnel Psychology* 34 (1981), pp. 77–87.

gency telephone operators.[11] A job analysis identified six critical knowledge, skill, and ability (KSA) dimensions for the job (communication skills, emotional control, judgment, cooperativeness, memory, and clerical/technical skills). A set of predictors was then specially constructed to assess job applicants on these KSA dimensions. The predictors included:

- A spelling test in which applicants received 10 tape-recorded telephone calls and had to accurately record the pertinent information from each call on a form.
- A test in which applicants had to accurately record information received from monitoring police units.
- A typing test for both speed and accuracy.
- A "situational interview" in which applicants were asked how they would behave in a series of job-related situations.
- A role-playing exercise in which applicants assumed the role of police and telephone operator taking calls from complainants.

In short, content validation is a flexible process for developing predictors and for providing some evidence about their relationship to the content of the job.

DECISION MAKING

Upon completion of a validation study, two sequential decisions must be made. The first is whether to now use the predictor in the selection process. Essentially, this decision involves judging how much utility the predictor would have to the organization. If the predictor is judged to have utility, the second decision involves the establishment of the hiring standards or requirements for the predictor. For example, if the predictor is a test, it is necessary to specify exactly how applicants' test scores will enter into the final selection decision.

Utility of a New Predictor

The *utility* of a new predictor is the amount of "payoff" (that is, benefits minus costs) its use is estimated to provide to the organization.[12] Utility estimates may take on both positive and negative values, with

---

[11] N. Schmitt and C. Ostroff, "Operationalizing the Behavioral Consistency Approach: Selection Test Development Based on a Content-Oriented Strategy," *Personnel Psychology* 39 (1986), pp. 91–108.

[12] Reviews and criticisms of utility concepts and procedures are in R. M. Guion and W. M. Gibson, "Personnel Selection and Placement," in *Annual Review of Psychology*, eds. M. R. Rosenzweig and L. W. Porter (Palo Alto, Calif.: Annual Reviews, Inc., 1988), p. 349–74; B. D.

positive values leading toward a decision to use the predictor and negative values indicating that the predictor should not be used. Both the benefits and costs may involve monetary and nonmonetary considerations.

On the benefit side, use of a new predictor may help the organization more accurately identify applicants who will have positive impacts on the P/HR outcomes if they are hired. This would show up, for example, in the form of higher performance and satisfaction levels. Another potential benefit might occur in the form of lower labor costs (this is explained below in more detail).

On the cost side, any new predictor must be administered to applicants, it must be scored, and the scores must be interpreted for purposes of making hiring decisions. Such factors will require additional P/HR staff time and money. More subtle costs may also be involved. Applicants might have negative reactions to the new predictor, for example, if it is viewed as too difficult or time consuming. These reactions could hinder attempts to get applicants to accept job offers, or in the long run hinder attempts to even get people to apply to the organization. In a different example, use of the new predictor could lead to the occurrence of adverse impact against women and/or minorities.

In short, utility estimates must be based on numerous considerations, all of which must be examined more or less simultaneously. Typically, such estimates are done judgmentally and in a "gut level" manner. Recently, however, sophisticated statistical models have been developed to aid in the utility estimation process. These models differ in the type of payoff they estimate, and in the factors they use to actually estimate the payoff. Both of these differences are discussed next in nontechnical terms.

Predictor payoffs

Use of a new predictor could possibly lead to several types of payoffs. One common one is an increase in the amount of employee effectiveness on a P/HR outcome. For example, assume the outcome is job performance, and that management considers 65 percent of current employees on a given job as satisfactory and the remaining 35 percent as less than satisfactory (the percentage of current employees considered satisfactory

Steffy and S. D. Maurer, "Conceptualizing and Measuring the Economic Effectiveness of Human Resource Activities," *Academy of Management Review* 13 (1988), pp. 271–86; J. R. Terborg and J. S. Russell, "The Economic Impact of Valid Employee Selection Practices for Entry-Level Management Under Typical, Best, and Worst Case Scenarios" in *Readings in Personnel and Human Resource Management*, 3d ed., eds. R. S. Schuler, S. A. Youngblood and V. L. Huber (St. Paul: West Publishing, 1988), pp. 530–41.

is defined as the *base rate*). If management now begins using a new predictor in the selection process, as new applicants are hired over time this could lead to an even greater percentage of satisfactory employees. Say this new percentage is estimated to be 85 percent satisfactory employees. If so, the base rate will increase by 20 percentage points (85 percent minus 65 percent), and this increase in the base rate is the estimated payoff in nonmonetary terms from using the new predictor.

A second way to treat payoff is to take a given base rate increase and then try to translate that increase into a monetary equivalent. The resulting estimates can be pleasantly surprising. For example, the life insurance industry estimated that by using a new predictor it had recently validated, the annual profit generated *per agent* would increase by more than $10,000. In another example, the Armco Company estimated that use of a new, valid, arm-strength test for selecting steelworkers had a utility of $9.1 million per year.[13]

A third approach to the notion of payoff is to start with the assumption that total output of a good or service is to remain constant (e.g., an insurance company might assume that the total number of policies sold in a year will not change). Now the payoff from using a new predictor will take the form of reducing the number of employees that will be needed to produce this constant level of output. For example, one study of federal government employees estimated that use of a new, valid, ability test over just one year would permit a 9 percent reduction in new employees hired; this reduction would yield a payroll savings of $231 million.[14]

Factors used to estimate payoff

The type of payoff to be estimated will influence which model is chosen to develop the utility estimate. And as noted, these models differ in the types of factors considered for making the estimate. Ignoring these complexities, examples of the types of factors that might be used include:

1. The empirical validity of the new predictor.
2. The number of applicants and number of new hires.
3. The selection ratio or hiring rate (number of new hires/number of applicants; this can range from .00 to 1.00).

---

[13] J. D. Arnold, J. M. Rauschenberger, W. G. Soubel, and R. M. Guion, "Validation and Utility of a Strength Test for Selecting Steelworkers," *Journal of Applied Psychology* 67 (1982), pp. 588–604; S. H. Brown, "Validity Generalization and Situational Moderation in the Life Insurance Industry," *Journal of Applied Psychology* 66 (1981), pp. 664–70.

[14] F. L. Schmidt, J. E. Hunter, A. N. Outerbridge, and M. H. Trattner, "The Economic Impact of Job Selection Methods on Size, Productivity, and Payroll Costs of the Federal Work Force: An Empirically Based Demonstration," *Personnel Psychology* 39 (1986), pp. 1–30.

4. Probable length of service of new hires.
5. Dollar value of an increase on the P/HR outcome, such as job performance.
6. Interest rates and corporate tax rates.
7. Recruitment and selection costs.
8. Salary and benefit costs of new employees.

Some or all of these, and even other factors may be formally incorporated into a utility model to estimate the likely utility or payoff from using a new predictor. Unfortunately, there is no one "best" utility model, and many problems remain with all of these models. Nonetheless, the models illustrate the wide range of factors that should be considered in approaching the decision to use or not use a new predictor. Doing this will help us better answer the question "Is it worth it"?

Establishment of Hiring Standards

A decision to use a predictor carries with it a need to decide the hiring standard that will be associated with it. If the predictor is a test, it is necessary to establish the minimum score that applicants must achieve to be hired. This minimum score is known as a *cutoff* or *cut score*. If the predictor is an interviewer's rating of applicants, a cut score must be established for the rating. If previous work experience is the predictor, the cut score will be in the form of minimum amount of experience necessary.

Whatever cut score is decided, there is another issue to be considered. Namely, how will the organization choose from among those applicants who score above the minimum?

Selection error concept

The level at which the cut score is established has substantial implications for selection error. To illustrate this, refer to Figure 10–6.

Figure 10–6 shows a scatter diagram of the relationship between predictor and criterion scores. In addition, lines A and B divide the scatter diagram into four quadrants. The horizontal line, A, represents the dividing line between being successful or unsuccessful on the criterion. The vertical line, B, represents a cut score on the predictor. Applicants who met or exceeded the score would be hired; applicants who scored below the cut score would be rejected.

Quadrant I represents people who scored above the cut score on the predictor and were successful on the criterion. Had the predictor been used for making selection decisions about these people, they would have

FIGURE 10–6

Scatter Diagram Showing Correct and Erroneous Selection Decisions

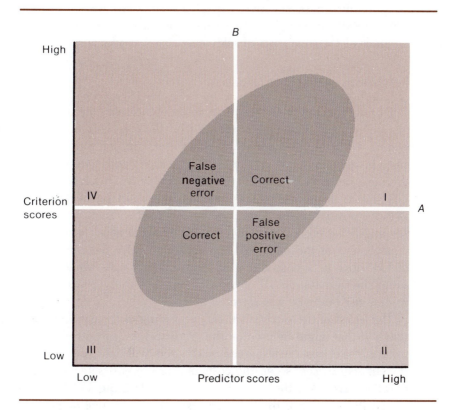

been hired, and these would represent correct selection decisions. Quadrant III contains people who scored below the cut score on the predictor and were unsuccessful. They would not have been hired, and these would have been correct selection decisions.

Quadrants II and IV represent selection error. In quadrant II are people who would have been hired (based on their predictor scores) but would have been unsuccessful on the criterion. These are *false positive* selection errors, also called *erroneous acceptances*. People in quadrant IV would not have been hired, but if they had been, they would have been successful. They represent *false negative* selection errors, also called *erroneous rejections*.

There are inherent trade-offs between false positive and false negative selection error. False positive error can be reduced by raising the cut score on the predictor. However, this will increase false negative errors. Conversely, lowering the cut score will reduce false negative error, but it will also increase false positive error.

Thus, establishment of any particular hiring standard needs to be based on the organization's relative willingness to commit false positive, as opposed to false negative, selection error. One way to express this willingness, and then derive a hiring standard, is to couch it in terms of minimizing the total costs of selection.

Hiring standards and cost minimization

During the external staffing process, continuing up to the actual placement of trained new employees on the job, certain costs are incurred. Some of these are actual, and others are potential costs. Actual costs involve those of recruitment, selection, and training. Potential costs are those that would be incurred if a selection error were made. They thus refer to the costs of false positive and false negative error.

False positive error costs may be incurred in such areas as record keeping, lowered productivity, damage to equipment, termination, and replacement of the unsuccessful employee. False negative error costs include loss to a competitor of an employee who would have been successful and the actual costs of obtaining an additional applicant to replace the one who was rejected.

The levels of these costs will vary according to the cut score or hiring standard that might be used on the predictor. As the cut score is raised, some of these costs will increase and others will decrease. Typically, as the cut score rises, so do the costs of recruitment, selection, and false negative error. On the other hand, costs of training and false positive error will decrease as the cut score rises. Hence, it will be necessary to establish a cut score that minimizes total costs—actual plus potential costs.[15]

Figure 10–7 shows a typical relationship between total costs and predictor cut scores. As the cut scores increases, total costs decrease for a while. However, total costs begin to increase again beyond point X on the predictor score, and they increase quite rapidly. Hence, the cut score that minimizes total costs is score X.

Naturally, the relationship between total costs and predictor scores will vary among situations, depending on the costs of the specific components. However, at some point total costs generally increase as the cut score increases. This means that the organization should usually be careful not to establish hiring standards at artificially high levels. Such standards are rarely cost effective.

---

[15] W. A. Sands, "A Method for Evaluating Alternative Recruitment-Selection Strategies: The CAPER Model," *Journal of Applied Psychology* 57 (1973), pp. 222–27.

FIGURE 10–7

Relationship between Predictor Scores and Total Staffing Costs

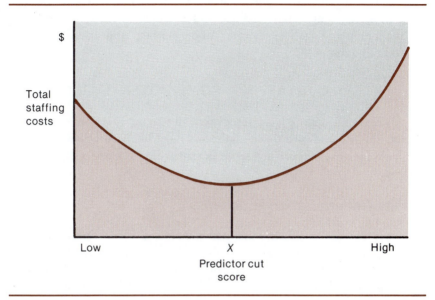

Applicants scoring above the minimum

Whatever cut score is established, there is a need to specify exactly how applicants scoring above it will be treated in terms of whether they are accepted or rejected. There are several possibilities: *ranking, grouping,* and *pass-fail.*

In the ranking procedure, applicants are rank-ordered from top to bottom according to their predictor scores. Hiring then starts with the highest scores and works on down the hiring list until all vacancies are filled.

Grouping involves placing applicants into categories—such as high, medium, and low—based on their predictor scores. Within each category, however, applicants are *not* rank-ordered. Hiring starts in the high category, based on predictor scores and other factors. These other factors may include information from other predictors, as well as affirmative action goals and timetables. After applicants in the high category have been exhausted, those in the medium category are considered, and so on.

With pass-fail systems, all applicants who score above the minimum are considered "qualified" and thus eligible to be hired. Their scores on the predictor will thus have little or no further impact on the selection decision. Instead, other factors will make the difference, including other predictors and affirmative action considerations.

None of the above approaches is inherently best. Each involves both advantages and disadvantages, and trade-offs have to be made. These will involve legal, economic, labor market, and social responsibility considerations.[16]

EXTERNAL STAFFING: SOME POTENTIAL LIMITATIONS

External staffing is a strategy for influencing P/HR outcomes. It seeks to identify and hire those applicants most likely to be effective employees. However, there are some potential limitations to this strategy.

Validity Generalization Problems

Is the validity of a predictor specific to a given job in the organization, or could its validity be generalized to the same (or a similar) job elsewhere? If validity is job specific, then validation ideally should occur each time before deciding whether to use a predictor. This means substantial time and cost to the organization, thus detracting from staffing as a viable strategy.

With *validity generalization*, however, a predictor could be used without being preceded by a validation study, provided this was for a type of job in which previous validity evidence for the predictor was favorable. Validation time and cost could thus be reduced.

The possibility that the validity of a predictor might generalize across similar settings (especially similar jobs and types of applicants) has generated considerable excitement and research. Unfortunately, the research results are not as promising as had been hoped for.[17] It simply is not clear whether the validity of a predictor does in fact generalize, and we are not certain either about why this may be the case. Until additional research results are available, caution is urged in thinking that validity generalizes and that one can thus avoid the need for conducting a validation study each time use of a predictor is being considered.

---

[16] W. F. Cascio, R. A. Alexander, and G. V. Barrett, "Settling Cutoff Scores: Legal, Psychometric, and Professional Issues and Guidelines," *Personnel Psychology* 41 (1988), pp. 1–24; C. F. Sproule, "Should Personnel Selection Tests Be Used on a Pass-Fail, Grouping, or Ranking Basis?" *Public Personnel Management* 13 (1984), pp. 375–94.

[17] M. J. Burke and N. S. Raju, "A Review of Validity Generalization Models and Procedures" in *Readings in Personnel and Human Resource Management;* Guion and Gibson, "Personnel Selection and Placement."

Validity Ceiling

Theoretically, the correlation between the predictor and criterion can range from -1.00 to $+1.00$. In practice, rarely does the validity coefficient exceed $r = .60$ in validation studies. Thus, there is a definite ceiling on validity to be expected from a predictor.

With definite limits on the ability of predictors to accurately predict an applicant's subsequent success on the job, other strategies must also be used for influencing P/HR outcomes. These would include many of the other P/HR activities, particularly development and compensation.

Predictor Unreliability

Reliability refers to the consistency with which something is measured. There are many ways to estimate it. For example, the same employment test could be given twice to a group of people, and the two sets of test scores could then be correlated. This is known as *test-retest reliability*. In another example, two employment interviewers could separately interview and then rate the probable job success of a group of applicants. The interviewers' ratings could then be compared, yielding an indication of *interrater reliability*.

Predictors usually lack reliability to some degree, meaning that there is inconsistency in the evaluation of job applicants. Such inconsistency in turn reduces our ability to accurately predict the likely success of applicants in the organization. Predictor unreliability thus contributes to the validity ceiling.

Unanticipated Changes

At the time a selection decision is made, there are certain givens surrounding the decision. The decision is based on an assessment of the applicant's current ability and motivation, relative to the current requirements and rewards of a particular job. However, changes can occur after the individual is hired, and these changes may be difficult to anticipate and take into account at the time of the initial selection decision.

Once in the organization, people's ability and/or motivation could change, thus affecting their contribution to the organization. Too, jobs may change in content, leading to differing job requirements and rewards. Such changes could also affect employee success. Finally, people normally switch jobs in the organization. External staffing is limited in its ability to deal with new employees' probable success on jobs to which they might move in the future. External staffing strategies thus need to be coupled closely with internal staffing strategies (see Chapter 12).

EXTERNAL STAFFING CONCEPTS AND EQUAL EMPLOYMENT OPPORTUNITY

External staffing activities have been subject to substantial legislation, regulation, and litigation regarding equal employment opportunity. The general issue has to do with claims that individuals may be illegally discriminated against based on such legally protected characteristics as race, sex, and age.

Title VII of the Civil Rights Act prohibits discrimination in staffing on the basis of race, color, sex, religion, and national origin. There are two permissible staffing practices, however, under Title VII. First, it is permissible to discriminate on the basis of sex, religion, and national origin (but not race or color) if doing so can be shown to be a bona fide occupational qualification (BFOQ) necessary for the operation of the business. Second, it is permissible to use a "professionally developed ability test," as long as the test is not designed, intended, or used to discriminate.

The Age Discrimination in Employment Act prohibits staffing discrimination based on age for individuals over age 40. An exception to this is permissible age discrimination when age can be shown to be a BFOQ.

Bona Fide Occupational Qualifications

One form of potential staffing discrimination is outright rejection of applicants based on a particular characteristic, such as sex. In this approach, mere possession of a characteristic is sufficient to disqualify the applicant from employment consideration. The characteristic thus functions as a rigidly applied predictor. Most of the time such a practice reflects true discrimination without any business purpose.

When the organization believes that discrimination based on a protected characteristic is a BFOQ, and a discrimination charge is filed against the organization, the burden of proof is on the organization to justify the claim in court. This is normally difficult, since the courts are interpreting BFOQ provisions narrowly. Unless specific, overwhelming evidence can be presented, the courts will not approve BFOQ claims. Examples of evidence generally *not* sufficient include claims of customer preference ("Our customers prefer women salespeople . . .") or gross gender characterizations ("Women cannot lift 30 pounds . . .").

The organization thus must examine its staffing policies for all jobs. Where applicants have been rejected based on sex, age, and so forth, these practices should cease immediately unless the organization can truly justify them through BFOQ provisions. Most of the time it will probably be concluded that such practices are not sufficiently justifiable to warrant their continuance.[18]

Testing and the Uniform Guidelines

Although Title VII permits the use of "professionally developed ability tests," the use of tests and other selection procedures could result in discriminatory effects known as "adverse impact." Adverse impact refers to differences in selection (hiring) rates for men and women, minorities and nonminorities, and so forth. For example, what if the selection rate for men on a particular job is 75 percent and 25 percent for women. Is this evidence of adverse impact? If so, what should be done about it? The 1978 *Uniform Guidelines on Employee Selection Procedures* (issued by the EEOC) attempts to provide the answers to these questions.[19]

Specific provisions

Determining adverse impact.   Virtually any type of predictor (test, interview, experience requirement, etc.) is considered a selection procedure. Moreover, selection refers to both external (hiring) and internal (e.g., promotion) selection decisions. The guidelines require that the organization check for, and maintain records on, possible adverse impact for all selection decisions involving virtually all selection procedures. This is to be done on a job-by-job basis, according to the four fifths or 80 percent rule.

The following is a general provision of the 80 percent rule for identifying adverse impact: "A selection rate for any race, sex, or ethnic group

---

[18] R. H. Faley, L. S. Kleinman, and M. L. Lengnick-Hall, "Age Discrimination and Personnel Psychology: A Review and Synthesis of the Legal Literature with Implications for Future Research," *Personnel Psychology* 37 (1984), pp. 327–50; M. F. Hill, Jr., and T. Bishop, "Aging and Employment: The BFOQ under ADEA," *Labor Law Journal* 34 (1983), pp. 763–75.

[19] For detailed discussions see R. H. Faley and L. S. Kleinman, "Misconceptions and Realities in the Implementation of Equal Employment Opportunity," in *Readings in Personnel and Human Resource Management*; Gatewood and Feild, *Human Resource Selection*; D. Yoder and P. D. Staudohar, "Testing and EEO: Getting Down to Cases," *Personnel Administrator* 29, no. 2 (1884), pp. 67–78.

which is less than four fifths (⅘), or 80 percent, of the rate for the group with the highest rate will generally be regarded . . . as evidence of adverse impact." For example, assume that for a given job the selection rates for men and women are .60 and .50, respectively, Here, adverse impact would probably not be inferred, since the women's rate is within 80 percent of the men's rate (that is, $.60 \times .80 = .48$). A selection rate for women below .48, however, would suggest adverse impact.

Coping with adverse impact.   Should instances of adverse impact be detected, the organization has two options for coping with them. The first option is to take steps to eliminate the adverse impact. This could be done by no longer using the predictor(s) causing the adverse impact. Another approach in this option would be to expand recruitment to identify more qualified applicants in the group for which adverse impact is occurring.

The second option is to attempt to justify the occurrence of the adverse impact by providing evidence that the predictor has acceptable validity. Choice of this option means that the organization must be able to show that it is in compliance with the validation standards put forth in the guidelines. These standards are very detailed, and they cover both content and empirical validation. Also, it should be noted that these validation standards place great emphasis on job analysis as part of any validation process.

Controversies

The guidelines have been, and continue to be, quite controversial. One source of controversy is simply the 80 percent rule itself. Some argue that it is too rigid and mechanical a procedure for determining adverse impact. People also differ on whether the 80 percent rule should be applied to each predictor in the selection process for a given job, or only to the final hiring rates that result from the total process. It is possible, for example, for a given predictor in the process to have adverse impact even though other predictors do not, thus possibly yielding no adverse impact overall.

A second controversy involves whether the validation requirements should apply to virtually all predictors. Some argue, for example, that requiring validation of the interview is too costly, and that it is not meaningful to do it in a technical sense.

Finally, in discrimination cases where the grievance/arbitration process (rather than litigation) is being used, the guidelines may carry little or no weight in the final decision about whether or not discrimination has occurred. Since the arbitrator handling the case is bound by different laws and legal standards, he or she frequently pays little attention to the guidelines.[20]

SUMMARY

External staffing activities are concerned with attempting to predict the likely effectiveness of individuals at the time they are job applicants. Many predictors are used to assess applicants' motivation and ability relative to job requirements and rewards.

Critical to the success of this strategy is examination of the validity of predictors through empirical or content validation. Empirical validation involves correlating scores on the predictor with scores on the criterion, either concurrently or predictively. The resultant correlation is then tested for statistical significance. If an acceptable level of statistical significance is reached, the results of the validation study may be generalized to future job applicants. In turn, it would then be legitimate to use the predictor for selecting future applicants.

Content validation may be thought of as a subset of empirical validation. It involves making a judgment about the likely relationship between the predictor and criterion, rather than a statistical analysis of the relationship.

The actual decision to use a predictor should be based on a judgment about its likely "payoff" or utility. Basically, this involves weighing the relative benefits and costs of using the predictor. Many factors typically should be taken into account in this decision.

If a predictor is judged useful, it can become part of the selection system. When this happens, a hiring standard or cut score must be established for it. At a minimum, the relative importance and cost of false positive and false negative selection errors should influence where the cut score is set. Ideally, a hiring standard will be established that minimizes total (actual plus potential) staffing costs.

As a strategy, external staffing has some potential limitations associated with it. For one thing, there is a ceiling on the validity of a given predictor, and the predictor's validity may be very specific. Also, there may be certain changes that cannot be anticipated at the time an initial selection decision is made. These involve changes in people, changes in job content, and people changing jobs over time.

---

[20] D. G. Gallagher and P. A. Veglahn, "Arbitral Standards in Cases Involving Testing Issues," *Labor Law Journal* 37 (1986), pp. 719–30.

Equal employment opportunity laws and regulations have substantial impacts on all external staffing activities. They greatly limit discrimination based on claims of bona fide occupational qualifications (BFOQs). When any selection procedure is having an adverse impact on one or more groups, the organization must comply with the regulations put forth in the "Uniform Guidelines on Employee Selection Procedures." The thrust of the guidelines is that the organization either eliminate the adverse impact or justify it by presenting evidence on the validity of the selection procedure. Detailed standards are given for conducting both empirical and content validation studies.

DISCUSSION QUESTIONS

1. Why is job analysis important for both empirical and content validation?
2. Under what circumstances is a new predictor likely to have high utility? Low utility?
3. What role should cost considerations play in the establishment of hiring standards?
4. When might an organization not use a ranking procedure for hiring applicants?
5. What are the basic provisions of the Uniform Guidelines on Employee Selection Procedures?
6. What factors might account for the validity ceiling?

11

External Staffing Processes

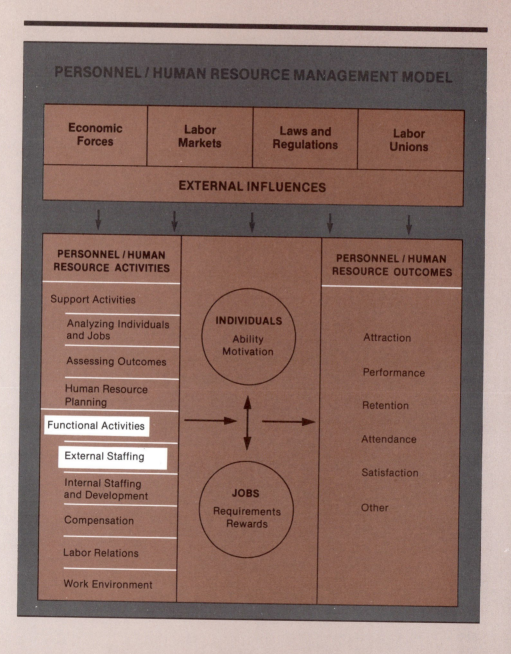

PERSONNEL / HUMAN RESOURCE MANAGEMENT MODEL

Economic Forces	Labor Markets	Laws and Regulations	Labor Unions

EXTERNAL INFLUENCES

PERSONNEL / HUMAN RESOURCE ACTIVITIES

Support Activities

Analyzing Individuals and Jobs

Assessing Outcomes

Human Resource Planning

Functional Activities

External Staffing

Internal Staffing and Development

Compensation

Labor Relations

Work Environment

INDIVIDUALS
Ability
Motivation

JOBS
Requirements
Rewards

PERSONNEL / HUMAN RESOURCE OUTCOMES

Attraction

Performance

Retention

Attendance

Satisfaction

Other

After reading this chapter, you should be able to speak to the questions posed in each of the following personnel/human resource incidents:

1. You have just been hired for the newly created job of personnel director for the state Division of Community Services. You have decided that one of your major tasks will be to guide the development of a systematic employee selection system for the division. Currently, selection decisions are made solely on the basis of an interview. You believe that other selection techniques should possibly be used. What other techniques might be used? What factors would you need to consider in choosing and using these techniques? How will you ensure that the system is consistent with equal employment opportunity laws and regulations?

2. A search and screen committee is responsible for developing a list of three candidates for the job of assistant professor of personnel/human resource management. You were appointed by the dean of the school of business as the student member of the committee. Before the first meeting of the committee, each member is to prepare a proposed process for evaluating candidates. What process would you propose? What parts of the process would you be willing to compromise on with other members?

3. Your company requires that all applicants complete an application blank during the selection process, and the same blank is used for all applicants. As staffing manager of the personnel department, you have been asked by your boss to consider the possibility of developing a separate blank for each major department. Would this be desirable? If you developed a new blank, how would you evaluate its effectiveness? What types of interactions with line management would be necessary?

4. The Beaverton Company manufactures equipment for automotive electrical systems. After a one-month training program, you have been appointed a first-level supervisor on the night shift. You have three vacancies in your department that you will need to fill soon, and the personnel department will send to you all applicants who survive the initial selection hurdles. You must interview each applicant and then decide which to hire. What types of questions will you ask? What should you do prior to actually interviewing applicants? What should you do at the completion of each interview?

The previous chapter dealt with the major concepts underlying external staffing activities and the general equal employment opportunity laws and regulations that affect these activities. In this chapter, staffing processes in practice are examined, as well as more specific equal employment opportunity issues.

Figure 11–1 shows a typical process a job applicant goes through preceding a hiring decision. Multiple predictors are used during the process, and some are used on more than one occasion (usually *application blanks and interviews*). The primary purpose of these predictors is to assess applicants' abilities and motivations relative to the requirements and rewards of the job. To the extent that this is done effectively, positive P/HR outcomes (for example, high job performance) will result.

Each of the predictors shown in Figure 11–1 is treated in this chapter. Descriptions and examples of each are provided, and what is known about their validity for predicting job success is summarized. Some of these predictors are especially affected by equal employment opportunity law, and the nature of these impacts is also noted.

Following the discussion of the individual predictors, attention is turned to administration of a total staffing system in the organization. Emphasis is placed on making the system work effectively and in a manner acceptable to both management and job applicants. These administrative concerns are important because the P/HR department has direct responsibility for the design, validation, operation, and control of the external staffing process.

FIGURE 11–1

Example of a Typical Staffing Process

1. Applicant completes application blank in the personnel department.
2. Personnel department conducts preliminary screening interview, looking for obvious disqualifying factors such as lack of appropriate training.
3. Applicant is administered one or more tests.
4. Personnel department conducts more thorough interview, using application-blank information, test results, and any references and recommendations.
5. Applicant has preemployment health test or completes a health questionnaire.
6. Applicant is interviewed by the supervisor of the vacant job; supervisor has access to all information about the applicant.
7. Final selection is made by the supervisor alone, or in conjunction with the personnel department.

SELECTION PREDICTORS

Tests

A test is any systematic, standardized procedure for obtaining information from individuals. In the case of selection predictors, the information pertains to applicants' abilities and/or motivations. Although this definition of a test could encompass almost any predictor, its use here is restricted to four major categories. These are ability tests, personality and interest tests, work sample tests, and honesty tests.

Ability tests

Ability tests measure characteristics in the individual representing, or likely to lead to acquiring, knowledge or skill. Thus, ability test results indicate what tests the applicant might be able to perform in the future, given the opportunity (for example, through training). Results from ability tests also suggest what tasks the applicant could currently perform.[1]

There are literally hundreds of ability tests available for use in organizations; they fall into three major categories: *cognitive, mechanical,* and *psychomotor*.

Cognitive tests.   Cognitive tests measure numerous abilities. Some of these tests are referred to as "general mental tests" because they measure ability characteristics that may be useful in many different types of situations and jobs. Other cognitive tests are referred to as "specific ability tests" since they assess characteristics that are more situation or job-specific.

As shown in Chapter 4, these specific abilities may be grouped into the following categories: verbal comprehension, word fluency, number aptitude, inductive reasoning, memory, spatial aptitude, and perceptual speed. Examples of typical test items for measuring these abilities are shown in Figure 11–2.

Mechanical tests.   Mechanical tests, although primarily cognitive in nature, have been developed mostly for semiskilled and skilled mechanical jobs. The first of these is a general mechanical ability that involves comprehension of mechanical relations, recognition of various tools and their uses, and the identification and use of mechanical principles. The

---

[1] R. D. Gatewood and H. S. Feild, *Human Resource Selection* (Hinsdale, Ill.: Dryden Press, 1987), pp. 383–418.

FIGURE 11–2

Test Items for Seven Major Cognitive Abilities

Verbal comprehension: to understand the meaning of words and their relations to each other; to comprehend readily and accurately what is read; measured by test items such as:

Which one of the following words means most nearly the same as *effusive?*
1. evasive
2. affluent
3. gushing
4. realistic
5. lethargic

Word fluency: to be fluent in naming or making words, such as making smaller words from the letters in a large one or playing anagrams; measured by test items such as:

Using the letters in the word *Minneapolis,* write as many four-letter words as you can in the next two minutes

_____
_____
_____
_____

_____

Number aptitude: to be speedy and accurate in making simple arithmetic calculations; measured by test items such as:

Carry out the following calculations:

346	8732	$422 \times 32 =$ _____
+722	−4843	$3630 \div 5 =$ _____

Inductive reasoning: to be able to discover a rule or principle and apply it to the solution of a problem, such as determining what is to come next in a series of numbers or words; measured by test items, such as:

What number should come next in the sequence of the following five numbers?
1 5 2 4 3
1. 7
2. 1
3. 2
4. 4
5. 3

Memory: to have a good rote memory for paired words, lists of numbers, and so forth; measured by test items such as:

The examinee may be given a list of letters paired with symbols such as:

A	*	E	?
B	,	F	;
C	☆	G	:
D	!	H	.

He is given a brief period to memorize the pairs. Then he is told to turn the page and write the appropriate symbols after each of the letters appearing there.

FIGURE 11–2 *(concluded)*

Spatial aptitude: to perceive fixed geometric relations among figures accurately and to be able to visualize their manipulation in space; measured by test items such as:

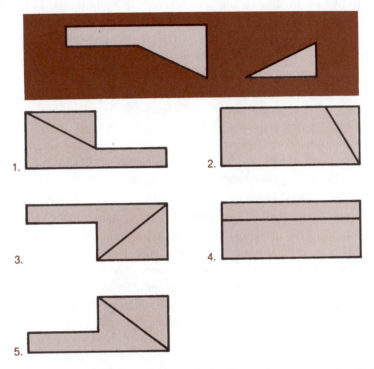

Which figure would result if the two pieces in the picture above were put together?

Perceptual speed: to perceive visual details quickly and accurately; measured by test items such as:

Make a check mark in front of each pair below in which the numbers are identical:
1. 367773 _____ 367713
2. 471352 _____ 471352
3. 581688 _____ 581688
4. 324579 _____ 334579
5. 875989 _____ 876898

Source: M. D. Dunnette, *Personnel Selection and Placement* (Belmont, Calif.: Wadsworth, 1966), pp. 47–49. Copyright © 1966 by Wadsworth, Inc. Reprinted by permission of the publisher, Brooks/Cole Publishing Company, Monterey, Calif.

other ability deals with spatial relations—the ability to visualize how parts fit together into a whole (see Figure 11–2).

   Psychomotor tests.   Psychomotor tests measure physical, not cognitive, ability. Finger dexterity and reaction time are examples of psychomotor skills these tests assess. Obviously, psychomotor tests are most relevant to jobs involving physical, as opposed to mental, tasks.

Personality and interest tests

Personality and interest tests seek to measure motivation.[2] Furthermore, with few exceptions, personality and interest tests have *not* been developed for use as employee selection techniques. Personality tests are typically intended for use as *diagnostic devices* (for example, to identify broad personality dimensions or mental disorders). Interest tests are used to provide people with information about their preferences for various activities and, in turn, such information can be of assistance in making occupational choices.

Personality tests.   Personality tests usually ask individuals to describe themselves in terms of traits or typical behaviors. As an example, the Ghiselli Self-Description Inventory has 64 pairs of trait adjectives.[3] For some pairs, the person is asked to choose the most descriptive adjectives; for others, the least descriptive adjective. Examples of pairs include:

_____ capable _____ sympathetic _____ defensive _____ weak

_____ discreet _____ patient   _____ touchy   _____ selfish

Responses yield scores on 13 broad personality dimensions, such as initiative, self-assurance, maturity, and achievement motivation.

Interest tests.   Interest tests measure the individual's preferences, or likes and dislikes, for a wide variety of activities. Two of the most widely known and used interest tests are the Strong Vocational Interest Blank and the Kuder Vocational Preference Record.

On the Kuder, for example, the individual is given a large number of sets of three activities. For each set, the person must check the activities he or she most and least prefers. A set might be:

_____ play baseball

_____ work a puzzle

_____ listen to music

Responses to the Kuder yield scores on 10 broad interest dimensions, such as outdoor, mechanical, scientific, social service, and literary.

Work sample tests

Work sample tests are, literally, samples of the work involved in the performance of a specific job.[4] In a sense, these tests may be thought of as miniature replicas of jobs. Underlying them is the assumption that the

---

[2] A. Anastasi, *Psychological Testing*, 6th edition, (New York: Macmillan, 1988), pp. 523–623.

[3] E. E. Ghiselli, *Explorations in Managerial Talent* (Pacific Palisades, Calif: Goodyear Publishing, 1971).

[4] Gatewood and Feild, *Human Resource Selection*, pp. 451–90.

FIGURE 11-3

Examples of Work Sample Tests Used in Selection

Test (Behavioral)	Job
Lathe Drill press Tool dexterity Screw board test Packaging	Machine operator
Shorthand Stenographic Typing	Clerical worker
Blueprint reading Tool indentification Installing belts Repair of gear box Installing a motor Vehicle repair	Mechanic
Tracing trouble in a complex circuit Inspection of electronic defects Electronics test	Electronics technician

Test (Knowledge and Skill)	Job
Report of recommendations for problem solution Small business manufacturing game Judgment and decision-making test Supervisory judgment about training, safety, performance evaluation	Manager or supervisor
Processing of mathematical data and evaluating hypotheses Basic information in chemistry Mathematical formulation and science judgment	Engineer or scientist
Oral fact finding Role playing of customer contacts Writing business letters Oral directions	Communication specialist

Source: Adapted from R. D. Gatewood and H. S. Feild, *Human Resource Selection* (Hinsdale, Ill.: Dryden Press, 1987), p. 456.

best predictor of job performance is a sample of that performance obtained under simulated, but realistic, work conditions.

Work samples are difficult to neatly categorize into types. About the best that can be done is to differentiate between *behavioral* work samples and work samples of *knowledge and skill*. Examples of each type are shown in Figure 11–3.

Behavioral work samples.   These tests measure samples of behavior involved in the performance of critical job tasks. Usually behavioral work samples involve the measurement of psychomotor-type skills. They differ from traditional psychomotor tests by being more job-specific and are frequently especially constructed for a single job in the organization.

Knowledge and skill work samples.   Knowledge and skill work samples measure factors one or more steps removed from actual job behavior. They focus on measuring the knowledge and skill presumed necessary for successful work behaviors. Figure 11–3 shows that such work samples are similar to ability tests. They are most appropriate for professional, technical, and administrative jobs and, like behavioral work samples, are usually especially constructed for the job in question.

Honesty tests

Employee theft of merchandise and cash is estimated to cost employers billions of dollars each year. This concern has led to increased reliance on honesty tests. Two major types are used—the lie detector (polygraph), and paper and pencil measures. With the lie detector, the test taker is interrogated (e.g., "Did you steal the ring from the window display?"), and his or her physiological changes from question to question are recorded. Such changes assumedly indicate whether the person is lying. Paper and pencil honesty tests ask people their attitudes and opinions about theft through a series of written test questions (e.g., "Should a person be fired for stealing $5?"). Responses to such questions presumably indicate how predisposed a person is toward stealing.

Validity of tests

Over the years, much work has been done investigating the validity of the various types of tests as predictors of P/HR outcomes. What follows are some general statements about the validity of these tests based on the accumulated evidence. It should be noted that exceptions to these conclusions are always possible in any given situation or job.

Starting with ability tests, the validity evidence for them is quite favorable.[5] They are reasonably valid predictors of both job performance and of success in training programs. This is true across a wide variety of jobs and occupations. Recent evidence also shows that general ability tests are oftentimes at least as valid as specific ability tests in predicting

---

[5] R. D. Arvey, "General Ability in Employment: A Discussion," *Journal of Vocational Behavior* 29 (1986), pp. 415–20; E. E. Ghiselli, "The Validity of Aptitude Tests in Personnel Selection," *Personnel Psychology* 26 (1973), pp. 461–77; J. E. Hunter and R. F. Hunter, "Validity and Utility of Alternative Predictors of Job Performance," *Psychological Bulletin* 96 (1984), pp. 72–98; R. R. Reilly and G. T. Chao, "Validity and Fairness of Some Alternative Employee Selection Procedures," *Personnel Psychology* 35 (1982), pp. 1–62.

job performance. All in all, the validity evidence indicates that ability tests warrant serious consideration for usage in selection systems.

On the other hand, personality and interest inventories are seldom valid predictors.[6] Few studies have obtained significant correlations between personality or interest test scores and job success criterion scores. One exception to this involves managerial and sales occupations, where the validity evidence is slightly more favorable. With this possible exception, there is little evidence to support the use of personality and interest tests in employee selection.

Validity evidence for work samples is very favorable for predicting both job performance and success in training programs.[7] Among these, behavioral work samples are better predictors of job performance, and knowledge and skill work samples are better in predicting training success.

Honesty tests and the validity evidence surrounding them are matters of considerable controversy.[8] Claims and counterclaims about their validity have a long history, and the debate shows no sign of ending any time soon. In the meantime, it is best to remain skeptical about honesty tests' validity for predicting employee theft.

Legal considerations

Any predictor may potentially have *adverse impact* resulting in significantly higher rates of rejection for some groups of applicants as a function of their race, sex, and so on. Evidence clearly shows that adverse impact is often a real problem with cognitive ability tests and job knowledge work samples.[9] Much less is known about the adverse impact of the other types of tests, though behavioral work samples may be relatively free from adverse impact effects.

When adverse impact occurs, the *Uniform Guidelines on Employee Selection Procedures* (see Chapter 10) provide for two ways to handle it. The first way is to justify it by demonstrating the validity of the selection

---

[6] E. E. Chiselli, "The Validity of Attitude Tests"; G. Gough, "Personality and Personality Assessment," in *Handbook of Industrial and Organization Psychology*, ed. M. D. Dunnette (Skokie, Ill.: Rand McNally, 1976); Hunter and Hunter, "Validity and Utility of Alternative Predictors of Job Performance."

[7] Hunter and Hunter, "Validity and Utility of Alternative Predictors of Job Performance"; Reilly and Chao, "Validity and Fairness of Some Alternative Employee Selection Procedures."

[8] P. R. Sackett and M. M. Harris, "Honesty Testing for Personnel Testing: A Review and Critique," *Personnel Psychology* 37 (1984), pp. 221–46.

[9] Hunter and Hunter, "Validity and Utility of Alternative Predictors of Job Performance"; J. E. Hunter and F. L. Schmidt, "Ability Tests: Economic Benefits Versus the Issue of Fairness," *Industrial Relations* 21 (1982), pp. 293–308.

ILLUSTRATION 11-1

Illinois to Reexamine Insurance Test for Bias

The State of Illinois and the Educational Testing Service, the major developer of standardized tests, agree to examine the potential discriminatory impact of the licensing examination for insurance agents. Settling an eight-year-old suit brought by the Golden Rule Insurance Company and five applicants for the test, the parties agree to a review of individual questions on the test for possible racial bias by an independent advisory panel and to see that future exams will eliminate those with the greatest gap between black and white test-takers.

The out-of-court agreement is likely to have a ripple effect resulting in challenges of other professional licensing exams, such as those for real estate agents, police and firefighters, and lawyers, J. Patrick Rooney, president of the Lawrenceville, Ill., company that initiated the suit, suggests. Unless ETS "voluntarily extends," the reforms called for in Illinois, "dozens of similar lawsuits" will be filed, predicts Chuck Stone, a former director of minority affairs at the testing service. The test that was challenged in Illinois—the multistate insurance licensing examination—currently is in use by 23 other states. "The settlement," Rooney says, "will remove some of the unfair obstacles that have prevented thousands of qualified blacks from becoming insurance agents."

Source: Bureau of National Affairs, "Daily Labor Report," November 29, 1984, p. 1.

---

device as a predictor of job success. The second way is modify the predictor, or eliminate it from use altogether. An out-of-court settlement involving an agreement to modify a licensing test for insurance agents is shown in Illustration 11-1.

Unfortunately, there can be some real trade-offs between using the most valid predictors possible and minimizing adverse impact.[10] For example, it was shown above that cognitive ability tests have high validity, but they also have strong adverse impact. Under these circumstances, failure to use the predictor will reduce adverse impact, but at a tremendous cost to the organization by failing to use a predictor that does a reasonable job of identifying applicants most likely to be successful on the job. These costs can be foregone by continuing to use the predictor, but at a cost of continued adverse impact. Each organization has to decide for itself how to deal with this trade-off.

Another legal consideration involves honesty tests. There is substantial controversy surrounding their usage, especially for the polygraph (lie detector). Part of the controversy involves questions of validity, discussed above, while the other part involves claims that honesty tests are an unwarranted invasion of applicants' privacy rights. Such controversies

---

[10] Ibid.

have caused some states to pass laws that ban, or strongly limit, usage of the lie detector for selection.[11]

A new federal law now prohibits most private (but not public) employers from using the lie detector for selection purposes. Whether such prohibitions will carry over to paper and pencil honesty tests remains to be seen.

Training and Experience Requirements

Minimum training and experience (T&E) requirements for applicants have long been an integral part of the staffing process. Training requirements usually refer to various types of educational attainment. These could be general, such as a college degree requirement; or they could be specific, outlining such requirements as type of major, types of coursework, overall gradepoint average, and gradepoint average in the major.

T&E requirements, especially specific ones, bear a close relationship to work samples. Training requirements represent a knowledge and skill work sample, since an educational requirement attempts to ensure that applicants have acquired these characteristics through formal training.

Experience requirements are usually stated in terms of previous job experience. They can focus on length of experience in a job, or they can state exactly what types of experiences the applicant must have.

Experience requirements typically contain both knowledge and skill, and behavioral, work samples, For example, if a staffing specialist job requires two years' previous experience, the presumption is that the applicant has experienced certain types of behaviors that staffing specialists engage in (for example, test validation). This requirement also attempts to ensure that the applicant has acquired certain knowledge and skill because of varied job experiences (for example, knowledge of various types of jobs).

Validity of training and experience requirements

Research shows that T&E requirements usually have very low validity as predictors of job success.[12] This conclusion, however, most applies to situations in which the requirements are very broad and general—such as "college degree" or "three years experience."

11 D. J. Herron, "Statutory Restrictions on Polygraph Testing in Employer-Employee Relationships," *Labor Law Journal* 37 (1986), pp. 632–38.

12 A. Howard, "College Experiences and Managerial Performance," *Journal of Applied Psychology* 71 (1986), pp. 527–52; M. A. McDaniel, F. L. Schmidt, and J. E. Hunter, "Job Experience Correlates of Job Performance," *Journal of Applied Psychology* 73 (1988), pp. 327–30.

FIGURE 11–4

One Dimension of the "Accomplishment Record" Inventory and an Example of a Response

---

USING KNOWLEDGE

Interpreting and synthesizing information to form legal strategies, approaches, lines of argument, etc.; developing new configurations of knowledge, innovative approaches, solutions, strategies, etc.; selecting the proper legal theory; using appropriate lines of argument, weighing alternatives and drawing sound conclusions.

Time Period: *1974–75*

General statement of what you accomplished:

I was given the task of transferring our antitrust investigation of _____ into a coherent set of pleadings presentable to _____ and the Commission for review and approval within the context of the Commission's involvement in shopping centers nationwide.

Description of exactly what you did:

I drafted the complaint and proposed order and wrote the underlying legal memo justifying all charges and proposed remedies. I wrote the memo to the Commission recommending approval of the consent agreement. For the first time, we applied antitrust principles to this novel factual situation.

Awards or formal recognition:

   none

The information verified by: *John _____, Compliance.*

Source: L. M. Hough, "Development and Evaluation of the 'Accomplishment Record' Method of Selecting and Promoting Professionals," *Journal of Applied Psychology* 69 (1984), pp. 135–46.

When T&E requirements are very specific and developed on the basis of thorough job analysis, chances for acceptable validity may be improved. One recent example of this is the development of an "Accomplishment Record" for attorneys.[13] The attorneys are asked to write down major accomplishments of theirs that illustrate their competence on eight performance dimensions. An example for the dimension "Using Knowledge" is in Figure 11–4. These are read and then rated by job experts, using predetermined rating scales. The final result is an "Accomplished Record" score on each performance dimension for a job applicant.

Another example is the "Preemployment Experience Questionnaire" that was developed by a large company in the communication industry.[14]

---

[13] L. M. Hough, "Development and Evaluation of the 'Accomplishment Record' Method of Selecting and Promoting Professionals," *Journal of Applied Psychology* 69 (1984), pp. 135–46.

[14] D. C. Myers and S. A. Fine, "Development of a Methodology to Obtain and Assess Applicant Experiences for Employment," *Public Personnel Management* 14 (1985), pp. 51–64.

Applicants complete the questionnaire, which contains more than 100 specific T&E questions. (There is a separate questionnaire for each job family, such as clerical, sales, and maintenance.) Responses to the questionnaire are scored, using a predetermined scoring key.

T&E requirements are likely candidates for adverse impact because not all members of society have historically had equal access to the acquisition of the relevant training and experience. Educational requirements have a more severe impact on minorities. Previous management experience requirements are often difficult for women to meet because of their historical lack of representation in managerial positions. Thus, T&E requirements should be carefully established and maintained only if they are truly necessary employment prerequisites.

References and Recommendations

References and letters of recommendation are used to assess the applicant's past job experiences and the effectiveness of the applicant in those experiences. Thus, a reference from a former employer could tell what the applicant did on a job and how well the person performed. Additionally, references often obtain a prediction from the person about the applicant's probability of success on the new job. This prediction may take into account not only previous work experience, but other factors as well.

Validity of references and recommendations

Few validation studies have been conducted on references and recommenations. Because of this, firm conclusions about their validity are difficult to draw. However, the little available validity evidence is not supportive of references and recommendations.[15] In all probability, references and recommendations tend to be mostly favorable and hence do not differentiate between good and poor job applicants. This problem might be overcome by specifying more precisely to reference providers the types of information desired and providing feedback to them on the value of the information they have provided.[16]

Legally, use of references creates potential problems of violating federal or state laws regarding privacy of, and employee access to,

---

[15] Hunter and Hunter, "Validity and Utility of Alternative Predictors."

[16] B. D. Wonder and K. S. Keleman, "Increasing the Value of Reference Information," *Personnel Administrator* 29, no. 3 (1984), pp. 98–103.

FIGURE 11-5

Guidelines for Defensible References

1. Don't volunteer information. Respond only to specific company or institutional inquiries and requests. Before responding, telephone the inquirer to check on the validity of the request.
2. Direct all communication only to persons who have a specific interest in that information.
3. State in the message that the information you are providing is confidential and should be treated as such. Use qualifying statements such as "providing information that was requested"; "relating this information only because it was requested"; or "providing information that is to be used for professional purposes only." Sentences such as these imply that information was not presented for the purpose of hurting or damaging a person's reputation.
4. Obtain written consent from the employee or student, if possible.
5. Provide only reference data that relates and pertains to the job and job performance in question.
6. Avoid vague statements, such as: "He was an average student"; "She was careless at times"; "He displayed an inability to work with others."
7. Document all released information. Use specific statements such as: "Mr. _____ received a grade of C—an average grade"; "Ms. _____ made an average of two bookkeeping errors each week"; or "This spring, four members of the work team wrote letters asking not to be placed on the shift with Mr. _____."
8. Clearly label all subjective statements based on personal opinions and feelings. Say "I believe . . ." whenever making a statement that is not fact.
9. When providing a negative or potentially negative statement, add the reason or reasons why, or specify the incidents that led you to this opinion.
10. Do not answer trap questions, such as "Would you rehire this person?"
11. Avoid answering questions that are asked "off the record."

Source: J. D. Bell, J. Castegnera, and J. P. Young, "Employment References: Do You Know the Law?" *Personnel Journal* 63, no. 2 (1984), pp. 32–36.

information.[17] A set of guidelines for minimizing the chances of these problems occurring is shown in Figure 11–5.

Application Blanks and Resumes

A typical application blank form is developed by the organization, and it requests the job applicant to provide information the organization deems important for making selection decisions. Types of information sought include education, job experiences, references, medical history, and personal data. A resume may provide the same types of information.

---

[17] J. D. Bell, J. Castegnera, and J. P. Young, "Employment References: Do You Know the Law?" *Personnel Journal* 63, no. 2 (1984), pp. 32–36.

Unlike the application blank, however, it is the job applicant and not the organization who determines what information to provide and in what format on a resume.

Validity of application blanks and resumes

Before discussing validity, it is necessary to address the issue of accuracy of information provided on application blanks and resumes. There is an obvious potential for job applicants to give distorted information, which could detract from validity and lead to erroneous selection decisions. Research indicates that distortion does in fact occur generally, and especially for information that cannot be verified or only verified at great time and expense.[18] When distortion is detected, organizations typically refuse to hire the applicant or terminate the employee if the distortion was not discovered until after the applicant had been hired.

Despite possible distortion problems, the validity evidence for application blanks is quite favorable for predicting both job performance and length of service.[19] Unfortunately, little is known about the validity of resumes. Since they may be more subject to distortion than application blanks, they should be used and treated cautiously.

Application blank information has been the object of considerable attention by the courts, and many states have passed laws limiting the types of biographical data that can be asked for job applicants.[20] Some potentially inappropriate questions for the application blanks (or the interview) and suggestions for converting them to more appropriate questions are shown in Figure 11–6.

It is not necessarily illegal to gather such information and in many instances the organization must have the information (for example, for insurance purposes and for maintaining required documentation on adverse impact). However, care must be taken to ensure that it does not inadvertently enter into the selection decision. Two ways to accomplish this are to gather the information on a form separate from the application blank before the hiring decision is made, or to obtain the information only after the hiring decision has been made.

---

[18] R. D. Broussard and D. E. Brannen, "Credential Distortions: Personnel Practitioners Give Their Views," *Personnel Administrator* 31, no. 6 (1986), pp. 129–46; Gatewood and Feild, *Human Resource Selection*, pp. 291–92.

[19] E. D. Hammer and L. S. Kleiman, "Getting to Know You," *Personnel Administrator* 88, no. 5 (1988), pp. 86–93; Hunter and Hunter, "Validity and Utility of Alternative Predictors"; Reilly and Chao, "Validity and Fairness of Alternative Employee Selection Procedures."

[20] Arvey, *Fairness in Selecting Employees*, pp. 187–222; C. M. Koen, Jr., "Application Forms: Keep Them Easy and Legal," *Personnel Journal* 63, no. 5 (1984), pp. 26–29; Gatewood and Feild, *Human Resource Selection*, pp. 277–98.

FIGURE 11-6

Suggested Conversions of Some Inappropriate Preemployment Inquiries

Inappropriate Inquiry	*More Appropriate Inquiry*
1. Do you have any handicaps?	1. Do you have any handicaps that might affect your ability to perform the duties of the job for which you are applying?
2. What is your maiden name? Have you been known by another name?	2. Have you used another last name in which your educational or employment records are filed?
3. Date of birth?	3. Are you over 18 and under 70?
4. If you served in the military, what was your discharge date?	4. What types of education and experience did you have in the military which relate to the job for which you are applying?
5. When did you attend high school? College?	5. Did you complete high school? Do you possess college degrees that relate to the job for which you are applying?
6. What is the minimum salary you are willing to accept?	6. If employed, are you willing to accept the approved salary for the job?
7. Have you ever been convicted of a criminal offense?	7. Have you, since 18, been convicted of a misdemeanor or felony, other than minor traffic violations? (Note: Each conviction will be judged in relation to time, seriousness and circumstances and will not necessarily bar you from employment).
8. List all of your clubs and/or organizational memberships.	8. List any organizations, clubs, societies or professional memberships that relate to the job for which you are applying.
9. Do you possess a valid driver's license?	9. If the job for which you are applying requires driving a state vehicle (see circular): Do you possess a valid driver's license?
10. Do you have any dependents or relatives who should be contacted in the event of an emergency.	10. Please provide the name, address, and telephone number of someone who should be contacted in the event of an emergency.

Source: D. D. Burrington, "A Review of State Government Employment Application Forms for Suspect Inquiries, *Public Personnel Management* 11 (1982), p. 59.

Health Exams

Increasingly organizations are recognizing that the health of their work forces can have an important bearing on employee effectiveness and labor costs. Employee health problems may have negative effects on the P/HR outcomes, particularly job performance and attendance. Labor costs may also be affected through increases in medical insurance and workers' compensation premiums.

One way to confront such problems is to attempt to select job applicants who are likely to pose the lowest health risks for the organization. This requires the use of various health exams in the selection process. Four are considered here: Preemployment physical exams, drug tests, AIDS tests, and genetic screening.[21]

Preemployment physical exam

This is typically a standard medical exam. In some cases it may be administered by the organization; at other times the applicant may be required to have his or her own physician conduct the exam.

The costs of regular preemployment physical exams by a physician have greatly increased. As a consequence, many organizations now use a health questionnaire instead. These questionnaires are completed at the time of application. Unless the applicant indicates serious medical problems on the questionnaire, there is no regular exam.

Drug tests

Drug tests seek to detect usage of substances such as alcohol, marijuana, and cocaine. Typically they involve examination of urine specimens. Positive test results normally lead to retesting, using the same or an alternative procedure, to confirm the initial findings. Many states have laws restricting usage of drug tests.

AIDS tests

Acquired Immune Deficiency Syndrome (AIDS) is a virus that infects people and has an incubation period that may be seven years or more. Should it become activated (present evidence suggests it does so in about 30 percent of cases), it results in death. The virus is usually transmitted to others through sexual contact, unclean needles used by intravenous drug users, or infected blood products used in transfusions. A positive test result only indicates that the person has been exposed to the AIDS virus. It does *not* indicate that the person has AIDS.

---

21 J. D. Olian, "New Approaches to Employment Screening: Body over Mind," in *Readings in Personnel and Human Resource Management*, 3d ed., eds. R. S. Schuler, S. A. Youngblood, and V. L. Huber (St. Paul: West Publishing, 1988).

Genetic screening

Because of their genetic makeup, some people are more predisposed toward certain diseases than others. And this may vary among people according to the type of disease in question. Often the onset of the disease may be triggered by exposure to certain chemical agents or toxins in the workplace. Genetic screening seeks to identify which people are more predisposed toward certain diseases. In this way job applicants may not be hired for, or placed on, jobs in which they would likely be exposed to the chemical agents and toxins to which they are especially susceptible.

Validity and other issues

Relatively little is known about the validity of the various health exams as predictors of the P/HR outcomes. This alone suggests that health exams should be used cautiously. Validity, however, is only the tip of the iceberg when it comes to health exams.

Such exams raise a host of other issues that need to be confronted when deciding whether to use health exams in the selection process.[22] Examples of these issues include (1) employee privacy rights, (2) federal (e.g. Vocational Rehabilitation Act) and state laws dealing with health and disability, (3) constitutional protections, such as the due process requirement, (4) confidentiality of obtained information, (5) labor contract provisions, (6) which job(s) to use the tests for, and (7) alternatives to testing, such as educational and employee assistance programs.

All of the above issues are quite complicated, and in many instances we are just beginning to confront them. Thus, decisions about usage of health exams should be made after careful consideration of such issues.

Employment Interview

The employment interview is a conversation with multiple purposes. Foremost among these is selection—that is, to gather information about applicants' abilities and motivations and then evaluate this information

---

[22] B. Heshizer and J. P. Muczyk, "Drug Testing at the Workplace: Balancing Individual, Organizational and Societal Rights," *Labor Law Journal* 39 (1988), pp. 342–57; L. Z. Lorber and J. R. Kirk, *Fear Itself: A Legal and Personnel Analysis of Drug Testing, AIDS, Secondary Smoke, VDTs* (Alexandria, Va.: ASPA Foundation, 1987); M. F. Masters, "Drug Testing in the Federal Sector," *Labor Law Journal* 39 (1988), pp. 312–19; D. W. Myers and P. S. Myers, "Arguments Involving AIDS Testing in the Workplace," *Labor Law Journal*, 38 (1987), pp. 582–90; M. P. Rowe, M. L. Russell-Einhorn, and J. N. Weinstein, "New Issues in Testing the Workforce: Genetic Diseases," *Labor Law Journal* 38 (1987), pp. 518–23; S. Vodanovich and M. Reyna, "Alternatives to Workplace Testing," *Personnel Administrator* 33, no. 5 (1988), pp. 78–85.

relative to job requirements and rewards. The interviewer usually also has information from other predictors, such as test scores and a completed application blank, which may serve as a basis for questioning by the interviewer. In addition, the interviewer often seeks unique information, such as the applicant's ability to communicate.

Informing the applicant about the job and organization is another purpose of the interview. Here, there may be attempts not only to inform, but also to persuade the applicant about the virtues of the job and organization (see Chapter 9). The interviewee may also use the interview to inform and persuade the organization about his/her qualities. These latter purposes are important, but the concern here is solely with the first purpose—use of the interview as a selection predictor.

Interview characteristics

Selection interviews vary along a number of dimensions.[23] Length is one. For some jobs (for example, unskilled), a brief 10- to 15-minute interview may be conducted, although considerably longer interviews are typical for higher-level jobs. Two- or three-hour interviews are not uncommon at the managerial and professional levels.

Interviews also differ in degree of *structure*. In a structured interview, all applicants are asked the same questions in the same order. There is little, if any, follow-up questioning. At the other end of the continuum is the unstructured interview. It is typically not well planned in advance, and interviewees will not be asked a common set of questions. The interviewer probes and "teases out" information from the interviewee.

Relevance of the interview to the content and requirements of the job also varies. Some interviewers ask only questions of direct relevance to the requirements and rewards of the job, such as regarding previous work experience on similar jobs and the types of rewards that were most satisfying in those jobs. Other interviewers tend to focus on more abstract issues and on attitudes about things that seem to have little job relevance (e.g., "What is the one thing in this world you would most like to do, and why?").

Interviews also differ in the number of interviewers present.[24] They are usually one-on-one in the private sector, but public-sector selection

---

[23] L. Summers, "What Makes You Think You Can Do This Job? A Look at Approaches to Selection Interviewing," *The Industrial-Organizational Psychologist* 21 (1983), pp. 15–25.

[24] D. J. Weston and D. L. Warmke, "Dispelling the Myths About Panel Interviews," *Personnel Administrator* 33, no. 5 (1988), pp. 109–11.

procedures often use group or panel interviews. Typically, there will be three interviewers on the panel, and all will actively participate in interviewing each applicant.

Finally, interviews vary in the degree to which the interviewers are required to make and record systematic evaluations of interviewees. At one extreme, no such requirements may exist. At the other extreme, the interviewer must make ratings of the interviewee on ability and/or motivation dimensions (e.g., interpersonal skills), as well as take notes about what the interviewee said and did in the interview. This latter approach is more logical, since it is then easier to subsequently compare interviewees for purposes of making selection decisions.

Validity of the employment interview

Research clearly shows that the typical interview lacks any reasonable degree of validity. It is one of the least, if not the least, valid of all predictors.[25]

This rather startling (to most people) evidence has caused researchers to try to identify factors that detract from the validity of the interview. Results of this research show that there are many such factors.[26] Examples of these factors include (1) interviewers making snap judgments about interviewees, (2) lack of interview structure, (3) lack of job-related questions, (4) weighting negative information about applicants too heavily, (5) failure to remember what the interviewee said, and (6) lack of a standardized procedure for recording evaluations of the interviewees.

Improving the employment interview

Coming out of such research findings have been attempts to alter the interviewing process to improve interview validity. Recommendations that emerge from these efforts include:[27]

1. Develop questions based on job analysis.
2. Ask the same questions of each applicant (that is, structure the interview).

---

[25] Gatewood and Feild, *Human Resource Selection;* Hunter and Hunter, "Validity and Utility of Alternative Predictors of Job Performance."

[26] F. L. Dipboye and T. M. Macan, "A Process View of the Selection/Recruitment Interview," in *Readings in Personnel and Human Resource Management*, pp. 217–32; Gatewood and Feild, *Human Resource Selection*, pp. 352–59.

[27] M. A. Campion, E. D. Pursell, and B. K. Brown, "Structured Interviewing: Raising the Psychometric Properties of the Employment Interview," *Personnel Psychology* 41 (1988), pp. 25–42; Gatewood and Feild, *Human Resource Selection*, pp. 359–63.

ILLUSTRATION 11–2

The following study is an illustration of the design, use, and evaluation of a standardized, job-relevant, interviewing procedure.

1. *The problem:* There was a need to design an interview procedure for hiring entry-level, labor-pool employees in a large paper and pulp mill.

2. *Job analysis:* Job analysis conferences were conducted with supervisors and job incumbents for 17 entry-level jobs. There were 25 knowledges, skills, and abilities (KSAs) identified that were common to all the jobs.

3. *The interview and rating scales:* A 20-question, 30-minute, structured panel interview was developed, based on the KSAs. Responses to each question were rated on a five-point, anchored, rating scale. Three of the questions, and anchored rating scales, were:

   a. Job knowledge question assessed mechanical comprehension: "When putting a piece of machinery back together after repairing it, why would you clean all the parts first?"

      (5) Particles of dust and dirt can cause wear on moving parts. Need to have parts clean to inspect for wear and damage.
      (3) Parts will go together easier. Equipment will run better.
      (1) So it will all be clean. I don't know.

   b. Simulation question assessed low-level reading ability: "Many of the jobs require the operation of a forklift. Please read this (90-word) forklift checkout procedure aloud."
      (5) Reads fluently pronouncing all words accurately.
      (3) Can read most words but hesitates.
      (1) Reads with great difficulty.

   c. Worker characteristic or willingness question assessed fear of heights: "Some jobs require climbing ladders to a height of a five-story building and going out on a catwalk to work. Give us your feeling about performing a task such as this."
      (5) Heights do not bother me. I have done similar work at heights in the past (and gives examples).
      (3) I do not think I am afraid of heights. I know that this would have to be done as part of the job.
      (1) I am afraid of heights. I would do it if absolutely necessary.

4. *The interviewers:* Many interview panel members were used. Each interview was conducted by a three-member panel, composed of two supervisors and a representative from the P/HR department.

5. *The evaluation:* To determine empirical validity, average interview ratings were correlated with total scores on a behavior-based performance appraisal rating that was made six months after date of hire. Utility and adverse impact analysis were also conducted.

6. *The results:* One hundred forty-nine of the 243 applicants were hired. The correlation between interview ratings and performance appraisal ratings for those hired was $r = .56$ ($p < .01$). Use of the interview was estimated to provide a utility gain in excess of $100,000 the first year. There was no adverse impact detected.

Source: M. A. Campion, E. D. Pursell, and B. K. Brown, "Structured Interviewing: Raising the Psychometric Properties of the Employment Interview," *Personnel Psychology* 41 (1988), pp. 25–42.

3. Develop rating scales for evaluating applicants, and anchor the scales for scoring answers with examples and illustrations.
4. Have an interview panel conduct the interviews, record answers, and rate the applicants.
5. Consistently administer the process to all applicants.
6. Train the interviewers.
7. Give special attention to utility and EEO considerations.

An example of an interviewing process that incorporates many of these suggestions, as well as its validity, utility, and EEO compliance, is shown in Illustration 11–2. As can be seen, the results of the process are quite favorable. They are also consistent with other such studies.[28] Thus, the recommendations above should receive serious consideration when designing and conducting the employment interview.

ADMINISTRATION OF STAFFING SYSTEMS

Predictor Usage

Many different types of predictors may be used in a staffing system. Usage patterns for a representative sample of 436 companies, by major job categories, are shown in Figure 11–7. As can be seen, references and interviews are by far the most extensively used. Also, with the exception of ability tests, usage levels are the same for all applicants, regardless of job category.

Choice of predictors to use for a given job or job category is governed by several factors. Especially important here are judgments about the likely utility of predictors and costs of administration (see Chapter 10). Also, the organization should consider the amount of adverse impact that might be caused by any predictor. Ideally, organizations should strive to use predictors with high utility, low cost, and no adverse impact. Reaching this ideal, however, often proves quite difficult.

Validation

It was shown in Chapter 10 that, other things equal, the greater the validity of a predictor, the greater the accuracy of selection decisions. Unfortunately, validation is seldom performed. For example, a survey of

---

[28] Examples include R. D. Arvey, H. E. Miller, R. Gould, and P. Burch, "Interview Validity for Selecting Sales Clerks," *Personnel Psychology* 40 (1987), pp. 1–12; J. A. Weekley and J. A. Gier, "Reliability and Validity of the Situational Interview for a Sales Position," *Journal of Applied Psychology* 72 (1987), pp. 484–87.

FIGURE 11-7
Selection Procedures Used for Outside Applicants to Positions in Seven Groups

	Percent of Companies						
	Unskilled Semiskilled (370)	Skilled (352)	Office Clerical (436)	Professional Technical (426)	Sales (244)	First-Level Supervisor (430)	Manager Executive (433)
Background information							
• Reference/record checks	83%	89%	92%	96%	94%	93%	94%
• Weighted application blank	8	8	8	9	7	8	8
• Investigation by outside agency	8	6	8	15	13	13	22
Interviews							
• Unstructured	72	71	72	72	72	71	71
• Structured	30	32	35	36	32	36	35
Ability testing							
• Skill performance test/work sample	9	20	73	7	1	2	2
• Mental ability test	7	11	13	9	7	6	5
• Job knowledge test	4	10	12	10	2	4	1
• Physical abilities test	4	3	*	3	—	—	—
• Assessment center	—	—	*	2	2	3	5
Other screening techniques							
• Medical examination	48	47	38	41	37	40	42
• Polygraph test/written honesty test	4	5	2	4	2	2	1
• Personality test	1	1	1	4	6	4	6
No answer/None used	2	1	—	*	2	1	1

Note: Percentages are based on the number of companies with employees in each job group.
* Less than 0.5 percent.
Source: Bureau of National Affairs, ASPA-BNA Survey No. 45—Employee Selection Procedures (Washington, D.C.: Bureau of National Affairs, 1983).

private and public organizations found that less than one fifth of them had conducted validation studies on the predictors they were using.[29] Failure to validate means that the organization does not know how effective its staffing system is in accurately identifying applicants who will be successful employees. It also means that the organization will have no evidence to use in defense of staffing discrimination charges.

Use of Multiple Predictors

The P/HR model emphasizes that each job has a set of ability requirements and rewards. Typically, these vary among jobs. Thus, predictors must be chosen to assess applicant ability and motivation relative to the requirements and rewards of the *specific job* in question.

For relatively unskilled jobs with few critical ability requirements, a single predictor may be sufficient. For more complex jobs, however, it is necessary to assess more applicant abilities through a variety of predictors. Staffing managerial jobs, for example, may involve multiple interviews, a series of specific T&E requirements, and a battery of tests.

When two or more predictors are used for a job, it is necessary to decide how scores are combined to make employment decisions. There are three possible approaches that may be taken: *multiple hurdles*, *compensatory*, and *combined*.

Multiple-hurdles approach

In a multiple-hurdles approach, each predictor serves as a hurdle the applicant must jump over before proceeding to the next one. Failure to pass any hurdle results in being rejected for the job. Underlying this approach is the assumption that the ability and/or motivation being assessed in a hurdle is so critical that inadequacy guarantees the person will be unsuccessful on the job. In other words, a lack of certain qualities cannot be compensated for by possessing other qualities.

This assumption sometimes applies for physical ability requirements. For example, adequate vision is obviously necessary for surgeons and airline pilots. With few exceptions, though, multiple hurdles should be used sparingly in staffing systems. Most jobs do not have truly absolute ability and motivation requirements.

---

[29] Bureau of National Affairs, ASPA-BNA Survey No. 45, *Employee Selection Procedures* (Washington, D.C.: Bureau of National Affairs, 1983).

Compensatory approach

As the name implies, in the compensatory approach applicants may have some characteristics that compensate for deficiencies in others. A variety of combinations of characteristics could lead to successful job performance. Thus, automatic rejection does not occur on discovery of a single deficiency. Not until completion of the selection process is a selection decision made, and it is based on information obtained from all of the predictors used.

The compensatory approach is more realistic than the multiple-hurdles approach for most requirements. Most ability and motivation characteristics can be traded off against each other insofar as they contribute to job success. Hence, use of a compensatory approach is generally to be recommended.

Combined approach

A combined approach uses both multiple-hurdles and compensatory approaches. It works like this. If a particular ability or motivation characteristic is considered essential for success, that characteristic is the first one assessed in the selection process. If deficient on the characteristic, the applicant is rejected. If not deficient, the applicant continues through the rest of the selection process, and a selection decision is made at the end of the process. In short, the combined approach starts with multiple hurdles and ends with a compensatory approach.

Selection Decisions

Both the personnel department and line management play a role in selection decisions, though line management usually makes the final selection decision. Line managers have an obvious stake in selection decisions since the selected employees will work directly for them. Consequently, they usually want an active part in decision making, particularly at later stages in the selection process when choices among applicants have been narrowed.

Although the personnel department must be sensitive to line management's needs for participation, its job is to take steps to ensure that selection decisions are made based on valid predictor information. Thus, if test scores warrant a heavy weight because of their validity, the personnel department must ensure that the test scores are considered in the final selection decisions.

Research shows that when we make decisions about other people, such as selection decisions, we may use several different heuristics (i.e., rules of thumb) to help us in making the decision.[30] This is especially likely to be the case for managers toward the end of the selection process, when the final applicants appear to be quite similar and the final selection decision is to be based on the interview. Unfortunately, these heuristics often have the effect of detracting from making the best (most accurate) selection decisions. Here, the P/HR department might well consider conducting training programs for managers in selection decision making. Some of the programs' content could focus on a description of common heuristics, the problems they create, and how to overcome them. The programs might also focus on giving managers practice with the organization's predictors and total selection system.

Training programs are often supplemented with direct control devices to ensure acceptable decision making. This requires monitoring of actual decisions by the personnel department. It may also require that a representative of the personnel department take part in all selection decisions. Such a stringent step could be justified based on equal employment opportunity compliance, as well as on maintaining accuracy in selection decision making.

Standardization

In standardized staffing systems, the gathering and evaluating of applicant information for a given job are performed uniformly. Standardization is desirable because it helps ensure that the staffing system will be reliable—that applicant information will be gathered and evaluated in a consistent manner. In turn, this may help improve the validity of the staffing system.

At a minimum, standardization requires that the same types of information be gathered from all applicants. In addition, conditions surrounding the administration of predictors must also be standardized. For example, when a test is administered, all applicants should be read the same set of directions and have the same time limit.

Finally, when applicant information is evaluated, standardized scoring systems are needed. This usually presents no problem with written tests, since they have a scoring key. Standardization may be more problematic with other predictors. For example, when an organization solicits references or letters of recommendation, the information is usually evaluated

---

[30] V. L. Huber, G. B. Northcraft, and M. A. Neale, "Foibles and Fallacies in Organizational Staffing Decisions," in *Readings in Personnel and Human Resource Management*, eds. Schuler et al., pp. 193–205.

in a highly subjective, nonstandardized fashion. This raises the distinct possibility that applicants may be evaluated on noncomparable bases. For example, one applicant's letter may focus on previous job experience, and another's may deal with personality characteristics.

Perhaps the greatest need for standardization occurs in the case of the employment interview, given its generally low reliability and validity. Illustration 11–2 above exemplifies a standardized approach to interviewing.

Equal Employment Opportunity

Under most circumstances, equal employment opportunity laws and regulations make it necessary for the personnel department to assume substantial responsibility for administration and control of the total external staffing process. Failure to comply with the laws and regulations can result in discrimination charges being filed against the organization, which may lead to costly litigation and settlements.

The personnel department evaluates the staffing process, job by job, for possible discrimination and *adverse impact* (see Chapter 10). This includes comparisons of *selection rates* for race and sex subgroups, as well as comparisons of minorities' and women's *utilization rates* relative to their availability in the labor market.

When staffing appears to be causing adverse impact, the personnel department must formulate strategies for dealing with it. One strategy involves the development and implementation of affirmative action plans (see Chapters 3 and 8). Another alternative is to justify adverse impact with validity evidence for the selection technique(s). Mechanisms for, and regulations applying to, the gathering of such evidence are discussed in the previous chapter. A final alternative is to use predictors with less adverse impact.

The strategies may be used in combination. For example, assume that a particular test for the job of management traineee is having an adverse impact on women. The organization can conduct a validation study to determine if the test is predictive of job success. However, even if the test is valid, the organization may seek to overcome its adverse impact through affirmative action. The latter requires special efforts to recruit more women applicants, with particular attention given to finding recruits who are likely to pass the test.

Regardless of strategies chosen, the personnel department is responsible for the implementation and use of staffing procedures that are consistent with the relevant laws and regulations. Crucial here is training for people who make staffing decisions—including members of the personnel department as well as managers.

Finally, the personnel department must monitor the staffing systems of the organization to ensure that they remain consistent with staffing goals, policies, and applicable regulations. The previously discussed regulations on selection procedures and on affirmative action contain numerous requirements for such monitoring (see Chapters 3, 8, 9 and 10).

Applicant Reactions to Staffing

Applying for a job and going through the selection process is an important event to job applicants. Naturally, they will form opinions about, and reactions to, the treatment they receive during the process. Such impacts may influence the probability they would accept a job offer, the "image" they form of the organization, whether they recommend to others that they apply for jobs with the organization, and the perceived fairness of the staffing system in terms of equal employment opportunity concerns.

Research has identified steps the organization can take to increase the chances of favorable applicant reactions.[31] These include:

1. Using personable recruiters who are knowledgeable about the job and organization.
2. Making prompt follow-ups with applicants after they have completed the selection process.
3. Gathering only applicant information that is highly job related.
4. Avoiding the collection of excessive information from applicants.
5. Providing applicants with accurate information about various job attributes (pay, location, type of work, etc.).

SUMMARY

To obtain samples of job applicants' abilities and motivations, organizations use many predictors. These include ability tests, personality and interest tests, work sample tests, honesty tests, training and experience (T&E) requirements, references and recommendations, application blanks, health exams, and the employment interview.

Substantial empirical validity evidence has accumulated for many of these predictors. Generally speaking, validity evidence is strongest for

---

[31] M. M. Harris and L. S. Fink, "A Field Study of Applicant Reactions to Employment Opportunities: Does the Recruiter Make a Difference?," *Personnel Psychology* 40 (1987), pp. 765–84; S. L. Rynes, H. G. Heneman III, and D. P. Schwab, "Individual Reactions to Organizational Recruiting: A Review," *Personnel Psychology* 33 (1980), pp. 529–42; M. S. Taylor and T. J. Bergmann, "Organizational Recruitment Activities and Applicants' Reactions at Different Stages of the Recruitment Process," *Personnel Psychology* 40 (1987), pp. 261–86.

ability tests, work sample tests, and application blanks. Relative to such predictors, the remaining predictors are of more questionable validity, particularly the interview. In some cases, though, there are examples of how validity could be improved, such as in the case of the interview and T&E requirements.

Any of the above predictors might have adverse impact on women and minorities. When this occurs, regulations require that the organization either justify it based on validity evidence or take steps to reduce it. Ideally, only predictors with relatively high validity and no adverse impact would be used in the organization's staffing systems.

Administration of staffing systems is the responsibility of the P/HR department, with input and participation by line management. Many issues are involved. Decisions need to be made about which predictors to use for each job or job category. Validation of the predictors is highly desirable, though often not done in practice. When multiple predictors are used for a job, the organization must establish a multiple-hurdles, compensatory, or combined staffing process. Accompanying this are clear specifications of the roles that line management will play in staffing and job offer decisions. This is especially important because of equal employment opportunity concerns, as well as the desirability of operating very standardized systems. Finally, all of this is based, in part, on recognition that job applicants can and do have definite reactions to staffing practices of the organization.

DISCUSSION QUESTIONS

1. Why might such a small percentage of organizations validate their selection techniques?
2. Why is it not advisable to have all selection decisions made by the personnel department?
3. What are some things an organization could do to improve the effectiveness of its interview process?
4. Why would an organization want to use a variety of selection techniques as opposed to only one? Are there any disadvantages to using multiple measures?
5. What are some potential limitations on the use of work samples?
6. Why do applicants form reactions to the staffing process itself? Should they not just be concerned about the job for which they are applying?

Case for Part Five

FOSSIL CHEMICAL

Background

Fossil Oil Corporation, one of the largest and most profitable of the energy conglomerates, began the 1980s with revenues just under $50 billion, assets of $26 billion, earnings close to $2 billion, and capital outlays of nearly $3 billion. Although clearly the dominant portion of Fossil's business lies in petroleum and other fossil fuels, they have recently undergone a major diversification effort into the chemical industry. This pursuit, characteristic of all the major oil producers, has been profitable for Fossil Corporation since the early 1960s. Over the last six years, Fossil Chemical has contributed an average of 6.2 percent to Fossil Corporation's total net income on only 4.1 percent of their total revenues. Fossil Chemical's profits have grown steadily at about 8 percent annually, and prospects for the future look bright.

Fossil Oil Corporation is sparing no expense to help develop and foster Fossil Chemical as a top-notch company in every way. Recently, the major management thrust has been to make the chemical division more capital intensive through facilities automation and computerization. In fact, over the last three years, there have been drastic changes in both the number and kinds of jobs being performed by employees. Most of this change has been piloted at a plant near Centralia, Illinois, positioned at the mouth of the Ohio and Mississippi Rivers. The latest change at the Centralia plant involves the job transformations of the system analyzer position.

The System Analyzer

Because chemical production involves highly integrated process technologies, someone is needed that can monitor all of the individual components simultaneously. The system analyzer is primarily responsible for this monitoring function. It is one of the most prestigious non-managerial jobs in the entire plant, and is becoming even more so.

FIGURE 1
Performance Dimensions

Maintaining spares and supplies.
1. Anticipates future need for parts and supplies and orders them.
2. Stocks parts and supplies in an orderly fashion.
3. Maintains and calibrates test equipment.

Troubleshooting.
4. Applies calibration standards to verify operation by subjecting the system to known standards.
5. Decides whether problem is in the sensor, in the processor, in the process stream, and/or in the sample system.
6. Uses troubleshooting guides in system manuals to determine the problem area.
7. Uses test equipment to diagnose problem.
8. Makes a general visual inspection of analyzer system as a first troubleshooting step.
9. Replaces components such as printed circuit boards and sensors to see if problem can be alleviated.

Revisions and new installations.
10. Makes minor piping changes such as size, routing, and additional filters.
11. Makes minor electrical changes such as installing switches, wires, and making terminal changes.
12. Uses common pipefitting tools.
13. Uses common electrical tools.
14. Reads installation drawings.

Record keeping.
15. Maintains system files showing historical record of work on each system.
16. Maintains loop files which show the application of the system.
17. Updates piping and instrument drawings if any changes are made.
18. Maintains Environmental Protection Agency records and log books.
19. Disassembles analyzers to perform repairs on-site or back to shop.
20. Replaces damaged parts such as filters, electronic components, light source, lenses, sensors, and values.
21. Uses diagnostic equipment such as oscilloscopes, ohmmeters, and decade boxes.
22. Tests and calibrates repaired equipment to ensure that it works properly.
23. Reads and follows written procedures from manuals.

Routine maintenance.
24. Observes indicators on systems to ensure that there is proper operation.
25. Adds reagents to systems (e.g., phosphoric acid, persulfate solution).
26. Decides whether the lab results or the system is correct regarding results (i.e., resolves discrepancies between lab and analyzer results).
27. Performs calibrations.

Formerly the position was classified as a semiskilled maintenance technician, but as the plant has become more computer automated, the requirements for the system analyzer job have become much more extensive. Knowledge of pneumatics, hydraulics, computer programming and electrical wiring are all increasingly critical aspects of this job. As these trends continue, the three men who currently hold the position will be incapable of performing adequately in the future. It is estimated that within two years, the tasks, duties, and responsibilities of the system analyzer will have changed over 65 percent. For these reasons, the decision was made to recruit and select three new people for the rapidly transforming position.

Job Analysis and New Position Analysis

The plant manager, Robert Cole, four senior staff engineers, and two personnel consultants formed a selection committee. They first conducted a job analysis for the new position of system analyzer. Although they had to project into the future regarding the specific nature of the job, they collectively felt they had created an accurate depiction of the requirements for someone who would occupy the position. Figure 1 shows a list of the major performance dimensions of the job accompanied by a subsample of specific tasks characteristic of each dimension.

From this list of tasks, the selection committee then delineated a set of personal qualities required for anyone who would hold the system analyzer position. These qualities included the 12 ability dimensions shown in Figure 2. The numbers beside the ability dimensions indicate the tasks (see Figure 1) to which they are related. The abilities marked with an asterisk (*) were considered by the committee to be "critical." Any

FIGURE 2
Abilities and Tasks

---

* Finger dexterity (3, 4, 7, 9, 10, 11, 12, 13, 19, 20, 21, 22, 25, 27)†
* Mechanical comprehension
  (3, 5, 6, 8, 9, 10, 12, 13, 7, 14, 19, 20, 22, 23, 24, 27, 11, 17)
* Numerical ability (11, 3, 4, 24, 10, 21, 12, 13, 14, 27)
* Spatial ability (2, 4, 5, 9, 10, 11, 14, 19, 20)
* Visual pursuit
  (3, 4, 5, 6, 7, 8, 9, 10, 11, 14, 16, 17, 19, 20, 21, 22, 27)
* Detection (2, 3, 5, 6, 8, 9, 10, 14, 19, 20, 23, 7)
  Oral comprehension (1, 2, 5, 6, 26, 7, 8, 9, 19, 21, 25)
  Written expression (1, 15, 16, 17, 18)
  Deductive reasoning
  (1, 5, 3, 6, 7, 8, 9, 4, 10, 11, 14, 19, 20, 21, 22, 23)
  Inductive reasoning
  (1, 3, 5, 6, 7, 8, 9, 10, 11, 19, 21, 20, 22, 2, 26, 27)
  Reading comprehension (3, 6, 14, 7, 22, 23, 21, 9, 27)
  Reading scales and tables (3, 4, 7, 8, 9, 21, 23, 24, 27, 2, 6, 14)

---

* Abilities considered critical by the committee.
† Task numbers identified in Figure 1.

applicant not scoring well on each of the critical dimensions would be considered unqualified for the job.

Anticipated Selection Process

The committee hoped to gain "new blood" for the redesigned system analyzer job and, therefore, wanted to recruit externally for the best available talent they could find. However, as a matter of policy, management also was deeply committed to the idea of promoting from within. After deliberation, they decided to recruit both internally and externally for the new position. They also decided to especially encourage current system analyzers to "reapply" for the job.

Because there was a two-year lead time before the new transformed position would be put in place, the committee was very careful not to include in the selection battery any skills or knowledge that could reasonably be trained within that two-year period. Only aptitude or ability factors were incorporated into the selection process, rather than achievement tests.

In a private session, a few of the selection committee members admitted candidly that they had serious doubts whether any woman or black currently in the relevant labor market would have requisite credentials to be competitive for the position. The three present system analyzers were white males. However, since Fossil Corporation had a rather unenviable history of employment discrimination charges, the decision was made to do no unnecessary prescreening of applicant qualifications, previous experience, and so on. This strategy was thought to encourage minorities and women to apply for the new position irrespective of their prior employment history.

It should be noted, however, that there was some concern about prejudice if a woman or black were to get the job. Word through the grapevine was that many did not consider a woman or black suitable for such a prestigious position. Moreover, several comments had been heard that a woman would not get down into the treatment tanks to check gauge readings.

All of these factors, taken together, made for a very sensitive selection process. Fossil's management, however, was dedicated to making the procedures and decisions fair and objective.

Applicants

Fifty-six employees applied for the new position of system analyzer. Twenty-one were female; 15 were black. Only two of the three current system analyzers reapplied for the new position. For now, the company

FIGURE 3

Primary Pool of Candidates

Candidate	Race	Sex	Internal or External Recruit	Finger Dexterity	Mechanical Comprehension	Numerical Ability	Spatial Ability	Visual Pursuit	Detection	Oral Comprehension	Written Expression	Deductive Reasoning	Inductive Reasoning	Reading Scales/Tables	Reading Comprehension	Total Score
Anderson, A.	W	M	—	80	60	67	66	67	62	74	80	67	72	75	65	835
Anderson, S.	W	M	E	67	78	74	70	76	62	80	69	71	76	78	82	883
Baldwin, T.	W	M	—	83	78	78	76	69	71	90	70	74	72	88	92	941
Bittner, D.	W	F	E	92	62	88	89	96	85	90	94	93	89	97	87	1062
Daniels, J.	B	F	E	87	97	89	61	94	93	75	90	85	96	85	80	1032
Egan, M.	W	M	—	92	88	72	72	78	79	69	76	81	83	81	78	949
Erwin, R.	B	F	E	93	80	76	98	76	88	93	92	93	78	81	92	1040
Fleming, L.	W	M	—	82	82	79	75	77	73	72	80	81	77	70	80	928
Gray, D.	W	F	E	82	76	76	71	69	80	62	76	75	74	78	67	886
Hastings, J.	W	F	E	65	75	72	67	80	74	62	47	66	67	60	80	815
James, T.	W	M	E	82	87	85	85	83	88	81	80	80	83	84	80	998
Johnson, J.	B	M	—	87	97	63	89	93	90	91	85	86	96	88	89	1054
Klein, H.	W	M	E	83	84	89	91	90	82	86	88	85	84	90	89	1031
Lopez, P.	W	M	E	89	81	77	93	92	91	88	78	98	80	80	76	1021
Miller, B.	W	M	E	91	82	78	93	80	94	89	77	95	77	81	92	1041
Myers, R.	B	M	—	76	72	78	81	80	72	73	77	75	79	82	82	927
Rom, D.	W	M	—	80	85	84	81	81	80	89	88	84	86	81	82	1001
Snell, S.	W	M	E	82	78	76	71	69	80	62	76	76	70	71	67	878
Weimes, J.	B	M	—	67	71	70	76	76	62	81	69	71	76	78	82	879
Wright, P.	W	M	—	80	60	57	56	57	62	74	80	69	72	75	65	807

Note: Scores are standardized and can range from 0 to 100 points.

had decided that an overall total score of 800 on the 12 tests would be the cutoff score in order for an applicant to be seriously considered for the system analyzer position. This cutoff resulted in the primary pool of 20 candidates shown in Figure 3. It should be noted that although each of the aptitude tests has been published, standardized (100 points possible for each test), and validated on other jobs, there are no normative data or validity information for the specific job of the system analyzer. Therefore, the defensibility of the test battery is consequently founded solely upon content validity judgments. Issues regarding the final cutoff scores and method for combining the multiple predictors are problematic for the selection committee.

Questions

1. How would you go about conducting a job analysis for a job that does not yet exist?

2. Do you think the ability dimensions chosen for selection are content valid? What other kinds of predictors might be generally useful for employee selection?

3. What reasons did the selection committee have for selecting only those factors that could not be acquired in a two-year training program? Were these reasons sound?

4. Should the concern for women getting down into the dirty treatment tanks have been a selection issue? How might you include this factor into a selection battery?

5. For the abilities termed "critical," what score should someone receive to be considered scoring "well" on that test (i.e., cutoff scores)? How should the test scores be combined (e.g., compensatory, multiple hurdle, combination)?

6. Which three candidates appear most qualified? What are your reservations if any about this recommendation?

7. Would this test battery and selection procedure be defensible in court?

PART SIX

Internal Staffing and Development

12

Internal Staffing and Career Management

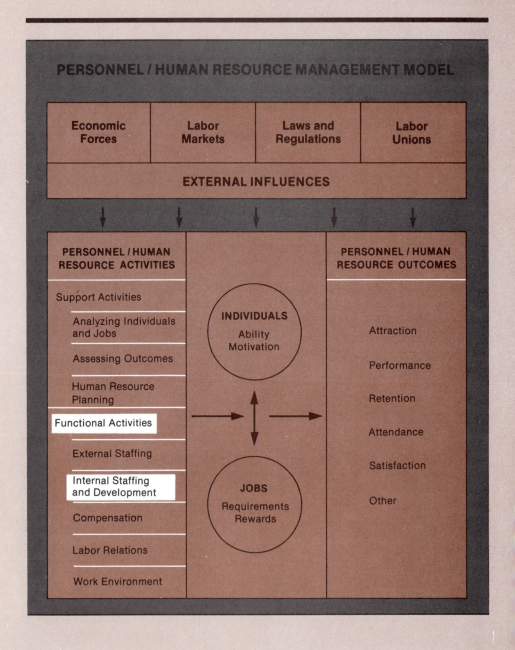

PERSONNEL / HUMAN RESOURCE MANAGEMENT MODEL

Economic Forces	Labor Markets	Laws and Regulations	Labor Unions

EXTERNAL INFLUENCES

PERSONNEL / HUMAN RESOURCE ACTIVITIES

Support Activities

   Analyzing Individuals and Jobs

   Assessing Outcomes

   Human Resource Planning

Functional Activities

   External Staffing

   Internal Staffing and Development

   Compensation

   Labor Relations

   Work Environment

INDIVIDUALS
Ability
Motivation

JOBS
Requirements
Rewards

PERSONNEL / HUMAN RESOURCE OUTCOMES

Attraction

Performance

Retention

Attendance

Satisfaction

Other

After reading this chapter, you should be able to speak to the questions posed in each of the following personnel/human resource incidents.

1. You are the director of the consumer products division of a medium-sized corporation. Your division has 20 middle-management jobs to fill during the coming year. Company policy says you must fill these jobs from within. But it is up to you to decide which of the more than 300 people in the division will be candidates for the positions and on what basis the final selections will be made. What options do you have in these matters? Which options would you choose? Why?

2. You manage a state hospital for the mentally retarded. Your division will begin phasing out the hospital in 6 months and within 18 months it will be closed entirely. You must develop a plan for dealing with the nearly 300 employees of the hospital. What would you like to know about the current policies of the state regarding such matters? Why? Assuming whatever policies you prefer, indicate what you would put in your plan, and why.

3. The head of a department with 48 employees comes to the P/HR department to see you about a problem. It seems that three of the superintendents who work under her are blocking promotion opportunities. The three men are all over 58 years of age; one is 66. All are doing acceptable work, although none is considered promotable. The department head is worried that she might lose some of her better younger employees if something is not done, and it is clear that she would really like to have at least a couple of the superintendents transferred, fired, or retired. What factors would you consider in deciding how to handle this situation? What would you do? Why?

4. To date your company has formulated no policy with respect to the use of temporary employees. As a consequence, you have a patchwork of practices in the various divisions and departments; some have no temporaries, while others use temporaries liberally (for as much as 25 percent of the total work force in some cases). Many of the temporaries come through agencies, others are hired from local colleges and universities, while still others have been enticed out of retirement. As an internal staffing specialist in the company, you have become concerned about this situation and are toying with the idea of recommending to top management that the company establish a uniform policy on the matter. Why might you be concerned? What factors would you consider in deciding whether to recommend a uniform policy? If you did recommend a uniform policy, what would it be? Why?

5. Jane Jones, a promising young engineer, comes to you as her supervisor and expresses concern about her future in the organization. She thinks she might like to get into management and is wondering about her chances of doing so within the next couple of years. You tell her not to worry about it. She is a good engineer, and the company has a history of taking care of its own. Later, you wonder about the way you handled the situation. What might you have done differently? What, if anything, should you have done differently? Why?

Recruitment and selection are only parts of organizational staffing activities. Many job vacancies that occur are not filled by new recruits, but by current employees through promotions and transfers. Further, job vacancies are not always the issue. Recurringly, as was shown in Chapter 8, employers face the prospect of employee surpluses rather than shortages and thus must either lay off some employees or find other, more creative, ways of avoiding or dealing with these surpluses.

Also, from time to time employers face performance and related behavioral problems that are amenable to staffing solutions, most commonly transfers to other jobs and, in extreme cases, discharge. And finally, employers' concerns about organizational vitality (including opportunities for promotions among younger employees) influence their choices of retirement options.

Figure 12–1 summarizes these internal staffing objectives and activities, and provides a framework for much of this chapter.

The chapter also deals with two other internal staffing issues. One concerns the use of alternative staffing or work scheduling arrangements, sometimes to meet special business needs and sometimes to accommodate employee preferences. The former includes use of temporary employees of various types and the latter such things as part-time work, flextime, and compressed workweeks. The remaining issue of interest in this chapter is career management, which is actually the flip side of internal staffing. Companies rely on career management to rationalize their internal staffing decisions and employees' responses to the choices they face. Comprehensive career management has three components: (1)

FIGURE 12–1

Internal Staffing Objectives and Activities

	Objectives			
Activities	Filling Job Vacancies Internally	Eliminating Employee Surpluses	Correcting Behavioral Problems	Renewing Organizational Vitality
Internal allocation processes				
• Promotion	×			
• Transfer	×	⊗	⊗	
Separation processes				
• Layoff (and alternatives)		×		
• Discharge (and alternatives)			×	
• Retirement		⊗		×

×—Activity is the primary means of attaining the objective.

⊗—Activity is a secondary means of attaining the objective.

career planning to help ensure that employees have career options that make sense from both an organizational and individual point of view, (2) career development to help prepare employees to make the most of the opportunities they are likely to have, and (3) career counseling to provide employees with the assistance they need to prevent or cope with career crises.

Internal staffing and career management are primarily undertaken to enhance organizational effectiveness in two ways. First, they are used to control employee flows and thus meet the organization's human resource requirements (see Chapter 8). Second, they are used to upgrade the general quality level of employees.[1] This is accomplished primarily by making the best possible matches between individuals and their jobs, not just once—as with external staffing—but several times over their careers. This happens when employers make a real effort to identify and select the best available employees for promotional and transfer opportunities, and, in the event of layoffs, identify and retain the highest performers and those with the most promising career prospects. It is also facilitated when employers face up to performance and other behavioral problems constructively using performance improvement and discipline programs where necessary, and ultimately discharging employees whose performance fails to improve.

It is also logical to assume that effective internal staffing and career management practices to some extent help attract high-quality employees and to a large extent help retain them by satisfying both their short- and long-term career needs, although the evidence on these points is less than conclusive.[2]

Of course, employers do not have a free hand in making internal staffing and career management decisions; as always (as the P/HR model shows), they are either helped or hindered by a variety of environmental factors. Growing businesses offer more career opportunities, and less threat of layoffs than declining ones. Firms operating in loose labor markets have more discretion than those operating in tight ones. Various pieces of legislation and regulations must be adhered to, most notably Title VII, EO 11246, and the Age Discrimination in Employment Act. And labor unions, where present, almost always push to have length of

---

[1] J. W. Boudreau, "Utility Analysis," in *Human Resource Management: Evolving Roles and Responsibilities, ASPA/BNA Handbook of Human Resource Management*, vol. 1, ed. L. Dyer (Washington, D.C.: Bureau of National Affairs, 1988).

[2] W. T. Markham, S. L. Harlan, and E. J. Hackett, "Promotion Opportunity in Organizations: Causes and Consequences," in *Research in Personnel and Human Resource Management*, vol. 5, ed. K. M. Rowland and G. R. Ferris (Greenwich, Conn.: JAI Press, 1987), pp. 261–73.

service (i.e., seniority) take precedence over performance in promotion, transfer, and layoff decisions.

In most companies, line managers are the ones ultimately responsible for making internal staffing decisions. When job vacancies develop, for example, managers one or two levels higher in the organization often decide who will be considered for these jobs (although some companies permit employees to nominate themselves) and almost always decide who will be offered the jobs. Conversely, when jobs become redundant, top management usually assumes responsibility for determining whether layoffs will occur and if so (in the absence of a relevant collective bargaining agreement) how they will be carried out. Lower-level managers then use these guidelines to decide who will actually be laid off. Responsibility for career management is usually jointly shared by employees and their managers.

The primary role of the personnel department in all this is to recommend policies and procedures, develop programs where needed, and provide guidance to line managers. Sometimes, human resource specialists assume partial responsibility for administering certain internal staffing and career management programs (e.g., outplacement and career planning, development, and counseling). And these staff specialists are also usually responsible for monitoring the internal staffing decisions made by line managers to ensure that policies and procedures are followed, that laws and labor contracts are adhered to, and that the desired results are being attained.

INTERNAL STAFFING

Filling Job Vacancies

When job vacancies are anticipated, several policy decisions must be made. A basic one involves the relevant candidate pool, that is, which jobs will be filled from outside through recruitment and selection (see Chapters 9, 10, and 11), which by moving current employees, and which by some combination of these. A second decision, where vacancies will be filled from within, is whether movement can occur only within each employee group (e.g., assistant manager to manager) or also across groups (e.g., production worker to first-level supervisor). A third decision is whether there will be cross-functional mobility (e.g., personnel to sales). A fourth is whether vacancies will be filled only through promotions (i.e., moves involving increased authority, responsibility, and pay) or if lateral transfers will also be used.

FIGURE 12–2

Typical Patterns of Promotions and Lateral Moves

From (Time 1) \ To (Time 2)	Manufacturing				Engineering				Losses	Total
	A	B	C	D	A	B	C	D		
Manufacturing A	.80								.20	1.00
B	.15	.75							.10	1.00
C	.05	.15	.60						.20	1.00
D			.30	.50					.20	1.00
Engineering A					.85				.15	1.00
B		.05			.10	.70			.15	1.00
C			.05		.05	.15	.60		.15	1.00
D						.05	.25	.55	.15	1.00
New entrants			.20†	.40*				.40†		1.00

* Of these, 30% are internal promotions from the hourly ranks, 70% are outside hires.

† All outside hires.

In practice, policies vary on all four points.[3] The patterns demonstrated in the transition matrix in Figure 12–2 are not atypical (recall the discussion of transition matrices in Chapter 8). Vacancies in the lowest (or entry) level job in engineering are filled entirely through new hires (mostly from college campuses). Vacancies in the lowest level job in manufacturing (i.e., first-level supervisors) are filled partly from outside and partly by promoting production workers up from the ranks. Vacancies in the second-level job in manufacturing—superintendent—are filled partly from outside and partly from inside by promoting first-level supervisors. Otherwise, nearly all vacancies in the second, third, and fourth-level positions are filled through promotion within functions. Exceptions are the few lateral moves from engineering to manufacturing in jobs B and C.

---

[3] Markham et al., "Promotion Opportunity," pp. 242–43. Also, for examples of actual company policy statements in this area, see Bureau of National Affairs, *Employee Promotion and Transfer Policies*, Personnel Policies Forum Survey No. 120 (Washington, D.C.: Bureau of National Affairs, 1978), pp. 27–40.

Most observers favor the use of internal moves whenever possible to fill upper-level jobs.[4] Cited advantages cut across most of the major P/HR management outcomes. The attraction of new employees is easier because they can be offered opportunities beyond the first job. Ability improves because the records of internal candidates are more readily judged against organizational selection critieria and because internal candidates have knowledge of organizational practices, which lowers job-learning time. Motivation improves because promotional opportunities are valent rewards to many people. Performance increases because both ability and motivation are improved. Retention is increased because employees can see opportunities to advance, and satisfaction increases when advancement does in fact materialize.

However, there are some potential problems. Exclusive reliance on internal movement may not always be possible, especially if an organization is growing rapidly or if it has done a poor job of preparing employees to assume new responsibilities. Also, it may not always be desirable, since it can lead to excessive inbreeding, foster the feared "organization man/woman," and cause stagnation due to the absence of new blood with fresh ideas.

Large, geographically dispersed organizations face yet another policy issue. To what extent will geographic transfers from one location to another be encouraged? Historically, such moves have always been rare among technical, clerical, and blue-collar employees. However, they have been anything but rare among professional and, especially, managerial personnel. The number slowed significantly in the early 1980s in response to an increase in costs (especially mortgage interest rates and real estate), the increasing number of dual career couples (now more than one half of the total), and a heightened awareness of quality of work-life issues. But the number of transfers rebounded sharply in the mid- and late-80s. Apparently the need is there, and most organizations have learned to live with the costs and to assuage employee concerns (more on this later).

Whatever the relative advantages and disadvantages, virtually all organizations of any size fill at least some job vacancies from within. This necessitates the development of policies and practices in at least five important areas: (1) recruiting internal candidates, (2) developing and validating predictors, (3) decision making, (4) administration, and (5) evaluation and control.[5]

---

[4] Markham et al., "Promotion Opportunity," pp. 231–42.

[5] M. London and S. A. Stumpf, *Managing Careers* (Reading, Mass.: Addison-Wesley Publishing, 1982), Ch. 7.

Identifying and recruiting internal candidates

Recruiting procedures for internal job candidates fall on a continuum from closed to open. In closed systems, the primary responsibility for locating candidates rests with the manager with the vacancy. The search may be conducted informally, based on the manager's personal knowledge of potential candidates. More broadly, other managers who may have potential candidates among their subordinates might also be included. A more formal process may come into play where replacement charts (see Chapter 8) are prepared. These charts can be consulted to identify individuals who have been designated as backups for the vacated job. Even more elaborate are the skills inventories used in a few organizations. These consist of computerized records of employees' education, work history, and key abilities and can be "searched" for matches whenever vacancies occur.[6]

Closed systems of internal recruitment, however formal, give managers considerable power. Those with vacancies determine which employees (if any) will receive serious consideration for the jobs, and those supervising potential candidates determine whether to allow their subordinates to be seriously considered.

Open systems reduce some of this power. Under such systems—often called "job posting"—managers with vacancies openly publicize them in designated areas and publications. Employees meeting the minimum qualifications are free to apply, sometimes without even having to inform their supervisors. All applicants receive full consideration and, usually, those who are unsuccessful are told why. This helps direct their development efforts should they want to try again.[7]

The decision about whether to lean toward a closed or an open-system approach to internal recruitment is based primarily on the staffing objectives an organization chooses to emphasize and on the organization's predominant norms and values. Speed and organization control are maximized through a closed system. An open system introduces an element of employee participation and more equal opportunity for women and minorities, but probably at some additional administrative cost.[8]

---

[6] B. D. Dunn, "The Skills Inventory: Second Generation," *Personnel*, September–October 1982, pp. 40–44.

[7] For a description of the job posting system used at Dow Jones & Co., see R. K. Broszeit, "If I Had My Druthers . . .: A Career Development Program," *Personnel Journal*, October 1986, pp. 84–90; see also, H. Z. Levine, "Job Posting Practices," *Personnel*, November–December 1984, pp. 48–52.

[8] Markham et al., "Promotion Opportunity," pp. 242–45.

Organizational preferences for internal recruitment systems appear to vary depending on the employee group involved. Among private employers, surveys show a preponderance of relatively closed systems among managerial employees and of relatively open ones among office and clerical and, especially, blue-collar employees. Usage of the two is about equal among professional and technical employees. Relatively open systems are more prevalent in public than in private employment and where employees are unionized.[9]

Developing and validating predictors

Many of the predictors used in selecting among internal (or among a combination of internal and external) job candidates are the same ones used in the external staffing process (see Chapter 11). Because internal job candidates already have organizational experience, certain additional predictors also may be used; these include seniority, performance and promotability ratings, and assessment center results.[10]

Seniority.   Seniority refers to an employee's accumulated service with an organization, subunit (e.g., a plant), department, or occupational group (e.g., electrician). The relative importance to be accorded seniority vis-à-vis other possible predictors in internal allocation decisions is an issue that every employer must face.

In unionized situations, the matter is resolved through collective bargaining. Generally, management favors a relatively moderate emphasis on seniority, while unions take the opposite view. More than 80 percent of all union contracts require that at least some consideration be given to seniority in promotion decisions; around one half state that it must be the major or only factor considered. Where employees are not unionized, the tendency is to consider seniority, but only informally, and to give it less weight. Even among managers, seniority appears to be only a minor factor in many promotion decisions.[11]

Many good arguments can be advanced in favor of considering seniority in internal staffing decisions. It can be measured reliably and relatively accurately; it may have content validity, since it reflects on-the-job experience; and it rewards loyalty. Still, content validity is

---

[9] Bureau of National Affairs, *Employee Promotion*, pp. 2–6.

[10] Markham et al., "Promotion Opportunity," pp. 245–53; London and Stumpf, *Managing Careers*, pp. 212–31.

[11] Bureau of National Affairs, "Basic Patterns in Seniority Provisions," *Daily Labor Report*, March 25, 1983, E1–E2; K. G. Abraham and J. L. Medoff, "Length of Service and Promotions in Union and Nonunion Work Groups," *Industrial and Labor Relations Review* 38 (1985), pp. 408–20; and D. Q. Mills, "Seniority versus Ability in Promotion Decisions," *Industrial and Labor Relations Review* 38 (1985), pp. 421–25.

questionable where previous jobs held do not resemble the one to which a move is proposed; and loyalty is not the same as job performance, nor does it necessarily reflect the ability or motivation to perform on a new job. Among a group of recently promoted female sewing machine operators, for example, interjob similarity (as well as performance on the former job) was found to be a valid predictor of performance on the new job, but seniority *per se* was not.[12]

Further, research has shown that excessive reliance on seniority often results in the identification of less qualified candidates. One study showed that 97 percent of the promotions in a unionized plant went to the most senior candidate, even though in 57 percent of the cases this was not the highest performer.[13] Even at the managerial level it has been found that significant percentages of high performing and high potential candidates are passed over in favor of those who have greater seniority.[14]

Generally, the courts have upheld the sacrosanct stature of seniority in promotion decisions under section 703(h) of Title VII of the Civil Rights Act. The effect of this in the case of women and minorities has been to exempt seniority from the usual requirement of demonstrated validity, even when there is evidence of adverse impact. An accused employer need show only that such a system was not established or was not applied with discriminatory intent.[15]

Performance and promotability.   Where there is a choice, most organizations give at least some credence to past performance when making promotion and transfer decisions. This tendency is so natural that it has the potential for being badly misused. A good record of performance on one job is not necessarily predictive of success on a future job, particularly where the two jobs do not share many common duties or responsibilities.

To get around this problem, many performance appraisal systems include ratings of employee promotability (and sometimes long-term

---

12 M. E. Gordon, J. L. Cofer, and P. M. Mccullough, "Relationships among Seniority, Past Performance, Interjob Similarity, and Trainability," *Journal of Applied Psychology* 71 (1986), pp. 518–21; and M. E. Gordon and W. J. Fitzgibbons, "Empirical Test of the Validity of Seniority as a Factor in Staffing Decisions," *Journal of Applied Psychology* 67 (1982), pp. 311–19.

13 Abraham and Medoff, "Length of Service."

14 Mills, "Seniority Versus Ability."

15 See Bureau of National Affairs, *Affirmative Action Today: A Legal and Practical Analysis* (Washington, D.C.: Bureau of National Affairs, 1986). For a lucid description of the definitive *Johnson* v. *Transportation Agency* case (which was decided after the preceding reference was published), see S. Taylor, Jr., "Supreme Court, 6–3, Extends Preferences in Employment for Women and Minorities," *New York Times*, March 26, 1987, p. 1. For a more general review of the issues involved, see M. E. Gordon and W. A. Johnson, "Seniority: A Review of Its Legal and Scientific Standing," *Personnel Psychology* 35 (1982), pp. 255–80.

potential) in addition to performance. In some situations (mostly managerial ones), periodic meetings of executives are held to update or verify
performance, promotability, and potential ratings; this is common in
succession planning programs (see Chapter 8).[16] In a similar vein, some
observers advocate the use of multiple-rater consensus procedures involving teams of superiors and peers.[17]

When used as predictors in promotion decisions, rating procedures, of
whatever type, must be held to the same standards of reliability and
validity as are standard predictors in selection decisions. This is both a
logical and a legal necessity. These are difficult standards for performance appraisals to meet, since they are not usually designed to predict
success on a future job; and indeed such ratings have not always fared
well in this context in court (see Chapter 6).

Assessment centers.   Assessment centers provide a means of systematically gathering and processing information concerning the promotability (as well as the development needs) of employees.

Illustration 12–1 describes a fairly typical assessment center and illustrates several important points about this approach.[18]

1.   Those assessed are usually lower- to middle-level managers.
2.   Multiple predictors are used, at least some of which are work
     samples (for example, in-baskets, leaderless group discussions). In
     this case, the predictors were based on careful job analysis, but
     this is not always true, thus raising legitimate questions of content
     validity.[19]
3.   Assessments are made off site to ensure standardized conditions.
4.   Multiple raters are used. They are carefully trained, and their
     ratings are made using standardized formats. All of this helps to
     ensure interrater reliability.

---

[16] For examples, see L. Dyer, R. A. Shafer, and P. J. Regan, Jr., "Human Resource
Planning at Corning Glass Works," and L. Dyer and N. O. Heyer, "Human Resource Planning
at IBM," both in *Human Resource Planning: A Case Study Reference Guide to the Tested
Practices of Five Major U.S. and Canadian Companies,* ed. L. Dyer (New York: Random
House, 1986).

[17] M. R. Edwards and J. R. Sproull, "Team Talent Assessment: Optimizing Assessee
Visibility and Assessment Accuracy," *Human Resource Planning* 8, no. 3 (1985), pp. 57–71.

[18] R. Klimoski and M. Brickner, "Why Do Assessment Centers Work: The Puzzle of
Assessment Center Validity," *Personnel Psychology* 40 (1987), pp. 243–60; S. Zedeck, "A
Process Analysis of the Assessment Center Method," in *Research in Organizational Behavior,*
vol 8, eds. L. L. Cummings and B. Staw (Greenwich, Conn.: JAI Press, 1986); V. Boehm,
"Assessment Centers and Management Development," in *Personnel Management,* eds. K. M.
Rowland and G. R. Ferris (Boston: Allyn and Bacon, 1982), pp. 327–62; and G. C. Thornton III
and W. C. Byham, *Assessment Centers and Managerial Performance* (New York: Academic
Press, 1982).

[19] P. R. Sackett, "Assessment Centers and Content Validity: Some Neglected Issues,"
Personnel Psychology 40 (1987), pp. 13–25.

ILLUSTRATION 12–1

An Assessment Center

The Company:

Gino's, Inc., an operator of fast-food shops with $200 million annual sales. Expanded rapidly in 1970s; in early years of expansion many managers were put in jobs they couldn't handle. Needed a way to better evaluate managerial potential. Settled on assessment center approach. Began in 1972; in first three years conducted 22 sessions with 264 participants.

The Program:

Patterned after AT&T (as many are). Features:

Two and one-half days at a secluded conference center.

Twelve participants per session. Participants are restaurant managers being assessed for potential to be area managers. Participants are selected by their supervisors, but attendance is voluntary.

Six observers per session. All are company managers who have participated in an earlier center and have received four days training in interviewing skills, behavior observation, and report writing.

Participants are assessed on 27 dimensions selected on the basis of job analysis. These include planning skills, subordinate development skills, management style, sensitivity, stress tolerance, and seven different communications skills.

Participants complete seven exercises and a personal interview.

Observers combine individual ratings into one final report per assessee. Final reports go to the participants and their supervisors. Final reports are important, but on-the-job behavior is still the most important factor in supervisory judgments of promotability.

Results have not been validated. Managerial reactions are generally favorable.

Cost $5,000 to $6,000 each session, not including participants' time.

A Session:

Prior to attending: Participants fill out background form involving self-evaluations and career plans. Supervisors provide performance ratings.

Day 1: In the morning, participants have personal interviews and prepare a seven-minute oral presentation concerning new products. In the afternoon, the oral presentations are made before five peers, two observers, and a videotape camera. Presentations are discussed by the group, and all participants rank each other's performances. Also, in the afternoon, two groups of six each participate in a group decision-making exercise. Again, performances are discussed and ranked. In the evening, the videotapes made earlier are discussed.

Day 2: In the morning, participants complete a 30-item in-basket exercise. In the afternoon, they participate in a creative-writing exercise in which they have three hours to write an essay on a broad topic relating to the company's future. In the evening, small groups work on four cases drawn from actual company experiences.

Day 3: In the morning, participants discuss their earlier performances on the in-basket and group decision-making exercises. The session ends at noon, but observers stay on for two days to discuss their ratings, to reach consensus, and to write their final reports.

Source: Adapted by permission of the publisher from K. Amundsen, "An Assessment Center at Work," *Personnel* 52, no. 2 (1975), pp. 29–36. © 1975 by AMACOM, a division of American Management Associations. All rights reserved.

5. Raters must reach consensus on ratees wherever possible.
6. Final reports may be used to make decisions about both internal selection and employee development, although assessment center results are rarely the only input in either area.
7. Assessment centers are costly, running from $600 to $5,000 per assessee, but the benefits have the potential to outweigh these costs by a substantial margin.

The precise number of organizations using assessment centers is unknown; estimates have exceeded 2,000.[20] A survey of 166 private and public organizations showed that between 10 and 14 percent were using assessment centers to identify supervisory talent among office, plant, and professional-technical employees.[21] Use is most common among large organizations, such as AT&T, IBM, GE, J. C. Penney, and Sears, Roebuck & Co.

Considerable research has been conducted to determine the reliability, validity, and fairness of assessment centers (unlike other promotion predictors). Most has been supportive.[22] Interrater reliability is generally high. Validity coefficients as high as 0.50 to 0.60 have been reported; the mean and median coefficients reported are between 0.30 and 0.40. Studies have generally found equal validities for men and women and for majority and minority candidates.

Despite these favorable results, the reliability, validity, and fairness of assessment centers in all situations cannot be assumed. They must be demonstrated through careful research in each unique situation. So, too, must one consider the utility (costs and benefits) of this relatively expensive approach.

Decision making

In theory, selecting among internal job candidates is the same as selecting among external job candidates. Thus, the procedures discussed in Chapter 10 with respect to combining and applying data gathered through various predictors are applicable and are not repeated here.

Frequently, the decision-making process with respect to internal placements is far less systematic than is desirable.[23] Common problems include the use of unvalidated predictors, inconsistent use of data across

---

[20] Boehm, "Assessment Centers."

[21] Bureau of National Affairs, *Employee Promotion*, p. 24.

[22] B. B. Gaugler, D. B. Rosenthal, G. C. Thornton III, and C. Bentson, "Meta-Analysis of Assessment Center Validity," *Journal of Applied Psychology* 72 (1987), pp. 493–511.

[23] Markham et al., "Promotion Opportunity," pp. 252–53.

decisions and even across candidates in the same decision situation, and the introduction of irrelevant data (such as politics, personality, and personal favoritism) into the decision-making process.

Administration

Once selected, internal candidates receive an offer stating such things as new salary, starting date, and relocation process and assistance. Organizational needs—expediency, for example—must be balanced against those of the individual and his or her family. Often the process is routine, involving a standard pay increase and a simple move to the next machine or a nearby office.

Geographic relocations can be particularly disruptive and, as noted earlier, expensive.[24] Many organizations routinely pay for one or two house-hunting trips to the new location, for moving household goods, and for temporary living expenses while employee and family are in transit. Becoming more common are such things as assistance in selling the employee's house (some companies will even buy it at a fair market value if it fails to sell within a certain period of time), low-cost loans to help with a down payment on a new house, mortgage differentials to offset the gap between the old and new rates, and housing-cost differentials to help offset higher taxes or living expenses in the new location (for a few years). Not all employers offer all of these forms of financial assistance, of course. Still, a recent survey showed that on average these items cost employers nearly $33,000 per move.[25]

Another, increasingly important, relocation inducement is job-hunting assistance for employee spouses. Sometimes this is as simple as a few phone calls by the personnel director at the receiving location. Other times it involves a referral to a local employment agency or headhunter. In several cities, relocation counseling centers have been set up by local chambers of commerce or other civic groups to help find jobs for spouses as well as to provide assistance with house hunting, locating suitable schools for children, and the like. Most operate at no charge to the employer or employee.[26]

---

[24] C. C. Pinder and K. G. Schroeder, "Time to Proficiency Following Job Transfers," *Academy of Management Journal*, 30 (1987), pp. 336–53; and C. C. Pinder and G. A. Walter, "Personnel Transfers and Employee Development," in *Research in Personnel and Human Resource Management*, vol 2, eds. K. M. Rowland and G. R. Ferris (Greenwich, Conn.: JAI Press, 1984).

[25] A. Layton, "Relocation: Consider the Service First, Not Price," *Personnel Journal*, February 1988, pp. 81–93.

[26] A. Trippel, "Relocation: Spouse Assistance Programs—Relocating Dual Career Families," *Personnel Journal*, October 1985, pp. 76–78; and K. F. Groh, "Counseling Centers Ease Adjustment to a New City," *Personnel Journal*, June 1984, pp. 88–92.

As mentioned earlier, financial and other forms of relocation assistance appear to have been generally successful in overcoming employee reluctance to move. Whether the payoff is worth the increasing costs is an interesting issue that seems not to have received much systematic assessment.

Evaluation and control

Monitoring of promotions and transfers can take many forms. In the short run, organizations follow up on each decision to ensure that established policies and procedures are followed. In the longer run, the monitoring of individual careers over time helps to assess whether worthy individuals, and especially women and minorities, are being regularly promoted or transferred as openings occur.

Still another approach takes place at the organizational level. The issue here is to determine if the general pattern of movements experienced over time are those expected, given existing personnel policies and/or collective bargaining agreements. One study that used transition matrices (such as the one in Figure 12-2) to trace internal movements in three firms over several years found that actual practices deviated from stated personnel policies and prevailing union contracts in many ways. Employees were hired from outside to fill jobs that were supposed to be filled only from within. Promotions occurred outside designated channels. Patterns of movements differed between whites and blacks and between men and women over time. These deviations reflected significant changes in organizational human resource requirements and in external labor market conditions, as well as tradition in defining typically "male" and "female" jobs.[27]

This is not to suggest that these organizations would have been better off had they rigorously adhered to existing policies and contracts (except, of course, in the case of women and minorities). Determining the costs and implications of the deviations would be the next step in evaluation. It is clear, however, that simply formulating policies and developing procedures is not enough. It is equally important to assess actual events against expected results and to correct dysfunctional deviations on a timely basis.

---

[27] T. A. Mahoney and G. T. Milkovich, "Internal Labor Markets: An Empirical Investigation," *Proceedings of the 32nd Annual Meeting of the Academy of Management*, 1972, pp. 203–6.

Eliminating Employee Surpluses

When human resource planning (HRP) suggests that an organization's labor costs are (or will be) out of line—or that product, technological, or other changes will result in the elimination of some jobs—the resulting human resource strategy can take many forms. Perhaps the most common approach is to declare some portion of the work force surplus, to be removed from the payroll through temporary or permanent layoffs. This is not the only possible approach, however. A major policy issue that nearly every organization must face or negotiate with the union is whether layoffs are to be thought of as a first or last resort. A related issue, where the policy is one of layoff-avoidance, is the nature of the alternatives that will be tried.[28]

A handful of U.S. corporations—probably no more than fifty—has "full-employment" policies with consequent commitments to shun layoffs.[29] A few others—surveys suggest the number may be as high as 10 percent—have policies or have signed labor contracts with provisions calling for layoffs only as a last resort and after several specified alternatives are invoked.[30] Many more undoubtedly have informal policies eschewing layoffs whenever possible, especially among employee groups that represent substantial company investments and that are difficult to replace.

The reasons are fairly obvious. First, many find it emotionally difficult to put people out of work, even temporarily. Second, employers can often "buy" greater employee flexibility (in adjusting to technological change, for example) when employees are not afraid of losing their jobs. Third, layoffs are costly. Employers lose at least some of their investments in the laid-off employees. In addition, there are more tangible costs. Figure 12–3 shows an example of these costs compiled for a six-month layoff of 134 production workers based on the experience of three manufacturing firms.[31]

---

[28] P. Osterman, "Turnover, Employment Security, and the Performance of the Firm," in *Human Resources and the Performance of the Firm*, eds. M. K. Kleiner, R. N. Block, M. Roomkin, and S. W. Salsburg (Madison, Wis.: Industrial Relations Research Association, 1987), pp. 275–318.

[29] L. Dyer, F. F. Foltman, and G. T. Milkovich, "Contemporary Employment Stabilization Practices," in *Human Resource Management and Industrial Relations: Text, Readings, and Cases*, eds. T. A. Kochan and T. A. Barocci (Boston: Little, Brown, 1985); and J. M. Rosow and R. Zager, *Employment Security in a Free Economy* (Elmsford, N.Y.: Pergamon Press, 1984).

[30] Osterman, "Turnover, Employment Security"; and Bureau of National Affairs, *Layoff and Unemployment Compensation Policies*, Personnel Policies Forum Survey No. 128 (Washington, D.C.: Bureau of National Affairs, March 1980).

[31] D. L. Ward, "The $34,000 Layoff," *Human Resource Planning* 5, no. 1 (1982), pp. 35–41.

FIGURE 12-3

Costs of Laying Off 135 Employees

Efficiency losses	$ 48,600
Cushioning payments	70,200
Administrative costs	6,075
Termination pay	79,650
State U.I. Comp. taxes	429,000
Total	$633,525

Source: D. L. Ward, "The $34,000 Layoff," *Human Resource Planning* 5, no. 1 (1982), pp. 35–41.

Efficiency losses ($48,600) represent lost production resulting from bumping (i.e., 484 employees who were not laid off had to be moved to other jobs because of the seniority provisions in labor contracts). Cushioning payments ($70,200) result from a contract provision protecting for 13 weeks the wages of employees bumped to lower-paying jobs. Clerical overtime and charges for the medical exams given to laid-off workers who had handled hazardous chemicals accounted for the bulk of the administrative costs ($6,075). Severance payments, referred to here as "termination pay," are significant ($79,650). By far the largest cost item, however, is the increase in state unemployment insurance taxes over what would have been paid had no layoff occurred: $429,000 spread over three years. Total cost to the employer: more than $600,000 (nearly $5,000 per laid-off employee).

There is reason to believe that in some circumstances the benefits of layoffs to employers are not worth the costs incurred.[32] A recent study conducted in the federal government, for example, found that the budgetary savings from layoffs were exceeded by the cost of those layoffs in six of the eight agencies studied. In half of these instances, the margin was more than $1 million.[33]

And, of course, there are costs to employees. A major one is the difference between wages that could have been earned and the level of unemployment compensation received (typically a drop of between 50 and 70 percent of wages and a loss of fringe benefits). In addition, there may be serious health problems, both physical and mental, that sometimes incur significant medical costs.[34]

---

[32] Osterman, "Turnover, Employment Security."

[33] U.S. General Accounting Office, "Reductions in Force Can Sometimes Be More Costly to Agencies Than Attrition and Furlough" (Washington, D.C.: U.S. General Accounting Office, July 24, 1985).

[34] For a vivid account of these difficulties, see A. Slote, *Termination: The Closing of the Baker Plant* (Ann Arbor, Mich.: Institute for Social Research, Survey Research Center, University of Michigan, 1969, reissued 1977).

Despite the costs and trauma involved, layoffs are a common phenomenon in the United States. Good data are difficult to come by, but surveys suggest that about half of all employers have laid off at least some employees at least once. Often the results are dramatic. During the downswings of the 1980s, for example, three to four million employees in a variety of industries were hit by layoffs. Some of these layoffs were temporary, but many were the permanent result of industrial restructuring, technological change, and a general need for businesses to pare labor costs in an effort to become more competitive with foreign firms.

Layoffs

Personnel professionals are the ones usually responsible for developing procedures governing layoffs, except in those cases where the issues are fully dealt with in a collective bargaining agreement. Areas that are covered include employee identification, notification, reassignments, and benefits and assistance.

Identifying employees for layoffs. As in the case of promotions, seniority and merit are the two criteria most commonly applied in layoff decisions.

And again, unions prefer seniority. Management rarely opposes its use, although the two parties often differ on the relative weight it should receive. Traditionally, about 90 percent of the labor contracts in the United States have required that seniority be used to some extent to determine order of layoff; nearly 60 percent have made it the sole criterion.[35] Unions also prefer that seniority units be relatively wide (e.g., covering a whole plant or geographic area) to protect the most senior workers irrespective of job assignments. Managements tend to prefer narrower units to minimize the efficiency losses and cushioning payments that can result from bumping across departments or jobs (see Figure 12–3). About one third of collective bargaining agreements covering 1,000 or more workers in the United States call for seniority units that cut across plants in cases of layoff.[36]

Merit is probably the governing factor in most nonunion situations, although seniority is rarely ignored. In one fairly typical company, for example, the layoff procedure covering nonunion engineers specifies the use of both merit and seniority to identify three groups of employees: (1)

---

[35] Bureau of National Affairs, *Basic Patterns in Union Contracts* (Washington, D.C.: Bureau of National Affairs, 1983).

[36] *Major Collective Bargaining Agreements: Plant Movement, Interplant Transfer, and Relocation Allowances*, Bulletin 1425–1430 (Washington, D.C.: Bureau of Labor Statistics, U.S. Department of Labor, 1981).

a protected group, including those with critical skills who have satisfactory or better performance records; (2) a dispensable group, consisting of those with unsatisfactory performance records; and (3) a swing group, which contains all other employees arrayed in order of seniority in their departments.

Layoffs, like other personnel decisions, can be done in a discriminatory manner. Further, they can pose a serious threat to the attainment of affirmative action goals and timetables in many organizations. This results when there are disproportionately higher layoff rates among women and minorities who, because they are newly hired, have relatively low seniority. Attempts by employers to achieve utilization rates after layoffs equal to those attained before by protecting less senior women and minorities have led in some cases to legal challenges by more senior white males who have been laid off. In cases where union and management have negotiated bona fide seniority systems neither established nor used with the intent to discriminate against women and minorities, the courts have recently tended to uphold the systems—even in the face of a deleterious affirmative action effect.[37]

In cases involving layoffs based on merit, however, organizations are on weaker ground for two reasons. First, merit is far more subjective than seniority both conceptually and as it is usually measured. Second, many companies fail to keep adequate records to support claims of poor performance, let alone the inability to perform whatever work may remain once layoffs occur.[38]

Notifying employees of layoff.   Advance notification of layoffs (particularly through plant closings) is a hotly debated issue. Some argue that employees should be notified of impending layoffs well in advance to help squelch rumors and reduce anxiety. Others contend that such advance notice hamstrings managerial decision making, results in slowdowns designed to stretch the available work, and increases absenteeism as employees take time off to search for new jobs. Unfortunately, there is very little research on this issue. One study, conducted among blue-collar employees in four plants, found no evidence that advance notice resulted in negative effects on either productivity or absenteeism.[39] Nonetheless, the debate goes on.

Notification practices vary widely. In general, organizations tend to

---

[37] Bureau of National Affairs, *Affirmative Action Today.*

[38] G. V. Barrett and M. C. Kernan, "Performance Appraisal and Terminations: A Review of Court Decisions Since *Brito* v. *Zia* with Implications for Personnel Practices," *Personnel Psychology* 40 (1987), pp. 489–503.

[39] R. Hershey, "Effects of Anticipated Job Loss on Employee Behavior," *Journal of Applied Psychology* 56 (1972), pp. 273–75.

give earlier warnings to salaried (exempt) than to hourly (nonexempt) employees. One week seems to be minimal for managerial, professional, technical, and clerical employees, with the norm being two weeks or longer (and often much longer). Same-day notice exists in some cases for blue-collar employees, although one to two weeks is more common.[40]

Employers are finding that they have increasingly less discretion in such matters. During the mid-80s a few states passed laws effectively mandating the period of advance notice, usually at 60 days. More important, the Worker Adjustment and Retraining Notification Act of 1988 requires most employers with 100 or more employees to provide at least 60 days notice of intention to downsize or close an operating unit or facility if the move is expected to: (1) result in significantly reduced working hours, layoffs of six months or more, or permanent terminations and (2) affect one third or more of the unit or facility's work force (or 500 or more employees irrespective of the size of the work force). In addition to the affected employees, notification must also go to the labor unions that represent these employees (if any) and to public officials in affected communities.

Reassignments.   After a layoff, some of the retained employees usually must be reassigned to new jobs. Where employees are unionized, bumping by seniority is common. Through bumping, as noted earlier, a relatively modest layoff can lead to a number of very costly lateral moves and demotions. Where discretion is possible, therefore, management generally prefers to maintain maximum flexibility to minimize the number of reassignments and to make them based on ability rather than seniority.

Benefits and assistance to laid-off employees.   Termination or severance pay is fairly common; surveys show that it is offered by about one half to two thirds of medium-sized and large employers. Somewhat fewer offer outplacement assistance, most commonly for managerial employees. Outplacement assistance can mean nothing more than assisting employees in registering with the state employment service or helping them prepare resumes. In full-scale programs, however, experienced counselors are brought in to work with laid-off employees to help them work through the trauma of job loss and to guide their subsequent job-search efforts.[41]

---

[40] Accurate data on advance notice are impossible to obtain because of the wide variety of interpretations given to the term in various studies. For a good overview, see S. P. Brown, "How Often Do Workers Receive Advance Notice of Layoffs?" *Monthly Labor Review*, June 1987, 13–17.

[41] Bureau of National Affairs, *Severance Benefits and Outplacement Services*, Personnel Policies Forum Survey No. 143 (Washington, D.C.: Bureau of National Affairs, 1986); H. Z. Levine, "Outplacement and Severance Pay Practices," *Personnel Journal*, September 1985, pp. 13–21.

In a very small number of highly visible industries (e.g., autos and steel) unions have been successful in negotiating supplementary unemployment benefits (SUB). In these cases, laid-off union members receive ongoing payments from an employer-financed fund to augment what is received through unemployment compensation. Payments are based on seniority and are available only for a specified period of time.

Since the passage of the Consolidated Omnibus Reconciliation Act (COBRA) in 1986 (see Chapter 16), employers have been required to continue employees' health care coverage even after layoffs, sometimes for as long as 36 months, depending on the circumstances. In addition, a few employers continue to provide life insurance coverage and other fringe benefits during layoffs. Many protect the seniority rights of laid-off employees for up to a year or more in case they are recalled. Recall typically occurs in reverse order of layoffs. Generally, it has been the labor unions that have taken the lead in negotiating benefits and other protections for laid-off employees.

Alternatives to layoffs

Layoffs meet the objective of reducing labor costs but, as noted, not without inducing other kinds of costs. Furthermore, they run the risk of decimating a work force that might well be needed as business conditions improve. For these reasons, and because they consider it the "right thing" to do, some employers, as previously mentioned, routinely manage in a manner designed to avoid layoffs.[42]

As shown in Figure 12–4, these employers use a variety of alternatives designed to manage both human resource requirements (i.e., labor demand) and human resource availabilities (i.e., labor supply) (see Chapter 8), and to do so when business is booming as well as when it is in a state of fluctuation or actually declining. In general, human resource requirements are evened out on the up side by shunning seasonal or short-run work, avoiding sharp increases in workload, and allocating some work to contractors. On the downside, requirements can be "artificially" propped up by calling back contracted work, producing for inventory rather than immediate sale and, in extreme cases, taking on such make-work projects as building upkeep, which tend to be deferred when business is good.

On the human resource availabilities side, the goals are, first, to avoid adding any more new people than is absolutely necessary during the good times and, second, to use alternative methods of spreading the

---

[42] Dyer et al., "Contemporary Employment"; and Rosow and Zager, *Employment Security*.

FIGURE 12–4

Alternatives to Layoffs

Focus	Actions Taken When Output Is		
	Increasing	Variable	Declining
To manage human resource requirements (demand)	Avoid business that appears to be short run or cyclical. Gear up slowly (IBM, LE, Lilly), Contract out some work (HP, IBM, Lilly)	Call in contracted work (HP, IBM, Lilly). Move work to people (IBM). Stretch productivity improvement programs. Pressure suppliers for more reliable deliveries (LE).	Call in contracted work (HP, IBM, Lilly). Produce for inventory (LE). "Create" work (HP, LE, Lilly).
To manage human resource availabilities (supply)	Add new jobs only as a last resort (HP, IBM, LE, Lilly). Use overtime (LE). Hire temporaries (all). Train to meet the future (HP, IBM, Lilly).	Move people to work/train—sometimes with ultimatum: Take it or leave it (all).	Freeze hiring (all). Cut overtime (all). Lay off temporaries (all). Encourage voluntary leave of absence, vacations (DG, HP, IBM). Encourage voluntary terminations (all). Tighten performance standards (all). Share the work—short week, fortnight, month (HP, LE). Encourage voluntary retirement (all). Cut pay (HP).

Note: In parentheses are examples of companies using the various approaches. DG is Data General Corp., HP is Hewlett Packard, IBM is International Business Machines, LE is Lincoln Electric, and Lilly is Eli Lilly.

Source: L. Dyer, F. Foltman, G. Milkovich, "Contemporary Employment Stabilization Practices" in *Human Resource Management and Industrial Relations: Text, Readings, and Cases*, eds. T. Kochan and T. Barocci (Boston: Little, Brown, 1985), pp. 203–14.

available work when business is bad. In the first case, effective HRP (see Chapter 8) and control can help prevent overhiring, as can the scheduling of overtime among current employees and the hiring of temporary employees. The use of temporary employees, in particular, has become an increasingly popular option in recent years. Sources include temporary help agencies, housewives and students, and even an organization's pool of retirees. As noted later in this chapter, such sources are usually tapped to staff temporary upsurges in business or to work on special projects.[43] Another slightly different twist is to use the good times to train employees for the flexibility that will be needed when times get tough.

As conditions worsen, employers managing to avoid layoffs typically follow an incremental approach. Initially, a hiring freeze is imposed (i.e., employees who leave are not replaced, a concept known as "attrition"), overtime is cut, and temporary employees are released. If this is not enough, employees may be asked to volunteer to take accrued vacations or leaves of absence or to resign (often with severance pay). Also, performance standards may be tightened to get rid of the so-called deadwood.

In extreme cases, induced early retirement, work sharing (e.g., four day workweeks, with the lost income offset to some extent in some states by unemployment compensation), or pay cuts may be resorted to. Recently, for example, when hard times hit the computer industry IBM was forced to reduce its work force and labor costs. It was able to do so without violating its practice of full employment, however. The most radical step was to temporarily sweeten the corporation's retirement plan (see Chapter 16). Under the arrangement, employees were permitted to retire up to five years earlier than usual with considerably enhanced pension checks. About 12,000 employees took advantage of the plan which, when combined with a hiring freeze and normal attrition, allowed the company to pare employment by about 16,000 over a two-year period (from a base of about 240,000 employees in the United States). Other measures taken by IBM to avoid layoffs included the elimination of overtime, the termination of temporary employees, calling back contracted work, encouraging employees to take accrued vacation, and prodigious amounts of training and nearly 20,000 personnel reassignments (mostly from staff and factory jobs into marketing, sales, and programming). The total costs of these measures is unknown, as is the

---

[43] "Flexible Scheduling and Staffing Helps Companies Meet Business Demands and Improve Employee Satisfaction: Report of the 1987 ASPA/CCH Survey," *Human Resource Management* (Washington, D.C.: Commerce Clearing House, June 26, 1987).

ILLUSTRATION 12-2

Using Union-Management Cooperation to Avoid Layoffs

The Situation

Xerox Corporation, facing increased competition and needing over $3 million in cost savings to become competitive, proposed to subcontract the manufacture of selected components, thereby closing a department and laying off 180 employees.

The Solution

Building on earlier cooperative efforts with management, the union (Local 14A of the Amalgamated Clothing and Textile Workers Union) proposed a joint union-management Study Action Team to search for cost savings and thus save the jobs. An eight-member team (six hourly employees, one engineer, and one manager) was established and given training, as well as the autonomy and staff assistance needed to analyze all aspects of the production process. The team held weekly meetings with a policy group made up of top managers and union leaders, solicited suggestions widely, and spent countless hours investigating and analyzing proposals. The process continued for six months.

The Results

The Study Action Team identified $3.7 million in cost savings ($3.2 million had been the target). Involved were such recommendations as stabilizing employee headcounts, redesigning jobs, tightening work standards, reducing scrap, and reducing overhead. Henceforth, employees would work in self-managing work teams (see Chapter 19), taking full responsibility for output, scheduling, purchasing, inspection, and repairs.

Management accepted the proposal, the changes were adopted over an eight-month period, and all 180 jobs were saved. Additional Study Action Teams were established in three new areas.

Source: P. Lazes and T. Constanza, "Cutting Costs without Layoffs through Union-Management Collaboration," *National Productivity Review*, Autumn 1983, pp. 362–70.

---

full value of the benefits; the payroll savings alone, however, amount to about $700 million per year.[44]

In general, the courts have ruled that early retirement plans, such as the one at IBM, are permissible under the Age Discrimination in Employment Act so long as they are truly voluntary and not designed with discriminatory intent.

Another approach to avoiding layoffs is to encourage employee ingenuity in locating new markets, developing new products, and/or finding other ways to cut costs. Illustration 12–2 describes a joint venture between Xerox and the Amalgamated Clothing and Textile Workers

---

[44] M. A. Harris, "A Lifetime at IBM Gets A Little Shorter for Some," *Business Week*, September 29, 1986, p. 40.

Union that was able to generate more than $3 million in cost savings and save 180 jobs.

Correcting Behavioral Problems: Employment-at-Will and Discharge

There are occasions when employees fail to meet performance standards or to abide by policies, procedures, and rules governing appropriate conduct on the job. Thus, it is necessary to develop, or negotiate where a union is present, means for coping with such situations.

Methods that are commonly applied can be classified into four categories: (1) preventive (such as better selection or promotion procedures), (2) corrective (such as training, counseling), (3) the use of rewards (such as praising improved behavior), and (4) the use of punishments or sanctions.[45] The last includes the use of discharge (otherwise known as "dismissal," "termination," or "firing"), an internal staffing solution that is the "capital punishment" of employment.

It is estimated that in the United States each year more than three million employees are discharged.[46] Despite the numbers, most discharges come hard and only as a last resort (more on this later). Managers and supervisors find them distasteful and difficult to do, and dismissed employees are increasingly successful in challenging their terminations through government agencies and the courts.

Withering away of employment at will

Under the "employment at will" doctrine, employers have historically been deemed free to fire employees at will. A Tennessee court decision in 1894 stated: "All may dismiss their employee(s) at will, be they many or few, for good cause, for no cause, or even for cause morally wrong. . . ." The doctrine still stands, but its effects have been eroded over the years in a number of ways.[47]

The Railway Labor Act (1926) and the National Labor Relations Act (Wagner Act, 1935) make it illegal to fire (or otherwise discriminate against) employees for engaging in union activities. Title VII of the Civil

---

[45] T. R. Mitchell and C. A. O'Reilly III, "Managing Poor Performance and Productivity in Organizations," in *Research in Personnel and Human Resource Management*, vol 1, eds. K. M. Rowland and G. R. Ferris (Greenwich, Conn.: JAI Press, 1983).

[46] J. Stieber, "Most U.S. Workers May Be Fired under the Employment-at-Will Doctrine," *Monthly Labor Review* 107 (1984), pp. 34–38,

[47] D. J. Koys, "The Employment-at-Will Doctrine: A Proposal," *Loyola University of Chicago Law Journal* 17, no. 2 (1986), pp. 259–74; S. M. Abbasi, K. W. Hollman, and J. H. Murrey, Jr., "Employment-at-Will: An Eroding Concept in Employment Relationships," *Labor Law Journal* 38, no. 1 (1987), pp. 261–79.

Rights Act (1964) forbids discharging employees on the basis of race, color, religion, national origin, or sex. Persons over the age of 40 are protected under the Age Discrimination in Employment Act (1967). The Occupational Safety and Health Act (1970) forbids the discharge of employees for filing complaints or charges with OSHA. Some states have passed laws protecting employees from dismissals for "whistle blowing" (that is, for bringing to light illegal activities by their employers). Federal, state, and local laws often state that government employees can be fired only for "just cause," and many unions have negotiated similar provisions in their labor contracts.

Recently, some courts have begun to interpret laws and legal concepts in ways that extend just cause protection.[48] These decisions fall in three categories. First are those that overturn dismissal decisions judged to be contrary to public policy (for example, those based on refusals to commit illegal acts ordered by employers). Second are situations in which the courts decide that employers have entered into implied contracts with their employees (for example, by using in their employee handbooks and personnel policies such phrases as "permanent employees" and "dismissal only for just cause"). Third are cases where employers are judged to have acted in bad faith or in a retaliatory manner (for example, by terminating long-service employees who have recently moved to new locations fully expecting to be kept on).

Increasingly, discharged employees are taking their former employers to court for wrongful discharge and winning, often with very large settlements. (The average settlement in California as far back as 1983 was over $500,000.)[49]

These developments have served to make it difficult and potentially expensive to fire employees. Many employers have reviewed existing policies and practices, or instituted new ones, to ensure that all dismissal decisions are at least legally defensible. This has led to a spate of books, articles, and seminars on managing employee discharges.[50]

Managing discharges

Employers interested in maintaining the right to terminate unsatisfactory employees should remove from all company documents (e.g., help-

---

[48] D. J. Koys, "State Court Disparity on Employment-at-Will," *Personnel Psychology* 40 (1987), pp. 565–77.

[49] K. B. Noble, "When Walking Papers Lead to Court," *New York Times*, October 13, 1985, p. E5.

[50] See, for example, T. J. Condon and R. H. Wolff, "Procedures That Safeguard Your Right to Fire," *Harvard Business Review*, November–December 1985, pp. 16–19; and J. G. Allen, ed., *Employee Termination Handbook* (New York: John Wiley & Sons, 1986).

wanted advertisements, recruiting brochures, employee handbooks) any unintentional statements of implied job security. Additionally, company policies reinforcing the right of discipline and discharge in cases of demonstrated incompetence or rule breaking should be established and communicated. Managers should be trained to resist the temptation to retaliate when employees report acts of questionable ethics or legality.

The ability to successfully dismiss for incompetence requires a well-designed, well-managed system of performance appraisal (see Chapter 6).[51] It also requires that, except in extreme cases, corrective action precedes dismissal. Thorough documentation must be maintained in all instances that may eventually result in discharge.

Virtually all employers, both union and nonunion, maintain systems of progressive discipline.[52] Figure 12–5 shows some of the more commonly included infractions and the percentages of responding firms that apply various types of penalties. The penalties range in severity from an oral warning or reprimand, through a written warning, to suspension without pay and, ultimately, dismissal (hence the term *progressive*). Relatively minor infractions (such as absenteeism), if not resolved, typically involve all four steps; more serious ones (such as theft) invoke immediate suspension or even dismissal.

Most companies require supervisors to consult with at least one other company official before taking disciplinary action. Multiple consultations typically are required in the case of the more severe penalties; most companies require the approval of personnel managers and, often, top-line managers before dismissals become final.

Among nonunion employers, about three quarters of all progressive discipline procedures contain an appeals procedure. Among those that are unionized, the figure is 98 percent. In the former case, the final decision is most likely to be made by a senior company official; in the latter, by an outside arbitrator. The appeals procedures appear to be used in virtually all companies having them, but the proportion of disciplinary actions that are appealed varies widely from firm to firm. On average, about one third of all dismissals are appealed; but in nearly 20 percent of the responding companies, the figure is 100 percent.

Research has shown that well-designed and carefully administered disciplinary procedures help to reduce absenteeism and turnover (both

---

[51] Barrett and Kernan, "Performance Appraisal and Terminations."

[52] The statistics reported in this section are taken from Bureau of National Affairs, *Employee Discipline and Discharge*, Personnel Policies Forum Survey No. 139 (Washington, D.C.: Bureau of National Affairs, January 1985), pp. 8–21.

FIGURE 12-5
Use of Progressive Discipline

Infraction	Four Steps: Oral Warning Written Warning Suspension Dismissal	Three Steps: Written Warning Suspension Dismissal	Two Steps: Suspension Dismissal	One Step: Dismissal	No Policy/ No Answer
Attendance Problems:					
Unexcused/excessive tardiness	82%	14%	—	—	4%
Excessive absences	77	18	1%	1%	3
Leaving work without permission	33	37	16	9	5
Performance/Production Problems:					
Failure to meet quantity/quality standards	64	25	5	1	5
Failure to follow safety precautions	38	35	11	5	11
Refusal to obey order or accept assignment	10	27	29	29	4
Unauthorized work stoppage	6	11	22	31	30
Honesty/Loyalty Issues:					
Failure to report injuries/accidents	32	28	13	3	23
Using company time/resources for personal gain	16	29	16	25	14
Falsification of work records	2	7	17	69	5
Theft of employer property	—	3	11	84	2
Workplace Behavior Problems:					
Violation of dress/grooming code	46	11	1	—	41
Smoking where/when prohibited	40	20	10	5	24
Sleeping on the job	20	27	30	18	5
Abusive/threatening language to supervisor	10	23	38	25	4
Fighting/physical assault	2	9	33	50	6
Possession of a weapon	—	7	18	62	13
Reporting to work under the influence of alcohol or drugs	8	18	43	29	3

Percent of Companies (Total = 222)

Source: *Employee Discipline and Discharge*, PPF Survey No. 139 (Washington, D.C.: Bureau of National Affairs, January 1985), pp. 17–18.

voluntary and involuntary), employee grievances, and wrongful discharge suits, and to enhance employee satisfaction.[53]

As suggested earlier, effective performance appraisal and disciplinary procedures are not the only means used to effectuate defensible dismissals. Among managerial and professional employees, organizations often negotiate mutually satisfactory departures that may involve severance allowances and outplacement assistance (see the earlier section on layoffs). These procedures help to ensure that the tenures of unsatisfactory employees are not prolonged. The probabilities of lawsuits are lessened, and transitions are smoothed for those who lose their jobs.

Retirement

With the passage of the Social Security Act in 1935, 65 became the so-called normal retirement age in the United States. However, the Age Discrimination in Employment Act now prohibits compulsory retirement. There are some exceptions to this prohibition: public safety personnel, college professors, and executives who will receive retirement benefits in excess of $44,000 per year.

Laws eliminating mandatory retirement do not necessarily result in retirements at older ages. Many companies encourage early retirement by offering either full or less than fully discounted pensions for those retiring at age 65 or younger. Almost none offer inducements for employees to stay on after age 65.

And, indeed, most employees retire before age 70.[54] Two thirds of companies report a trend toward early retirement; 86 percent report that the average age of their retirees is below 65; among 51 percent, it is below age 62. Comparable figures in 1972 were 58 and 23 percent. Nationally, the labor force participation rate of those older than 60 has been declining steadily for many years, although the rate of decline began to slow in 1983.

Opinions vary about whether these policies and patterns are good or bad for the companies involved (not to mention the individuals, and society more broadly). Some argue that they are necessary to preserve organizational vitality. Others are quick to point out, however, that older

[53] D. N. Campbell, R. L. Fleming, and R. C. Grote, "Discipline without Punishment—at Last," *Harvard Business Review*, July–August 1985, pp. 162–78; R. D. Arvey, G. A. Davis, and S. M. Nelson, "Use of Discipline in an Organization: A Field Study," *Journal of Applied Psychology*, 69 (1984), pp. 448–60.

[54] R. C. Ford and M. D. Fottler, "Flexible Retirement: Slowing Early Retirement of Productive Older Employees," *Human Resource Planning* 8, no. 3 (1985), pp. 147–56.

employees are not necessarily less productive than their younger counterparts, and indeed there are great individual differences in the rates at
which people age physiologically and in the extent to which they experience decrements in job performance over time.[55] Thus, the potential
payoff depends to a large extent on the numbers and relative capabilities
of the older and younger employees involved and the likelihood that the
least capable employees are the ones who retire early. Financial benefits
accrue to the extent that higher-paid older employees are replaced by
lower-paid younger ones. These benefits are offset by the costs of additional pension payments, special inducements, and the recruiting and
training of replacements.

Given the "graying of America," many observers are predicting future
labor shortages that only older employees can fill and thus are calling for
a reversal of the trend toward earlier retirements. Clearly, the relative
balance of the aforementioned costs and benefits will be shifting over
time and this, in turn, requires frequent reexaminations of retirement
policies and practices, as well as of a wide variety of other issues
pertaining to the management of older employees.[56]

Retirement assistance

For some employees, retirement is a difficult experience.[57] To help
ease the transition, many organizations adopt programs of assistance for
their potential or actual retirees.

Most prevalent are programs that offer preretirement counseling on
retirement financing and lifestyles. A few organizations have phased
retirement programs, which offer older employees increasing amounts of
time off through reduced workweeks, extended vacations, or job sharing.
Postretirement contacts between employers and retirees are becoming
increasingly common. Some companies provide professional assistance
(e.g., counseling) for their retirees. Others sponsor and host social or
service events, and (as noted earlier) a few rely on their retirees as
sources of temporary employees to help protect full employment and to
meet special business needs.

As the retirement decision becomes increasingly individualized, such
programs are likely to multiply.

---

[55] D. A. Waldman and B. J. Avolio, "A Meta-Analysis of Age Differences in Job Performance," *Journal of Applied Psychology* 71 (1986), pp. 33–38.

[56] R. C. Ford and M. D. Fottler, "Flexible Retirement."

[57] T. A. Beehr, "The Process of Retirement: A Review and Recommendations for Further
Investigation," *Personnel Psychology* 39, 1986, pp. 31–55.

ALTERNATIVE STAFFING ARRANGEMENTS

Employers often find it desirable to establish a degree of flexibility in staffing arrangements. One reason, noted earlier, is to reduce the risk of layoffs among regular employees when business downturns occur. Another is to meet temporary increases in demand for the firms' products or services. And a third is to comply with the desires of some employees for whom regular, full-time employment may be difficult (e.g., single parents of young children). Flexibility is difficult to achieve when all employees are hired to work regular hours, full time, and for the long term.

Thus, as Figure 12–6 shows, employers institute various forms of alternative staffing arrangements for some portions of their work forces. These tend to be of two basic types: (1) alternative work arrangements and (2) alternative scheduling arrangements.[58]

Alternative staffing arrangements are as old as work itself. Available evidence, however, suggests that they are becoming increasingly popular and systematized. In part this is a response to increasingly competitive (and hence uncertain) business conditions, and in part it reflects greater diversity and asssertiveness among today's employees.

Alternative Work Arrangements: Temporary Help, Short-Term Hires, On-Call Employees, Homework[59]

Employers with increasing human resource requirements, but a reluctance to incur the risks associated with adding regular employees, have two alternatives. They can, in effect, lease the needed talent from agencies that specialize in supplying temporary employees, such as Kelly (formerly Kelly Girl) or Manpower. Or they can hire it directly, but with the understanding that the arrangement is for a limited duration. Studies show that about three quarters of all employers use the former alternative, while up to two thirds use some variant of the latter (see Figure 12–6).

The increased use of temporary help agencies is well documented. In 1970, such agencies employed fewer than 200,000 people for placement; in 1986, the figure was approaching a million. Further, the pattern is changing. In the early years the placements were almost exclusively in clerical and secretarial positions and in unskilled blue-collar jobs. Now employers are also using temporary help agencies to meet short-term

---

[58] Bureau of National Affairs, *The Changing Workplace: New Directions in Staffing and Scheduling* (Washington, D.C.: Bureau of National Affairs, 1986).

[59] Statistics reprinted in this section are from Bureau of National Affairs, *The Changing Workplace*.

FIGURE 12–6
Alternative Staffing and Scheduling Arrangements

Method	Definition	Percent of Employers Using
Alternative Work Arrangements		
● Agency temporaries	● Individuals employed through a temporary help agency to work for the responding organization. Examples: accountants, clerical help, laborers, maintenance workers, nurses.	77
● Short-term hires	● Employees hired either for a specific time or a specific project. Examples: extra staff hired by retailers during the Christmas season, students hired for the summer, employees hired for a one-time event.	64
● On-call employees	● Individuals in a pool of employees who are called on an as-needed basis. Examples: laborers supplied by a union hiring hall, retirees who are available to work a few days a month.	36
● Homework	● Work is performed at home rather than traditional workplace.	?
Alternative Scheduling Arrangements		
● Part-time	● Scheduling employees to work fewer hours than on a regular work schedule. A variation is job sharing, a situation in which two (or more) employees share a full-time job.	? (Around 15% use job sharing)
● Flextime	● Employees have some degree of flexibility to decide the hours they work. Usually, there is a core period that all employees must work and then flexibility on each side with respect to starting and quitting times. All employees are expected to work a full day, week, or month.	22–35
● Compressed work week	● Compressing a full week's work into three, or more usually, four days. A variant is 5 9-hour days one week, followed by 4 9-hour days the next.	1–15

Source: Bureau of National Affairs. *The Changing Workplace: New Directions in Staffing and Scheduling* (Washington, D.C.: Bureau of National Affairs, 1986).

needs for technical and professional personnel such as accountants, data processing specialists, nurses, engineers and, to a lesser extent lawyers, doctors, and even managers and executives.

In general, employers seem to be satisfied with the use of temporary employees. Certainly, they value the enhanced flexibility. Some also report labor cost advantages since temporary employees are often paid less and offered fewer fringe benefits than regular employees, but in general seem to be just about as productive. But, these conditions do not always hold. Temporary help agencies often charge a premium for their services (in part because some of them provide fringe benefits to those they place), and some companies experience lower levels of performance among temporary employees.

Most employers have policies controlling the use of temporaries. In one study, nearly two thirds of the respondents limited them to less than 5 percent of total employment, while only one twentieth allowed them to exceed 25 percent of the work force. Reasons given for not using more temporaries included difficulty in controlling the quality of work (45 percent), higher costs (32 percent), restrictions in union contracts (26 percent), and difficulty in coordinating work (21 percent).

Clearly, many employees value the flexibility and variety associated with temporary employment. Research suggests, however, that between one third and two thirds of temporary employees would trade this flexibility and variety for the job security, enhanced pay and fringe benefits, and status associated with more permanent employment if they had the opportunity. And, indeed, many job seekers use temporary employment as a means of shopping for, and proving their ability to do, regular jobs.

Some observers fear that employers' increasing reliance on temporary employees is contributing to the gradual development of a permanent underclass of the underemployed. But others cite forecasts of labor market developments (see Chapter 3) suggesting that the traditional sources of people willing to take temporary work will soon be drying up, thereby putting an upper limit on this approach to flexible staffing for many employers.

Still another arrangement that provides employer flexibility is home work. There are many variations; it is estimated, for example, that as many as 23 million Americans do at least some work at home. But, the one that provides flexible staffing (as opposed to just flexible hours for the individuals involved) is the increasing practice of arranging with (mostly) women to perform clerical and computerized tasks such as word processing and claims processing in their homes. In many (but not all) cases flexibility and lower costs are achieved by treating these individuals as independent contractors rather than employees, thus facilitating the variation of their work loads; by basing their fees on the amount of work performed rather than on the number of hours worked (or paying a fixed salary); and by providing few if any fringe benefits.

Again, home work—or "telecommuting" as it is called when computers are involved—is an attractive alternative for some people, most notably parents with young children who need the income but prefer not to leave home and the handicapped for whom it is difficult to leave home. But the practice is not without controversy, stirred up mostly by labor union leaders and legislators who remember the exploitation of home workers in the garment industry before such arrangements were outlawed in the 1940s. Given the relatively small number of companies and individuals involved, there have been a surprisingly large number of court cases challenging the right of employers to treat home workers as independent contractors. It is unclear how this matter will be resolved, but at any rate it is likely to be a long time before home work, or telecommuting, achieves significance as an alternative staffing arrangement.

Alternative Work Schedules: Part-Time, Flextime, Compressed Workweek

Most employers operate with a standard five-day, 40 (or so) hour workweek for most employees. Many, however, also rely in part on part-time employees, and, as a consequence, there are over 20 million Americans who work less than 35 hours per week. These are mostly women and those who are either very young or very old. Almost two thirds of the men who work part time, for example, are between the ages of 16 and 24 or age 65 and older. Most part-timers probably prefer this arrangement (to leave time free for child care, going to school, and leisure-time activities), although some are forced into it because of the lack of full-time work.[60]

Employers rely on part-timers for flexibility in staffing and to keep costs down. Twenty percent of the work force at Federal Express, for example, works part time, mostly between 11 P.M. and 4 A.M., to facilitate overnight delivery schedules. Most of these part-timers are students and moonlighters (i.e., those working second jobs). Although Federal Express pays part-timers the same as comparable full-timers (a somewhat uncommon practice), it provides part-timers with fewer and less generous fringe benefits, a clear-cut cost savings. Further, the use of part-timers helps cut down on overtime among full-time employees, which also saves money.

A variation on part-time work is job sharing, an arrangement through which two (or occasionally more) employees share a single job. This is usually done where jobs are full time, but some employees prefer to work only part time. It is most common in clerical and blue-collar jobs

---

[60] H. R. Hamel, "New Data Series on Involuntary Part-Time Work", *Monthly Labor Review* 108, no. 3 (1985), pp. 42–43.

where the work is relatively routine and the coordination of the work relatively easy. About 15 percent of the nation's employers are reported to be using job sharing, although most of them probably have only a few employees involved (see Figure 12–6).

A more common arrangement, which serves some of the same purposes, is flextime. Here employees work full time, but have some degree of latitude in arranging their hours (this, of course, simply formalizes the informal treatment of many professional and managerial employees). Under the most common arrangement all employees are required to be present during some core period (say between 10 A.M. and 4 P.M.), but are free to determine their own starting and quitting times. Variations include flexibility across the workweek or even across the work month. Such arrangements may help employers attract and retain certain employees that otherwise could not be enticed to work full time (such as working mothers). And there is some evidence to suggest that they help cut down on absenteeism, the use of leave time, and overtime. In general, however, after an initial blush, flextime apparently has little or no effect on performance or productivity, although problems of coverage and supervision can arise. Employees report great satisfaction with flextime.[61]

Another, relatively uncommon, variation in work scheduling is the compressed workweek. Here 40 or so hours of work are compressed into four or even three days per week, thus yielding a greater number of days for leisure or moonlighting. Obviously, many jobs do not lend themselves to this type of schedule. Further, research has shown it to have no distinct advantages over more conventional arrangements in terms of the common P/HR outcomes. And it is opposed by many (although not all) labor unions as a regression from the eight-hour day (unless, of course, it is accompanied by a reduction in the total number of work hours in a week or month). For all these reasons, the compressed workweek is unlikely to spread very far or very fast.

CAREER MANAGEMENT

The moment an individual accepts a job with an employer, his or her organizational career begins. It may last only a few hours or days (as is

---

[61] D. A. Ralston and M. F. Flanagan, "The Effect of Flexitime on Turnover and Absenteeism for Male and Female Employees," *Journal of Vocational Behavior* 26 (1985), pp. 206–17; V. K. Narayanan and R. Nath, "The Influence of Group Cohesiveness on Some Changes Induced by Flexitime: A Quasi-Experiment," *Journal of Applied Behavioral Science* 20 (1984), pp. 265–76.

sometimes the case, for example, with temporary employees) or continue for 30 or 40 years; it may involve only a single job in a single field in a single location or a series of several, usually progressively higher-level, jobs in many different areas (e.g., manufacturing, sales, finance, personnel) located throughout the country or, increasingly, the world. To a large extent, the duration and pattern of individuals' organizational careers are shaped by organizations' internal staffing decisions which determine the nature of the career opportunities that are (or are not) offered. But, of course, individuals have much to say about their own careers, partly through the actions they take to develop or create opportunities for movement and advancement and partly through their responses to the various opportunities that materialize.

All employers must decide how systematic to be in planning employees' careers and how much effort to put into facilitating their career moves and career adjustments. A number of authors have pointed out the potential advantages of a comprehensive effort:

- Easier attraction of high-quality employees.
- Less undesirable turnover, because the best employees are more satisfied with their career progression and opportunities.
- Higher performance, since individuals are continually better matched with available jobs.
- Better affirmative action results as women and minorities are systematically prepared for, and moved into, higher-level jobs.[62]

Many argue that high-quality career management is more critical now than ever before because of the clash of two antithetical trends. On the one hand, as a result of the post-World-War-II baby boom, huge numbers of people are moving into the critical midcareer stage (see Chapter 3). On the other hand, as a result of recent competitive pressures and the accompanying restructuring and downsizing, many traditional career opportunities have dried up, particularly in large corporations. The results? First, many baby-boomers have or will become plateaued or derailed from their inexorable marches to the top. Second, all the jammed-up baby-boomers are further jamming up the ambitious younger employees below them in the corporate hierarchy, who suddenly find themselves all dressed up with no place to go. The problem? How to cope with the career needs of the individuals in these various

---

[62] The arguments are everywhere; see, for example, London and Stumpf, *Managing Careers*, pp. 97–100. But, data are sparse; a recent and oft-cited work in the field, for example, reports none on the effects of career management programs: D. T. Hall and Associates, *Career Development in Organizations* (San Francisco: Jossey-Bass, 1986).

groups in such a way that the best and the brightest are first, retained and second, refrained from retiring on the job.[63]

When asked, most organizations claim to be actively involved in trying to solve these problems. On examination, however, many of their efforts are found to be less than fully developed and quite fragmentary; and most are still focused on only a small proportion of employees, usually fast-track or high-potential managers and professionals and—to a lesser extent—minorities and women as part of affirmative action efforts.[64]

But, recognizing the need, an increasing number of organizations express an interest in making a greater effort to develop comprehensive career-management programs which address the concerns of a fuller range of employees and include the three major components: planning, development, and counseling.

Career Planning

Career planning is the process that individuals use to assess their opportunities and their strengths and weaknesses and to develop goals and action plans that will move their careers in desired directions. Although individuals ultimately must assume responsibility for their own career planning, there is much that organizations can do to help.

Organizational component

Organizations contribute by making available to employees information about potential career opportunities and organizational perceptions of their current readiness or long-term potential to avail themselves of these opportunities.

Potential career opportunities are identified by delineating possible career paths, job requirements, and estimates of future job openings. Career paths are typically aimed at focal jobs to which many people aspire (e.g., senior scientist, plant manager, group manager, vice president of personnel). Typical paths may be described using historical data, such as those displayed in the transition matrix shown in Figure 12–2. Another method develops career paths consisting of logical job progressions based on knowledge, skill, and ability requirements. Information about jobs and their requirements is obtained through job analysis (as described in Chapter 3). Illustration 12–3 shows career paths based on

---

[63] M. London and S. A. Stumpf, "Individual and Organizational Career Development in Changing Times," in *Career Development*, D. T. Hall and Associates.

[64] T. G. Gutteridge, "Organizational Career Development Systems: The State of the Practice," in *Career Development*, D. T. Hall and Associates.

ILLUSTRATION 12–3

Career Paths in an Insurance Company

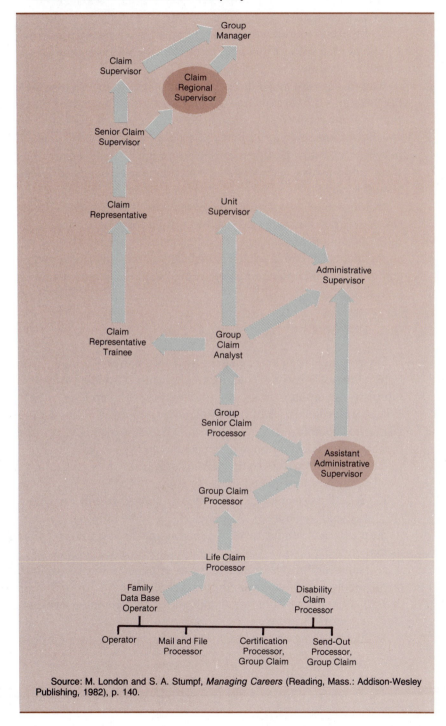

Source: M. London and S. A. Stumpf, *Managing Careers* (Reading, Mass.: Addison-Wesley Publishing, 1982), p. 140.

knowledge and skill progressions leading to three focal jobs—administrative supervisor, unit supervisor, and group manager—in a large insurance company.

To be useful in individual decision making, career path information is supplemented with estimates of future job openings generated by human resource planning (see Chapter 8).

Employees also need to know their chances of progressing. Most organizations rely heavily on supervisors to assess the career potential of their subordinates and to communicate the results of these assessments, usually through the performance-appraisal process (see Chapter 6). Supervisors may also be asked to decide on next career moves (if any) for their subordinates and on the developmental activities in which they should engage.

Other processes, including assessment centers (discussed earlier in this chapter) and managerial reviews and succession planning (see Chapter 8), supplement the supervisors' information base. The aim of these supplements is to use a pooled knowledge base to identify high potentials and to ensure that planned career moves and development activities are carried out.

Individual component

Savvy employees also engage in their own career planning. Organizations offer assistance in the form of planning guides or workbooks, interactive computer programs, conferences with supervisors or trained P/HR professionals, and career-planning seminars. Illustration 12–4 shows how employees and their supervisors work together on career planning in a telecommunications company.

As is clear from Illustration 12–4, a typical career-planning process usually involves four major steps.[65]

1. A self-assessment of one's values, long-term concerns, interests, strengths, and weaknesses. Also included may be ratings of one's current performance and longer-term career potential as assessed by the organization.

2. Information gathering about career opportunities both inside the organization (available through the career-pathing process described earlier) and out (available from family members, friends, business associates, and written sources).

3. Establishing career goals, at least for the foreseeable future. It is

---

[65] M. London and E. M. Mone, *Career Management and Survival In The Workplace* (San Francisco: Jossey-Bass, 1987).

ILLUSTRATION 12–4

Career Planning Program in a Telecommunications Company

Objective: To help identify "best fits" to a marketing role

First Step: Identification of Key Marketing Skills/Attributes

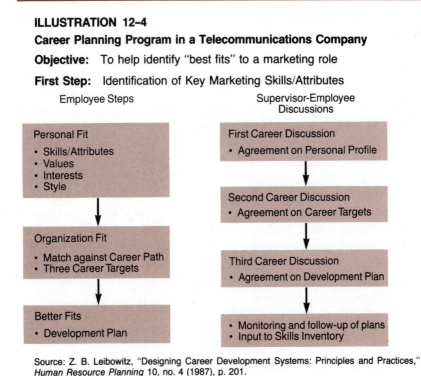

Source: Z. B. Leibowitz, "Designing Career Development Systems: Principles and Practices," *Human Resource Planning* 10, no. 4 (1987), p. 201.

at this point that one must genuinely face the facts generated in the preceding steps.

4.   Developing action plans to achieve career goals within established timeframes.

Career Development

Career development is the process through which the action plans are implemented. Developmental activities include all of the off- and on-the-job training techniques to be discussed in Chapter 13. One might engage in classroom training in-house or at universities, or opt for special job or task force assignments or, especially early in the career, job rotation. Lateral moves and promotions are more difficult to use for developmental purposes. Managers with vacancies have their own objectives to meet and may be reluctant to fill openings with candidates designated for career development rather than with those who have the best skills to do the jobs.

Career development is where individual career plans encounter organizational realities. Sometimes there is congruence, and sometimes not. In the latter case, the individual has three alternatives: to stay on and attempt to show those making the assessments and developmental assignments that they are wrong, to reassess career plans, or to seek opportunities elsewhere. Realizing that the third alternative is sometimes best for the employer as well as the employee, some organizations routinely adopt as part of career development the possibility of a mutual parting of the ways, greased perhaps by separation pay and outplacement assistance (as discussed earlier in this chapter).

It is essential that career development be fully integrated with internal staffing activities.[66] A number of observers have documented the negative effects that can occur when employees who have been told of their bright prospects and treated to extensive developmental activities are regularly passed over for advancement. This most typically happens when the assessors (e.g., supervisors) are too low in the hierarchy to influence promotion decisions, and no well-placed individual or group is overseeing both processes.

Career Counseling

Much has been written about the personal problems that can arise as a result of certain career events.[67] Most recognizable, perhaps, are the problems of career plateauing and career bottlenecks mentioned earlier. Others include the difficulties encountered when ambitious individual career plans do not square with organizational assessments of career potential, or (less commonly) when the opposite occurs. Slightly more subtle, but nonetheless highly visible these days, are the problems faced by women in traditionally male careers and by couples involved with dual careers. Least recognizable may be the career crises befalling some individuals as new task and emotional demands are encountered when making the transition from one career stage to another or as they fail to make these transitions when they should (see Figure 12–7).

Apparently, most employees who encounter these types of career problems successfully cope with them without outside help. Occasionally, the problems become overwhelming and begin to interfere with effective job performance. Although supervisors can be trained to recog-

---

[66] M. A. VonGlinow, M. J. Driver, K. Brousseau, and J. B. Prince, "The Design of a Career-Oriented Human Resource System," *Academy of Management Review* 8 (1983), pp. 23–32.

[67] See, for example, London and Mone, *Career Management and Survival*, especially Chapters 10 through 14.

FIGURE 12-7

Career Stages and Their Task and Emotional Needs

Stage	Task Needs	Emotional Needs
Trial	Varied job activities	Make preliminary job choices
	Self-exploration	Settling down
Establishment and or advancement	Job challenge	Deal with rivalry and competition; face failures
	Develop competence in a specialty area	Deal with work-family conflicts
	Develop creativity and innovation	Support
	Rotate into new area after 3 to 4 years	Autonomy
Midcareer	Technical updating	Express feelings about midlife
	Develop skills in training and coaching others (younger employees)	Reorganize thinking about self in relation to work, family, and community
	Rotation into new job requiring new skills	
	Develop broader view of work and own role in organization	Reduce self-indulgence and competitiveness
Late career	Plan for retirement	Support and counseling to see one's work as a platform for others
	Shift from power role to one of consultation and guidance	Develop sense of identity in extraorganizational activities
	Identify and develop successors	
	Begin activities outside the organization	

From D. T. Hall and M. Morgan, "Career Development and Planning," in *Contemporary Problems in Personnel,* rev. ed., ed. W. C. Hamner and F. Schmidt (Chicago: St. Clair Press, 1977), p. 218.

nize and properly diagnose such situations, most are unequipped to handle them. Rather, the services of trained counselors are called for.[68] Thus, as part of a complete career-management program, many organizations retain the names of such counselors so that timely referrals can be made. Very large organizations may even have such counselors on their

---

[68] P. C. Cairo, "Counseling in Industry: A Selected Review of the Literature," *Personnel Psychology* 36 (1983), pp. 1–18.

P/HR staffs (see also employee assistance programs described in Chapter 20).

An Example of a Career-Management System

When career planning, career development, and career counseling are combined in the appropriate sequence, a comprehensive career management system is created. Illustration 12–5 provides an example taken from Xerox Corporation.[69]

Evaluating Career Management

One would think that organizations adopting comprehensive career management systems, or pieces thereof, would be interested in knowing whether they work.

- Are they used by employees?
- Do they provide accurate and useful information?
- Do employees receive the developmental activities they need?
- Are employees' career plans realized?
- Are promotion and transfer decisions improved?
- Do employees experience fewer or less severe career problems than they did before?
- Do employees who participate have more successful careers than those who do not?
- Are the results worth the costs incurred?

Actually, as noted earlier, little research has been conducted on these issues and what has been conducted has often lacked methodological rigor. The findings, however, have generally been supportive of career management activities. Employee reactions have been favorable, and improvements in retention and performance have been found. Crocker National Bank assessed the utility of its program and concluded that the returns in the form of reduced turnover, lower replacement costs, and improved professional growth were nearly $2 million in excess of program costs.[70]

Additional evaluation work is sorely needed to determine the generalizability of these findings and to ascertain the conditions under which employers and employees are most likely to benefit from career management activities.

---

[69] For a further description of the system at Xerox, plus others, see Gutteridge, "Organizational Career Development Systems" and London and Stumpf, *Managing Careers*, Ch. 5.

[70] Gutteridge, "Organizational Career Development Systems."

ILLUSTRATION 12-5

Career Management at Xerox

Overview:
  Integrated programs involving career planning, career development, and
  career counseling.
  Developed and implemented by Human Resource Department.
  Available to all employees. Strictly voluntary. Approximately 25 percent
  participation rate.

Career Planning:
  Organizational—primarily the responsibility of a separate unit, Human
  Resource Planning. Emphasis is on the identification of employees with
  management potential and replacement planning. Employees so identified are encouraged to institute developmental action plans (see below).
  Individual—ultimately the employee's responsibility. Company offers
  help and guidance. Three stage program:

  1. "Honest self evaluation"—involves in-depth exploration by the em-
     ployee of his or her needs, wants, strengths, experiences, and train-
     ing. Done through specially designed workbooks and workshops.
  2. "Career choice knowledge"—involves an exploration of the business
     outlook, realistic career options, career paths, job requirements, and
     selection standards through videotapes, write-in forms through which
     employees can request specific job information, and a counseling
     staff.
  3. "Developmental action planning"—using data from stages 1 and 2,
     employees and their supervisors identify target job(s) and develop-
     mental steps.

  Some slippage occurs between organizational and individual career planning because organizational career planning is not done for all employees. Sometimes leads to overly ambitious individual career plans that
  must be trimmed back.

Career Development:
  Career pathing for all jobs communicated through a career path manual.
  Job posting.
  Instructional tapes and workshops for supervisors.

Career Counseling:
  Done by supervisors and staff.
  Early emphasis on minorities and women through special panel discus-
  sions.
  More recent emphasis on individuals in midcareer.

Evaluation:
  Employee surveys to determine attitudes toward career planning and
  perceptions of assistance available to help do career planning.
  Staff follow-up of workshop participants to assess individual career plans
  and perceived value of workshop.
  Supervisory follow-up of individual career plans to determine extent of
  movement toward goals, value of developmental activities, and so
  forth.

Source: Case study done by Lorna Rosenblith and Barbara Sinclair, Cornell University, 1978.
Special thanks to Dr. Harold Tragash and Mr. Roy Semplenski of Xerox.

SUMMARY

Organizations have been likened to anthills because of the constant flurry of activity going on inside: at any given time in a medium-sized to large organization there may be in the works a hundred or more promotions, a couple of dozen relocations, a plant or office shutdown, a half-dozen retirement parties, and so on. Making sense of and managing this activity is the essence of internal staffing.

The primary concern, of course, is to ensure that the organization's ongoing human resource requirements are met on a timely basis. To some extent this always involves filling job vacancies created by growth and employee losses of various kinds, often, for both philosophical and efficiency reasons, through promotions and transfers from within. Thus, in addition to having mechanisms for identifying where the vacancies will occur and for developing employees to fill them, all organizations have to have ways of handling these promotions and transfers, that is, some means of identifying candidates, deciding among candidates, easing transitions across jobs, and monitoring all this activity from an organizational, individual, and legal perspective. Developing and administering policies, programs, and procedures to do these things is a big part of what internal staffing is all about.

Another part is dealing with the spector or reality of employee surpluses. Many companies work hard to avoid the reality. They carefully control the numbers of regular employees added to the payroll during the good times—often by relying on overtime and the use of temporary and part-time employees—and do their best to anticipate and manage the necessary adjustments when times turn bad. Even with the best of intentions, however, many organizations find that layoffs cannot be avoided. Thus, another important element of internal staffing is preparing for, and if necessary managing through, this eventuality. Again, it is a matter of deciding on the factors that determine who goes and who stays (e.g., merit or seniority), the assistance that is to be provided those who go (e.g., severance pay and outplacement), and the procedures to be used to minimize the disruption among those who stay.

The balancing acts would be tough enough even if all employees could be relied on to do their jobs effectively and to obey the rules. Unfortunately, they cannot, so another facet of internal staffing is anticipating and dealing with performance and behavioral problems. Basically, this is a matter of having a carefully designed and well-understood disciplinary procedure, as well as policies governing employee discharges. As the common-law concept of employment-at-will continues to erode, it is imperative that all managers know when and how to (and not to) fire employees and that they be carefully monitored in these activities.

And then there is retirement. With rare exceptions, organizations can no longer force employees to retire at any age. Most, however, are not enamored with the prospect of employees hanging on forever, and so find it desirable to develop retirement policies and pension plan provisions designed to entice and facilitate retirements at specific ages (e.g., 62 or 65). In a comparatively recent development, it turns out that older workers, whose numbers are growing, are increasingly being enlisted in ongoing battles to balance human resource requirements and availabilities. On the downswings, more and more employers are turning to special, one-time early retirement programs to help balance their work forces and avoid layoffs among younger employees. On the upswings, retirees are increasingly being relied on as on-call, temporary employees to carry out special projects and meet other short-term needs.

Labor market considerations, especially the huge influx of working women with children, are inducing still other kinds of flexibilities in internal staffing and work scheduling. Flextime is probably the most widespread phenomenon; others include job sharing and working at home.

Career management certainly has been buffeted by current turmoil and experimentation in internal staffing. On the one hand, the uncertainty increases the need for better career management and on the other, makes it increasingly difficult to do. On balance, it appears that employees have become less willing to rely on their employers either for career stability or career assistance. Thus, while many organizations continue to provide organizational career planning and assistance with individual career planning, development, and counseling, most emphasize more than ever that ultimately employees must assume responsibility for managing their own careers.

DISCUSSION QUESTIONS

1.   What is the nature of the relationships among internal staffing, alternative work arrangements, and career management?

2.   What does an organization gain and give up when it goes from a closed to an open approach to internal recruiting? Under what conditions might an organization want to do this? Not do it?

3.   Since seniority is so easy to measure, why shouldn't all organizations simply use it to decide who will get promoted, transferred, and laid off (if necessary)?

4.   What are the costs of layoffs? The benefits? Under what conditions might an organization be quite happy to engage in periodic layoffs?

5.   A restaurant chain does not want to fool around with performance problems. Thus, anyone whose performance is judged to be below par or who violates any

policy or rule, no matter how minor, is simply fired—no warning, no disciplinary procedure, and no appeal. Does this seem like a good idea? Why or why not?

6.   Under the recent amendment to the Age Discrimination in Employment Act, college and universities are still permitted to force professors to retire at age 70 until 1992. Why should mandatory retirement be permitted for college professors when it is forbidden for just about everyone else? What policies and practices should colleges and universities follow until 1992? Thereafter? Why?

7.   Every company should use temporary employees. Discuss.

8.   Why should companies fool around with work schedules just to accommodate certain people who don't want to or say they can't work regular hours like everyone else?

9.   In these times of such great uncertainty, companies might as well forget about career management. Discuss.

10.   How can organizations ever hope to attain some degree of consistency in their internal staffing decisions when in actuality virtually all such decisions are made by line managers who can do just about anything they really want to?

13

Employee Development

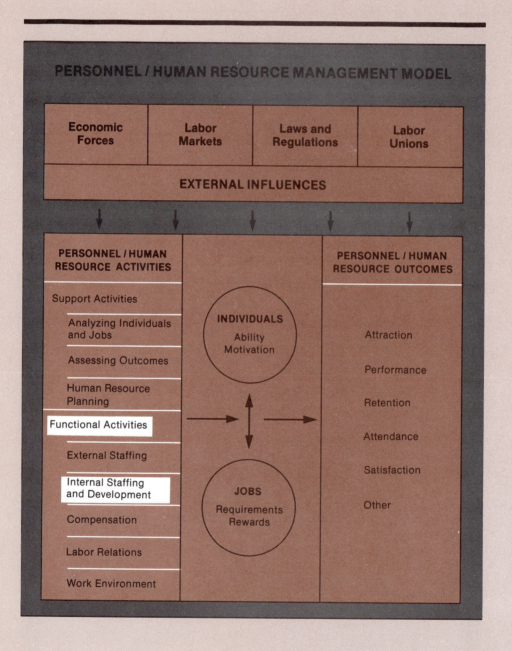

PERSONNEL / HUMAN RESOURCE MANAGEMENT MODEL

Economic Forces	Labor Markets	Laws and Regulations	Labor Unions

EXTERNAL INFLUENCES

PERSONNEL / HUMAN RESOURCE ACTIVITIES

Support Activities

Analyzing Individuals and Jobs

Assessing Outcomes

Human Resource Planning

Functional Activities

External Staffing

Internal Staffing and Development

Compensation

Labor Relations

Work Environment

INDIVIDUALS
Ability
Motivation

JOBS
Requirements
Rewards

PERSONNEL / HUMAN RESOURCE OUTCOMES

Attraction

Performance

Retention

Attendance

Satisfaction

Other

After reading this chapter, you should be able to speak to the questions posed in each of the following personnel/human resource incidents:

1. The Holstein Milk Company produces and distributes milk in a variety of containers. One of the distribution channels involves delivery by truck to various warehouses. Each truck has a driver and a helper, both of whom are paid on a commission basis according to amount of stock delivered. An important job duty is to rotate the stock in the truck at least three times a day to ensure consistency of temperature for the milk. The supervisor of these drivers and helpers has learned that they do not rotate the stock, and consequently fears that some of the delivered milk may spoil too quickly. Thinking that this problem might be solved by some sort of training for them, the supervisor calls you, the training and development director, to discuss this possibility. When you meet with the supervisor, what questions will you ask? What points might you make, and why?

2. You are the personnel administrator of County General Hospital. A new performance appraisal system is about to be introduced among the 42 managerial and supervisory personnel at the hospital. It is important to you that the system get off to a good start. One task you have decided is necessary is to train all raters in the use of the system, and you have allocated $6,000 to do this. You must now design the training program. What type of program would you run?

3. You are a recent college graduate who is a management trainee. You have been assigned to an experienced manager for orientation and on-the-job training. During the first three months, you are assigned a number of projects, most of which you complete on a timely basis, but little communication passes between your mentor and you. You go to him and express concern about the situation. His response is: "Oh, yeah! Well, what do you expect me to do?" How would you go about answering his question?

4. You are a training specialist with XYZ Corporation and, in support of the company's new push on quality, you have designed a three-day workshop on quality control for the supervisors and operators in the various manufacturing plants. You have just finished presenting your creation to the vice president of manufacturing and her response was: "How do I know this is a good idea? It costs a lot to take that many people out of the plants and send them all to Boise for three days. How will I know if I'm getting my money's worth?" Now you've got to come up with a response. What would it be?

Chapters 10 through 12 have emphasized the importance of selecting and promoting new employees wisely and of carefully planning and managing their organizational careers. However, no amount of expertise and effort in external and internal staffing will ensure a 100 percent success rate on new hires or a forever perfect match between job requirements and individual abilities.

- Sara Raines shows up for her first day at work nervous and unsure of herself. She is well trained in her field, but the plant looks so big and imposing, and everyone there is a complete stranger. Will she be able to fit in?
- John Boudoir has never seemed to catch onto his job. He tries hard, but his output is only about one half that of his fellow employees.
- Professor Leon M. Grits is getting along in years, and the world seems to be passing him by. There have been many new developments in his field, but he is still using the same old yellowed lecture notes he prepared several years ago.
- Dawn Neehoff is a hard-charging salesperson with her eye on a management job. Her supervisors believe she has the potential to be an excellent manager, but right now she lacks management skills.

Situations such as these may call for employee development, which can be defined as a planned process of learning experiences intended to enhance employees' contributions to organizational goals. In terms of our overall P/HR model, the purpose of employee development is to improve individual abilities and bring them more in line with existing or anticipated job requirements. As the above examples show, the more immediate goals of particular learning experiences are usually one or more of the following:[1]

- To orient new employees to the organization and their jobs.
- To improve employees' performance levels on their present jobs.
- To enable employees to maintain performance levels as their present jobs change.
- To prepare employees for new jobs.

To be effective, employee development requires close cooperation between line management and the P/HR department. Line managers often assume responsibility for helping to decide which employees are in

---

[1] L. Nadler, *Corporate Human Resource Development: A Management Tool* (New York: Van Nostrand Reinhold, 1980), pp. 23–26.

need of development and the type of development that is needed. They may also be called on to take an active part in their subordinates' development, either on the job (for example, through coaching) or off (for example, as teachers in the classroom). They must also be continually aware of their own developmental needs and periodically participate in training themselves.

P/HR managers and specialists usually take responsibility for developing general policy regarding employee development and for administering the overall effort, as well as various training programs. Thus, they work with line managers to diagnose training needs, recommend budgeting levels to top management, maintain lists of outside (e.g., university) programs that employees might attend, set up, and sometimes conduct, in-company training programs, and evaluate the overall employee development effort and specific training programs that are offered.

Environmental factors exert considerable influence on the nature of the training that organizations provide. Certain types of training—for example, updates by physicians and attorneys—are required by law. Other sorts of training are encouraged by law. Under the Job Training Partnership Act (JTPA) of 1983, for example, the federal government subsidizes local area and employer-provided training for the unemployed. In the act's first year, more than $3 billion was spent to prepare tens of thousands of the unemployed for such jobs as nurses' aides, secretaries, machinists, mechanics, telephone installers, accountants, and engineers.[2] Although JTPA funding has decreased by 7 percent in constant dollars since 1983, more than $17 billion was spent from 1983 to 1987. For 1988, the JTPA appropriation was $4.4 billion.[3] Another approach is being tried in various states, where excess cash that has accumulated in unemployment insurance funds is used to retrain displaced employees; once these individuals have been hired, trained, and placed in new jobs for a period of time, their employers are reimbursed for the costs of the training provided.

Many employers provide special training for women and minorities— and their supervisors—under voluntary, negotiated, and court-imposed affirmative action plans.

Labor unions frequently bargain for training. There are long-standing apprenticeship programs that have been negotiated in the building trades and elsewhere, often with support from the federal and state governments. General Motors and the United Automobile Workers

---

[2] "JTPA: A New Approach to Training the Disadvantaged," *News* (No. 84–433)(Washington, D.C.: United States Department of Labor), October 15, 1984.

[3] S. Levitan and F. Gallo, *A Second Chance: Training For Jobs* (Kalamazoo, Mich.: The W.E. Upjohn Institute for Employment Research, 1988).

(UAW) recently established a National Human Resource Center (HRC) in Cincinnati, Ohio, to train employees displaced by plant closings.[4] In 1986, AT&T and the Communications Workers of America (CWA) set up a unique joint venture called The Alliance to help employees cope with technological changes. During the first year of operation, The Alliance has reached more than 4,000 employees—both active and displaced—by providing programs such as short-term skills training, self-directed job search training, technical training, relocation counseling, and so on.[5]

Finally, the amount and nature of training provided is greatly affected by labor market conditions. When skills are in short supply, training budgets increase, and vice versa, reflecting employers' vacillations on the "make versus buy" option.

In this chapter, attention is focused on the prevalence and nature of employee development, on an overall model of the process, and on the various action steps inherent in the model. These actions steps include identifying employee development needs, formulating employee development plans, designing and conducting training programs, and evaluating the results.

PREVALENCE AND NATURE

All organizations engage in employee development. Available evidence suggests that this activity is becoming increasingly important in the face of ever more intensive international competition, deregulation, accelerated technological change, and the inexorable march toward the postindustrial society.[6] Training is one way to develop a more flexible work force. According to a recent study,[7] technological change is the driving force behind much of today's training, especially in technical areas. In a period of high turbulence, training and development is a must for such companies as IBM and Hewlett-Packard, which are committed to full employment. Without continuous learning and investment in training, these companies could not make the constant internal adjustments needed to avoid layoffs.[8]

---

[4] D. Feldman, "Helping Displaced Workers: The UAW-G.M. Human Resource Center," *Personnel* 65, March 1988, pp. 34–36.

[5] *The Alliance: Securing the Future Together* (Somerset, N.J.: The Alliance for Employee Growth and Development, Inc., 1987).

[6] See, for example, P. Choate and J. K. Linger, *The High-Flex Society* (New York: Alfred A. Knopf, 1986).

[7] E. Stephan, G. E. Mills, R. W. Pace, and L. Ralphs, "HRD in the Fortune 500," *Training and Development Journal* 42, January 1988, pp. 26–32.

[8] Work in America Institute, "The Continuous Learning/Employment Security Connection," *Report* (Scarsdale, N.Y.: Work In America Institute, 1987).

Most employee development is carried out on the job, and most of this is done informally.[9] Still, a study of 1,006 employers in seven different industries found that more than two thirds engaged in some type of formal training. The median expenditure was between $75 and $100 per employee.[10] Larger companies that are more employee oriented spend many times as much. It is reported that IBM, for example, has a training and development budget in excess of $700 million, which averages out to nearly $2,000 per employee.

IBM and other companies—Xerox, AT&T, GE, GM, Wang and Motorola—operate their own "universities," in which a wide variety of technical and managerial subjects are taught.[11] Collectively, U.S. organizations with 50 or more employees were estimated to have spent $32 billion to train about 38.8 million employees in 1987. In total these employees received 1.2 billion hours of training.[12]

Is this money well spent? Although the organizations involved apparently think so, the fact is that the benefits of employee development are largely taken on faith. Evaluation efforts have lagged. Yet we know that it is extremely difficult to design developmental experiences that will result in desired learning, let alone changed behavior leading to better organizational results. Adequate theory and research to guide the process are emerging only slowly, and organizations have been somewhat slow to capitalize on that which has become available.[13] In fact, of all the P/HR activities, employee development has been the one to be most consistently seduced by the alluring array of fads and folderol offered by consultants and "educators."

The costs of this promiscuous behavior are becoming ever more apparent, however, forcing P/HR professionals to ensure that their employee development efforts are (1) directed toward organizational and P/HR management objectives, (2) undertaken only when they are the most effective way to attain these objectives, (3) solidly designed, using the latest state of the art, and (4) carefully administered and thoroughly evaluated.

---

[9] A. P. Carnevale and H. Goldstein, *Employee Training: Its Changing Role and an Analysis of New Data* (Washington, D.C.: American Society for Training and Development, 1983).

[10] Prentice-Hall Editorial Staff, *Employee Training: Personnel Management: Policies and Practices Series* (Englewood Cliffs, N.J.: Prentice-Hall, 1979).

[11] "Schooling for Survival," *Time*, February 11, 1985, pp. 74–75; and K. B. Noble, "Where Xerox Hones Skills," Spring Survey of Education (Section 12), *New York Times*, April 14, 1985, p. 49+.

[12] C. Lee, "Training Magazine's Industry Report 1987," *Training* 24, October 1987, pp. 33–35; and C. Lee, "Where the Training Dollars Go," *Training* 24, October 1987, pp. 51–52.

[13] G. P. Latham, "Human Resource Training and Development," *Annual Review of Psychology* 39 (1988), pp. 545–82.

FIGURE 13-1

The Employee Development Process

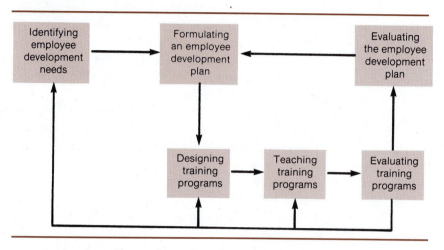

EMPLOYEE DEVELOPMENT AS A PROCESS

Like many other P/HR activities, employee development is best thought of as a process consisting of several interrelated phases or steps.[14] Figure 13-1 shows the major features of the process. The process begins with a series of ongoing analyses to determine the extent and nature of an organization's employee development needs. With these needs clarified, it is then possible to put together an employee development plan that shows overall objectives, program priorities, and resource allocations, and indicates who will be trained in what, by whom, and when.

Each potential trainee can then be matched with a training opportunity, which might occur in-house or out, on the job or off. As each program is developed, consideration is normally given to the instructional objectives that should be met, program content, and the delivery system (i.e., training technique(s)) to be used. Then the actual training takes place. Finally, there is evaluation. It is necessary to know first if the various training programs met their instructional objectives and at what cost and then to know if the total effort was successful in fulfilling the overall objectives that were set out in the employee development plan. The results of the evaluations are fed back to those who will be planning, developing, and delivering future programs.

---

[14] I. L. Goldstein, *Training in Organizations: Needs Assessment, Development, and Evaluation*, 2d ed. (Monterey, Calif.: Brooks/Cole Publishing, 1986).

IDENTIFYING EMPLOYEE DEVELOPMENT NEEDS

The first step in the employee development process is to diagnose needs. These needs consist of actual and potential performance discrepancies that are important to the organization and that can be remedied as effectively and efficiently by training as by any other means. As this definition suggests. the diagnosis phase is designed to answer several questions: (1) Does an actual or potential performance discrepancy exist? (2) Is it important to the organization? (3) Is it correctable through training? (4) Is training the most cost-effective solution available?[15]

Does a Performance Discrepancy Exist?

A performance discrepancy is a gap between attained and desired performance. Actual performance discrepancies are apparent in the cases of Sara Raines, John Boudoir, and Professor Grits noted earlier in this chapter. Dawn Neehof, on the other hand, represents a potential performance discrepancy.

The identification of performance discrepancies is somewhat analogous to detective work.[16] Various data sources are searched for possible leads, and the more promising ones are pursued until a decision can be made. Figure 13–2 lists several of the more common sources of leads.[17] They vary depending on whether the level of analysis is organizational or individual and whether the focus is on the present or the future. Organizational analysis techniques are most likely to turn up actual or potential performance discrepancies among managers or supervisors because they show which units are failing, or are likely to fail, to meet performance standards (e.g., which units have low productivity or high turnover). The person analysis techniques apply more generally across the board.

Not surprisingly, between actual and potential performance discrepancies, the first are easier to identify. They require only data on current performance and an appropriate standard. To uncover potential performance discrepancies, three types of information, are required: (1) Are current jobs going to change, particularly in their ability requirements? (2) Which individuals will (or might) be moving to new jobs? (3) Will those people whose jobs will change or who will be changing jobs have

---

15 R. F. Mager and P. Pipe, *Analyzing Performance Problems* (Belmont, Calif: Pitman Learning, 1984), pp. 7–57. The following section owes much to this insightful and delightful book.

16 F. L. Ulschak, *Human Resource Development: The Theory and Practice of Need Assessment* (Reston, Va.: Reston Publishing, 1983).

17 See Latham, "Human Resource Training."

FIGURE 13–2

Sources Used to Identify Performance Discrepancies

	Type of Performance Discrepancy	
Type of Analysis	*Actual*	*Potential*
Organization analysis	Unit output, productivity, and cost records.	Business plans (new products or services, new processes or technologies, etc.)
	Absenteeism records or reports.	
	Turnover records or reports.	Human resource plans.
	Grievance records or reports.	Organization development plans.
	Safety records or reports.	Delphi technique.
	Employee attitude surveys.	Affirmative action plans (anticipated utilization rates).
	Exit interviews.	
	Affirmative action plans (current utilization rates).	
Person analysis	Performance ratings or objective indexes.	Promotability and potential ratings.
	Skill tests.	Individual development plans.
	Assessment center results.	Career plans.
	Surveys:	Surveys:
	Self.	Self.
	Peers.	Peers.
	Supervisors.	Supervisors.
	Observation.	

the necessary abilities to perform effectively once the transformations are complete? Obviously, there is much speculation here, which no doubt helps to explain why most training is aimed at solving actual performance discrepancies.

Is the Performance Discrepancy Important?

A performance discrepancy is important if it has potentially negative consequences for the organization. Obviously, the importance of performance discrepancies depends to some extent on who is making the judgment. Two questions, however, are suggested to help keep the issue in perspective. One is, why is the performance discrepancy important? The other is, what would happen if it were ignored?

A performance discrepancy can be ignored if the answer to the first question bears no relationship to significant organizational outcomes. Certain behaviors of employees, for example, may drive managers up the wall, but if they have no effect on output, productivity, costs, and so forth, they may best be ignored (although the supervisors may need training on stress management). Further support for ignoring a performance discrepancy emerges if the answer to the second question is "nothing much." Some performance discrepancies take care of themselves with time, particularly if they were not very important to begin with. But many are too important and persistent to ignore, and these are the ones requiring further analysis.

Is Employee Development a Potential Solution?

Employee development is a potential solution to an important performance discrepancy when (1) the discrepancy is caused by a lack of ability rather than a lack of motivation to perform (there are better ways to deal with motivational problems), (2) the individual(s) involved have the aptitude and motivation needed to learn how to do the job better (the importance of "trainability" is palpable,[18] although it can sometimes be overcome by clever training design), (3) supervisors and peers are supportive of the desired behaviors (the effort will be wasted if learning is not reinforced on the job).[19]

Discerning the extent to which these three conditions are met is no easy task. The first two require direct knowledge of the individual(s) involved: Has this type of work been successfully performed before? Could it be done now if the individual's job depended on it? If the answer to these two questions is no, employee development is a definite possibility. It is still helpful to dig a little further: Has this type of material been learned before? Are the basic aptitudes there? Is there an important reason—for example, job retention—why the individual(s) should want to learn?

The third condition involves what is known as transfer of training. It often takes some careful organizational diagnosis to determine supervisory and peer attitudes toward employee development and the extent to which the prevailing climate is supportive of new ideas and behaviors. If conditions appear to be negative, often the best solution is not to give up on employee development, but to extend it to an entire work group through a process known as organization development (OD).

Is Employee Development the Preferred Solution?

Employee development may be a potential solution, but not a preferred one. It is to be preferred only when it is a relatively cost-effective

---

[18] For a review of the literature on trainability, see K. N. Wexley, "Personnel Training," *Annual Review of Psychology* 35 (1984), p. 527.

[19] The classic study here is E. A. Fleishman, "Leadership Climate, Human Relations Training, and Supervisory Behavior," *Personnel Psychology* 6 (1953), pp. 205–22. For a recent review of the goings-on since, see Wexley, "Personnel Training."

means of correcting an important performance discrepancy. Other possible solutions may include a job change, the introduction of such work aids as special instructional sheets or computational devices, or creativity. Illustration 13–1 provides a particularly poignant example of the use of creativity in the place of a potentially expensive training program.

ILLUSTRATION 13–1

On the Effectiveness of Not Holding a Formal Training Course

The Situation:

In a major manufacturer of textiles considerable pressure was being put on the training director to hold a course for supervisors on the union contract. Managers contended that because the union stewards knew the contract better than the supervisors, the company was being bamboozled from time to time.

Diagnosis suggested to the training director, however, that this situation bothered managers far more than it bothered the supervisors. Thus, one essential ingredient for successful training, motivation, appeared to be lacking. In addition, the textile industry was in a slump, and every extra cost was examined with great care.

The Solution:

Rather than confront management with the probable futility of a training course, the training director decided to commission the development of a test to determine what the supervisors knew about the contract. He alleged that such a test would provide baseline data to make training more efficient.

To simulate on-the-job conditions, supervisors would be able to consult their contracts and each other during the test. To provide an incentive, the company president agreed to provide a steak dinner for the best performing supervisor and his manager. The training director also encouraged and successfully brought about sizable side bets among supervisors and managers from different mills. The test was deliberately made comprehensive and difficult.

Tests were delivered simultaneously to all mills at 8:00 one morning. At 8:05 the test writer's phone began to ring; it did not stop for a week. Supervisors and their managers held exam-taking sessions before work, during breaks, during lunch, after work, and at night. The activity was frenzied. Everyone protested that each question had two, three, or even four correct answers.

Results:

Within a week all tests were in and all were perfect or near perfect. Two weeks later, the president hosted a steak dinner for all 75 supervisors and their managers. During the cocktail hour and during and after dinner, the test writer was surrounded by indignant supervisors quoting sections of the contract verbatim to support contentions that certain test questions were unfair.

No formal training course was ever given. Management pressure for such a course disappeared.

Source: P. Thayer and W. McGehee, "On the Effectiveness of Not Holding a Formal Training Course," *Personnel Psychology* 30 (1977), pp. 455–56.

When Does It Not Matter?

It would be inappropriate, to say the least, to leave the impression that all or even most training results from a careful needs analysis of the type just described. As noted earlier, some training is legally or contractually required and must be given whether or not it is truly needed. Often employee development needs are simply assumed; many companies, for example, give all new employees a standard orientation program. Many others—IBM is one—require all newly appointed managers irrespective of education or experience to attend an intensive training program (usually centered on personnel matters) shortly after assuming their new jobs.

Sometimes employees hear about programs being offered, perhaps by professional associations or universities, and, discerning or assuming their own employee development needs, nominate themselves for attendance. Not uncommon either are training programs that are offered at the insistence of an influential manager ("All the boys at the country club have one") or because they are hot on the training circuit. Finally, there are the boondoggles—that is, done-for-fun programs usually justified by the need to raise or maintain morale.

FORMULATING THE EMPLOYEE DEVELOPMENT PLAN

It might be thought that as employee development needs are identified, the next step would be to develop appropriate training programs. However, since needs typically exceed available resources, it is usually necessary to formulate a strategy for meeting as many of them as possible with available staff, facilities, and funds.

The allocation process is conceptually straightforward. First, overall objectives are set, for example, to bring all first level supervisors up to date on their equal employment opportunity obligations, to provide all fast-track managers with the training called for by their career development plans, and the like. Then, employee development needs are assigned priorities, resources are allocated in priority order until they are exhausted, and surviving in-house programs are integrated into a working plan.

In reality, priorities are seldom clear-cut. First priority typically must go to employee development needs that are legally or contractually required (such as programs to upgrade women and minorities, or apprenticeship programs for trade union members). After these needs are met, however, matters become less clear-cut as resource and sometimes delicate political considerations come into play. Decision makers must balance many factors—estimates of benefit-cost ratios, estimates of prob-

able program success, managers' demands, and employee desires—
using a heavy dose of professional judgment.

Once priorities are determined, they may be codified in the form of an
employee development plan that shows (1) who will be trained, (2) the
programs, (3) time frames, (4) person(s) responsible, and (5) resources
and facilities to be used. Some plans are laid out for specific individuals,
but most are organized around programs.

Program listings and time frames may be communicated through
various channels. The study of 1,006 employers referred to earlier found
that nearly two thirds of the respondents relied primarily on managers to
do this, since they were the ones who usually selected program participants. About half of the respondents prepared booklets or flyers listing
scheduled programs, posted notices on bulletin boards, and/or published
the information in more general employee publications.[20]

DESIGNING TRAINING PROGRAMS

As Figure 13–1 shows, once an employee development plan is drawn
up, it is then necessary to design the various training programs that will
be offered or to rework, if necessary, those that have been offered
before. In each case, this involves setting instructional objectives, determining program content, and deciding on training methods and techniques. The design work may be done by specially designated training
professionals, especially for programs to be offered several times, or left
to individual instructors.

Setting Instructional Objectives

Instructional objectives are statements of what trainees should know,
believe, be able to do, do, or accomplish when a program is over. They
guide the selection of program content, and to some extent guide selection of methods and techniques. They also serve as the criteria against
which a program can be evaluated when it is over (a point to be discussed
later in this chapter).

Instructional objectives usually emerge from a needs analysis or the
program developer's understanding of the trainees' jobs (as determined
perhaps through job analysis) or the subject matter at hand. Mastery
modeling provides a relatively systematic approach to the identification

---

[20] Prentice-Hall, *Employee Training.*

of areas in which instructional objectives need to be set.[21] This approach requires the program developer to delineate for relevant jobs the behaviors of highly competent performers and to develop detailed descriptions of the knowledge and skills through which these individuals maintain their mastery.

Complete instructional objectives contain three elements: (1) a statement of desired performance, (2) an indication of any important conditions under which the desired performance is to occur, and (3) a criterion of acceptable performance that is suitable, if possible, for measurement.[22] They can take one or more of the following forms:

1. Knowledge objectives refer to the material participants are expected to know when the program is over.
2. Attitudinal objectives state the beliefs and convictions that participants are expected to hold as a result of the program.
3. Skill objectives describe the kinds of behaviors participants should be able to demonstrate under learning conditions.
4. Job behavior objectives indicate the desired responses of participants once they are back on the job.
5. Organizational results objectives state changes in profitability, sales, service, efficiency, costs, employee turnover, and the like that should result from the program.

Figure 13–3 shows how each type of objective might be stated for a training program on performance appraisal.

As this figure shows, a given training program may have multiple instructional objectives. Generally, short-run instructional objectives are stated in terms of knowledge, attitudes, or skills, with job behaviors being more intermediate in length and organizational results longer run. In many cases, the link between a training program and improved organizational results is so tenuous that it is unrealistic to set such objectives. Rather, it must be assumed that if trainees change their job behavior, the results will be beneficial to the organization.

Determining Program Content

Program content refers to the material to be covered and to the general sequence in which it will be presented. The two primary deter-

---

[21] D. F. Barr, "More Needs Analysis," *Training and Development Journal* 34 (1980), pp. 70–74; M. London and S. A. Stumpf, *Managing Careers* (Reading, Mass.: Addison-Wesley Publishing, 1982), pp. 174–78; and Wexley, "Personnel Training."

[22] R. F. Mager, *Preparing Instructional Objectives* (Belmont, Calif.: Pitman Learning, 1984), pp. 19–88.

FiGURE 13–3

Examples of Instructional Objectives

Type of Objective	Examples
Knowledge	All trainees will understand, and be able to attain a grade of 80 or better on a test designed to measure the principles of performance appraisal, including types, uses, assessment procedures, errors and their avoidance, providing feedback, and EEO issues.
Attitudes	All trainees will believe that performance appraisal is important to effective management and that every employee has a right to receive an accurate appraisal annually. To be judged by their statements in class and their behavior back on the job.
Skills	All trainees will be able accurately to appraise three videotaped examples of employee performance. All trainees will be able to provide high-quality feedback to these "subordinates" in role playing.
Job behavior	All trainees will provide all of their subordinates with high-quality appraisals within six months after completion of training.
Organizational results	All trainees' work groups will improve their performance levels by 5 percent during the first year following training.

minants of program content are instructional objectives and the information base that is available on the subject. When instructional objectives are specific to a particular job, job descriptions and specifications can serve as the information base (this is what training people usually call task or operation analysis). When they relate more to a broad field, general "theory" must be relied on. Sometimes both can be used. For the program in Figure 13–3, for example, the designer might first study the managers' jobs to determine how performance appraisal is to be used and then selectively choose from among the theoretical materials available on performance appraisal.

Program content should match job content inasmuch as possible for both practical and legal reasons. Practically, the greater the content validity, the more effective and efficient training can be—since no essential material is omitted, and no irrelevant material is included. Also, it helps to foster the transfer of training back to the job. Content validity is also a legal necessity, since training is often a prerequisite to job selection or assignment, and in this context it falls under Title VII of the Civil Rights Act as well as the *Uniform Guidelines on Employee Selection Procedures.*[23]

---

[23] J. S. Russell, A Review of Fair Employment Cases in the Field of Training," *Personnel Psychology* 37 (1984), pp. 261–76.

In recent years, systematic processes have been developed that enable "subject matter experts" to translate the behavioral content and knowledge and skills requirements of jobs into training program content.[24] So far, these have found greatest application on technical and service jobs (e.g., Coast Guard radio operator and police officer) rather than at professional or managerial levels. In these cases, however, statistical analyses have shown a high degree of fit,[25] and extensions are expected to higher-level jobs.[26]

In addition to job content, potential participants also influence training program content. Most material can and should be adjusted in level of difficulty and rate of presentation to be consistent with the participants' current state of understanding and their abilities to learn. This is one reason it is so important to assess trainability when employee development needs are determined.

A final determinant concerns the designer's beliefs about learning. One key issue involves *whole* versus *part* learning, that is, whether material is to be presented all at once and then repeated in total, or is to be broken into smaller elements, each to be mastered before the next is tackled. Generally, part learning is preferable, particularly when the material is complex.[27] Also, it is generally agreed that the transfer of training problem is lessened if material is presented in the same sequence in which it will be used on the job.[28] This is why it is important for designers to study job descriptions and the actual work performance of trainees.

Selecting Instructional Techniques

With instructional objectives and program content firmly in mind, consideration can be given to the techniques that will be used for the actual training. Deciding on the best approaches is more art than science. The decision is often constrained by the number of people who must be trained, budgetary considerations, the availability of facilities

---

[24] For a brief description, see Wexley, "Personnel Training."

[25] D. A. Bownas, M. J. Bosshardt, and L. F. Donnelly, "A Quantitative Approach to Evaluating Training Curriculum Content Sampling Adequacy," *Personnel Psychology* 38 (1985), pp. 117–31; and J. K. Ford and S. P. Wroten, "Introducing New Methods for Conducting Training Evaluation and for Linking Training Evaluation to Program Redesign," *Personnel Psychology* 37 (1984), pp. 651–65.

[26] W. H. Macey, "Linking Training Needs Assessment to Training Program Design." Paper presented at the 90th annual meeting of the American Psychological Association, Washington, D.C., 1982.

[27] K. N. Wexley and G. P. Latham, *Developing and Training Human Resources in Organizations* (Glenview, Ill.: Scott, Foresman, 1981), pp. 59–61.

[28] Wexley and Latham, *Developing and Training*, pp. 74–75.

and technologies (e.g., audiovisual aids, computers, and so on), and the experience and flexibility of the trainer(s).

With respect to techniques, program designers must first decide whether training should take place off the job or on. Within these two broad categories, choices must then be made about specific approaches.

Off-the-job training techniques

Figure 13–4 shows the major types of off-the-job training techniques. For convenience, these are divided into three types: (1) information presentation, (2) information processing, and (3) simulation.

Information presentation techniques.   These are preferred when instructional objectives focus on knowledge, the content is not too complex, participants are relatively capable and self-motivated, large

FIGURE 13–4
Off-the-Job Employee Development Methods and Techniques

Category	Methods and Techniques
1. Information presentation techniques—designed primarily to impart information with a minimum amount of activity by the learner.	a. Reading list. b. Correspondence course. c. Film. d. Lecture. e. Panel discussion. f. Programmed or computer-based instruction—material to be learned is presented in a series of carefully planned steps either in a booklet or on a screen. Learners move at their own pace, answering preprogrammed questions when ready. Answers are immediately "graded." Correct responses are reinforced, and the learner moves to new material. Incorrect responses require that the material be repeated.
2. Information-processing techniques—designed to involve groups of learners in the generation and discussion of material to be learned.	a. Conference or discussion group—a problem is presented to a group of learners who are expected to discuss the issues and reach a conclusion. Usually a leader provides guidance and feedback. b. T (training) group—similar to the conference or discussion group technique, except that attention is focused on the behavior of the group and the learners' behavior as part of the group rather than on a substantive problem. Emphasis is on open and honest communications, especially concerning personal feelings.

FIGURE 13–4 *(concluded)*

Category	Methods and Techniques
3. Simulation techniques—designed to represent the work environment to a greater or lesser degree and to actually involve the learner (experiential learning)	a. Incident/case—similar to the conference or discussion group technique, except that real organizational problems rather than general problems are used as the basic stimulus for discussion.
	b. Role playing—trainees are assigned and act out organizational roles, usually followed by trainer or group feedback. Sometimes involves role reversals—for example, a white supervisor playing the role of a minority employee and vice versa.
	c. In-basket—the trainee assumes a role and makes a set of decisions as presented in an in-basket filled with customer complaints, operating problems, personnel difficulties, and the like. In follow-up discussion, the trainee receives feedback from the trainer.
	d. Vestibule—a duplicate work operation is set up independent of the usual work site. Trainees learn under realistic situations but apart from production pressures.
	e. Mock-up—the essential aspects of a work environment are duplicated, usually in a manner that allows specific problems to be introduced. Classic example is the Link trainer used to train airline pilots.
	f. Business game—attempts to simulate the economic functioning of an entire organization either manually or on a computer. Trainees make decisions concerning market strategies, pricing, staffing levels, and so forth and observe the results on sales, profits, and so on.

numbers are to be trained, and the budget is limited (except in the case of programmed or computer-based instruction, where developmental costs may be quite high). These techniques provide a relatively efficient way to organize and present a large volume of material to a great many people in a limited period of time. The problem is that they are very much trainer (or technology) centered, and thus they may not appeal to adult learners who are used to taking a more active role in their own development.[29] Furthermore, most of them (programmed or computer-

---

[29] D. W. Lacey, R. J. Lee and L. J. Wallace, "Training and Development," in *Personnel Management,* eds. K. M. Rowland and G. R. Ferris (Boston: Allyn & Bacon, 1982).

based instruction aside) provide few opportunities for pacing the material to allow for individual differences in learning rates. Still, it is rare not to have at least some lecture time (perhaps augmented by films or panel discussions) to introduce concepts and organize or summarize material that has been dealt with using other instructional techniques.

Among the information presentation techniques, computer-based instruction is clearly in the ascendancy. This, of course, parallels the sharp increase in the use of computers in P/HR more generally. It also reflects the value of this approach, particularly in the development of technical skills. Research has shown significant reductions in learning time and instructional costs over more conventional training techniques, with no significant differences in learning or subsequent job performance.[30]

Information processing techniques. Such techniques, particularly conference or discussion groups, are particularly well suited as adjuncts when the objective is to enhance knowledge—especially when the material is complex, the participants are experienced or lacking in self-motivation, and the number of trainees is (or can be made) manageable. An application of this approach may be found in many introductory personnel courses where lectures are supplemented by weekly discussion sessions allowing for in-depth exploration of the material. Information-processing techniques may also be somewhat effective in changing attitudes. Research has shown that simply presenting information has relatively little effect on attitudes, but group discussions can be more effective in this respect because trainees feel peer pressure to change, and the new attitudes can be reinforced by the group.[31] A relatively common use of this approach has been to eliminate sexist or racist attitudes on the part of white male supervisors soon to be assigned women or minority subordinates for the first time. New skills, particularly communications and interpersonal skills, may also be learned through information-processing techniques, either directly or as a by-product; this is the main purpose of T-groups, for example.

Simulation techniques. When it comes to developing skills, however, simulation techniques generally are most effective. The reason for this may be summed up in one word: *practice.* Manual or motor skills are sharpened through vestibule training and the use of mock-ups; leadership and supervisory skills can be honed through the use of role playing; and problem-solving and decision-making skills are developed

---

[30] Wexley, "Personnel Training," pp. 534–36.

[31] For an interesting discussion, see J. P. Campbell, M. D. Dunnette, E. E. Lawler III, and K. E. Weick, Jr., *Managerial Behavior, Performance, and Effectiveness* (New York: McGraw-Hill, 1970), p. 254. This book is a classic and should be read by every serious student of management and management development.

through cases, in-basket exercises, and business games. Illustration 13–2, for example, describes Looking Glass, a currently popular business game.

One simulation technique—role playing—may be as effective in changing attitudes as in developing skills. This is accomplished through role reversals (e.g., by assigning blacks to play whites and vice versa). Trainees are thus forced to engage in discrepant behavior and to defend actions stemming from attitudes that are foreign to those held before training. This approach has been found particularly effective when the new attitudes are reinforced on the job.

Often the three major types of off-the-job training techniques—infor-

---

ILLUSTRATION 13-2

Looking Glass: Example of a Business Game

Looking Glass is a business game created by the Center for Creative Leadership in Greensboro, North Carolina, and used by some of America's largest corporations—AT&T, Dow Jones, Union Pacific, Monsanto—to train managers for a wide variety of purposes. AT&T, for example, uses it to teach middle managers to cope with the ambiguities of deregulation. Dow Jones's purpose is to encourage managers from different segments of the company to get to know one another and, thus, enhance cooperation on the job. Union Pacific has a similar intent. Monsanto uses it as part of a management course designed to lure scientists into executive jobs (it is supposed to dispel stereotypes of managers as uncreative drones).

Looking Glass is a make-believe glass manufacturing company with $200 million in annual sales and 4,000 employees. It comes replete with hundreds of pages and descriptive material: financial records and reports, marketing research results, memos. Managers participate 20 at a time, "working" in an elaborately staged environment consisting of a suite of offices, large meeting rooms, a telephone network, and a distribution system for memos. The idea is to recreate the "hectic disorder" of a typical work environment.

Memos are used to present participants with a myriad of problems, 99 in all, concerning such situations as possible acquisitions, plant locations, lagging production, and poor financial results. Unlike many such games, the idea is not to make more money than other teams, but rather to identify and solve the various problems. In the process, managers' styles and decision-making and communications skills, as well as the quality of team interactions, are exposed to close scrutiny.

The one-day simulation is followed by a one-day debriefing during which participants receive feedback from the many trainers who are on the scene and from each other. This, it is hoped, will lead to the motivation to improve.

Usually conducted as part of a one-week management development program at a cost of $1,500 per participant, Looking Glass is not cheap. Is it worth it? Unfortunately, no solid evidence is available one way or the other. But participants continue to come: Over 4,000 have played the game thus far.

Source: P. Petre, "Games that Teach You to Manage," *Fortune*, October 29, 1984, pp. 65–72.

mation presentation, information processing, and simulation—are used in various combinations during a single training program. To cite one example, the objectives of the training programs described in Illustration 13–4 were to improve managers' understanding of the performance appraisal process and to improve the quality of their performance appraisal ratings and feedback sessions. One program involved only an information presentation technique—computer-aided instruction (CAI). The other added to CAI a 12-hour workshop that combined information presentation (lectures, videotapes), information processing (group discussions), and simulation (role playing) techniques. As might be expected, the CAI alone was as effective as the CAI plus the workshop (CAIW) in improving trainees' knowledge and rating skills, but the latter was more effective in improving quality of their on-the-job appraisal feedback.

Behavior modeling is an increasingly popular training approach.[32] One of its attractive features is the use of all three types of off-the-job training techniques in a single integrated package. Another is the incorporation of role modeling and social reinforcement techniques, as well as specific actions to facilitate the transfer of training.

In behavior modeling, program content is usually based on careful job analysis, and is presented in logical modules, each with its own "learning points." In each module, trainees observe desired behaviors in films and videotapes and reinforce and practice these behaviors in group discussions and role-playing exercises. Constant feedback is provided by trainers and fellow trainees during group discussions and role playing. At the end of each module, trainees are provided copies of key "learning points," given instructions on how to use them on the job, and instructed to do so soon and often. At the beginning of the next module, they are asked to report on their successes and failures. (Sometimes supervisors are also trained on how to reinforce trainees who exhibit desired behaviors on the job.)

Not surprisingly, given the strong theoretical base and comprehensiveness of behavior modeling, the available research suggests that it is often quite successful, especially in increasing knowledge and skills and in changing attitudes. Mixed findings with respect to job behaviors and results, however, have led some to suggest the need to ensure that considerable posttraining reinforcement is provided to increase the moti-

---

[32] First popularized by G. P. Goldstein and M. Sorcher, *Changing Supervisory Behavior* (New York: Pergamon Press, 1974). See also Wexley and Latham, *Developing and Training*, pp. 176–79; and Latham, "Human Resource Training," pp. 569–71. A recent review of 70 studies on the effectiveness of management training found behavior modeling to be a particularly effective approach; see M. J Burke and R. R. Day, "A Cumulative Study of the Effectiveness of Managerial Training," *Journal of Applied Psychology* 71 (1986), pp. 232–46.

vation to apply newly attained abilities once trainees return to their jobs.[33]

On-the-job training techniques

Figure 13–5 shows the major types of training techniques that take place on the job. Rather than attempting to change job behavior by changing knowledge, attitudes, or skills in a more or less artificial environment, these techniques attempt to change job behavior more directly while employees remain on their jobs or take on special assignments or tasks. On-the-job training is often used to supplement off-the-job training in the interest of facilitating the otherwise often elusive improvements in job behavior and organizational results.

On-the-job training is widespread; one study showed, for example, that about three fourths of the respondents were involved with it in a planned way.[34] Of course, its usage is limited to situations where mistakes can be tolerated. Airlines pilots and surgeons, for example, get to practice on the job only after their skills have been sharply honed using off-the-job simulation techniques.

Normally, a trade-off exists between off- and on-the-job training techniques. Off-the-job training is relatively efficient from the standpoint of learning, but relatively inefficient in transferring learning from the classroom to the job. On-the-job techniques present few transfer-of-training problems. At the same time, on-the-job learning may be particularly inefficient for two reasons. One concerns a lack of control over program content, which is determined by day-to-day job demands. The other concerns supervisory or peer trainers, who normally have many responsibilities in addition to employee development and who may receive little training for the task and no rewards for doing it well. A story is told, for example, about chicken catchers who work in nine-person crews and who are paid on a group incentive plan according to the number of birds they catch and crate. These employees deeply resent the introduction of trainees on their crews because the training task detracts from the catching task, and everyone's pay goes down.[35]

---

[33] J. S. Russell, K. N. Wexley, and J. E. Hunter, "Questioning the Effectiveness of Behavior Modeling Training in an Industrial Setting, *Personnel Psychology* 37 (1984), pp. 465–81. For more on the transfer of learning from off-the-job training to on-the-job performance, see K. N. Wexley and T. T. Baldwin, "Posttraining Strategies for Facilitating Positive Transfer: An Empirical Exploration," *Academy of Management Journal* 29 (1986), pp. 503–20; and Latham, "Human Resource Training," p. 575–76.

[34] H. Gorlin, *Personnel Practices I: Recruitment, Placement, Training, Communication.* Conference Board Information Bulletin No. 89 (New York: The Conference Board, 1981).

[35] Wexley and Latham, *Developing and Training*, p. 108.

FIGURE 13–5

On-the-Job Employee Development Methods and Techniques

Category	*Methods and Techniques*
1. Techniques based on actual job assignment	a. Coaching. This method has been described as the process of ensuring that employee development occurs in the day-to-day supervisor-subordinate relationship. Basically, in coaching, the supervisor acts much as a tutor in an academic setting. His/her function is to serve as a favorable role model and to facilitate the learning process by providing guidance, assistance, feedback, and reinforcement.
	b. Job Instruction Training (JIT). It consists in training the supervisors who in turn train the employees (especially white- and blue-collar employees as well as technicians). Supervisors are trained to follow instructions such as (1) preparing the trainee; (2) demonstrating the job; (3) having the trainee perform the job; and (4) checking frequently the trainee's performance.
2. Techniques based on temporary job assignments	a. Special assignments. A common method of employee development, involves putting trainees on special committees, projects, or jobs, usually on a temporary basis. Often the purpose is to give the trainees an opportunity to work on special problems to which they otherwise would not become exposed. This approach often is combined with coaching.
	b. Job rotation involves the systematic movement of trainees through a predetermined set of jobs, usually with the objective of providing exposure to many parts of an organization and to a variety of functional areas. It may be combined with coaching at each stop. Often newly hired college graduates are involved in job rotation before receiving permanent assignments. Another common usage: to provide broad exposure to fast-track managers whose career plans suggest they will reach general management positions.

All of this is not to suggest that on-the-job training cannot be effective. It clearly can be effective, but the oft-heard shibboleth that one learns by doing is a gross oversimplification of the facts. One effectively and efficiently learns by doing only when the situation is carefully managed and when continual guidance and assistance are provided by skilled mentors who have the time and motivation necessary to do the job.

TEACHING

The ability to teach, as every college student knows, is an attribute not possessed by all. It is extraordinarily difficult to transform an ordinary manager or training specialist into a spellbinding lecturer, discussion leader, or coach. But a few general principles have emerged from research and practice that trainers can use to good advantage in the classroom or on the job. These principles, if consistently and carefully applied, help trainers facilitate learning by building on whatever ability and motivation trainees bring to the task.

The principles fall into the following general categories: goal setting, material presentation, practice, feedback, and classroom demeanor.

Goal Setting

Goals are powerful spurs to performance in training as well as other settings.[36] They help cognitively because trainees know what is expected of them. They also help motivationally by energizing, directing, and sustaining effort toward their accomplishment. Instructional objectives can be communicated to trainees and, if accepted, can serve as their goals as well as the trainer's. Since instructional objectives may be seen as rather general and remote, trainers usually find it desirable as well to set subgoals along the way. Subgoals can be time based: By the end of the morning, you should be able to complete an arc weld that is both solid and pleasing to the eye. Or they may be content based (when part learning is employed): On completion of this section of the course, you should be able to compute three validity coefficients from raw data sets with 100 percent accuracy.

Research suggests that instructional objectives (or subgoals) are most effective in enhancing performance when they are specific (it is not optimal simply to tell trainees to do their best) and challenging. Challenging objectives are those that stretch the abilities of the trainees but are not so difficult that they are seen as impossible to reach and thus not worth striving for. Setting challenging subgoals for trainees is a challenging subgoal for trainers.

Actually, it may be possible in some cases to short-circuit the arduous task of setting objectives. Research has shown that at least in some cases

---

[36] Latham, "Human Resource Training," pp. 567–71.

simply telling trainees that they have high success potential has a positive effect on their training performance. Why is not entirely clear, although the effect is probably to cause the trainees to set higher goals for themselves than they otherwise would and to work hard to achieve these goals and avoid "failure." The effect appears to be stronger among men than among women.

A related phenomenon is the so-called Pygmalion effect.[37] Here the communication regarding potential is with trainers rather than trainees, but the result is the same.[38] The trainers apparently develop higher expectations of the anointed trainees and subconsciously communicate these expectations and act in a more supportive manner during training. Further research is necessary to ascertain how best to persuade trainers that all their trainees have high potential or, failing this, to discover, harness, and make conscious those trainer behaviors that are responsible for the salubrious results.

Material Presentation

In general, material should be presented to trainees in the way that will be most meaningful and easily understood. The trainer can take a giant step in this direction at the outset of a program and the beginning of each subpart by providing trainees with an overview of the material to be learned. This helps to highlight goals (or subgoals) and to tie the pieces of the material together. Then the material should be presented in a logical order, recognizing that the trainer may not totally control this when discussion and other participative training techniques are used.

Attempts to develop "natural" hierarchies of cognitive skills for presentation purposes have thus far met with mixed results.[39] Attempts have yet to be made with respect to other types of skills, knowledge, or attitudes.

Practice

A key to learning is practice. Practice enables trainees to shape appropriate responses to behaviors in an environment where mistakes are not too costly.

---

[37] E. Eden and G. Ravid, "Pygmalion versus Self-Expectancy: Effects of Instructor- and Self-Expectancy on Trainee Performance," *Organizational Behavior and Human Performance* 30 (1982), pp. 351–64.

[38] Eden and Ravid, "Pygmalion"; and D. Eden, "Self-Fulfilling Prophecy as a Management Tool: Harnessing Pygmalion," *Academy of Management Review* 9 (1984), pp. 64–73.

[39] Wexley, "Personnel Training," p. 529.

Should practice be massed or spaced over time? Prevailing opinion seems to suggest that practice sessions should be spaced whenever possible.[40] It is not entirely clear why, although it may have something to do with minimizing fatigue. The notion of spaced practice is entirely consistent with designing program content in parts and setting subgoals for each part. Often practice can be done cumulatively: At the end of part 1 of a training program, the skills learned in that part are practiced; at the end of part 2, the skills learned in parts 1 and 2 are practiced; and so on. This apparently helps learning when the material covered in the various parts is interrelated and likely to be required in its entirety on the job.

How much practice is enough? Available evidence suggests that there can be both too much and too little, but that the right amount (alas!) varies from situation to situation.[41] For most tasks, it is probably sufficient to continue practice until trainees are able to demonstrate satisfactory levels of performance several times within tolerable limits of error. For tasks that are encountered only infrequently on the job, are performed under stressful conditions, and are critical—for example, the use of firearms by police officers or emergency procedures by airline pilots— trainers use the concept of overlearning. That is, they continue practice far beyond the point of ordinary proficiency. The purpose of this is to build up such a strong stimulus-response connection in the trainees' minds that the learned skills will be invoked almost automatically if and when the trainee is actually faced with an armed suspect or a malfunctioning jet engine.

Feedback

In training, as elsewhere, feedback is important to performance because it helps keep learning on track and because it can serve as a form of reward or punishment to foster motivation. This is particularly true in self-paced, as opposed to externally paced, learning environments. Some feedback comes from the learning task itself as practice is successfully carried out and goals and subgoals are attained. Other feedback comes from the trainer and/or fellow trainees in the form of verbal instructions, praise, or criticism. Returning to the concepts of expectancy theory (see Chapter 5), feedback is expected to motivate to the extent it is positively valent to trainees and is linked closely enough to desired behaviors to develop strong instrumentality perceptions.

"Rules" for the provision of verbal feedback can be derived from these

---

[40] Wexley and Latham, *Developing and Training*, p. 59.
[41] Wexley, "Personnel Training," p. 529.

concepts. For example, although verbal feedback can be either positive or negative, positive tends to be more effective in shaping behavior. Negative feedback, especially if it is critical in tone, can generate defensive rather than desired behaviors by trainees. Furthermore, when negative feedback is in order, it is better given by trainers, who have legitimacy in the training situation, than by fellow trainees.[42] Both positive and negative feedback should be as specific as possible to clarify expectations and eliminate ambiguity. "That isn't quite right," is not quite right. "Lighting that cigarette while working with inflammable cleaning solvent could get us all killed and should never be done again" is better. Finally, verbal feedback should be provided as soon as practicable after the act that is being acknowledged; a close linkage helps to increase instrumentality perceptions.

Experienced trainers point out that great individual differences in the need for verbal feedback usually exist in any group of trainees. Some seem to adjust their behaviors and maintain their motivation with only task feedback, and others require considerable feedback from the trainer.

Classroom Demeanor

Classroom trainers should behave in a professional manner, employing the best available training techniques and teaching methods and treating trainees fairly and ethically. Many observers believe that trainers should think of themselves as models for trainees by demonstrating desired behaviors whenever possible, working hard to eliminate annoying habits that retard learning, and developing a repertoire of knowledge and skills that can be brought to bear in varying situations almost on demand.[43]

All of this is to suggest that effective teachers are, to some extent at least, made, not born. For this reason, significant portions of many employee development efforts are programs designed to train the trainers. Such efforts probably represent money well spent whether training is to take place off or on the job.[44]

---

[42] D. R. Ilgen, C. D. Fisher, and M. S. Taylor, "Consequences of Individual Feedback on Behavior in Organizations," *Journal of Applied Psychology* 64 (1979), pp. 349–71; and Latham, "Human Resource Training," pp. 567–76.

[43] R. F. Mager, *Developing Attitude toward Learning*, 2d ed. (Belmont, Calif.: Pitman Learning, 1984), especially Chapters 7 and 10. Readers of this book will find, of course, that their instructors measure up well against these standards.

[44] Model "training the trainer" programs are discussed by Wexley and Latham, *Developing and Training*, pp. 18–21 and 107–11.

EVALUATING EMPLOYEE DEVELOPMENT PROGRAMS

Evaluation is the final formal phase of the employee development process (see Figure 13–1). As the preceding discussion suggests, evaluation actually takes place at two levels—first, to determine if the various training programs were successful and, second, to assess the extent to which the overall employee development process met its goals. Evaluation results can be made available to those responsible for developing and carrying out future training programs and employee development efforts in an attempt to facilitate improvement (as shown in Figure 13–1). When positive, they also can be used to justify the existence of the employee development activity to top-level P/HR and line managers.

Trainers and employee development managers are often sharply criticized for not doing better jobs of evaluating their programs. In point of fact, however, they probably are no worse than other P/HR specialists and managers in this respect, and most of them undoubtedly do about as much as can be expected given the pressures of their jobs and the resources at their disposal. Most seem to feel (apparently correctly) that management would rather see 10 training programs that appear to be meeting important employee development needs than 6 or 8 that have been rigorously evaluated (some, perhaps, with negative results). Further, many know that negative results can be, and often are, used not in the "spirit of inquiry" but in the "spirit of retribution."

None of this condones present practices, but it does serve to direct whatever blame is in order to the right place—that is, on P/HR and line managers who are content to take training on faith rather than allocate a portion of available resources in a positive way toward eventual improvement.

Evaluating Training Programs

Since training programs are discrete events, it is possible to evaluate each one separately. At a basic level, this can be done by obtaining trainee reactions to the program. At a more advanced level, the task is to determine with as much confidence as possible (1) how much change in knowledge, attitudes, skills, job behaviors, or organizational results occurred among the participants in the program, and (2) to what extent this change can reasonably be attributed to their participation in the program. Inasmuch as possible, these questions are answered in a way that provides maximum information for those who must develop future programs.

What was the participant reaction?

Participant reaction is usually assessed during or immediately following a training program either through interviews or questionnaires. An example would be the course evaluations completed by college students at many universities at the end of each semester. Assessed are such things as how well the program was liked, aspects that facilitated or retarded learning (e.g., habits of the trainer), most and least relevant topics covered, and probable usefulness once trainees return to their jobs.

Since it is easy to do, participant reaction is by far the most frequently used approach to training evaluation.[45] And the results can be useful to trainers, particularly in spotting major deficiencies in course content, training techniques, and trainers. Positive results can also be helpful in garnering management support for a program, although negative ones can just as easily lead to premature termination of a program that is much needed and could be made to work. The big weakness of this approach is that it provides no solid indication of whether any learning or behavioral change occurred. Thus, if these are objectives of the program, participant reaction must be regarded as at best an adjunct to other, more sophisticated methods of evaluation, all of which begin with an assessment of change.

How much change occurred?

To assess change requires comparable measures of evaluation criteria before and after training occurs. This requires trainers to decide what criteria to use, how to measure them, and when to measure them.

Criteria.   Actually, the choice of evaluation criteria occurs before training when instructional objectives are set because the two concepts are synonymous. Programs are evaluated based on what the trainer sets out to do. Thus, relevant criteria include learning in terms of knowledge, attitudes, or skills; behavioral change on the job; and/or improvements or decrements in organizational results.

Measures.   Learning can be measured using paper and pencil tests (for knowledge), questionnaires (for attitudes), or work sample tests (for skills). Behavioral change is assessed by means of such performance measures as indicators of individual output (e.g., units produced or dollar sales) or one of the many forms of performance appraisal. Various

---

[45] L. Digman, "How Companies Evaluate Management Development Programs," *Human Resource Management* 19 (1980), pp. 9–13.

types of reports can be used to measure organizational results; examples include profit-and-loss statements, unit output reports, cost reports, and turnover records. The ultimate measure in organizational results is utility, that is, an assessment of the dollar benefits accruing from such things as increased sales or reduced costs in comparison with the dollar costs of the program.

Timing. Since evaluation is concerned with change, it follows that the appropriate criterion measures must be obtained both before and after the program takes place. How much before and after varies with the type of measure(s) under consideration. Generally, assessments of knowledge, attitudes, and skills are obtained shortly before and immediately after the program. Measures of job performance are taken from some typical period a few weeks or months before the program and again a few weeks or months after trainees have returned to the job. Similarly, measures of organizational results are taken from some typical period a few weeks or months before the program, but are not taken again until several months after trainees have returned to the job, since it typically will take a while before behavioral changes can be expected to result in, say, improved profits or reduced turnover.

The approaches to training evaluation that use before-and-after criterion measures are shown at the top of Figure 13–6.[46] The first is called the before-and-after design, and the second is the time series design. The main difference is that in the former before and after measures of the evaluation criteria are taken only once each, and in the latter they are taken several times each. The advantage of the time series design is that it enables the evaluator to determine if there were upward or downward trends in the criterion measures before training that should be taken into account when assessing the program's effect. One disadvantage is that the design is difficult to use for knowledge, attitudinal, and skills criteria. (How many tests or questionnaires can trainees be expected to put up with?) A second disadvantage is the high costs of multiple measures.

Both the before-and-after and the time series designs show whether change has occurred, but neither can provide much assurance that the change is attributable to the training program. The change could have resulted from a number of alternative factors, particularly alterations at the workplace. For example, during a training program to change the attitudes of white supervisors toward black employees, many of the latter may be hired for the first time. If supervisory attitudes change, the question arises as to whether the change is due to the training experience

---

[46] For an outstanding treatment of this topic that goes well beyond the issues raised here, see T. D. Cook and D. T. Campbell, *Quasi-Experimentation: Design and Analysis Issues for Field Settings* (Skokie, Ill.: Rand McNally, 1979).

FIGURE 13–6
Training Evaluation Designs

Name	Number Groups	Process
1. Before and After	1	M_B (T) M_A
2. Time Series	1	M_{B1} M_{B2} M_{B3} M_{Bn} (T) M_{A1} M_{A2} M_{A3} M_{An}
3. Before and After with	1	(R) M_B (T) M_A
Control Group	2	(R) M_B M_A
4. Time Series with	1	(R) M_{B1} M_{B2} M_{B3} M_{Bn} (T) M_{A1} M_{A2} M_{A3} M_{An}
Control Group	2	(R) M_{B1} M_{B2} M_{B3} M_{Bn} M_{A1} M_{A2} M_{A3} M_{An}
5. After Only with	1	(R) (T) M_A
Control Group	2	(R) M_A
6. Solomon Four	1	(R) M_B (T) M_A
Group	2	(R) M_B M_A
	3	(R) (T) M_A
	4	(R) M_A

(T) = Training.
M_B = Measurement of criteria before training.
M_A = Measurement of criteria after training.
(R) = Random assignment of employees to training and control groups.

or is something that would have occurred without the expense of training simply through the increased exposure to black employees.

Can the change be attributed to the training program?

How does an evaluator determine whether a program is, in fact, responsible for observed change? The usual approach is to use a control group whenever feasible. A control group consists of employees who are as much like the trainees as possible except that they do not participate in the training program.

Examples 3 and 4 in Figure 13–6 show the most common designs of this type, which really are nothing more than the two designs discussed earlier with control groups added. In these designs, members of both groups are subjected to the same criteria measures, and the results are compared. If the trainees improve more than the members of the control group, the training program gets the credit. Figure 13–7 shows the power of both the time series and the time series with control group designs. In the case shown, a before-and-after design (with measures at, say M_{B4} and M_{A2}) would indicate that the program had a slight positive effect. However, a time series analysis (part A of Figure 13–7) shows that the performance improvement represents only the continuation of a general upward trend resulting possibly from increased job experience. Thus, it might be concluded that the training had no effect. Add a control group (part B of Figure 13–7), however, and this possibility is discredited, since its performance fell off dramatically during the period following the training. Since the trainees show an improvement, and the control group does not, the ultimate conclusion is that the training program was indeed effective in meeting its instructional objective. Other, even more elaborate, designs are possible (see, for instance, designs 5 and 6 in Figure 13–6).

Evaluation designs involving control groups and the random assign-

FIGURE 13–7
Results from a Hypothetical Training Program

(A) Time series only

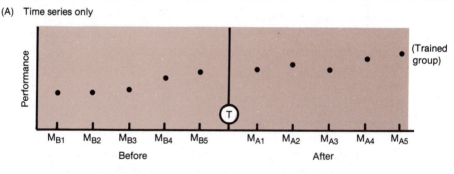

(B) Time series with control group

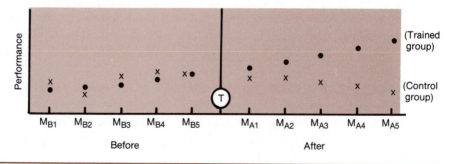

Source: Adapted from K. N. Wexley and G. P. Latham, *Developing and Training Human Resources in Organizations* (Glenview, Ill.: Scott, Foresman, 1981), pp. 94–95.

ment of employees to training and control groups are rare in practice. Often, there is no comparable group of employees to use for control purposes. Even where there is such a group, management is often unwilling to withhold (or delay) training for them just for the sake of evaulation. Similarly, management may be unwilling to tolerate random assignment of employees to training and control groups, preferring to retain control over who is trained and when. Nonetheless, it is often worthwhile to evaluate training programs with a less sophisticated design than not to evaluate them at all. CIGNA Corporation, for instance, was able to demonstrate a bottom-line effect of a management development program with a simple before-and-after design (number 1 in Figure 13–6).[47]

Illustration 13–3 describes an evaluation design that is about as sophisticated as they come (without getting into cost-benefit analysis, described below). In this example (1) the instructional objectives involved knowledge, skills, and job behaviors; (2) evaluation involved all three types of instructional objectives, plus trainees' reactions; (3) reactions were measured with a questionnaire, knowledge with a paper and pencil test, skills with a work sample test (role playing), and job behavior with performance appraisal; (4) the evaluation design is an after only with control group and random assignment (number 5 in Figure 13–6); and (5) the training was judged successful. The reactions were favorable, the trained group improved its performance more than the control group on all three criterion measures, and the control group caught up once it was trained.

Was the training worth the effort?

As noted earlier, in training designed to affect job performance and organizational results, the ultimate evaluation questions evolve around utility. More specifically, is the gain to the organization in increased performance enough greater than the cost of the training to justify the investment? Answering this question requires that dollar values be placed on various levels of performance and that various training costs be computed.

Training costs are fairly easy to compute. They consist of nonrecurring and recurring expenses. Nonrecurring costs are those associated with the development of training programs (such as the materials used by the developer and his or her salary), while recurring costs are those associ-

[47] B. Paquet, E. Kasl, L. Weinstein, and W. Waite, "The Bottom Line," *Training and Development Journal* 41 (May 1987), pp. 27–33.

ILLUSTRATION 13–3

Example of Training Program Evaluation

The Situation:

In a large international company, a training program was undertaken to improve leadership skills among the first-level supervisors. The program consisted of two hours of training each week for nine weeks. The sessions focused on: (1) orienting a new employee, (2) giving recognition, (3) motivating a poor performer, (4) correcting poor work habits, (5) discussing potential disciplinary action, (6) reducing absenteeism, (7) handling a complaining employee, (8) reducing turnover, and (9) overcoming resistance to change.

Each training session followed the same format: (1) an introduction to the topic by the trainers, (2) presentation of a film demonstrating effective behaviors, (3) group discussion of the film, and (4) role-playing with class feedback. In addition, trainees were encouraged to use the learned skills with one or more employees during the following week and to report the results during the next session. Problems were role-played and discussed. Superintendents to whom the supervisors reported were given an accelerated training program and encouraged to reinforce desirable behaviors by their subordinates on the job.

The Evaluation:

The evaluation design was (mostly) an after only with control group and random assignments, involving the first 20 supervisors to be trained and a like number of controls. The evaluation criteria, in addition to reactions measured by questionnaire, were: knowledge learning measured by a specially constructed paper and pencil test, skills learning measured by evaluations of role plays, and job behavior change measured with performance appraisals. Timing of the measures was as follows: reactions—immediately following and eight months after the training; knowledge learning—six months after training; skills learning—three months after training; and job behaviors—one month before (an exception to the overall design) and one year after the training.

The Results:

Trainees expressed high opinions of the program both immediately after training and eight months later. They also scored significantly better than the controls on both the knowledge and skills tests. And although the two groups had been rated the same on performance before training, the trained group was significantly better after. Further, when the control group was eventually trained, it caught up to the original group on all of the criteria.

The conclusion: "Leadership skills can be taught in a relatively short time period (i.e., 18 hours), providing that the trainees are given a model to follow, are given a specific set of goals or guidelines, are given an opportunity to perfect the skills, are given feedback as to the effectiveness of their behavior, and are reinforced with praise for applying the acquired skills on the job" (p. 245).

Source: G. P. Latham and L. M. Saari, "Application of Social-Learning Theory to Training Supervisors through Behavior Modeling," *Journal of Applied Psychology* 64 (1979), pp. 239–46. Copyright 1979 by the American Psychological Association. Reprinted/adapted by permission of the publisher and author.

ated with conducting such programs. Recurring costs can be further broken down into those that are fixed (such as facilities) and those that are variable (such as handouts provided to trainees, trainees' salaries while they are off the job).

While training costs are fairly easy to conceptualize and compute, the same is not true of the gains from training. How much, for example, is the performance improvement noted in Illustration 13–3 worth to the company involved? How would this be determined? The estimation of gains requires that evaluators not only place a dollar value on various levels of performance, but also take into account several factors that can affect these dollar values (e.g., the diminishing effect of training over time, and turnover rate among those who have been trained). Major conceptual and methodological advances in the measurement of training benefits have been made in recent years, but actual applications are few.[48] In a rare application, it was shown that a training program to develop the managerial skills of 65 bank supervisors that cost $50,000 to run returned two to three times that much (depending on the assumptions made) in three to five years.[49]

So far utility analysis has generally focused on hypothetical illustrations and simulations and on cost comparisons across training methods designed to accomplish comparable results (these are considered later).[50] However, this is an emerging field of P/HR research that eventually will help training managers estimate the cost effectiveness of their work and make better training decisions (for example, deciding which group of employees to train first or the smallest number of participants needed to justify a particular program). Thus, further field work is eagerly anticipated.[51]

Evaluating the Overall Employee Development Effort

In addition to evaluating each training program, some attention must be devoted to an assessment of the overall employee development effort. This type of evaluation helps to guide decisions concerning planning, programming, and budgeting.

---

[48] J. Boudreau, "Utility Analysis," in *Human Resource Management: Evolving Roles and Responsibilities, ASPA/BNA Handbook of Human Resource Management*, vol 1, ed. L. Dyer (Washington, D.C.: Bureau of National Affairs, 1988).

[49] J. E. Mathieu and L. Leonard, Jr., "Applying Utility Concepts to a Training Program in Supervisory Skills: A Time-Based Approach," *Academy of Management Journal* 30 (1987), pp. 316–35.

[50] W. F. Cascio, *Costing Human Resources: The Financial Impact of Behavior in Organizations*, 2d ed. (Boston: Kent Publishing, 1987).

[51] But, not by everyone. For a dissenting view, see Latham, "Human Resource Training," pp. 559–62.

Three issues are of concern at this point: effectiveness, efficiency, and EEO/AA results.

Effectiveness

The logical starting place for an evaluation of effectiveness is the data obtained through training program evaluations. If some programs did not meet their instructional objectives, the result is likely to be unmet employee development needs. It is also possible for every program to meet its instructional objectives and, yet, for the overall effort to leave some employee development needs unmet.

The latter situation occurs because of problems in the first two steps of the employee development process (see Figure 13–1). For example, important employee development needs may have been overlooked, or slippage may have occurred in the process of translating employee development needs into the employee development plan. Moreover, some of the programs called for in the employee development plan may not have been conducted, perhaps because of more pressing matters.

Efficiency

In the short run, the question of efficiency can be dealt with through the budget by asking whether employee development needs were met with available resources. In the longer run, however, it is important to know whether some of these needs might be met at a lower cost.

This question requires that forethought be given to evaluation before program implementation. The strategy is to conduct two or more pilot programs using different methods but aimed at the same employee development need and to compare the outcome in terms of results and effectiveness. Where feasible, this approach can provide extremely valuable information on which to base future decisions concerning program choice. An example of this type of evaluation is provided in Illustration 13–4.

Equal employment opportunity/affirmative action

In addition to effectiveness and efficiency, EEO/AA results are important criteria for judging the contribution of an employee development effort. Was all training conducted in a nondiscriminatory manner? And, for affirmative action employers, to what extent did it contribute to the attainment of AA goals and timetables?

To answer the first question P/HR professionals continually examine relevant records to ensure that:

ILLUSTRATION 13–4

Comparing the Relative Effectiveness of Alternative Employee Development Programs

The Situation

From a large multinational corporation, 260 managers located in the same metropolitan area were selected for training in performance appraisal (PA).

The Programs

All trainees participated in a computer-assisted instruction (CAI) course, which consisted of a textbook composed of six chapters, each of which was followed by four, 30-minute CAI learning activities on the relevant topic. In the latter, trainees were presented with case studies followed by questions involving judgments about the way PA was being handled or the PA actions they would take.

In addition to CAI, 111 of the managers also participated in a 12-hour behavioral modeling workshop (CAIW) in groups of 12 to 15. The first half day of the workshop consisted of an introduction and lectures on six "learning points" (preparation, nonverbal communication, active listening, giving positive and negative feedback, receiving feedback, reducing defensiveness). The next day was skills oriented and consisted of videotapes showing supervisors modeling the six "learning points," group discussions of the videotapes, and 20-minute role plays, which were videotaped and critiqued by trainers and other trainees.

The Evaluation Design

To evaluate the training, the after only with control group design (number 5 in Figure 13–6) was used. After training the two trained groups (CAI and CAIW) were compared against each other, and both of them were compared with an untrained control group consisting of 142 managers. (Since no before measures were taken, assignments to the three groups were made randomly; the purpose of this was to make it unlikely that the three groups differed before training.)

1. On- and off-the-job training is well distributed and not overly concentrated in geographic areas or occupations dominated by white males (as it tends to be).[52]

2. Women and minorities participate in training—and particularly in training that is a prerequisite to promotion or to pay increases—in numbers roughly proportional to their representation in the employee group(s) from which trainees are drawn.

3. Women and minorities successfully complete training in numbers roughly proportional to their representation in the appropriate trainee groups.

---

[52] Carnavale and Goldstein, *Employer Training.*

ILLUSTRATION 13-4 *(concluded)*

The criteria were of three types: knowledge, attitudes, and job behavior. Tests and questionnaires were used to measure knowledge of PA principles and attitudes toward PAs. Two aspects of job behavior were assessed: (1) the accuracy and thoroughness with which the managers rated their subordinates' performance and (2) the quality of PA feedback they provided their subordinates.

The Results

Knowledge of PA principles was higher for the two trained groups than for the control group, and there was no difference between the two trained groups in this respect. In other words, training improved understanding, and CAI alone was as effective in this respect as CAIW.

Attitudes toward PA did not differ among the three groups; the training had no effect here.

Job performance was affected variably. Accuracy and thoroughness of PAs were no higher for the trained groups than for the untrained groups. Quality of PA feedback provided, however, was higher for the trained than for the untrained groups, and highest for the CAIW group. That is, this aspect of job performance was improved by CAI, but even more so when the workshop was added.

The Conclusion

CAI helped some; CAIW helped a little more, especially on the feedback dimension. But, the study has a couple of serious flaws (as most do). First, the situation made it impossible to do the workshop without CAI, thus the efficacy of the two could not be directly compared. Second, no cost benefit data were obtained. So, it's difficult to say with any certainty whether the incremental increase in the quality of PA feedback was worth the obvious added expense of the workshop.

Source: B. L. Davis and M. K. Mount, "Effectiveness of Performance Appraisal Training Using Computer-Assisted Instruction and Behavior Modeling," *Personnel Psychology* 37 (1984), pp. 439–52.

---

4. Women and minorities perform as well and stay on the job as long as comparable white males.

Failures in any of these four areas do not necessarily mean that illegal discrimination has occurred. They do raise red flags, however, indicative of the need for further investigation into causes.[53] Both Title VII of the Civil Rights Act and *The Uniform Guidelines on Employee Selection Procedures* prohibit the use of sex and race as criteria for determining access to, or the completion of, training.

Affirmative action employers constantly monitor training activities

---

[53] Russell, "A Review of Fair Employment Cases."

against their affirmative action plans (AAPs) to ensure that promised programs are being delivered. They monitor situations of persistent underutilization for determining factors. There are many such factors, but at least two are training related. Sometimes special training that women and minorities may need to qualify for certain jobs has not been highlighted or provided. In other cases, managers and supervisors who make training and promotion decisions have been trained neither in the law nor in the special obligations attendant to affirmative action plans.

SUMMARY

Employee development is a planned process designed to provide employees with learning experiences that enhance their contributions to organizational goals. The process consists of several interrelated phases or steps.

The first is to identify employee development needs, that is, actual or potential performance discrepancies that are important to the organization and that can be remedied at least as effectively and efficiently by training as by any other means.

Once employee development needs are identified, an employee development plan is formulated specifying overall objectives, as well as who will be trained, major training programs, time frames, person(s) responsible, and resources and facilities to be used. Then individual training programs can be designed. Here trainers establish their instructional objectives and then decide on the material that will be taught and the methods and techniques that will be used to teach it.

Training can take place off the job or on. Off-the-job training tends to be relatively efficient from the standpoint of learning, but relatively inefficient in transferring learning from the classroom to the job. On-the-job training is just the opposite in nature.

In teaching, trainers have learned to use various principles to facilitate learning and the transfer of learning. These include goal setting, the meaningful organization of material, the organization of practice, the provision of feedback to trainees, and the use of appropriate classroom demeanor.

Employee development efforts and training programs must be systematically evaluated to determine whether objectives and learning goals are being met.

DISCUSSION QUESTIONS

1. When is employee development an appropriate solution for correcting a performance discrepancy? When is another solution more appropriate?

2. What are the various forms of instructional objectives? Think of a training problem, and state some possible objectives.

3. Why do trainers appear to be relatively unaffected by advancements in training theory and research? What can be done to overcome this problem?

4. To what extent can needs assessment be facilitated by the use of information flowing from the career management system discussed in Chapter 12?

5. What can be done to ensure that on-the-job training does not become too informal and haphazard?

6. Why is cooperation between management and unions more likely in solving training problems than in coping with other P/HR problems?

7. In what ways does utility analysis provide advantages over more traditional approaches to training evaluation? Where is it likely to be most useful? Least useful?

Case for Part Six

ARTHUR C. KAPLAN AND COMPANY

Background

Arthur C. Kaplan and Company (AC Kaplan), one of the major "Big Eight" accounting firms, is an international organization that provides accounting, auditing, and tax services in addition to developing management information systems and conducting a broad range of business consulting activities. Their client list numbers in the tens of thousands and ranges from small businesses to Fortune 500 companies. Kaplan's contracts include industrial organizations, financial and educational institutions, government, hospitals and religious organizations as well. The firm has offices in 52 U.S. cities and covers 31 nations. World headquarters are in London, with U.S. headquarters in New York City. The company employs almost 20,000 people, the vast majority of whom are young aggressive CPAs.

In light of the tremendous growth of the consulting industry, AC Kaplan has ambitious plans for expanding the firm. It is estimated that in the next five years alone they will need 900 new managers and about 200 new partners. Because AC Kaplan maintains a policy of promotion from within, these people will come mainly from the ranks of entry-level accountants. There is plenty of incentive for these young professionals to do well; starting salaries for partners average $125,000 (although normally no one reaches partner status until he or she has been with the firm for 10 years).

Training and Development

Given the critical importance of professional talent in the highly labor-intensive consulting business, AC Kaplan has devoted millions of dollars over the years to create in-house educational and training facilities that are the envy of the industry. The most observable indicator of this dedication is the very plush Corporate Education and Development Center (CEDC) in Rye, New York, 30 minutes north of New York City.

The 27-acre center provides living and meeting accommodations for approximately 500 persons and includes an impressive facility of class-rooms, conference rooms, libraries, and even a television studio. The center also employs a staff of nearly 50 instructors, mostly field managers who rotate on a two-year basis into the CEDC.

Every new Kaplan employee spends two weeks at CEDC before receiving a total of three additional months of training at one of nine other regional facilities in either Atlanta, Boston, Cleveland, Chicago, Dallas, Denver, Los Angeles, Portland, or St. Louis. All told, AC Kaplan and Company spends almost $1,200 per employee for training and education each year.

The majority of this investment is on technical and procedural training for entry-level accountants (e.g., accounting and finance, auditing, tax, business writing, time management). Additionally, employees receive extensive training in the specific industries where they will predomi-nantly work (e.g., oil and gas, manufacturing, banking, health care). The senior staff is particularly aware that AC Kaplan's public image is largely a function of the actions and work quality of their first-level associates. They clearly recognize the importance of an expert work force and try to spare no expense in this regard.

Employee Performance

While AC Kaplan affords many opportunities to their employees and spends a great deal of money on professional development, they in turn expect a great deal from their employees. Especially in the first two years, it is not at all uncommon for a beginning CPA to work 60–70 hours per week. The schedules and traveling are often grueling, and the rewards in the first few years are typically not commensurate. For example, salaries are generally in the mid-$20,000s and the benefit package is only average for a firm of AC Kaplan's size and revenue base. The greater payoffs, as indicated before, come when one achieves part-ner status, but not much earlier.

Nevertheless, AC Kaplan has little trouble attracting aggressive ener-getic students generally right out of college who are eager to "pay their dues" for corporate success in a major firm. Occasionally, however, this aggressiveness has come across as being boorish and callous with clients, especially in the health care and real estate industries. There are even situations where clients have discontinued business with AC Kaplan *not* because of their level of expertise, but because of the "fast-in, fast-out style of big-time consulting." While in most cases, Kaplan employees gradually learn to interpret the subtleties of client needs, occasionally (and increasingly), employees have been let go due to their lack of interpersonal acumen.

In view of the importance of interpersonal competence at Kaplan, some of the training staff have suggested that more attention should be placed on interpersonal development of entering employees. But others on staff point out that only two years ago a series of lectures was put into the training program dealing with client and customer relations. The consensus has been that that program addition had not been well received. They simply do not feel the added expense would be justified. In fact, there is a growing group of senior partners who believe too much is already being spent on education and training, since so many of those trained employees subsequently leave to take jobs with other companies.

The Training and Development Dilemma

Not surprisingly, there is an increasing debate regarding the role and importance of education and training at Arthur C. Kaplan and Company. It is difficult to know which parts of the current programs are good and which are not. Likewise, it is a problem determining if additional training is needed. As Anthony Blaine, one of the training directors summarized it: "For years we've been throwing tons of training at these people, but we aren't sure if it's the right kind, if it's too much, or even if they're catching what we're throwing! We've got to start coming up with some good questions, and then figure out some pretty intelligent answers."

Questions

1. Does a performance discrepancy exist?
2. Is it important to the firm?
3. Will training correct the problem?
4. Is training cost effective for AC Kaplan?
5. Is AC Kaplan training the right knowledge and skills? How would they determine this ahead of time?
6. Are they using the most effective techniques, especially with regard to the training for client and customer service? What technique changes would you recommend?
7. How should AC Kaplan decide specifically *who* needs training? Is it advisable or more cost efficient to send everyone through the program?
8. How would they determine whether their education and training programs are of sufficient utility? How would you specifically evaluate the programs (e.g., design, criteria)?

PART SEVEN

Compensation

14

Pay Level and Pay Structure

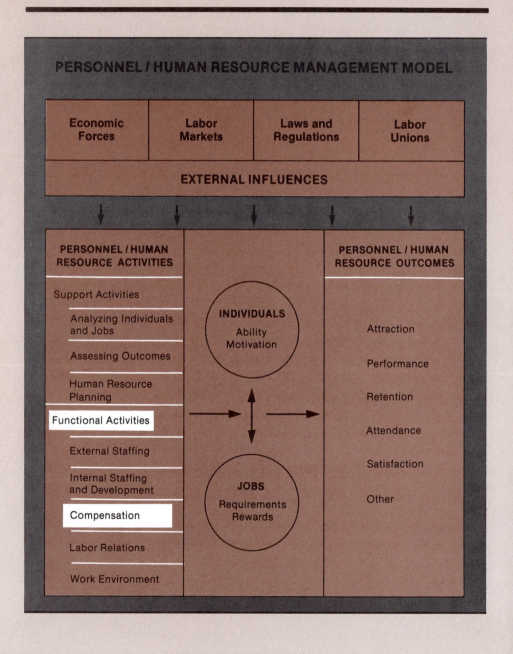

PERSONNEL / HUMAN RESOURCE MANAGEMENT MODEL

Economic Forces	Labor Markets	Laws and Regulations	Labor Unions

EXTERNAL INFLUENCES

PERSONNEL / HUMAN RESOURCE ACTIVITIES

Support Activities

Analyzing Individuals and Jobs

Assessing Outcomes

Human Resource Planning

Functional Activities

External Staffing

Internal Staffing and Development

Compensation

Labor Relations

Work Environment

INDIVIDUALS

Ability
Motivation

JOBS

Requirements
Rewards

PERSONNEL / HUMAN RESOURCE OUTCOMES

Attraction

Performance

Retention

Attendance

Satisfaction

Other

After reading this chapter, you should be able to speak to the questions posed in each of the following personnel/human resource incidents.

1. As the new manager of the personnel department in a large department store, you feel that a disproportionate amount of supervisory and personnel department time is being taken up with complaints about pay. Upon investigation, you discover that most of the complaints deal with alleged internal inequities, that is, with situations in which employees feel that their pay is out of line with that of others, given the work they do. You further discover that the store never has done formal job evaluation. The general policy has been to "pay the market." You consider the use of formal job evaluation and a systematic salary survey to price jobs. What factors would you weigh in deciding whether to go with this more formal approach? Assuming you decided to go ahead, what process would you follow in implementing job evaluation and pricing the jobs?

2. You are the human resource manager of a profitable electronics firm. Over the years, the wage structure for the roughly 500 production jobs has evolved through bargaining with the union that represents your production employees. Not much thought has been given to equity, either internal or external—although given the firms' profitability, wages are high relative to the market.

Recently, no doubt because of interest in comparable worth, the union argues that a point factor job evaluation plan should be installed as a way to eliminate inequities in the wage structure. Specifically, it argues that the predominantly female assembly jobs are underpaid relative to the predominantly male skilled maintenance jobs. The union expresses an interest in working toward the elimination of the inequities in the next negotiating session.

Given the information, what is your general reaction to the union's position? Given the profitability of the firm and the relatively high wage rates paid, is there any reason to oppose the union's request? Any reasons to agree with the union?

3. You recently purchased a defunct laundry and have converted it to a fast food, "McDonald's type" store in Montello, Wisconsin. Other than yourself, there will only be two jobs, short-order cook and server. You expect business to be quite brisk in the summer (you expect to employ up to 12 employees) when nearby Buffalo Lake attracts a serious fishing crowd from all over the midwest. During the winter, however, you expect to close for about four months to do some ice fishing on your own.

Given these facts, how would you go about developing pay policies for your part-time employees? What information would you try to obtain? How would you decide if your pay policies were satisfactory?

Employee compensation, the subject of this and the next two chapters, comes in two main forms: direct and indirect. Direct compensation refers to wages and salaries or, more simply, pay.[1] Indirect compensation refers to the various types of benefits that organizations provide. Examples include vacations, paid holidays, health insurance, life insurance, and pension plans.

Organizations often establish pay policies of two general kinds. One involves compensation for the jobs that employees perform, and the other applies to individuals or groups of employees who hold the jobs. Typically, then, pay depends partly on the job and partly on characteristics of employees, such as length of service or level of performance on the job. The present chapter addresses organizational pay policies for jobs. Individual and group pay policies are considered in Chapter 15, and benefits are covered in Chapter 16.

Compensation is a subject that is near and dear to employers and employees alike. To employers, it is both a potentially powerful influence on employees' behaviors and attitudes and a (usually significant) cost. To employees, it is a reward that is a source of both economic and psychological income. The task facing the employer is to allocate this reward in a way that optimizes the returns on dollars spent in employee motivation to join the organization, perform effectively, stay, and attend work regularly, and in employee satisfaction.

Accomplishing this task is not easy. As one compensation scholar has stated, "There are no objectively right answers to what an individual should be paid."[2] Less reverently, columnist Nicholas von Hoffman has said, "Ultimately, a man or woman is worth whatever some damn fool will pay." Thus, there are entertainers, athletes, and executives who make well in excess of $1 million a year, college professors who are paid somewhat less generously, and college students who toil away in cafeterias, libraries, and the like for little more than the minimum wage. Organizations devise policies and procedures to attempt to bring order to this seemingly chaotic situation.

However, they do not have an entirely free hand in these matters. Federal and state governments play a role; Chapter 3 discussed several laws and regulations that affect compensation administration, including

---

[1] The terms *wage* and *salary* are used interchangeably throughout these chapters—although in practice the term *wage* often refers to an hourly rate of pay, and *salary* is used to describe a weekly or monthly rate. Blue-collar and some clerical employees generally are paid a wage, and other employees tend to receive a salary. Exceptions are found in such companies as IBM, Texas Instruments, Polaroid, Avon Products, and Gillette, where all employees are salaried.

[2] E. E. Lawler III, *Pay and Organization Development.* (Reading, Mass.: Addison-Wesley Publishing, 1982), p. 33.

the Fair Labor Standards Act, the Walsh-Healy Act, the Davis-Bacon Act, the Employee Retirement Income Security Act, Title VII, and the Equal Pay Act.[3] In addition, labor unions bargain for more pay and benefits and often for a greater degree of control over compensation administration procedures. They also bargain over and subsequently use the right to grieve compensation decisions considered unwarranted or unfair. Labor markets play a part also. Employers can ignore the wages and salaries paid by others for their types of jobs only at the peril of being unable to fill jobs in high demand or losing valuable employees to other employers.[4]

Generally, the P/HR function recommends policy positions to top management and designs and administers the pay procedures that guide day-to-day decision making. P/HR managers also may become involved in some of the decision making, particularly in questionable or potentially troublesome cases, such as those involving equal employment opportunity issues. When line managers make the decisions, the P/HR function usually reviews them and takes action to correct those that are inconsistent with established policies and procedures.

Because compensation costs are usually considerable and apparent, top management typically takes a direct interest in this P/HR activity. It establishes compensation policy regarding such fundamental issues as pay levels vis-à-vis other employers, amounts of money to be allocated for pay increases and benefits, criteria to be used in allocating pay increases, and types of benefits to be offered. Other line managers generally decide such matters as starting rates for new employees and sizes of pay increases for their subordinates following existing policies and practices. Exceptions to these generalizations are found among many public employers where basic policy is established by legislative bodies, and standard procedures greatly restrict or even eliminate management discretion in decision making.[5]

In sum, compensation is an area in which the vested interests and influences of management, employees, the public, labor unions, and

---

[3] For a more complete discussion of public policy regarding pay, see F. S. Hills, *Compensation Decision Making*, (Chicago: Dryden Press, 1987), pp. 105–34; G. T. Milkovich and J. M. Newman, *Compensation*, 2d ed. (Plano, Tex.: Business Publications, 1987), pp. 452–73; or M. J. Wallace, Jr., and C. H. Fay, *Compensation Theory and Practice*, 2d ed (Boston: Kent Publishing, 1988), pp. 92–108.

[4] For discussions of the effects of unions and labor markets on pay, see G. H. Hildebrand, "External Influences and the Determination of the Internal Wage Structure," in *Internal Wage Structure*, ed. J. L. Meji (Amsterdam: North Holland Market System); and H. R. Northrup, "Wage Setting and Collective Bargaining," in *Comparable Worth: Issues and Alternatives*, 2d ed., ed. E. R. Livernash (Washington, D.C.: Equal Employment Advisory Council, 1984).

[5] For more on the various responsibilities of personnel/human resource specialists and line managers, see N. F. Crandall, "Wage and Salary Administrative Practices and Decision Process," *Journal of Management* 5 (1979), pp. 71–90.

labor markets are often at odds and must be delicately balanced. It is also an area in which many key issues remain unanswered, and many important decisions must be made based on best judgment or conventional wisdom rather than on firm insights gained through systematic theoretical formulations or empirical research. As a result, present practices vary widely.

However, all organizations must make certain basic decisions. For example, will the same policies and practices prevail among all units (for example, divisions, departments, and plants) and employee groups (such as top executives, other managers, various professional groups, technicians, clerical employees, and blue-collar workers), or will they vary? The answer depends on the overall objectives to be accomplished through pay, the nature of the organization (e.g., centralized or decentralized), and general custom. Often, top corporate executives are in one pay system. Top division managers may be in that system, or they may be in separate systems tailored to divisional needs. Middle managers may be in yet another, sometimes standardized throughout the corporation and sometimes customized by division. The other employee groups mentioned above are usually treated separately also. Exceptions abound, however, as in the federal government, wherein nearly all employees in all functions and at all levels (except very top managers and certain skilled trades people) are in a single plan.

In each case, however, the basic pay-setting process is the same. As noted above, it involves two major decision areas, one having to do with establishing the pay structure (wages or salaries) to be attached to the various jobs involved and the other with establishing the pay that each person will receive within that structure. The present chapter deals with managerial decisions involved in setting pay rates for jobs. Three major issues are considered. The first has to do with the way employers develop job hierarchies or structures for pay purposes; the second deals with the way organizations assign job pay rates to the hierarchy; the third involves consequences of inequities in pay structures. A special concern of certain groups has to do with possible pay inequities between wages received by women and those received by men, the so-called *comparable worth* controversy. Comparable worth is addressed in this chapter, since pay solutions to the inequities claimed have focused on changing employer pay structures for jobs.

DEVELOPING JOB HIERARCHIES

In formal organizations, all employees are assigned a collection of tasks that in total make up their jobs. Furthermore, in most organizations policy dictates that pay, at least in part, shall reflect the content of the jobs that employees perform. Given this policy, it is incumbent on wage and salary specialists to develop and administer procedures to price jobs.

The Equity Criterion

Most people probably agree that jobs of greater value to an organization should carry higher rates of pay than jobs of lesser value. The challenge, of course, is to determine which jobs are worth more and which less, and how much more or less. These decisions must be reasonably acceptable to employers and employees alike. Compensation specialists have come to view the acceptability of job hierarchies largely in two kinds of equity comparisons—external and internal.[6] Such comparisons are used by both employers and employees to judge the fairness of wages paid for jobs.

One comparison typically made when judging the acceptability of a job hierarchy and resulting pay structure is comparing pay rates in the organization with pay rates for similar jobs in other organizations. This external comparison relates the employers' wages to wages in the labor market. Compensation managers are concerned with external comparisons in part because of the need to keep pay and labor costs competitive. This is especially important when the organization must compete aggressively for sales of its products or services. In part, it is also important to attract and retain a labor force, since employees also make external comparisons.

Typically, employees and employers also compare the equity of job hierarchies and pay structures internally. That is, they judge whether the content of jobs (e.g., skill required to perform the job duties) higher in the hierarchy is greater than the content of jobs lower in the hierarchy. These internal comparisons take on special significance when external comparisons are difficult to make as, for example, when there are no similar jobs found in other organizations.

These two comparisons present a challenge for compensation managers because they are not necessarily very highly related.[7] For example, external labor market changes may require a substantial wage increase for an occupation because of a large increase in labor demanded by employers. This change in external equity can occur without any change

---

[6] Hills, *Compensation Decision Making*, pp. 13–14; Wallace and Fay, *Compensation Theory*, pp. 46–65.

[7] D. P. Schwab, "Determining the Worth of Work," *Society* 22, no. 5 (1985), pp. 61–67.

FIGURE 14–1
The Job Evaluation Process

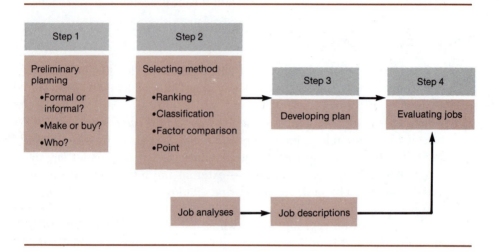

in internal equity (i.e., the content of the job). In other situations, internal equity might change, but no corresponding change occurs in external equity comparisons.

A set of procedures has evolved over time that is used to achieve an acceptable balance between external and internal equity considerations. These procedures include *job evaluation*, used to obtain a structure of jobs for the purpose of establishing pay rates for those jobs. They also include procedures for linking job evaluation results to market wage rates as determined by *wage surveys*. These procedures are discussed in the following two sections.

Arranging Jobs in a Hierarchy: Job Evaluation

A number of judgments and decisions must be made by compensation specialists in conducting job evaluation. Steps in the process leading to the development of a job hierarchy for purposes of pay are shown in Figure 14–1.[8]

---

[8] The following discussion is necessarily brief; for more, see any standard wage and salary text—for example, Hills, *Compensation Decision Making*, pp. 139–221. Then see D. P. Schwab, "Job Evaluation and Pay Setting: Concepts and Practices," in Livernash, *Comparable Worth*.

Step 1: Preliminary planning

In preliminary planning, the first issue is whether to conduct job evaluation formally or informally. The informal approach involves little more than an intuitive ranking of jobs, as the proprietor of a small grocery store might do when deciding that the stock clerks will make less than the checkout clerks, who will make less than the assistant manager. Formal job evaluation involves the relatively systematic application of standards and decision rules to rank or rate jobs. The formal approach takes longer and costs more, but probably yields superior results in all but very small organizations. One survey found that formal job evaluation was used by about three fourths of the 158 organizations studied.[9]

Given a decision favoring formal job evaluation, organizations must further decide whether to make or buy a plan. Two well-known pre-packaged plans are the Hay Plan, developed for managerial jobs by a consulting firm, and the National Electrical Manufacturers Association (NEMA) plan, for production jobs. However, there is often a good reason to develop a plan specifically for one's own organization.[10] Prepackaged plans were developed largely in the 1940s and 1950s and largely for manufacturing firms. What was appropriate in manufacturing then is likely not appropriate now for many firms such as those in the service and public sectors.

A third issue in preliminary planning is that of who should perform job evaluations. A good case can be made for using committees representing not only management, but also persons covered by the system.[11] First, more accurate evaluations may result when people with different perspectives provide information about jobs. Second, participation in the process can help increase acceptance of the evaluation results.

Step 2: Selecting a job evaluation plan

Four common job evaluation methods are available: (1) ranking, (2) classification, (3) factor comparison, and (4) point. The point method is by far the most widely used, however, probably because it combines the

---

[9] Bureau of National Affairs, *Job Evaluation Policies and Procedures,* Personnel Policies Forum, Survey No. 113 (Washington, D.C.: Bureau of National Affairs, 1976), pp. 1–2. Crandall, "Practices," found 80 percent.

[10] A. J. Candrilli and R. D. Armagast, "The Case for Effective Point-Factor Job Evaluation, Viewpoint 2," *Compensation and Benefits Review* no. 2 (1987), pp. 49–54.

[11] Milkovich and Newman, *Compensation,* pp. 155–57.

apparent precision of quantification with a degree of simplicity that makes the results relatively easy to explain to employees.[12]

All subsequent examples in this section involve the point method. Readers interested in exploring the other job evaluation methods are encouraged to consult any standard wage and salary text.[13]

Step 3: Developing the plan

In formal job evaluation plans, a job hierarchy is developed by comparing the content of various jobs against specified standards using a predetermined procedure. In the point method, the standards are set forth in the form of *compensable factors.*

Compensable factors are nothing more than job dimensions involving such things as ability requirements (such as experience required) and working conditions. Usually, they reflect a combination of factors believed to be (1) significantly related to job importance or contribution to organizational goals, and (2) significant to employees in their estimations of job worth. In the Hay Plan mentioned earlier, the compensable factors are know-how, problem solving, and accountability. In the NEMA plan, they are skill, effort, responsibility, and working conditions.

Point plans tend to have between 3 and 10 compensable factors. Available research clearly shows that in any given situation only two or three factors are likely to be important in the results attained.[14] More are used, however, because experience suggests that employees reject the notion that their jobs can be competently valued using only two or three factors.

Once compensable factors are decided on, they are defined and weighted and broken into degrees that, in turn, are defined and assigned point values. Despite occasional attempts at rationalization and even computerization, this process generally remains a highly subjective one in which there is a strong tendency to borrow freely from existing job evaluation plans.

Factors, degrees, definitions, and weights are set forth in a job evaluation model. Figure 14–2 shows one page from a more or less typical

---

[12] The relative popularity of the various job evaluation methods has not changed for many years. One survey found the following usage pattern: ranking—14 percent; classification—24 percent; factor comparison—33 percent; and point—53 percent (the figures total more than 100 percent because many organizations use different methods among different employee groups). See Bureau of National Affairs, *Job Evaluation Policies,* pp. 2–3.

[13] See footnote 3.

[14] For a review of this research, see D. P. Schwab, "Job Evaluation Research and Research Needs," in *New Directions for Comparable Worth,* ed. H. I. Hartmann (Washington, D.C.: National Academy Press, 1985), pp. 37–52.

FIGURE 14–2

An Excerpt from a Job Evaluation Manual

Compensable Factor: Importance and Scope of Decisions

Consider the consequences of the decisions and the impact they are likely to have on the education of individual children as well as on the educational system itself. Consider also the number of people and schools affected by the decisions. Do not consider the fact that decisions have to be approved by higher echelons before implementation.

Weight: 20 percent

Degree 1: Decisions have a relatively small impact on individual children and on the educational system itself; errors would result in embarrassing but short-term problems; few people would be affected. 4 points.

Degree 2: Some decisions could have fairly important consequences either for individual children or for some aspects of the educational system; most errors, however, would be quickly and/or easily detected and then corrected, decisions would not affect more than 300 persons. 8 points.

Degree 3: Many decisions could have important consequences either because their impact on individual children is deep or because they influence important aspects of the educational system; impact could be felt on as many as 1,000 persons; some errors could easily go undetected and result in relatively serious problems. 12 points.

Degree 4: Many decisions have a great deal of importance both for individual children and for the system itself; as many as 2,000 persons could be affected in one or several buildings; serious errors could be made and go uncorrected for a long time. 16 points.

Degree 5: Decisions have very serious and long-term consequences, both on individual children and on critical aspects of the educational system; such decisions would affect a great number of people throughout the district; errors could result in serious impediments to the progress of education and/or in significant financial loss. 20 points.

---

manual; this one is used to evaluate administrative jobs in a public school district. Shown is the compensable factor, "Importance and Scope of Decisions," along with its definition and weight (20 percent, that is, 20 out of a total of 100 points across all factors). Note that this factor is divided into five degrees, representing equally spaced gradations. This particular point plan has eight other compensable factors: education and special training (with a 5 percent weight), experience (15 percent), complexity of duties (10 percent), autonomy (10 percent), nature of supervision (10 percent) number of subordinates (15 percent), contacts and communications (10 percent), and pressures and volume of work (5 percent).

Step 4: Evaluating jobs

Jobs cannot be adequately evaluated without accurate, up-to-date information about job duties and responsibilities. Thus, as Figure 14–1 suggests, concurrent with steps 1 through 3 of the job evaluation process, the usual practice is to conduct job analyses and prepare written job descriptions (see Chapter 4). Often members of the job evaluation committee also observe the job and interview incumbents and supervisors to obtain additional information for the evaluation.[15]

In a point system, jobs are evaluated factor by factor. In each case, job content is compared against the various degree definitions, and the best fit is decided on. The job is then assigned the corresponding number of points on that factor. For example, on the factor "Importance and Scope of Decision," the job of principal of a small school might be matched with degree 3 and receive 12 points. This process continues across all factors. When completed, the points assigned to the various factors are totaled. When all jobs have been similarly evaluated, the point totals represent the resulting job hierarchy.

Generally, it is preferable for evaluations to be done independently by two or more evaluators or even groups. This alows for a reliability check on the evaluations. Research suggests that disagreements frequently exist between raters about the number of points to be assigned to the various compensable factors and, to a lesser extent, the various jobs.[16] Causes of the unreliability are not well understood, although a significant factor probably is lack of familiarity with job content.[17] Where disagreements exist, the reasons can be explored, more information about the job(s) can be gathered (if necessary), and the differences resolved through discussion. This, in turn, probably serves to improve the overall validity of the resulting job hierarchy.

PRICING A JOB HIERARCHY

Linking Internal and External Criteria

The steps discussed to this point emphasize the internal equity component of the pay-setting process. Jobs are scaled on compensable factors that have to do with the content of work performed. A hierarchy is

---

[15] D. P. Schwab and R. Grams, "Sex-Related Errors in Job Evaluation: A 'Real-World' Test," *Journal of Applied Psychology* 70 (1985), pp. 533–39.

[16] For a review of research see Schwab, "Job Evaluation Research and Research Needs." For an example of a study investigation on the reliability of individual judgments, see D. C. Doverspike, G. V. Barrett, and R. A. Alexander, "Generalizability Analysis of a Point-Method Job Evaluation Instrument," *Journal of Applied Psychology* 68 (1983), pp. 476–83. For an example of a study on the reliability of group judgments in job evaluation, see D. P. Schwab and H. G. Heneman III, "Assessment of a Consensus-Based Multiple Information Source Job Evaluation System," *Journal of Applied Psychology* 71 (1986), pp. 354–56.

[17] D. C. Hahn and R. L. Dipboye, "Effects of Training and Information on the Accuracy and Reliability of Job Evaluations," *Journal of Applied Psychology* 73 (1988), pp. 146–53.

FIGURE 14-3
Job Evaluation Development and Implementation

Development (Performed on Key Jobs)
    Identification of compensable factors.
    Evaluation of key jobs.
    Statistical weighting of compensable factors on key jobs.
    Modification of the statistical model to obtain a correspondence between key job
        wages and job evaluation results.
Implementation (Performed on Nonkey Jobs)
    Modified statistical model applied to nonkey jobs.
    Development of the wage structure.

Source: Adapted from Donald P. Schwab, "Determining the Worth of Work," *Society* 22(25) (1985), p. 64.

established based on the total points obtained on the compensable factors. How then does external equity get into the process?

External equity is accounted for when pay rates are assigned to the jobs in the hierarchy. As with job evaluation itself, there are many ways that organizations accomplish this task. The procedure described here is the most formal method for linking pay rates to the job hierarchy.[18] Some employers, especially smaller ones, use less formal procedures. Whether formal or informal, however, organizations link job evaluation results closely to the external market. The acceptability of job evaluation hinges in large part on whether the results are consistent with the ranking of the same jobs in the external labor markets.[19]

Organizations that formally link job evaluation to external wage rates often first make a distinction between *key* or *benchmark* jobs and all others. Key jobs are ones that are relatively stable in content and are found in many different organizations. Entry-level jobs typically fall into this category, as do most jobs the organization considers especially important because they involve essential skills or because they use a large number of employees.

As Figure 14-3 shows, these key jobs are evaluated first, and the statistical relationship between the job evaluation results and wages is observed. Where discrepancies between job evaluation results and wages are found (e.g., where engineering jobs that are highly paid are evaluated lower than marketing jobs that are less highly paid), the job

---

[18] For a more detailed discussion of methods linking job evaluation results to external wages, see Schwab, "Job Evaluation," p. 62–67.

[19] E. R. Livernash, "The Internal Wage Structure," in G. W. Taylor and F. C. Pierson, *New Concepts in Wage Determination* (New York: McGraw-Hill, 1957).

evaluation plan may be modified by changing either compensable factors or their weights. Such adjustments are made until the relationship between total key job scores from the evaluation system corresponds satisfactorily to the wages for those key jobs. As Figure 14–3 shows, implementation of the plan then takes place on nonkey jobs using the statistical model developed on key jobs. In this way, the plan is used to determine wages for nonkey jobs.

This procedure is similar to the empirical validation of a selection predictor (see Chapter 10). Key jobs serve as the validation sample; wages for those key jobs represent the criteria that are correlated with total job evaluation scores (the "predictor"). The resulting mathematical model, which weights the job evaluation system by how well it "predicts" market wages, is then used to array the nonkey jobs in a hierarchy for purposes of pay. This procedure thus brings market influences into the organization to determine wages for nonkey jobs where external markets are weak or nonexistent.

Developing a Pay Structure

The steps described to this point result in a hierarchy of jobs, both key and nonkey, arrayed based on the total weighted scores from the job evaluation. A number of additional decisions remain before actual pay rates are assigned to jobs. These include decisions regarding (1) whether to pay each job separately or collapse them into a lesser number of pay grades, (2) whether to establish a single rate of pay or a rate range for jobs, (3) what the actual rates of pay, or the minimum and maximum of the rate ranges, will be, and (4) how to handle current wages or salaries that are out of line.

Jobs versus pay grades

If an organization has only a few jobs and the distinctions among them are clear (for example, they have received a significantly different number of points evaluated), the decision might be made to establish a different rate of pay or rate range for each one. Where there are many jobs and the distinctions among some of them are slight, both prudence (born in the knowledge that job evaluation is hardly an error-free process) and administrative convenience dictate that similar jobs be lumped into a single pay grade. Unfortunately, no general rules exist to help decide when pay grades are desirable or, when desirable, how many a particular pay plan should have. Plans exist with as few as 3 and as many as 60. Figure 14–4 (column 1) shows how 10 administrative jobs in a public school district were grouped into 4 pay grades. (This is obviously a

FIGURE 14-4
Pricing a Job Hierarchy

Benchmark Jobs and Point Values		(1) Develop Pay Grades		(2) Obtain Survey Data			(3) Adjust Midpoint to Fit Organization	(4) Establish Rate Ranges Midpoint ± 15%
Jobs	Points	Grade	Points	Minimum	Midpoint	Maximum		
A	37	I	35–49	$ 16,100	$ 17,600	$ 19,100	$15,500	$13,200–$17,800
B	45			(12,500)	(14,400)	(16,300)		
C	49							
D	56	II	50–64	18,000	20,100	22,200	17,400	14,800–20,000
E	58			(13,700)	(16,000)	(18,300)		
F	59							
G	69	III	65–79	19,500	21,800	24,100	19,300	16,400–22,200
H	87			(15,000)	(18,100)	(21,200)		
I	90	IV	80–94	21,000	24,200	27,400	21,200	18,000–24,400
J	91			(17,500)	(20,000)	(22,500)		

Source: Adapted from T. H. Patten, Jr., *Pay: Employee Compensation and Incentive Plans* (New York: Free Press, 1977), p. 276. Copyright © 1977 by The Free Press, a Division of Macmillan Publishing Co., Inc.

simplified example, since most organizations have many jobs and, typically, more pay grades.)

Single rate versus rate range

Policymakers in an organization might decide as a matter of convenience to establish a single pay rate for a given job or pay grade. For example, the small grocer cited earlier could choose to pay all stock clerks the prevailing minimum wage regardless of any differences among them in training, length of service (seniority), or performance. This is not common, because it fails to allow for the recognition of the personal characteristics that most employers and employees think should be recognized and rewarded. Where differences in individual inputs or performance are to be recognized, it is necessary to establish for each job a rate range, that is, a minimum and a maximum amount that any incumbent can be paid as long as he/she holds that job. Criteria used for individual employee movement through rate ranges and objectives employers seek to achieve with such ranges are discussed in Chapter 15.

Determining actual rates or rate ranges

At this point, a major policy issue is encountered. It is the matter of *pay level*. Will the organization pay wages and salaries that are above, roughly equal to, or below those established for comparable jobs in other organizations?

It is sometimes thought that organizations have little flexibility in this respect, since wages and salaries must be responsive to external labor supply and demand. However, in actuality, pay rates for a given job in a given labor market often vary substantially across organizations, suggesting a fair amount of room for discretion.[20]

Thus, policymakers must decide whether to be wage leaders, wage followers, or neither. A major factor in this decision is the organization's financial condition—its ability or inability to pay. The ability to pay does not ensure that wages or salaries will be relatively high, but an inability to pay usually ensures that they will be relatively low. Factors pushing wages and salaries up toward the maximum an organization can afford to pay include labor unions (or the desire to remain nonunion), tight labor markets, a policy of "creaming" certain labor markets, and the desire to enhance organizational status or prestige.

---

[20] S. L. Rynes and G. T. Milkovich, "Wage Surveys: Dispelling Some Myths about the 'Market Wage'," *Personnel Psychology* 39 (1986), pp. 71–90.

In deciding what rates to establish, as well as deciding that key job wages will serve as an adequate criterion in policy capturing (see above), an organization will typically use a *wage* or *salary survey*.[21] An organization may conduct its own survey or rely on one or more of the many surveys available from such sources as the American Management Association, the American Compensation Association, various industry groups, and the U.S. Bureau of Labor Statistics.

Conducting a wage or salary survey is a time-consuming and demanding process. Care must be exercised to ensure that the organizations surveyed are those with which labor market competition exists; that the jobs covered by the survey are comparable to those being priced; that data are current; and that data are collected, analyzed, and interpreted accurately.[22] Errors at any point can be extremely costly.

However obtained, survey data are compared with the organization's own wages or salaries to facilitate analysis and interpretation. As shown in Figure 14-4 (column 2), common comparisons include minimum, median, and maximum rates (here the salaries in parentheses are the organization's current rates; the others are from a salary survey). The purpose of these comparisons is to suggest appropriate wage and salary adjustments consistent with organizational policy. Note in Figure 14-4 (column 3) that the school district involved raised its median salaries somewhat above previous levels (the salaries in parentheses in the middle of column 2). Also note that the new rates are well below those paid in the labor market (the other salaries in the middle of column 2). In this case, this policy was possible because the district is relatively poor and because it traditionally has experienced little trouble in attracting and retaining competent administrators. Moreover, the administrators' union lacked the power to force salaries higher.

When rate ranges (rather than single rates) are called for, decisions must be made about the range from minimum to maximum values and the degree of overlap that will exist between jobs or labor grades. Commonly, ranges vary from 10 to 25 percent (approximately 5 to 12.5 percent above and below the median), 25 to 35 percent, and 50 to 100 percent for blue-collar, clerical, and managerial jobs, respectively. Regarding overlap, it is often suggested that the maximum rate of any given pay grade should be no higher than the minimum rate of the grade two levels above it in the hierarchy. These are at best guidelines; in practice, conditions may well dictate other conclusions.

---

[21] Bureau of National Affairs, *Job Evaluation Policies*, pp. 9–11; Crandall, "Practices," p. 76.

[22] For a more complete discussion of wage and salary surveys, see Hills, *Compensation Decision Making*, pp. 225–57; Milkovich and Newman, *Compensation*, pp. 215–52.

Notice in Figure 14-4 (column 4) that both guidelines are violated. These are managerial jobs, yet the width of the rate ranges is only 30 percent, and the overlap is considerable. These decisions serve to flatten the salary structure and, of course, save money.

A relatively flat structure was possible in this situation for a variety of reasons: Administrators rarely are hired into pay grades III and IV, little turnover is experienced at these levels, large within-grade "merit" increases are the exception rather than the rule, and most promotions involve movements across two pay grades (thus, even a flat structure allows for promotional pay increases and room for some salary growth on the new job). In this particular case, labor market and other conditions were such that the employer's financial circumstance was very influential in determining the range within and the overlap between labor grades.

In other circumstances, labor market conditions are more compelling, for example, when the organization must compete actively with other employers for a labor force. In these situations, it would be best to link key job wages closely to market rates and then relate nonkey job wages to them. In contrast, the process described in the school district example gives relatively more weight to job content, since the job hierarchy is determined for all jobs before any pricing is done.

In summary, job evaluation and the usual processes used to price jobs are not to be regarded as sacrosanct mechanisms for determining job worth. Rather, they are administrative conveniences that are quite judgmental and somewhat error prone. Judgments must be made with respect to the choices of compensable factors, factor weights, key jobs (where used), appropriate labor market comparisons, and the relative weights to be accorded job content vis-à-vis market rates. Errors can creep into job analysis, evaluation results, and surveys.

The challenge for policymakers and salary administrators is to ensure that the judgments are made reasonably. In part, reasonableness pertains to the salary outcomes, errors are to be minimized. Yet errors are inevitable. Consequently, compensation managers must also attempt to ensure that the processes used to achieve the outcomes appear to be fair by all those affected by the system.[23]

---

[23] The significance of equity in the process used to set wages and salaries is discussed in Livernash, "The Internal Wage Structure." For a recent discussion of the importance of equitable procedures in personnel, see R. Folger and J. Greenberg, "Procedural Justice: An Interpretive Analysis of Personnel Systems," in *Research in Personnel and Human Resource Management*, vol. 3, eds. K. M. Rowland and G. R. Ferris (Greenwich, Conn.: JAI Press, 1985), pp. 141–83.

Out-of-line rates

Figure 14–5 shows the pay structure that results from the data shown in Figure 14–4 (columns 3 and 4). Also shown are the current salaries of 21 school administrators. Notice that three of these salaries fall outside the new labor grade ranges.

The two salaries above the range are referred to as "red-circle rates." Ordinarily, they would not be reduced, but would persist until the

FIGURE 14–5
A Pay Structure

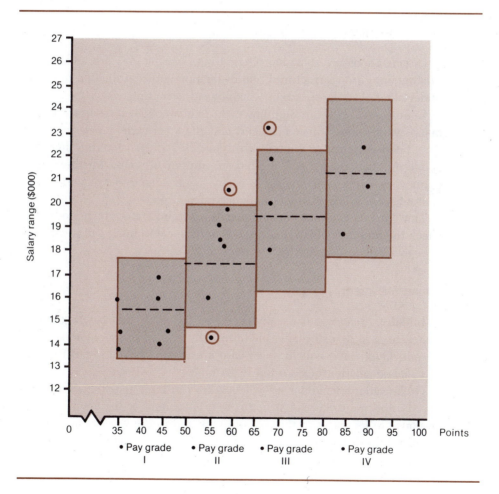

employees involved left the organization or until future adjustments in the pay structure brought them into line.[24] The salary falling below its range, however, ordinarily would be increased immediately to the minimum of the range. A policy of not reducing red-circle rates, while immediately increasing low rates, is intended to foster employee acceptance of the new pay structure.

Administering and Controlling the Pay Structure

Once a pay structure is in place, it must be administered and controlled. It is necessary to be concerned with the integrity of both the job hierarchy and the established pay rates or rate ranges.

Maintaining the integrity of the job hierarchy

Organizations are dynamic. Over time, as new jobs are added and existing ones are restructured, job evaluation and reevaluation must be undertaken. To a large extent, this process is routine.

Control must be exercised, however, to guard against an upward drift in job evaluations.[25] Since managers and employees are human, jobs that have been enriched in content are typically reported for reevaluation, and those that have been diluted in content are not. Furthermore, employees—and their managers—have been known to exaggerate job content in an attempt to attain higher rates of pay.

Thus, it is the job of wage and salary administrators to periodically check the accuracy of job descriptions and the continuing validity of the ever-evolving job hierarchy.

Maintaining the integrity of pay rates and rate ranges

Initially, great care is usually exercised to ensure that pay levels and structures are as externally and internally equitable as circumstances permit. Over time, equally great care must be exercised to ensure that established relationships do not deteriorate.

Organizations maintain wage levels by routinely making across-the-board adjustments to pay structures on an annual or biannual basis in response to increases in the cost of living and in the wages and salaries paid by other employers (as indicated by updated wage or salary sur-

---

[24] P. R. Reed and M. J. Kroll, "Red-Circle Employees: A Wage Scale Dilemma," *Personnel Journal* 66 (1987), pp. 92–95.

[25] J. R. Schuster, "How to Control Job Evaluation Inflation," *Personnel Administrator* 30, no. 6 (1985), pp. 167–73.

veys). Some unions have been successful in negotiating automatic cost-of-living adjustments (COLA) through so-called escalator clauses. A common contract clause requires the employer to match every 0.4 point increase in the consumer price index (CPI) with a one-cent-per-hour increase in union members' pay.

Periodic adjustments in pay levels can create distortions in pay structures, usually in the form of unwanted compression. For example, adjustments involving fixed money amounts (rather than percentages) flatten existing structures and erode the relative advantages of those in the upper pay grades. Moreover, negotiated increases or escalators can destroy traditional relationships between the pay of unionized and nonunionized employees.

No totally satisfactory solution to those problems exists. Organizational policymakers and wage and salary administrators continually face the challenge of balancing the benefits of retaining established pay structures against the costs of doing so.

CONSEQUENCES OF INEQUITABLE PAY STRUCTURES

Behavioral Responses

How important is it for compensation managers to establish and maintain equitable pay structures? What are the consequences of inequitable pay structures in employee responses in the work environment? Compensation specialists and scholars alike believe that employees do react strongly and negatively unless organizations are able to establish and maintain equitable pay structures.

A number of theories have been put forth that explicitly predict individual responses to inequitable situations. The best known, formulated by J. Stacy Adams,[26] focuses on inequity arising from any social exchange (e.g., work, family) situation. Other models have been offered that focus exclusively on employment and primarily on the importance of pay in judging what is equitable or inequitable.[27] Although these theo-

---

[26] J. S. Adams, "Inequity in Social Exchange," in *Advances in Experimental Social Psychology*, 2d ed., ed. L. Berkowitz (New York: Academic Press, 1965). For a recent statement of the theory, see R. P. Vecchio, "Predicting Worker Performance in Equitable Settings," *Academy of Management Review* 7 (1985), pp. 103–10. For a broader perspective on equity, see J. Greenberg, "A Taxonomy of Organizational Justice Theories," *Academy of Management Review* 12 (1987), pp. 9–22.

[27] E. Jaques, *Equitable Payment* (New York: John Wiley & Sons, 1961); M. Patchen, *The Choice of Wage Comparisons* (Englewood Cliffs, N.J.: Prentice-Hall, 1961). See also R. Richardson, *Fair Pay and Work* (Carbondale: Southern Illinois University Press, 1971), for research and a statement of Jaques's theory.

ries differ in detail, all predict that employees will respond to feelings of inequity with dissatisfaction and motivation to change the situation (e.g., employee turnover to escape the inequity).

There is some research to support these kinds of predictions.[28] Pay dissatisfaction can in fact lead to lower job performance under some circumstances. Length of service and attendance are also adversely affected by pay dissatisfaction. Finally, the greater the pay dissatisfaction, the greater the probability that employees will vote for union representation in a certification election.

One case study of the job evaluation system used in the west coast airframe industry during and following World War II provides an especially insightful analysis of difficulties in maintaining equitable wage differentials.[29] The investigators noted that "[t]he most difficult and pervasive problem in the administration of job description and evaluation . . . arose from the frequent conflicts between measures of external and measures of internal equity."[30] This potential conflict between internal and external equity also poses the greatest problem in the comparable worth controversy, as is shown in the next section.

Comparable Worth

Currently the most controversial equity issue regarding job hierarchies and pay structures involves comparable worth. Advocates question the external equity of present pay structures and recommend that internal equity using job evaluation be given greater attention. Critics, alternatively, argue that such changes in pay-setting practices could deleteriously distort market wage structures.

Underlying issues

Comparable worth and *pay equity* are terms that have come to stand for improving wage rates of predominantly female jobs relative to those of predominantly male jobs.[31] The issue is whether secretarial and nursing jobs, for example, should pay as much as male-dominated jobs

---

[28] H. G. Heneman III, "Pay Satisfaction," in *Research in Personnel and Human Resources Management*, vol. 3, eds. K. M. Rowland and G. Ferris (Greenwich, Conn.: JAI Press, 1985), pp. 115–39.

[29] C. Kerr and L. H. Fisher, "Effects of Environment and Administration on Job Evaluation," *Harvard Business Review* 28, no. 3 (1950), pp. 76–96.

[30] Kerr and Fisher, "Effects of Environment," p. 81.

[31] By current convention, jobs with 70 percent or more women are called "female jobs;" those with 70 percent or more men are called "male jobs." This convention is followed throughout this section.

requiring equal training and skill levels. On average, women earn about 72 percent of what men earn, and this differential has increased about 10 percent in the last 10 years.[32] Advocates of comparable worth argue that at least part of the differential is due to discrimination. Others, however, argue that the differential is not a result of discrimination, or at least that the research evidence is insufficient to conclude that discrimination is involved.[33]

One reason it is difficult to determine whether discrimination is involved is that men and women tend to perform different jobs. Women tend to be concentrated in clerical, education, health care, and service sector jobs. For example, female jobs account for only 9 percent of federal government general schedule and federal wage survey jobs, although nearly 40 percent of federal employees are women. Male jobs, alternatively, account for 74 percent of these federal jobs.[34]

The reasons for these differences in job concentration are also disputed. Advocates argue that women have been segregated into low-paying jobs by employer practices (which is illegal under Title VII of the Civil Rights Act). Critics argue that women and men have different preferences and that these differences, not discrimination, account for the differing concentrations.[35] These differences in how the observed labor market statistics should be interpreted go a long way in explaining the comparable worth controversy.

Proposed solution

Advocates have recommended greater use of job evaluation as the mechanism to achieve pay equity. This recommendation is motivated in part by the lack of conspicuous alternatives to job evaluation and in part by successes advocates have experienced with job evaluation in litigation

---

[32] G. T. Milkovich, "The Nature of the Earnings Gap," *Pay Equity*, ed. D. E. Friedman (New York: Conference Board, 1988), pp. 8–10.

[33] For an advocate's position see, for example, D. T. Treiman and H. I. Hartmann, eds., *Women, Work, and Wages: Equal Pay for Jobs of Equal Value* (Washington, D.C.: National Academy Press, 1981). A critical position is offered by Milkovich, "The Emerging Debate." The U.S. Civil Rights Commission concluded from hearings it conducted in 1984 that research has not established gender-based pay discrimination (J. S. Lublin, "Use of Comparable-Worth Idea to Fight Job Sex Bias Opposed by Rights Panel," *The Wall Street Journal*, April 12, 1985, p. 48).

[34] "Options for Conducting a Pay Equity Study of Federal Pay and Classification Systems," *Report by the Comptroller General of the United States* (Washington D.C.: U.S. Government Priting Office, 1985).

[35] For an advocate's view see, for example, P. England, "Explanations of Job Segregation and the Sex Gap in Pay," *Comparable Worth: Issue for the 80s*, vol. 1 (Washington, D.C.: U.S. Civil Rights Commission, 1984), pp. 54–64. A critical perspective is offered by S. W. Polachek, "Women in the Economy: Perspectives on Gender Inequality," *Comparable Worth: Issue for the 80s*, vol. 1 (Washington, D.C.: U.S. Civil Rights Commission, 1984), pp. 34–53.

and legislation (see below). Recall, however, that organizations currently link job evaluation results to market wages either formally or informally. To the extent that market wages are biased, as advocates conclude, the practice simply perpetuates pay discrimination in the organization.[36] Thus, advocates propose the use of job evaluation, but with a twist or two.

First, they note that organizations often use multiple job evaluation systems, which makes it difficult to compare female and male jobs. For example, female office jobs may be in one system, and male production jobs may be in another. Thus, advocates recommend the use of the same job evaluation system for all jobs in an organization or governmental unit. Point systems are preferred to other job evaluation systems because of their allegedly greater objectivity.

Second, advocates propose developing separate pay analysis for men's jobs and women's jobs. Figure 14–6 illustrates what advocates expect to find when such a procedure is followed.[37] It shows that traditional men's jobs, on average, receive higher pay than traditional women's jobs, holding constant the number of job evaluation points. Confronted with these sorts of results, advocates would raise the pay rates of female jobs to the male rate for any given level of job evaluation points. They reason that such a procedure would eliminate the market bias against female job pay.

Critics of comparable worth, not surprisingly, disagree with this procedure. They argue that the underlying premise—there is pay discrimination in the market—has not been established. They also argue that job evaluation is too subjective to be relied on so exclusively in the pay-setting process. In particular, they believe that job evaluation, used as the advocates propose, would seriously distort the market-based system of pay determination, with resulting dysfunctional consequences for the entire economy.

Where does the issue stand?

The federal level.   Presently there is no comparable worth law at the federal level. The Equal Pay Act applies only when men and women

---

[36] D. P. Schwab and D. W. Wichern, "Systematic Bias in Job Evaluation and Market Wages: Implications for the Comparable Worth Debate," *Journal of Applied Psychology* 68 (1983), pp. 60–69.

[37] Comments by N. Rothchild, commissioner of Employee Relations for the State of Minnesota, at the 6th Annual Industrial Relations Alumni Meeting (St. Paul, Minn., October 11, 1984).

FIGURE 14–6
Pay Lines for Female and Male Jobs

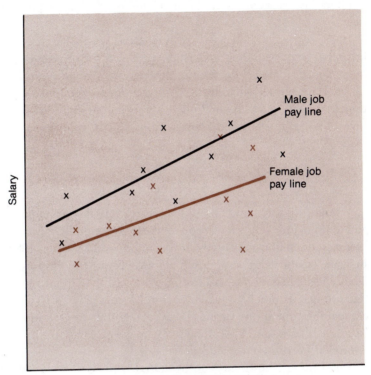

Job evaluation points

perform the same job.[38] Since comparable worth advocates seek to compare jobs that are not the same, the Equal Pay Act has little relevance to the issue.

In *Gunther* v. *County of Washington*, the Supreme Court ruled that Title VII of the Civil Rights Act could be used to deal with cases where the jobs held by men and women were not equal. However, in reaching that conclusion, the Court explicitly did not endorse comparable worth.

Though different district and appellate courts have come to different conclusions, the following generalizations seemed warranted. First, courts are reluctant to get into pay determination cases because of the complexity of the issues involved. Second, they generally agree that the

---

[38] For a review of equal pay litigation, see E. A. Cooper and G. V. Barrett, "Equal Pay and Gender: Implications of Court Cases for Personnel Practices," *Academy of Management Review* 9 (1984), pp. 84–94.

employer's use of the external market to determine pay rates is acceptable, even though this may result in lower pay for female jobs. Finally, they will conclude that pay discrimination has occurred if the employer deliberately treats women and men differently in pay policies or practices.

State and local initiatives.   Comparable worth has received a more favorable hearing among some states and local governments. Some states (e.g., Iowa, Idaho, Minnesota, New Mexico, Washington, and South Dakota) are already increasing pay rates for public employees in traditionally female jobs. Several other states are studying public pay structures to see if equity or comparable worth adjustments should be made.[39]

Prospects for the future

Women's groups and some unions strongly favor comparable worth, and employers and their representatives generally oppose it.[40] The Democratic platform called for its implementation in 1984, and the Reagan administration opposed it. However, the dispute transcends labor and management, and even politics. Employment status and prestige are just as much at stake as are relative pay rates.[41] Consequently, comparable worth pits various employee groups on opposite sides of the issue as Illustration 14–1 shows. To make predictions about how this issue will be resolved would be very risky.

Some things, however, can be stated with confidence. Women have become a significant portion of the labor force. They are expected to constitute half the labor force by the end of this decade.[42] Until the differential in wages between men and women decreases, women will likely advocate changes in the employment environment. Whether success comes through legislation mandating comparable worth or through alternative procedures, such as collective bargaining, pressure will be put on employers and compensation managers.

Consequently, organizations need to examine their pay policies carefully in view of this new challenge. Pay rates of male and female jobs

---

[39] An interesting study of comparable worth implementation in Iowa is reported by P. F. Orazem and J. P. Mattila, "Comparable Worth and the Structure of Earnings: The Iowa Case," in *Pay Equity: Empirical Inquiries*, eds. R. T. Michael and H. I. Hartmann (Washington, D.C.: National Academy Press, forthcoming).

[40] For a variety of current views on comparable worth see Friedman, *Pay Equity.*

[41] T. A. Mahoney, "The Comparable Worth Construct: A Societal Perspective," in *Research in Organizational Behavior*, vol. 9, eds. B. Staw and L. L. Cummings (Greenwich, Conn.: JAI Press, 1987), pp. 209–45.

[42] G. S. Becker, "How the Market Acted Affirmatively for Women," *Business Week*, (N. 2894), May 13, 1985, p. 10.

ILLUSTRATION 14–1

Advocates point to Minnesota as a good example of how comparable worth can be implemented without a great deal of expense or fuss. Critics in the business community, as might be expected, point to many difficulties that have and might yet emerge.

Perhaps most interesting, not all public employees are happy with the Minnesota law, even though it is explicitly designed to raise wages of female jobs without corresponding cuts in wage rates of male jobs. Police and firefighter unions are lobbying the legislature to be excluded from the legislation. Firefighters, especially, seem to be upset with being classified at the same level as librarians. One fireman commented that he "knows a librarian's job is very dangerous—a book could fall on her head."

An analogous sentiment was expressed in Princeton, Minnesota, a prairie town that implemented comparable worth for its three female employees even before required by state law. One woman, the bookkeeper, received a 39 percent hourly wage increase to match the pay of male street sweepers. She bought a bottle of wine to celebrate and commented. "It's about time we moved out of the 1950s and got past the idea that women are just working for money to buy nylons." Not all Princeton citizens felt the same way. In a local cafe the waitress, wife of a street sweeper, refused to serve the bookkeeper. She said "the bookkeeper can sweep the streets (around city hall)."

The views expressed by police, firefighters, and the spouse of the street sweeper illustrate that pay rates mean far more than income for purchasing goods and services. Pay differentials reflect status and importance in our society. Changes in differentials mean changes in status, rewarding for those who improve, threatening for those who lose.

Source: C. Trost, "In Minnesota, 'Pay Equity' Passes Test, but Foes See Trouble Ahead," *The Wall Street Journal*, April 10, 1985, p. 21.

should be studied to determine if differentials may be discriminatory. Certainly, pay practices should be examined to make sure that the administration of pay does not discriminate against any group.

SUMMARY

Wage and salary administration is a pervasive P/HR activity. Employers are continually challenged to develop pay policies and procedures that enable them to attract, motivate, retain, and satisfy employees while remaining within the parameters established by public policy, labor unions, labor markets, and the organization's ability to pay.

To meet the challenge, a variety of wage and salary systems has been developed. Some of these, discussed in this chapter, apply to jobs. In developing job hierarchies and subsequent pay structures, organizations must be concerned about external and internal equity. Maintaining external equity is important as a way of remaining competitive with other organizations as well as to attract and retain a labor force. Internal equity is significant to both employees and managers since it reflects the contribution of various jobs to the organization.

Developing and maintaining pay structures that are both internally and externally equitable is difficult because the two forms of equity need not be highly related nor move in the same direction through time. Over the years, procedures have been established to deal with many of the problems encountered. Still, many problems seem to defy satisfactory solution.

Particularly problematic at present are the challenges associated with the comparable worth controversy. Laws and interpretations of those laws are evolving rapidly in this area. Compensation administrators must be alert to such changes and must be especially sensitive to the need for equitable pay structures for all employee groups.

DISCUSSION QUESTIONS

1. Describe the process involved in establishing a pay structure.
2. How can an organization determine its pay level?
3. Should a compensation manager be more concerned about internal or external equity? Why?
4. What is meant by the expression "comparable worth"? How have courts viewed the issue?
5. What are the implications, if any, of market wage bias against predominantly female jobs for the way organizations conventionally do job evaluation?

15

Pay Systems and Their Consequences

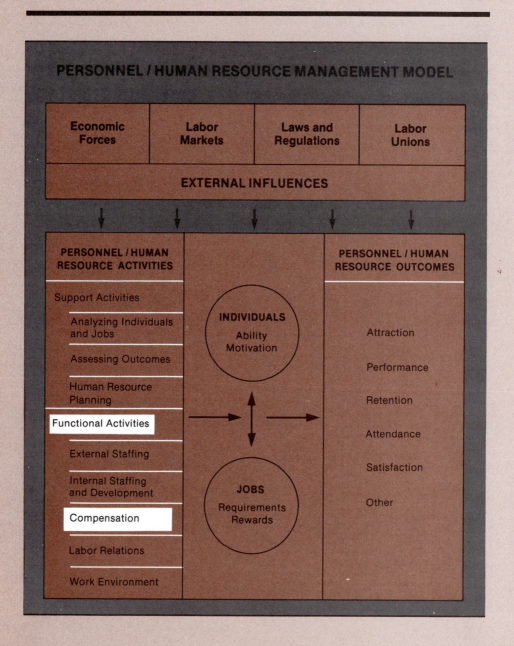

PERSONNEL / HUMAN RESOURCE MANAGEMENT MODEL

Economic Forces	Labor Markets	Laws and Regulations	Labor Unions

EXTERNAL INFLUENCES

PERSONNEL / HUMAN RESOURCE ACTIVITIES

Support Activities

Analyzing Individuals and Jobs

Assessing Outcomes

Human Resource Planning

Functional Activities

External Staffing

Internal Staffing and Development

Compensation

Labor Relations

Work Environment

INDIVIDUALS
Ability
Motivation

JOBS
Requirements
Rewards

PERSONNEL / HUMAN RESOURCE OUTCOMES

Attraction

Performance

Retention

Attendance

Satisfaction

Other

After reading this chapter, you should be able to speak to the questions posed in each of the following personnel/human resource incidents:

1. You are the manager of a small plant (200 employees) that manufactures paint under contract to three major retail chains. Productivity in the plant has slipped about 3 percent per year over the past three years, putting a severe squeeze on profits. You have read that incentive plans are effective in increasing productivity and reducing labor costs, and you feel that this might be the way for you to go. What factors would you consider in deciding whether to try an incentive system? What kind of system would you be most inclined to try? Assuming that you tried this type of system, what kinds of problems do you think you would encounter?

2. Assume you have just been appointed dean at your school. In about six months, you will have to make the annual adjustment to faculty salaries. Last year your predecessor granted an across-the-board increase of 8 percent to all members of the faculty. Would you be inclined to follow the same practice? What alternatives would you consider, and which would you choose?

3. The hospital that employs you has a difficult time with the unionized support personnel who do laundry, wash dishes, clean vacant rooms, and so on. There is no difficulty hiring people for these jobs, and turnover is unusually low. Nevertheless, absenteeism is excessive. On Mondays, Fridays, and the weekends, especially, it is often hard to staff the jobs that need doing.

At present, these employees are making an average of $6.50 an hour, which is about 50 cents above the market rate according to the latest hospital wage survey. Wages are higher than the hospital would like, largely because most of the employees are "old timers" and have accumulated many pay increases (which depend mostly on length of service). In addition, these employees receive a much better fringe-benefits package than is typical in other organizations.

As compensation manager, you are asked to evaluate this situation. What changes would you consider making in pay administration to alleviate the problems specified?

4. Your division of a large manufacturing organization has experienced more than its share of personnel difficulties. Production-employee turnover and absenteeism are higher, and satisfaction and performance are lower than in other divisions of the company. Your production manager has suggested that all production employees in the plant be given an across-the-board pay increase as a way of overcoming these difficulties. How do you evaluate this proposal? Why might it not be effective?

The previous chapter discussed issues involved with payment for jobs. The major concern for compensation managers is to obtain and maintain equitable pay structures for jobs, regardless of the individuals performing those jobs. However, as noted, organizations typically also establish pay policies that pertain to individuals in the jobs. Pay ranges are developed around the job rates to allow for individual pay variability.

Organizations establish individual or groups-of-employees pay policies to help achieve the objectives of our general model. Especially important are the performance and satisfaction outcomes, although pay policies are also aimed at influencing employee attendance and retention. The present chapter describes individual and group pay policies and the consequences of those policies on employee behaviors.

Since pay systems are designed to influence the motivation of some employee behavior (e.g., performance), a brief review of the motivation model presented in Chapter 5 is necessary. According to the expectancy model, motivation to engage in a behavior depends on: (1) *expectancy* perceptions (beliefs about the relationship between effort and the behavior), (2) *instrumentality* perceptions (beliefs about the connection between the behavior levels and rewards, such as pay), and (3) *valence* (the value of the rewards). An employee is motivated toward a behavior to the extent that expectancies for the behavior are high (s/he believes the behavior is attainable), instrumentalities are high (s/he believes rewards will result because of the behavior), and s/he values whatever rewards are, in fact, dependent on the behavior.

Since pay is a reward, the expectancy model predicts it will help motivate a behavior if employees (1) regard it as valent and (2) believe that its attainment depends on engaging in the behavior. Since it has already been established that pay is generally valent to the typical employee (see Chapter 5), the critical issue regarding the motivational properties of pay has to do with instrumentality perceptions. Other things being equal, pay policies that foster employee beliefs that pay depends on their behavior will motivate that behavior.

INDIVIDUAL AND GROUP PAY SYSTEMS

To a greater or lesser degree, the pay systems described below are all designed to link individual pay to some behavior(s) the organization seeks from its employees. In practice, three basic approaches are found often in combination. Most commonly, rate ranges for jobs and criteria for levels within the range are decided. Then either the criteria themselves or decision makers (usually managers) determine how much any given employee will earn.[1] This is the *conventional* approach. With the *incentive* approach, a single base rate is established for each job, but employees have an opportunity to earn more depending on what they or their work groups produce. Here the organization establishes (or negotiates) the "rules" (for example, in addition to the base rate, an appliance salesperson in a department store may be paid 25 percent of his/her sales). Within these rules, individual employees or groups of employees actually determine their own pay. A third approach, *gain sharing*, is used in conjunction with one of the other two. It provides a bonus based on some organizational criterion, such as cost savings or profits. Here again, the organization determines (or negotiates) the rules, and actual amounts received by employees are determined through some combination of their own efforts, managerial proficiency, and fortune.

Conventional Pay Systems

Prevailing criteria in conventional pay systems are the personal characteristics employees bring to the job and their performance while on the job, or some combination of these. Systems using these three criteria are referred to as input, merit, and mixed, respectively.

Input systems

Theoretically, any personal characteristic employees bring to their job might be regarded as an input for which they should be paid. In practice, seniority prevails over all others, although job skills is a criterion used in certain circumstances.

Seniority systems.   In seniority systems employees are placed in and move through rate ranges solely based on their length of service. Such systems may motivate length of service, but there is no reason to believe that they motivate employee performance (beyond whatever level may be required to keep the job). As a result, management generally opposes this approach, at least in principle.[2] In practice, however, it is frequently found among blue-collar jobs and often for clerical ones because (1) such

---

[1] *Wage and Salary Administration*, Personnel Policies Forum Survey, No. 131 (Washington, D.C.: Bureau of National Affairs, 1981), pp. 5–12; M. E. Personick, "White-Collar Pay Determination under Range-of-Rate Systems," *Monthly Labor Review* 107, no. 12 (1984), pp. 25–30.

[2] C. O'Dell, *People Performance and Pay* (Houston, Tex.: American Productivity Center, 1987); C. Peck, *Pay and Performance: The Interaction of Compensation and Performance Appraisal*, Research Bulletin, No. 155 (New York: The Conference Board, 1984).

jobs often do not require or permit large individual differences in performance levels (the classic case being jobs on assembly lines); (2) management is not willing to put in the time and effort necessary to obtain accurate measures of performance among these employees; (3) employees in these jobs frequently believe that seniority is a more appropriate criterion than performance to use in determining pay;[3] and (4) this is where most unionized employees are found, and unions frequently bargain for seniority systems.[4]

Most seniority systems provide for automatic progression through rate ranges by means of a series of steps. A more or less typical system in the electronics industry starts assemblers at $8 per hour. On completion of a six-month probationary period, successful employees progress to $8.80. Other automatic increases are given at the end of one ($9.80), two ($10.80), and five ($13.00) years. (Of course, these rates are subject to change as the entire pay structure is adjusted because of inflation and changes in labor market rates.)

Pay-for-knowledge systems.   Recently a number of organizations have begun to pay employees for the number of job skills they acquire. The Topeka plant of General Foods Corporation provides an example.[5] Here, the system is used as part of a larger effort of workplace redesign (see Chapter 19). New production employees earn a standard entry rate and thereafter progress one pay grade for each new job they learn until all the jobs in the plant have been mastered (a process that typically takes about two years). Employees are paid the rate appropriate for the skills they have learned regardless of the job they may be performing at any given time.

Organizations appear to have two major objectives for installing pay-for-knowledge systems.[6] First, they provide greater flexibility. Changes in product demand and production technology can be more easily handled because employees have a broader range of skills. Absenteeism and even turnover can also be more easily accommodated with a broadly skilled work force. Second, largely due to the increased flexibility, fewer

---

[3] E. E. Lawler III, *Pay and Organizational Effectiveness: A Psychological View* (New York: McGraw-Hill, 1971), pp. 159–62.

[4] *Wage and Salary Administration*, p. 13.

[5] E. E. Lawler III, *Pay and Organizational Development* (Reading, Mass.: Addison-Wesley Publishing, 1981), pp. 65–69.

[6] G. D. Jenkins, Jr., and N. Gupta, "The Payoffs of Paying for Knowledge," *Labor-Management Corporation Brief* (Washington, D.C.: U.S. Department of Labor, 1985); H. Tosi and L. Tosi, "What Managers Need to Know about Knowledge-Based Pay," *Organizational Dynamics* 14 no. 3 (1986), pp. 52–64.

employees are necessary to perform the work activities of the organization.

These advantages of pay-for-knowledge systems come at a price,
however. Because employees are paid for the skills they have acquired,
whether they use these skills or not, hourly wage costs per employee are
higher in such systems. Further, the organization typically has to spend
substantially more on training than in alternative pay systems. Thus, a
firm considering the use of a pay-for-knowledge system has to determine
whether its technology and product demand can benefit from the increased flexibility that such systems appear to offer.

Output systems

Merit systems.

In merit plans, pay increases are determined by job
performance rather than seniority. The objective, of course, is to use pay
to motivate high levels of performance by increasing the instrumentality
perceptions of employees. To do this successfully requires a reasonably
accurate performance appraisal system (see Chapter 6), and some means
of translating performance ratings into pay increases. With respect to the
last point, relevant issues involve the size and timing of pay increases and
the form they take.

Considering size, the basic question is, how much of a difference
makes a difference? A merit increase must exceed some threshold value
before employees feel they are really receiving something worthwhile.
Investigators studying this issue have labeled the threshold value a "just-
noticeable difference" (JND). A 20 percent salary increase would surely
be noticeable; a 4 percent increase might not be. In general, JND salary
increases appear to depend on present income.[7] Higher-paid employees
must receive a larger dollar increment to regard it as a real pay increase
than must those earning a smaller amount.

Organizations tend to set up pay ranges that are consistent with these
findings. For example, a survey of pay plans for white-collar employees
found that the width of the salary range for highly paid administrative
and professional employees averaged more than 50 percent. The highest
salary in a range exceeded the lowest salary by more than 50 percent.
Among clerical positions, the range generally averaged less than 45

---

[7] Studies on JNDs include H. G. Heneman III and R. A. Ellis, "Correlates of Just
Noticeable Differences in Pay Increases," *Industrial Relations Research Association*, Proceedings of the 1982 Meeting, Milwaukee, Wis., April 1982; P. Varadarajan and C. Futrell, "Factors
Affecting Perceptions of Smallest Meaningful Pay Increases," *Industrial Relations* 23 (1984), pp.
278–86.

percent.[8] On the other hand, another survey found that actual wages paid employees varied less than the total range width. For example, the actual spread between highest and lowest paid employees in given technical and professional occupations averaged about 30 percent.[9]

With respect to timing, motivation theory suggests that the best results are achieved when rewards immediately follow desired behaviors. But this is impractical in merit pay plans, since performance cannot be reviewed daily, weekly, or even monthly. Common practice involves once-a-year review,[10] although new employees are often evaluated after their first six months of employment.

In merit systems one's pay increment in any given time period is usually built into the subsequent base salary. This creates a potential problem because employees may eventually move out of the salary range for their jobs. To help prevent this situation, organizations often employ a merit pay matrix, as shown in Figure 15–1. Note that it specifies the (1) size of salary increases to be associated with various performance levels (with increases ranging from 5 to 15 percent), and (2) length of time that should elapse between merit increases (usually 10 to 12 months). Also note that the performance-pay linkage is not direct in this company; rather, it is moderated by an employee's position in his/her rate range.[11]

One-shot bonus systems.   Even with a merit pay matrix, evidence suggests that the relationship between pay and performance can deteriorate substantially in a conventional merit system.[12] As an alternative, some organizations are moving to one-shot bonus systems, so named because the increment one earns in any time period is not carried forward to subsequent time periods. General Motors has recently begun to use one-shot bonuses among its office employees in an attempt to keep pay more closely in line with performance.[13]

---

[8] Personick, "White-Collar Pay Determination."

[9] J. E. Buckley, "Wage Differences among Workers in the Same Job and Establishment," *Monthly Labor Review* 108, no. 3 (1985), pp. 11–16.

[10] Personick, "White-Collar Pay Determination."

[11] There is evidence that employees and managers believe merit increases should be lower for more highly paid individuals in the salary range. M. H. Birnbaum, "Perceived Equity of Salary Policies," *Journal of Applied Psychology* 68 (1983), pp. 49–59; P. D. Sherer, D. P. Schwab, and H. G. Heneman III, "Policy Capturing Managerial Salary Raise Decisions," *Personnel Psychology* 46 (1987), pp. 27–38.

[12] D. P. Schwab, and C. Olson, "Pay-Performance Relationships as a Function of Pay-for-Performance Policies and Practices." Paper presented at the National Academy of Management Meetings, Anaheim, Calif., August 1988).

[13] J. M. Schlesinger, "GM's New Compensation Plan Reflects General Trend Tying Pay to Performance," *The Wall Street Journal*, January 26, 1988.

FIGURE 15–1

A Salary Increment Matrix from a Merit Pay System

Range position (compa-ratio)‡		Outstanding† Limit*	Excellent Limit*	Good	Fair	Unsatisfactory
Maximum	120	6% 10 months	6% 12 months		Review with salary administration	
	112	9% 10 months	6% 12 months	5% 12 months		
Midpoint	104 100	11% 10 months	9% 12 months	6% 12 months	5% 12 months	
	96	13% 10 months	11% 12 months	8% 12 months	5% 12 months	
Minimum	88	15% 10 months	13% 12 months	10% 12 months	6% 10 months	
	80	Outstanding†	Excellent	Good	Fair	Unsatisfactory
			Performance			

Note: Increases in less than the number of months indicated are exceptions. Below minimum increases provide for 6–9 months of time worked using 80–88 compa-ratio percentages. Applies to full-time permanent employees.

* Percentage increase limited by range maximum. Minimum of 4 percent increase suggested when range adjustment permits.

† Very selective usage expected.

‡ Compa-ratio is actual salary divided by midpoint of range.

Used with permission of Corning Glass Works.

Mixed systems

In mixed systems, individual rates of pay are determined by a combination of criteria, typically a combination of seniority and merit. Some mixed systems involve only modest modifications of the seniority principle. This is the case in systems where automatic progressions prevail with the provisions that increases may be withheld for unsatisfactory performance or accelerated for outstanding performance. Another common system involves the use of automatic progression up to the midpoints of rate ranges (considered the going rate for satisfactory performance) and merit increases thereafter.

Mixed systems often evolve from merit systems that are not carefully controlled. For example, managers may juggle performance ratings to manipulate the pay increases of their subordinates. Managers are sometimes reluctant to differentiate among employees for fear that doing so may lead to intragroup competition and hostility.[14] Another common practice is for organizations to apply the label "merit increases" to general increases that all employees receive. Obviously, both of these practices tend to weaken the performance-pay linkage; many organizations that claim to have merit pay systems in fact have systems that are mixed.

Administering and controlling conventional pay systems

Two issues that arise in the administration and control of conventional pay systems have to do with planning and monitoring merit increases and establishing beginning salaries for new employees.

Managing merit increases. Line managers usually make individual merit pay decisions. As previously noted, these decisions have a way of transforming merit pay into mixed plans in the absence of controls. Personnel/human resource departments use many different measures to monitor managers' merit pay allocations, including checks to ensure that (1) all increases given are justified by performance ratings, (2) all employees receive merit reviews (although not necessarily raises) when due, (3) merit increases are distributed in a manner consistent with established norms, (4) employees are not discriminated against because of race, color, creed, national origin, sex, or age, and (5) budgets are not exceeded.

Controlling starting rates. Usually, rate ranges are established with the idea that new employees will be hired at the bottom of the ranges. When labor markets become tight, however, organizations often experience difficulties in hiring certain kinds of employees, and line managers begin to hire—or request to hire—at higher than usual rates.[15] This creates dissatisfaction and pressures for adjustments from existing employees in the same and adjacent pay grades. If these adjustments are made, employees in the lower pay grades (where most of the hiring occurs) begin to become bunched toward the upper end of their ranges. *Wage* or *salary compression* is the term usually given to this situation.

Two-tier wage systems represent the opposite of wage compression. In such systems new employees are hired at a wage below the existing

---

[14] S. E. Markham, "Pay-for-Performance Dilemma Revisited: Empirical Example of the Importance of Group Effects," *Journal of Applied Psychology* 73 (1988), pp. 172–80.

[15] C. C. Hoffmann, "Multiple-Pay Systems: Are They Worth the Risk?" *Compensation and Benefits Review* 19, no. 1 (1987), pp. 36–46.

range minimum. Two-tier systems have been implemented largely during the 1980s, usually in union-management negotiated labor agreements (see also Chapter 18).[16]

Both of these deviations from standard practice illustrate the effects of external markets. Compression is a consequence of skill shortages in the labor market. The two-tier system is a consequence of surpluses in the external labor market combined with increased product market competition. Both present problems for management since they contribute to feelings of inequity among employees.

The administration and control of conventional pay plans are enhanced by well-developed and clearly articulated pay policies and procedures. Ensuring that compensation objectives are met and that policies and procedures are adhered to is a major task in the face of the various internal and external forces at work. Clearly, at this time, totally satisfactory solutions are lacking despite several decades of experience with conventional pay plans.

Incentive Pay Systems

Like merit pay plans, individual and group incentive pay systems are adopted to enhance employee motivation to perform. While merit pay plans attempt to motivate by relating periodic pay increases to employee performance ratings, most incentive pay plans tie day-to-day earnings directly and automatically to relatively objective indexes of individual or group performance.[17] In individual incentive pay plans, it is individual performance that is measured and rewarded. These plans vary widely, however, with respect to performance measures used and the specific linkages established between performance and pay.

Piece-rate plans pay directly for units of output produced. A simple example is a situation in which students coding research data are paid $1 for each questionnaire completed. Production bonus plans pay for time saved. In many automobile repair shops, for example, standard times are beaten. Thus, a mechanic who completes a four-hour brake job in, say, three hours earns 33 percent over standard (four hours pay for three hours work).

---

[16] S. M. Jacoby and D. J. B. Mitchell, "Management Attitudes toward Two-Tier Pay Plans," *Journal of Labor Research* 7 (1986), pp. 221–37.

[17] Confusion surrounds the term *incentive* as it is used in the pay context. Broadly, the term is used to refer to pay that is held out as a potential future reward if certain behaviors are carried out or certain objectives are met (e.g., to refer to the merit pay increase that will be forthcoming if a faculty member proves to be an effective classroom teacher). Here, however, the term is being used much more narrowly to describe two generic forms of pay plans in which a *specific amount of money* is attached to *physical measures of employee or work group output.*

Commission plans are found among salespeople. Most are similar to piece-rate plans except that payment is made for sales rather than for production. Some commission plans resemble production bonus plans in that they provide extra compensation for sales beyond an established quota.

Parallels of piece-rate, production bonus, and commission plans are found at the group level. Group incentive pay plans are less common than individual plans but are found where teamwork and cooperation are essential to produce goods or services or to make sales.

Prevalence

From a motivational standpoint, individual and, to a lesser extent, group incentive pay plans are more appealing than merit pay plans because the linkage between performance and pay is much more direct and unambiguous, thus enhancing instrumentality perceptions. Such plans, however, are applicable only in a relatively limited number of situations, most notably where employee or group output can be counted or assessed in dollar terms. Moreover, they are difficult to develop, administer, and control.

As a consequence, individual and group incentive pay systems are found among only a minority of the nation's work force. They are most prevalent among blue-collar production workers and salespeople. Estimates vary, but it appears that as many as one third and three fourths of the nation's employers use such systems among at least some of their blue-collar workers and salespeople, respectively.[18]

Developing a plan

Although variations exist, the basic process involved in developing an individual or group incentive pay plan is well documented. It is as follows:

Step 1.   Establish minimum job rates. This is done using the same process as is used to price jobs under conventional pay plans. It is necessary to ensure a minimum standard of living for all employees and

---

[18] The figures for blue-collar workers are from the Bureau of National Affairs, *Wage and Salary Administration;* N. W. Carlson, "Time Rates Tighten Their Grip on Manufacturing Industries," *Monthly Labor Review* 105, no. 5 (1982), pp. 15–22. The figures for salespeople are from J. P. Steinbrink, "How to Pay Your Sales Force," *Harvard Business Review* 56, no. 4 (1978), pp. 111–22.

to avoid violations of the Fair Labor Standards Act (FLSA) and other minimum-wage laws.

Step 2.   Establish performance standards. In individual incentive plans, this usually is done by industrial engineers using time and motion studies.[19] In group incentive and commission plans, it is more likely that tradition and judgment will be relied upon.

Step 3.   Determine incentive rates. It must be decided how much will be paid per piece produced, unit of time saved, or sales volume generated. Often, a plan offers the best workers an opportunity to make 15 to 35 percent more than standard.

Step 4.   Establish a process for changing standards. Usually, changes should be made only when conditions change (for example, a new machine or procedure is introduced).

Step 5.   Establish a mechanism through which complaints and grievances can quickly be processed.

Step 6.   Try out the plan on an experimental basis before adopting it officially.

Step 7.   Communicate all of the above to employees. Plans that are not understood or believed are in for rough going. Involving employees in steps 1 to 4 may facilitate understanding and acceptance of the plan.

Administering and controlling incentive pay systems

It may be that Murphy had individual and group incentive pay plans in mind when he formulated his famous law, "Anything that can go wrong *will*." Setting performance standards and incentive rates requires considerable judgment, even when time and motion study is used. Since no organization is static, a watchful eye must be maintained to ensure that the original standards and rates remain "reasonable." Constantly comparing the earnings of employees on incentives with the earnings of those around them, particularly their supervisors, helps accomplish this.

The administration of incentive systems is also problematic because employees are motivated to "beat the game" by keeping standards low so that they can maximize their pay with a minimum of effort. As a consequence, an adversarial relationship may develop between employees and managers responsible for the pay system. These competing objectives

---

[19] Time and motion study is a complex process. Interested readers are encouraged to consult H. G. Zollitsch, "Productivity, Time Study, and Incentive Pay Plans," in *ASPA Handbook of Personnel and Industrial Relations*, eds. D. Yoder and H. G. Heneman, Jr. (Washington, D.C.: Bureau of National Affairs, 1979).

continually challenge compensation specialists as they attempt to effectively administer and control individual and group incentive systems.

Gain-Sharing Plans

Gain-sharing plans use various measures of organizational performance to determine the size of periodic bonus payments employees will receive. Such plans are never the sole source of employee compensation. Rather, they are adjuncts to conventional pay plans or to individual or group incentive plans. Typically, the measure of organizational performance focused on is either cost savings or profits.

Cost-savings plans

Plans focusing on cost savings come in many forms. The prototype, however, is the Scanlon Plan, conceived in 1937.[20] In the Scanlon Plan, bonuses are determined based on labor cost savings over some base rate. The incentive is to reduce labor costs below the norm.

Consider an example. Assume that a Scanlon Plan company determines that historically labor costs have equaled 50 percent of the value of production. Assume further that in a given month the value of production is $100,000, and the actual labor costs are $40,000—a 20 percent improvement over the norm of $50,000. The $10,000 savings goes into the incentive pool—perhaps 20 percent of which would be retained as a reserve (to cover bad months) and perhaps another 20 percent would accrue to management. The remainder would go to the employees. In the example, $6,000 would be available to distribute across a payroll of $40,000. Thus, each employee would receive a bonus equal to 15 percent ($6,000/$40,000) of his/her pay for the month.

Scanlon and other cost-savings plans do not rely solely on the cash bonus to mobilize employees. When such plans are installed, a number of interlocking committees are established throughout the organization. At Dana Corporation, for example, production committees typically consist of the supervisor, a tool engineer, and two to four representatives elected by the departmental employees. Production committees, in turn, report to a plant steering committee.[21] These committees (1) generate suggestions for achieving cost savings, (2) evaluate similar

---

[20] G. Strauss, "Participatory and Gainsharing Systems: History and Hope." Paper presented at Wingspread Conference on Pay and Participation, 1986.

[21] H. Gorlin and L. Schein, *Innovations in Managing Human Resources* (New York: The Conference Board, 1984), p. 10.

suggestions that emanate from employees not on the committees, and (3) foster communications and cooperation between management, employees, and (where present) labor union leaders. In other words, these plans represent a form of organization development (see Chapter 19) as much as a method of compensation.

Cost savings plans such as Scanlon, Rucker, and Improshare have received a great deal of attention in recent years, and their use is increasing somewhat.[22] Nevertheless, relatively few firms have adopted such plans to date. The available evidence on these plans generally shows favorable results in cost savings, suggestions made, cooperative climate attained, and the like, although some have been unsuccessful.[23] Best results seem to be attained when employees actively participate in the program and when top management is committed to the plan's success.[24]

Profit-sharing plans

More widespread than cost-savings plans are profit-sharing plans in which organizations set aside some percentage of their annual earnings for distribution to employees. The intent is to promote a sense of partnership and sharing in the organization's fate and to motivate higher levels of performance and lower levels of turnover.

Profit-sharing plans come in many forms. In some, profit shares are distributed annually; in others, payment is deferred until employees retire. Many profit-sharing plans cover all employees, but some pertain only to top executives and, perhaps, selected middle managers. A profit-sharing plan can be added to an organization with little or no change otherwise. However, in the best known of these plans, that of the Lincoln Electric Company, profit sharing is an integral part of a performance management system that includes tight cost controls, an individual incentive plan, productivity committees, and a no layoff policy.[25]

The popularity of profit sharing ebbs and flows with the business cycle. One estimate puts usage at about 20 percent of moderate- and

---

[22] Strauss, "Participatory and Gainsharing."

[23] For a review of this research, see H. Thierry, "Payment by Results Systems: A Review of Research 1945–1985, *Applied Psychology: An Internal Review* 36 (1987), pp. 91–108; and M. Schuster, *Union-Management Cooperation: Structure, Process, and Impact* (Kalamazoo, Mich.: W. E. Upjohn Institute for Employment Research, 1984).

[24] J. K. White, "The Scanlon Plan: Causes and Correlates of Success," *Academy of Management Journal* 22 (1979), pp. 292–312; and B. E. Morre and T. L. Ross, *The Scanlon Way to Improved Productivity* (New York: Wiley-Interscience, 1978).

[25] On Lincoln Electric, see R. Zager, "Managing Guaranteed Employment," *Harvard Business Review* 56, no. 3 (1978), pp. 103–15.

large-sized private-sector firms.[26] Testimonials to the virtues of profit-sharing plans are legion. Reliable research on their effectiveness, however, is nearly nonexistent.[27] However, it is probable that in terms of motivating performance, profit-sharing plans are less effective than are cost-savings plans. This is because the link between employees' efforts and company profit levels is generally weak, but the link between employees' efforts and labor cost savings is much more direct.

EMPLOYEE RESPONSES TO PAY SYSTEMS

It is clear that organizations use a wide variety of payment methods designed to reward individuals "above and beyond" the particular job they perform. They do this in an effort to influence employees' behaviors and attitudes in a manner favorable to the objectives of the organization, specifically to achieve the personnel/human resource outcomes of our general model.

Attraction of new employees is likely to be influenced to some extent by individual pay policies and practices. Job seekers who have a choice between two or more job alternatives might express an interest in just how their pay may be expected to increase in time, if hired. However, most job seekers—because they lack alternative opportunities or lack sufficient information—probably place most emphasis on starting pay level (amount).

Pay policies and practices aimed at individuals have their fullest impact on employees after they enter the organization and begin working. From the organization's perspective, these pay policies and practices are particularly relevant as they may influence employee performance, attendance, retention, and satisfaction. Each of these P/HR outcomes is discussed below.

Performance

As noted, the expectancy model suggests that the performance levels of individuals depend on their ability and motivation. As a reward, pay will motivate high performance to the extent that pay policies foster employee beliefs that pay depends on high performance.

In Chapter 5, it was argued that employee instrumentality percep-

---

[26] *Productivity Improvement Programs*, Personnel Policies Forum, No. 138 (Washington, D.C.: Bureau of National Affairs, 1984), p. 7.

[27] G. W. Florkowski, "The Organizational Impact of Profit Sharing," *Academy of Management Review* 12 (1987), pp. 622–36.

FIGURE 15–2
Size of Incentive Group and Group Productivity

Productivity

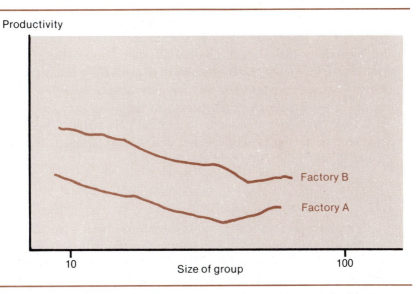

Source: H. Campbell, "Group Incentive Payment Schemes: The Effects of Lack of Understanding and of Group Size," *Occupational Psychology* 26 (1952), pp. 15–21.

tions depend largely on the objective links between a behavior and the rewards in question. Thus, the major determinant of how compensation influences motivation to perform depends on the actual relationship between performance and pay. Systems that link high performance to pay can be expected to motivate high performance. Other things being equal, the stronger the linkage, the higher the motivation. It is apparent in considering the pay systems described above that individual incentive systems, if properly administered, objectively link pay most closely to performance. Thus, individual incentive systems should be most motivating. Somewhat less motivating are group incentive systems because individual pay depends on the performance of the group, not the individual directly. The larger the group, the lower is the individual's performance-pay link, and hence the lower the motivation. To illustrate, Figure 15–2 shows the relationships between productivity and the number of employees in incentive groups for two automobile manufacturing plants.[28] In addition to the decline in productivity as size increased,

---

[28] H. Campbell, "Group Incentive Payment Schemes: The Effects of Lack of Understanding and Group Size," *Occupational Psychology* 26 (1952), pp. 15–21.

employees in larger groups have more difficulty determining the groups' productivity. This serves to weaken individual instrumentality perceptions.

The value of merit and mixed systems for motivating employee performance is somewhat controversial, as might be expected given the problems with such systems identified earlier. Some of the pros and cons are listed in Figure 15–3. In short, if properly administered and if employees are responsive to pay for performance systems, merit plans can help motivate high performance. At the other extreme are systems that make no effort to objectively link pay and performance. Seniority systems are illustrative of those not designed to motivate high performance, although they may motivate retention.

Does pay motivate?

Over the years a great many organizations have tried to determine whether pay can be used to motivate high performance. Although by no means universally successful, such investigations have frequently found that pay can be administered in ways that yield higher employee productivity. Moreover, the manner in which pay appears to operate is generally consistent with the predictions made by the expectancy model.

Many investigations have been performed on individual incentive systems, often contrasting them with group incentives of job-based systems.[29] Results generally show that employees paid on individual incentive systems produce at higher levels than employees on job-based systems. One review of field studies found that the median performance improvement following the introduction of an individual incentive plan

---

[29] For general reviews, see Thierry, "Payment by Results"; L. D. Dyer and D. P. Schwab, "Personnel/Human Resource Management Research," Chapter 5 in *Industrial Relations Research in the 1970s: Review and Appraisal*, eds. T. A. Kochan, D. J. B. Mitchell, and L. D. Dyer (Madison, Wis.: Industrial Relations Research Association, IRRA Series, 1982); A. N. Nash and S. J. Carroll, Jr., *The Management of Compensation* (Monterey, Calif.: Brooks/Cole Publishing, 1975), pp. 199–202; R. L. Opsahl and M. D. Dunnette, "The Role of Financial Compensation in Industrial Motivation," *Psychological Bulletin* 66 (1966), pp. 94–118. A few examples of recent investigations of incentive pay plans include D. J. Campbell, "The Effects of Goal-Contingent Payment on the Performance of a Complex Task," *Personnel Psychology* 37 (1984), pp. 23–40; W. E. Scott, J. Farh and P. M. Podsakoff, "The Effects of 'Intrinsic' and "Extrinsic' Reinforcement Contingencies on Task Behavior," *Decision Processes* 41 (1988), pp. 405–25; F. Luthans, R. Paul, and D. Baker, "An Experimental Analysis of the Impact of Contingent Reinforcement on Salespersons' Performance Behavior," *Journal of Applied Psychology* 66 (1981), pp. 314–23; P. Sari and G. P. Lutham, "Employee Reactions to Continuous and Variable Ratio Reinforcement Schedules Involving a Monetary Incentive," *Journal of Applied Psychology* 67 (1982), pp. 506–8.

FIGURE 15–3
The Pros and Cons of Merit Systems

Pros:

1. Employees prefer that their pay be based on their performance.
2. If an average wage is given to each employee, then high performers, the people that the organization wishes to retain, will be dissatisfied with their pay and may leave the organization.
3. If merit pay is not included as a component of the total compensation package, then performance is not being rewarded, and only membership is being rewarded. This provides an incentive for poor performers to remain with the organization.
4. Merit pay plans are based on a number of well-established theories (expectancy theory and reinforcement theory).
5. There have been a number of empirical studies demonstrating the effectiveness of merit pay.
6. Merit pay will work when it is administered properly.
7. Motivation through merit pay is one way to increase productivity in the United States.
8. There are valid methods of performance appraisal that can be used. In addition, the measurement of performance is becoming easier, with the advent of management information systems and the continuing decentralization and diversification of American companies.
9. Merit pay is increasingly important during periods of inflation.
10. There is more openness and employee participation in some pay plans.
11. Merit pay distinguishes between high- and low-performing employees.
12. Merit pay is an excellent source of performance feedback to the employee.

Cons:

1. It is difficult to make accurate performance ratings.
2. Merit pay plans are costly and difficult to administer.
3. Merit pay has little meaning during periods of high inflation.
4. Differences in merit pay between high and low performers are very small.
5. There are problems with the theories used to support merit pay (expectancy theory and reinforcement theory).
6. Merit pay has not worked for the federal government, and it may not work for executives.
7. Merit pay threatens the self-esteem of employees because they overestimate their own performance and, as a result, feel underrewarded. A decrease in self-esteem may decrease performance.
8. Too much emphasis is placed on money as a motivator at the exclusion of other motivators coming from the job itself.
9. Labor unions prefer basing pay on seniority rather than on merit.
10. Emphasis is placed on satisfaction with pay rather than on job performance; an attempt is made to keep all employees satisfied, including low performers.
11. Relative to the size of base pay, merit pay is very small and therefore has little meaning to employees.
12. Conflicts are created when a competitive reward system like merit pay is used.
13. Emphasis is placed upon individual performance to the exclusion of group performance.

Source: Adapted from R. L. Heneman, "Pay for Performance: Exploring the Merit System," *Work in America Institute Studies in Productivity* (New York: Pergamon Press, 1984), pp. 5–6.

was 30 percent.[30] Individual incentive systems also often result in higher productivity than group incentive systems. Moreover, when employees are switched from a job-based to an individual incentive system, productivity tends to increase. Illustration 15–1 describes an individual incentive system and the cost implications of its installation. Although employees earned more money under the incentive system than before, the firm's actual labor costs declined because of increased performance levels.

When pay systems fail to motivate

Despite the many successful applications, there are instances when incentive and merit systems fail, sometimes in a spectacular fashion. There are many reasons any particular system may fail to generate the intended results, but several common problems deserve elaboration.[31]

One pervasive problem has to do with measurement. Any system that purports to reward for performance must first be able to measure performance. As Chapter 6 points out, this requirement is often hard to satisfy. Even in cases where employees produce or sell an identifiable product, as is typical where individual and group incentive systems exist, measures are often less satisfactory than desired.[32] The problem is even greater in merit systems since many organizations that purport to base pay increases on past performance do not even have formal performance appraisals.[33]

Obviously, pay rewards cannot be closely connected to performance when the last is not measured accurately. Employee instrumentality perceptions are necessarily weakened. As a consequence, poor performance measurement almost certainly reduces the motivational potential of an incentive or merit system.

---

[30] E. A. Locke, D. B. Feren, V. M. McCaleb, K. N. Shaw, and A. T. Denny, "The Relative Effectiveness of Form Methods of Motivating Employee Performance," in *Changes in Working Life*, eds. K. D. Duncan, M. M. Gruneberg, and D. Wallis (New York: John Wiley & Sons, 1980), pp. 363–88. Performance gains from the introduction of pay incentives exceeded gains from the installation of goal-setting programs, job enrichment, or participation plans. Somewhat less powerful effects were obtained in a review by R. A. Guzzo, R. D. Jette, and R. A. Katzell, "The Effects of Psychologically Based Intervention Programs on Worker Productivity: A Meta-Analysis," *Personnel Psychology* 38 (1985), pp. 275–91.

[31] Problems that may crop up in incentive pay administration are elaborated on by W. C. Hamner, "How to Ruin Motivation with Pay," *Compensation Review* 7, no. 3 (1975), pp. 17–27; and W. F. Whyte, *Money and Motivation* (New York: Harper & Row, 1955).

[32] H. G. Zollitsch, "Productivity, Time Study and Incentive Pay Plans," in *ASPA Handbook of Personnel and Industrial Relations*, eds. D. Yoder and H. G. Heneman, Jr. (Washington, D.C.: Bureau of National Affairs, 1979), pp. 51–74.

[33] W. A. Evans, "Pay for Performance: Fact or Fable," *Personnel Journal* 49 (1970), pp. 726–31.

ILLUSTRATION 15–1

Increasing Beaver-Trapping Productivity

A lumbering firm located in the Northwest was interested in increasing the productivity of its trappers. These men, members of a union, were employed to trap and kill beavers, animals that chew down and hence destroy trees that the firm was interested in harvesting.

Before the new pay system was implemented, the company calculated that the cost to trap a beaver averaged $16.75. This included the trappers' hourly wage of $5, fringe benefits, and transportation to and from the field.

As a way of increasing productivity, the company proposed to the union that the trappers receive a bonus of $1 for each beaver trapped to be paid over and above the hourly rate. Trappers were to take the beavers caught to the supervisor, who would then pay them the appropriate bonus on the spot. (Actually the system was somewhat more complicated than this. Nevertheless, the average bonus paid was $1 per beaver). The union agreed to try this new system on an experimental basis and helped the company explain the system to the employees.

The investigation of the incentive system took place over a two-month period. Trapping performance under the new system increased dramatically. Even though the company added the bonus expense, the cost of trapping a beaver dropped to $12.86 (a reduction of 23 percent). During the two-month period, the employees caught 2,006 beavers. Thus, although the trappers received over $2,000 more than under the hourly system, the firm saved $7,703 compared to the cost of an equivalent number of beavers trapped on the hourly system.

The experience of this company is not unique. Nevertheless, several factors that were probably very important to the success of the program should be considered. First, the company carefully got the unqualified support of the trappers' union. Had the union not been convinced of the value of the system, it might well have been able to convince the trappers not to accept it. Second, the system was carefully explained to the trappers themselves. The employees in this case were enthusiastic about the system before it was implemented.

Another important component of the plan was the fact that the output (trapped beavers) was an easily measured output. There were no questions about when work was successfully performed. Moreover, the trappers worked by themselves; their success was not dependent on the performance of other employees. Finally, beaver trapping is a task where greater effort can lead to greater performance. Were this not true, no pay system, no matter how motivating, could lead to higher productivity.

Source: G. P. Latham and D. L. Dossett, "Designing Incentive Plans for Unionized Employees: A Comparison of Continuous and Variable Ratio Reinforcement Schedules," *Personnel Psychology* 31 (1978), pp. 47–62.

Motivation problems also occur frequently as a result of the standard-setting process. When standards are inequitable (some employees earn more than others because of the standards rather than true differences in performance), instrumentality perceptions are sure to suffer. *Quota restriction,* deliberately holding production to some level below maximum output, for example, often reflects employee attempts to maintain existing production standards as a way of keeping current pay-perform-ance linkages.

No system is faultless; to some extent problems of measurement and standard setting are inherent in any incentive or merit system. It is imperative, therefore, that an organization obtain employee acceptance of the pay system. One important requirement is to make sure employ-ees understand it. Helpful in this regard is a system that is relatively simple.[34] Employee participation in the development of the pay plan also may serve to gain employee acceptance.[35]

Attendance

Chapter 7 discussed the significance of employee attendance and the costs associated with absenteeism. The questions addressed in this sec-tion are (1) can pay be administered to help reduce absenteeism and (2) if so, what components of pay are most critical?

In answering these questions, it may be helpful to recall the model of at-tendance developed in Chapter 7. Employee attendance depends on both ability (such as the employees' health) and motivation. As in the case of performance, pay is not assumed to influence ability to attend. Thus, pay is influential to the extent that it influences motivation to attend.

To some extent, the motivation model used to describe performance is also applicable for employee attendance. Thus, pay policies that strengthen the instrumentality between attendance and pay are likely to motivate attendance. For example, New York Life Insurance Company permits each employee who has attended every day for a quarter of the year to participate in a lottery for savings bonds of up to $200.[36] Perfect attendance for the year permits participation in a lottery where winners can obtain bonds up to $1,000. In the first year of operation this plan was associated with a 21 percent decline in absenteeism among employees eligible to participate.

Other companies have also generally found that pay linked con-tingently to attendance can reduce absenteeism.[37] However, it should

---

[34] C. Dammann and E. E. Lawler III, "Employee Reactions to a Pay Incentive Plan," *Journal of Applied Psychology* 58 (1973), pp. 263–72.

[35] G. D. Jenkins, Jr., and E. E. Lawler III, "Impact on Employee Participation in Pay Plan Development," *Organizational Behavior and Human Performance* 28 (1981), pp. 111–28.

[36] A. Halcrow, "Incentive! How Three Companies Cut Costs," *Personnel Journal* 65 no. 2 (1986), pp. 12–13.

[37] L. M. Schmitz and H. G. Heneman, "The Effectiveness of Positive Reinforcement Programs in Reducing Employee Absenteeism," *Personnel Administrator* 25, no. 9 (1980), pp. 87–93. One survey reported that 25 percent of firms have incentive programs to reduce absenteeism; see B. Martin and M. Magnus, "Recognizing Reward Programs," *Personnel Journal* 65, no. 12 (1986), pp. 65–76.

not be assumed that any incentive system will influence attendance. For example, a small manufacturer of textile products installed a plan for its production employees. The plan provided a $25 bonus for employees if they had no more than three hours of unexcused lost time for each quarter of the calendar year.[38] To its dismay, the firm found that, although the percentage of employees with less than three hours of absenteeism increased (it had to pay $7,500 in bonuses the first year), overall absenteeism also *increased* by more than 12 percent. While it is not possible to determine why this system failed, a probable explanation includes the relatively small bonus coupled with the long time (three months) necessary to obtain it.

Retention

Another P/HR outcome where pay programs are likely to be of significance pertains to employee retention, or its opposite, turnover. Pay is most likely to influence the *voluntary* dimension of turnover (that is, turnover within the control of the employee rather than the organization).

Pay levels and turnover

The model reported in Chapter 7 indicated that voluntary turnover depended on employee perceptions of the *desirability* and *ease* of movement. Individuals typically seek to improve their employment conditions when they change jobs (that is, perceived desirability of movement). Their ability to accomplish this obviously depends on a number of personal and labor-market factors, but it is often found that job seekers improve their pay levels if they obtain a new job before they leave their present employer.[39]

These types of findings suggest that the organization's *pay level* is a potentially important direct influence on voluntary turnover. At least some employees appear to compare their pay with pay levels available in other organizations. When better pay is available elsewhere, there is a tendency to quit one's employer and accept the job with the higher pay

---

[38] G. O. Schneller IV and R. E. Kopelman, "Using Incentives to Increase Absenteeism: A Plan that Backfired," *Compensation Review* 15, no. 3 (1983), pp. 40–45.

[39] For a summary of research findings, see H. S. Parnes, *Research on Labor Mobility* (New York: Social Sciences Research Council, 1954), pp. 154–87. It should also be noted that if employees quit a job without another job or leave an employer involuntarily, the wage they obtain on their next job is often lower than the previous one. See, for example, T. G. Gutteridge, "Labor Market Adaptations of Displaced Technical Professionals," *Industrial and Labor Relations Review* 31 (1978), pp. 460–73.

opportunity. Not all employees are concerned enough about pay to act this way,[40] but organizations must be aware that paying low wages will quite possibly result in higher voluntary turnover.[41]

Benefits and turnover

In general, one might suspect that the impact of benefits on voluntary turnover is less than the impact of pay levels because benefits are often less visible and make up less of total compensation than direct pay. There is, however, an important exception to this expectation, namely pensions. Specifically, when the employee's pension is *nonvested*, the employee loses the accrued value of the benefits if s/he leaves the organization before retirement (see Chapter 16). Thus, one would expect a reduced likelihood of voluntary turnover. Studies on employee mobility tend to support this expectation.[42] However, there is little evidence indicating that nonvested pensions serve to reduce turnover in comparison to vested ones.

Satisfaction

In Chapter 7, a model was developed suggesting that satisfaction depended on an evaluation contrasting what one actually experiences at work with one's values or standards of what should be experienced. Thus, in the case of pay satisfaction, the simple model predicts that employees compare their pay with what they believe their pay should be. This representation, however, is an oversimplification because employees may make such judgments about each pay component.[43] For example, in evaluating one's experience against one's standards, an employee may find the pay level satisfying but benefits dissatisfying.[44]

---

[40] While there is little question about the relationship between pay level and voluntary turnover, its strength has been extensively debated by those who study labor markets. See H. S. Parnes, "Labor Force Participation and Labor Mobility," in *A Review of Industrial Relations Research* vol. 1, ed. G. G. Somers (Madison, Wis.: Industrial Relations Research Association, 1970), pp. 1–78.

[41] For a study offering support of this conclusion, see O. S. Mitchell, "Fringe Benefits and the Cost of Changing Jobs," *Industrial and Labor Relations Review* 37 (1983), pp. 70–78.

[42] See ibid; O. S. Mitchell, "Fringe Benefits and Labor Mobility," *Journal of Human Resources* 17 (1982), pp. 286–98; B. R. Schiller and R. D. Weiss, "The Impact of Private Pensions on Firm Attachment," *Review of Economics and Statistics* 61 (1979), pp. 369–80.

[43] H. G. Heneman III and D. P. Schwab, "Work and Rewards Theory," in *ASPA Handbook*, eds. Yoder and Heneman (Washington, D.C.: Bureau of National Affairs, 1979), pp. 1–22.

[44] Even this perspective may be too simple. A recent study found the structure of satisfaction with pay varied by the type of pay system under which employees worked. See V. Scarpello, V. Huber, and R. J. Vandenberg, "Compensation Satisfaction: Its Measurement and Dimensionality," *Journal of Applied Psychology* 73 (1988), pp. 163–71.

Some of the major pay issues as they apply to employee satisfaction are discussed below.

Pay level

Both the model and intuition would predict that the higher the amount of pay an employee receives, the greater the satisfaction. Indeed, this relationship has been observed across a wide variety of employees ranging from blue-collar employees to managers.[45] However, the relationship is not too strong. One reason for the modest relationship is evidence that the way the organization administers its pay level influences pay satisfaction. In particular, employees bring a variety of factors to bear when deciding what their pay should be.[46] For example, such factors as one's performance level and job responsibilities, what others receive, and changes in the cost of living can all be viewed by employees as appropriate standards for deciding the pay they should receive.

Since there appear to be substantial differences between employees in how important they consider these criteria,[47] persons earning identical amounts could experience very different levels of satisfaction. One employee earning $28,000 annually, for example, may be dissatisfied because s/he evaluates that amount against a previous, higher-paid job. Another employee earning the same amount may be quite satisfied because s/he evaluates the salary relative to others doing the same type of work.

Pay system

The type of pay system may influence employees' pay satisfaction because employees often have standards regarding the appropriate pay-

---

[45] For a review see H. G. Heneman III, "Pay Satisfaction," in *Research in Personnel and Human Resources Management*, vol. 3, eds. K. Rowland and J. Ferris (Greenwich, Conn.: JAI Press), 1985. For an investigation of U. S. and Canadian managers that found a positive relationship between pay level and satisfaction, see L. D. Dyer and R. Theriault, "The Determinants of Pay Satisfaction," *Journal of Applied Psychology* 61 (1976), pp. 596–604. For an investigation on blue-collar employees that obtained a similar relationship, see D. P. Schwab and M. J. Wallace, Jr., "Correlates of Employee Satisfaction with Pay," *Industrial Relations* 13 (1974), pp. 78–89.

[46] L. D. Dyer, D. P. Schwab, and R. D. Theriault, "Managerial Perceptions Regarding Salary Increase Criteria," *Personnel Psychology* 29 (1976), pp. 233–42; H. G. Heneman III, D. P. Schwab, J. T. Standal, and R. B. Peterson, "Pay Comparisons: Dimensionality and Predictability," *Academy of Management Proceedings* 38 (1978), pp. 211–15; F. S. Hills, "The Relevant Other in Pay Comparisons," *Industrial Relations* 19 (1980), pp. 345–51; R. W. Scholl, E. A. Cooper and J. F. McKenna, "Referent Selection in Determining Equity Perceptions: Differential Effects on Behavioral and Attitudinal Outcomes," *Personnel Psychology* 40 (1987), pp. 113–24.

[47] See, especially, Heneman et al., "Pay Comparisons," and Hills, "Relevant Others."

ment system. If employees believe that their pay should be based on length of service, a system that rewards more senior employees with greater pay will, other things being equal, be satisfying. Alternatively, some form of merit or incentive system may be most satisfying if employees believe that they should be paid based on their performance.

Several investigations have been conducted examining the basis on which managers believe they should be paid.[48] These suggest that managers believe performance (implying some sort of merit or incentive system) should be more important than seniority. Studies of blue-collar employees, alternatively, show that they are sometimes less satisfied working under incentive systems than when paid on a job-based or seniority system.[49]

An interesting possibility arises from all of this, namely, that the pay system may have a different impact on employee motivation (and hence performance) than it has on satisfaction. In particular, the evidence reviewed earlier suggested that pay incentives typically have a positive impact on employee performance. At the same time, however, such systems may have a negative impact on employee satisfaction with pay. An investigation of blue-collar assemblers and manufacturing employees that found this to be true is described in Illustration 15–2. Consequently, the organization must be very careful in its choice of a pay system to consider all the potential impacts such a decision has on employee behaviors and attitudes.

Benefits

As is pointed out in Chapter 16, benefits now account for a large percentage of total compensation. As a consequence, one might expect that benefits would influence employee satisfaction in a fashion similar to pay level. One recent investigation using a national sample of heads of households studied whether having or not having each of 12 specific

---

[48] Dyer et al., "Managerial Perceptions"; and E. E. Lawler III, "Manager's Attitudes Toward How Their Pay Is and Should Be Determined," *Journal of Applied Psychology* 50 (1966), pp. 273–79.

[49] Schwab and Wallace, "Correlates of Satisfaction." The organization may be able to influence the factors employees use in evaluating the adequacy of their pay levels to some extent. Specifically, one study found that employees were more likely to view performance as a legitimate basis for pay when their organizations rewarded performance through merit pay increases (L. A. Krefting, "Differences in Orientations toward Pay Increases," *Industrial Relations* 19 (1980), pp. 81–87). The differences among employees may thus be partially due to organizational practices, since managers more often than blue-collar employees are subject to merit systems.

ILLUSTRATION 15–2

Pay Systems, Motivation, and Satisfaction

An incentive pay system should enhance motivation to perform (relative to hourly based systems) by strengthening instrumentality perceptions linking performance and pay. That is, employees on incentive systems should believe a closer connection exists between their performance and the pay they receive than employees paid by the hours they work. At the same time, however, it has been stated that at least some employees may find incentive systems to be less satisfying.

These possibilities were investigated at a large consumer-goods organization located in the Midwest. Interestingly, the firm used three systems of pay for its nearly 3,000 production employees. Those personally responsible for output (such as assemblers of small parts) were paid individual incentives. Group incentives were used for employees who were collectively responsible for some product. Finally, hourly pay was provided for employees (such as maintenance employees) not directly responsible for any product.

The company conducted an attitude survey on a sample of these employees. Among the questions asked were items about motivation to be a high performer as defined in the expectancy model. In addition, employees completed both the Minnesota Satisfaction Questionnaire (MSQ) and the Job Descriptive Index (JDI), questionnaires described in Chapter 6.

The groups studied and the questions asked thus allowed a comparison of the motivation and satisfaction implications of the three pay systems: (1) individual incentive, (2) group incentive, and (3) hourly pay. The major results are shown in the accompanying figure.

Average Motivation and Satisfaction within Each Pay System

| | Pay System | | |
	Individual Incentive	Group Incentive	Hourly Pay
Attitude			
Motivation			
Instrumentality-link between pay and performance	4.46	3.95	2.03
Satisfaction with pay			
MSQ	7.20	6.21	8.69
JDI	4.10	3.89	6.44

Note, first, that instrumentality perceptions linking pay and performance were highest in the individual incentive group, next highest in the group incentive, and lowest among hourly paid employees. All three groups were significantly different from each other.

A very different picture emerges, however, when one looks at satisfaction employees expressed about their pay. Here, using either the MSQ or JDI (and controlling for differences in pay level), hourly paid were significantly

ILLUSTRATION 15–2 (*concluded*)

more satisfied than either incentive groups. Group incentive employees were least satisfied (significantly less than the individual incentive group on the MSQ).

It is important to keep in mind that these results were obtained in a single organization. The findings might not generalize to other organizations (using different types of incentive systems) or to different kinds of employees. Nevertheless, the results offer compelling evidence that pay policies having a desirable impact on one personnel outcome may have undesirable effects on some other outcome.

Such a possibility means that managers must be careful to evaluate their policies and practices against all employee outcomes of concern. In the present instance, for example, the firm was experiencing a very high level of voluntary employee turnover. Perhaps the motivational advantages of the incentive system were more than offset by the disadvantage of employee dissatisfaction and possible resulting turnover.

Source: From D. P. Schwab, "Conflicting Impacts of Pay on Employee Motivation and Satisfaction," *Personnel Journal* 53 (1974), pp. 196–200. Adapted with permission *Personnel Journal,* copyright March 1974.

benefits influenced satisfaction.[50] Six of the benefits had a significant effect on satisfaction even after the effect of pay level was taken into account. The more important the benefit in explaining satisfaction, the more costly the benefit to employers.

DEVELOPING AND ADMINISTRATING PAY SYSTEMS

The discussion to this point has shown how various pay components can be expected to have an impact on each of a number of human resource outcomes. There is, as indicated, much support for each linkage discussed. However, compensation managers must think beyond these simple relationships when developing or changing pay systems for a group of employees or for the entire organization. Attention needs be given to issues that transcend specific pay systems or relationships between pay systems and specific employee behaviors.

Strategic and Cultural Perspectives

Recent research and thinking on compensation has attempted to link pay systems to broader organizational objectives and values. While still

---

[50] C. J. Berger, "The Effects of Fringe Benefits on Satisfaction." Paper presented at the National Academy Meetings, Dallas, August 1983. For another study with similar findings, see G. F. Dreher, "Predicting the Salary Satisfaction of Exempt Employees," *Personnel Psychology* 34 (1981), pp. 579–89.

new, and thus admittedly speculative, these perspectives offer promise of value in designing and modifying pay systems to meet the objectives of the organization.

A perspective that has received substantial attention seeks to examine how the overall strategic objectives of the business might appropriately shape pay systems, especially for managers.[51] One approach differentiates organizational strategy into two categories: defender and prospector.[52] Defender strategy is appropriate when a firm is concerned with maintaining an already developed market share. In such firms emphasis is placed on efficient production through close management control. Compensation systems consistent with this strategy include frequent measurement of employees using quantitative measures of performance.[53] Among production employees gain-sharing plans might well be considered.

Prospector firms are more concerned with developing new markets. Strategic emphasis in such firms focuses on innovatively developing new products. Compensation systems in prospector firms should be designed to foster innovation among both managers and production employees.[54] More qualitatively oriented merit systems for managers might better fit organizations with prospector strategies. Pay-for-knowledge systems among production employees might also be appropriate in such firms.

Compensation systems have also recently been studied in terms of organizational culture. Organizational cultures are often related to, but are not necessarily identical with, business strategy. Culture represents the values shared by members of the organization.[55]

A recent study found that business firms could be differentiated based on their culture, and that these differences were related to the type of pay systems used.[56] One type of culture was characterized by long-term relationships between employee and organization; internal promotions were the norm. Pay systems in such organizations tended to emphasize interdependence, subjective performance assessment, and rewards for longevity with the firm.

---

[51] See, for example, S. J. Carroll, "Business Strategies and Compensation Systems," eds. D. B. Balkin and L. R. Gomez-Mejia, *New Perspectives on Compensation* (Englewood Cliffs, N.J.: Prentice-Hall, 1987), pp. 343–55; E. M. Hufnagel, "Developing Strategic Compensation Plans," *Human Resource Management* 26 (1987), pp. 93–108.

[52] P. E. Miles and C. C. Snow, *Organizational Strategy, Structure and Process* (New York: McGraw-Hill, 1978).

[53] Carroll, "Business Strategies and Compensation Systems."

[54] Ibid.

[55] See, for example, H. M. Trice and H. M. Beyer, "Studying Organizational Cultures through Rites and Ceremonials," *Academy of Management Review* 9 (1984), p. 654.

[56] J. L. Kerr and J. W. Slocum, Jr., "Linking Reward Systems and Organizational Cultures," *Academy of Management Executive* (1987), pp. 99–108.

A second cultural type identified in this study focused more on quantitative aspects of performance. There was less emphasis on long-term employee relationships with the organization and more hiring from the external market as opposed to internal promotion. Again, these cultural differences were reflected in the pay systems employed. To a greater degree, pay systems reflected an emphasis on performance objectively measured. Pay systems were more contractual, less based on loyalty between employees and employer.

Implications for Pay Systems

While there are clear similarities between the strategic and cultural approaches to understanding pay systems, differences are also apparent. At this point it is too early to suggest which perspective will ultimately prove more useful. Both, however, can help managers think about pay objectives and their implications for the design of pay systems. Often different pay practices can be implemented that are of about equal apparent cost but have different effects on personnel outcomes. For example, consider two alternative ways of paying jobs—I through IV, as shown in Figure 15–4. Assuming equal numbers of employees on each job, methods A and B result in the same total wage cost to management.

FIGURE 15–4
Two Hypothetical Pay Structures

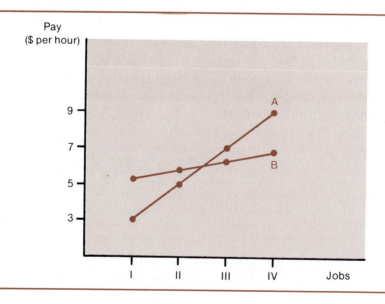

However, the expected behavioral consequences vary. Since pay structure A differentiates between the pay levels of the jobs to a greater degree than B, it probably provides greater motivation for employees to seek promotion and thus a long-term future with the organization. Structure A is consistent with the first organizational culture described.

As another example, consider two ways of moving persons through a pay range on some job. In one, promotion to the midpoint of the range depends on passing a probationary review and then is based solely on seniority. Only after reaching the midpoint can employees receive raises based on a merit review. In the other system, all salary increases depend on a merit review. Again there need be no difference in the direct cost to the organization. Nevertheless, the former encourages acceptable performance and provides security and an adequate income for acceptable performers. The latter encourages high performance. However, if only the best performers receive merit increases, the latter system may also encourage turnover among acceptable (although not high-performing) employees.

Any structure or system may be best in certain situations. The challenge for management is to decide on the objectives desired, the culture to be fostered, and then plan accordingly. Does the organization want to pay to ease recruiting difficulties and, if so, for what jobs? Does it want to encourage only the best performers, or are average performers also valued? Does management seek to motivate employees for promotions, or are there limited promotional opportunities available? Decisions of this sort will likely benefit by attending to the strategic objectives of the overall business.

SUMMARY

Pay potentially influences all of the major P/HR outcomes considered in this book. Compensation managers use a variety of individual pay procedures to influence these outcomes in ways favorable to the organization. Some, such as seniority-based conventional systems, encourage retention; others, such as individual incentive systems, are aimed primarily at enhancing motivation to perform.

Research clearly shows that these alternative pay systems do influence employees, often as the behavioral models discussed in this book predict. But the evidence also demonstrates that pay systems often fail to work as expected, or have consequences that were unintended and unexpected. For the compensation manager, this suggests the importance of establishing objectives for pay system implementation or change, making sure that all employee outcomes are considered, not just ones of immediate concern. Once the system is established with policies and practices, close monitoring is necessary to see that the objectives are achieved in an acceptable fashion.

DISCUSSION QUESTIONS

1. What are the unique problems encountered in the administration and control of merit pay plans, and how can they be dealt with?

2. Why may highly paid employees be dissatisfied with their pay?

3. Why do incentive pay systems sometimes fail to motivate high performance?

4. What pay components are most important for influencing attendance and length of service? Why?

5. Compare and contrast the major types of individual pay systems in objectives, procedures, and advantages and disadvantages.

6. How does an organization go about developing an incentive pay system? How is this different from a cost-savings plan?

16

Benefits

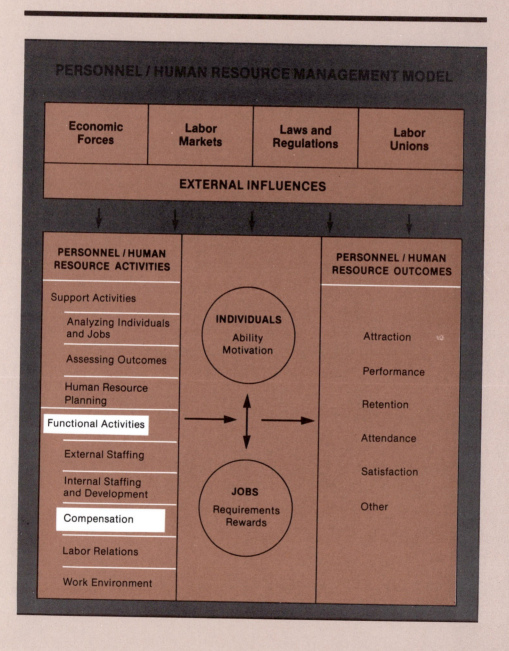

PERSONNEL / HUMAN RESOURCE MANAGEMENT MODEL

Economic Forces	Labor Markets	Laws and Regulations	Labor Unions

EXTERNAL INFLUENCES

PERSONNEL / HUMAN RESOURCE ACTIVITIES

Support Activities

Analyzing Individuals and Jobs

Assessing Outcomes

Human Resource Planning

Functional Activities

External Staffing

Internal Staffing and Development

Compensation

Labor Relations

Work Environment

INDIVIDUALS
Ability
Motivation

JOBS
Requirements
Rewards

PERSONNEL / HUMAN RESOURCE OUTCOMES

Attraction

Performance

Retention

Attendance

Satisfaction

Other

After reading this chapter, you should be able to speak to the questions posed in each of the following personnel/human resource incidents:

1. Jean Deutschmeister is the general manager of Holroyd Molded Plastics (HMP), a medium-sized plastics manufacturer. The main plant is located in a large urban area. While the area is heavily unionized, the company has remained nonunion even though it employs many production employees.

She has recently acquired data that shows the HMP has experienced a sharp increase in the cost of compensation benefits. Twenty years ago when the firm started, the average employee earned about $6,000 and the average cost of benefits was about $1,000 per employee. Since then, direct pay has increased two and a half times to an average of $15,000, and benefit costs have increased four times to $4,200 per employee. To what extent should these figures be of concern to her? What might explain the increase? Do you see any possible benefits occurring as a result of these increases?

2. The union that represents the office employees in Teachers Independent Retirement Equitable Development Society, the insurance company for which you work, is negotiating for a dental insurance plan. It has indicated some willingness to trade direct pay roughly comparable in cost to the cost of insurance for the first year. The company labor negotiator, Andy Burgee, has come to you, as benefits manager, with the union proposal. He is inclined to go along with the union but is interested in your reactions. What kind of issues would be appropriate to consider in a decision of this sort?

3. John Wyemaster is responsible for all personnel/human resource activities in Regal Industrial Press, a medium-sized printing company. Recently, RIP was acquired by Reflection Press, a large media conglomerate that coincidentally had its own printing operations. The new owners have decided to merge the two printing companies. Many of RIP's employees are senior to the employees of Reflection Press's printing companies, but will be laid off as a result of the merger. What would be an appropriate severance benefit for him to propose to management? What legal issues, if any, are involved in the takeover and consolidation?

The previous two chapters dealt with the administration of direct cash payments made to jobs and individuals. This chapter extends the discussion to employee benefits. Benefits are the provision of indirect compensation to the employee in forms such as health and life insurance, pension plans, pay for time not worked (such as holidays, vacations, and breaks), and family and social welfare benefits and services.

The bases for providing benefits do not conform to the distinction between jobs and individuals used to discuss direct compensation. Some benefits depend on organizational membership (e.g., holidays, health insurance). All employees in an organization typically have the same number of holidays and similar health insurance protection regardless of job assignment, seniority, or pay level. Other benefits, such as the number of days of vacation, usually depend on how long an employee has been with the organization. The size of pensions and the value of life insurance, along with a number of other benefits, depend on the employee's salary, which depends on both job and personal characteristics.

Benefits are a significant portion of total labor costs. As such, employers are concerned with the basis for incurring a benefit cost. Benefit costs might roughly be separated into two categories: person-tied and wage-tied. Person-tied benefit costs are incurred when additional employees are added. For example, health insurance premiums are dependent on the number of covered employees on the payroll at the beginning of the premium period. On the other hand, wage-tied costs increase as pay increases. Holiday and vacation pay are examples since the pay for time not worked is compensated at the employees' current pay rate.

Before 1930, employee benefits were no more than 3 percent of total compensation. Beginning in the 1930s and 1940s, however, benefits have been provided on a much larger scale. Figure 16–1 shows U.S. Chamber of Commerce estimates of benefits as a percent of direct pay over past years. This survey estimates the average hourly cost of benefits at $4.96 and the yearly cost at $10,283. Average cost as a percent of payroll in 1986 was 39.6 percent.[1]

Several implications can be drawn from an examination of Figure 16–1. First, benefits have expanded rapidly in nearly every category. The next section will briefly explore reasons for this growth. Second, a substantial number of different types of benefits is provided by employers. Consequently, the second major section of this chapter will describe major types of compensation benefits. Included is a discussion of public regulation applicable to the various benefit types. Third, the variety, expense, and rapid growth of benefits require that management very

---

[1] *Employee Benefits 1986* (Washington, D.C.: U.S. Chamber of Commerce, 1987), p. 5.

FIGURE 16–1

Employee Benefits, 1929 to 1986 as a Percent of Direct Compensation

Type of Payment	1929	1955	1965	1975	1986
			(Percent of Wages and Salaries)		
1. Legally required	0.8%	3.3%	5.3%	8.4%	11.1%
Old-Age, Survivors, Disability, and Health Insurance (FICA taxes)	0	1.4	2.3	4.6	5.9
Unemployment Compensation	0	0.7	1.0	0.8	1.2
Workers' compensation	0.6	0.5	0.7	1.0	1.0
Government employees retirement	0.2	0.5	1.0	1.7	2.8
Other	0	0.2	0.3	0.3	0.2
2. Agreed-upon	0.4	3.6	4.6	7.4	9.7
Pensions	0.2	2.2	2.3	3.6	2.8
Insurance	0.1	1.1	2.0	3.4	5.6
Other	0.1	0.3	0.3	0.4	1.3
3. Rest periods	1.0	3.0	3.1	3.7	3.3
4. Time not worked	0.7	5.9	7.3	9.4	10.2
Vacations	0.3	3.0	3.8	4.8	5.2
Holidays	0.3	2.0	2.5	3.2	3.1
Sick leave	0.1	0.8	0.8	1.2	1.4
Other	0	0.1	0.2	0.2	0.5
5. Bonuses, profit-sharing, etc.	0.1	1.2	1.2	1.1	1.2
Total benefit payments	3.0%	17.0%	21.5%	30.0%	35.5%
			(Billion Dollars)		
Wages and salaries	$50.4	$210.4	$358.4	$806.6	$2,089.0
Total benefit payments	$ 1.5	$ 36.0	$ 77.0	$240.0	$ 741.6

Source: *Employee Benefits 1987* (Washington, D.C.: U.S. Chamber of Commerce, 1987), p. 27.

carefully administer policies in this area. The final section deals with this important topic.

THE DEVELOPMENT OF COMPENSATION BENEFITS

Given the substantial growth in benefits documented in Figure 16–1, it should come as no surprise that all parties to the employment process (employees, organizations, unions, and the public through regulation) have contributed to the expansion. At the outset, however, it should be recognized that economic factors have influenced the thinking of all participants. The economic changes that occurred during the depression of the 1930s were particularly important. Before that time, providing for one's economic security was assumed to be an individual responsibility.

This view was challenged and modified by the events of the 1930s. As unemployment soared beyond 25 percent of the labor force, it became obvious that economic well-being was often determined by events over which employees had little control. Economic conditions were very influential in shaping the thinking of all people concerned with employment. In addition, however, each party has special self-interests served by increases in compensation benefits.

Employee Attitudes about Benefits

From the employees' perspective, increased benefits typically do not come without a corresponding cost. Specifically, employees can assume some trade-off between benefits and direct compensation. Increases in the former may be achieved at the expense of increases in the latter.

Despite this trade-off, most employees prefer receiving certain types of benefits rather than direct pay. There are several good economic reasons for choosing some increased benefits at the expense of direct pay. Health and life insurance can generally be purchased by the employer at group rates, which are typically lower than those the employee would have to pay. However, there is some evidence that employees significantly undervalue the magnitude of employer payments for their benefits or their market value. Benefits that require employee contribution, however, are more highly valued by employees.[2] This is important for employers to recognize when deciding the degree of participation employees should have in the construction and operation of benefit plans.

Progressive federal and state income tax rates also affect preferences. With progressive rates, income taxes accelerate faster than the rate of increased earnings. Any procedure that permits an equivalent increase in pay to be taxed at a lower rate or not taxed at all would be highly desirable from the employees' point of view. Most benefits either are not taxed (such as health insurance) or taxes are deferred to a time when the individual's marginal rate is likely to be lower (such as pensions).

Tax laws are very complex and are revised frequently. The taxable status of many benefits is constantly under review by tax authorities. P/HR departments that attempt to reduce employee taxes through the design of benefit programs must keep abreast of any such tax changes.[3]

---

[2] M. Wilson, G. B. Northcraft, and M. A. Neale, "The Perceived Value of Fringe Benefits," *Personnel Psychology* 38 (1985), 309–20.

[3] *Compensation and Benefits Review,* a quarterly journal published by the American Management Association, frequently reviews tax changes and court decisions applicable to employee benefits.

Employer Attitudes about Benefits

To some extent, employers' willingness to provide benefits has paralleled employee preferences for them. Employers also desire to reduce employees' income tax burden so that increases in compensation will have positive effects. It is often assumed that policies that conform to employee desires will enhance P/HR outcomes, especially length of service and satisfaction.[4] When unemployment rates are low an attractive benefits package may be helpful in attracting a work force.

Research on the effect of benefit types and levels on employer performance is just beginning and some results will be noted in this chapter. On a general level, recent evidence finds that pension plans offered by employers are not related to a relative reduction in pay, nor are they associated with either reduced profitability or increased productivity.[5]

Union Perspectives on Benefits

Unions also have reinforced employees' desires for benefits. Following an appeals court decision in 1948 affirming that benefits were a form of wages, and thus a mandatory bargaining issue, unions pushed hard for indirect benefits. Often these demands explicitly recognized a trade-off of direct pay increases for greater indirect benefits.

In part, union pressure for increased benefits was motivated by inter-union competition. Intense rivalry between unions during the 1940s encouraged attempts to win more attractive benefit packages for their members. Benefits may have exceeded their straight monetary value for unions (and their predominantly blue-collar membership), because benefits were rewards traditionally associated with white-collar and managerial employees. The effect of unionization on benefit levels relative to nonunion employees will be explored in Chapter 17.

Government Encouragement of Benefit Growth

The United States has historically lagged behind European nations in protecting citizens from uncertainties that interfere with income security, such as illness, accidents, unemployment, and retirement. Beginning in the 1930s, several laws and regulations were passed that require

---

[4] As noted in Chapter 15, benefits do appear to have a substantial impact on employee satisfaction.

[5] S. G. Allen and R. L. Clark, "Pensions and Firm Performance," in *Human Resources and the Performance of the Firm*, eds. M. M. Kleiner, R. N. Block, M. Roomkin, and S. W. Salsburg (Madison, Wis.: Industrial Relations Research Association, 1987), pp. 195–242.

employers to provide certain mandatory benefits to protect employees against major types of employment insecurity. These include mandatory pensions, survivors' benefits, health benefits, and income security for the unemployed as a part of the Social Security Act of 1935 (as amended); and insurance protection to cover costs of work-related accidents and illnesses covered in state workers' compensation laws (to be discussed in Chapter 20). The general rationale underlying these requirements is that society has an obligation to provide basic protections to the nation's work force.

In addition to these mandatory benefits, legislation is aimed at regulating certain types of benefits and their administration. These include private pension plan regulations, health care continuation, taxability and tax deductibility, and prohibitions against age and sex discrimination. Interestingly, wage controls imposed during World War II stimulated the growth of benefits. Designed to hold down inflation by limiting direct pay increases, the controls encouraged increased indirect benefits because the last were not covered by the controls.

It is impossible to state just which of the above factors has been most responsible for the relative increase in benefits. By and large, employees, employers, unions, and the government have reinforced each other. However, laws and regulations that mandate certain benefits and regulate voluntary benefits, together with unintended effects on benefits resulting from other laws, have probably been the most significant causes of their growth.

TYPES OF MAJOR BENEFITS

Organizations provide an amazing range of benefits. Benefits are available to employees while on the job (e.g., coffee breaks and washup time) and off the job (e.g., tuition reimbursements and vacation payments). In addition, many benefits are provided to employees' families or survivors in the event of death. The discussion below focuses on major benefits to which organizations contribute a substantial amount of resources or on newly developing benefits that are increasingly important to employees.

Payments for Time Not Worked

Historically, organizations paid employees only for the time that they actually spent on the job. Over the years, however, payment for a certain amount of time away from work has become common. The two major types of paid days off are (1) vacations and (2) specific days, such as holidays and days to perform civic or personal activities. The two types differ in eligibility. Amount of vacation time usually depends on length of service and possibly salary or job level. Paid holidays, however, are usually available to all employees on an equal basis.

Vacations

Vacation length generally depends on employee length of service with the organization. In medium and large firms, employees with 15 years of service average 18.5 days of paid vacation each year; those with 10 years of service average about 16 days.[6] Until 1980, vacation periods were increasing, and years of service necessary to be eligible were decreasing.[7] However, this trend has halted.[8]

Holidays

The number of holidays granted by employers has also stabilized recently, with the modal number being 10.[9] Where employees must work on holidays, premium pay (time and half or greater) is usually earned and/or another day is granted in lieu of the holiday. Specific holidays paid by nearly all employers are Christmas, New Year's, Thanksgiving, Independence Day, Labor Day, and Memorial Day.

Other paid days off

Most organizations also provide paid days off for jury duty and reserve military assignments. Some employers continue pay during military leave and/or supplement military or jury pay to bring pay levels up to employees' regular rates. Most employers provide paid funeral leave with three days being the modal benefit. Only about 25 percent of employees are currently entitled to paid personal leave.[10] About 70 percent provide paid sick leave. There is a wide range of practices for granting sick leave, with some employers providing it on a case-by-case basis and others allowing employees a certain number of days per year that are accruable, in some cases, if unused. The modal number of days

---

[6] U.S. Department of Labor, Bureau of Labor Statistics, *Employee Benefits in Medium and Large Firms, 1986* (Washington, D.C.: U.S. Department of Labor, 1987), p. 7.

[7] M. Meyer, "Profile of Employee Benefits: 1981 Edition," *The Conference Board*, Report No. 813, 1981, p. 50.

[8] *Employee Benefits in Medium and Large Firms*, p. 3.

[9] Ibid., p. 8.

[10] Ibid., pp. 10–11.

of sick leave to which employees are entitled each year in organizations where employers who grant them is about ten.[11] Other paid time off occurs at work and takes the form of breaks, washup time, and the like.

Insurance Benefits

Employers provide or subsidize a variety of insurance vehicles for employees. These include health insurance, life insurance, disability insurance, and other employment related plans. By law, however, employers may not offer group insurance plans for automobiles, dwellings, and the like as nontaxable benefits.

Health insurance

With the substantial recent expansion in medical costs, health insurance protection is an attractive (but expensive) benefit. Nearly three fourths of employees in the private sector are covered by health insurance plans.[12] About 80 percent of public employees are also covered.

Two types of health insurance plans are typical; often employers offer both. The base plan usually provides for specific medical services with maximum benefits for each type of service. Major medical plans provide coverage for a broad range of health-related services up to some maximum, such as $250,000. The last plans usually also have some standard deductible amount ($50 to $500) that must be paid by the employee.

Where federally certified health maintenance organizations (HMOs) are available, employers with over 25 employees who offer health insurance must provide this as an option. Employers are not required to make larger payments to HMOs than they would to their regular insurance carrier, however.

Since a large majority of households in the United States is covered by employer provided health care, breaks or changes in employment or marital status could leave individuals uncovered by insurance and unable to purchase replacements at the attractive group rates offered to employers. The Consolidated Omnibus Budget Reconciliation Act of 1985 (COBRA) requires that employers allow laid-off employees to purchase insurance through the group for up to 18 months, and up to 36 months for divorced or surviving spouses, or spouses of employees who are eligible for medicare coverage.

Most employers enable retired employees to continue to participate

---

[11] Ibid., p. 16.
[12] *Daily Labor Report*, September 11, 1981, p. 1.

FIGURE 16-2

Coverage of Selected Types of Medical Care: Percent of Full-Time Participants in Health Care Benefit Plans, Medium and Large Firms, 1984–86

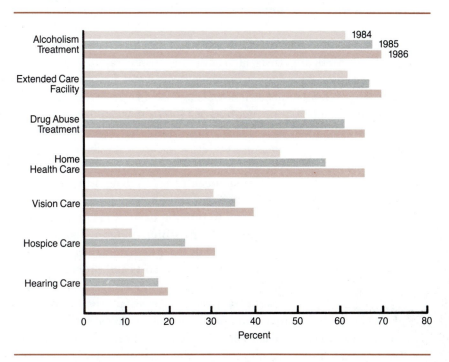

Source: U. S. Department of Labor, Bureau of Labor Statistics, *Employee Benefits in Medium and Large Firms, 1986 (Washington, D.C.: U.S. Government Printing Office) p. 30.*

in the plan while coordinating benefits with medicare. Presently employed individuals who are old enough to qualify for medicare may not be dropped from the plan, and must be allowed to use their employer-paid insurance as the primary payer in the event of a claim.

There are variations in what is covered by employers under their health insurance plans. Generally hospitalization and surgical coverage are provided. Increasingly, alcoholism treatment, extended care, drug abuse treatment, home health care, vision care, hearing care, and hospice care are being added. Some plans also cover mental health care.[13] Figure 16–2 illustrates the recent growth in the availability of different types of coverage.

When health insurance was first introduced as a benefit, employees

---

[13] *Employee Benefits in Medium and Large Firms,* pp. 27–33.

often paid a portion of the insurance premiums (contributory plans). Many were replaced with noncontributory plans (the employer paying the entire premium) until the early 1980s. The trend now appears to be a shift toward contributory plans to hold down insurance premium costs for employers.[14]

The average cost per employee of health benefits in 1987 was $1,985.[15] With the costs of health care rising rapidly, employers are increasing the amount that employees must pay before insurance takes over the payment of major medical expenses. In 1986, over 35 percent of plan participants had deductibles of $150 or more annually as compared to less than 8 percent in 1979, while those with $50 or less deductible coverage declined from just under 30 percent to about 12 percent.[16] Additionally, increasing numbers of plans are requiring second opinions for elective surgery, offering incentives for diagnostic testing before rather than after hospitalization and the like.[17]

A variety of vehicles is used to provide or fund health care coverage. The most ubiquitous are the Blue Cross/Blue Shield Associations. These contract with doctors and hospitals to provide services. Participants know that they will receive care at agreed costs and providers know that they will be paid. Private insurance companies also provide group coverage. Normally, a schedule of payments is established and employee claims up to the approved amount for various medical treatments will be paid. These insurers usually handle the claims process as well as paying the benefits, reducing the load on the employer. HMOs are prepaid plans in which a monthly membership (or premium) entitles the covered member to health care provided by a group health practice or individual affiliated physicians and hospitals. Preferred provider organizations (PPOs) are health care providers that have contracted with employers to provide health care at discount rates. Higher volume associated with the discount is beneficial to the provider. Employees who choose not to use the PPO are usually required to pay the difference in costs, if any. Finally, employers may self-insure, especially if they are very large. This usually reduces costs, but increases claims work and potentially creates conflicts between employees who have problems with their providers and the organization that is providing payment. Some self-insuring com-

---

[14] Ibid., p. 28.

[15] *Employee Relations Weekly*, March 14, 1988, p. 507.

[16] *Employee Benefits in Medium and Large Firms*, p. 28.

[17] R. W. Frumkin, "Health Insurance Trends in Cost Control and Coverage," *Monthly Labor Review* 109 (September 1986), pp. 3–8.

panies carry stop-loss insurance that covers claims over a certain amount for a given employee (e.g., $25,000 in a year).[18]

Dental insurance

Dental insurance was added rapidly to employee health protection plans in the 1970s and early 1980s. However, in the last five years, coverage has topped out at about 75 percent of employees in large and medium-sized firms. Unlike many health care plans, the employee must make payments before the insurance comes into force. Further, there are likely to be lifetime limits on elective procedures such as orthodontics, and extra employee payments for first-class repairs such as gold crowns.[19]

Sickness and disability insurance

Workers' compensation provides payments for permanent or temporary work-related disabilities, usually up to about two thirds of an individual's earnings with a legislated maximum in each state. Social security also provides payments to covered individuals in the event of permanent nonwork-related disabilities. These payments are not subject to federal income tax until a certain limit is reached.

Employers also typically provide income maintenance protection for all employees with 10 or more years of service in the event an accident or illness prevents them from working.[20] Generally, employers pay for coverage that provides payments up to 26 weeks at 60 percent of base pay. In addition, long-term income maintenance plans are provided for the majority of managerial and office employees. These plans are designed to provide a reduced form of income for employees unable to return to work permanently. The payments are generally coordinated with workers' compensation and/or social security so that the employee receives no more than about 75 percent of the amount that would have been earned through employment if not disabled.[21]

---

[18] For more details see R. M. McCaffery, *Employee Benefit Programs: A Total Compensation Perspective* (Boston, Mass.: PWS-Kent, 1988), pp. 69–78; and B. T. Beam, Jr., and J. J. McFadden, *Employee Benefits*, 2d ed. (Homewood, Ill.: Richard D. Irwin, 1988), pp. 144–60 and pp. 237–50.

[19] *Employee Benefits in Medium and Large Firms*, pp. 28–30.

[20] Ibid., pp. 12–14.

[21] McCaffery, *Employee Benefit Programs*, pp. 87–91.

Life insurance

Life insurance, providing benefits to employees' survivors in the event of death before retirement, is now broadly applicable to both private and public employees. The size of benefits usually depends on the employees' direct pay, typically one or two times an employee's yearly salary.[22] In addition, many organizations provide employees with the opportunity to continue life insurance protection after retirement.[23]

Under recent tax law changes, the premium cost of employer-paid life insurance that exceeds $50,000 annually is a taxable benefit. This would result in a tax liability for any employee on a "two-times earnings" plan who made over $25,000 annually.

As employees age, costs of a given amount of term life insurance increase. The Age Discrimination in Employment Act (ADEA) allows employers to reduce life insurance coverage after age 65 at either 8 percent per year or through a one-time 35 percent reduction.[24] Further, many states require, and most group life insurance plans allow, employees to convert their group plan to an individual policy when they terminate or retire.[25]

Retirement Benefits

Providing income for years in retirement is becoming more and more important with the gradual extension of life expectancy. Pensions provide income after retirement and until death based on the employee's years of work and direct pay. Most employees participate in a pension program mandated by the Social Security Act of 1935. Many are also covered by nonmandatory private plans. In addition, most employers offer some form of health insurance to retirees.

Mandatory pensions

The pension benefits of social security are financed by equal employer and employee contributions based on the level of compensation earned by the employee. From the passage of the act until 1949, the maximum yearly contribution by either employer or employee was $30. Since then, however, social security taxes have increased substantially, necessitated by the expansion in the number of people eligible to receive benefits

---

[22] *Employee Benefits in Medium and Large Firms,* p. 32–33.
[23] Ibid.
[24] McCaffery, *Employee Benefit Programs,* p. 97.
[25] Ibid., p. 98.

(many of whom have not contributed to the program) and in the benefit levels.

The Social Security Financing Act of 1977 and subsequent amendments in 1983 increased taxes substantially to keep the system solvent. In 1988 employees paid 7.51 percent up to an increase of $45,000 for a maximum tax of $3,379.50. The base earnings level increases each year using the formula shown in Chapter 3. The tax rate increases to 7.65 percent in 1990. The employee tax is matched by an equal employer contribution.

The act currently provides full retirement benefits when a covered employee reaches age 65 (reduced benefits are available if one retires at age 62). The 1983 amendments increase the minimum age at which one can receive full benefits to 67 in the year 2027. The amount of benefits depends on past work experience and earnings. Social security provides other benefits in addition to pensions, including health services for people older than 65 (medicare), survivor benefits to families with children under age 18, and benefits for employees who are totally disabled before age 65.

Private pension plans

The income provided by social security is often insufficient to provide the standard of living most employees have become accustomed to while working. As an illustration, employees under age 31 earning more than $40,000 per year can expect to receive about $850 per month, in today's dollars, if they retire at age 65.[26] The 1983 amendments reduced benefits somewhat, and further reductions may occur in the future.[27]

Many organizations provide benefits in addition to those mandated by social security. About 90 percent of employees in medium and large firms are covered by pension plans.[28] For office personnel, benefits almost always depend on length of service and salary level. This is also typical of nonoffice employee plans, but a substantial minority of the latter base benefits exclusively on length of service.[29]

Although private pensions are very attractive benefits, the income they provide generally falls short of preretirement earning levels. As Figure 16–3 shows, less than one third of employees who are covered by

---

[26] R. L. Rose, "Retirement Planning Should Begin with Early Look at Social Security," *The Wall Street Journal*, April 5, 1985, p. 31.

[27] R. J. Myers, "The Effects of the 1983 Social Security Amendments," in *The Handbook of Employee Benefits: Design, Funding and Administration*, ed. J. S. Rosenbloom (Homewood, Ill.: Dow Jones-Irwin, 1984) pp. 1063–74.

[28] *Employee Benefits in Medium and Large Firms*, p. 2.

[29] M. Meyer, Profile of Employee Benefits," p. 28.

FIGURE 16–3

Monthly Benefits under Private Defined Benefit Pension Plans: Distribution of Participants Assuming Earnings of $30,000 in the Final Year of Work, Medium and Large Firms, 1986

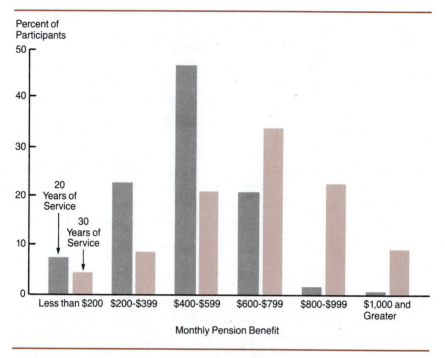

Source: U. S. Department of Labor, Bureau of Labor Statistics, *Employee Benefits in Medium and Large Firms, 1986* (Washington, D.C.: U.S. Government Printing Office), p. 56.

defined benefit pension plans and who retire with 30 years of service receive as much as $800 monthly from their plans.

Inflation rates in the 1970s and early 1980s have also taken a heavy toll on the value of private pension benefits. Unlike social security, most private pension plans are not indexed to the cost of living, although about 40 percent of employers increased benefits during 1981–1985.[30]

Regulation of Private Pensions

Unfortunately, employees participating in private pension plans have not always been assured of obtaining benefits at retirement. In some

---

[30] *Employee Benefits in Medium and Large Firms*, p. 57.

cases, benefits were lost if the employee left the organization before retirement. In others, the plan went out of existence before the employee received benefits. These and other difficulties led to the passage of the Employee Retirement Income Security Act (ERISA) in 1974, the Retirement Equity Act of 1984, and the Consolidated Omnibus Budget Reconciliation Act (COBRA) clauses that amend it.[31] ERISA was designed to regulate the administration of the roughly 400,000 private-sector pension plans in the United States. ERISA does not require employers to provide private benefits to employees. If, however, the employer chooses to have a private pension plan, it must conform to ERISA requirements, which fall into five major categories.[32]

Eligibility to participate.   Before ERISA, pension plans varied regarding when an employee was eligible to participate in the program. As amended, the law requires that all employee earnings from age 21 be factored into the benefits equation. Service from age 18 must be considered toward vesting. Only 1,000 hours of work are required during the year so that many part-time employees, who were often not covered before, are eligible to participate.

Vesting and portability.   ERISA requires that pension plans eventually lead to full vesting (that is, providing full benefits even if employment is terminated before retirement). There are two alternatives an employer can choose. One provides 100 percent vesting when each employee achieves five years of service with the employer. Another provides 20 percent vesting at three years increased by 20 percent per year until the employee is fully vested at seven years.

Portability refers to the employee's right to transfer accumulated pension funds from one employer or to an individual retirement account (IRA) with job changes. ERISA permits tax-free transfers in these situations.

Funding.   ERISA requires that pension plans be funded yearly, based on an actuarial projection of future benefits required. Where existing plans do not conform to ERISA's funding requirements, they must be brought up to standard in no more than 40 years from the passage of the act.

Fiduciary responsibility.   ERISA also increases the legal obligations of those responsible for administering the pension funds. Administrators are required to manage the funds solely for the welfare of the benefici-

---

[31] G. Rueben, "Developments in Industrial Relations," *Monthly Labor Review* 106, no. 8 (1983), p. 47.

[32] A more detailed description of ERISA is provided by D. L. Salisbury, "Regulatory Environment of Employee Benefit Plans," in *The Handbook of Employee Benefits: Design, Funding and Administration* ed. J. S. Rosenbloom (Homewood, Ill.: Dow Jones-Irwin, 1988), pp. 32–44.

aries. Investments are expected to be diversified to reduce risks of loss. To encourage conformance, the law makes pension administrators personally responsible for failure to meet regulations in this area.

Termination of pension plans. To prevent losses through terminations of pension plans, the Pension Benefit Guarantee Corporation (PBGC) was established. It receives a yearly premium for each covered employee to form a reserve fund. The fund is to be used to protect the pensions of employees who are in organizations that fail to provide the intended benefits. The act was amended in 1980 to include multiemployer plans.[33] Such plans currently cover about 9 million employees and are expected to cover more than 16 million by the year 2000.[34] The PBGC is potentially vulnerable to major losses given the intended termination of LTV Steel's plans in connection with its bankruptcy.[35] These plans are severely underfunded.

Types of Plans

The passage of ERISA and favorable tax treatment for salary reduction plans have spawned a large variety of retirement funding options. The primary categories include *defined benefit, defined contribution,* and *salary reduction plans.*

Defined benefit plans. A defined benefit plan establishes a particular pension payment for retirees, usually based on length of service and salary level at retirement. For example, an employee may receive a benefit of $25 per month for each year of service; or an employee may receive 1.5 percent of the average of his or her last five year's salary times number of years of service.

Defined benefit plans require that the employer set aside an amount each year that will cover the future service costs of the pension plan. Among other things that have to be considered are the rate at which employees are becoming vested in the plan, the rate of turnover of employees (especially given their ages), the likely life expectancies of future retirees, the levels of returns on the pension plan's investments, and other variables.

About 75 percent of surveyed firms have defined benefit plans. Most plans base benefit levels on terminal earnings. The modal formula provides about 1.5 to 1.75 percent of an employee's terminal pay times the number of years of service.[36] This would mean that an employee who

---

[33] *Daily Labor Report,* September 29, 1980, p. 1.

[34] U.S. Department of Labor, *Office of Information News,* October 15, 1980, p. 1.

[35] *Employee Relations Weekly,* September 28, 1987, p. 1195.

[36] *Employee Benefits in Medium and Large Firms,* pp. 59–64.

retired at a salary of $30,000 with 30 years of service would receive about $14,580 per year. Under current tax law, the maximum benefit that can be paid from a qualified defined benefit plan is $90,000 (indexed to inflation).[37]

Defined contribution plans.   A large and increasing number of firms provide defined contribution pension plans. Under these plans, the employer makes a contribution toward each employee's retirement under an established formula. For example, an employer might contribute 5 percent of an employee's straight-time income each year; or an employer might allocate 5 percent of its aftertax profits to be divided among employees in proportion to their salaries as a percent of total base pay.

Defined contribution plans reduce the risks employers encounter during cyclical economic changes since they do not have to fund to meet a prescribed benefit level. On the other hand, if the investment vehicles in which the plan's funds are invested do particularly well, the employee benefits since, unlike the defined benefit plan, the employer cannot recoup funds from an "overfunded" plan. There is, by definition, no overfunding or underfunding in a defined contributions plan. Under current tax law, the maximum contribution that an employer can make to a qualified plan is 25 percent of an employee's pay or $30,000 per year, whichever is less.

Employees with greater education and tenure are more likely to be covered by pension plans, while higher income employees are more likely to have a defined contribution plan. Defined benefit plans are more likely among larger and less profitable firms, and those that are unionized.[38]

Salary reduction plans.   During the 1980s a variety of salary reduction plans was encouraged under tax law reforms. Some of these were restricted following the 1986 Tax Reform Act, but most are still available at reduced levels. The most widely used have been so-called [Section] 401(k) plans. Under 401(k), employees are allowed to reduce their taxable income by up to $7,000 annually. Employers often add inducements for lower-paid employees to participate since the reductions of highly compensated employees cannot be subtracted from income unless certain nondiscrimination tests are met.[39] Individual retirement accounts

---

[37] For details on the effects of the 1986 Tax Reform Act on retirement programs and other compensation, see J. H. Schechter, "The Tax Reform Act of 1986: Its Impact on Compensation and Benefits," *Compensation and Benefits Review* 19 (1987), pp. 11–32; for information on new funding requirements for defined benefit plans, see A Task Force of Consultants, "The Omnibus Budget Reconciliation Act of 1987: What it Means to Pensions and Employee Benefits, *Compensation and Benefits Review* 20 (1988), pp. 14–32.

[38] R. A. Luzadis, "Defined Benefit, Defined Contribution, or No Pension?" *Proceedings of the Industrial Relations Research Association* 39 (1986), pp. 222–25.

[39] Schechter, "The Tax Reform Act of 1986."

(IRAs) are substantially limited by the latest reforms. Employees who are not covered by employer contributions equal to $2,000 annually may fund an IRA with an amount that, when combined with employer contributions, equals $2,000 for couples with incomes under $40,000 annually.

Pensions and employee knowledge

Employees can easily look at the front of their paychecks each pay period and see their level of direct pay. But where an employee is covered by a defined benefit plan, all that is known is the formula that will apply to future benefits—perhaps 30 years from now. Thus, little is known about the cost or ultimate value. Evidence suggests that a great deal of misinformation exists among employees about their pension plans. Generally, unionized employees, higher-income workers, better educated employees, and more senior employees are more accurately informed about their future benefits.[40] Employers may not receive the incentive value from their pension structure that they desire if employees do not know or understand the trade-offs between early and normal retirement, the levels of benefits they will receive, or the effective level of their compensation if they continue to work after they become entitled to pension benefits.

Early retirement

The proportion of the labor force that continues employment past age 65 has dropped steadily since 1950 from about 50 percent to less than 16 percent in 1986. Among men between 55 and 59, the participation rate has fallen to 79 percent. Early retirees are more likely to be in ill health, and to be earning less than their counterparts in similar jobs or at similar age levels.[41] Employers have increasingly offered early retirement during the 1980s as they attempted to downsize their work forces. Whether this trend continues into the 1990s is presently unknown, but the decreasing number of new entrants into the labor force will probably mean a reduction in early retirement options. Illustration 16–1 shows the results of an AT&T study of its early retirees and their characteristics.

---

[40] O. S. Mitchell, "Worker Knowledge of Pension Provisions," *Journal of Labor Economics* 6 (1988), 21–37.

[41] *Older Americans in the Workforce: Challenges and Solutions* (Washington, D.C.: Bureau of National Affairs, 1987), pp. 59–78.

ILLUSTRATION 16–1

AT&T Study Shows Early Retirees Share a Range of Character Traits

Who jumps at early-retirement incentive programs? What distinguishes them from managers who remain? These questions are growing pertinent as more companies, looking to cut their work forces, resort to financial sweeteners to induce workers to quit ahead of schedule.

More money, of course, is one answer; early retirees are usually better equipped financially to leave a sure income, and the incentive bonus removes any doubt. But in a recent study, industrial psychologists at American Telephone & Telegraph Co. found managers who accepted early retirement viewed life and work quite differently than those who stayed.

Although some of what the researchers found was obvious . . . [t]hey were, for instance, less religious, more involved in leisure activities, less proud of their work and, generally, disenchanted with their bosses and the company . . . [N]o meaningful difference in overall job performance existed between those who stayed and those who retired early.

"You lose a lot of good performers and you lose a lot of lousy performers," Ann Howard [a former AT&T psychologist who headed the research] says. But in terms of their attitude, she adds, "You're better off in the sense that you've lost the ones who don't feel as good about the company."

. . . The early retirees were . . . more likely to have given up on further promotions, rating higher on a scale researchers call realism of expectations. "I don't think I have a bad attitude," said one manager, but "it's just that reality set in. I had to turn down better jobs because I didn't want to move, so I have faced up to the reality that I am where I'll be for the rest of my life."

Source: Abridged from Larry Reibstein, "AT&T Study Shows Early Retirees Share a Range of Character Traits," *The Wall Street Journal*, September 4, 1987, p. 13.

Income Maintenance

A large number of employees change organizations each year. These changes are often accompanied by a short stretch of unemployment. Many other employees, especially in construction and cyclical manufacturing industries, are laid off temporarily now and again (see Chapter 12). Several programs have been developed to provide income during such periods, since either form of joblessness can create severe economic hardships.

Mandatory maintenance benefits

Besides making pensions mandatory, the Social Security Act of 1935 also established unemployment compensation through state-administered systems that provide benefits to employees who become unemployed. These benefits are aimed at providing income while the individual searches for a new job. Presently, an insured job seeker recovers about one half of preunemployment income through direct payments and reduced taxes.

Each state has its own specific regulations. Generally speaking, however, eligibility to receive unemployment compensation benefits requires that an employee worked for a covered employer (most are) for a sufficient time to qualify for benefits, had lost a job through no personal fault, be seeking a job, and be willing to accept a suitable (similar to previous) job. About half of the unemployed satisfy these requirements.[42]

Recently, there has been a lot of controversy regarding the effect of unemployment compensation on the job-search behavior of the unemployed. The available evidence suggests that increases in benefits tend to modestly increase the time unemployed between jobs.[43] It is not known to what extent this increase is due to (1) reduced search activity on the part of the job seeker, or (2) the possibility that the benefits allow job seekers to hold out for better jobs. Unfortunately, the administration of benefits is not particularly accurate, with one study reporting about 26 percent of payments incorrectly calculated with overpayments far outnumbering underpayments. Most of the overpayments appear to be related to claimants falsely stating that they had been looking for jobs.[44]

Unemployment benefits are financed by a tax on employers. Presently, the federal tax is 0.8 percent on the first $7,000 of employee earnings. However, states can increase the base, and increase or reduce the tax (to a minimum of 0.8 percent) depending on their experiences with unemployment claims in the state and from the specific employer. Thus there may be a wide range of rates and bases between states and within states across employers. Benefit levels are determined by the states as well. Thus an unemployed worker might collect substantially different sums in different states. Given that the tax is based on experience with the claims levied against employers, organizations are encouraged to stabilize employment to reduce their unemployment compensation taxes.

---

[42] G. F. Fields, "Direct Labor Market Effects of Unemployment Insurance," *Industrial Relations* 16 (1977), pp. 1–14.

[43] Reviews of research on the effects of unemployment can be found in Fields, "Labor Market Effects," and F. Welch, "What Have We Learned from Empirical Studies of Unemployment Insurance?" *Industrial and Labor Relations Review* 30 (1977), pp. 451–61.

[44] J. L. Kingston, P. L. Burgess, and R. D. St. Louis, "Unemployment Insurance Overpayments: Evidence and Implications," *Industrial and Labor Relations Review* 39 (1986), pp. 323–36.

Voluntary income maintenance benefits

Besides the protection provided by unemployment compensation, some organizations have attempted to provide additional income security for employees through private plans. Fairly common are organizations that provide termination or severance pay for laid-off employees (see Chapter 12). These benefits are granted most frequently for involuntary terminations due to either performance or economic conditions. The median cost of recent severance payments is about $2,500.[45] A few organizations guarantee employees' employment or pay for some future period up to a year. Figure 16–4 displays a sample of current reasons for granting severance benefits.

In the manufacturing sector, some firms provide supplementary unemployment benefits (SUB) to employees who are laid off.[46] The United Auto Workers first negotiated such a plan with Ford Motor Company in 1955. Eligibility is tied to eligibility for unemployment compensation, and benefits are based on seniority and reduced by other income received while unemployed. Senior employees can obtain 95 percent of their take-home pay from a combination of unemployment compensation and SUB.

Private maintenance plans are highly significant to employees who receive them. Nevertheless, income security beyond unemployment compensation is atypical. Organizations have been very reluctant to provide such plans because the costs depend largely on economic factors that are difficult to anticipate.

Employee Welfare Programs

A variety of employee welfare programs has been developed over the past two decades. The primary types include Employee Assistance Programs (EAPs), wellness programs, child care, and (the newest) elder care.

Employee assistance programs

EAPs vary substantially in the problems with which they deal. At their most basic, they focus on alcohol and drug abuse problems that directly influence on-the-job behavior. Some employers make them

---

[45] "Severance Benefits and Outplacement Services," *Personnel Policies Forum*, no. 143 (December 1986), p. 9.

[46] A. Freedman, *Security Bargains Reconsidered: SUB, Severance Pay, Guaranteed Work.* (New York: The Conference Board, 1978), no. 736.

FIGURE 16–4

Circumstances and Eligibility for Severance Benefits

| | Percent of Companies | | | | | |
| | | By industry | | | By Size | |
(Number of Companies)	All Cos.	Mfg.	Nonmfg.	Nonbus.	Lg.	Sm.
	(112)	(62)	(29)	(21)	(54)	(58)
Circumstances in which severance benefits are provided:						
Discharge or permanent layoff for economic reasons	93%	94%	90%	95%	91%	95%
Discharge for poor job performance	33	39	31	19	26	40
Discharge for disability	12	16	—	14	11	12
Voluntary resignation	8	6	7	14	7	9
Retirement with pension	7	8	—	14	6	7
Retirement without pension	6	10	—	5	6	7
Elimination of position	5	2	10	10	4	7
Discharge for misconduct	5	6	7	—	6	5
Other	8	8	10	5	7	9
Severance plan covers:*						
All employees	58	42	72	86	61	55
Some employees	41	58	28	10	39	43
No response	1	—	—	5	—	2
Minimum service required for severance pay eligibility:*						
None	39	44	34	33	43	36
One year	28	27	14	48	26	29
Six months	15	11	31	5	22	9
Three months	9	11	—	14	6	12
Other	9	6	21	—	4	14

* Percentages may not add to 100 due to rounding.
Note: Percentages are based on companies that have a formal severance pay plan.

Source: "Severance Benefits and Outplacement Services," *Personnel Policies Forum,* no. 143 (December 1986), p. 4.

available as a safe haven for employees to seek help before performance problems overwhelm them and lead to their discharges. Other programs encourage employees to use the resource for anything that is troubling them—off or on the job. If the organization does not have available the resource to deal with the problem, it will be provided or the employee will be referred to an appropriate source.

EAPs have grown rapidly recently, but they are not without problems. At this point there is no certification or credentialing for EAP personnel or counselors, and malpractice is a potential problem. Employees have occasionally suspected that their problems would be revealed to their supervisors, but this suspicion has declined recently and unions have become more positive about EAPs. Problems may also exist where EAPs refer an employee for treatment and his/her insurer does not agree that the condition exists. This may be particularly true when the employee is an HMO member.[47] Illustration 16–2 gives an idea of some of the services and processes of Control Data Corporation's program.

Wellness programs

Several organizations have installed programs to encourage healthy behavior. These include exercise and weight control programs, smoking cessation programs, and the like. Relatively few data are presently available regarding their effectiveness.[48] However, Control Data Corporation recently reported the results of a four-year study of 15,000 employees. Among other things found in the study was that health care costs were 11 percent higher for obese than thin employees; that employees who routinely used seatbelts averaged 54 percent fewer days in the hospital (regardless of the reason for hospitalization); that employees whose exercise was less than the equivalent of a half-mile walk per week had costs 114 percent higher than those with the equivalent of one and one-half miles; and that smokers of one or more packs of cigarettes a day had claims 118 percent higher than nonsmokers.[49]

Child care

As the labor force participation of women has increased substantially over the last 20 years, there has been a corresponding increase in the demand for day care for children. As of 1980, about one third of mothers with three year olds were in the labor force with this proportion increasing to 85 percent for mothers of five year olds. Children of working

---

[47] *Employee Assistance Programs: Benefits, Problems, and Prospects* (Washington, D.C.: Bureau of National Affairs, 1987).

[48] R. A. Wolfe, D. O. Ulrich, and D. F. Parker, "Employee Health Management Programs: Review, Critique, and Research Agenda, *Journal of Management* 13 (1987), 603–16.

[49] F. E. James, "Study Lays Groundwork for Tying Health Costs to Workers' Behavior," *The Wall Street Journal*, April 14, 1987, p. 35.

ILLUSTRATION 16–2

The 800-Number

Control Data Corporation, headquartered in Minneapolis, runs its own in-house EAP program and also markets the service to about 90 subscriber companies, ranging in size from 12 employees to 40,000. The total employee population served, including Control Data, is about 225,000.

David Robinson, director of Control Data's Employee Advisory Resource (or EAR R) describes the program as "low barrier access."The primary means of using the program is via the telephone. Robinson explained the advantages of the system:

- *Cost is low,* ranging from $12 to $20 per year per head.
- *The "window of vulnerability" is generally fairly small,* in that if the person calls when he or she is hurting the most, the biggest impact is made. The EAR R program maintains a staff of experts covering the gamut of problems, and the toll-free number is answered 24 hours a day, seven days a week.
- *The client doesn't have to look a counselor in the eye* or feel uncomfortable waiting in the waiting room. Robinson said an informal study at Control Data indicated fewer than 10 percent of employees wanted face-to-face contact immediately.

Robinson said the service consists of:

- *Basic assessment:* short-term counseling via the active listening model.
- *Basic referral:* referral to other treatment resources if needed. When people call in, he said, "they get a live counselor and they can talk as long as they want. Or they can request to be seen by one of our over 120 associates across the nation, either clinics or treatment centers we have agreements with, and they can get a free session there."

In addition, Robinson said, the program has a sophisticated nationwide referral resource database on line all the time. He said the database has more than 3,000 resources and is constantly being updated.

Robinson said that out of every 100 people who call, about 25 have work-related problems. The rest of the 75 are ranked in the following order: half-hour consultation with attorneys; financial counseling; drugs and alcohol; relationships; and mental health.

Robinson said close to 90 percent of calls are self-referred, because the program is promoted as being voluntary and totally confidential.

Source: *Employee Assistance Programs: Benefits, Problems, and Prospects* (Washington, D.C.: Bureau of National Affairs, 1987), pp. 19–20.

mothers are more likely to be enrolled in preschool programs, particularly among women with more education and higher incomes. Particularly difficult problems exist for parents of newborns since only about 40 percent of employers of working mothers provide any paid maternity leave.[50]

Relatively few employers provide child care benefits to employees.

---

[50] S. B. Kamerman, "Child-care Services: A National Picture," *Monthly Labor Review* 106 (December 1983), pp. 35–39.

Some questions exist about the benefit-cost ratio and many employers believe that a relatively small proportion of their work forces would make use of this benefit. Where it has been offered, it has usually been included within a cafeteria or flexible benefit plan (see below).[51] For those employers who do offer benefits, most provide subsidies rather than in-house care. Those who do offer on-site premises are more frequently in the health care industry or other situations hiring larger proportions of women employees.

To the extent that child care reduces turnover and attendant staffing costs, and curbs absenteeism that might result in either lower productivity or excess staffing, it can be a substantially cost-effective benefit to both the employee and the employer. A variety of implementation problems exist for in-house programs, however, including recruiting and establishing compensation programs for employed child care workers.[52]

Elder care

A handful of companies have begun to provide assistance to employees in caring for their elderly parents. Among the services include information regarding nursing homes and other medical and custodial care facilities, access to group insurance for extended care benefits, flexible spending accounts for dependent care, day-care centers for the elderly, and counseling services.[53]

The Travelers Companies surveyed employees who were over 30 in 1985 and found that about 20 percent of them provided care for an older person for an average of 10.2 hours per week (16.1 for women, 5.3 for men). About 40 percent had school-age children at home. They indicated that care giving for the elderly caused conflicts with their other responsibilities. Care giving responsibilities occurred primarily as the result of an illness of the older person and/or declining health. In many cases, the health situation of the person cared for was unlikely to improve since the average age of recipients was 77. Illustration 16–3 capsulizes some of the initiatives The Travelers took as a result of their survey.

BENEFITS ADMINISTRATION

The previous section discussed a wide variety of benefit programs offered to employees. Many of these are required by law, and others are

---

[51] *Employers and Child Care: Development of a New Employee Benefit* (Washington, D.C.: Bureau of National Affairs, 1984).

[52] For substantial details about implementing programs, see B. Adolf and K. Rose, *The Employer's Guide to Child Care* (New York: Praeger Publishers, 1985).

[53] *Elder Care—A Growing Concern* (Lincolnshire, Ill.: Hewitt Associates, 1987).

ILLUSTRATION 16–3

Elder Care Initiatives at The Travelers Companies

In June of 1985, the Travelers Insurance Companies surveyed a random sample of their home office employees age 30 and over . . . Survey results revealed that 28 percent of these employees were providing some type of elder care, with an average of 10 hours per week being spent on care giving. On average, elder care had been provided for five and one-half years. Combined with job and other family responsibilities, survey respondents indicated that providing care to an aging relative was stressful.

As a result, Travelers has introduced various programs aimed at helping employees who are care givers. Community agencies, home care services, and referral agencies took part in the annual *care giver fair*. In addition, Travelers' employee assistance program regularly conducts *educational workshops* on elder care, and runs a *noontime peer support group. Additional information* is available through articles in the company's newsletter, videos, and a library section for books on elder care. *Flexible hours* also are available to employees and can be changed daily or weekly with an employee's supervisor.

Source: *Elder Care—a Growing Concern* (Lincolnshire, Ill.: Hewitt Associates, 1987), pp. 6–7.

regulated if offered. Employees and their unions are very much concerned with, and often involved in, the benefits process. The variety of benefits offered, their cost, the number of interested groups, and regulation make the administration of benefits a source of considerable managerial effort.

Five administrative issues deserve special mention. The first involves the choice of objectives in establishing benefits and the evaluation procedures to be employed. The second involves the controlling of benefit costs. Third is the desirability of possibly providing benefit choices to employees. Fourth is the need to communicate benefit information to employees. Finally, managers must be concerned about tax law reforms.

Benefit Objectives and Evaluations

In establishing objectives, management may consider several factors.[54] Among these are matters of organizational values, such as an assessment of organizational responsibility for employee security. Somewhat more concrete (especially if assessed systematically through sur-

---

[54] The discussion of objectives is based on S. T. Pritchett, "Cost-Value Analysis of Employee Benefits: An MBO Approach," *Compensation Review* 7, no. 4 (1975), pp. 31–37.

FIGURE 16–5
Hypothetical Benefit Objectives

1. The organization will provide a package of benefits that, when integrated with compulsory social programs, will provide economic security at approximately 75 percent of a long-term employee's standard of living prior to any adversities. (Employees who want additional economic security should arrange additional insurance and investment plans on an individual basis.) Paid rest periods, leisure time, and other nonsecurity benefits will be maintained at a level competitive with similar employers in the geographical area.

2. With the joint objectives of recognizing differences among individuals and maintaining an administratively feasible program, economic security benefits will be tailored, where practical, to two classes of employees—employees without dependents and employees with dependents. Employee needs and wants related to the life cycle will be recognized in pension, survivor, and disability income plans.

3. In recognition of the tax advantage to employees, the entire cost of benefits consistent with the standards set in Objective 1, above, will be borne by the organization.

4. A triennial survey will be made of employee attitudes toward the benefits package. The results, from a random sample of employees, will be considered when changes are made in plan design.

5. Each employee will receive an annual statement itemizing the level of his/her benefits, the total of employer contributions to his/her benefits, and any changes since the previous year in benefit levels and costs.

6. Benefits negotiated for union employees will be simultaneously extended to non-represented employees.

7. Costs of benefits will be monitored annually in accordance with a cost-analysis system approved by the vice president of finance.

8. Surveys of employee attitudes, turnover rates, available current studies of benefit programs for other firms, and the recommendations of an objective consultant on employee benefits will be reviewed triennially to ascertain the need, if any, for changes in the objectives, design, and insurers or other outside administrators of the program.

Source: Reprinted, by permission of the publisher, from S. T. Pritchett "Cost-Value Analysis of Employee Benefits: An MBO Approach," *Compensation Review*, Fourth Quarter 1975. © 1975 by AMACOM, a division of American Management Associations, 31–37. All rights reserved.

veys) are employee preferences for benefits. P/HR outcomes such as attendance, length of service, and performance should be important considerations in the objective-setting process. Finally, when setting objectives, organizations have to consider their ability to pay for benefits. Figure 16–5 provides a hypothetical example of objectives that might emerge from a consideration of these factors.

Evaluation of existing or proposed benefits should be made against the same factors that led to the objectives in the first place. Costs of the benefits are one important component of the evaluation process. In addition, an assessment of the effects, or an estimate of the probable effects, of the benefits needs to be made.

As a somewhat oversimplified illustration of the process that might be employed, consider some issues in evaluating the desirability of a new benefit. Suppose the benefit has been proposed primarily as a way of attracting new employees into the organization. It would be appropriate first to determine if the organization really has a recruitment problem. If so, the probability of the benefit easing the problem needs to be estimated. A survey of practices in other organizations might be helpful in making this estimate.[55]

Even if it is decided that recruiting is a problem and that this benefit would help ameliorate the problem, its introduction is not necessarily warranted. At this point, the cost of the benefit should be considered against the cost and potential benefits of alternative P/HR activities that may attract employees. A change in recruiting practices, for example, might be a less expensive but equally effective way of accomplishing the same objective.

One thing that deserves special mention is the relative permanence of benefits. Once benefits are installed, organizations find it extremely difficult to eliminate them. Although adding a benefit may not improve P/HR outcomes, its removal may very well have detrimental effects. It is imperative, therefore, that the probable result of a new benefit be assessed before implementation.

Controlling Benefit Costs

Mention has already been made about the significance of costs when a new benefit is considered. Costs of existing benefits are also at issue. Indeed, one of top management's major concerns has been the cost of employee benefits, especially the cost of health care. In 1983, health care costs reached 10 percent of the gross national product. In 1986, employers contributed $100 billion to these costs through various health care plans, an increase of over 275 percent from just eight years earlier.[56]

Unfortunately for management, some of the increased costs associated with benefits are entirely out of administrative control, since the programs are mandatory, and the benefit levels are established by federal and state governments. Changes in social security taxes, for example, resulted in a 31 percent increase in employer contributions for highly paid employees between 1983 and 1986.

---

[55] M. J. Wallace, Jr., and C. H. Fay, *Compensation Theory and Practice*, 2d ed. (Boston: Kent, 1988), pp. 198–99.

[56] For an update on benefit costs, see "Benefits Shock," *U.S. News & World Report*, March 28, 1988, pp. 62–74.

Regulation of voluntary benefits also typically serves to raise costs. ERISA is a good illustration. Necessary changes in employee eligibility for pensions, as well as vesting and funding changes, are almost certain to increase pension costs to the employer.

Even some unregulated benefits have been thought to be outside the immediate cost control of management because the service is provided by other institutions. An especially significant example, health services, has already been noted. Organizations have aggressively sought in the past few years to reduce health care costs. Overall, the most frequently used cost containment procedures have been (1) preadmission hospital testing, (2) second opinions before surgery, (3) higher deductibles, (4) management financial reports, and (5) required audits for health care plans.[57]

Chrysler Corporation, which has a very comprehensive health care plan, has gone even further. By aggressively confronting hospitals and physicians in the Detroit area, Chrysler was able to cut 12 percent, or $58 million, from its health care costs in 1984.[58] Other large firms are engaging in the same type of activity.[59]

Cafeteria-Style Benefit Plans

Another popular approach to benefits administration is the cafeteria-style benefit plan. Such plans provide basic protection for employees and then allow employees some flexibility in augmenting basic benefits or choosing others. The basic general fixed and flexible benefits of the Educational Testing Service (ETS) plan is shown in Figure 16–6. Employees with less than 10 years service are given 3 percent of their salary, and those with 10 or more years service receive 6 percent to allocate to the flexible options.[60]

One major reason for the increased popularity of flexible benefit plans among organizations is their cost-cutting potential. Figure 16–7, which shows Xerox's reasons for starting a flexible benefits program, makes this clear. But there are other good reasons for the dramatic increase in such

[57] H. D. Spring, "Medical Benefit Plan Costs," *Personnel Administrator* 29, no. 12 (1984), pp. 64–72.

[58] "Chrysler Eyes Further Curbs in Employee Health Expenses," *Today's Summary and Analysis*, April 2, 1985, p. 2.

[59] See R. A. Formisano, "The Future of Employee Benefits," in *The Risk Management Revolution*, eds. D. R. Anderson and H. F. Kloman (Homewood, Ill.: Richard D. Irwin, 1987).

[60] "By Design," *Employee Benefit Plan Review* 38, no. 7 (1984), pp. 10, 20.

FIGURE 16–6

Fixed and Flexible Benefits at ETS

Fixed
    Health care coverage
    Life insurance
    Disability benefits
    Vacation pay
    Pension plan

Flexible
    Additional life insurance
    Optional health plan (higher deductibles)
    Health plan for dependents
    Dental care
    Additional vacation
    Dependent care
    Additional retirement benefits
    Cash

Source: "By Design," *Employee Benefit Plan Review* 38, no. 7 (1984), pp. 10, 20.

plans. (In 1980 there were just 8 such plans; there are now well over 150.)[61]

One important consideration is the legal liberalization and clarification of cafeteria-style plans in 1984. Before 1984, the Internal Revenue Service (IRS) ruled that if employees could choose between nontaxable benefits and cash, the entire package was taxable. Congress has now changed this ruling so that only the cash portion of the benefit package is taxed.[62] This clarification and liberalization should greatly stimulate the development of cafeteria-style plans.

Yet another underlying reason for flexible benefit programs results from changing demographics of the labor force (see Chapter 3) and changing lifestyles.[63] Employee needs differ far more now than when married males dominated the work force. A young married employee with small children might, for example, reasonably choose a package that emphasized direct pay and health insurance. An older, high-salary employee, alternatively, might choose a package that emphasized deferring benefits until after retirement.

Employers may, however, run the risk of encountering higher benefit costs when employees make their choices. It stands to reason that employees will choose those benefits they are most likely to use. For

---

[61] D. Gifford, "The Status of Flexible Compensation," *Personnel Administrator* 29, no. 4 (1984), pp. 19–26.

[62] "Flexible Benefits," *Employee Benefit Plan Review* 39, no. 7 (1985), pp. 8–13.

[63] Ibid. See also Formisano, "The Future of Employee Benefits."

FIGURE 16-7
Xerox Goals for Flexible Benefits

1. Reduce costs.
2. Protect employees against catastrophic health expenses, while recognizing that Xerox utilization was becoming excessive.
3. Modify health care behavior.
4. Succeed in bargaining.
5. Develop a fair and long-term benefits-cost solution.

Source: "Flexible Benefits," *Employee Benefit Plan Review* 39, no. 10 (1985), p. 13.

example, sick employees will opt for more health insurance; younger employees may trade some health care for increased vacations, requiring that more employees be hired. Insurance carriers will experience more claims and rates will increase.[64]

Communicating Employee Benefits

One advantage of a cafeteria-style benefit plan stems from the fact that it forces employees to think about their choices, and hence to learn about what benefits they actually have. It is ironic to note that benefits, despite their significance and cost, are often not very well understood by employees. Since benefits do not have the immediacy of the weekly or monthly paycheck, employees may be unaware of the types and specific levels of the benefits they are eligible to receive. Obviously, benefits cannot have positive impacts on P/HR outcomes unless employees are knowledgeable about them.

To overcome this lack of knowledge, organizations are appropriately expanding their efforts to communicate to employees about benefits. One survey found a large increase in the number of organizations with formal benefit communication programs.[65] Part of this increase is undoubtedly due to the employee-reporting requirements of ERISA,[66] but part reflects management's desire to have employees realize the scope of benefits provided.

Certain benefits, such as health and life insurance, are fairly easy to communicate. Both the employer contribution and the benefits to be received by the employee can be readily determined. Other benefits,

---

[64] R. Ostuw, "The Cost of Adverse Selection under Flexible Benefits Programs," *Compensation and Benefits Management* 3 (Winter 1987), pp. 53–55.

[65] "Informing Workers: More Firms Turn to Benefit-Communication Plans," *The Wall Street Journal*, April 18, 1979, p. 1.

[66] T. Martinez and R. V. Nally, "Communication and Disclosure of Employee Benefit Plans," in Rosenbloom, *Handbook of Employee Benefits*, pp. 926–946.

ILLUSTRATION 16–4

Employee Benefits Fair

Concerned about the lack of information employees had regarding their benefits, the personnel department of a small hospital in Coon Rapids, Minnesota, decided to hold a benefits fair. The department hoped that the carnival atmosphere of a fair would contribute some enthusiasm to a topic of something less than overwhelming interest to most employees.

The event, scheduled on payday (paychecks were passed out at the entrance to increase attendance), was held in a large room in the hospital. Booths were set up and run by representatives from the health insurer, savings plan, tax-sheltered annuity plan, and credit union. These representatives were available to answer employee questions about any of their benefits.

To add some levity to the occasion, carnival music, free snacks, helium balloons, and clowns were provided. One game booth was set up containing a dart board (with pictures of the administrative staff). Employees who hit a picture and correctly answered a benefits question got a prize. Administrators further showed their support by playing the clowns, filling balloons, and staffing the snack bar and game booth.

Was the fair a success? More than 64 percent of the employees attended. A follow-up questionnaire indicated that participants believed they learned quite a bit or more about their benefits (unfortunately, there is no way of knowing whether or not this is true).

Source: S. N. Gerberding, "Communicate Your Benefits Program through an Employee Fair," *Personnel Administrator* 28, no 5 (1983), pp. 51–53.

especially those that are deferred, are more difficult to communicate. Pensions, for example, usually depend partly on earnings just before retirement. Thus, it is impossible to specify the exact value until that time. The survey mentioned earlier found that many organizations are now providing individual counseling with employees to facilitate benefit understanding.[67] These sorts of communication efforts are generally the responsibility of P/HR specialists. Illustration 16–4 describes such an effort.

Tax Reform Considerations

The Tax Reform Act of 1986 substantially tightened the requirements for the qualification of employee benefit programs as taxable business expenses and nontaxable to employees. The law defines two classes of employees: highly compensated (HCE) and nonhighly compensated (NHCE). A highly compensated employee is anyone who (1) owns 5 or

---

[67] "Informing Workers."

more percent of the company; (2) earns more than $75,000; (3) earns more than $50,000 and is in the top 20 percent of pay; or (4) is an officer of the company and earns more than $45,000. To be qualified as a taxable business expense at least 50 percent of employees eligible for the benefit must not be HCEs, at least 90 percent of NHCEs must be allowed to participate, and if they participate they must receive at least 50 percent of the benefits.[68]

EQUAL EMPLOYMENT OPPORTUNITY

Benefits must be administered to conform to equal employment opportunity laws and regulations. Of special significance are sex discrimination provisions in Title VII of the Civil Rights Act and the Age Discrimination in Employment Act.

Sex Discrimination

Pregnancy discrimination

Title VII was initially silent on whether pregnancy should be considered as a disability analogous to other nonoccupational disabilities typically covered by employee health insurance plans.[69] In *Gilbert* v. *General Electric*, the Supreme Court ruled that pregnancy need not be included in plans covering other nonoccupational disabilities. To reverse this ruling, Congress passed the Pregnancy Discrimination Act (PDA) to amend Title VII in 1978. It requires that pregnancy and pregnancy-related disabilities be treated similarly to other disabilities.

In *Newport News Shipbuilding* v. *EEOC*, the Supreme Court extended the PDA to include spouses of employees. This shipbuilder had a comprehensive health plan for employees' families that did not cover pregnancy. The court ruled such a plan was discriminatory.[70]

PDA and *Newport News* have major impacts on major medical and hospitalization plans, temporary disability benefits, and sick leave plans. Employers who offer these benefits must include pregnancy as a covered condition. One study found that many smaller employers were still not in compliance with the PDA in 1981.[71]

---

[68] Beam and McFadden, *Employee Benefits*, pp. 73–74.

[69] J. P. Kohl and P. S. Greenlaw, "The Pregnancy Discrimination Act: Compliance Problems," *Compensation Review* 15, no. 6 (1983), pp. 65–71.

[70] Rueben, "Developments in Industrial Relations," p. 40.

[71] Ibid.

Employers in some states are required to provide an unpaid leave period for pregnant workers, as required by state laws. Those laws have been upheld by the Supreme Court in *California Federal Savings & Loan Association* v. *Guerra*.

Pension discrimination

Another important and difficult discrimination issue involving sex has to do with pensions. Since women live longer than men, on average, they need to receive retirement benefits longer. How is this added cost to be paid for? Historically, it has been done by having women contribute more than men toward their pension (unequal contributions) or by having women receive a lower monthly benefit (unequal benefits).

Such practices are now illegal. In *Los Angeles Department of Water and Power* v. *Manhart* the Supreme Court said unequal contributions were illegal under Title VII; and in *Arizona* v. *Norris* the Court concluded unequal benefits were illegal.[72] Changes in ERISA made during 1984 were designed to make it easier for women to become eligible for pensions.[73]

Age Discrimination

The Age Discrimination in Employment Act influences the way in which employee benefits are administered. First, employees must be allowed to continue participation in pension programs regardless of age. Second, employers must provide life insurance to employees over age 65 to 70 if they provide such insurance to younger employees, but they can reduce the benefit amount to reflect increased insurance costs. Third, employers must allow employees over age 65 to continue participation in health insurance programs rather than requiring them to use medicare.

SUMMARY

During the past 40 years, there has been phenomenal growth in the number and types of benefits offered to employees. Many factors have contributed to this growth, but perhaps most influential has been the change in attitudes resulting from the economic climate of the 1930s. This climate aided government, unions, employees, and even employers

---

[72] Ibid., p. 36.

[73] G. Rueben, "Developments in Industrial Relations," *Monthly Labor Review* 107, no. 10 (1984), p. 47.

to view economic security as an appropriate area of organizational responsibility.

Currently, the largest benefit expenditures are for holidays and vacations, pensions, and health insurance. In the case of health plans, organizations have taken strong steps recently to keep costs under control. Voluntary and mandatory benefits are now almost 40 percent of total compensation.

P/HR responsibilities for benefits are substantial. These involve day-to-day administration, as well as the evaluation of costs and returns of benefits and the communication of benefits to employees.

A significant factor to keep in mind regarding benefits is the continued growth expected for the foreseeable future. Increases in longevity, increases in the number of elderly, improvements in health care (with attendant cost implications), and preferences for and expectations of greater time away from work are but examples of the factors operating to continue the increase in benefits and their costs. P/HR management will be required to monitor the effect of these changes carefully to keep benefit costs within the organization's ability to pay.

DISCUSSION QUESTIONS

1. In what ways has government regulation stimulated the growth of benefits?
2. Why might employees be interested in increased benefits, even when it can mean less direct pay?
3. Why do organizations have relatively little control over the costs of some benefits?
4. Why would employers be interested in providing additional benefits?
5. What types of benefits have traditionally been administered to men and women unequally? Are such differences still permitted?
6. What factors might an organization consider when deciding whether to adopt a cafeteria-style benefit plan?

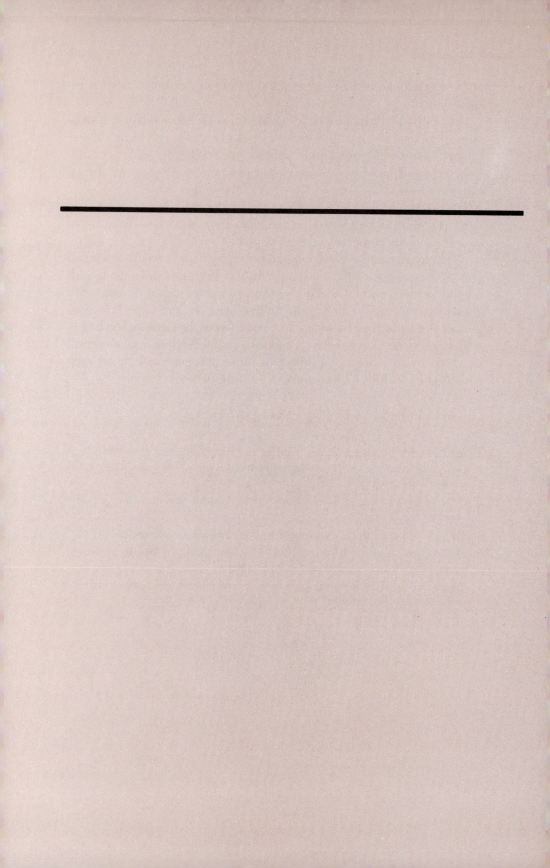

Case for Part Seven

CONSOLIDATED CHICKEN PRODUCTS

Introduction

Tom Pruitt had looked forward to his new job at Consolidated Chicken Products. When he took the job as personnel director three months ago, it had all seemed so perfect. He never dreamed that he would face a decision that might cost him his job.

History

Tom Pruitt earned his B.A. in psychology from the University of Wisconsin and M.B.A. from Penn State University. After his graduation he took a job with Kellogg's in central Michigan. It was an entry-level personnel position, but the job-rotation management training allowed him to get his feet wet in a number of different areas of personnel: selection, compensation, training, and Equal Employment Opportunity.

After having rotated through the one-and-a-half-year training program, Tom decided to settle into the compensation area. For the next couple of years he was involved in all aspects of compensation. He had performed a number of job evaluations, but been integrally involved in designing the benefit package for the production workers, and had gained valuable experience in designing executive compensation packages. It was this experience that landed him the job as personnel director at Consolidated Chicken Products (CCP).

CCP was a family-managed and -owned firm that produced chicken products. Fred Fordyce, Sr., was the principal owner and chief executive officer of the company. His oldest son, Fred, Jr., was the president of the company, while his daughter Lindsey and youngest son, Jeffrey, were in charge of the company newsletter and the processing plant respectively.

The company owned the farms on which the chickens were raised as well as the processing plant where they were slaughtered and packaged.

The company was started by Fred, Sr., over 15 years ago, but the company's rapid growth did not begin until five years ago. Sales last year had been just over $20 million, which was a 20 percent increase over the year before. In addition, they expected another 20 percent increase for 1985. Although the sales were increasing, the return on investment was not. This was due to the company's strategy of keeping the price competitive. They felt that as the market would continue to grow, they could increase their sales through their low price. This strategy had also kept the company from being very cash rich. Most of the profits were funneled back into the plant in the form of new technology.

Two factors explained the growth in CCP's sales. First, the country's newfound concern with health had increased the demand for chicken. Second, recent technological advances in the processing plant, combined with their utilization of low-priced labor, had enabled the company to maintain its low price strategy, which had paid off so far.

The work force was also growing, especially in the processing plant where there were now 120 employees. It was more the technological change, however, than the work force growth that necessitated bringing in a personnel director. The changing technology had also changed the content of some of the jobs, and the company felt that a compensation system needed to be developed. They were not interested in developing selection tests since most of the applicants were friends or relatives of the present employees. In addition, they saw little need for developing any selection systems since the labor market was very favorable from the company's standpoint. The unemployment level was about 10 percent.

The first month of work seemed very uneventful, as Tom was just learning to find his way around. It was not until the second month that he really began to get to work on the compensation system. As he studied the jobs, it appeared that they seemed to fall into three labor grades with about equal numbers of people in each grade. At the beginning of the third month, while in the process of performing the job evaluation, he discovered two very interesting issues. First, of the 100 production workers in the plant, 30 were female. All of the women were being paid about 60 percent as much as their male counterparts. For example, on one job, the man performing it was being paid $8.23 while the woman doing the exact same work was paid only $4.55. (See Table 1.)

The second issue dealt with the pay of the women in the office. When looking at the secretarial jobs (which were entirely staffed by women), the job evaluation showed the jobs to be worth 425 points. Although this was based on a separate job evaluation system that was only examining office jobs, under the plant system this point total would fall into the high range of plant labor grade 1. This labor grade had a pay range of $4.05 to

TABLE 1
Results of Job Evaluation for Plant Jobs

Labor Grade	Points	Pay Range	Average Men	Average Women
1	350–450	$4.05–7.50	$7.02	$4.05
2	450–550	$4.25–8.00	$7.57	$4.25
3	550–650	$4.55–8.75	$8.25	$4.50

TABLE 2
Results of Job Evaluation for Office Jobs

Labor Grade	Points	Pay Range	Average
1	300–400	$3.65–4.15	$3.75
2	400–500	$3.85–4.35	$4.15

$7.50 and yet the average pay for the secretaries was $4.15 with a high of $4.35. (See Table 2.)

He brought up the pay discrepancy between males and females to Fred, Sr. Fred seemed completely unconcerned. "Oh, don't you worry about that, Tom. Heck, we're paying them more than they could make anywhere else in this area. If you ask them, they'll tell you that they're satisfied with their wages." In a way, Tom knew that Fred, Sr., was right. The unemployment rate in the area for women was about 25 percent, and even those who were employed usually worked for minimum wage. With regard to the issue of the pay of the secretaries, Fred, Sr., said basically the same thing. He felt he was paying them more than a fair wage.

Tom was faced with a decision. It seemed that he had three options. First, he could let things go on like they were, and everyone would be happy but himself. Second, he could try to convince the company to change its practice, but he felt strongly that this would do no good. Finally, he could take the role of a whistle-blower by calling in the EEOC to investigate the situation.

Questions

1. Is there a reasonable basis for believing that the company is discriminating against women?

2. Is there reason to believe that women could file an equal pay lawsuit? How about a comparable worth lawsuit? What additional information would be useful?

3. What would be the consequences of each of Tom's options to all of the people involved (e.g., women, men in the plant, the company, his family)?

4. How has the company's strategy affected its human resource policies?

5. Should cultural norms affect compensation systems?

6. Should satisfaction with the pay be the only criterion for evaluating the compensation system? If no, what other variables should be considered?

PART EIGHT

Labor Relations

17

Labor Unions

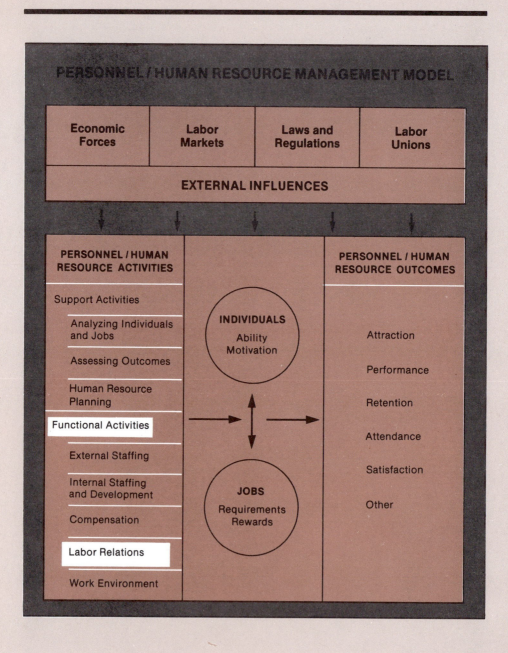

PERSONNEL / HUMAN RESOURCE MANAGEMENT MODEL

Economic Forces	Labor Markets	Laws and Regulations	Labor Unions

EXTERNAL INFLUENCES

PERSONNEL / HUMAN RESOURCE ACTIVITIES

Support Activities

Analyzing Individuals and Jobs

Assessing Outcomes

Human Resource Planning

Functional Activities

External Staffing

Internal Staffing and Development

Compensation

Labor Relations

Work Environment

INDIVIDUALS
Ability
Motivation

JOBS
Requirements
Rewards

PERSONNEL / HUMAN RESOURCE OUTCOMES

Attraction

Performance

Retention

Attendance

Satisfaction

Other

After reading this chapter you should be able to speak to the questions posed in each of the following personnel/human resource incidents:

1. The National Labor Relations Board has just notified your company that the United Steelworkers of America has filed a petition seeking to represent your company's production and maintenance employees at its Central City machinery fabrication plant. The company has never had any of its employees represented by a union and would like to preserve this situation. Casey Clausen, the plant manager at Central City, has proposed moving production to another plant and laying off some employees to counteract the union's organizing campaign. You have been asked to make a recommendation regarding this strategy. You are also asked to frame the outline of the employer campaign against union representation. What strategies and tactics could you use, and how effective do you think they would be? What conduct would be likely to lead to unfair labor practice charges?

2. In the same situation in incident 1 above, your company's board of directors has indicated a disbelief that its employees would want to organize and blames the petition on the work of outside union agitators. The company's president, Ford Holroyd, has been asked to prepare a short report and presentation for the board on the situation. You have been asked to develop background information for the presentation. What general information would give you a clue about where to look for specific company problems? What evidence would tell you that the push came from the outside, if it did? What situations would predict success or failure for the organizing campaign?

3. You are the president of Local 359 of the United Electrical Workers. You are presiding over your local's monthly meeting and have just turned to new business. One of the members, Neal Young, argues that the local should drop out of the national union. He sees affiliation as a big drain on the treasury, since half the $15 monthly dues goes to the national headquarters. He complains that the national never does anything for 359. Would you counter his arguments? If so, how?

This chapter covers the development, philosophy, and goals of the labor movement; the changing environment in which collective bargaining takes place; federal labor law and administration, the organizational structure of organized labor, the process by which employees become represented by labor unions, and the effects of labor unions. Organized labor is an important external influence in employment, influencing the decisions of both P/HR and line managers. Managers do not deal directly with employees on many issues where they are unionized. In nonunion situations, the practice of P/HR management is constrained primarily by laws and regulations and the current state of the labor market. In organizations with unions, a collective bargaining agreement spells out the rights and duties of both employers and employees.

Under U.S. labor laws, employers whose employees are represented by a union are required to negotiate on wages, hours, and terms and conditions of employment. Management cannot unilaterally alter any of these (even to the supposed benefit of the union member). Furthermore, the results of negotiations with the union tend to spill over to nonunion employees in the same and other organizations to reduce the desires of these employees to organize.

Unions also form a powerful political subgroup that lobbies legislative bodies for positions it has been unable to win at the bargaining table. An example of this was labor's successful push for occupational safety and health standards and enforcement (see Chapter 20 for details).

THE DEVELOPMENT OF LABOR UNIONS

Unions developed as a reaction to the use of management decision-making power in ways employees thought were excessive or illegitimate. This reaction has centered most often on basic economic issues. They also have been highly involved in establishing ownership rights in jobs by increasing job security and limiting the rights of employers to transfer, lay off, or dismiss their members. Unions frequently develop because employees are frustrated in achieving important goals on an individual basis, and unionizing is the only countervailing technique available to achieve these goals.

A set of persisting ideas underlies the philosophy, development, and goals of the American labor movement. These include obtaining a greater return for those who actually produce goods and services for society and a reduction in the inequality of the distribution of economic opportunities in society. The labor movement and its leaders have generally felt that unless democratic institutions like labor unions could have a voice in employment and public policy issues, education would be elitist and hence major portions of the nation's income would go to a relatively small proportion of the population.[1]

Historical Roots

In 1794, the first labor conflict in the United States involved a strike over a wage cut by the Philadelphia Cordwainers (shoemakers). Employers requested that the strike should be enjoined, arguing that collective pressure to restore wage cuts was an illegal conspiracy in restraint of trade. Under the existing common law, the court upheld the employers and involved employees were fined.

The *conspiracy doctrine* interpretation regarding union activities held until a Massachusetts court ruled in 1842 that unions were not illegal conspiracies *per se*, but that a union's conduct would establish its legality.[2] This decision was a limited victory for unions, however, since most of their activities were considered illegal under 19th-century interpretations.

Development of national organizations

Before the Civil War, a few small unions of skilled workers had been established. But, until the National Labor Union (NLU) was established in 1866, no organization had gathered them into a single labor organization. However, the NLU was not only concerned with employment issues, but also advocated social reforms such as women's suffrage and easy credit. Many members did not practice a trade but saw the union as a vehicle for social change. Its failure to maintain union member involvement helped lead to its demise in 1872.

The Knights of Labor, organized in Philadelphia in 1869, was the second labor organization of national scope. Workers were organized on a city-by-city basis, since the Knights' creed held that workers had common interests that overrode craft distinctions. The Knights differed from present unions by disavowing strikes as a bargaining tactic. Ironically, the organization achieved its greatest membership as the result of strikes against several railroads in 1882 and 1883. After their success, many new members joined in hopes that they would be able to wrest the same types of concessions from their employers that had been won from

---

[1] M. F. Neufeld, "The Persistence of Ideas in the American Labor Movement: The Heritage of the 1830s," *Industrial and Labor Relations Review* 36 (1982), pp. 207–20.

[2] For a discussion of the conspiracy doctrine, see J. S. Williams, ed., *Labor Relations and the Law*, 3d ed. (Boston: Little, Brown, 1965), pp. 18–23.

the rail carriers. The leadership, however, pursued long-run social goals rather than redressing day-to-day grievances.

The Knights of Labor declined rapidly after 1886. Differences in perspectives between the leadership, the rank and file, and an antagonistic press that sought to link the labor movement to anarchy and terrorism contributed to the decline.

The American Federation of Labor

As the Knights of Labor began its slide to obscurity, the American Federation of Labor (AFL) was born. It differed from its predecessors in several respects, but the most important lay in its pragmatic orientation toward relations between employees and employers. AFL affiliates enrolled only members of the craft they represented, and bargained for changes in wages, hours, and working conditions rather than developing broad social goals.

The success of AFL unions while others failed resulted from two tactics. First, they concentrated on job oriented issues. Second, they were *craft* (employees in a single occupation) rather than *industrial* (all employees in a given industry) unions. Attempts to establish enduring industrial unions failed consistently until the 1930s. Ideological positions of industrial union organizers were strongly resisted by public opinion; and low bargaining power due to the steady influx of immigrants who sought unskilled jobs contributed to their failure. The pragmatic orientation of the AFL founders is shown in the congressional testimony portrayed in Illustration 17–1.

The Congress of Industrial Organizations

Until several factors coalesced in the 1930s, industrial unions were not viable. These included (1) the Depression and its impact on wages and employment, (2) legislation facilitating organization, (3) the emergence of strong industrially oriented leaders, and (4) the virtual end of immigration, which had lowered the bargaining power of unskilled industrial workers.

The Congress of Industrial Organizations (CIO) was born in 1935. Its strategy was to organize all workers in a given plant or company rather than to focus on a craft. Resistance was encountered from most employers. Early successes in organizing in the auto and rubber industries resulted from the use of the sit-down strike, in which workers refused to leave the premises until employers met their demands for recognition.

ILLUSTRATION 17-1

Testimony Regarding the Labor Movement by Samuel Gompers, President of the AFL before Congress

Q.   Well, is it not true that there is capital and capital; there is productive capital and there is capital which is not engaged, not embarked in any industry which employs labor?

A.   Then it is not capital; it is wealth, but not capital.

Q.   I see your distinction; but the capital that is employed in productive industry sustains very close relation with labor, so there ought to be a very great harmony of interests between the owners of that capital and the owners of labor?

A.   There has never yet existed identity of interests between the buyer and seller of an article. If you have anything to sell and I want to buy it your interest and mine are not identical.

Q.   Is there not a possibility that the day will come when they will be substantially identical, when they recognize each other's rights?

A.   I should regard that upon the same plane as I would the panaceas that are offered by our populists, socialists, anarchists, and single-tax friends, as very remote and very far removed, if that time should ever come, I am perfectly satisfied to fight the battles of today, of those here, and those that come tomorrow, so their conditions may be improved, and they may be better prepared to fight in the contests or solve the problems that may be presented to them. The hope for a perfect millenium—well, it don't come every night; it don't come with the twinkling of the eye; it is a matter which we have got to work out, and every step that the workers make or take, every vantage point gained, is a solution in itself. I have often inquired of men who have ready-made patent solutions of this social problem, and I want to say to you, sir, that I have them offered to me on an average of two or three a week, and they are all equally unsatisfactory. I maintain that we are solving the problem every day; we are solving the problems that confront us. One would imagine by what is considered as the solution of the problem that it is going to fall among us, that a world cataclysm is going to take place; that there is going to be a social revolution; that we will go to bed one night under the present system and the morrow morning wake up with the revolution in full blast, and the next day organize a Heaven on earth. This is not the way progress is made; that is not the way the social evolution is brought about; that is not the way the human family are going to have interests advanced. We are solving the problem day after day. As we get an hour's more leisure every day it means millions of golden hours, of opportunities, to the human family. As we get 25 cents a day wages increase it means another solution, another problem solved, and brings us nearer the time when a greater degree of justice and fair dealing will obtain among men.

Source: From the testimony of Samuel Gompers, president of the AFL, in U.S. Congress, House, *Report of the Industrial Commission on the Relations and Conditions of Capital and Labor Employed in Manufacturers and General Business*, 56th Congress, 2d sess., House Doc. 495 (Washington, D.C.: U.S. Government Printing Office, 1901), pp. 654–55.

The merger of the AFL and CIO

The passage of the Taft-Hartley Act (see below) in 1947 created penalties for competition between unions for members. In 1954, both ratified a no-raid agreement, suspending attempts to organize workers belonging to an affiliated union of the other. In 1955, the federations merged to form the AFL–CIO.

Membership in labor organizations

Membership has been falling since 1979.[3] Whether this trend will continue is open to speculation. Much of the change is due to declining employment in heavily unionized industries.[4] If unionized firms existing

FIGURE 17–1

Percent of Nonfarm Work Force Organized in the U.S.

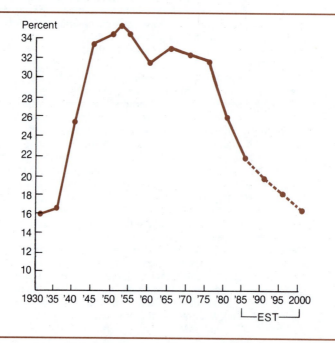

Note: Leo Troy and Nel Shevlin *Union Sourcebook* IRDIS, West Orange, N.J.; 1985–2000 Projections, Richard B. Freeman of Harvard University, BW

Source: J. Hoerr, "Beyond Unions," *Business Week,* July 8, 1985, p. 72.

---

[3] E. C. Kokkelenberg and D. R. Sockell, "Union Membership in the United States, 1973–1981," *Industrial and Labor Relations Review* 38 (1985), pp. 497–543.

[4] W. T. Dickens and J. S. Leonard, "Accounting for the Decline in Union Membership, 1950–1980," *Industrial and Labor Relations Review* 38 (1985), pp. 323–34. For a more detailed

FIGURE 17-2
Union Membership Proportions by Industry

50 percent and over

1. Railroads
2. Postal
3. Automobiles
4. Primary metals
5. Transportation equipment

40 to 49.9 percent

6. Communications
7. Paper
8. Stone, clay, and glass products
9. Other public utilities
10. Aircraft
11. Other transportation
12. Other transportation equipment

30 to 39.9 percent

13. Food
14. Local government
15. Fabricated metals
16. Education
17. Petroleum products
18. Mining
19. Construction
20. Tobacco products
21. Ordnance

20 to 29.9 percent

22. Rubber and plastics
23. Machinery

24. Furniture
25. Electrical equipment
26. State government
27. Chemicals
28. Apparel
29. Leather
30. Printing

10 to 19.9 percent

31. Miscellaneous services
32. Federal government
33. Lumber
34. Hospitals
35. Miscellaneous manufacturing
36. Textiles
37. Entertainment and recreation
38. Personal services
39. Forestry and fisheries
40. Welfare and religious
41. Instruments
42. Wholesale trade
43. Business and repair services
44. Medical

Less than 10 percent

45. Retail trades
46. Insurance and real estate
47. Agriculture
48. Banking and finance
49. Private household services

Source: J. A. Fossum, *Labor Relations: Development, Structure, Process,* 4th ed. (Homewood, Ill.: BPI/Irwin, 1989), p. 476.

in the same industry as nonunion firms have higher wage costs, they are either more vulnerable to closure or would require productivity increases to balance increasing wage costs. Frequently the reaction to increased wages is to substitute capital for labor in the long run. Figure 17–1 shows that both the relative proportion and absolute numbers of the labor force who are union members is declining. Figure 17–2 shows that the proportion of unionized employees varies substantially by industry.

look at the employment changes of unionized and nonunion workers, see L. T. Adams, "Changing Employment Patterns of Organized Workers," *Monthly Labor Review* 108 (February 1985), pp. 25–31.

THE CHANGING ECONOMIC ENVIRONMENT

Employees' jobs depend ultimately on consumers' purchases of goods and services. Occupations that are required by the economy vary with the tastes and needs of society. As new products that have attractive characteristics or are less expensive substitutes are introduced, certain industries or firms increase or decrease their demand for employees. For example, the time-saving capabilities of air travel led to an increase in the demand for pilots, mechanics, flight attendants, and the like—and a decrease in railroad engineers, conductors, porters, and others. Ticket agents and baggage handlers were needed by both industries, but within each, demand increased or decreased. Since the demand for information-processing technology and personal services is increasing, the demand for labor in the service and finance sectors is increasing while it has declined in mining and durable goods industries. Those occupations and industries in which employees are represented by unions happen to be experiencing the greatest relative decline.

In this section, the effects of several economic trends on union membership and bargaining power will be examined.

Mechanization

Employers frequently make decisions about how plants will be equipped. Some durable goods manufacturers have installed industrial robots that manufacture products at a lower cost than the labor they replaced. Sometimes technological changes do not eliminate labor but reduce its need. For example, new aircraft that require only two cockpit personnel rather than three reduce the demand for pilots. The manner in which something is produced also has an influence on the need for employees. For example, strip mining is much less labor intensive than is underground mining. Thus the use of labor changes as the result of innovations that reduce the cost of equipment relative to labor, and wage increases that do the same.

Foreign Competition

Low-wage foreign competition reduces the need for domestic labor when capital investment in plants is relatively small or the labor cost differentials between domestic and foreign labor are large. A large amount of production in small appliances and electronic components has moved to Far Eastern countries, such as Taiwan and Korea, because of the labor cost advantages in them relative to the United States. Total employment in the economy may remain stable, with companies involved in importing adding workers as domestic producers cut back.

Deregulation

Deregulation allows firms to compete on prices and enables new firms to enter previously regulated industries, such as trucking, airlines, and long-distance phone carriers. The new entrants often hire employees at pay rates below those negotiated by unions with established companies. The lower labor costs allow the new entrants to offer goods and services at lower prices to gain a foothold in the market. Deregulation also allows organizations to eliminate less profitable operations. Rail carriers are selling less heavily traveled routes to so-called short lines. These small carriers usually operate at lower wage levels with smaller crews and may be nonunion. The major carriers maintain that they cannot operate these profitably under current labor agreements or that they are less profitable than other investment opportunities.

Regulated firms could act as monopolies and pass the costs of wage increases on to consumers, since prices were not in competition. For example, long-distance rates were regulated by the Federal Communications Commission, which allowed AT&T to earn an "adequate" return on its investment. When labor costs increased, they were passed on to the consumer in higher rates to allow an equivalent return.

If new firms in deregulated industries are nonunion, or if entrepreneurs can enter easily (as in trucking), unionized employees will often be unable to command the wages or job security they had in the past.

LABOR LAW

There are five major federal laws regulating private-sector labor-management relations (for an overview, see Chapter 3). These are the Norris-LaGuardia, Wagner, Taft-Hartley, Railway Labor, and Landrum-Griffin Acts. In the public sector, state and local government employees are covered by state laws; and the federal civil service is covered by the Civil Service Reform Act of 1978.[5]

---

[5] For an expanded treatment of federal labor law, see J. A. Fossum, *Labor Relations: Development, Structure, Process*, 4th ed. (Homewood, Ill.: BPI/Irwin, 1989), pp. 64–78.

Railway Labor Act

The Railway Labor Act, passed in 1926, guarantees the rights of railway and air transportation employees to choose whether to be represented by a union and to engage in union activities. It differs from later legislation by specifying methods for resolving disputes over the form or the interpretation of the contract. The resolution of contract disputes under the Railway Labor Act has often led to the creation of emergency boards and actions by Congress to legislate settlements to avoid strikes. Many of these disputes resulted from technological changes that eliminated the need for certain occupations.

Norris-LaGuardia Act

The Norris-LaGuardia Act, passed in 1932, applies to all private sector employers and labor organizations. It forbids so-called yellow-dog contracts, in which an applicant or employee agrees not to become a member of a union in exchange for continued employment. Federal court judges are forbidden from enjoining lawful union activities unless there is a clear and present danger to life or property, and the damage to the union from the issuance of the injunction is substantially less than the potential damage to others.

Wagner Act

With the passage of the Wagner Act in 1936, organized labor received the tools that were necessary to put it on a more roughly equal footing with management. The act (later amended by the Taft-Hartley Act in 1947) had three major thrusts. First, it recognized an employee's right to engage in union activities, to organize, and to bargain collectively without the interference or coercion of the employer. Second, where a majority of employees in a given unit desired union representation, it required the employer to collectively bargain with the union regarding wages, hours, and terms and conditions of employment. Third, the legislation established the National Labor Relations Board (NLRB) to conduct union representation elections and to investigate unfair labor practices and remedy them.

Employers strongly resisted the early implementation of the act, but by 1937, unions were beginning to gain bargaining rights. This came about as a result of a Supreme Court decision upholding the constitutionality of the statute, the recognition by U.S. Steel of the Steelworkers

Organizing Committee as the representative of its production employees, and the successful use of sit-down strikes to organize the auto and
rubber industries.

Taft-Hartley Act

The Taft-Hartley Act was passed in 1947 over President Truman's
veto. The major thrust of the legislation was to balance the powers of
labor and management in the collective bargaining relationship. Because
employees had so little power to organize and bargain before the passage
of the Wagner Act, the earlier legislation restricted only employer
activities. As unions became more powerful, some argued that there was
no recognition of individual rights in relation to union rights and that
unions had unbridled power to engage in many activities that gave them
an unfair advantage in the bargaining relationship. Taft-Hartley was
aimed at providing a balance.

Coverage

The Taft-Hartley Act applies to employers and employees in the
private sector (and postal workers) except for those covered by the
Railway Labor Act. Coverage does not apply to supervisors, independent
contractors, agricultural or domestic workers, or family members employed by an owner. Professional employees cannot be included in a
bargaining unit with nonprofessionals without their majority consent.

Unfair labor practices

Employers may not establish or assist labor organizations. They may
not discriminate in staffing decisions based on union membership, but
unions and managements can negotiate contract clauses requiring union
membership as a condition of continued employment, once hiring has
occurred. Employers cannot refuse to bargain with the union over issues
related to wages, hours, terms, and conditions of employment.

Unions cannot require an employer to discriminate against an employee based on union nonmembership except where the contract requires membership. Unions may not strike to force an employer to cease
handling nonunion goods (except in contract construction) or a variety of
other activities related to bargaining or organizing.

Both parties have the mutual duty to bargain in good faith at the
request of the other on mandatory issues. Bargaining does not simply

mean the process of achieving a contract, but includes its administration and interpretation as well.

Representation

If a majority of employees in a unit desires representation, the union represents all, whether they are members or voted for the union. It is the *exclusive representative* and *bargaining agent* for employees in the unit.

Other provisions

Taft-Hartley established the Federal Mediation and Conciliation Service (FMCS), which has two major responsibilities. First, it receives notifications of contract expirations and offers services to the parties to assist them in settling contracts without work stoppages. Second, it is responsible for maintaining a roster of arbitrators who are qualified to decide contract interpretation disputes the parties are unable to resolve themselves.

Section 14b is a controversial provision, enabling states to enact *right-to-work* laws. These laws forbid employers and unions from agreeing to union shop clauses in contracts. A union shop clause is a form of union security in which new employees are required to join the union after some probationary period as a condition of continued employment. Proponents of these laws argue that employees should be free to join or not join a union based on their own personal beliefs rather than being coerced by a contractual agreement. Opponents argue that nonmembers are free riders and that in a democratic society persons frequently must belong to jurisdictions (like cities) in which they did not vote for the present officers. Figure 17–3 has a column showing what levels of union security are permissible in most right-to-work-law states.

Landrum-Griffin Act

The Landrum-Griffin Act resulted from Senate investigations into labor racketeering in the late 1950s. The findings demonstrated that most of the labor movement and collective bargaining relationships were operating as public policy intended, but a few unions and employers were denying employees' rights to representation and due process.

To remedy these problems, the act established a bill of rights for union members that requires equal rights in voting and other union activities, freedom of speech in union matters, the right to vote on dues increases, and the right to sue their unions. Union and management

FIGURE 17–3
Levels of Union Security and Right-to-Work Laws

Level of Security and Definition	Permissibility with Right-to-Work Law
Closed shop—Person must be a member of the representing union before being considered for employment. Illegal.	No
Union shop—Person must become a member of the representing union after a period of time as specified by the collective bargaining agreement, but in no event less than 30 days, except 7 days in construction industry.	No
Agency shop—Person need not become a member of the representing union but must pay a service charge for representation, in lieu of dues.	No
Maintenance-of-membership—Person must remain a member of the representing union once joined.	No
Checkoff—Person may request that the employer deduct union dues from pay and forward directly to the representing union.	Yes

officials are forbidden from having financial dealings with each other, and union officers are required to report annually the financial transactions they may have with a company in which union members are represented (even including the purchase and sale of stock). National unions were restricted from taking over their local unions except in cases of failure to conduct affairs democratically, failure to carry out a collective bargaining agreement, corruption, or financial mismanagement. National unions are also required to have constitutional conventions at which officers are elected at least every five years. Locals must hold elections at least every three years.

Landrum-Griffin also made some minor changes to Taft-Hartley in specifying that *secondary boycotts* by unions would be unfair labor practices. A secondary boycott occurs when a union asks firms or other unions to cease doing business with an employer who is handling a struck product. The union can ask that the struck product not be used or sold but cannot ask persons to refuse to patronize someone who handles it.

Civil Service Reform Act, Title VII

Collective bargaining in the federal government was originally permitted by Executive Order 10988 issued by President Kennedy in 1961.[6]

---

[6] For a comprehensive examination of the development and operation of labor relations in the federal sector under the executive orders, see M. A. Nesbitt, *Labor Relations in the Federal Government Service* (Washington, D.C.: Bureau of National Affairs, 1976).

The executive order was replaced by the Civil Service Reform Act. Unions are forbidden to strike or to make demands in economic and staffing areas without the consent of the agency. The act established the Federal Labor Relations authority (FLRA) to monitor labor-management relations in the federal government, such as the NLRB does in the private sector. Arbitration of unresolved grievances under the contract is required with the award binding both labor and management.[7]

The first real test of the law occurred when the Professional Air Traffic Controllers Organization (PATCO) struck in August 1981. President Reagan refused to negotiate with them while they were on strike and ordered a return to work within 48 hours or their rights to federal employment would be forfeited. Those who failed to return were terminated. PATCO's right to represent government employees was also terminated, since the act forbids either the advocacy of, or actual, work stoppages.

Administrative Bodies

Labor legislation has created four major administrative agencies. The Railway Labor Act created the National Mediation Board; the Wagner Act, the NLRB; the Taft-Hartley Act, the FMCS; and the Civil Service Reform Act, the FLRA. These agencies have different roles to fulfill and different ways in which they operate. The FMCS is essentially a responsive organization. When contract negotiation is difficult, the parties may ask for mediation assistance. Mediators are experienced in bargaining, and their goal is to achieve a settlement. The NLRB responds to alleged unfair labor practices and questions regarding the majority status of union representation. The NLRB is made up of several regional offices with the regional director having responsibility to determine how charges are to be handled. Where charges are neither dismissed nor informally settled with the parties, an administrative law judge hears the case and renders a decision. Final determination is made by the appointed members of the NLRB. The FLRA operates in a similar manner.

Members of the NLRB are appointed by the president and confirmed by the Senate. The general counsel of the NLRB, also a political appointee, has a major say in the types of cases the NLRB will hear. The members of the NLRB interpret provisions of the Taft-Hartley Act and render decisions that can be enforced by or appealed to a circuit court of appeals.

---

[7] For an analysis of the legislation and the operation of the Federal Labor Relations Authority, see H. B. Frazier III, "Labor-Management Relations in the Federal Government," *Labor Law Journal* 30 (1979), pp. 131–38.

If the NLRB is politicized by the appointment process, neither unions nor employers can count much on the stability of its decisions. Recent evidence suggests that Democratic members appointed by a Democratic president were 12 percent more likely to rule in favor of unions than were members who were appointed by a president who was not of their political party. Republican appointees of a Republican president were 20 percent less likely to rule in favor of unions than this same comparison group.[8]

Wide swings in decisions influenced by the political composition of the NLRB may lead the parties either to avoid legal means for dealing with labor-management conflicts or to charge each other with unfair practices whenever the composition changes, in the hope of getting a reversal of a precedent.[9]

Besides the history and philosophy of the labor movement and the legal environment in which collective bargaining takes place, the economic environment has an influence on the paths that labor and management are able to take in forging labor agreements and practicing industrial relations.

UNION STRUCTURES

The labor movement's organization structure is very similar to a government's. A comparison would show that as governments operate on different levels, in different manners, and service multiple and overlapping constituencies, so do the various labor organizations. The three major levels are (1) the national or international union, (2) the local union, and (3) the labor federation. There are also state and city central federations, but these are more often involved with political than employment issues.

The National Union

National unions are established to represent employees in particular jurisdictions. Examples of national unions are the United Steelworkers of America (an industrial union) and the International Brotherhood of Electrical Workers (a craft union). Affiliated with national unions are numerous local unions. The present trend, however, is for unions to move away from traditional jurisdictions and toward organizing many trades or industries. The Teamsters Union is the prime example of a national

---

[8] W. N. Cooke and F. H. Gautschi III, "Political Bias in NLRB Unfair Labor Practice Decisions," *Industrial and Labor Relations Review* 36 (1982), pp. 539–49.

[9] Ibid.

union that takes this approach, having less than one third of its membership in the trucking industry. Some unions have established separate divisions for organizing specific groups such as the UAW's efforts toward private university nonacademic employees and the Service Employees (SEIU) Local 925 (nine-to-five) clerical organizing unit.

The national union's power resides in two bases. First, it has the power to charter new local unions and direct existing ones. Second, it has the power to affiliate with or withdraw from such labor federations as the AFL–CIO.

Most national unions are governed by their periodic conventions. The nationals' power stems from their constitutions, which are reviewed and amended by the national conventions. National officers are elected during these conventions. The executive board and the president answer to this body.

Day-to-day operations of the national union are handled via two different types of organizational approaches. The first is functional, with departments organized to handle particular services, such as legal, organizing, and arbitration. The second approach is in recognition of the union's relationship to employers in representing employees. Nationals frequently have departments to deal with particular industries or major employers. For example, in the Steelworkers there is a nonferrous metal representative to its industry conference; in the UAW, there is a General Motors Department.

Some of the services and activities provided by the nationals include organizing workers in unorganized areas or industries; industrywide collective bargaining and/or assistance to local bargainers; strike assistance, including economic benefits; legislative, legal, and lobbying activities; research and education; communications to members; benefit and pension plan administration; and contract interpretation and grievance assistance.

Local Unions

Local unions represent employees within a given geographical area. In the industrial sector, a local is frequently confined to one plant of a given organization in an area (e.g., there are several UAW locals representing General Motors employees in Flint, Michigan) or in all plants of an organization in a given geographical area (such as several plants of Honeywell, Inc., located in Minneapolis, Minnesota, and represented by Teamsters Local 1145), or to employees of many small organizations in a given geographical area (e.g., several establishments where employees are represented by UAW Local 12 in Toledo, Ohio).

A local union chartered by a national union must conform to requirements laid down in the national union constitution. National unions retain and exercise the power to approve or disapprove settlements negotiated at the local level, to pass on the legitimacy of strikes, to require dues payments to the national, to review local imposition of discipline on members, to supervise local elections, to audit local financial affairs, and to remove local officers and place the local under *trusteeship* if national rules are violated.

Locals are not passive and powerless, however. Most activities that directly affect union members are conducted on the local level. Among the functions of the local union are negotiation of labor contracts; administration of the agreement; pursuit and adjustment of grievances alleging contract violations; organization of workers in the local area; operation of union hiring halls; and social, community, and public relations activities.

The activities of the local are carried out by representatives elected by the membership. In locals where workers are employed in a single organization, the union's activities are directed by the *president*, and members are represented on the shop floor by *stewards*. If a member believes that the contract has been violated by the company, assistance may be sought from the steward. The steward acts as an advocate, contract interpreter, and reviewer of company policy implementation.

Where the union membership is dispersed across employers (particularly within the building trades), the local will probably elect a *business agent* to conduct its day-to-day affairs. The business agent handles hiring hall problems, inspects job sites to ensure that the employer is abiding by the contract, and handles union-related problems for individual members.

The AFL–CIO

The AFL–CIO is a labor federation made up of most national unions, state federations, and city central unions, and some local labor unions which are unaffiliated with a national. The federation has the power to expel or deny membership to constituents who fail to abide by the federation's constitution.

Some of the activities of the labor federation include political action and lobbying, organizing nonunion employees, research and education, resolving jurisdictional disputes between members, publications and

FIGURE 17–4
Structural Organization of the American Federation of Labor and Congress of Industrial Organizations

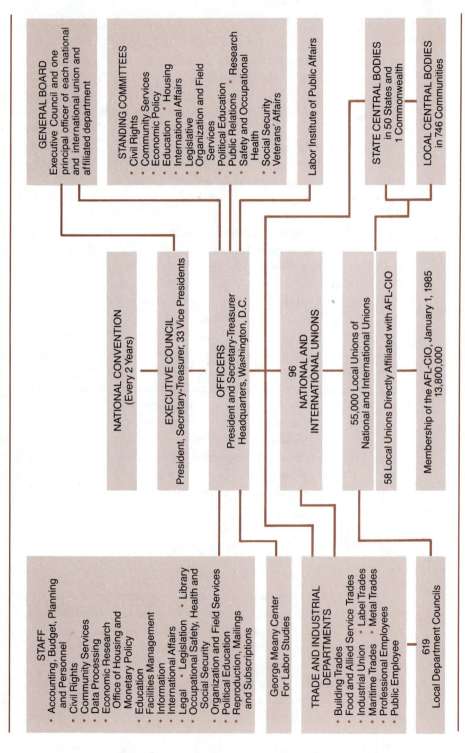

584

communications, and legal proceedings and interpretations. Figure 17–4 is an organizational chart of the AFL–CIO.

National Union Mergers

Recently there has been a number of mergers between national unions.[10] The largest has been the formation of the United Food and Commercial Workers through the merger of the Retail Clerks and the Amalgamated Meat Cutters. This and other recent mergers are shown in Figure 17–5. The AFL–CIO encourages mergers to increase union bargaining power and concentrate more resources on organizing new members.

Unions merge for many of the same reasons as businesses. In some instances, their work is interdependent, and the ability to meet the needs of members requires taking into consideration the operation of the other. In other instances, merging competing unions allows a more efficient use of resources. Finally, some unions absorb others simply to increase their size, at the same time perhaps increasing their efficiency.[11] Mergers among competing unions increase during periods of economic adversity.

Union Democracy

Relative to business and other employing organizations, unions are highly democratic, since their members elect the leadership. Unlike employing organizations, unions are forbidden by law from discriminating against members who vocally object to the current leadership. On the other hand, there is no requirement that a union must foster a two-party system even though it is a political organization.

Union members do have a unique set of democratic mechanisms to reflect the will of the membership, however. Under the concept of dual governance, union members are first entitled to be represented or unrepresented through an NLRB election. Second, they are entitled to elect their leaders and to ratify offered contracts. Thus, although the democracy does not necessarily equal two-party politics, substantial safeguards for member choices exist.[12]

---

[10] G. N. Chaison, "Union Growth and Union Mergers," *Industrial Relations* 20 (1981), pp. 98–108; L. T. Adams, "Labor Organization Mergers 1979–84; Adapting to Change," *Monthly Labor Review* 107, no. 9 (1984), pp. 21–27.

[11] J. Freeman and J. Brittain, "Union Merger Process and the Industrial Environment," *Industrial Relations* 16 (1977), pp. 173–85.

[12] See A. H. Cook, *Union Democracy: Practice and Ideal* (Ithaca, N.Y.: New York State School of Industrial and Labor Relations, Cornell University, 1963).

FIGURE 17–5

Recent Merger Activity among National Unions (chronology of major labor organization mergers, January 1979 to April 1984)

Date	Organization and Affiliation	Membership at Time of Merger
1979	Amalgamated Clothing and Textile Workers Union (AFL–CIO) merged with United Shoe Workers of America (AFL–CIO)	475,000 25,000
	Retail Clerks International Union (AFL–CIO)	735,000
	Amalgamated Meat Cutters and Butcher Workmen of North America (AFL–CIO)	500,000
	Formed the United Food and Commercial Workers International Union (AFL–CIO)	
	International Union, United Automobile, Aerospace and Agricultural Implement Workers of America (AFL–CIO) merged with	1,499,000
	Distributive Workers of America (Ind.)	35,000
1980	United Food and Commercial Workers International Union (AFL–CIO) merged with	1,300,000
	Barbers, Beauticians and Allied Industries International Association (AFL–CIO)	27,000
1982	Aluminum, Brick, and Clay Workers International Union (AFL–CIO)	40,000
	United Glass and Ceramic Workers of America (AFL–CIO)	28,000
	Formed the Aluminum Brick and Glass Workers International Union (AFL–CIO)	
1982	Service Employees International Union (AFL–CIO) merged with	650,000
	National Association of Government Employees (Ind.)	100,000
1983	International Printing and Graphic Communications Union (AFL–CIO)	112,000
	Graphic Arts International Union (AFL–CIO)	82,500
	Formed the Graphic Communications International Union	
1984	Service Employees International Union (AFL–CIO) merged with	750,000
	California State Employees Association (AGE)	50,000
	American Federation of State, County and Municipal Employees (AFL–CIO) merged with	1,130,000
	Ohio Association of Public School Employees (Ind.)	25,000
1984	International Brotherhood of Boilermakers, Iron Ship Builders, Blacksmiths, Forgers and Helpers (AFL–CIO) merged with	134,000
	United Cement, Lime and Gypsum Workers International Union (AFL–CIO)	29,000

Source: L. T. Adams, "Labor Organization Mergers 1979–84; Adapting to Change," *Monthly Labor Review* 107 no. 4 (1984), pp. 23–24.

National Unions and Public Policy

Representation is aimed at enhancing union members' employment outcomes through collective bargaining. Unions also serve the needs of their members through attempts to influence public policy. Some are aimed at membership interests in particular industries, while others are aimed at improving the lot of the membership as a whole or an identifiable subgroup across industries.

Examples of public policy initiatives that cut across industries include labor's support of occupational safety and health legislation, increases in the minimum wage, opposition to lower minimum wages for younger workers, and the reduction of pay inequality between men and women.

As competition changes within industries, unions may engage in political activity to restrict the options of employers in cutting employment. Where domestic markets have opened to foreign competition (e.g., autos and steel), lower wage costs among foreign competitors may reduce the demand for domestic unionized employees, and unions push for protective legislation in the form of tariffs, domestic content laws, or reregulation.

The political activities of national unions have increased markedly in the 1980s. Activity is greatest among unions involved with public employers and those in which executive boards are democratically chosen.[13] Political action committees (PACs) have been important vehicles for providing financial support to election campaigns of individuals thought to be friendly to the viewpoints of the PACs. PAC contributions to a candidate who subsequently becomes or remains an incumbent are related directly to roll-call voting records and indirectly to the number of candidates elected.[14] PACs do not, however, give contributions to all who support their causes. Contributions to candidates appear to depend on the willingness of the organization to give, the compatibility of the candidate's ideology with that of the contributing PAC, the probability of the candidate's winning (with more given when the race is close), and the magnitude of the vote margin the candidate had in the last election (if an incumbent).[15] They also appear to be related to the closeness of an incumbent's committee assignment to interests of labor, voting record, and electoral security.[16]

---

[13] M. F. Masters and J. T. Delaney, "The Causes of Union Political Involvement," *Journal of Labor Research* 6 (1985), pp. 341–62.

[14] G. M. Saltzman, "Congressional Voting on Labor Issues: The Role of PACs," *Industrial and Labor Relations Review* 40 (1987), pp. 163–79.

[15] A. Wilhite and J. Theilmann, "Unions, Corporations, and Political Campaign Contributions: The 1982 House Elections," *Journal of Labor Research* 7 (1986), pp. 175–86.

[16] K. B. Grier and M. C. Munger, "The Impact of Legislator Attributes on Interest-Group Campaign Contributions," *Journal of Labor Research* 7 (1986), pp. 349–59.

While unions (and corporations) are heavily involved in PAC activities, their members or employees' attitudes toward issues appear to be varied, and in the case of unions, are less liberal than the positions espoused by their unions' PACs. Further, it appears that the PACs are more successful in influencing legislative outcomes peripheral to labor's interest, such as education, rather than directly affecting its environment, such as labor law reform.[17]

MAJOR ACTIVITIES OF UNIONS

The overriding activity of labor unions is the representation of members through collective bargaining agreements. The first major activity is organizing a majority of employees within a work unit. A second major activity is negotiating with the employer over the terms and conditions of the employment relationship. This activity establishes rules and governance systems, a job structure with wage rates and internal staffing patterns, and a system for resolving disputes about the meaning of the rules. The third major activity is the joint administration of the agreement with management. The union generally takes a proactive role in negotiations, but it is usually reactive in contract administration. It acts as a police force to identify situations in which management oversteps its authority and as a prosecutor if management refuses to stop the activity and/or redress the wrong. Organizing activities will be examined in this chapter, and negotiating and administration will be covered in the next.

THE MOTIVATION TO JOIN UNIONS

Why do employees join unions? In Chapter 5 it was suggested that individuals perform acts that they believe will result in outcomes they prefer and prevent outcomes they would like to avoid. Extended to the situation in which individuals consider unions, this means that unions would be preferred when one believes that unions can accomplish preferred outcomes one cannot accomplish alone. Evidence from a national survey suggests that employees in the United States believe that unions are likely to obtain important outcomes for them.[18] Figure 17–6 shows the areas where these beliefs exist.

---

[17] M. F. Masters and J. T. Delaney, "Union Political Activities: A Review of the Empirical Literature," *Industrial and Labor Relations Review* 40 (1987), pp. 336–53.

[18] T. A. Kochan, "How American Workers View Labor Unions," *Monthly Labor Review* 103 (1979), pp. 22–31; J. Hoerr, "Beyond Unions."

FIGURE 17–6

American Workers' Beliefs about Trade Unions (in percent)*

Beliefs	Strongly Agree	Agree	Neither Agree nor Disagree	Disagree	Strongly Disagree
Instrumental beliefs					
Protect workers against unfair practice	20.5%	63.0%	3.4%	11.2%	2.0%
Improve job security	19.2	61.0	2.8	14.5	2.5
Improve wages	18.9	67.6	3.2	8.7	1.7
Give members their money's (dues) worth	6.9	38.5	6.3	36.9	11.3

* In the survey, 1,515 workers were polled.

Source: Thomas A. Kochan, "How American Workers View Labor Unions," *Monthly Labor Review*, April 1979, p. 24.

ORGANIZING AND REPRESENTATION

It has been suggested that labor unions form because employees are frustrated in gaining important rewards.[19] In an attempt to reduce dissatisfaction associated with this frustration, organizing may occur. In what areas does dissatisfaction appear to have the greatest impact on organizing activity and in voting for the union in a representation election?

One study of 250 units of a nationwide retailing firm found that attitude measures taken 3 to 15 months before any organizing activity predicted the level of later organizing attempts. Those units that had more union organizing activity were not as satisfied with their supervision, their co-workers, their career future, the amount of work required, their physical surroundings, and the type of work accomplished.[20]

Another study of more than 1,000 employees who voted in 33 union representation elections conducted by the NLRB in different Midwest firms indicates that attitudes are strongly related to the direction of

---

[19] This approach is explained in detail in R. Stagner and H. Rosen, *Psychology of Union-Management Relations* (Belmont, Calif.: Wadsworth, 1965).

[20] W. C. Hamner and F. J. Smith, "Work Attitudes as Predictors of Unionization Activity," *Journal of Applied Psychology* 63 (1978), pp. 415–21.

voting.[21] A recent analysis of reported and unreported research on union organizing finds that the individual's voting decision is most strongly influenced by dissatisfaction with management's administration of the employment relationship and beliefs that the union will successfully address employee concerns.[22]

Organizing Campaigns

Organizing campaigns may be initiated by either employees or organizers employed by the union. Employees are likely to organize when they are dissatisfied with conditions in their organizations. Union organizers may have to convince employees that they are dissatisfied if organizing is to be successful.

There are differing legal rights for employee and nonemployee (outsider) organizers in organizing campaigns. Employee organizers may solicit fellow employees to join the union during nonworking time on company premises, but in most cases, an outsider can be barred from this type of activity.

The organizing campaign generally continues until a majority of employees has signed *authorization cards* stating that they want to be represented by the union. (The NLRB will normally conduct a representation election if 30 percent or more of employees have signed these cards.) When the union believes that it has a majority, it may ask the employer to voluntarily recognize it. Most often the employer refuses, and the union petitions the NLRB to conduct a *representation election*.

Bargaining unit determination

When a petition is received, the NLRB conducts a hearing to determine an appropriate *bargaining unit*, that is, the group of employees the union will represent if it wins. If both the union and company agree, a *consent election* is held. If they disagree, the NLRB determines the appropriate unit. The results of the election will bar another for at least one year.

---

[21] J. Getman, S. Goldberg, and J. B. Herman, *Union Representation Elections: Law and Reality* (New York: Russell Sage Foundation, 1976). For a review of this study and others, see H. G. Heneman III and M. H. Sandver, "Prediction of the Union Election Outcome: A Review and Critical Analysis of the Research," *Industrial and Labor Relations Review* 37 (1983), 537–59.

[22] S. L. Premack and J. E. Hunter, "Individual Unionization Decisions," *Psychological Bulletin*, 103 (1988), pp. 223–34.

Bargaining unit determination is a critical issue for both the employer and the union because it can greatly influence the outcome of the election and the bargaining power of the parties if the union wins. Employers most often opt for plantwide bargaining units, feeling that this offers the greatest chance for defeating the union and for avoiding the possibility of a small subgroup of employees tying up the entire organization in bargaining. Unions seek to represent a subset of employees in a plant where they have traditionally represented one occupational classification.

Except in consent elections, the NLRB decides the makeup of the bargaining unit and has used the following criteria in determinations:

1. *Community of interests.* Members are likely to have similar goals in bargaining.
2. *Geographical proximity.* Ease or difficulty of representation of employees in several locations of one organization.
3. *Employer's administrative or territorial divisions.* Separate managements may be difficult to coordinate for one representative.
4. *Functional integration.* Employees whose duties go together in a logical manner to produce a single product or service.
5. *Interchange of employees.* Traditional transfer policies of the organization.
6. *Bargaining history.* Typical patterns for other employers in the same industry.
7. *Employee desires.* Interests in a broad or narrow unit.
8. *Extent of organization.* Degree to which a particular unit has been organized relative to other units in the same organization.[23]

Representation elections

Organizing campaigns take place in a highly charged atmosphere. Both sides use tactics they believe will convince employees to vote for or against representation.

The union generally seeks to keep organizing activity secret until it has established a foothold. The union forwards its case through present employees who favor organization, personal visits to employees' homes, and off-hours union meetings.

---

[23] J. E. Abodeely, R. C. Hammer, and A. L. Sandler, *The NLRB and the Appropriate Bargaining Unit*, rev. ed., Labor Relations and Public Policy Series, Report No. 3 (Philadelphia: Industrial Research Unit, Department of Industry, Wharton School of Finance and Commerce, University of Pennsylvania, 1981).

Management has some advantages once the organizing campaign becomes known, since it can use company time to communicate antiunion information. However, according to law, no threats or promises about what will happen if the union is elected or defeated may be communicated, and the employer cannot make unplanned changes in wages, hours, and terms and conditions of employment until the election has been certified. Generally, the union need not be granted use of the premises or time to respond unless the employer has broad rules that essentially eliminate contact among employees at work. Management may also make mailings to employees and instruct supervisors to hold informal meetings in work groups to communicate specific antiunion information.

The NLRB supervises most representation elections. These are usually *certification elections.* Management is likely to try to delay the election as long as possible, since evidence suggests the union's support erodes at the rate of about 2.5 percent per month during delays.[24] Delays also contribute to both reduced participation in elections and proportions of prounion votes.[25] If the union receives a majority of the votes cast, the board certifies it as the employees' exclusive representative. If the company wins a majority, any union is barred from seeking an election for a one-year period.

After an election, the losing party may object to the winner's campaign tactics. For example, the union may have signed up more than 50 percent of the employees during the authorization card campaign, yet lost the election. If union leaders think the company committed unfair labor practices to destroy the majority, it may file a charge with the NLRB asking that the election be set aside. On the other hand, if the union wins, management may refuse to bargain with the union, believing that the union does not actually represent a majority of the employees. The NLRB must then decide whether to require the employer to bargain or to set aside the election.[26] Figure 17–7 represents a model that summarizes the organizing and representation election process.

---

[24] R. Prosten, "The Longest Season: Union Organizing in the Last Decade, a/k/a How Come One Team Has to Play with Its Shoelaces Tied Together?" *Proceedings of the Industrial Relations Research Association,* 1978, pp. 240–49.

[25] G. Florkowski and M. Schuster, "Predicting the Decisions to Vote and Support Unions in Certification Elections: An Integrated Perspective," *Journal of Labor Research* 8 (1987), pp. 191–207.

[26] In 1948, the NLRB ruled that a representation election should provide "a laboratory in which an experiment may be conducted, under conditions nearly as ideal as possible, to determine the uninhibited desires of employees." Several tactics violate the laboratory conditions standard. These include: interrogation of employees about union activities, implementing unplanned improvements in wages and benefits, discharges or demotions for union activity, captive audience speeches less than 24 hours before an election, and a promised reduction in dues for persons joining the union before the election.

FIGURE 17-7
Sequence of Organizing Events

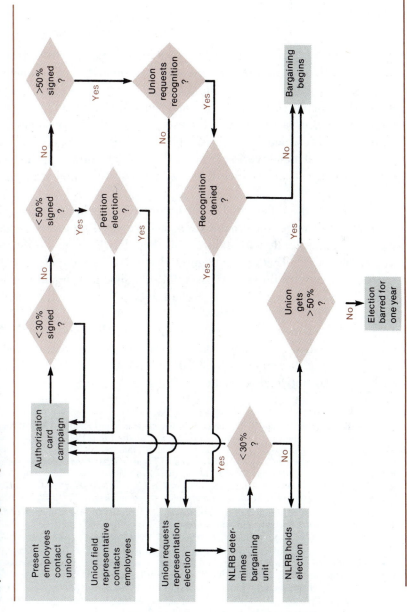

Source: J. A. Fossum, *Labor Relations: Development, Structure, Process,* 4th ed. (Homewood, Ill.: BPI/Irwin, 1989). p. 109.

Decertification elections

Occasionally, the NLRB conducts *decertification elections*, wherein employees currently represented by a union vote on whether they wish to remain represented. If a majority votes against the union, it loses its right to represent the employees.

THE EFFECT OF CAMPAIGN TACTICS

Management usually conducts a vigorous campaign to defeat the union. Usually, several letters are sent to employees; meetings with supervisors are held; split paychecks are written, with regular pay and union dues listed separately; and mass meetings with employees are often held. Other tactics include the use of outside labor consultants who help devise a resistance campaign, special training programs for supervisors, and legal maneuvering to delay the election. Research shows that such resistance tactics reduce the likelihood of the union winning the election.[27]

The greater the differential between union wages in an industry and the employer's wage, the greater resistance will be. Employer resistance increases more rapidly with differentials than desires for unionization by the employees.[28] Evidence suggests that an active union avoidance strategy for new facilities decreases the likelihood of organizing from about 15 percent to 1 percent.[29] Neutrality is quite likely to lead to representation.[30]

Some managements purposely commit unfair labor practices to blunt an organizing drive. An analysis has pointed out that the cost to employers of restoring discriminatorily fired union activists to their jobs with back pay is far outweighed by the potential costs of wage increases in a

[27] See K. F. Murrmann and A. A. Porter, "Employer Campaign Tactics and NLRB Election Outcomes: Some Preliminary Evidence," *Proceedings of the Industrial Relations Research Association* (1982), pp. 67–72; and J. Lawler, "Labor-Management Consultants in Union Organizing Campaigns: Do They Make a Difference?" *Proceedings of the Industrial Relations Research Association* (1981), pp. 374–80; Getman, Goldberg, and Herman, *Union Representation Elections;* W. T. Dickens, "The Effect of Company Campaigns on Certification Elections: Law and Reality Once Again," *Industrial and Labor Relations Review* 37 (1983), pp. 560–75.

[28] R. B. Freeman, "The Effect of the Union Wage Differential on Management Opposition and Union Organizing Success," *American Economic Review* 76 (1986), pp. 92–96.

[29] T. A. Kochan, R. B. McKersie, and J. Chalykoff, "The Effects of Corporate Strategy and Workplace Innovations on Union Representation," *Industrial and Labor Relations Review* 39 (1986), pp. 487–501; see also J. J. Lawler and R. West, "Impact of Union-Avoidance Strategy in Representation Elections," *Industrial Relations* 24 (1985), pp. 406–20.

[30] See Jeanne M. Brett, "Why Employees Want Unions," *Organizational Dynamics* 8, no. 4 (Spring 1980), p. 54; and A. H. Raskin, "Management Comes out Swinging," *Proceedings of the Industrial Relations Research Association*, (1978), pp. 223–32.

union contract if they were to be organized.[31] Employers may "learn" that the consequences for unlawful discrimination are slight since these practices appear most prevalent where unionization is pervasive and among employers who had previously violated the labor acts.[32] Further evidence suggests that discrimination by employers against employees for engaging in union activities decreases the probability of a union victory by 17 percent on the average.[33]

THE EFFECTS OF LABOR UNIONS

Unions are organized to assist in the accomplishment of outcomes sought by employees. They have two major goals—the increased financial well-being of present members and the addition of new members through organizing and/or increased employment. This may cause problems since it might be expected that present employees will prefer additional income to greater membership.[34] Conflict between these two goals may explain why substantial layoffs were necessary in some industries before members were willing to accept actual pay cuts during contract bargaining. Since contracts have to be ratified by a majority of the members, until the majority's employment was at risk it would not agree to a cut in its wage levels.

Unions involved in organizing are more likely to be in industries where the proportion of employees organized is not extremely large. Where organizing has been successful in the past, the international union is more likely to presently concentrate on representation activities.[35] The economic returns to employees from union representation in most industries are substantially greater than the costs of organizing to the union.[36] Thus, the union may recoup its investment through the payment of union dues, and the employee receives at least a one-time boost in wage levels compared to nonunion employees.

---

[31] C. R. Greer and S. A. Martin, "Calculative Strategy Decisions during Union Organizing Campaigns," *Sloan Management Review* 19, no. 2 (1978), pp. 61–74.

[32] M. M. Kleiner, "Unionism and Employer Discrimination: Analysis of 8(a)(3) Violations," *Industrial Relations* 23 (1984), pp. 234–43.

[33] W. N. Cooke, "The Rising Toll of Discrimination Against Union Activists," *Industrial Relations* 24 (1985), pp. 421–42.

[34] A. M. Cartter, *Theory of Wages and Employment* (Homewood, Ill.: Richard D. Irwin, 1959), pp. 88–94.

[35] R. N. Block, "Union Organizing and Allocation of Union Resources," *Industrial and Labor Relations Review*, 34 (1980), pp. 110–13.

[36] P. B. Voos, "Union Organizing: Costs and Benefits," *Industrial and Labor Relations Review* 36 (1983), pp. 576–91.

Effects on Employers

Besides income and membership, there may be a number of other operational goals and effects of unions on employers. Unions generally bargain for wage increases. The available evidence shows that union wages are higher than in comparable nonunion firms.[37] The package of benefits employees receive under union contracts is a larger proportion of total compensation than in nonunion firms, and a substantially larger portion of total benefits is in the form of deferred payments that build up or become more valuable with seniority (e.g., pensions and health insurance).[38] Pay structures in unionized organizations are generally flatter than in nonunion firms, and the pay increase systems are most often based on job level and seniority, and less often on performance or other measures devised by management.[39] Wage practices in unionized organizations tend to be copied by nonunion organizations.[40] However, there is limited spillover of union wage gains to other employee groups within an organization.[41]

Turnover in union establishments is lower than in nonunion organizations, while internal mobility is greater.[42] Union contracts systematize the promotion process, with seniority usually playing a major role in promotion decisions. Thus, employees build up greater expected returns as they increase their length of service.

Unionized employees are older and more experienced, other things being equal, than their nonunion counterparts. Estimates indicate that human capital per worker (knowledges, skills, and abilities related to the job) is about 6 percent higher in unionized settings.[43] These effects indicate the production worker quality in union establishments is 11

---

[37] R. B. Freeman and J. L. Medoff, "The Impact of Collective Bargaining: Illusion or Reality?" in *U.S. Industrial Relations 1950–1980: A Critical Assessment*, eds. J. Stieber, R. B. McKersie, and D. Q. Mills (Madison, Wis.: Industrial Relations Research Association, 1981), pp. 47–98.

[38] R. B. Freeman, "The Effect of Unionism on Fringe Benefits," *Industrial and Labor Relations Review* 35 (1981), pp. 489–509.

[39] R. B. Freeman, "Union Wage Practices and Wage Dispersion within Establishments," *Industrial and Labor Relations Review* 36 (1982), pp. 3–21.

[40] S. Vroman, "The Direction of Wage Spillovers in Manufacturing," *Industrial and Labor Relations Review* 36 (1982), pp. 102–12.

[41] L. J. Solnick, "The Effect of Blue Collar Unions on White Collar Wages and Fringe Benefits," *Industrial and Labor Relations Review* 38 (1985), pp. 236–43.

[42] R. B. Freeman, "Individual Mobility and Union Voice in the Labor Market," *American Economic Review* 66 (1976), pp. 361–68; R. N. Block, "The Impact of Seniority Provisions on the Manufacturing Quit Rate," *Industrial and Labor Relations Review* 32 (1978), pp. 474–88; and C. A. Olson and C. J. Berger, "The Relationship between Seniority, Ability, and the Promotion of Union and Nonunion Workers," in *Advances in Industrial and Labor Relations*, vol. 1, eds. D. B. Lipsky and J. M. Douglas (Greenwich, Conn.: JAI Press, 1983), pp. 91–129.

[43] R. B. Freeman and J. L. Medoff, "The Impact of Collective Bargaining."

percent higher, while nonproduction worker quality is lower by 8 percent.[44] Unionized employees have higher productivity levels than their nonunion counterparts. A number of explanations may be offered. First, employers need to seek efficiency if they are paying higher wage rates. Second, if experience contributes to productivity, the lower turnover of unionized employers would contribute to productivity gains. Third, where wage increase systems are negotiated collectively and promotions are based on seniority, there is no motive on the part of an individual employee to withhold information or training from another employee because the two would not compete for the same job.

Despite these higher productivity levels, unionized firms are not as profitable as nonunion organizations. In large part this is because investments in capital in union organizations is greater, and the returns to greater productivity of employees do not entirely offset the costs of these increased investments.[45]

Effects on Employees

Unions particularly increase the pay levels of younger and less well educated employees. These higher pay levels are accompanied by a somewhat greater level of unemployment among younger and minority job seekers in areas where unions have established relatively high local pay levels.[46]

For applicants who do not initially obtain union employment, the passage of time makes union jobs less attractive since opportunities for promotion within bargaining units are at least partially related to seniority.[47] However, employers with represented work forces are no more likely than others to hire applicants who seem to be innately stable.[48] Lower turnover is also probably related to the fact that wage premiums for taking a unionized job are about 3 to 8 percent, but losses from leaving one are about 7 to 11 percent.[49]

---

[44] Ibid.

[45] R. S. Ruback and M. B. Zimmerman, "Unionization and Profitability: Evidence from Capital Markets," *Journal of Political Economy* 92 (1984), pp. 1134–57. For a comprehensive review of union effects on firm performance see B. E. Becker and C. A. Olson, "Labor Relations and Firm Performance" in *Human Resources and the Performance of the Firm*, eds. M. M. Kleiner, R. N. Block, M. Roomkin and S. W. Salsburg (Madison, Wis.: Industrial Relations Research Association, 1987), pp. 43–86.

[46] R. B. Freeman and J. L. Medoff, *What Do Unions Do?* (New York: Basic Books, 1984).

[47] J. S. Abowd and H. S. Farber, "Job Queues and the Union Status of Workers," *Industrial and Labor Relations Review* 36 (1983), pp. 354–67.

[48] R. B. Freeman, "The Effect of Unionism on Worker Attachment to Firms," *Journal of Labor Research* 1 (1980), pp. 29–61.

[49] J. D. Cunningham and E. Donovan, "Patterns of Union Membership and Relative Wages," *Journal of Labor Research* 7 (1986), pp. 127–44.

Layoff and discharge likelihoods are not changed by unionization,[50] but unionized employees who are laid off are much less likely to quit while awaiting recall than nonunion employees. Thus, in the absence of supplemental unemployment benefit packages, unionized employers have a cost advantage, since recall costs are lower due to fewer vacancies and training of new employees, which would result from quits. Management is provided an opportunity to store labor for future demand at relatively minimal costs.[51]

The satisfaction of unionized employees is not higher than that of nonunion employees, even though their wage levels are higher.[52] There may be two explanations for this phenomenon. First, union leaders might be expected to fan job dissatisfaction to increase member interests in negotiating improvements. Second, a recent poll found that employees are not dissatisfied with their jobs, but a substantial number are dissatisfied with their employers.[53] This is understandable if unions are a reaction to employer policies and practices that are opposite to employee desires.

Satisfied union members are also more likely to be satisfied with management, although the union is seen as more important among less satisfied employees.[54] Commitment to the union appears to be related, in order, to the following factors; loyalty, responsibility to the union, willingness to work for the union, and belief in unionism.[55] Commitment to the union and the employer has been demonstrated to be independent. Simultaneous (dual) commitment to the employer and the union has been found to be related to both individual differences,[56] and a positive labor relations climate.[57] Union stewards were found to have dual commitment, but generally higher commitment to the union than the employer.[58]

[50] Ibid.

[51] J. L. Medoff, "Layoffs and Alternatives under Trade Unions in U.S. Manufacturing," *American Economic Review* 69 (1979), pp. 380–95.

[52] C. J. Berger, C. A. Olson, and J. W. Boudreau, "Effects of Unions on Job Satisfaction: The Role of Work-Related Values and Perceived Rewards," *Organizational Behavior and Human Performance* 31 (1983), pp. 289–324.

[53] J. Hoerr, "Beyond Unions," *Business Week*, July 8, 1985, pp. 72–77.

[54] M. E. Gordon, J. W. Philpot, R. E. Burt, C. A. Thompson, and W. E. Spiller, "Commitment to the Union: Development of a Measure and an Examination of Its Correlates," *Journal of Applied Psychology* 65 (1980), pp. 479–99.

[55] R. T. Ladd, M. E. Gordon, L. L. Beauvais, and R. L. Morgan, "Union Commitment: Replication and Extension," *Journal of Applied Psychology* 67 (1982), pp. 640–44.

[56] C. V. Fukami and E. W. Larson, "Commitment to Company and Union: Parallel Models," *Journal of Applied Psychology* 69 (1984), pp. 367–71.

[57] H. L. Angle and J. L. Perry, "Dual Commitment and Labor-Management Climates," *Academy of Management Journal* 29 (1986), pp. 31–50.

[58] J. E. Martin, J. M. Magenau, and M. F. Peterson, "Variables Related to Patterns of Union Stewards' Commitment," *Journal of Labor Research* 7 (1986), pp. 323–36.

SUMMARY

Labor unions have existed in the United States for more than 200 years, but it is only since the 1930s that they have claimed a large membership and have bargained collectively in a relatively stable environment. Successful labor organizations in the United States have attended primarily to their members' needs and have not been overly concerned about taking a particular political approach. Basic overall goals of unions generally include the enhancement of their members' economic welfare and the security of their jobs.

Labor law plays an important part in the practice of collective bargaining. Most U.S. laws have their roots in the Depression and have been passed to facilitate collective bargaining and balance the powers of labor and management.

There are three basic levels of union organizations. The most powerful are the national unions, which charter and assist local unions and affiliate with the AFL–CIO. The local union handles grass-roots issues on a day-to-day basis and is probably the institution with which the union's members tend to identify themselves. The AFL–CIO is a voluntary federation of most of the country's national unions and broadly sets and communicates the policies of the labor movement.

Employees join unions because they see them as vehicles for accomplishing important objectives they consider unachievable otherwise. When employees organize, strategies and tactics of both employers and unions are aimed at communicating the advantages both groups see in their own preferred outcomes. If employees choose to be represented, the union then assumes the role of an agent in negotiating and administering provisions of employment relating to wages, hours and terms and conditions of employment.

DISCUSSION QUESTIONS

1. What do you think might be the advantages and disadvantages for labor organizations of becoming primarily a political movement, as opposed to remaining primarily concerned with bargaining terms and conditions of employment?

2. Under the rules of most national unions, local unions do not have the power to completely ratify contracts, call strikes, or engage in some other activities. What are the pros and cons of this structural arrangement?

3. Organizing campaigns are closely regulated by the NLRB. What are the possible consequences of a change in the NLRB policy to permit no-holds-barred campaigning?

4. Given that the impact of unions on organizations does not appear to be particularly negative, why do managements resist union organizing campaigns so strongly?

18

Labor-Management Relations

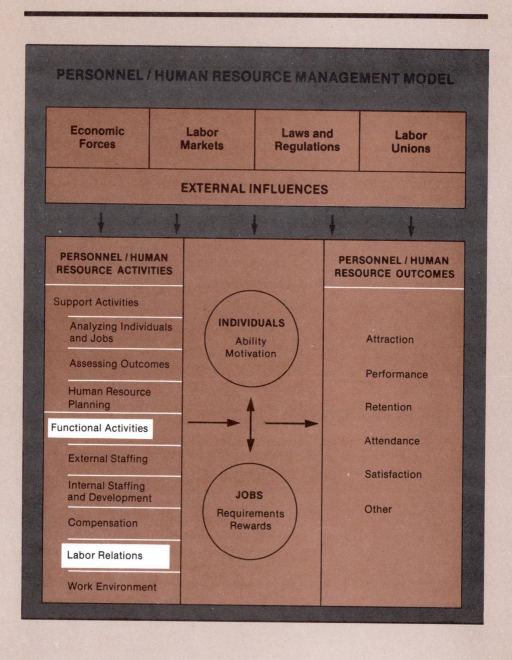

PERSONNEL / HUMAN RESOURCE MANAGEMENT MODEL

Economic Forces	Labor Markets	Laws and Regulations	Labor Unions

EXTERNAL INFLUENCES

PERSONNEL / HUMAN RESOURCE ACTIVITIES

Support Activities

Analyzing Individuals and Jobs

Assessing Outcomes

Human Resource Planning

Functional Activities

External Staffing

Internal Staffing and Development

Compensation

Labor Relations

Work Environment

INDIVIDUALS
Ability
Motivation

JOBS
Requirements
Rewards

PERSONNEL / HUMAN RESOURCE OUTCOMES

Attraction

Performance

Retention

Attendance

Satisfaction

Other

After reading this chapter you should be able to speak to the questions posed in each of the following personnel/human resource incidents:

1. As the personnel director of JB Truck Lines, a regional carrier based in Lake Dalton, Arkansas, you are preparing to negotiate a new contract for your truck drivers with their representatives, the International Brotherhood of Teamsters. The president, Merle C. Creeger, believes that substantial expansion of the business that he began by trucking hogs to markets in Memphis is possible because business activity in the area is increasing. However, it is likely that owner-operators might buy new equipment to compete with JB Lines if this happens. Meanwhile, the Teamsters are demanding a pay increase for the drivers now employed. You are considering asking the union to accept a two-tier wage system that will grant modest increases to present employees but will create a new entry-level wage about 40 percent below the present level. New drivers would probably require at least 10 years to make the wages of present drivers under the system. Although it would allow expansion and free up funds for pay increases, you are uncertain how to sell this to the union. What should your strategy be?

2. You are the regional personnel representative for the New England region of the Handy Andy convenience store chain. All of the stores are owned by the chain and managed by employees of the chain. Handy Andy has 20 stores in the Boston area. Employees in 12 of these stores are represented by a local of the United Food and Commercial Workers. There are about 80 convenience stores in the whole Boston area, and about 60 of these have represented employees. This morning you were approached by a representative from the Boston Convenience Retailers Aid Board who asked Handy Andy to join with other convenience stores in multiemployer bargaining with the UFCW during the next negotiations. Preliminary exploration with the UFCW reveals that they would not object to this arrangement. Should you join this multiemployer effort? What are the advantages and risks of taking this approach?

3. You are the vice president of industrial relations for the Gütwurst Sausage Company, a nationwide processor, packer, and marketer of processed meat products. Like the rest of the packing industry, price competition in sausage products has increased markedly over the past several years. Three years ago, when the last contract was negotiated with the Packinghouse Workers, a wage concession from $11 per hour to $9.25 was negotiated. Fringe benefit costs are worth an additional $3.10 per hour. Studies that your department has conducted

(continued)

with the finance department indicate that labor rates must be cut to $11 (wages and fringes) to remain competitive. Union members are still dissatisfied as the result of the last wage cut, and several union locals in your 20 plants have elected militant local leaders. You need the reduction in labor costs, but you want to avoid any bad publicity that could negatively influence the sale of your branded products, which make up more than 50 percent of Gütwurst's revenues. What type of package should you propose to the union? What do you think will be necessary to gain agreement on concessions of this magnitude? What other alternatives would you propose to management?

4.   You are a personnel analyst in the municipal employee relations department of a large southern city. Your supervisor, Sharon Guenther, has asked that you put together a proposal that would outline the type of program the city should provide to hear and act on the grievances of its employees, none of whom are presently organized. Where would you go for information? What has worked in other organizations? What pitfalls would you want to avoid?

The previous chapter dealt with the formation, evolution, and structure of labor unions, as well as the legal environment for labor relations. In this chapter, the ongoing collective bargaining relationship is explored. Although the P/HR model casts labor unions as an external influence, once collective bargaining has begun, both labor and management are affected by the labor market and the market for the goods and services produced by the employer. These external influences will be examined in their effects on the scope and outcome of the contract the parties negotiate. The parties are also governed in their relationship to laws and regulations. Just as these forbid labor and management from coercing or discriminating against employees in their involvement with or avoidance of labor organizations, they also regulate the conduct of collective bargaining. The outcome of negotiations is also influenced by the bargaining power of the parties, the manner in which bargaining between the parties is organized, and the issues each thinks are important in bargaining.

Negotiation and *administration* are the two activities that primarily occupy the parties in collective bargaining. The processes involved in preparing for negotiation, the costs associated with various contract demands, the tactics used in negotiating, and factors related to preferences of the parties will be examined. Administration involves the day-to-day management of the collective bargaining relationship. The means used to deal with disputes during the term of the contract will be examined.

Other issues that will be covered include procedures followed when the parties fail to agree on a contract (impasses) and when they disagree on contract interpretation. Although many organizations have substantial numbers of employees who are unorganized, they still pay attention to and adopt methods that are used in unionized organizations. Employee relations in nonunion firms will thus also be examined.

THE ENVIRONMENT FOR BARGAINING

Products and services are created by combining raw materials, capital, and labor. The demand for them is derived from the final demand for the products and services. If labor were to become more productive (perhaps through additional training) while equipment prices remained the same, an employer would substitute labor for capital. Where labor costs increase or capital prices decline, capital will be substituted for labor. When the prices of products and services decline, the amount of labor, capital, and raw materials that can be purchased with the sales revenue also declines.

Wages are influenced both by the demand for products and services and by the relative factor prices included within these products and services. Recent changes in the structure of product and service markets have had a major effect on revenue and profit levels of some employers and the wage levels of both unionized and nonunion employees. Three of these changes are examined next. They will be followed with an examination of the effects of legal requirements, bargaining power, and bargaining structure.

Deregulation

Major changes have occurred in the structure of the airline, trucking, and telecommunications industries over the 1980s as a result of legal deregulation. Before a relaxation in regulations, tariffs and prices were regulated by federal agencies (Civil Aeronautics Board and Interstate Commerce Commission). Besides the regulation of prices, permission to serve particular geographical areas was allocated to only a few transportation companies. Thus, an air traveler or a shipper might have only two or three choices of carriers between, say, St. Louis and Louisville, at a fixed price from each. A transportation company seeking to serve this route would have to secure government permission before beginning operations. For those firms serving a particular route, price competition was impossible, so they needed to distinguish themselves in such other areas as schedules, food services, and so on.

Following deregulation, new firms entered the market, and both new and existing firms could choose which routes they intended to serve. This meant several new competitors on routes that had been highly profitable to the previous permission holders. The new entrants frequently hired employees at lower wage rates than their previously regulated competitors who had had little motivation to hold down wage costs, since they could not previously compete on price. Suppose total costs of a 1,000-mile airline flight were $5,000 for fuel, $2,500 for labor, and $2,500 for the interest and debt retirement on capital. If 80 passengers took the flight at a price of $150 per ticket before deregulation, the total cost would be $10,000, the total revenue would be $12,000, and the profit would be $2,000 per flight. Now suppose that after deregulation two discount carriers begin flying the same route. The previously regulated carrier has to cut ticket prices to $120 to remain competitive. If the fuel, labor, and capital costs remain at $10,000, the carrier will lose $400 per flight at this ticket rate unless ridership increases. Fuel and capital prices are outside the carrier's control; thus labor costs must be reduced or the run abandoned, unless ridership increases substantially. Labor and management must bargain over labor cost control and reduction to meet deregulation effects.

Foreign Competition

Basic industries have been dominated historically by a small number of domestic producers. For example, American Motors, Chrysler, Ford, and General Motors produced essentially all of the passenger vehicles sold in the United States before 1960. To the extent that their prices were essentially similar, consumers could only choose between them based on product attributes. In the late 1950s foreign producers began to introduce vehicles that were smaller than any produced by domestic manufacturers. When the vehicle market swung toward models of this size, domestic manufacturers found themselves in a competitive market, both on product attributes and price. Then, in the early 1980s, as the U.S. dollar appreciated against foreign currencies, relative costs of imported goods decreased. To continue to compete, labor costs needed to be reduced. Pay concessions in the steel and auto industry are typical of those negotiated as a result of foreign competition.

Nonunion Entries

Other industries have seen a major influx of new domestic producers who have been able to compete on both labor and capital costs. This is perhaps most apparent in the meat-packing industry wherein large, heavily concentrated processors have essentially vanished. These have been supplanted by smaller nonunion processors who offer lower wages and more services to wholesalers. By having more custom cutting done at the packing plant, supermarket chains can reduce their butcher labor costs—even though they pay more for the finished cut. For example, assume that a 400-pound side of beef cost a supermarket $500 from a large unionized supplier and $490 from a smaller nonunion supplier. There would be a natural tendency to prefer the smaller supplier. However, assume further that there is another $100 in labor costs for eight hours work by butchers for the grocer to divide the side into retail cuts. If the packing plant would do half of this at $36 (nonunion) or $48 (union), the cost differential favoring the nonunion operation spreads from $10 per side to $22. To continue to compete, the union operation must cut costs.

FIGURE 18–1

Sequence of Business Strategy Decisions Affected by Product Market Change

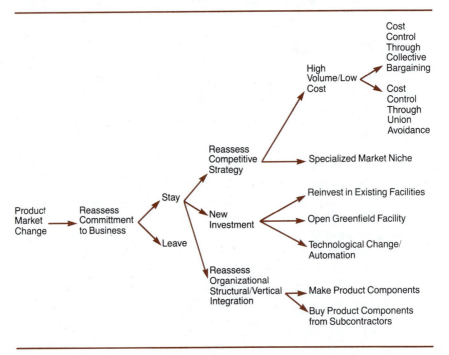

Source: T. A. Kochan, H. C. Katz, and R. B. McKersie, *The Transformation of American Industrial Relations* (New York: Basic Books, 1986), p. 66.

Besides nonunion entries, some organizations have expanded policies or objectives to reduce the proportion of their employees who are unionized.[1] By reducing investment in unionized plants and opening or expanding nonunion operations, the employer reduces the proportion of production that is paid through negotiated wage rates and that might be vulnerable to strikes. An organization makes a variety of assessments about its environment and product market in formulating a strategy. As Figure 18–1 shows, some of the choices of a strategy to pursue involve collective bargaining approaches or union avoidance, plant and equipment investment decisions, and making components or purchasing them from suppliers.[2] All of these influence the bargaining power of the employer as is noted later.

[1] A. Freedman, *The New Look in Wage Policy and Employee Relations* (New York: Conference Board, 1985), pp. 5–6.

[2] T. A. Kochan, H. C. Katz, and R. B. McKersie, *The Transformation of American Industrial Relations* (New York: Basic Books, 1986), pp. 65–75.

Legal Requirements to Bargain

Under federal labor law, private-sector employers whose employees are represented and unions who are their bargaining agents are required to meet at reasonable times and places to negotiate and administer agreements that cover wages, hours, and terms and conditions of employment. This means that an employer with represented employees may not unilaterally change employment aspects in any of these mandatory areas. Employers and unions cannot refuse to discuss these issues with their opposite numbers either before or during a contract period. The law does not require, however, that they reach an agreement regarding any of these issues. Figure 18–2 lists many of the bargaining issues that have been held by the courts and the NLRB to be mandatory for bargaining when raised by either party.

Bargaining Power

Bargaining power influences the shape of the final contract and might be conceived of as "my costs of disagreeing on your terms relative to my cost of agreeing on your terms."[3] For example, where costs cannot be easily passed on to consumers, the cost of a 5 percent wage increase might lead to a 10 percent reduction in total revenues or the erosion of the profit margin necessary for survival. An employer in this situation would have great bargaining power. On the other hand, suppose there was company resistance to a 5 percent wage increase. If resistance would cause a strike and enable competitors to capture market share sufficient to erode profits, and if such erosion would more than equal the cost of the 5 percent increase, the company would have little bargaining power.

Bargaining power is influenced by the perishability of products (food, travel, etc.) that would not be produced if a strike occurred, the timing of a strike (turkey processors before Thanksgiving), the production technology (automated phone service), the availability of substitutes (nonpublic secondary education), and the availability of striker replacements (skill and training required as well as labor market conditions).

Bargaining Structure

Bargaining outcomes are also influenced by the scope and level of the parties to the bargaining process. Smaller employers within a given industry in a particular geographical area will often bargain together with

---

[3] N. W. Chamberlain and D. E. Cullen, *The Labor Sector*, 2d ed. (New York: McGraw-Hill, 1971), p. 227.

FIGURE 18–2

Items Mandatory for Bargaining

Wages
Hours
Discharge
Arbitration
Holidays—paid
Vacations—paid
Duration of agreement
Grievance procedure
Layoff plan
Reinstatement of economic strikers
Change of payment from hourly base to
    salary base
Union security and checkoff
Work rules
Merit wage increase
Work schedule
Lunch periods
Rest periods
Pension plan
Retirement age
Bonus payments
Price of meals provided by company
Group insurance—health, accident, life
Promotions
Seniority
Layoffs
Transfers
Work assignments and transfers
No-strike clause
Piece rates
Stock purchase plan
Workloads
Change of employee status to indepen-
    dent contractors
Motor carrier—union agreement provid-
    ing that carriers use own equipment
    before leasing outside equipment
Overtime pay
Agency shop
Sick leave
Employers insistence on clause giving
    arbitrator right to enforce award

Management rights clause
Cancellation of seniority upon relocation
    of plant
Discounts on company products
Shift differentials
Contract clause providing for supervisors
    keeping seniority in unit
Procedures for income tax withholding
Severance pay
Nondiscriminatory hiring hall
Plant rules
Safety
Prohibition against supervisor doing unit
    work
Superseniority for union stewards
Checkoff
Partial plant closing
Hunting on employer forest reserve
    where previously granted
Plant closedown and relocation
Change in operations resulting in re-
    classifying workers from incentive to
    straight time, or cut work force, or in-
    stallation of cost-saving machine
Plant closing
Job-posting procedures
Plant reopening
Employee physical examination
Union security
Bargaining over "bar list"
Truck rentals—minimum rental to be paid
    by carriers to employee-owned vehi-
    cles
Musician price lists
Arrangement for negotiation
Change in insurance carrier and benefits
Profit sharing plan
Company houses
Subcontracting
Discriminatory racial policies
Production ceiling imposed by union
Most favored national clause
Vended food products

Source: R. Richardson, "Positive Collective Bargaining," in *ASPA Handbook of Personnel and Industrial Relations,* eds. D. Yoder and H. G. Heneman, Jr., (Washington, D.C.: Bureau of National Affairs, 1979), pp. 7–120—7–121.

a single union. For example, grocery stores in a large city may form a *multiemployer bargaining unit* to contract with meat cutters represented by the United Food and Commercial Workers. The rationale behind this coalition formation is that the costs of the wage increase may be passed through to consumers simultaneously. Stores will not have to compete based on labor cost differentials per job. Wages have thus been taken out of competition for the union.

Occasionally, industrywide bargaining also occurs. For example, Trucking Management, Inc. negotiates a national master freight agreement between employers it represents and the Teamsters Union. The Bituminous Coal Operators Association negotiates a contract with the United Mine Workers. However, these industrywide contracts, as well as companywide contracts, have begun to disappear as wage-job security issues peculiar to particular plant locations have become more important to both unions and employers. However, where the union expects to get trade-offs in return for concessions, negotiations still tend to take place at a companywide level.[4]

ISSUES IN BARGAINING

Bargaining issues can be divided into wage and nonwage categories. Both have economic consequences. The following sections detail types and prevalence of issues.

Wage Issues in Bargaining

Wage issues affect one or more of the characteristics of pay: level, structure, form, or system.[5] Figure 18–3 shows the recent prevalence of several economic issue clauses in labor contracts.

Pay level issues

Pay level issues require that the union or employer choose a comparison organization or occupation whose pay is to be imitated. As was noted in the bargaining structure section, imitation was more frequent in the past. As Figure 18–4 shows, the primary influences on wage-bargaining targets of employers would include industry patterns, productivity or

---

[4] P. Cappelli, "Concession Bargaining and the National Economy," *Proceedings of the Industrial Relations Research Association* 35 (1982), pp. 362–71.

[5] H. G. Heneman III and D. P. Schwab, "Work and Rewards Theory," in *ASPA Handbook of Personnel and Industrial Relations*, eds. D. Yoder and H. G. Heneman, Jr. (Washington, D.C.: Bureau of National Affairs, 1979), pp. 6–1—6–2.

FIGURE 18–3

Basic Wage Clauses in Contracts (1986)

Clause	Percent Containing Clause
Insurance	
Accidental death and dismemberment	74
Dental care	79
Doctors' visits	54
Hospitalization	79
Life	96
Long-term disability	21
Major medical	74
Maternity benefits	54
Miscellaneous medical expenses	61
Optical care	40
Prescription drugs	35
Sickness and accident	83
Surgical	77
Pensions	
Early retirement	98
Noncontributory plans	95
Some provision	99
Income maintenance	
Severance pay	41
Some provision	52
Supplemental unemployment benefits	16
Wages	
Deferred increases	80
Cost-of-living adjustments	38
Wage reopeners	10
Shift differentials	86
Incentive plans	33
Job classification procedures	57
Hiring rates	15
Wage progression	42
Two-tier structure	17

Source: *Collective Bargaining Negotiation and Contracts* (Washington, D.C. Bureau of National Affairs, updated as necessary).

labor-cost trends in the company, expected profitability of the company, and local labor market conditions and wage rates. Companies that have a master contract covering several operations are somewhat more concerned with labor cost trends and less concerned with local labor market conditions.[6]

---

[6] Freedman, *New Look in Wage Policy,* p. 10.

FIGURE 18-4

Most Important Influences on Wage and Benefit Targets, by Industry

Factor	Manufacturing	Utilities	Transportation and Communication	Trade
	100%*	100%*	100%*	100%*
Industry patterns	18	25	26	4
Productivity or labor-cost trends in this company	20	14	30	24
Expected profits of this company	18	11	17	28
Local labor-market conditions and wage rates	20	17	9	12
Internal (company) wage patterns (historical)	7	11	—	4
Influence of this settlement on other wage settlements and/or nonunion wage levels	2	6	—	8
Consumer price index increases	2	8	4	4
Potential losses from a strike	4	—	4	8
Major union settlements in other industries	3	3	4	—
National labor market conditions and wage rates	6	6	4	—
Internal (company) benefit patterns (historical)	—	—	—	8

* Details do not add to 100 percent because of rounding.

Source: A Freedman, *The New Look in Wage Policy and Employee Relations* (New York: Conference Board, 1985), p. 10.

Pay structure issues

Pay structure is an important issue for both the employer and the union. Structural differences are often necessary to attract and retain employees in jobs with greater demands, an issue of concern to employers. Union members also have beliefs about the relative worth of jobs and may form political coalitions if they believe the contract does not equitably reward groups to which they belong. Contract settlements often include across-the-board, cents per hour increases. These compress the pay structure over time by reducing the relative pay differentials between jobs. Comparable worth (see Chapter 14) is an emerging collective bargaining issue that seeks to rearrange the structure of pay for jobs dominated by women as compared with those of men. Strikes (see Illustration 18-1) and union-sponsored litigation make this an important

ILLUSTRATION 18–1

Strike over "Comparable Worth" Ends

What was perhaps the first strike in U.S. history over the "comparable worth" approach to ending unwarranted pay disparities between men and women has ended. A two-year agreement between 2,000 members of (AFSCME) Local 101 and the city of San Jose, California, provided for a $1.5-million fund to be used to narrow such unwarranted pay differences. Also, employees are to receive a 7.5 percent salary increase effective immediately, and an 8 percent increase in 1982.

The comparable worth theory contends that "traditional" female jobs generally pay less than "traditional" male jobs, even if the jobs are of comparable worth to society. The controversy was accelerated when a city-initiated study indicated that the city's female employees were generally paid less than the male employees holding jobs of comparable worth. The comparisons were made by assigning "grade points" to jobs, based on the "know-how, accountability, problem solving, and working conditions" involved.

San Jose Mayor Janet Gray Hayes backed the special pay adjustment for women, calling comparable worth "the new civil rights issue . . . the woman's issue of the 1980s." Hayes said that the weeklong strike had started because the union wanted the city council to make spending commitments extending beyond the council's term of office. The union had been seeking a total commitment of $3.2 million for pay adjustments over a four-year period.

Source: "Developments in Labor Relations," *Monthly Labor Review*, September 1981, p. 51.

issue for unions representing largely female constituencies in bargaining units where several job classifications are represented.

Substantial differences exist in pay and job structure approaches by employers as compared to the 1970s. For example, in one study of a company with both union and nonunion plants, the new nonunion plants had only 6 job classifications as compared to 96 in the union plants, 7 wage grades as compared to 14, and 1 maintenance class as compared to 11.[7] More employers are also attempting to negotiate skill-based pay plans in which employees are not paid according to job classification but in relation to the numbers and types of skills they have learned and can demonstrate. These methods enhance the flexibility of the employer in responding to changing product mixes and schedules.[8]

---

[7] A. Verma, "Union and Nonunion Industrial Relations at the Plant Level." Unpublished doctoral dissertation, Sloan School of Management, Massachusetts Institute of Technology, 1983.

[8] Kochan et al., *Transformation of Industrial Relations*, pp. 96–106.

Pay form

In the past, the choice of specific benefits was generally left up to the union once the total size of an economic settlement had been reached. The rationale for this was that the union should be expected to know the preferences of its membership, and its structuring of the package should improve chances for ratification.

However, this has now changed, since often benefit levels rather than contributions are specified in the contract. This leads to potential unknowns in costs. For example, health insurance premiums are largely out of the control of the employer so that a benefit that might cost $150 per employee per month at the beginning of a contract could conceivably increase by two thirds during the life of the agreement. Benefits that are tied to seniority escalate in cost as a work force matures and larger proportions of employees become entitled to a specific benefit.

Pay system

In unionized organizations, changes in pay are most frequently determined by seniority and job level. Other methods that are used include incentive pay systems, cost-of-living increases based on changes in the consumer price index, and supplementary unemployment benefits. All of these are subjects of bargaining.

Union effects on pay

Other things held equal, unions appear to have effects on the level, structure, form, and system of pay. In terms of pay level, there have been wide swings in the degree to which unionized workers (relative to nonunion ones) are paid a premium ranging from a high of 46 percent in the early 1930s to a low of 2 percent in the late 1940s.[9] Premiums were greater during recessions and narrowed during inflation due to the rigidity of rates in long-term contracts.[10] The effects of wage gains are substantially greater for increased unionization within an industry than for increased unionization within an occupation. The size of industrial effects is inversely related to the level of competition in the industry, while occupational effects are most pronounced through increased union

---

[9] G. Johnson, "Changes over Time in the Union/Nonunion Wage Differential in the United States." Unpublished paper, University of Michigan, February 1981, Table 2.

[10] D. J. B. Mitchell, *Unions, Wages, and Inflation* (Washington, D.C.: Brookings Institution, 1980), pp. 80–83.

representation at the local labor market level.[11] A variety of effects of unions on pay level occur, with the advantage going to individuals who have less education, are nonwhite, younger or older, male, short tenure, transport operatives, and laborers.[12] Evidence also finds that becoming unionized, remaining unionized, or becoming employed in unionized organizations is associated with higher wages.[13] There is also evidence that wage gains in the union sector tend to "spill over" (cause) subsequent increases in the nonunion sector of the same industries.[14] The role

FIGURE 18-5
Recent Evidence on Union/Nonunion Differences in Pay

Compensation	Finding
Wage rates	All else (measurable) the same, union/nonunion hourly wage differential is between 10 percent and 20 percent.
Fringes	All else the same, union/nonunion hourly fringe differential is between 20 percent and 30 percent. The fringe share of compensation is higher at a given level of compensation.
Wage dispersion	Wage inequality is much lower among union members than among comparable nonmembers, and total wage dispersion appears to be lowered by unionism.
Wage structure	Wage differentials between workers who are different in terms of race, age, service, skill level, and education appear to be lower under collective bargaining
Cyclical responsiveness of wage rates	Union wages are less responsive to labor market conditions than nonunion wages.
Determinants of compensation differential	Other things equal, the union compensation advantage is higher the greater the percent of a market's workers who are organized. The effects of market concentration on wage differentials is unclear. The differentials appear to be very large in some regulated markets. They appear to decline as firm size increases.

Source: R. B. Freeman and J. L. Medoff, "The Impact of Collective Bargaining: Illusion or Reality?" in *U.S. Industrial Relations 1950–1980: A Critical Assessment*, eds. J. Stieber, R. B. McKersie, and D. Q. Mills (Madison, Wis.: Industrial Relations Research Association, 1981), p. 50.

---

[11] W. J. Moore, R. J. Newman, and J. Cunningham, "The Effect of the Extent of Unionism on Union and Nonunion Wages," *Journal of Labor Research* 6 (1985), pp. 21–44.

[12] R. B. Freeman and J. L. Medoff, *What Do Unions Do?* (New York: Basic Books, 1984), p. 49.

[13] Ibid., pp. 46–47.

[14] S. Vroman, "The Direction of Wage Spillovers in Manufacturing," *Industrial and Labor Relations Review* 36 (1982), pp. 102–12.

of unions can also be to raise wages from a below-average position to one of equivalence with others.[15] A study of wage levels in firms that faced an organizing drive found that pay levels in the year subsequent to the drive were higher than a control group that saw no union activity. Firms in which organizing activity took place had pay levels lower than those that did not before the drive began.[16]

Pay structures in unionized organizations are generally flatter than their nonunion counterparts by about 22 percent.[17] One of the areas in which unions appear to have the greatest influence is pay form. The proportion of wages going to benefits is higher in unionized organizations, with the greatest preferences for insurance, pay for time not worked, overtime premiums, and pensions.[18] In the pay system area, unionized organizations use fewer performance-based pay plans and more pay plans with automatic increases tied to job level and seniority changes.[19] A summary of the effects is shown in Figure 18–5.

Nonwage Bargaining Issues

Noneconomic issues deal with hours and terms and conditions of employment. Seniority is highly involved with some issues, and others are aimed at restricting management's authority to make decisions on certain work-related issues. The relative prevalence of noneconomic issues in recent contracts is shown in Figure 18–6.

Job security

Many contracts provide increased "ownership" in employment as the individual gains seniority. When layoffs occur, the most senior employees are retained in their jobs. When everyone in a given job would be laid off, employees with higher seniority than persons in other jobs may be given a chance to *bump* if they are qualified for the jobs to which they wish to move.

---

[15] See O. Ashenfelter and G. E. Johnson, "Unionism, Relative Wages, and Labor Quality in U.S. Manufacturing Industries," *International Economic Review* 13 (1972), pp. 488–507.

[16] R. B. Freeman and M. M. Kleiner, "The Impact of New Unionization on Wages and Working Conditions: A Longitudinal Study of Establishments under NLRB Elections," *Journal of Labor Economics*, in press.

[17] R. B. Freeman, "Union Wage Practices and Wage Dispersion within Establishments," *Industrial and Labor Relations Review* 36 (1982), pp. 3–21.

[18] R. B. Freeman, "The Effect of Unionism on Fringe Benefits," *Industrial and Labor Relations Review* 34 (1981), pp. 489–509.

[19] Freeman, "Union Wage Practices."

FIGURE 18–6

Basic Nonwage Clauses in Contracts (1986)

Clause	Percent containing clause	Clause	Percent containing clause
Contract term		*Layoff, rehiring, and work sharing*	
1 year	3	Seniority as criterion	89
2 years	13	Seniority as sole factor	49
3 years	79	Notice to employees required	50
4 or more years	5	No minimum	6
Contract reopeners	14	1–2 days	22
Automatic renewal	86	3–4 days	15
Discipline and discharge		5–6 days	17
General grounds for discharge	94	7 or more	16
Specific grounds for discharge	74	Bumping permitted	60
Grievance and arbitration		Manufacturing contracts	74
Steps specified	99	Nonmanufacturing contracts	39
Arbitration as final step	99	Recall	82
Hours and overtime		Work sharing	18
Daily work schedules	83	*Leaves of absence*	
Weekly work schedules	60	Personal	72
Overtime premiums	96	Union	77
Daily overtime	93	Maternity	36
Sixth day premiums	24	Funeral	84
Seventh day premiums	26	Civic	82
Pyramiding of overtime		Paid sick	28
prohibited	64	Unpaid sick	52
Distribution of overtime work	68	Military	72
Acceptance of overtime	25	*Management and union rights*	
Restrictions on overtime	38	Management rights statement	100
Weekend premiums	70	Restrictions on management	89
Lunch, rest, and cleanup	60	Subcontracting	54
Waiting time entails	20	Supervisory work	59
Standby time	5	Technological change	25
Travel time	23	Plant shutdown or relocation	26
Voting time	7	In-plant union representation	55
Holidays		Union access to plant	56
None specified	1	Union bulletin boards	69
Less than 7	2	Union right to information	71
7, 7½	6	Union activity on company time	36
8, 8½	8	Union-management cooperation	45
9, 9½	9	*Seniority*	
10, 10½	23	Probationary periods at hire	82
11, 11½	18	Loss of seniority	80
12 or more	33	Seniority lists	69
Eligibility for holiday pay	86	As factor in promotions	73

FIGURE 18–6   *(concluded)*

Clause	Percent containing clause	Clause	Percent containing clause
Seniority (cont.)		*Vacations*	
As factor in transfers	53	Three weeks or more	89
Status of supervisors	31	Four weeks or more	84
		Five weeks or more	62
Strikes and lockouts		Six weeks or more	22
Unconditional pledges (strikes)	59	Based on service	90
Unconditional pledge (lockouts)	66	Work requirement for eligibility	50
Limitation of union liability	39	Vacation scheduling by	
Penalties for strikers	40	management	87
Picket line observance	28	*Working conditions and safety*	
		Occupational safety and health	84
Union security		Hazardous work acceptance	26
Union shop	60	Safety and health committees	49
Modified union shop	14	Safety equipment provided	44
Agency shop	10	*Guarantees against discrimination*	
Maintenance of membership	4	Guarantees mentioned	96
Hiring provisions	25	EEO pledges	18
Checkoff	90		

Source: *Collective Bargaining Negotiation and Contracts*, 1986 data.

Seniority also usually entitles one to have first choice on movement to jobs with greater responsibility and higher pay or to jobs with more desirable characteristics, such as type of effort and shift assignment.

Hours of work

One of the earliest issues unions fought for was a shorter workday and workweek. There are two obvious reasons for this position. First, employee fatigue and lack of leisure time helped foster unionization. Second, shorter hours for present employees may require an employer to hire more people to get out the work. This increases employment and expands union membership. Ironically, although employees are generally in favor, unions have opposed innovative work schedules such as the four-day 40-hour week and the three-day 36-hour week.[20] It is probably

---

[20] See, for example, J. L. Pierce, J. W. Newstrom, R. B. Dunham and A. E. Barber, *Alternative Work Schedules* (Boston: Allyn and Bacon, 1989); and H. R. Northrup, J. T. Wilson, and K. M. Rose, "The 12–Hour Shift in the Petroleum and Chemical Industries," *Industrial and Labor Relations Review* 32 (1979), pp. 312–36.

difficult to argue that long days are fatiguing but then later agree to go to long days and a short week.[21]

Unions have often introduced contract clauses to penalize employers for scheduling overtime by requiring premiums greater than (or earlier than) those required by law, such as double the pay for weekend work. They have also gotten employers to agree that mandatory overtime cannot exceed a certain number of hours in a given week.

Shift pay differentials are usually paid to employees who work outside of the day shift. Entitlement to certain shift schedules may be based on seniority.

A current major issue in hours of work relates to pay for time not worked. Most contracts provide that vacation time increases as seniority builds up. More senior work forces accumulate a great deal of vacation. Contracts that provide for paid time off become expensive to employers. Considering that 2,080 hours (52 40-hour weeks) is the normal work year, if an employee were to receive 10 holidays, 10 paid personal holidays, 5 sick days, and 4 weeks of vacation, 360 paid hours would not be worked. This is more than 15 percent of the total available. This is a major reason contract concessions frequently include "givebacks" in this area.

Management and union rights

Management rights clauses seek to retain unilateral control for management in some mandatory bargaining issue areas. These might include such things as retaining the ability to subcontract at will, the right to introduce technological changes that might have an impact on employment, the right to allow supervisors to perform work of union employees in certain situations, and the right to decide when and at what volume to operate.

Clauses also recognize the right of the union to represent employees, to assign stewards who have some freedom to investigate problems, to have access to broad areas of the plant, and to provide information to employees. Union security issues (see Chapter 17) are also covered within this area.

Discipline and discharge

Usually, the management rights clause retains for management the authority to impose discipline for work-related offenses. Management

---

[21] Northrup et al., "The 12-Hour Shift."

also retains the right to make reasonable rules for workplace conduct and to take action on violations. Management is expected, however, to be consistent in the application of discipline, across persons and infractions.

Grievance procedures

Grievance procedures specify the rights of union members if they believe the contract has been violated. Several steps for the resolution of grievances are provided with the ultimate step most often involving binding arbitration. These procedures usually require that each step be handled within a specified length of time. It is the union's responsibility to pursue a grievance if it believes a contract violation has occurred.

Contracts often contain no-strike clauses. This means that the union agrees to forego its right to strike during the agreement. The clause is the quid pro quo for binding arbitration as a final step in the grievance process.

THE NEGOTIATING PROCESS

The negotiating process requires preparing demands and offers by both parties, deciding what strategies and tactics to use, and convincing the parties being represented (labor and management) that a proposed agreement should be ratified rather than having a strike. Contract cost estimates play an important role in virtually all stages of the process.

Preparation for Negotiations

Federal law requires employers and unions to notify each other and the Federal Mediation and Conciliation Service within a 60-day period before the end of an agreement if they intend to negotiate changes. The laws also require the parties to meet at reasonable times and places and to bargain in good faith toward an agreement. The ambiguity of the term *good faith* is both a curse and a blessing. It would be almost impossible to define, a priori, what constitutes good faith bargaining; but at the same time, the looseness of the definition has allowed parties to implement innovative bargaining processes with little fear that they would be held to be illegal *per se*. Current interpretations of good faith depend on the "totality of conduct" of the parties rather than on isolated practices.

Bargaining preparation varies substantially among organizations, being more thorough as the size of the organization (both management and union) and the length of the bargaining relationship increase. Management does not want to be "surprised" by an unforeseen union demand,

FIGURE 18-7

Management Planning for Negotiations

	8 to 12 Months before Contract Expires	4 to 8 Months	1 to 4 Months Prior to Commencement of Negotiations	During Negotiations	Postnegotiations
Local unit management	1. Assigns responsibilities for community surveys estimating union demands and employee attitude. 2. Assesses the total corporate community and union compensation/benefit plans. 3. Assesses union/employee motivation and goals for impending negotiations.	1. Develops with division management, corporate E.R., and corporate insurance to project alternate benefit proposals that are to be designed and costed. 2. Continues all steps in the planning process.	1. Secures division approval of strategy, negotiating plans, and cost estimates	1. Continues negotiations, clears significant cost variances from plan with division management. 2. Integrates benefit negotiations with all other items. 3. Secures agreement in accord with plan. 4. Agrees with union on method and expense to inform employees of new contract terms.	1. Evaluates previous negotiations against plan within 30 days. 2. Assigns responsibilities for the planning process so as to integrate with the division's plans. 3. Identifies tentative objectives for next contract. 4. Completes wage/benefit adjustment form.
Division headquarters management	1. Assures local unit is preparing for negotiations. 2. Plans through annual financial plan to project impact of inventory buildup, possible settlement costs, etc. 3. Identifies internal responsibilities and relationships (corporate, law, E.R., insurance, benefits, etc.). 4. Keeps corporate employee relations informed.	1. Coordinates the development of strategy and negotiating plan, consulting with corporate employee relations and benefits. 2. Develops with local management, corporate E.R., and insurance to project alternative benefit proposals that are to be designed and costed. 3. Makes broad judgment on impact on company of expected proposals in relation to division and corporate goals, strategy, and plans. 4. Evaluates plans to control costs and deviations from plan/strategy.	1. Approves negotiating plan strategy. 2. Clears benefit and corporate policy variances from plan with corporate employee relations. 3. Communicates progress to senior management and corporate employee relations. 4. Approves cost variances from plan. 5. Identifies strike issues.	1. Provides—in addition to those points in "1 to 4 months" column—identification of "end" position and supports local negotiators in maintaining such position.	1. Evaluates all aspects of the previous negotiations within 45 days. 2. Identifies and communicates all long-range needs to executive management and corporate employee relations. 3. Integrates planning process in the division of growth plan.

Corporate employee relations	1. Advises division and local management of union's national position on economics, benefits, and other issues. 2. Counsels on any anticipated conflict with corporate policy, other divisions, etc. 3. Provides available historical information pertinent to planning.	1. Assists division, local management, and corporate insurance in projecting and preparing alternate benefit proposals that are to be designed and costed. 2. Keeps division and local unit informed of any external developments having impact on its planning.	1. Consults with division on strategy and plans; available for on-the-scene assistance or to consult with international union officers; recommends corporate point of view on issues. 2. Approves all variances from corporate personnel policy and benefit plan proposals. 3. Assures that all issues are resolved at the required levels.	1. Provides same as "1 to 4 months" column. 2. Identifies to division management potential problems having corporate impact; if necessary, advises corporate management of unresolved major issues.	1. Counsels with union and/or unit management on negotiating experiences and/or evaluation of new contract. 2. Informs other units of results. 3. Initiates needed objectives for study policy change or corporate decision.
Corporate law department	1. Counsels on request.	1. Counsels on request and reviews current contract as required. 2. Approves benefit plan drafts to assure legal compliance.	1. Counsels and drafts contract language on request. 2. Makes counsel available to review contract language before signing.	1. Provides same as "1 to 4 months" column.	1. Reviews new contracts for possible problems; advises division and corporate employee relations.

Source: A. Freedman, *Managing Labor Relations* (New York: The Conference Board, 1979), p. 24.

so it analyzes union responses to the present agreement expressed in the form of grievances, issues lost or modified at the last negotiation by the union, and the patterns of settlements won elsewhere in the industry or the economy in general.[22] Figure 18–7 shows a fairly complex timetable of duties and responsibilities for one management team before negotiations.

To prepare for bargaining sessions, unions hold membership meetings to incorporate demands for changes made by individuals or groups. Since the union is a political organization, the leadership is expected to be responsive to its members and incorporate their expressed preferences in the union's demands.

Strategies and Tactics

As bargaining begins, the side proposing the negotiations (usually the union) generally presents its demands first. The other side (usually management) responds by communicating its initial position and rationale for taking that approach. Many demands made by the union are not anticipated to become part of the agreement but may be used to trade off for other issues later. These indicate to management what is becoming important to the union or represent individual worker demands included to satisfy the political advocacy role requirement of the union. As negotiations continue, certain issues may be decided and positions initialed, and both parties may modify their positions. It is customary that once a position has been modified, the party stating a modification will not retreat to an earlier position at a later time.

During the negotiations, there may be table pounding and stubborn remarks. There may also be examples of cooperation and compliments for an opponent. Information on bargaining positions is shared, particularly where one side or another is adamant in adhering to a particular bargaining position. Figure 18–8 contains examples of seemingly stubborn and apparently cooperative behavior. These examples of negotiator behavior are directed at influencing the attitudes of the opponents toward the negotiator or the bargaining position represented by the negotiator. Illustration 18–2 is an excerpt of the IUE's opening statement in the 1982 GE negotiations. Note the conciliatory and firm nature of the statement at different points.

---

[22] See A. Freedman, *Managing Labor Relations* (New York: Conference Board, 1979); and M. S. Ryder, C. M. Rehmus, and S. Cohen, *Management Preparation for Collective Bargaining* (Homewood, Ill.: Dow Jones-Irwin, 1966).

FIGURE 18–8

Examples of Attitudinal Structuring in Bargaining

Deemphasizing Differences

"Who won?" was the question as the two parties proceeded to the next room for the formal announcement and picture taking (after the completion of the 1955 Ford Motor–UAW negotiations). "We both won," Reuther replied. "We are extremely happy to announce that we have arrived at an agreement. . . . Both the company and the union have worked very hard and very sincerely at the bargaining table."

Source: B. M. Selekman, S. K. Selekman, and S. H. Fuller, *Problems in Labor Relations*, 2d ed. (New York: McGraw-Hill, 1956), pp. 428–29.

Conferring Status on Opponent

Management negotiators speaking to a mediator: "They love to have these things (negotiations) go on till say 12 o'clock Saturday and then have a meeting in union hall at 12:15 Saturday. And they stroll in there and get up on stage, you know, all sleepy-eyed from being up late that night. They were really pooped, and they looked worse than they were. These people just ate it up. 'Those stalwarts in there, struggling for us.'"

Source: A. Douglas, *Industrial Peacemaking* (New York: Columbia University Press, 1982), p. 331.

Dissociation of Tactics from Person

Management negotiator during bargaining: "I have found that your union representatives, even when they were angry and sore and mean—and they get that way just the way we get that way, because we are all human—even their worst moments, they were all men whose word could be trusted."

Source: Selekman, et al., *Problems*, p. 550.

Rewarding Opponent's Behavior

Management negotiator during bargaining: "I might inquire as to the job-evaluation committee. I want to say that you people have gone along in pretty fine style there. It is new to you and the reason you are doing well is because you have an open mind."

Source: Douglas, *Industrial Peacemaking*, p. 255.

Punishing Opponent's Behavior

A union delegate to management: "We have been very reasonable this year; if the company does not take advantage of it, *things will be different.* It appears to me that the company is not sincere; General Motors has settled, John Deere has settled, and yet the company has done nothing."

Source: R. E. Walton and R. B. McKersie, *A Behavior Theory of Labor Negotiations* (New York: McGraw-Hill, 1965), p. 254.

Management negotiator to union: "We have tried not to create for ourselves too much of a bargaining position and have confined ourselves to a reasonable number of points. Frankly, you made some proposals that I don't think any of you, in your wildest dreams, expect to get. So cut out the clowning and get down to business."

Source: Selekman et al., *Problems*, p. 536.

Source: All excerpts are contained in R. E. Walton and R. B. McKersie, *A Behavioral Theory of Labor Negotiations* (New York: McGraw-Hill, 1965), pp. 230, 238, 247, 250, 254, 259. Copyright 1965. Reproduced with permission.

ILLUSTRATION 18-2

Portions of the IUE Opening Statement for the 1982 GE Negotiations

We on the IUE negotiating committee are pleased to be here and once again beginning the process of negotiating a national agreement with General Electric beneficial both to the workers we represent and to the company.

We note familiar faces on GE's side of the table, and particularly Bill Angell, as chief negotiator for the company. Bill, your presence adds to our optimism that these negotiations will be carried through successfully.

Our optimism is based on the recent history of IUE–GE relations, during which the parties have negotiated three consecutive national contracts with no work stoppage or lockout.

IUE and GE were prone to fight all the time. Our conflicts were waged on the picket line, in the courts, before the NLRB, and in the press.

This is no longer the case.

While continuing to vigorously carry out our responsibilities to our respective constituencies, both union and company have respected the problems and positions of the opposite side. As a result, we have achieved understanding without surrender on either side. . . .

So, in this strange bargaining year, which some say is not a union year and we say is not a company year, we will be listening for GE's responses. In recent rounds of talks, we have come to expect straight answers and hard bargaining. I hope that is the way you will approach these negotiations, avoiding regressive ideas, which can only have the effect of laying down the gauntlet to our side.

Cooperation, not confrontation, is our aim. In that spirit, let's get on with the job of negotiating a contract that benefits your employees represented by IUE, as they deserve, that enables GE to continue to prosper, that solves problems, and that advances the union-management relationship.

Source: Statement of IUE President Fitzmaurice, Essex House, New York, May 5, 1982, as reported in *Daily Labor Report*, No. 86, May 4, 1982, F-1–F-2.

There is nothing in the labor acts or their interpretation that can compel either party to change its position during bargaining. However, the unmoving party would be expected to provide a justification for its positions and may easily refute a charge of refusing to bargain in good faith if it demonstrates that it has made counteroffers in other areas.

Negotiation of a contract the first time around is often difficult, particularly if a bitter organizing campaign preceded it. Employers who use delaying tactics and discrimination against union leaders and who are in low-wage industries are less likely to reach a settlement. National union involvement in local negotiations increases the likelihood of reaching a settlement. Just as in the organizing areas, delays by the NLRB in processing refusal to bargain charges work to the union's disadvantage.[23]

---

[23] W. N. Cooke, "The Failure to Negotiate First Contracts: Determinants and Policy Implications," *Industrial and Labor Relations Review* 38 (1985), pp. 163–78.

Costing Contracts

Both sides, but particularly management, need to know the potential costs of various contract demands. The effects of a wage demand may be relatively straightforward, but many other issues are more difficult to cost, and a wage increase itself may have complex ramifications depending on pay system and form provisions. The entitlement to certain benefits (e.g., longer vacations, vested pensions, etc.) is frequently associated with seniority. As a work force gains longer tenure, the cost per employee for benefits may escalate more rapidly than pay for time worked.

One area of concern relates to the differences in costing arrangements associated with *defined benefit* as compared to *defined contribution* insurance and pension plans (see Chapter 16). A defined benefit plan indicates what the employee will be entitled to at some future period. The cost depends on the level of use and the percentage of employees who become entitled to the benefit. In a defined contribution plan, costs are more clearly known because the organization contributes at a specified rate (e.g., $2 per $100 straight-time earnings for pensions).

Pay for time not worked is another area that causes difficulties. Where overtime is required to replace the lost time, more time off may cost at least time and one half. Where there is slack time among present employees (as in repair occupations or departments), cost penalties may not occur with modest increases in paid time off.[24]

Recent Contract Outcomes and Concessions

Since 1980, contract provisions have changed markedly. Wage increases have been held to very low levels (the 1987 increase in the first year of newly negotiated contracts was 2.6 percent).[25] Employees covered by many contracts have agreed to major wage concessions. Major industries in which concessions have occurred include trucking, airlines, steel, autos, and meat packing. In return, they have received a voice in management decision making (for example, United Auto Worker membership on Chrysler Corporation's board of directors), stock ownership

---

[24] For further information see M. H. Granof, *How to Cost Your Labor Contract* (Washington, D.C.: Bureau of National Affairs, 1973); J. A. Fossum, *Labor Relations: Development, Structure, Process*, 4th ed. (Homewood, Ill.: BPI/Irwin, 1989); G. Daniels and K. Gagala, *Labor Guide to Negotiating Wages and Benefits* (Reston, Va.: Reston Publishing, 1985); and R. E. Allen and T. J. Keaveny, "Costing out a Wage and Benefit Package," *Compensation Review* 15, no. 2 (1983), pp. 27–39.

[25] *Employee Relations Weekly*, February 8, 1988, pp. 179–80.

(for example, Eastern Airlines), and "lifetime" job security (for example, Ford Motor).

A number of recent contracts also create a *two-tier wage structure*. Two-tier pay plans are an effort by employers to lower their wage costs by decreasing the starting rate offered to newly hired employees. Two types of plans exist. The first starts employees at a lower rate and requires a longer time period to reach top rates than for present employees. The second creates a permanent differential with newly hired employees never expected to earn the top rate of present employees. Managements would benefit most in situations where turnover was high or the company planned to expand. The rate of change would be most rapid in situations where retirement rates were also increasing. Both the employer and the union might expect problems when the lower-tier employment levels began to exceed half of the total. Successful implementation of these plans appears to require careful employee communications and assurances that job security will be enhanced.[26] This policy goes against the union philosophy of "equal pay for equal work" but protects the wage levels of present employees from further concessions.

Wage concessions were resisted during the early periods of economic downturns. It was not until large proportions of represented workers in enterprises faced job loss that they were agreed to. The willingness to concede on pay to obtain job security for a majority of employees is probably related to the political necessity of the union to represent the "median voter" in its unit.[27] Until at least half of bargaining unit members were threatened with job loss, the unit as a whole would probably be unwilling to agree to concessions. In general, a contract must be acceptable to the "median voter" to gain the votes necessary for ratification.

Bargaining Impasses

If the negotiators become stalled and are unable to find a common ground for a new contract, an *impasse* is said to exist. Two major mechanisms are available to break an impasse. First, a *work stoppage* may take place to inflict an economic loss on the other party for failing to agree to one's terms. Second, both parties can seek the assistance of an uninvolved third party, called a "mediator."

---

[26] Kochan et al., *Transformation of Industrial Relations*, pp. 132, 170.

[27] M. D. White, "The Intra-Unit Wage Structure and Unions: A Median Voter Model," *Industrial and Labor Relations Review* 35 (1982), pp. 565–77.

Work stoppages

Strikes occurring after the expiration of the contract, called "economic strikes," pressure an employer to agree to the union's terms. "Unfair labor practice strikes" are engaged in to get the employer to conform to the labor acts. "Wildcat strikes" are unauthorized walkouts during the contract in violation of a no-strike clause in the labor contract. In most cases, employers are free to discipline employees involved in a wildcat strike. Where a strike is purely economic, employers can replace strikers with new hires but cannot refuse to hire strikers who unconditionally return to work as long as vacancies exist. Unfair labor practice strikers maintain their status as employees regardless of employer conduct. In most cases involving economic strikes, employers do not hire replacements and, at the conclusion of the strike, regular employees return to work.

A companion tool available to employers is the *lockout*. This occurs when the employer closes down and refuses to offer work until a contract is signed. An employer may lock out employees in a bargaining dispute if (1) an impasse has occurred, (2) a legitimate economic interest is served, (3) employees are not permanently discharged or replaced, and (4) no intent to discourage membership and activity in a union is involved.

Although unions and employers in the private sector may engage in strikes and lockouts, this is not generally true in the public sector. Federal and most state laws forbid public employees from striking. Some states permit employees to strike if they are in "nonessential" jobs.

Mediation

With or without an impasse, the parties in the negotiations can request the assistance of a mediator through the Federal Mediation and Conciliation Service. Mediators are experienced neutrals whose job it is to assist the parties in arriving at a solution. The mediator has no power to impose a settlement but acts to counsel the parties, reopen communication channels, clarify offers to each of the parties, attempt to find an overlapping settlement range if one exists, and suggest strategies and tactics that will lead to a mutually acceptable settlement.[28]

---

[28] See W. E. Simkin, *Mediation and the Dynamics of Collective Bargaining* (Washington, D.C.: Bureau of National Affairs, 1971); A. Douglas, *Industrial Peacemaking* (New York: Columbia University Press, 1962); and D. M. Kolb, "Roles Mediators Play: Contrasts and Comparisons in State and Federal Mediation Practice," *Industrial Relations* 20 (1981), pp. 1–17.

Approving an Agreement

Once a tentative agreement has been reached, the union negotiating team must secure a ratification vote by the membership. When meeting with the membership, the union negotiator may recommend acceptance or rejection. In most cases, acceptance is recommended, but rejection may be recommended where the union wishes to strengthen its bargaining power.

If the rank and file vote for acceptance, the contract is approved (usually subject to national union approval) and goes into effect. If the rank and file reject the contract, the union team may go back to try to get more or attempt to more completely communicate the terms of the proposed agreement and have a revote. The last may happen when the union team is convinced that management will not alter its position. Recently, contract rejections have increased, mainly in concession situations.[29] When this occurs, gaining an agreement is difficult because a majority of union members may no longer support its leaders.

Public Sector Differences

In the public sector, many states that allow bargaining but outlaw strikes require *binding arbitration* of disputes. Other states require *fact finding* or *voluntary arbitration* instead. In an effort to reduce the use of arbitration, final-offer arbitration has been implemented in some states. In final-offer arbitration each party presents its positions and the arbitrator is required to choose the positions of one or the other party without compromise. This supposedly results in an extreme contract that the loser would do anything to avoid in the future.[30]

Some jurisdictions opt for an entire-package approach (Massachusetts and Wisconsin), while others use an issue-by-issue approach (e.g., Michigan). Selection of an entire package increases the responsibility for making a reasonable final offer submission, since one unreasonable issue in an otherwise reasonable package may tip the scales toward the other party's offer in the mind of the arbitrator.

The most recent evidence does not support the idea that arbitration use increases over time.[31] In fact, it appears that the opposite is the case.

---

[29] *Business Week*, August 11, 1986, p. 72.

[30] C. M. Stevens, "Is Compulsory Arbitration Compatible with Bargaining? *Industrial Relations* 5 (1966), pp. 38–50.

[31] J. R. Chelius and M. M. Extejt, "The Narcotic Effect of Impasse Resolution Procedures," *Industrial and Labor Relations Review* 38 (1985), pp. 629–38.

Arbitration is used more widely when it becomes available, but less often after it has been experienced.

In both the private and public sectors, when an agreement is reached and the contract is ratified, labor and management return to their everyday roles in the administration of the agreement. Occasionally, disputes about the interpretation of the contract, objections about discipline imposed for contract infractions, and union reactions to management initiatives will require both parties to sit down on an ad hoc basis and resolve their differences. This is the process of *contract administration*.

CONTRACT ADMINISTRATION

The reason for contracting is to specify the relationship that the parties hope will exist during the term of the agreement. However, situations may arise in which supervisors or other management representatives may breach the contract terms, changing conditions may lead management to alter its production technology thereby affecting union members' jobs, or the parties may simply disagree about the interpretation of a contract clause.

Unlike contract negotiations where the union is more likely to demand changes, contract administration and problems involved are likely to stem from management initiatives. Under the contract, management acts and the union reacts. Management may discipline an employee, make a change in existing conditions, or change an individual employee's job or method of payment, and the union may perceive these types of changes as contract violations.

Given that these instances may occur and that in most cases the only union recourse to management action would be to strike, labor and management have devised *grievance procedures* to resolve differences between the parties during the life of the contract.

Grievance Procedures

Grievance procedures usually provide that if a member of the bargaining unit believes the contract has been violated, the member will contact a union steward about the grievance. The steward confronts the employee's supervisor with the grievance, and both may attempt to resolve it within the contract terms. Some organizations so not allow supervisors to adjust grievances because they do not want the firm bound to a precedent set by lower levels of supervision.

FIGURE 18–9

An Example of a Grievance Procedure Clause

ARTICLE 9. GRIEVANCE PROCEDURE AND NO-STRIKE AGREEMENT

9.01   DEPARTMENTAL REPRESENTATIVES. The UNION may designate representatives for each section on each shift and in each department for the purpose of handling grievances which may arise in that department. The UNION will inform the production personnel office in writing, as to the names of the authorized representatives. Should differences arise as to the intent and application of the provisions of this Agreement, there shall be no strike, lockout, slowdown, or work stoppage of any kind, and the controversy shall be settled in accordance with the following grievance procedures:

9.02   GRIEVANCES.

Step 1.   The employee and the departmental steward, if the employee desires, shall take the matter up with his foreman. If no settlement is reached in Step 1 within two working days, the grievance shall be reduced to writing on the form provided for that purpose.

Step 2.   The written grievance shall be presented to the foreman or the general foreman and a copy sent to the production personnel office. Within two working days after receipt of the grievance, the general foreman shall hold a meeting, unless mutually agreed otherwise, with the foreman, the employee, and the departmental steward and the chief steward.

Step 3.   If no settlement is reached in Step 2, the written grievance shall be presented to the departmental superintendent, who shall hold a meeting within five working days of the original receipt of the grievance in Step 2 unless mutually agreed otherwise. Those in attendance shall normally be the departmental superintendent, the general foreman, the foreman, the employee, the chief steward, departmental steward, a member of the production personnel department, the president of the UNION or his representative and the divisional committeeman.

Step 4.   If no settlement is reached in Step 3, the UNION COMMITTEE and an international representative of the UNION shall meet with the MANAGEMENT COMMITTEE for the purpose of settling the matter.

Step 5.   If no settlement is reached in Step 4, the matter shall be referred to an arbitrator. A representative of the UNION shall meet within five working days with a representative of the COMPANY for the purpose of selecting an arbitrator. If an arbitrator cannot be agreed upon within five working days after Step 4, a request for a list of arbitrators shall be sent to the Federal Mediation & Conciliation Service. Upon obtaining the list, an arbitrator shall be selected within five working days. Prior to arbitration, a representative of the UNION shall meet with a representative of the COMPANY to reduce to writing wherever possible the actual issue to be arbitrated. The decision of the arbitrator shall be final and binding on all parties. The salary, if any, of the arbitrator and any necessary expense incident to the arbitration shall be paid jointly by the COMPANY and the UNION.

9.03   In order to assure the prompt settlement of grievances as close to their source as possible, it is mutually agreed that the above steps shall be followed strictly in the order listed and no step shall be used until all previous steps have been exhausted. A settlement reached between the COMPANY and the UNION in any step of this procedure shall terminate the grievance and shall be final and binding on both parties.

FIGURE 18–9 *(concluded)*

9.04   The arbitrator shall not have authority to modify, change, or amend any of the terms or provisions of this Agreement, or to add to or delete from this Agreement.

9.05   The UNION will not cause or permit its members to cause or take part in any sit-down, stay-in, or slowdown in any plant of the COMPANY or any curtailment of work or restriction of production or interference with the operations of the COMPANY.

9.06   The UNION will not cause or permit its members to cause or take part in any strike of any of the COMPANY's operations, except where the strike has been fully authorized as provided in the constitution of the international union.

Source: J. A. Fossum, *Labor Relations: Development, Structure, Process* 4th ed. (Homewood, Ill.: BPI/Irwin, 1989), p. 377.

If the grievance is not resolved at this level, the union steward or local union officer and a company P/HR representative meet to resolve it. This is the point at which most differences are settled. If there is no resolution at this step, most contracts provide for a high-level manager and a national union official to decide the grievance. If agreement fails here, the grievance is usually submitted to an outside third party for voluntary binding arbitration. There are some variations in the number of steps and the time necessary to go through each step, but Figure 18–9 is representative of a typical grievance procedure spelled out in a contract.

Union and Management Organization for Contract Administration

The local union generally designates a negotiating committee that decides which issues in bargaining and contract administration are most important to pursue. The day-to-day representatives of the negotiating committee are the union's appointed or elected stewards. They receive and help prepare grievances of union members for presentation to management. The local union may receive assistance in advanced states of the grievance procedure from international union representatives or officers.

Management is represented at the first level by its supervisors. Industrial relations representatives are available for providing advice and resolution of routine cases not settled between the supervisor and the steward. Grievances not settled at lower steps of the procedure will be handled by higher-level plant industrial relations managers or corporate-level representatives.

Types of Grievances

Grievances arise for a variety of reasons, but perhaps the most prevalent are over the following issues.[32]

Custom and practice

Many practices are not explicitly spelled out in the contract but have grown up over time. For example, it may be customary to allow washup time at the end of a shift. If management changes procedures, a grievance may result. Practice, even though not spelled out, may take on the form of a contract clause particularly if management has cited it as a reason not to grant other concessions during negotiations. The whole issue of past practice is extremely complex and occupies a great deal of attention from arbitrators.

Rule violations

Work rules are often spelled out in contracts or supplementary materials. When an employee violates one, s/he is subject to discipline. There may be a dispute regarding whether the violation occurred and, if so, whether the discipline is excessive for the violation.

Insubordination

Violations of orders or refusal to perform work assigned leads to insubordination charges. Generally, employees are expected to perform the required work and then grieve its assignment rather than refuse to do it. There may be instances, such as safety situations, where employees may rightfully refuse to perform the work under the contract.

Absenteeism

Excessive absenteeism is frequently a cause for discipline. Grievances generally occur where employees are not treated consistently or where the discipline is seen as being excessive for the level of absences.

---

[32] K. L. Sovereign and M. F. Bognanno, "Positive Contract Administration," in *ASPA Handbook of Personnel and Industrial Relations*, eds. D. Yoder and H. G. Heneman, Jr. (Washington, D.C.: Bureau of National Affairs, 1979), pp. 7-137—7-171.

Dishonesty

Cases of theft usually result in discharge. Most grievances here relate to searches and seizures and other alleged violations of evidentiary procedures.

Substance abuse

Employees may be disciplined and/or discharged for drug use on company premises or where their performance is negatively influenced by prior acute or chronic use of intoxicants. Substance abuse is frequently involved with absence behavior.

Effects of Grievances on Employers and Employees

Both employers and employees are influenced by the filing, processing, and outcome of grievances. For example, in one governmental agency, employees who filed two grievances within one rating period received lower performance ratings, but winning or losing the grievance was not associated with the rating. Employees who filed a second grievance were more likely to receive a disciplinary sanction and losing a second grievance was associated with an increased probability of quitting. From the standpoint of the employer, grievance filing was associated with higher absenteeism and fewer production hours.[33]

High grievance levels are associated with a conflictual labor relations climate. Evidence across 118 bargaining units in 1976–77 followed up by a study of 18 units in 1979–80 found that high grievance rates were associated with conflictual rather than cooperative labor relations.[34] A study of 10 paper mills (9 unionized and 1 nonunion) found that higher grievances were associated with lower plant productivity. The presence of a grievance procedure (only in the union mills) was associated, however, with higher productivity, perhaps because employees had an outlet for complaints that would operate while production continued.[35]

----

[33] B. S. Klaas, H. G. Heneman III, and C. A. Olson, "Grievance Activity and Its Consequences: A Study of the Grievance System and Its Impact on Employee Behavior." Unpublished paper, University of South Carolina, 1988.

[34] J. Gandz and J. D. Whitehead, "The Relationship between Industrial Relations Climate and Grievance Initiation and Resolution," *Proceedings of the Industrial Relations Research Association* (1981), pp. 320–28.

[35] C. Ichniowski, "The Effects of Grievance Activity on Productivity," *Industrial and Labor Relations Review* 40 (1986), pp. 75–89.

A study of public-sector management and union representatives found that explicit performance and disciplinary standards were associated with higher grievance rates. Rivalry between unions representing employees within the same organization increased grievances. Positive attitudes and a willingness to compromise by management were related to lower rates, but consultation with the union about items of mutual interest did not reduce grievances.[36]

The resolution of a grievance provides information to the parties that might assist the resolution of subsequent cases at lower levels. Evidence suggests that only management uses prior decisions as a basis for their initial decisions on a grievance. The higher the level of settlement of a grievance, the more likely the parties are to use formal settlements of previous grievances as settlements. Earlier decisions are used most frequently as precedents in discipline and work assignment cases.[37]

Arbitration

Arbitration is invoked after the parties fail to agree on a resolution for a grievance. An arbitrator is empowered by the contract to make an award that is binding on both parties. The award may incorporate such things as back pay, reinstatement, and upholding management's actions.

Depending on the way the contract is written, the parties may use a *permanent umpire* or appoint an ad hoc arbitrator. Most agreements using a permanent umpire are with large bargaining units having mature bargaining relationships. In an ad hoc arbitration, the parties usually ask the American Arbitration Association or the Federal Mediation and Conciliation Service to supply a list of qualified arbitrators from which the parties may choose a mutually agreeable arbitrator.

The arbitrator is generally experienced in labor-management relations and is often either a labor lawyer, university professor of industrial relations, or a former labor or management official now arbitrating full time.

When the arbitrator receives a notification of appointment, a mutually acceptable hearing date is agreed to and the parties provide a hearing facility, court reporter (if necessary), and the witnesses they expect to call. The arbitrator may ask for prehearing briefs from the parties to get a clearer idea of the differences between the parties. During the hearing, both parties present their witnesses and documentary evidence. Cross-

---

[36] C. E. Labig, Jr. and I. B. Helburn. "Union and Management Policy Influences on Grievance Initiation," *Journal of Labor Research* 7 (1986), pp. 269–84.

[37] T. R. Knight, "Feedback and Grievance Resolution," *Industrial and Labor Relations Review* 39 (1986), pp. 585–98.

examination also takes place. No formal rules of evidence are required as they are in a judicial proceeding, but the arbitrator evaluates the source and credibility of the evidence.[38] After the hearing, the parties may submit posthearing briefs. The arbitrator then considers the evidence, the contract clause in dispute, and the powers granted to arbitrators under the labor agreement and then renders an award. In the rare instance where the losing party fails to honor the award, it will almost invariably be enforced after petitioning a federal district court.

Arbitration provides a method for settling contractual disputes without having to resort to work stoppages. It has been quite effective in meeting the needs of the parties, but the cost (which is equally shared between labor and management), and the time delays involved in some cases may sometimes interfere with access to and immediacy of due process procedures.

Union members have employment rights (over and above legal rights) as specified in their collective bargaining agreement. They also clearly know the means that are available for settling grievances that may occur. But what guarantees exist for employees in nonunion organizations? This area is explored next.

EMPLOYEE RELATIONS IN THE NONUNION ORGANIZATION

In Chapter 17, it was pointed out that fewer than 20 percent of all employees in the United States are union members. When union penetration was discussed, it was noted that the percentage of employees organized by industry varies widely. Many of the problems unions handle for employees also occur for nonunion employees. Represented employees have a contractual right to demand that actions by management be reviewed on a bilateral basis, but nonunion employees do not have this same negotiated right.

There are two types of situations in which employers may be engaged in nonunion labor relations. First, the firm or a division or location may be partially organized—some employees are represented and others are not (e.g., production employees are represented, clericals and professionals are not). Second, the firm may be totally unorganized. Given these situations, how do P/HR managers handle employee relations in the nonunion organization?

---

[38] See M. Hill, Jr. and A. V. Sinicropi, *Evidence in Arbitration*, 2d ed. (Washington, D.C.: Bureau of National Affairs, 1987).

Partially Organized Establishments

Many of the activities undertaken in labor relations in the partially organized establishment are also done in the totally unrepresented firm. Most of the practices unique to this type involve compensation and hours of work. For example, pay rates and benefit packages for unorganized employees are typically readjusted to conform to the negotiated package for bargaining unit employees (with minor exceptions).[39]

Unorganized Establishments

In several of the most basic industries, blue-collar employees of almost all major corporations are almost completely organized. In other industries some companies have little or no organization. Why do these differences exist?

An intensive study of large nonunion organizations concluded that these could be divided into two broad categories: *philosophy-laden* and *doctrinaire*. A philosophy-laden organization appears to be nonunion as a byproduct of its employee relations approach. Employees receive or are entitled to all of the protections a union might offer because management believes that this approach should be taken. In doctrinaire organizations, the management believes that it would be better off operating without a union, so it implements those programs that it feels will help to avoid organization.[40]

Pay programs in the unorganized establishments tended to be market leaders and were clearly communicated to employees. Philosophy-laden companies tended to have merit pay systems for blue-collar employees, and doctrinaire companies followed patterns bargained for comparison employers.[41]

More open promotional systems with job posting were frequent in nonunion organizations. Job security was enhanced by a greater use of subcontracting and temporary employment to cover periods of increased demand for products or services.[42]

---

[39] For more information, see *Policies for Unorganized Employees* (Washington, D.C.: Bureau of National Affairs, 1979).

[40] F. K. Foulkes, *Personnel Policies in Large Nonunion Companies* (Englewood Cliffs, N.J.: Prentice-Hall, 1980), pp. 45–46.

[41] Ibid., pp. 149–89.

[42] Ibid., pp. 99–122.

Grievance Procedures

Employee relations procedures in unorganized establishments are developed to ensure opportunities for due process for employees who believe that management has acted unfairly. Employers frequently establish procedures that allow employees access to superiors. In many instances, however, the ultimate authority in deciding the merit of the complaint is a high-level management official. This procedure will have little credibility if it is excessively controlled by management.

Several methods to reduce the possibility of employee cynicism about management's commitment to neutral grievance procedures in the non-union organization have been devised. For example, IBM has operated a system that allows employees direct anonymous access to high-level management on complaints. When complaints are received, investigations are required, and the remedial action to be taken, if any, is communicated back to the grievant. Follow-up is monitored by high-level management.

Many firms have created an ombudsman position to resolve grievances. Although technically an employee of the firm, this person has certain prescribed latitudes for taking action or requiring that certain decisions are made. If an employee is not satisfied with a proposed management solution where ombudsmen exist, the employee can insist on exhausting that remedy. Another innovative approach is the creation of an employee review board to act as an impartial group to resolve outstanding grievances.

THE IMPACT OF COLLECTIVE BARGAINING ON P/HR ACTIVITIES

In Chapter 1, it was pointed out that the organization of P/HR departments was responsive to the external and internal environments in which they operate. A union is an external influence that clearly alters the internal environment and modifies the P/HR activities for the organization. It also modifies the types and levels of line personnel decisions management can make.

The analysis of jobs continues in its importance in an organized situation, since the information may be necessary for work-rule and job evaluation disputes, for slotting new jobs into the wage structure, and for designing selection procedures for external staffing.

Assessing outcomes will probably decline in importance, except for such readily quantified indicators as absences and disciplinary actions.

Since unions usually demand that seniority be used as the criterion for most staffing and pay decisions, it is simply wasted effort to collect performance information for personnel decision making.

Personnel planning and external staffing grow in importance. Personnel planning is more critical because the costs of layoffs usually are greater under a contract with such provisions as supplementary unemployment benefits. External staffing grows in importance because this is the only bargaining unit level decision the employer unilaterally makes. As job rights associated with seniority accrue, a less productive employee becomes increasingly difficult to discharge.

Internal staffing for bargaining unit members will probably be spelled out by the contract. The contract will probably also spell out promotional ladders and jobs for which the employer must first exhaust internal candidate pools before engaging in external staffing. Training may still be largely within the employer's discretion, but opportunities for developmental upgrading programs may be included in the contract.

Compensation will also be spelled out in the contract, and the role of a compensation specialist will likely revolve around job evaluation.

Labor relations and safety and health will increase in importance to service contracted requirements and to interpret the contract for line management. Much of the character of activities will be reactive in a unionized situation. However, there is recent evidence that line managers are becoming more involved in P/HR activities and are taking a proactive role in restructuring the employment relationship.[43]

LABOR-MANAGEMENT RELATIONS AND EQUAL EMPLOYMENT OPPORTUNITY

Title VII of the 1964 Civil Rights Act applies to unions as well as employers. Most unions do not have a hand in initial hiring decisions, since the labor acts allow only contract-construction bargaining agreements to require union membership as a condition of employment. But unions do bargain over promotion rules, and they are required to exclusively represent all employees within a bargaining unit. Thus, both contracts and their administration can contribute to possible discrimination.

This section will cover the present requirements involving organized labor in the area of promotions and seniority, affirmative action, and representation in grievance administration and its role in exclusive representation under the contract.

---

[43] Kochan et al., *Transformation of Industrial Relations.*

Promotions and Seniority

Most collective bargaining agreements specify that many employment decisions be based on seniority. Collective bargaining agreements often define two different types of seniority: plant and departmental. Plant seniority is generally used as a basis for making such compensation decisions as entitlement to vacations, salary increases, and pension benefits. Departmental seniority is most often used as a basis for such employment decisions as layoffs, promotions, and job assignments. Plant seniority dates from a person's initial hire date with the organization, and departmental seniority dates from the initial date of assignment to a given unit within the organization (such as a machine shop in a manufacturing plant). The Supreme Court has called plantwide and departmental seniority systems that operate on these bases "benefit-status" and "competitive-status" seniority, respectively.

When a person accepts a promotion from one department to go to another, competitive-status seniority frequently begins as of that date. Thus, the individual accepting a promotion becomes more vulnerable to layoff due to the forfeiture of seniority accrued on a previously held job. Ironically, this means that there is a greater risk for a senior individual to bid on a promotion than for a junior person.

Before the 1964 Civil Rights Act, employers frequently created segregated jobs. After the passage of the act, minorities who had built up seniority rights in these jobs were often reluctant to bid on new jobs to avoid giving up their departmental seniority. Despite the "lock-in" effects such systems have, they have been ruled legal by the Supreme Court as long as there is no intention to discriminate.[44]

Affirmative Action

Since unions are directly covered by Title VII, and many federal contractors covered by Executive Order 11246 are unionized, unions are vitally affected by affirmative action laws and regulations. This is true whether the affirmative action is voluntary, part of an out-of-court settlement (consent decree), or part of a court-imposed (remedial) plan.

In all of these instances, unions have definite affirmative action obligations. Cooperation with the employer and the courts is thus not only desirable but required. Figure 18–10 describes the major components of affirmative action activity for one major union—the International Union

---

[44] M. Graham, "Seniority Systems and Title VII: Reanalysis and Redirection," *Employee Relations Law Journal* 9 (1983), pp. 81–97.

FIGURE 18–10

Affirmative Action Activity for a Union

Briefly, the IUE Title VII Compliance Program emphasizes the elimination of systemic discrimination and consists of the following elements: (1) an educational program for both staff and our membership; (2) a systematic review of the number and status of minority members and females at each of our plants; (3) a systematic review of all collective bargaining contracts and plant practices to determine whether specific kinds of discrimination exist, and (4) *most important,* requests to employers for detailed information broken down by race, sex, and national origin, relating to hiring (including the job grade given to each new hire), promotion, and upgrading policies, initial assignments, wage rates, segregation of job classifications, and seniority; copies of the employer's affirmative action plan (AAP) and work force analysis; and copies and information concerning the status of all charges filed against them under the Equal Pay Act, Title VII, Executive Order 11246, and state FEP laws.

After analyzing the data, if we conclude that discrimination exists, the IUE: (1) requests bargaining with employers to eliminate the illegal practices or contract provisions; (2) files NLRB refusal-to-bargain charges against employers who refuse to supply information or to agree to eliminate the illegal provisions; and (3) follows up these demands by filing Title VII charges and lawsuits under Title VII and E. O. 11246.

Source: W. Newman and C. W. Wilson, "The Union Role in Affirmative Action," *Labor Law Journal* 32 (1981), pp. 323–42. Published and copyrighted 1981 by Commerce Clearing House, Inc., 4025 W. Peterson Avenue, Chicago, IL 60646.

of Electrical, Radio, and Machine Workers (IUE). It should be noted, though, that people claim unions have been much more resistant to affirmative action than is implied in the IUE example.[45]

Fair Representation

Since a union is the exclusive representative of all members of the bargaining unit, whether union members or not, it is important that everyone has equal access to rights under the contract. A number of decisions has required that unions represent minorities on an equal basis when compared with majorities. This does not mean, however, that minorities (or majorities) are entitled to exhaust all steps of a grievance procedure for any alleged contract violation if the union determines that it is without merit.

A grievance claiming discrimination is somewhat different than others.[46] The individual is entitled to use the grievance procedure within

---

[45] See H. Hill, "The AFL–CIO and the Black Worker: Twenty-Five Years after the Merger," *Journal of Intergroup Relations* 10 (1982), pp. 5–78.

[46] E. G. Wrong, "The Social Responsibility of Arbitrators in Title VII Disputes," *Labor Law Journal* 32 (1981), pp. 630–35; E. G. Wrong, "Arbitrators' Determinations of Reverse Discrimination or Affirmative Action Cases," *Labor Law Journal* 35 (1984), pp. 587–93.

the contract if there is an equal opportunity clause but is also entitled to file a charge with the EEOC if the grievance is denied at any step, including arbitration.

SUMMARY

The economic environment influences the outcomes of collective bargaining. Recent changes—deregulation, foreign competition, and nonunion entries into product and service markets—have reduced the bargaining power of labor unions. Besides the economic environment, the structure of bargaining influences outcomes. Where employers and unions bargain on a multiemployer basis, and where entry to the industry is costly, wage increases can more easily be passed on to consumers.

Bargaining issues are related to wages, hours, and terms and conditions of employment. Wage issues relate to the level, structure, form, and system with which pay changes will take place. Unionized workplaces generally have higher pay levels, flatter structures, a greater percentage of pay in the form of benefits, and increases based on job level and seniority. Nonwage issues relate to union and management rights, grievance procedures, hours of work, and the like.

Before negotiations, the parties assess their environments and identify contract terms that require changes. They also devise strategies for convincing each other regarding the necessity for change and also for gaining consensus on agreements within their own constituencies. Proposed contract provisions are costed to determine their effect on the organization. Where agreements are not reached, impasse procedures may be applied—mediation and arbitration in the public sector, for example—or the union might strike.

During periods of adversity, unions and managements may cooperate to jointly improve the survivability of the employer and the security of employees' jobs. Contract administration is involved with the interpretation of the contract and handling disputes during its effective period. Grievance procedures are used to handle union member claims of contract violations. A variety of situations may lead to grievances. If the parties cannot agree on a settlement, third-party arbitrators hear the case and render a binding award.

DISCUSSION QUESTIONS

1. What is a grievance procedure? How does it work, and what methods help to ensure union members' individual rights during its use?

2. What circumstances would lead a union membership to reject a contract negotiated with their employers by its leadership?

3. Why do unions appear to avoid concessions until it is absolutely necessary?

4. What advantages would a union find in allowing a group of employers to negotiate a single multiemployer agreement with it?

5. What conditions are necessary for mediation to be able to break a bargaining impasse?

Case for Part Eight

UNITED CASTINGS

Introduction

United Castings is a small foundry supplying to the major automobile companies. The company's financial performance has been suffering as has the morale among the employees, especially with regard to management-labor relations. The owners have not been satisfied with the return on investment of the company and have privately expressed interest in selling it. In addition, the union contract expires in three months. Both the management and union bargaining committees are now planning their strategies for the upcoming negotiations. Following is more detailed information of the industry, area, union, and owners.

Industry Conditions

The foundry industry in North America is comprised of a large number of small foundries. These foundries' competition for business is usually based on ability to meet product specifications, ability to insure delivery, and price. United Castings presently sells almost exclusively to the automobile industry. This causes two problems. First, the company is subject to the same cyclical fluctuations in demand as the auto industry. Second, being United Castings' sole means of support, the auto companies have great power over the company in determining the terms and conditions of the exchange. For example, the auto companies presently demand a price of $3.99 for a brake disc that last year sold for $4.02 and five years ago sold for $4.13.

Another important aspect of the foundry industry is that it is very capital intensive. Payroll costs tend to be between 20 and 30 percent of sales. Wages in the industry average about $7.25 per hour with an additional benefit package of about $3.50 per hour.

Area Conditions

United Castings is located in a small town in northern Michigan. The unemployment rate in the area is approximately 18 percent. In addition, inflation in the area has been running at about 7 percent each year. A majority of the employed members of the town work in the iron mines owned and operated by Continental Steel Company. This company is known for having a terrible labor relations situation, exemplified by extremely autocratic behavior on the part of management, and feather-bedding and sabotage on the part of the union. In the past four years there have been 10 wildcat strikes at the mine, and each strike has resulted in violent activities. The average wage at Continental, however, is $9.25 per hour plus another $4 in benefits. The employees attribute their higher pay level to their militant union activities.

Compared to the situation at Continental, the owners of United Castings are very happy with their labor-management situation. Because the town is very small and isolated, management employees and union workers often cross paths away from the workplace. Due to the size of the company, management (including the owners) usually knows all the employees by name.

Of the 135 employees on United Castings' payroll, approximately 100 are production workers represented by the United Steel Workers of America. The USW has generally been a moderately militant union, although the local at United Castings has never been involved in violent strikes. The last three contract negotiations, however, have resulted in strikes before coming to a settlement. The last strike lasted almost two weeks.

The employees are in unskilled and semiskilled jobs. Their average wage rate is $7.51 per hour. In addition to wages, the union members receive a benefit package worth another $3 per hour. The union membership sees no way that they can accept less than a 7 percent increase in wages in the next contract negotiations, and they feel so strongly about this that they have authorized the bargaining committee to call a strike if the committee sees fit to do so.

Owners

Hal Lichtenfeld and Paul Wagner founded United Castings in 1963. Hal is 60 years old and is the chief executive officer of the company. He worked in the automobile industry during the 40s and 50s with Ford where he was in charge of training managers and first-line supervisors in human relations skills.

Paul's background is in engineering. He received both a bachelor's and master's degree in engineering from the Massachusetts Institute of Technology. He is 45 years old and is the president of the company.

Hal and Paul are very secretive in their bookkeeping. Since it is a privately held company, only their accountant and the government have any idea of how the company is performing. In fact, for one potential contract, they decided to cancel the order rather than reveal their financial performance data to the client.

In United Castings' first year of operation, they showed an 11 percent ROI on sales of $14 million. In 1973 their ROI peaked at 14 percent on sales of $60 million. During this time the number of employees increased from 60 to 90. Since that time the sales have continued to increase ($110 million), the asset base has increased ($12 million), and the work force has increased (135 employees), however, the ROI has consistently decreased to last year's level of 10 percent. In addition, projections for the following year show only a 9.5 percent ROI. The owners feel that anything less than 11 percent ROI is unacceptable, because they believe that their money could be invested elsewhere to ensure at least that amount in return. They suspect that the union will demand a 7 percent raise in the upcoming negotiations. However, they would like to keep the raise to no more than 2.5 percent.

The profits are not the only thing that has decreased. The owners state that they are unhappy with the work situation as well as the financial performance. "I used to enjoy going to work every day and seeing the guys (employees)," says Hal. "But now I dread showing up each day because I know I'm going to have some complaints or conflicts to deal with. It's just not fun anymore."

Due to the decreasing profitability of the company and the owners' loss of enjoyment in running it, they have recently discussed selling out and investing their money in a place where they might receive a higher return.

Summary

The upcoming contract negotiations will have an important impact on the success or failure of the company, and both the union and management see these negotiations as very important for ensuring that their needs will be met.

Once again, it is important to stress that the union knows nothing about the financial performance of the company, nor do they know the owners' feelings about the possible divestiture of it.

Questions

1. Place yourself in the position of the union, and given what it knows about the enterprise, what strategies or arguments would you make for getting your desired wage increase?

2. Place yourself in the position of the management. What strategies or arguments can you develop for negotiating a contract that will be acceptable to you?

3. What if the union decides to strike? What will be the negative outcomes for the union membership? What will be the negative outcomes for management? Think in both the short and long term.

4. As an objective third party, how valid are the positions of both parties?

5. What would be the advantages/disadvantages of Hal and Paul's policy of not making their books open?

6. What are the implications of the industry being capital intensive for the upcoming negotiations?

7. If you were called in as a mediator in this situation, what would you do to facilitate the successful negotiation of the new contract?

8. In addition to the short-term problem of negotiating a contract, think about the long-term viability of the enterprise. If you were called in as a consultant, what problems would you identify, and what recommendations would you make?

PART NINE

Work Environment

19

Work and Workplace Design

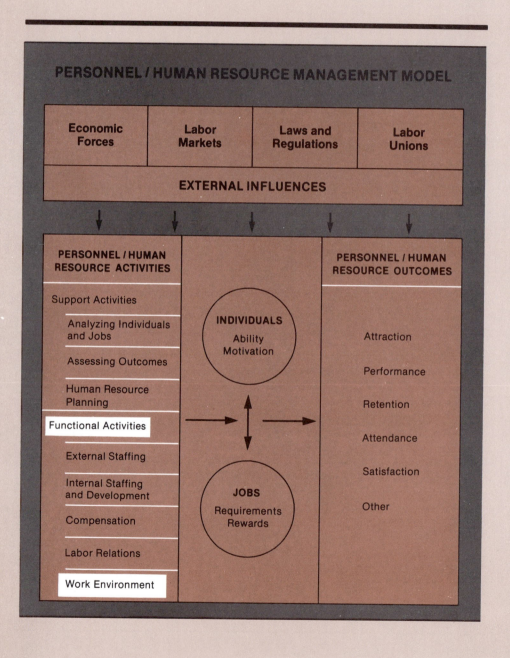

PERSONNEL / HUMAN RESOURCE MANAGEMENT MODEL

Economic Forces	Labor Markets	Laws and Regulations	Labor Unions

EXTERNAL INFLUENCES

PERSONNEL / HUMAN RESOURCE ACTIVITIES

Support Activities

Analyzing Individuals and Jobs

Assessing Outcomes

Human Resource Planning

Functional Activities

External Staffing

Internal Staffing and Development

Compensation

Labor Relations

Work Environment

INDIVIDUALS
Ability
Motivation

JOBS
Requirements
Rewards

PERSONNEL / HUMAN RESOURCE OUTCOMES

Attraction

Performance

Retention

Attendance

Satisfaction

Other

After reading this chapter, you should be able to speak to the questions posed in each of the following personnel/human resource incidents:

1. National Digital Products Corporation is a major producer of computer peripheral devices for mainframe computer manufacturers. The vice president for manufacturing, David Neumeier, has just returned from a computer industry trade association convention where he attended a program on job design. The speaker, Professor Laura Lou Cunnings of Southeastern University, advocated the use of job enrichment to improve productivity in the data processing manufacturing industry. Neumeier was so enthused by the presentation that he wants you, his director of personnel, to suggest ways in which job enrichment can be implemented in NDPC and to get the process started. What more would you want to know about the situation before making any suggestions? Under what conditions would you proceed? Under what conditions would you attempt to talk Neumeier out of proceeding? If you did go ahead, what would you try to do? Why? How?

2. The APC Pharmaceutical Corporation is considering the implementation of a management-by-objectives (MBO) program for all of its managerial and professional employees. As a member of the firm's training and development department, you sit on the MBO implementation team. What recommendations should you make concerning the design of the MBO process? What role, if any, should participation play in the processes of implementation and in the ongoing operation of MBO? What potential difficulties should the organization prepare itself for? How should implementation proceed?

3. The manager of a large office for PYA Insurance Company has heard about the quality-of-work-life (QWL) programs at General Motors and elsewhere and thinks that some form of employee involvement might help increase productivity and improve quality in the office. She has announced that beginning next Monday supervisors will be more participative and employees will start forming quality circles (QCs). What do you think of the manager's approach? What, if anything, should she have done differently?

4. You are serving on the start-up team for a new distribution facility that your company intends to open in Burlington, Vermont in about a year. The team is undecided about whether the facility should be managed using a traditional approach to work and workplace design or as a high-involvement work system (HIWS). The team leader has asked you to draw up "ideal types" showing what these two approaches might look like. Do it.

Traditionally, the role of personnel has been to enhance P/HR management outcomes by designing and administering policies and procedures to (1) fill job vacancies on a timely basis with individuals who possess the abilities and motivation needed to fulfill existing job requirements; (2) avoid if possible, and otherwise manage, employee surpluses; (3) assist employees in developing their abilities and motivation to better carry out their present jobs or prepare for future jobs; (4) offer rewards, such as pay and promotions, to enhance employee motivation; and (5) support these activities through careful planning, job analysis, and performance appraisal. Personnel managers and specialists have tended to take work and the work environment pretty much as given, and to attempt to select and develop people to fit it. Another approach, though, is to shift the emphasis to the other side and attempt to change the nature of the work and workplace as well.

It has long been known that employees' behavior and attitudes are affected by the nature of the work they do and the environment they do it in. Over time, much experimentation and research have taken place in attempts to discover optimal designs of work and workplaces for maximum organizational and employee results. In recent years, both the quantity and scope of this experimentation have increased in the face of heightened concerns over international competition, lagging productivity and product quality, and new expectations with respect to the quality of working life. To a large extent, these developments have been driven by two sets of not terribly well-documented beliefs: (1) that traditional approaches to work and workplace design are out of step with the needs and expectations of today's better educated, more liberated, and less passive employees and (2) that work redesign, especially that which enhances employee participation and involvement in the workplace, is the best (some would say only) way to restore America's competitiveness in the world economy.[1]

At a minimum P/HR professionals have found it necessary to stay abreast of experimentation in this area. Many have gone further and have emerged as leaders of work restructuring efforts in their companies.[2]

The relative newness and fluidity of their activities, however, preclude precise definition or description. In general, they tend to evolve around one (or more) of three major building blocks: *goal setting, job*

---

[1] See, for example, E. E. Lawler III, *High Involvement Management* (San Francisco: Jossey-Bass Publishers, 1986), Ch. 2 and 3.

[2] M. Beer and B. A. Spector, "Human Resource Management: The Integration of Industrial Relations and Organization Development," in *Research in Personnel and Human Resource Management*, vol 2, eds. K. M. Rowland and G. R. Ferris (Greenwich, Conn.: JAI Press, 1984); and M. A. Frohman, "Human Resource Management and the Bottom Line: Evidence of the Connection," *Human Resource Management* 23 (1984), 315–34.

design, and *participative work groups.* Sometimes a change in one or two of these areas constitutes the entire program. In other instances, modifications in these areas are enhanced into full-blown high-involvement work systems, with changes in organization structure and employee communications, as well as the traditional P/HR activities of staffing, development, compensation, and labor relations. In the latter cases, the intent is to create comprehensive human resource strategies that are consistent with organizational environments and employee expectations and are mutually reinforcing internally.[3]

This chapter explores the subject of work and workplace design with an emphasis on the three major building blocks and variations in systemic programs. In each case, the focus is on description, underlying theory and research, actual applications and, where possible, results in P/HR management and organizational outcomes. Following this, the concept of high-involvement work systems is explored.

GOAL SETTING

Goal setting is a straightforward approach to work design. Goals (targets, deadlines, etc.), when employees accept them, (1) direct attention and action, (2) mobilize effort, (3) encourage persistence toward task accomplishment, and (4) encourage the development of strategies for task accomplishment. The result, under the right conditions, is improved employee performance.[4]

Not just any goals or circumstances will do.[5] In general, more difficult ("stretch") goals are better than easy goals, although the relationship breaks down when goals are extremely difficult, probably because em-

---

[3] L. Dyer and G. W. Holder, "A Strategic Perspective of Human Resource Management," in *Human Resource Management: Evolving Roles and Responsibilities,* ASPA/BNA Handbook of Human Resource Management, vol 1, ed. L. Dyer (Washington, D.C.: Bureau of National Affairs, 1988), pp. 1–46; Lawler, *High Involvement Management;* and R. E. Walton, "From Control to Commitment in the Workplace," *Harvard Business Review,* March–April 1985, pp. 77–84.

[4] E. A. Locke and G. P. Latham, *Goal Setting: A Motivational Technique That Works* (Englewood Cliffs, N.J.: Prentice-Hall, 1984); G. P. Latham, "The Role of Goal Setting in Human Resource Management," in *Research in Personnel and Human Resource Management,* vol 1, eds. K. M. Rowland and G. R. Ferris (Greenwich, Conn.: JAI Press, 1983), pp. 169–200.

[5] R. E. Wood, A. J. Mento, and E. A. Locke, "Task Complexity as a Moderator of Goal Effects: A Meta Analysis," *Journal of Applied Psychology* 72 (1987), pp. 416–25; A. J. Mento, R. P. Steel and R. J. Karren, "A Meta-Analytic Study of the Effects of Goal Setting on Task Performance," *Organizational Behavior and Human Decision Processes* 39 (1987), pp. 52–83; M. E. Tubbs, "Goal Setting: A Meta-Analytic Examination of the Empirical Evidence," *Journal of Applied Psychology* 71 (1986), pp. 474–83; and E. A. Locke, K. N. Shaw, L. M. Saari, and G. P. Latham, "Goal Setting and Task Performance: 1969–1980," *Psychological Bulletin* 90 (1981), pp. 125–52.

ployees reject them. Further, specific goals result in higher performance than general ("do your best") goals. Finally, when tasks are complex, clarity of goals is also related to improved performance.

Many writers assert the beneficial effects of having employees participate in setting their goals rather than having supervisors set them unilaterally. It is argued that employees are more likely to understand and internalize goals they have helped to establish. The logic is impeccable, but the evidence is mixed.[6] Assigned goals often work, although participation can be helpful when other aspects of work are done participatively and when tasks are particularly ambiguous or complex.

An important aspect that often accompanies goal setting is feedback. In general, the performance effect of difficult and specific goals is enhanced when employees are apprised of their progress toward these goals.[7] Evidence from a variety of contexts suggests that feedback is most beneficial when it is timely, specific, instructive (i.e., directional), and supportive (i.e., accompanied by praise and other forms of recognition).[8]

The apparent efficacy and simplicity of goal setting make it a popular approach to management. Applications vary in many ways, although they tend to fall in two broad categories: prosaic programs and management by objectives (MBO).

Prosaic Programs

Much of the goal setting that takes place in work settings is done informally, almost casually; a common example is the use of deadlines. Much more systematic is the use of industrial engineering and related techniques to establish output and sales quotas for individual and group incentives plans (see Chapter 15). Falling between these two extremes is the use of relatively unadorned goal setting (with feedback) for performance improvement purposes.

Illustration 19–1 describes a reasonably typical application. Notice that the goals are unilaterally and judgmentally set by a first-line manager who attempts to make them "difficult but attainable." Regular feedback is provided, and in an open forum where social pressure and

---

[6] Mento et al., "A Meta-Analytic Study"; and Tubbs, "Goal Setting."

[7] See T. Matsui, T. Kakuyama, and M. L. U. Onglatco, "Effects of Goals and Feedback on Performance in Groups," *Journal of Applied Psychology* 72 (1987), pp. 407–15; and Mento et al., "A Meta-Analytic Study."

[8] C. C. Pinder, *Work Motivation: Theory, Issues, and Applications* (Glenview, Ill.: Scott, Foresman, 1984), pp. 214–16; and D. R. Ilgen, C. D. Fisher, and M. S. Taylor, "Consequences of Individual Feedback on Behavior in Organizations," *Journal of Applied Psychology* 64 (1979), pp. 349–71.

ILLUSTRATION 19–1
Goal Setting and Productivity

The Situation:

A logging company was experiencing backlogs because its truck drivers were often not at pickup points when needed. The challenge was to increase the number of trips each driver made each day.

The Program:

Preliminary diagnosis suggested the possible usefulness of a goal-setting program. Before implementation, however, discussions were held with the union to assure the acceptability of this approach and to establish the following ground rules: (1) the program must be voluntary, (2) there can be no special rewards or punishments associated with the program, (3) supervisors are encouraged to be supportive and may differentially praise those who attain goals, and (4) there must be no reduction in force as a result of the program.

Each Friday, the first-line supervisor of the 39 truckers involved assigned to each a goal for the following week, expressed in terms of average number of trips per day to and from a logging site and the mill. The goals were designed to be "difficult but attainable," taking into account such factors as (1) distance, (2) road conditions, (3) size of the timber being logged, and (4) driver skill. The weekly goals ranged from an average of three to seven trips per day. At the end of each day, the actual number of trips made was posted on a centrally located bulletin board.

Care was taken to explain carefully to the drivers the nature of, and the union's concurrence with, the program prior to its implementation.

The Results:

Following implementation many changes in the driver's behaviors were observed: increased use of radios to coordinate effort, frequent checking of the bulletin board, bragging about goal attainment, and the awarding of (self-purchased) gold stars for goal attainment.

Average number of trips per day increased from 3.55 (five-week average) before implementation of the program to 4.08 (18 week average) afterward. (Comparable averages for a control group were 3.49 and 3.34.) Accumulated across 39 drivers over 18 weeks the .53 increase in trips per day translates into more than 1,800 more trips in total.

On the 19th week, the company hired an industrial engineering firm to establish more systematic goal-setting procedures and staffing levels. This was done without consultation with the union. The anxiety produced by the resulting stop watches and goals (expressed in terms of "percent expected miles" rather than trips per day) resulted in a wildcat strike. The strike was resolved only after the company reaffirmed the previously established conditions and agreed to a two-month trial period after which the union could reject the new program if not satisfied. The program survived the trial and was still in operation a year later.

Source: G. P. Latham and L. M. Saari, "The Importance of Union Acceptance for Productivity Improvement through Goal Setting," *Personnel Psychology* 35 (1982), pp. 781–87.

recognition can work. By prior agreement with the union, the program is low key, voluntary, and not associated in any way with the allocation of rewards or punishments (save managerial praise). Still, the performance effects are considerable.

Scores of studies have been conducted on goal setting, and the overwhelming majority have found positive effects on performance. The magnitude of these effects, however, varies from a low of about 9 percent to a high of about 18 percent depending on the conditions, whether feedback was provided, and the like.[9] Notice that the goal setting program described in Illustration 19–1 resulted in performance increases toward the upper end of this range.

Management by Objectives

MBO is a formalized approach to management that incorporates elements of goal setting and is usually implemented among managers rather than clerical or blue-collar employees. There are no good statistics on its prevalence, but casual observation suggests there are few organizations of any size that have not tried MBO among at least some managers (sometimes emphasizing the performance enhancement aspects and sometimes the performance appraisal aspects discussed in Chapter 6).[10]

A complete MBO system contains the following elements: organizational goal setting and planning by top management, overall organizational commitment to goal-setting methods, mutual goal setting between superiors and subordinates, frequent reviews of performance, feedback on goal accomplishment and some degree of freedom in determining the best means for individual accomplishment of the goals.[11]

Figure 19–1 shows the essential features of an MBO system. Note that this approach presupposes that an organization has determined its long-range goals and the methods it intends to use to get there. Without these goals and their communication, successive managerial levels cannot integrate their goals with the overall strategy of the organization.

Specific individual goals are expected to be set between superiors and subordinates, with both having input about what are appropriate levels of goal accomplishment. (This is participation in goal setting.) Superiors

---

[9] Wood et al., "Task Complexity"; Mento et al., "A Meta-Analytic Study"; and Locke et al., "Goal Setting and Task Performance."

[10] J. S. Kane and K. A. Freeman, "MBO and Performance Appraisal: A Mixture That's Not a Solution, Part I," *Personnel* 63 (December 1986), pp. 26–36; and J. S. Kane and K. A. Freeman, "MBO and Performance Appraisal: A Mixture That's Not a Solution, Part II," *Personnel* 64 (February 1987), pp. 26–32.

[11] G. S. Odiorne, *MBO II* (Belmont, Calif.: Pitman Publishers, 1979).

FIGURE 19–1
Processes in an MBO System

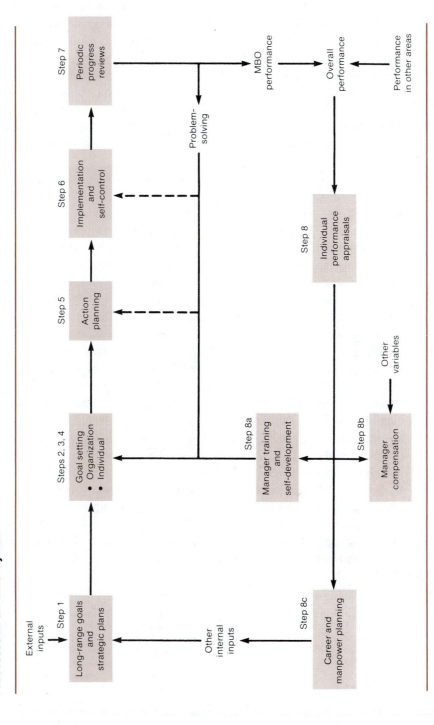

Source: A. P. Raia, *Managing by Objectives* (Glenview, Ill.: Scott, Foresman, 1974), pp. 21–22.

need to be particularly concerned about establishing achievable goals that are difficult and specific, and providing resources necessary for goal accomplishment. After goals have been established, action plans describing the activities necessary to reach the goals are constructed. Individual managers then implement and control the activities to reach the objectives. Periodically, they receive progress reviews. If progress is unsatisfactory, problem solving is undertaken to determine what should be done differently for goal accomplishment, what may not have been done that was considered necessary, or whether the goals were simply too difficult.

Reviews between superiors and subordinates help to assess and improve performance. Combining data on goal accomplishment with that obtained through behaviorally oriented performance measures is particularly useful.[12] Appraisals lead to suggested development activities to handle remedial problems or capitalize on the subordinate's potential, assist in human resource planning (HRP) and in career management for subordinates, as well as in establishing merit pay increases. This completes a cycle and provides the internal data necessary for updating long-range goals for the next cycle of goal setting and so forth.

This is an idealized example of an MBO system. One study found that even those who advocate MBO agreed no more than 34 percent of the time on what was involved in the goal-setting process, and only 14 percent of the time on the specification of characteristics that goals should reflect. A similar lack of agreement was obtained for how the appraisal process should be conducted.[13]

Intensive field studies of MBO systems show many problems in their implementation and administration.[14] The failure rate is fairly high. Where employees work in volatile environments or on projects with uncertain outcomes, MBO may not be appropriate. In other settings, however, it may succeed if care is taken in its introduction to ensure top management support and widespread acceptance, and in its administration to provide managers and subordinates with the skills and support needed to operate in such a "rational" and participative manner.

---

[12] It has been suggested that focusing on results alone without examining the behaviors that contribute to the results, or the behaviors that may be necessary in other jobs, reduces the effectiveness of performance measurements and feedback. See M. Beer and R. A. Ruh, "Employee Growth Through Performance Management," *Harvard Business Review* 54 (July–August 1976), pp. 59–66.

[13] M. L. McConkie, "A Clarification of the Goal Setting and Appraisal Process in MBO," *Academy of Management Review* 4 (1979), pp. 29–40.

[14] Pinder, *Work Motivation*, pp. 174–181; and J. N. Kondrasuk, "Studies in MBO Effectiveness," *Academy of Management Review* 6 (1981), pp. 419–30.

JOB DESIGN

Jobs are collections of tasks. To some extent in a given work situation the number and nature of tasks to be performed are defined and constrained by technology and the related work environment. However, within some bounds, organizations or individuals exercise discretion in specifying the precise character of the tasks performed and even more in deciding how these tasks are combined to form various jobs.[15]

Of major importance are the individuals who are to perform the jobs. As our model shows, the best results are obtained when job design is consistent with the abilities and reward preferences of employees. Jobs with narrow scopes (that is, containing relatively few simple tasks) require relatively little ability to perform but offer relatively few rewards associated with the work itself. Such jobs are best filled with individuals who have little training or experience and low needs for job challenge. The opposite is true of jobs with wide scopes.

Approaches to Job Design

The traditional approach to job design has been job simplification, for which technology and tradition are the driving factors. This approach creates jobs with narrow scopes, particularly at clerical and blue-collar levels. Because of low ability requirements, selection and training for such jobs is relatively easy. This is not true of motivation (or control), however, which has to be generated from sources other than the work itself.

More recently, there have been deliberate attempts to widen the scopes of many jobs through job enrichment. The hope is that more will be gained on the motivation side than will be lost as a result of the additional costs of attracting and developing employees with higher levels of ability needed to perform enriched jobs.

Job simplification

An enduring feature since the early days of the Industrial Revolution, job simplification was codified (as "the division of labor") by Adam Smith as early as 1776. At the turn of this century, the concept was turned into a movement by Frederick Winslow Taylor and fellow advocates of so-

---

[15] M. A. Campion and P. W. Thayer, "Job Design: Approaches, Outcomes, and Tradeoffs," *Organizational Dynamics* 15 (Winter 1987), pp. 66–79; and M. A. Campion and P. W. Thayer, "Development and Field Evaluation of an Interdisciplinary Measure of Job Design," *Journal of Applied Psychology* 70 (1985), pp. 29–43.

called scientific management.[16] It endures today through the work of many industrial engineers.

The basic approach is to discover methods for making tasks as simple and as easy to learn as possible. The emphasis is on minimizing ability requirements. The usual result is a sharp division of labor among several employees with few tasks assigned to any one. Employees are trained in the one best way to perform the work. Motivation is assumed to be taken care of by other means, such as incentive systems. Assembly-line jobs are perhaps the archetypes of job simplification.

Job enrichment

Job enrichment approaches job design from a motivational perspective.[17] The idea is to create jobs that are inherently motivating and thus to a large extent self-controlling. The job characteristics model shown in Figure 19–2, is a well-known approach.[18] It suggests that high internal work motivation (and satisfaction) result from three psychological states: (1) experienced meaningfulness of work, (2) experienced responsibility for outcomes of the work, and (3) knowledge of the actual results of the work activities. The first of these is said to result from jobs that are high in skill variety (involve many different types of tasks), task identity (result in the completion of a whole and identifiable piece of work), and task significance (have substantial effect on the lives of others). Autonomy (discretion in carrying out the work) and feedback (information about performance) are thought to cause the second and third, respectively.[19]

Consistent with earlier comments, the model suggests that these results occur only among certain individuals, namely, those who have the abilities required to perform enriched jobs, strong needs for challenge and accomplishments (growth) on the job, and a reasonable degree of satisfaction with their job contexts (for example, the degree of job security, pay, supervision, co-workers, etc.).

Among employees who meet these conditions, how are jobs actually enriched to provide more skill variety, task identity, task significance,

---

[16] F. W. Taylor, *The Principles of Scientific Management* (New York: W. W. Norton, 1967, originally published in 1911); and E. A. Locke, "The Ideas of Frederick W. Taylor: An Evaluation," *Academy of Management Review* 7 (1982), pp. 14–24.

[17] R. W. Griffin, "Toward an Integrated Theory of Task Design," in *Research in Personnel and Human Resource Management*, vol. 9, ed. K. M. Rowland and G. R. Ferris (Greenwich, Conn.: JAI Press, 1987), pp. 79–120; Campion and Thayer, "Job Design"; and R. W. Griffen, *Task Design: An Integrative Approach* (Glenview, Ill: Scott, Foresman, 1982), Ch. 3.

[18] J. R. Hackman and G. R. Oldham, *Work Redesign* (Reading, Mass.: Addison-Wesley Publishing, 1980), Ch. 4.

[19] Recall that the five core dimensions and the Job Diagnostic Survey (JDS) that is designed to measure employee perceptions of jobs on these dimensions were discussed in Chapter 5.

FIGURE 19–2
Job Characteristics Model

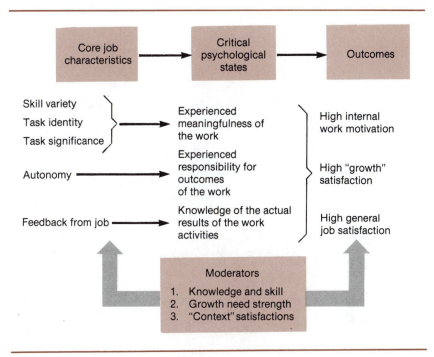

Source: J. R. Hackman and G. R. Oldham, *Work Redesign* (Reading, Mass.: Addison-Wesley Publishing, 1980), p. 90.

autonomy, and feedback? The change process is complex, but Figure 19–3 shows the essentials.[20] First, more tasks are added; second, these are selected to form natural work units (e.g., so as to serve an entire set of clients or geographic territory). Third, employees are put in direct contact with the internal or external "clients" from whom they receive and to whom they provide work or work products. Fourth, jobs are vertically loaded, that is, employees are given discretion in setting work schedules, determining work methods, and inspecting their own work. Finally, means are established to allow employees regularly to gain knowledge of how well they are doing.

As an example, consider a small bakery. An assembly-line approach to baking might give way to a team approach in which all employees have a hand in planning production schedules, ordering supplies, preparing recipes, baking, and inspecting the final products.

---

[20] Hackman and Oldham, *Job Redesign*, Ch. 5 and 6.

FIGURE 19-3

Links between Implementing Principles and the Core Job Characteristics

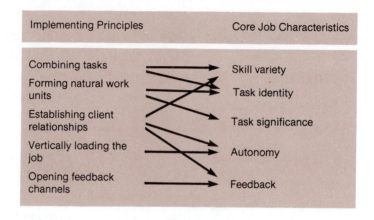

Source: J. R. Hackman and G. R. Oldham, *Work Redesign* (Reading, Mass.: Addison-Wesley Publishing, 1980), p. 135.

Effects of Changes in Job Design

Research shows that both job simplification and job enrichment currently are alive and well. A survey of 195 firms, for example, showed that within the past five years 29 percent had tried the former and 27 percent the latter in attempts to improve organizational productivity.[21]

Most of the research on the effectiveness of job design has focused on job enrichment, and more specifically on the job characteristics model.[22] In general, this research has been quite supportive. Across a great number of studies, job enrichment has been found to result in enhanced work motivation and higher levels of job performance, increased job satisfaction (and especially satisfaction with the opportunity to grow on the job), and lower levels of absenteeism. In fewer studies, it has also

---

[21] Bureau of National Affairs, *Productivity Improvement Programs*, Personnel Policies Forum Survey No. 138 (Washington, D.C.: Bureau of National Affairs, 1984), pp. 11–12.

[22] For recent reviews, see Y. Fried and G. R. Ferris, "The Validity of the Job Characteristics Model: A Review and Meta-Analysis," *Personnel Psychology* 40 (1987), pp. 287–322; E. F. Stone, "Job Scope-Job Satisfaction and Job Scope-Job Performance Relationships," in *Generalizing from Laboratory to Field Settings*, ed. E. A. Locke (Lexington, Mass.: D. C. Heath, 1986), pp. 189–206; B. T. Loehr, R. A. Noe, N. L. Moeller, and M. P. Fitzgerald, "A Meta-Analysis of the Relation of Job Characteristics and Job Satisfaction," *Journal of Applied Psychology* 70 (1985), pp. 280–89; and P. E. Spector, "Higher Order Need Strength as a Moderator of the Job Scope-Employee Outcome Relationship: A Meta-Analysis," *Journal of Occupational Psychology* 58 (1985), pp. 119–27.

been shown to result in lower levels of voluntary turnover (one review, for example, found job enrichment to be twice as effective as realistic job previews [see Chapter 9] in this respect).[23] Further, as the job characteristics model suggests (refer again to Figure 19–2), these effects are stronger among those high in growth-need strength than among those low on this attribute.

Among the core job characteristics, feedback has a consistent and considerable positive effect on all the P/HR outcomes (recall that feedback also enhances the performance effects of goals). In addition, task identity is particularly helpful in increasing motivation and performance, as are skill variety and autonomy in reducing absenteeism. All appear to enhance job satisfaction. (No comparable data are available with respect to turnover.)

Despite the preponderance of positive results, it must be remembered that the choice between job simplification and job enrichment always involves trade-offs. Neither approach has been shown to be clearly superior in all respects under all circumstances. Rather, each has its costs and benefits in various situations. Thus, in part the choice hinges on the costs management is willing to incur and the benefits it wishes to pursue. But, even though the costs are usually quite clear, the probability of attaining, and the value of, the various benefits often are not. Hence, the final decision often depends a good deal more on management's dominant values, beliefs about employees, and explicit or implicit theories of work motivation than on the evidence itself.[24] Perhaps this is why the survey noted earlier showed an even split between the two approaches among firms that have recently turned to job design in an attempt to enhance their competitiveness and bottom-line results.

PARTICIPATIVE WORK GROUPS

Closely related to the issue of job design is the issue of decision making. Specifically, which decisions should be made at various levels of the hierarchy? By what mechanisms should these decisions be made? What roles will be played by whom?

The traditional view (again codified by the advocates of scientific management and consistent with the tenets of job simplification) is that managers decide and workers do. Participation can be said to occur whenever this tradition is broken and lower-level employees become

---

[23] G. M. McEvoy and W. F. Cascio, "Strategies for Reducing Employee Turnover: A Meta-Analysis," *Journal of Applied Psychology* 70 (1985), pp. 342–53.

[24] Campion and Thayer, "Job Design"; and Campion and Thayer, "Development and Field Evaluation."

involved in organizational decision making. Its forms are many. It can be voluntary or imposed (on management), occur at all organizational levels or only at relatively low levels, involve many decisions or few, be advisory or binding, and so forth.

In many European countries, participation is mandated by law. Employee representatives (typically trade union leaders) sit on corporate boards of directors and on high-level works councils and routinely become involved in a wide range of policy decisions. The legislation usually does not apply to day-to-day operations, however, and here the amount and nature of participation varies widely from country to country and within countries from firm to firm. In Japan, participation is oriented toward operational decisions with the intent of gaining consensus within and across work groups on most matters of significance.

In the United States, managers for years eschewed both the European and Japanese models, and by and large avoided participation in any form (except through collective bargaining where employees were unionized). More recently, the obvious success of overseas competitors in many U.S. markets has led to a greater willingness to experiment in many areas, including participation. With a few notable exceptions (e.g., Chrysler where a union representative sits on the board of directors), this experimentation has more closely followed the Japanese than the European model. Specific types of experimentation include participative decision making, quality circles, and self-managing work teams.

Participative Decision Making

Figure 19–4 traces the mechanisms through which participative decision making (PDM) is said to affect employee behavior and attitudes and, in turn, organizational results. It suggests that participation improves both employee ability and motivation. Ability is improved primarily through communication and information sharing, which results in more informed employees who are better able to contribute creative ideas to the success of the enterprise. Motivation is improved in part because employees tend to set higher goals participatively than management does unilaterally (recall the motivational value of "stretch" goals) and in part because the process causes individuals to become ego involved and committed and to exert pressure on themselves and their co-workers to ensure that their decisions are sound and their goals are met. The act of participating can also increase employees' sense of trust and control, which may lower their resistance to new ways of doing things. On the attitudinal side, some find that participation (like job enrichment) meets their needs for challenge and accomplishment (growth), causing satisfac-

FIGURE 19–4
Proposed Effects and Mechanisms of PDM

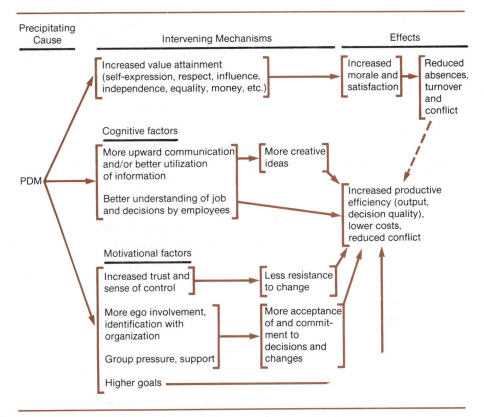

Source: E. A. Locke and D. M. Schweiger, "Participation in Decision Making: One More Look," in *Research in Organizational Behavior,* ed. B. M. Staw (Greenwich, Conn.: JAI Press, 1979), p. 279.

tion to increase and a consequent decline in the tendency to be absent or leave.[25]

The question is, does participation actually produce these results? A number of careful surveys of the research on this issue have been inconclusive; sometimes it does, but often it does not.[26] Such equivocal

[25] D. M. Schweiger and C. R. Leana, "Participation in Decision Making," in *Generalizing from Laboratory to Field Settings,* ed. E. A. Locke, pp. 147–66.

[26] J. L. Cotton, D. A. Vollrath, K. L. Froggatt, M. L. Lengnick-Hall, and K. R. Jennings, "Employee Participation: Diverse Forms and Different Outcomes," *Academy of Management Review* 13 (1988), pp. 8–22; E. A. Locke, D. M. Schweiger, and G. P. Latham, "Participation in Decision Making: When Should It Be Used?" *Organizational Dynamics* 14 (1986), pp. 65–79; J. A. Wagner and R. Z. Gooding, "Shared Influence and Organizational Behavior: A Meta-Analysis of Situational Variables Expected to Moderate Participation-Outcome Relationships," *Academy of Management Journal* 30 (1987), pp. 524–41; and K. I. Miller and P. R. Monge, "Participation, Satisfaction, and Productivity: A Meta-Analytic Review," *Academy of Management Journal* 29 (1986), pp. 727–53.

findings have encouraged some researchers to differentiate among the various forms of participation and compare and contrast the effects of each.[27] Others have chosen to focus not on the forms *per se* but rather on the circumstances under which the various forms might be expected to, or actually do, succeed or fail.[28] Still others have emphasized the problems of implementation and suggested that it is these rather than any inherent deficiencies in the concept of participation that account for the mixed record so far.[29] In truth, however, no one so far has done a very effective job of unraveling the nature and effects of the various cognitive, motivational, and attitudinal processes delineated in Figure 19–4. And the battle over participation, or employee involvement as it is increasingly called, is being fought more on ideological than on empirical grounds.

In the meantime, practitioners keep trying. In the previously cited survey of productivity improvement efforts, 44 percent of the 195 respondents had introduced and put considerable effort into the design and implementation of participation programs during the previous five years.[30] These efforts took many forms, but more than half were quality circles.

Quality Circles

Quality circles (QCs), yet another Japanese export, are groups of employees that meet regularly to work on problems affecting a work area.[31] They exist outside the normal organizational hierarchy, and their powers are to recommend but not implement solutions. Figure 19–5 enumerates the more common features of QCs, and Illustration 19–2 describes a simple but successful application in a telephone company.

Structures vary, but extensive QC programs such as the ones at Xerox and Inland Steel consist of a steering committee (which contains union leaders if employees are organized), professional or highly trained facilitators, circle leaders who (increasingly come from the rank and file), and circle members (usually 3 to 13; the average is 9) who are volunteers.

---

[27] Cotton et al., "Employee Participation."

[28] Locke et al., "Participation in Decision Making."

[29] See, for example, J. P. Muczyk and B. C. Reimann, "Has Participative Management Been Oversold?" *Personnel* 64 (May 1987), pp. 52–56; and S. A. Mohrman and G. E. Ledford, "The Design and Use of Effective Employee Participation Groups: Implications for Human Resource Management," *Human Resource Management* 24 (1985), pp. 413–28.

[30] Bureau of National Affairs, *Productivity Improvement Programs*, pp. 11–12. Note that the same study found considerably lower percentages for both job simplification or job enrichment, and a comparable figure for these two approaches to job design taken together.

[31] For a description, see Lawler, *High Involvement Management*, Ch. 4.

FIGURE 19-5

Typical Characteristics of Quality Circles

Objectives:
* To attain employee involvement in the identification and solution of problems relating to such issues as productivity or costs, quality, and conditions of work (e.g., housekeeping, safety).
* To improve results in these areas.

Organization:
* Each QC consists of a leader or coordinator, who is usually not from management, and 3 to 13 other employees (the average is around 9) from a single work unit or area.
* An organization may have many QCs that are assisted by one or more facilitators, usually a professional who is trained in group process skills.
* Since QCs have no formal authority, they require few changes in basic operating structures or procedures. There is usually little downward sharing of information about company plans, operating results, or finances.

Membership:
* Participation is voluntary.
* Most QCs are in manufacturing operations and involve blue-collar employees, although increasingly they are being adopted in service industries and are involving white-collar (but not managerial) employees.

Scope:
* QCs usually select the problems they will work on (within the scope of their own work area) although sometimes they are formed to tackle a particular issue. Certain topics (e.g., personnel matters, provisions of labor contracts) are taboo.
* QCs have no budgets and no direct control over any organizational resources, although often their recommendations involve the expenditure of funds.

Training:
* QC leaders or coordinators receive training in group facilitation skills.
* QC members receive training in group process, problem solving, and communication skills and may receive training in specialized areas such as statistical quality control techniques. Ten to 20 hours of training per individual is common.

Meetings:
* QCs meet weekly or biweekly for an hour or two, although the meetings may become more frequent or lengthy as they become immersed in a particular issue or involved in preparing a presentation to management.
* Meetings take place on company time, although some may be scheduled for after hours.

Rewards for Participation and Performance
* Monetary rewards above and beyond normal compensation are rare.
* Nonmonetary rewards—awards, plaques, banquets—are common. Often a lot of hoopla—team names, emblazoned caps and t-shirts, etc.—accompany QC formations.
* The big reward, however, is the satisfaction that comes from successfully tackling significant problems, making presentations to management, and having suggestions adopted, implemented, and (it is hoped) succeed.

Source: E. E. Lawler III, *High Involvement Management* (San Francisco: Jossey-Bass Publishers, 1986), pp. 46–50.

ILLUSTRATION 19–2

A Quality Circle Application

The case presented here is based on the work of a quality circle of telephone operators in a large bank. They handled an average of 500 customer calls daily.

- *Identifying and Selecting a Problem.* Bank surveys had indicated that callers tended to become irritated when the phone rang six or more times before it was answered. Because first impressions are important to customers, the circle decided to solve these two related problems:

  —Delays in answering.
  —Unnecessary switching from extension to extension.

- *Analyzing the Problem.* The circle first discussed the present system of answering calls and the potential reasons for making the customer wait.

Because the operators did not have information that indicated which were the most likely causes, they devised check sheets to record the number of delayed calls over a two-week period, and the reason for the delay. The categories were:

A—only one of the two operators at each station.
B—receiving party not present.
C—no one present in department receiving call.
D—department or name of receiving party not given.
E—other.

These data were arranged in a Pareto chart, shown on p. 671. The chart clearly indicates that almost half of the delayed calls occurred when one of the two department operators was not on duty.

- *Generating Potential Solutions.* Using brainstorming, the circle generated several potential solutions designed to solve the primary causes of the problem. Their suggestions:

  —Always have two operators on duty at each station.
  —Have employees leave messages when leaving desks.
  —Compile a directory of staff members and job titles.

- *Selecting and Planning Solution.* The circle reached consensus on all three recommendations. To make the recommendations viable, it was necessary to plan how they could be implemented. To ensure that there were always two operators on duty at each station, the circle suggested a three-shift lunch instead of the current two shifts. This would make it easier to cover the open position during lunch with another member of the clerical staff. To encourage employees to leave messages when they were to be away from their desks, their cooperation was requested at the regular staff meeting. Posters were also placed around the offices to publicize the new practice. Finally, the circle undertook production of the directory, which was designed especially to help operators locate the appropriate employee for a given incoming call.

ILLUSTRATION 19–2 *(concluded)*

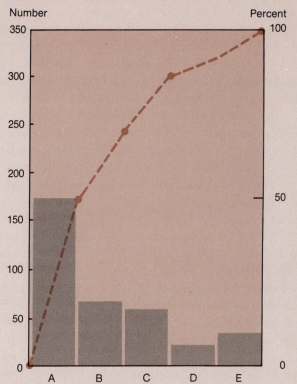

Frequency of Causes of Telephone Delays

- *Implementing Solution.* The circle's recommendations were approved by management and implemented according to the plan.

- *Evaluating Solution.* To determine the effectiveness of the solution, the circle collected additional data two months after implementation. The total number of delayed calls was dramatically reduced; furthermore, there were no "vital few" causes responsible. The identified problem was solved.

Source: Reprinted in, and taken from H. Gorlin and L. Schein, *Innovations in Managing Human Resources* (New York: The Conference Board, 1984), pp. 6 and 7.

QC programs require some up-front managerial commitment, since facilitators, circle leaders, and circle members must be trained. The circles take some time to get organized and become productive, but from a participation standpoint they are relatively innocuous since management typically controls location, size, and the problems on which the groups work. Most are advisory only; management retains the right to reject their advice (although, of course, frequent resort to this right would soon quell employee interest).[32]

A best guess is that nationwide QCs are in use in most of the Fortune 500 companies and in many government agencies as well. Their newness, however, means that they have yet to be extensively evaluated. Many successful applications have been reported by such corporations as Ford, TRW, Honeywell, Westinghouse, Digital Equipment Corporation, and AT&T. A recent review of 33 more or less systematic studies of QC effectiveness turned up mixed results at best.[33] Only 12 of the studies focused on such hard outcomes as productivity, costs, and quality (ostensibly the targets of QCs), and only four of these showed uniformly positive results. Usually it took from four to eight months before benefits began exceeding costs. Research cited elsewhere suggests that most of the benefits come through the improved work methods and procedures that the QCs suggest.[34]

Employee attitudes (such as job satisfaction) were examined in 30 of the 33 studies mentioned above, and 13 showed uniformly positive results among the QC participants. Some found a deterioration in the attitudes of those not participating in QCs.

Obviously, the infusion of QCs into American industry and governmental agencies has not always been easy. Reported difficulties include lack of volunteers to participate; inability of volunteers to absorb the training; excessive turnover among participants; resistance and even hostility on the part of non-participants, supervisors, and middle managers; too little attention to organizational outcomes and too much to individual ones; and results that fail to meet (perhaps inflated) expectations. Disillusionment and cynicism may develop among participants if management dictates the terms and conditions of participation, the scope of the QCs' activities, and the ultimate power to decide if, when, and how the recommendations of the QCs will be implemented.[35]

Solutions to sustaining QCs may lie in expanding the scope of the problems with which they deal, their decision-making power, or both,

---

[32] R. Griffen, "Consequences of Quality Circles in an Industrial Setting: A Longitudinal Assessment," *Academy of Management Journal* 31 (1988), pp. 338–58; K. Bradley and S. Hill, "Quality Circles and Managerial Interests," *Industrial Relations* 26 (1987), pp. 68–82; and G. W. Meyer and R. G. Stott, "Quality Circles: Panacea or Pandora's Box," *Organizational Dynamics* 13 (1985), pp. 34–50.

[33] M. R. Barrick and R. A. Alexander, "A Review of Quality Circle Efficacy and the Existence of Positive-Findings Bias," *Personnel Psychology* 40 (1987), pp. 579–92.

[34] Lawler, *High Involvement Management*, Ch. 4.

[35] Griffen, "Consequences of Quality Circles"; Lawler, *High Involvement Management*, Ch. 4; and Meyer and Stott, "Quality Circles."

FIGURE 19–6

A Comparison of Quality Circles and Self-Managing Work Teams

	Participation Concept	
Characteristic	Quality Circles	Self-Managing Teams
Implementation.	Mostly in mature plants.	Mostly in new, "greenfield" sites.
Ease of start-up.	Moderate in ease and speed.	Much more difficult and lengthy.
Participation.	Usually totally voluntary.	Usually not voluntary, but individual participation levels vary.
Membership.	Subset of work group.	The entire work group.
Leadership.	Initial leader, frequently a supervisor, may be elected or appointed by management.	Internal leader elected; external leader appointed by management.
Type and frequency of problems.	One at a time, usually a larger issue for a long period, selected from a wide range.	Many small day-to-day issues, selected from a wider range.
Implementation authority.	Usually recommend; sometimes implement.	Usually implement.
Motivational impact.	Moderate to strong.	Stronger.
Relationship to existing organization.	An overlay.	Largely replaces existing organizations.

Source: H. P. Sims, Jr. and J. W. Dean, Jr., "Beyond Quality Circles: Self-Managing Work Teams," *Personnel*, January 1985, pp. 25–32.

that is, in getting deeper into employee involvement through self-managing work teams.[36]

Self-Managing Work Teams

Self-managing work teams (SMWTs) are groups of employees given responsibility for managing and operating their own particular pieces of a business. The development of SMWTs is analogous to job enrichment, but at the group level. SMWTs are responsible for planning the work to be done, organizing themselves to get it done, selecting team members and assigning them to jobs, providing their own "supervision" (traditional supervisors, if present, usually serve as group facilitators, not

---

[36] Some (see H. P. Sims, Jr. and J. W. Dean, Jr., "Beyond Quality Circles: Self-Managing Teams," *Personnel* 62 [January 1985], pp. 25–32) argue that this is a natural evolution. Others (see E. E. Lawler III and S. A. Mohrman, "Quality Circles After the Fad," *Harvard Business Review* 85 [January–February 1985], pp. 65–71 and Lawler, *High Involvement Management*) take the opposite position, stating that organizations that want self-managing work teams should start with them.

ILLUSTRATION 19–3

The Use of SMWTs at Keithley Instruments

The Situation:

Keithley Instruments, located in Solon, Ohio, designs and manufactures sophisticated electronic measurement instruments. In 1982 sales were $33 million, profits were $1.5 million, and the company had nearly 500 employees.

In 1979 the company was facing increasing competition coupled with slowdowns in productivity levels, particularly in manufacturing. After an appropriate diagnosis, the vice president of manufacturing and his staff decided to convert the function to the use of self-managing work teams (SMWTs).

The Conversion:

From a traditional assembly-line approach, the manufacturing process was redesigned. The new layout was organized in such a way that teams of employees—usually around 12—could start, complete, and inspect entire instruments as single units. Team members could see how their work related to the completion of the final products and were in positions to assist others as the need arose.

Over time, 12 product teams were assembled. Each had responsibility for setting team goals and reviewing progress against these goals. A steady stream of information was provided the teams and how well the product was selling, what was being done to redesign it, and the like.

Initially, product team members were volunteers, although everyone in manufacturing was eventually assigned to a team. Team members received training in: (1) products, production methods, and costs; (2) team building (e.g., goal setting, problem solving, and communication); and (3) team procedures and goals. Team supervisors were carefully selected and trained in such areas as: (1) the role of supervision, (2) motivation, (3) performance appraisal, (4) counseling, and (5) team management.

The conversion was done deliberately, taking 2½ years to complete. Throughout this period, the vice president of personnel served as process consultant to facilitate the introduction of change.

The Results:

Between 1979 (the base year) and 1983 (the final team was formed in June 1982):

- Productivity (output per manufacturing employee) doubled.
- Product quality (measured by in-warranty repair rates) improved by 15 percent.
- Raw material and work in process inventories fell about 50 and 30 percent, respectively, even though total output rose by 80 percent.
- Absenteeism fell by 80 percent.
- Employees and supervisors reported significantly higher job satisfaction.

Since 1983, other teams have been formed elsewhere in the organization; some, which operate more as QCs (task forces), cut across functions and organizational levels.

Source: M. A. Frohman, "Human Resource Management and the Bottom Line: Evidence of the Connection," *Human Resource Management* 23 (1984), pp. 315–34.

managers), resolving team conflicts, and exercising quality control. Figure 19–6 provides a comparison between QCs and SMWTs.

In SMWTs everyone participates, not just volunteers. All relevant work issues are addressed, not just those given by management. SMWTs are an integral part of their organizations (indeed to their members they are the organization). Once teams decide, they implement; management is consulted only when the decisions transcend the bounds of their budgetary authority or impinge on the work of other teams.[37] Illustration 19–3 describes the workings of the SMWT approach.

Given the "radical" nature of SMWTs, considerable nurturing is necessary to make them work. Team members must be thoroughly trained, not only in technical matters, but also in group process skills. Supervisors must be trained for their new roles as facilitators and reinforced for giving up their authority in favor of the team approach. The quantity and quality of information flowing to the teams needs to be uniformly high. Often, particularly in the early stages, the assistance of outside consultants is required for SMWTs to function efficiently. Management must exercise a great deal of faith, particularly in the early going, as their norms and values are continually assaulted by "subordinates" with little more than a promise of future payoffs somewhere down the road.

Thus, it is not surprising that SMWTs are far less common than QCs. Only 200 or so plants or offices are said to be operating this way in the United States. Evaluations are rare. Productivity improvements and cost savings of 20 to 40 percent are claimed, but as yet not substantiated.[38] One recent and particularly well-designed study in a small British factory found that while SMWTs did result in enhanced job satisfaction, this form of work organization did not appreciably affect employee motivation, performance, or voluntary turnover (although involuntary turnover was higher as slackers were more easily identified). The factory experienced productivity and cost benefits, however, because of improved work methods and reductions in the number of supervisors and other forms of indirect labor.[39]

One clear result from the early case studies is the inability of SMWTs to survive very long within traditional organizational frameworks. The

[37] Lawler, *High Involvement Management*, Ch. 7; Sims and Dean, "Beyond Quality Circles."

[38] C. C. Manz and H. P. Sims, Jr., "Leading Workers to Lead Themselves: The External Leadership of Self-Managing Work Teams," *Administrative Science Quarterly* 32 (1987), pp. 106–28; Sims and Dean, "Beyond Quality Circles."

[39] T. D. Wall, J. K. Nigel, P. R. Jackson, and C. W. Clegg, "Outcomes of Autonomous Work Groups: A Long-Term Field Experiment," *Academy of Management Journal* 29 (1986), pp. 280–304.

clash of styles and needs has led in some instances to the abandonment of SMWTs and in others to a comprehensive restructuring (or initial structuring) of host organizations to create a "social system" that is inherently consistent and reinforcing. Such efforts rest on a participative base that is intended to enhance employee motivation and satisfaction, as well as self and social control.

HIGH-INVOLVEMENT WORK SYSTEMS

The systemic approaches to workplace design are often called high-involvement work systems (HIWS).[40] They are comprehensive, consciously created combinations of the building blocks just discussed, several traditional P/HR activities (especially compensation and labor relations), and other organizational features.[41] Figure 19–7 highlights the various components that are typically involved by contrasting a more traditional ("investment") strategy with the HIWS approach. Note that the HIWS is characterized by "stretch" goals, including expectations of considerable initiative and creativity on the part of all employees and a high degree of identification with work. The main means of attaining these goals is a work system organized around enriched jobs and/or SMWTs with minimal supervision. Supporting features include considerable investment in training, skill-based pay, a high degree of emphasis on employee relations (communications, grievance procedures, and the like), cooperative labor relations, and careful selection to choose employees who will fit into this type of "social system."

To date, no fully developed theory of HIWSs has been put forth. Thus, there is much art in choosing and combining components for the best results in employee behaviors and attitudes and organizational outcomes.

Undaunted, however, a number of organizations have pushed ahead. The result is a potpourri of experimental programs that defy neat classification. Here they are organized around major "entry points": SMWTs, rewards, labor relations, and new plant start-ups (or "greenfield sites").[42]

---

[40] Lawler, *High Involvement Management*, Ch. 8, 10, 11, and 12. A *commitment system* is the term preferred by R. E. Walton, "From Control to Commitment in the Workplace," *Harvard Business Review* 85 (March–April 1985), pp. 77–84.

[41] Dyer and Holder, "A Strategic Perspective."

[42] What follows relies heavily on Lawler, *High Involvement Management;* and S. A. Mohrman and E. E. Lawler III, "Quality of Work Life," in *Research in Personnel and Human Resource Management*, vol. 2, eds. K. M. Rowland and G. R. Ferris (Greenwich, Conn.: JAI Press, 1984), pp. 219–260.

FIGURE 19–7
Systematic Work Design Strategies

Goals	Inducement	Involvement (QWL)
Contribution	Some initiative and creativity, very high performance standards, modest flexibility	Very high initiative and creativity, high performance expectations, high flexibility
Composition	Lean headcount (core and buffer), low skill mix, minimal staffs	Comfortable headcounts (core and buffer), high skill mix, minimal staffs
Competence	Adequate	Very high
Commitment	High, instrumental	High, identification with work and company
Means		
Staffing	Careful selection, few career options, use of temps, (minimal layoffs)	Careful selection, some career development, much flex, minimal (or no) layoffs
Development	Minimal	*Extensive, continuous learning
Rewards	*Flat structure, high-variable, piece-rate, profit sharing, minimal benefits	Flat structure, high-partially variable, skill-based, gain-sharing, flex benefits
Work system	Narrow jobs, employee paced, individualized	*Enriched jobs, self-managed work teams
Supervision	Minimal, directive	*Minimal, facilitative
Employee relations	Some communication, some voice, egalitarian	Much communication, high voice, some due process, some employee assistance, egalitarian
Labor relations	Union avoidance, or conflict	Union avoidance, and or cooperative
Govt. relations	Compliance	Compliance

* Indicates priority program areas.

Source: L. Dyer and G. W. Holder, "A Strategic Perspective of Human Resource Management," in *Human Resource Management: Evolving Roles and Responsibilities, ASPA/BNA Handbook of Human Resource Management,* vol. 1, ed. L. Dyer (Washington, D.C.: Bureau of National Affairs, 1988), pp. 20 and 21.

Approaches Centering on SMWTs

This is the most common approach. It begins with the establishment of a SMWT or two, usually in manufacturing or major clerical operations. If success if experienced, additional SMWTs are added. Illustrative is the situation at Keithley Instruments, as described in Illustration 19–3.

As SMWTs become operational, jobs tend to become enriched. Responsibilities for planning, coordination, and control are added. By virtue of exposure, if not design, team members become cross-trained (they learn one anothers' jobs) and become more or less interchangeable.

Job rotation often follows. For a while, the rewards associated with participation, job enrichment, and cross-training may be enough to sustain employee interest. Eventually, however, especially in the face of higher productivity and profits, pressures begin to build for the addition of more tangible rewards. One possible answer, especially if cross-training and job rotation have caught on, is skill-based pay (see Chapter 15). This pays participants more as they learn new jobs. Organization-based bonus plans, especially gain sharing and profit sharing, are other possible responses. Often, in the spirit of the program, responsibility for the choice and design of new reward systems is allocated to a task force consisting of representatives from several organizational levels.

Training pervades the program. Employees learn new technical and group process skills. Group members learn to work together, groups learn to work with one another, and management learns (or tries to learn) how to operate in more participative and egalitarian ways.

Approaches Centering on Rewards

Older, but less common, systemic approaches to HIWS use reward systems—and especially gain sharing—as entry points. These approaches become systemic when participative features are added over and above the financial rewards. The Scanlon Plan, which is decidedly not new, is the best-known program of this type (see Chapter 15).

In the Scanlon Plan, periodic bonuses are paid, based on labor cost savings over a predetermined base rate. The intent is to align the interests of management and employees toward improved organizational performance, since both stand to gain. An important feature, however, is the establishment of interlocking plant-level committees to establish and monitor the base rate and to generate and evaluate suggestions for improving productivity and otherwise cutting costs. Participation on these committees cuts across functional and organizational lines. In addition, employees often participate on special task forces formed to follow up on special issues.

Communication becomes more open under these conditions, since employees require timely and accurate information on the status of the suggestions made, as well as the financial performance of their units. Extensive training in financial and operating matters and in group process skills is usually provided.

Illustration 19–4 describes Motorola's participative management program (PMP), which is a systemic approach that centers on both SMWTs and rewards. Among production employees at Motorola, gain sharing (a

ILLUSTRATION 19–4

A Systemic Approach to Workplace Design at Motorola

The Situation:

Motorola is a major manufacturer of electronics products that employs 57,000 employees in the United States. The company is under considerable competitive pressure from the Japanese. Major elements of its competitive strategy are to control prices through improved productivity and to enhance customer satisfaction through high product quality. Both are pursued, in part, through the company's participative management program (PMP).

The Program:

PMP is a comprehensive, two-part effort that centers on self-managing work teams (SMWTs) and group bonus plans. PMP I focuses on manufacturing employees and PMP II focuses on nonmanufacturing employees.

Plan I employees are divided into groups of 50 to 250 people around product lines. Group goals are established by a subgroup composed of directs, their supervisors, and support personnel. Goals are established in five areas: (1) costs, (2) quality, (3) deliveries (against schedules), (4) inventory levels, and (5) housekeeping and safety. Employees work in smaller groups. In addition, each product group has working committees consisting of a manager and several employees. These committees meet as frequently as necessary to review problems with costs, quality, deliveries, inventories, and housekeeping, and to suggest solutions. Recommendations are forwarded to steering committees, consisting of cross sections of employees, for review and approval. Employees at all levels receive considerable training to prepare them to meet the high standards of performance and to work effectively in a participative environment.

PMP I employees are paid competitive wages. In addition, they are eligible for monthly bonuses of up to 41 percent based in part on product group performance against goals and in part on the suggestions they make for improvements in operations.

PMP II employees are those in engineering, marketing, product development, accounting, and so forth. They, too, work in groups and have the potential to earn bonuses (paid quarterly rather than monthly). Bonuses are based in part on the earnings of the profit center in which they work and in part on their groups' performance against nonfinancial goals. Nonfinancial goals are established annually by the work groups in conjunction with a management steering committee (in a process resembling a group-based management-by-objectives program). Feedback against performance is frequent to encourage a sense of accomplishment (or nonaccomplishment) in the groups.

In addition, the company runs an active suggestion ("I recommend") system.

PMP is monitored and evaluated by the personnel function, and continually modified based on the results.

The Results:

Motorola's CEO calls the results of PMP "truly impressive" citing in one instance cost savings of $3 million in an electroplating operation and in

---

ILLUSTRATION 19–4 *(concluded)*

another a 33 percent increase in output with a substantial reduction in the number of employees involved. Also cited are anecdotes showing less need for supervision, increased cooperation among employees, and decreased turnover.

However, the road to increased participation is tough, and not all managers survive the rigors of sharp questioning by employees and the need to avoid the exercise of position power.

Source: W. J. Weisz, "Employee Involvement: How It Works at Motorola," *Personnel,* February 1985, pp. 29–33.

---

group-oriented bonus plan) predominates; other employees are rewarded through a combination of profit sharing and gain sharing. Though strictly speaking this is not a Scanlon Plan, it has many similar features.

Approaches Centering on Labor Relations

Some HIWSs have been undertaken as cooperative efforts between managements and unions. Best publicized are those undertaken jointly by the United Auto Workers and General Motors (known as Quality of Worklife or QWL) and Ford (known as Employee Involvement, or EI), although about 100 other such efforts are also in operation. Generally, the publicly stated purposes of these programs are to improve union-management relations and enhance the quality of working life, although it is unlikely that management would long participate without anticipating productivity, quality, and profit payoffs as well.

Some unions—notably the United Auto Workers, the United Steelworkers, the Communications Workers of America, and the Newspaper Guild—actively endorse and participate in such programs. The AFL–CIO cautiously endorses them. Many unions eschew them, however, as management speed-up techniques or union-busting tactics. (The last view is not entirely without merit. To cite one example, CUE, an educational subsidiary of the National Association of Manufacturers, openly promotes HIWSs as union-avoidance devices.)[43]

Where joint programs are undertaken, they usually are governed by one or more union-management committees that set the ground rules and oversee the process. Goals and the principle of joint ownership are

---

[43] C. A. Thorpe, *Making Participative Management Part of Your Winning Strategy* (Washington, D.C.: CUE/NAM, 1985).

established (although parties retain the right to withdraw at any time). Areas considered off limits, if any, are clearly defined.

Change processes vary, although most involve joint committees at plant and department levels to do diagnoses and to plan and implement change. Early efforts often focus on housekeeping and the work environment (heating, lighting, ventilation); subsequent evolution may be to more substantive matters of joint concern (e.g., safety) and to the nature of the work itself.

Key to the success of joint programs is the skillful management of the many political problems that can arise, particularly on the union side. Some union members fear the concept; others may come to feel left out if pilot projects are undertaken in work areas other than their own; still others may fail to have their expectations met and become disillusioned. Such developments as these put considerable pressures on union leaders (who are, after all, elected officials), making it difficult to evolve preliminary efforts into generally more cooperative union-management relationships. It can be done, though; QWL has survived at General Motors for more than a decade.

Approaches Centering on Start-Ups

Occasionally, companies (sometimes with unions) have attempted to adopt HIWSs right from the start in new plants or facilities ("greenfield sites"). The best known of these have been undertaken in manufacturing plants by General Motors, Procter & Gamble, General Foods, Cummins Engine, and H. J. Heinz. Illustration 19–5 provides an example from Westinghouse.

ILLUSTRATION 19–5

HIWS in a Start-Up Plant

Westinghouse has seen the future, and it is in College Station, Texas. There the company is shaping its factory of tomorrow. With 500 nonunion employees—a mere one tenth the work force at a traditional plant—it is easier to manage. And the employees earn salaries rather than hourly pay and get raises based on tests of their skills. "They are at the frontier of new plant design in structuring work and compensation," says Thomas A. Kochan, a labor expert at the Massachusetts Institute of Technology.

The goal: to make electronic assemblies for military radar more cheaply by integrating the work force with $19 million in automated equipment. The results: impressive. Costs for manufacturing a circuit assembly at College Station are half what they are in traditional plants. In a plant in Baltimore, each worker builds one and a half such assemblies each day. In College Station, with the help of two Seiko robots, each worker builds a dozen.

ILLUSTRATION 19–5 *(concluded)*

The key, says Westinghouse, is not the robots but the people. Employees work in teams of 8 to 12. Members devise their own solutions to problems. Teams measure daily how each person's performance compares with that of other members and how the team's performance compares with the plant's. Joseph L. Johnson, 28, a robotics technician, says that is a big change from a previous hourly factory job where he cared only about "picking up my paycheck." Here, peer pressure "makes sure you get the job done."

The pay system is different, too. Unlike union plants, where raises often are pegged to seniority, College Station workers who score well on skills tests can boost their pay to $1,550 a month from a $960 base in three years.

The changes have forced the company to seek a new kind of employee. Applicants must submit to interviews and tests that measure initiative, ability to take advice, creativity, and skills. Only about 5 percent are hired.

College Station's start in 1983 was rocky. Westinghouse rejected entire batches of bad parts, and dismissals of inefficient workers boosted turnover to 22 percent. The company became more selective in hiring and overhauled its training program. Productivity has shot up, and turnover is down to 4 percent.

Westinghouse faces a tougher battle changing older plants. The College Station approach rankles some union officials, who see it as a symbol of how the company has abandoned longtime workers. And even in nonunion plants, workers have trouble adapting. At its Columbia, South Carolina, nuclear-fuel facility, only 23 workers were selected from the work force for jobs on a 70-person automated line that functions next to the conventional assembly line.

"We have 600 people from a traditional culture, and we've got to lead them into a new form of operation," says Robert T. Graulty, a plant manager. How well Westinghouse does at Columbia will go a long way toward determining how well it does as a world competitor.

Source: Gregory L. Miles, "The Plant of Tomorrow Is in Texas Today," *Business Week,* July 28, 1986.

Lacking the baggage of existing systems and relationships, the designers of these programs have been free to go all out. The right-hand column of Figure 19–7 is a rather accurate representation of what most have tried to do. Participation often begins in the early stages as lower-level employees are added to design teams. Technology (equipment layout, etc.) is adjusted as necessary to accommodate job enrichment and SMWTs. Pay is skill based, and all employees are salaried. (Gain sharing often comes only after the operation is fully functioning.) Information systems are elaborate, policies and perquisites (parking, cafeterias) are egalitarian, and teamwork, cooperation, openness, and trust are touted and reinforced from day one. SMWTs are often free to choose their own members (subject, of course to EEO/AA requirements), and team members and managers receive considerable training in group processes and the act of managing participatively. A spirit of learning is instilled to permit experimentation as the effort proceeds.

Anecdotal evidence suggests that over time at least some "new design" organizations experience a "regression" from some of the basic tenets of HIWSs. If more careful research substantiates this tendency, it may suggest areas in need of alteration in the "ideal type" and concurrently contribute to the development of much needed theory in this field.

Evaluation

The total number of firms or employees affected by some form of involvement or QWL strategy is unknown. Estimates range as high as 1,000 firms and up to one fifth of the U.S. labor force.[44] If this number is anywhere near accurate, it is unfortunate that so little has been done by way of evaluative research.

There are a number of anecdotal case studies, which generally are supportive (see, for example, Illustrations 19–3 and 19–4), but few studies meet the standards for evaluation research set out in Chapter 13. One clear exception showed a positive effect of a HIWS on employee motivaton and satisfaction and significant improvements in safety in a coal mine. However, neither absenteeism nor the number of grievances declined, and productivity did not increase. And the program was eventually abandoned because of political problems in the union.[45] (A not uncommon fate, HIWSs have a high mortality rate.)[46]

Another excellent study examined the effects of the General Motors–United Auto Workers QWL programs in 18 plants over a 10-year period. Again, the results were equivocal. Although active QWL programs resulted in some improvements in the industrial relations climate (lower absenteeism, discipline, and grievances) and in product quality, productivity was only marginally higher.[47]

Given the paucity of solid research, the generally anemic results turned up in well-designed studies, and ample anecdotal evidence of the

[44] W. J. Gershenfeld, "Employee Participation in Firm Decisions," in *Human Resources and the Performance of the Firm*, eds. M. M. Kleiner, R. N. Block, M. Roomkin, and S. W. Salsburg (Madison, Wis.: Industrial Relations Association, 1987), pp. 123–58.

[45] P. S. Goodman, *Assessing Organizational Change: The Rushton Quality of Work Experiment* (New York: John Wiley & Sons, 1979).

[46] Gershenfeld, "Employee Participation."

[47] H. C. Katz, T. A. Kochan, and K. R. Gobeille, "Industrial Relations Performance, Economic Performance, and QWL Programs: An Interplant Analysis," *Industrial and Labor Relations Review* 37 (1983), pp. 3–17.

risks and difficulties associated with HIWSs—a reasonable question is, will the experimentation continue? The answer is almost certainly yes. The track record of the more traditional approaches to workplace design is under attack. Advocates for change abound, and a number of very large and influential companies—General Motors, Ford, Motorola, Honeywell, TRW, 3M, Dana, Eaton, Manufacturers Hanover Trust— are committed to trying new ways.

SUMMARY

Steadfastly, P/HR managers and specialists have channeled their energies into such activities as recruitment, selection, training, compensation, and labor relations, and have for the most part left matters of work and workplace design to others, or to chance. Increasingly, however, this posture is becoming difficult to sustain in the face of pressures for enhanced corporate competitiveness, evolving employee expectations about their jobs and employment, and emerging theory and research demonstrating the potential positive results to be gained from new and creative approaches to work and workplace design.

Many organizations have tried various forms of goal-setting programs, ranging from the deceptively simple (such as the one described in Figure 19–1) to the obviously complex (such as some MBO systems). While the results have been mixed, this is probably attributable more to problems of implementation than to flaws in the underlying theory.

Job design, too, has come in for considerable scrutiny. Interestingly, among organizations making specific efforts in this area job simplification and job enrichment appear to be tried in about equal numbers. Most of the evaluative research has focused on job enrichment, however, and usually with quite positive results with respect to both employee behaviors and attitudes.

The basic philosophy underlying job enrichment has been seized upon and expanded by a number of authors pushing one form or another of participative management or employee involvement. These efforts, along with a general dissatisfaction with the status quo, has led to considerable experimentation in this arena. The applications take many forms. From the least to most complex and intrusive on traditional hierarchical organizational structures, they include quality circles (QCs), self-managing work teams (SMWTs), and high-involvement work systems (HIWSs).

One or more of these has been tried in a substantial proportion of the Fortune 500 firms and a good many smaller organizations as well. While much remains to be learned about them, some things are clear: (1) whatever the form, employee involvement is not easy to sustain and many, perhaps most, efforts fail within a few months or years; (2) those efforts that survive long enough to be evaluated have produced mixed results (often because of problems in implementation); (3) the effects on employee attitudes (such as job satisfaction) are generally stronger than the effects on employee motivation, or performance, or other behaviors; (4) there are often improvements in organizational effectiveness (productivity, product and service quality, etc.) even without noticeable effects on employee motivation or performance, probably as a result of employees working smarter rather than harder; and (5) QCs and SMWTs have a difficult time surviving in an otherwise nonparticipative work environment.

The last conclusion has led many to propose and delineate full-blown, participatively oriented human resource strategies incorporating not only work and workplace design, but also the more traditional P/HR activities. It remains to be seen, however, under what conditions these HIWSs will provide results superior to those that can be obtained with other equally well-designed and well-managed P/HR strategies.

DISCUSSION QUESTIONS

1. Why, generally, do difficult goals enhance performance more than "do your best" goals? Under what conditions might this not hold true? Why?

2. Given the power of goal setting, why do organizations have so much difficulty with MBO?

3. Think of several jobs. How would you determine whether these jobs needed to be enriched? If they needed it, how would you go about enriching them? Can you think of jobs that simply cannot be enriched? What are the organizational implications of this?

4. Discuss the essential differences between QCs and SMWTs. Why might QCs be a good first step toward the development of SMWTs? Why not?

5. Why have advocates of participative management increasingly drifted away from QCs and SMWTs alone to take up the cause of a systemic approach to workplace design?

6. Given an organization that is attempting to manage participatively and has in place joint goal setting, enriched jobs, and SMWTs, describe how these efforts might be hindered and helped by P/HR policies and practices in each of the following areas: external staffing, internal staffing, employee development, and compensation.

7. Assuming that most union leaders are interested in improving the quality of their members' working lives, why do so many of them oppose QWL (and similar) HIWSs?

20

Occupational Safety and Health

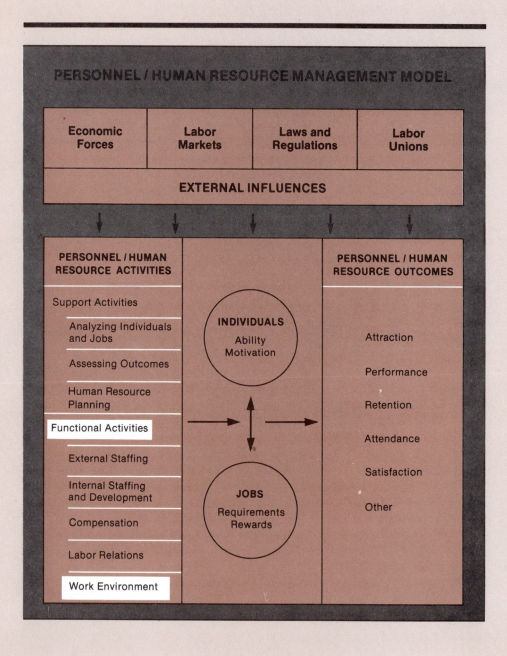

PERSONNEL / HUMAN RESOURCE MANAGEMENT MODEL

Economic Forces	Labor Markets	Laws and Regulations	Labor Unions

EXTERNAL INFLUENCES

PERSONNEL / HUMAN RESOURCE ACTIVITIES

Support Activities

Analyzing Individuals and Jobs

Assessing Outcomes

Human Resource Planning

Functional Activities

External Staffing

Internal Staffing and Development

Compensation

Labor Relations

Work Environment

INDIVIDUALS
Ability
Motivation

JOBS
Requirements
Rewards

PERSONNEL / HUMAN RESOURCE OUTCOMES

Attraction

Performance

Retention

Attendance

Satisfaction

Other

After reading this chapter, you should be able to speak to the questions posed in each of the following personnel/human resource incidents:

1. The Highrise Corporation manufactures many types of explosives for commercial use. In this volatile business, the company is attentive to safety issues. Noticing a slight downturn in Highrise's safety record over the past year, the personnel director has prepared a proposal for a new employee safety-training program. The proposal has been circulated to all managers for comment. As supervisor of the dynamite section, you receive the proposal and a request for comments. What factors would you take into account in framing your comments? Why?

2. The Federated Bank of Algoma is a large commercial bank and is a relatively safe place to work. Accidents do occur at the bank, but not very often. Because of this, top management has decided there is no need for any type of formal safety or health program. In fact, no one in the company has any designated safety responsibilities, except for one personnel specialist (your subordinate) who has responsibility for ensuring compliance with federal record-keeping requirements. Should you, as personnel director, recommend that the bank develop and implement a formal safety program? If so, what should the components of the program be? Should the bank consider adoption of a health program as well? If so, what should the components be?

3. The Quickhouse Corporation manufactures prefabricated houses and erects them on the buyer's building site. Employees work with many different types of equipment and handle large housing components. Prompted by the recent death of an employee who was crushed by a falling beam, the president has decided to crack down on accidents in the plant. To accomplish this, the president is seriously considering issuing a policy that says the first time an employee has an accident resulting in a lost-time injury, the employee will be fired. As vice president for personnel, the president asks your opinion on: How effective is this policy likely to be in improving Quickhouse's safety performance? What factors are most important in influencing the effectiveness of safety programs?

Attention to occupational safety and health seeks to reduce the occurrence of work-related illness, injury, and death. Not only are these important P/HR outcomes in their own right, but they may have an impact on other outcomes as well. For example, an accident threatens the employee's level of job performance and, if serious enough, impairs the employee's attendance record.

Society's concern for safety and health is shown by the laws that have been passed to deal with these items. Workers' compensation laws provide economic benefits to employees suffering illness and injury; the Occupational Safety and Health Act attempts to prevent safety and health problems through the development and enforcement of safety standards to which the organization must comply. In this chapter, these laws are explained in some detail.

Underlying all safety and health concerns is a need for measurement of the incidence and cost of accidents. Without the data these measures provide, efforts at planning, directing, and evaluating safety programs are greatly hampered. Hence, these activities also are treated in this chapter.

Safety programs are oriented toward the reduction of accidents. An *accident* is defined as the unintentional occurrence of physical damage to an object (such as machinery) or an injury to an individual. Accidents are caused by unsafe employee behaviors and/or unsafe working conditions. As discussed in this chapter, there are various types of programs to change unsafe behaviors and conditions, thereby reducing accidents. Top management and safety committees both play prominent roles in these efforts.

Health programs are more concerned with employee illness than with injury. Although the organizational outcomes resulting from an illness and an injury are frequently similar, an illness seldom results from a single incident, and the magnitude of a single incident is not sufficient to cause an injury. An illness typically builds up over a period of years (for example, black lung disease among coal miners), it may have no harmful effects for some time, and the harmful effects may never be outwardly visible. Occupational health is a technical medical area so that only an overview of environmental health hazards, employee stress, and the physically handicapped employee is provided in this chapter.

The severity and complexity of safety and health problems in many organizations require the personnel or safety department to take the lead in the development, administration, and evaluation of safety and health programs. At the same time, top management must recognize that its support for these programs is vital to their success.

LAWS AND REGULATIONS

The legal framework for occupational safety and health evolved from workers' compensation (WC) laws that provide benefits to employees should they suffer a work-related illness or injury, and laws that attempt to prevent the occurrence of injury and illness through the establishment and enforcement of safety and health standards. Of the latter, the most notable is the federal Occupational Safety and Health Act (OSHAct), although many states also have laws with a similar thrust. Provisions of WC laws and OSHAct are described and evaluated below (see Chapter 3 for a tabular overview).

Workers' Compensation Laws

WC laws are based on the concept of *liability without fault*, which means that an injured employee should be provided economic benefits regardless of who causes the accident. Since WC laws are state laws, their provisions vary considerably. Despite this, they do share some common general provisions regarding coverage, eligibility for benefits, types of benefits, and the financing of benefits.

To be covered by a WC law (and thus eligible for benefits), an employee must work in a covered occupation for a covered employer. Coverage is far from universal since all states have exemptions from their law. Also, the covered employee must suffer a work-related injury or illness to be eligible for benefits.[1]

Exactly what is considered "work related" varies among states. Generally, however, there has been a broadening of the definition to include not only physical problems, but stress-related mental and emotional problems as well. Claims for such disabilities occur most frequently in clerical and white-collar jobs that are routine and mechanical.[2]

Three types of benefits are typically provided—death benefits, medical payments, and wage-replacement benefits. Death benefits are a lump-sum, one-time benefit paid to the survivor of an employee killed on the job. Medical benefits provide payment for physician, surgeon, hospital, and rehabilitation costs incurred by the injured employee. To

---

[1] J. V. Grimaldi and R. H. Simonds, *Safety Management*, 4th ed. (Homewood, Ill: Richard D. Irwin, 1984); J. W. Hunt, *The Law of the Workplace* (Washington, D.C.: Bureau of National Affairs, 1984).

[2] "Employers Facing Increase in Workplace Stress Claims," *Daily Labor Report* (Washington, D.C.: Bureau of National Affairs, December 17, 1986), pp. 1–2.

tide employees over until they are able to return to work, wage-replacement benefits are also provided.

WC is essentially an insurance system. Benefits are financed by premiums paid by the employer. The size of the premium is partly determined by the safety record of the industry involved. Premium size also frequently depends on the individual employer's own safety record. This feature is known as *experience rating*. Its purpose is to provide employers with an economic incentive to improve their safety records.

Occupational Safety and Health Act (OSHAct)

Purpose

The primary intent of WC was to compensate employees for accidents, not to prevent accidents from occurring. Recognizing this, many states developed and enforced safety standards for employers as a way of trying to reduce accidents.

Pressure for national uniformity resulted in the passage of the OSHAct in 1970. The OSHAct's primary purpose is to reduce occupational injury, illness, and death through the establishment and enforcement of safety standards. These standards pertain to potentially unsafe work conditions employees may be exposed to.

Each covered employer has a *general duty* to furnish each employee "employment and a place of employment which are free from recognized hazards that are causing or are likely to cause death or serious physical harm to the employee."[3] Employers also have the *special duty* of complying with all safety standards developed under the act. Employees have a duty to comply with the law and safety standards, but unlike employers, they are not subject to any penalties for noncompliance.

Basic provisions of the OSHAct

Coverage.   Private employers (with few exceptions) engaged in a business affecting interstate commerce are covered by the OSHAct, and there is no exemption for small employers. Federal, state, and local governments are exempt, however.

Administration.   To administer the OSHAct, the Occupational Safety and Health Administration (OSHA) was created as an administrative agency located within the Department of Labor. The act also created the

---

[3] J. Ledvinka, *Federal Regulation of Personnel and Human Resource Management*, 2d ed. (Boston: Kent, 1989).

National Institute for Occupational Safety and Health (NIOSH). NIOSH assists in the development of safety and health standards, conducts basic research on the causes and prevention of occupational injury and illness, and develops educational programs.

Safety and health standards.   A large number of specific and intricate standards have been issued covering a wide array of potential environmental hazards, such as compressed gas, materials handling and storage, power tools, welding, machinery and machine guards, and toxic substances.

Compliance inspections.   Safety standards are enforced by OSHA through compliance inspections conducted by specially trained compliance officers (COs). These inspections can occur to investigate a complaint about an unsafe condition filed by an employee (the employer is prohibited from discriminating against an employee for lodging a complaint), or OSHA can itself initiate periodic inspections on a targeted basis. The choice of organizations for inspection is primarily within the discretion of the OSHA.

Violations and penalties.   After an inspection, the compliance officer prepares a report outlining probable violations, proposed penalties (fines), and proposed corrections of violations within certain time periods. The report is issued to the CO's superior, who reviews it, makes any necessary modifications, and then gives the report to the employer.

Appeals.   Citations for violations of safety standards, penalties, and ordered corrections are appealable. There is a lengthy appeals procedure, leading up to the Occupational Safety and Health Review Commission. Adverse commission decisions are appealable in federal courts.

State plans.   The OSHAct provides that states may develop and administer their own programs if they choose. Such states must submit a proposed program to the Secretary of Labor for approval. There are many criteria for approval, the most important being that the program must be judged "at least as effective" as the federal program.

Impact and effectiveness

Surveys indicate that the OSHAct has had many impacts on organization safety policies and practices. Prominent among these are equipment changes, increased safety planning and training, creation of formal units to administer safety programs, establishment of safety committees, expanded medical facilities and staff, and greater use of safety inspection systems.[4]

---

[4] B. G. Bricar and H. D. Hopkins, "How Does Your Company Respond to OSHA?" *Personnel Administrator* 28, no. 4 (1983), pp. 53–60.

Have these types of changes resulted in reduced illness, injury, and death? This is a highly debatable question.[5] Proponents point out that the overall accident incidence rate (see Figure 20–1) has decreased since the passage of the OSHAct. Opponents say the decline is due to factors other than the OSHAct, such as an increase in the average age of the work force and changing economic conditions. They also note that administration of the OSHAct lacks effectiveness. Problems include outdated safety standards, lack of new standards, an inadequate number of inspections, small fines for violations, and inaccurate data reporting by employers. Criticisms like these suggest there may be considerable room for improving the effectiveness of the OSHAct.

ACCIDENT MEASUREMENT

Accident measurement involves the assessment of accident rates and costs. Without adequate measurement, safety and health efforts in the organization may be greatly hampered for several reasons. First, a lack of data makes it difficult to identify causes of accidents. Second, management may be unaware of the severity of some safety problems. Third, without baseline figures on accident rates, meaningful goals for improving safety cannot be established. Finally, without measures, evaluation of the effectiveness of safety programs is difficult. In short, adequate measurement and data are the basic prerequisites for an organization's safety program.

Accident Incidence Rate

With passage of the OSHAct, the fundamental accident statistic reported by the Department of Labor is the incidence rate. This rate provides an expression of various accident experiences per 100 full-time workers. Most commonly, these experiences are number of injuries (includes both lost-workday and no-lost-workday injuries), number of lost-workday injuries, and number of lost workdays. The first two are expressions of *accident frequency* rates, and the last is an indicator of accident *severity*. In formula terms:

$$\text{Incidence rate} = \frac{N}{EH} \times 200,000$$

---

[5] J. Mendeloff, "The Hazards of Rating Workplace Safety," *The Wall Street Journal*, February 11, 1988, p. 22.

where

N = Number of injuries, lost-workday injuries, or lost work-days.

EH = Total employee hours worked in year.

$200,000$ = Equivalent of 100 full-time employees (each working 40 hours per week, 50 weeks per year).

Based on records employers are required to keep, incidence rate data are generated by the Department of Labor. They show that the overall incidence rate has declined from 10.6 in 1973 to 7.7 in 1986 (see Figure 20–1). This decline was primarily due to a decrease in the incidence rate for cases without lost workdays. Additional data (not shown) indicate substantial industry differences in incidence rates, with agriculture and mining having some of the highest rates, and finance and insurance having among the lowest rates. Also, regardless of industry, the rates are much higher for medium-sized (50–100 employees) organizations than for large and small ones. Finally, note in Figure 20–1 that there has been a substantial decline in the fatality rate.

FIGURE 20–1
Occupational Injury and Fatality Rates

Year	Injuries* Total Cases	Cases with Lost Workdays	Cases without Lost Workdays	Number of Lost Workdays	Fatalities† Total	Manufac-turing	Con-struction
1973	10.6	3.3	7.3	51.2	—	—	—
1974	10.0	3.4	6.6	53.1	9.8	—	—
1975	8.8	3.2	5.6	54.6	9.4	—	—
1976	8.9	3.4	5.5	57.8	7.9	—	—
1977	9.0	3.7	5.3	60.0	9.1	—	—
1978	9.2	4.0	5.2	62.1	8.2	5.9	30.6
1979	9.2	4.2	5.0	66.2	8.6	5.4	30.6
1980	8.5	3.9	4.6	63.7	7.7	5.5	26.4
1981	8.1	3.7	4.4	60.4	7.6	5.1	26.8
1982	7.6	3.4	4.1	57.5	7.4	4.2	25.2
1983	7.5	3.4	4.1	57.2	5.6	4.1	22.3
1984	7.8	3.6	4.2	61.8	6.4	4.3	20.2
1985	7.7	3.6	4.2	63.3	6.2	4.1	27.2
1986	7.7	3.6	4.2	63.9	5.9	4.2	17.9

* Per 100 full-time workers.   † Per 100,000 workers; figures for earlier years not comparable.

Source: Bureau of Labor Statistics, Department of Labor.

It is not only legally required but desirable that the organization calculate and report incidence rates on a periodic basis. This facilitates a comparison of the organization's rates with similar types of organizations. It also permits an internal analysis of the organization's own trends in incidence rates over time as a way of spotting problem areas and of evaluating the effectiveness of programs undertaken to reduce the problems.

Accident Costs

Industrial accidents take a high monetary toll. It is estimated that they cost more than $32 *billion* each year. This figure includes wage losses, insurance administrative costs, medical costs, fire losses, and time lost by employees who were not involved in the accident.[6]

At the organization level, accident costs can be broken down into those that are *insured* and *uninsured*. Insured costs include premiums for workers' compensation and employer-provided medical insurance. Uninsured costs include wage payments, time lost, lost productivity, and physical damage costs. When all these costs are considered, even seemingly minor accidents can be quite significant.

The calculation of accident cost figures, like incidence rates, is a desirable practice for the personnel or safety department. In addition to having all the same advantages of incidence rate data, costs data are readily communicable to, and interpretable by, top management. In turn, this facilitates the gathering of top-management support for safety programs.

SAFETY PROGRAMS

The ultimate objective of safety programs is to reduce accidents. Though sharing this common objective, safety programs very considerably in breadth and depth among organizations.[7] This is partially due to the wide differences in accident experiences among industries. Even within industries, however, there are differences in the importance attached, and resources committed, to safety programs.

Many issues confront any safety program—the role of top management, the role of safety committees, identifying causes of accidents, and reducing accidents. Each of these issues is treated below and, whenever

---

[6] National Safety Council. *Accident Facts* (Washington, D.C.: U.S. Government Printing Office, 1982).

[7] M. J Smith, H. H. Cohen, A. Cohen, and R. J. Cleveland, "Characteristics of Successful Safety Programs," *Journal of Safety Research* 10 (1978), pp. 5–15.

possible, effective versus ineffective practices are discussed. Unfortunately, evidence about the effectiveness of some of these practices is
sparse, and this fact should be borne in mind.

The Role of Top Management

Pressure for production, efficiency, and profits can all serve to encourage unsafe conditions and behaviors. Since these pressures ultimately
come from top management, it would seem that top management's
stance toward safety could have an important bearing on the organization's safety record.

Many studies have investigated the role and effectiveness of top
management in safety programs and accident reductions. The results of
these studies clearly and consistently show that top management commitment to, and active involvement in, safety programs is crucial to
program effectiveness. Indeed, this is probably the single most important factor influencing how effective safety programs are.

Top-management commitment and involvement can take many forms.
Examples uncovered in the relevant studies include:

1. Appointment of a safety officer with high-level rank and authority.
2. Evaluation of supervisors based on the safety records of their
   subordinates.
3. Conduct of safety inspections by top management.
4. Review of safety activity results against predetermined safety
   standards on periodic basis by top management.
5. Insistence on a detailed, high-quality safety record-keeping system.
6. Inclusion of safety figures and reports in company board meetings.

The Role of Safety Committees

Safety programs are frequently coordinated through one or more
safety committees. The existence of safety committees is often evidence
of top management support for the safety program. Committees typically
assume a number of functions, such as recommending safety policies to
top management, developing safety rules and regulations, conducting
safety inspections, training new employees in safety procedures, and
sponsoring safety campaigns.

Employees, safety specialists, and line managers are all likely to serve
as committee members. Employee representation may serve to encourage employee commitment to the safety program. Moreover, employees

are an invaluable source of information and suggestions for identifying and changing unsafe conditions or acts.

Where employees are represented by a union, a formalized joint labor-management safety committee is usually found.[8] Unions believe that safety is too important an issue to be left to unilateral management discretion. The specific details of labor's role in the committee and the total safety program are usually spelled out in the labor contract.

Identifying Causes of Accidents

To reduce accidents their causes must be identified. At the most general level, accidents are attributable to unsafe employee behaviors or acts, unsafe working conditions, or a combination of these. Notice that luck is not mentioned as an accident cause. Luck may influence whether an unsafe act or condition will lead to an accident, but luck *per se* does not actually cause the accident.

Incredibly large numbers of potentially unsafe behaviors and conditions exist. Some general examples of each of these are shown in Figure 20–2. Note that there are two major categories of unsafe conditions— physical and environmental. Since unsafe environmental conditions are usually more of a health than a safety hazard, they are treated more extensively in the section on occupational health.

Whenever an accident occurs, it should be reported and investigated as soon as possible to identify its cause(s). Doing this not only serves to obtain information while the event is still fresh in people's minds, but it also allows for the identification of factors that may need immediate change if further accidents are to be avoided (for example, employees not wearing safety glasses, oil spills on the floor, a broken guardrail).

On completion of the investigation, a thorough report must be made, identifying and recording as precisely as possible the causes of the accident. The greater the precision, the greater the potential usefulness of the information for suggesting necessary changes in unsafe behaviors and conditions.

Reports of individual accidents may be analyzed and aggregated for purposes of learning more about causes of accidents in general. For example, data could be analyzed by department or division as a way of identifying high- and low-accident units in the organization. Armed with this information, organizations could plan a thorough investigation of the

---

[8] For further description and evaluation, see T. A. Kochan, L. Dyer, and D. B. Lipsky, *The Effectiveness of Union-Management Safety and Health Committees* (Kalamazoo, Mich.: The W. E. Upjohn Institute for Employment Research, 1977).

FIGURE 20–2

Examples of Unsafe Behaviors and Unsafe Conditions

Unsafe Behaviors:
Working unsafely (for example, improper lifting).
Performing operations for which supervisory approval has not been granted.
Removing safety devices or altering their operation so they are ineffective.
Operating at unsafe speeds.
Using unsafe or improper equipment.
Horseplay.
Failure to use safety attire and protective devices.

Unsafe Physical Conditions:
Inadequate mechanical guarding.
Defective conditions of equipment.
Unsafe design or construction.
Hazardous process, operation, or arrangement (that is, unsafe piling, stacking, storing; congested aisle space; and so forth).
Unsafe dress or apparel and lack of protective equipment, such as gloves and safety goggles.

Unsafe Environmental Conditions:
Physical: noise, heat, vibration, radiation.
Chemical: dust, fumes and gases, toxic materials and chemicals, and carcinogens (cancer-causing agents).
Biological: bacteria, fungi, and insects.
Stress: caused by physical and chemical hazards, as well as psychological factors.

factors that differentiate high- and low-accident units. Results of this investigation could be used as input into safety improvement programs.

Another useful form of analysis would be to determine the percentages of accidents due to unsafe behaviors and unsafe conditions. Little is actually known about the proportions of accidents that could be attributed to unsafe behaviors as compared with unsafe conditions, or the factors that may influence these proportions (for example, type of job, type of employee, type of safety inspection program).

This information would be extremely useful in developing strategies for safety programs and the relative commitment of resources to those programs. For example, if the vast majority of accidents are found to be due to unsafe behaviors, the thrust of safety efforts and resources will need to be oriented to the implementation of programs to change these behaviors, such as staffing and training programs. Alternatively, if more accidents are due to unsafe conditions than to unsafe behaviors, this suggests a different strategy. The important point is that knowledge of the relative importance of unsafe behaviors and conditions in causing accidents can make a significant contribution to shaping programs for reducing accidents.

Reducing Accidents

Programs to change unsafe behaviors

Organizations typically use a variety of specific programs to reduce accidents by changing unsafe employee behaviors. These programs include staffing, training, safety rules and control procedures, and incentive systems.

Staffing. The concept of *accident proneness* suggests that certain employees are consistently more likely to have accidents than other employees, due to an occurrence of more unsafe behaviors. Based on this concept, one approach to reducing unsafe acts is to hire employees who are least likely to engage in them. This, however, requires an ability to identify characteristics of individuals that are in fact predictive of the probability of engaging in unsafe acts. Thus, it is necessary to conduct validation studies (see Chapter 10) to identify useful predictors of people's safety records.

There have been many such attempts involving the following types of predictors: age, length of service, vision, hearing, perceptual skills, motor skills, such personality characteristics as risk propensity, intelligence, and fatigue. With two exceptions, the results of these studies are spotty.[9]

The first exception involves age and length of service. Irrespective of length of service, the younger the employee, the higher the accident rate. Controlling for age, accident rates decrease as length of service increases. In fact, the incidence rate is substantially higher in the first month of employment than in all subsequent months of employment, regardless of age.[10] Together, these data suggest that young, inexperienced employees are particularly prone to accidents.

The other exception involves certain physical characteristics, such as vision and hearing. As might be expected, such characteristics are predictive of accidents in those jobs in which these abilities are critical job requirements.

Training. Organizations usually conduct safety training for both supervisors and employees. A typical program for supervisors includes such topics as safety rules and regulations, enforcement, safety control

---

[9] A. R. Hale and M. Hale, *A Review of the Industrial Accident Research Literature* (London: Her Majesty's Stationary Office, 1972), pp. 32–70; E. J. McCormick and D. J. Ilgen, *Industrial Psychology* (Englewood Cliffs, N.J.: Prentice-Hall, 1980), pp. 404–525.

[10] N. Root, "Injuries at Work Are Fewer among Older Employees," *Monthly Labor Review* 104, no. 3 (1981), pp. 30–34; F. Siskind, "Another Look at the Link between Work Injuries and Job Experience," *Monthly Labor Review* 105, no. 2 (1982), pp. 38–41.

procedures, recognition of hazards, and disciplinary problems. As with all types of training, what is taught must be constantly reinforced once supervisors are back on the job. Here, the previously noted importance of top-management involvement in safety efforts is quite relevant, for it is top management that can underscore the importance of safety to supervisors and hold them responsible for the safety of their subordinates.[11]

For employees, safety training programs should focus on instructions and practice in performing the job safely. Unfortunately, evidence suggests that the typical program falls far short of such content.[12] There may be only a brief informal orientation to the job for new employees in which safety is but one of many topics. General safety rules may be covered, but little said about job-specific rules. Supervisors may openly encourage employees to ignore safety rules and procedures that were taught in training in order to meet production goals.

Such occurrences are most unfortunate. If employee training is to be at all effective in reducing accidents, it must be consistent with guidelines for designing and conducting any training program (see Chapter 13). Moreover, the learning that occurs must be constantly reinforced on the job, particularly by supervisors.

Recently, the OSHA has been placing greater emphasis on training as a strategy for reducing accidents. There is now an OSHA Training Institute that conducts training programs for employers and others. Also, voluntary guidelines for training programs have been issued by OSHA. An overview of their content is shown in Illustration 20-1. Note that they are consistent with the general training principles presented in Chapter 13.

Safety rules and controls.   Most organizations have safety rules that typically indicate what employees both should and should not do. Safety handbooks that spell out the rules and the types of penalties for noncompliance (for example, written warning, discharge) are often given to employees. Also, safety posters may be prominently displayed, exhorting employee to "Think Safety" or "Put Safety First, Not Last."

These sorts of activities would seem to have some possibilities for curbing unsafe behaviors, but little is known about their effectiveness. There are factors that may severely limit it. Employees may fail to read the rules (or forget the ones they do read). Supervisors may neglect to

---

[11] For an example and evaluation of such programs, see F. E. Fiedler, C. H. Bell, M. M. Chemers, and P. Dennis, "Improving Mine Productivity and Safety Through Management Training and Organization Development: A Comparative Study," *Basic and Applied Social Psychology* 5, no. 1 (1984), pp. 1–18.

[12] Smith et al., "Characteristics of Successful Safety Programs."

ILLUSTRATION 20–1

OSHA's Voluntary Training Guidelines

1. *Determine if training is needed.* The first step in the training process is to determine whether a problem can be solved by training. Information shows that all skill deficiencies are not solvable through training.
2. *Identify training needs.* Analyze the employee's duties and what he or she needs in order to perform the job.
3. *Identify goals and objectives.* The employer can prepare instructional objectives once a list of specific job knowledge and skill deficiencies of the employees selected for training is made. This will tell employers what employees should do, do better, or stop doing.
4. *Develop learning activities.* Once the employer has stated precisely what the objectives for the training program are, learning activities must be identified and described. These activities enable employees to demonstrate that they have acquired the desired skills and knowledge. Factors which will help determine the type of learning activity to be incorporated into the training include: the training resources available to the employer; the kind of skills or knowledge to be learned; and whether the learning should be oriented toward physical skills or mental attitudes.
5. *Conduct the training.* The first four outlined steps will prepare the employer to conduct the training. The employer should: *(a)* provide overviews of the material to be learned; *(b)* relate each specific item of knowledge or skill to the ultimate purpose of the training; *(c)* relate the specific items of knowledge or skill to the employee's goals, interests, or experience.
6. *Evaluate program effectiveness.* This step is necessary to ensure that the training program is accomplishing its goals. Among the recommended methods of evaluating training are trainee opinion, supervisors' observations, and workplace improvements.
7. *Improve the program.* If a significant number of employees did not meet the expected levels of knowledge and skill, it may be necessary to revise the training program based on feedback from the worker, supervisor, or others. A step-by-step examination of the training process will help the employer to determine where course revision is necessary.

Source: Occupational Safety and Health Administration, 1984.

communicate and enforce the rules. Moreover, many of the rules tend to be general, and thus specific unsafe behaviors may go unnoticed and uncorrected.

One way to overcome such problems is to think of the need for safety control procedures, rather than just safety rules (see Figure 20–3).[13] In this approach, each job is thoroughly analyzed to identify the specific steps or procedures used in performing the job. For each step, possible

---

[13] D. A. Spartz, "A Challenge and an Answer: Job Control Procedures Standard," *Professional Safety* 23, no. 3 (1978), pp. 45–47,

FIGURE 20–3
Safe Behavior Control Procedure

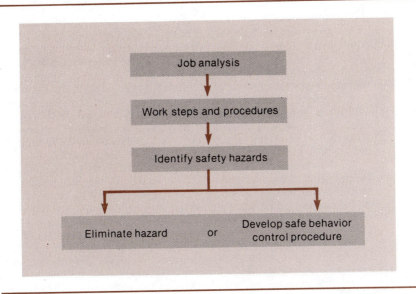

safety hazards are identified, and a decision is made about whether each hazard can be eliminated. If it cannot be eliminated, a specific safety-control procedure is established that will ensure a safe behavior if it is followed. Thus, the emphasis is on identifying and showing the employee, in a positive manner, what the person can do to engage in safe behaviors. To maximize the effectiveness of this approach, it probably has to be coupled with an incentive system that will motivate employees to follow the procedures.

Incentive systems.   Motivating employees to engage in safe behaviors has long been used as a strategy for reducing accidents. Probably the best example of this has been the use of safety contests. Here, departments may compete against each other for the best safety record, or they may compete against their own previous safety record. Note that these programs presuppose both a systematic accident measurement procedure and a detailed system of providing timely feedback on accidents to employees.

Even more elaborate safety incentive programs have been used. For example, a manufacturing company developed a plantwide safety contest around the theme of a horse race. The contest involved a modified betting scheme (with handicaps based on previous safety records), complete with supporting billboards and posters and a special letter sent to

ILLUSTRATION 20-2

Use of Positive Reinforcement and Feedback to Change Unsafe Behaviors

1.   The problem: A wholesale bakery lacked any type of formal safety program, and it was experiencing a dramatic increase in the injury frequency rate. It was felt that employees were committing too many unsafe acts that could result in accidents. A program of positive reinforcement and feedback was then planned as a way of decreasing employees' unsafe behavior.

2.   Observing unsafe behaviors: A very detailed observation code of safe and unsafe behaviors by employees in two departments was developed. The code was then used by numerous people to systematically observe the occurrence of safe and unsafe behaviors by these employees before, during, and after the conclusion of the safety program.

3.   The safety program: In a training program, employees were shown slides that illustrated unsafe behaviors, each of which was followed by a slide showing the corresponding safe behavior. They were also shown data on the percentage of safe behaviors in their department, and a goal of 90 percent safe behaviors was established. A feedback chart was put in each department; posted on it was the percentage of safe behaviors in each observation period. Supervisors received training in positive reinforcement techniques; the training emphasized the use of verbal praise when safe behaviors were observed.

4.   Effectiveness of the program: The percentage of safe behaviors in the two departments was determined before and during the program. To determine if any changes really were due to the program, the program was first introduced to one department and then was introduced to the second department after eight weeks. If the program caused the changes, the percentage of safe behaviors should increase after and not before the program was introduced in each department. As an additional confirmation, the program was discontinued and the percentage of safe behaviors decreased, indicating again that the program caused the changes. The average percentages of safe behaviors were as follows:

	Before Program	During Program	Program Discontinued
Wrapping department	70.0	95.8	70.8
Makeup department	77.6	99.3	72.3

Thus, the program appears to have been quite effective in improving safe behaviors.

Souce: J. Komaki, K. D. Barwick, and L. R. Scott, "A Behavioral Approach to Occupational Safety: Pinpointing and Reinforcing Safe Performance in a Food Manufacturing Plant," *Journal of Applied Psychology* 63 (1978), pp. 434-45. Copyright 1978 by the American Psychological Association. Reprinted by permission of the publisher and author.

employees. Other companies are implementing cash award programs to reward employees for safe work habits.[14]

Results of recent research suggest that incentive programs do in fact have excellent potential for reducing accidents. Illustration 20-2 contains

[14] P. C. Witbeck, "Cashing in on Safety," *National Safety News* 116, no. 6 (1977), pp. 87-89; *The Wall Street Journal*, January 27, 1987, p. 1.

one example. Developed for employees of a bakery, this program emphasized a detailed specification of safe and unsafe behaviors. Employees then received extensive feedback on, and reinforcement for, safe behavior. The favorable results obtained with this program have also been obtained in similar programs for bus drivers, paper mill employees, and farm machinery manufacturing employees.[15]

Finally, it should be noted that recent research has identified a positive relationship between employee attendance and their subsequent safety records.[16] This suggests that incentive systems to improve employee attendance (see Chapter 7) may also have another benefit, namely, improved safety.

Programs to change unsafe conditions

Along with programs to change unsafe behaviors, programs to change unsafe conditions also are appropriate in the organization's overall safety strategy. The specific components of programs to change unsafe conditions vary from situation to situation, but there are four basic elements that are a part of most programs. As shown in Figure 20–4, these elements are defining unsafe conditions, identifying unsafe conditions, taking corrective action, and establishing adequate controls. Each of these is elaborated on below.

Defining unsafe conditions.   Obviously, it is necessary to define what constitutes unsafe conditions before they can be changed. Doing so is primarily a matter of establishing safety standards, many of which have now been set up under the OSHAct. OSHAct standards are minimum standards to which the organization must comply; the organization may want to establish more stringent standards or establish standards not covered by the federal standards.

Identifying unsafe conditions.   Periodic inspection must be made to determine which conditions do not meet safety standards. The inspection system is a crucial element, for evidence clearly shows that the more thorough and systematic the inspection, the better the safety performance of the organization. The inspection may involve a visual "tour" of the facility, as well as a detailed analysis of the previously described

---

[15] D. J. Fellner and B. Sulzer-Azaroff, "Increasing Industrial Safety Practices and Conditions through Posted Feedback," *Journal of Safety Research* 15 (1984), pp. 7–21; R. D. Haynes, R. C. Pine, and H. G. Fitch, "Reducing Accident Rates with Organizational Behavior Modification," *Academy of Management Journal* 25 (1982), pp. 407–16; R. A. Weber, J. A. Wallin, and J. S. Chhokar, "Reducing Industrial Accidents: A Behavioral Experiment," *Industrial Relations* 23 (1984), pp. 119–25.

[16] P. S. Goodman and S. Garber, "Absenteeism and Accidents in a Dangerous Environment: An Empirical Analysis of Underground Coal Mines," *Journal of Applied Psychology* 73 (1988), pp. 81–86.

FIGURE 20–4

Elements of Safety Programs to Change Unsafe Conditions

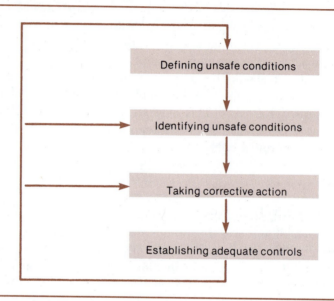

individual accident reports. In either event, it will be necessary to
determine both unsafe conditions and why they exist as the basis for then
taking corrective action.

Taking corrective action.   After identifying unsafe conditions, corrective action must be planned and implemented. In some instances this
will be fairly straightforward. At other times, however, corrective action
plans may be exceedingly complex, particularly if they involve extended
periods of time and such large financial resources as the purchase of new
machinery or equipment. Here, the corrective action plans must be
considered and meshed with overall organizational planning.

Establishing adequate controls.   Corrective actions may not necessarily be effective in reducing accidents. Some corrective actions may fail
because they were based on initially inadequate or inappropriate standards. In other instances, employees themselves may seek to circumvent
the changes, such as by removing a guardrail from a machine. Again, the
need for inspection and recordkeeping is clear, this time as mechanisms
for program control. Actually, records will be useful in all of the first
three components of the program, and this is the reason for the feedback
loops in Figure 20–4.

OCCUPATIONAL HEALTH

The above safety programs focus on reducing accidents, but the field of occupational health primarily seeks to reduce and ultimately prevent the occurrence of work-related illnesses and diseases. Traditionally, the major concern was the abatement of health hazards in the employee's immediate work environment. However, the field has now expanded to deal with the problems of employee stress. Also, the needs and problems of the physically handicapped are receiving increasing attention.

Environmental Health Hazards

As shown in Figure 20–2, employees may be subject to physical, chemical, biological, and stress health hazards. The actual amount of exposure to these hazards varies considerably among industries, particularly in the case of physical and chemical hazards.

Detection of health hazards requires constant monitoring of the work environment and of the employee. With the vast number of hazards in existence, such monitoring is complex and costly. Monitoring employee health (for example, through periodic health exams) not only may be useful as a diagnostic device for subsequent treatment of the employee, but is also invaluable in discovering new health hazards. For example, this is how it was learned that asbestos fibers, frequently encountered among workers in shipbuilding, were a serious health hazard that caused severe respiratory problems.

Passage of the OSHAct and the subsequent development of safety and health standards have had an impact on both employee and work environment monitoring.[17] In addition, organizations have strengthened existing, and introduced many new, methods of hazard control.

New problems and issues involving health hazards seem to constantly appear. Four illustrations of this phenomenon are health care employees, reproductive hazards, video display terminals, and smoking.

Health care employees

Ironically, our ability to enhance people's health and life expectancy comes about through potentially unhealthy work conditions in such health care facilities as hospitals and nursing homes. Health care employ-

---

[17] A. Freedman, *Industrial Response to Health Risk* (New York: The Conference Board, 1981).

ees are susceptible to health risks by hazardous chemicals, contaminated materials, and radiation. A hospital employee is 41 percent more likely than the average employee to need time off the job due to serious injury or illness. Because of these problems, health care employees are becoming more health-hazard conscious by pressing for safer work environments through their unions and through lobbying for better health legislation and standards.[18]

Reproductive hazards

It is becoming increasingly clear that there are potential hazards in the workplace that may affect employees' ability to reproduce or cause harm to a fetus.[19] Examples include various solvents used in the paint and electronics (especially computer-chip production) industries. While such reproductive threats may involve both men and women, women are more likely to be affected.

Dealing with such potential hazards raises difficult questions. For example, should employers be permitted to not assign pregnant or fertile women to such jobs? If so, is this not a form of sex discrimination? Or should pregnant or fertile women have the right to refuse to (or insist they should) perform these jobs. Few companies have policies dealing with such questions. It is clear, however, that policies will have to be developed to address the problems created by reproductive health hazards.

Video display terminals

More than 28 million employees—clerical workers, typesetters, writers, managers, and others—use video display terminals (VDTs) in their jobs, and that number will continue to increase. Many undesirable health effects have allegedly resulted from VDT usage. Included here are eyestrain, fatigue, muscular problems, and pregnancy complications due to radiation exposure. Evidence on these effects is scanty and inconclusive. Despite this, people are seeking changes. Some unions, for example, are seeking requirements for shielding employees from radia-

---

[18] J. S. Lublin, "As Job Hazards Increase, Hospital Unions Push Employers, U.S. for Better Protection," *The Wall Street Journal*, August 8, 1983, p. 17.

[19] B. Meier, "Companies Wrestle with Threats to Workers' Reproductive Health," *The Wall Street Journal*, February 5, 1987, p. 21; S. S. Paskal, "Dilemma: Save the Fetus or Sue the Employer?" *Labor Law Journal* 39 (1988), pp. 323–41.

tion, rest breaks, regular eye exams, and transfer rights for pregnant women to jobs not involving VDTs. Demands for such changes seem likely to continue.[20]

Smoking

Smoking has rapidly become a burning issue for many organizations.[21] In part, this is due to heightened concern for the health of smokers, as well as possible increases in health care insurance premiums for them. The concern is also due to nonsmokers, who claim they have a right to a smoke-free work environment, or at least an environment in which smoking is severely restricted.

Organizations are just recently confronting these issues and developing policies to deal with them. Examples of policies include (1) an absolute ban on smoking at work, (2) refusal to hire people who smoke,

---

FIGURE 20–5
Recommendations for Policy Development Regarding Smoking

---

1. Get a commitment from top management to the policy development and enforcement.

2. If there are relevant industry standards or state and local laws, ensure that any policy development complies with them.

3. Where there are unions, get them involved at an early stage.

4. Smoking policies may need to be tailored to specific facilities and even parts of facilities.

5. Involve a cross section of the company's work force in formulating the policy. All levels of employees and smokers, nonsmokers, and former smokers should be involved.

6. A survey of employees' attitudes and smoking habits is a logical step after the committee is formed.

7. Any policy that is developed should be circulated throughout the company. Consistent enforcement of the policy once it is implemented is as important as the policy itself.

Source: D. D. Schein, "Should Employers Restrict Smoking in the Workplace?" *Labor Law Journal* 38 (1987), pp. 173–78.

---

[20] "Greater Use of VDTs Brings Problems Along with Gains," *Daily Labor Report* (Washington, D.C.: Bureau of National Affairs, August 3, 1987), pp. 1–2; L. Z. Lorber and J. R. Kirk, *Fear Itself: A Legal and Personnel Analysis of Drug Testing, AIDS, Secondary Smoke, VDTs,* (Arlington, Va.: ASPA Foundation, 1987).

[21] Lorber and Kirk, *Fear Itself*; L. Reibstein, "Forced to Consider Smoking Issue, Firms Produce Disparate Policies," *The Wall Street Journal*, February 10, 1987, p. 41.

(3) establishment of restricted areas (such as bathrooms and cafeterias) where smoking is permitted, (4) allowing smoking in private offices, and (5) allowing smoking outdoors. Another obvious possibility is to simply have a "smoking as usual" policy. Recommendations for policy development are shown in Figure 20–5.

Employee Stress

Some employees may not feel capable of adequately responding to demands of their job and the work environment. When this happens, employees are said to experience job *stress,* and they may have a number of adverse reactions to it. Figure 20–6 illustrates the basic causes and consequences of stress.[22]

Potential sources or causes of stress are referred to as *stressors.* They include characteristics of the organization (e.g., reward systems), the job (e.g., task variety), and the individual (e.g., personality type). Although extensive lists of examples could be developed for each of these three categories of stressors, it is important to remember that they are only *potential* stressors. This is true for two reasons. First, research has not conclusively established links between all possible stressors and employee reactions to them. Second, there are individual differences among employees in how well they cope with a given stressor.[23]

Figure 20–6 shows that there may be both organizational and individual *coping mechanisms* that will help an employee to adjust to a stressor. Consider an employee who fails to receive a desired promotion. The organization may have a performance feedback and career development program that will provide reasons for not getting the promotion, as well as systematic plans for developing a promotable employee. At the individual level, the employee may cope by concluding that the promotion was not so desirable after all. To understand differences in reactions to stressors, the variety of coping mechanisms must be examined.[24] Any

---

[22] Based on treatments by A. P. Brief, R. S. Schuler, and M. Van Sell, *Managing Job Stress* (Boston: Little, Brown, 1981); and J. M. Ivancevich and M. T. Matteson, *Stress and Work* (Glenview, Ill.: Scott, Foresman, 1980).

[23] Examples of recent stress studies include S. Kirmeyer and T. W. Dougherty, "Work Load, Tension, and Coping: Moderating Effects of Supervisor Support," *Personnel Psychology* 41 (1988), pp. 125–39; S. J. Motowidlo, J. S. Packard, and M. R. Manning, "Occupational Stress: Its Causes and Consequences for Job Performance," *Journal of Applied Psychology* 71 (1986), pp. 618–29; D. W. Russell, E. Altmeier, and D. Van Velzen, "Job Related Stress, Social Support, and Burnout among Classroom Teachers," *Journal of Applied Psychology* 72 (1987), pp. 269–74; R. I. Sutton and A. Rafaeli, "Characteristics of Work Stations as Potential Occupational Stressors," *Academy of Management Journal* 30 (1987), pp. 260–76.

[24] J. C. Latack, "Coping with Job Stress: Measures and Future Directions for Scale Development," *Journal of Applied Psychology* 71 (1986), pp. 377–85.

FIGURE 20–6
The Nature of Stress

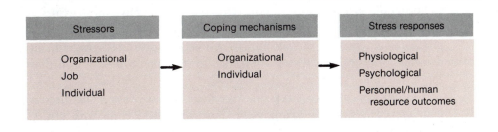

given stressor could cause many different reactions among employees, depending on the availability and employee use of various coping mechanisms.

Finally, Figure 20–6 shows that employees may react to experienced stress in a number of ways. Physiologically, indicators of stress would include high blood pressure, sweating, excessive eating or loss of appetite, and alcoholism and other drug abuse. At the psychological level, examples of stress indicators are nervousness, depression, anxiety, low self-esteem, and feelings of being "burned out." Finally, all of the P/HR outcomes may be adversely affected by stress.[25]

In summary, virtually any facet of organizational life is a potential source of employee stress, and employees may exhibit numerous reactions to stressors. Such reactions, however, are tempered by how people cope with them. Recognition of this latter fact has led organizations to experiment with developing stress reduction and health ("wellness") programs for employees.

Stress reduction programs

Given the complex causes and effects of stress, as well as wide differences among employees in their reactions to it, how can the organi-

[25] T. A. Beehr and J. E. Newman, "Job Stress, Employee Health, and Organizational Effectiveness: A Facet Analysis, Model, and Literature Review," *Personnel Psychology* 31 (1978), pp. 665–700; J. E. Newman and T. A. Beehr, "Personal and Organizational Strategies for Handling Job Stress: A Review of Research and Opinion," *Personnel Psychology* 32 (1979), pp. 1–44; M. J. Kavanaugh, M. W. Hurst, and R. Rose "The Relationship between Job Satisfaction and Psychiatric Health Symptoms for Air Traffic Controllers," *Personnel Psychology* 34 (1981), p. 692–708; J. M. Ivancevich, M. T. Matteson, and C. Preston, "Occupational Stress, Type A Behavior, and Physical Well-Being," *Academy of Management Journal* 25 (1982), pp. 373–91.

zation reduce stress levels for its employees? One approach is to minimize the occurrence of stressors in the organization. Indeed, the previously described accident reduction and environmental health control programs are attempts to reduce the presence of physical stressors in the employee's work environment. At a more general level, this approach would suggest that all human resource policies and programs be designed and evaluated partially from the standpoint of how well they serve to reduce stressor levels.

Another approach to stress management would be to work directly with employees, emphasizing how they can better cope with stress. Organizations are increasingly providing such coping mechanisms in the form of employee assistance programs (EAPs). The overall objective of these programs is to provide treatment to "troubled employees" so that they will be able to function normally and remain as productive members of the organization. Such programs do not always require that the cause of problems stems from the work environment for employees to be eligible for assistance.

Originally, EAPs were established to deal with problems of employee alcoholism. The treatment of alcoholism remains an important component of a typical EAP, but other activities are now also incorporated into an EAP. A survey of EAP characteristics in organizations found that, in addition to alcoholism treatment, 70 percent or more of the organizations offered (1) drug abuse programs, (2) emotional counseling, (3) family and marital counseling, (4) financial counseling, (5) legal counseling, and (6) career counseling. Overall, 21 percent of the responding organizations had an EAP.[26]

Sound assessments of the effectiveness of EAPs are hard to come by, so their promise has yet to be demonstrated.[27] Some anecdotal evidence about EAP effectiveness, and problems confronting EAPs, is presented in Illustration 20–3.

Health ("wellness") programs

Health programs in organizations are designed to improve employees' physical well-being. By doing so, it is hoped that there will be positive impacts on the P/HR outcomes. In addition, reductions in health care

[26] R. C. Ford and F. S. McLaughlin, "Employee Assistance Programs: A Descriptive Survey of ASPA Members," *Personnel Administrator* 26, no. 9 (1981), pp. 29–36.

[27] C. H. Grimes, *EAP Research* (Troy, Mich.: Performance Resource Press, 1984); R. M. Weiss, "Writing Under the Influence: Science versus Fiction in the Analysis of Corporate Alcoholism Programs," *Personnel Psychology* 40 (1987), pp. 341–56.

ILLUSTRATION 20–3

Employee Assistance Plans

No one knows exactly how many employee assistance programs (EAPs) currently exist, but Tom Delaney, executive director of the Association of Labor-Management Administrators and Consultants on Alcoholism, puts the figure at about 8,000. He is convinced that most do an excellent job of what they are set up to do—ease employee problems and improve job performance.

Three problems currently confronting EAPs, according to Delaney, are difficulties in establishing the programs at small businesses, emphasis by alcohol and mental health agencies on costly inpatient care, and an increasing intrusion of physical fitness and "quality-of-life"-type projects into EAPs. Inpatient care is driving up costs, he says, commenting that "everyone with a drinking problem doesn't need" an intensive 28-day confinement that costs up to $12,000.

Small businesses are a great challenge to EAP expansion because of comparatively high costs, a general antipathy by both management and workers based partly on fear of breaches of confidentiality, and logistics problems stemming from the isolated locations of many small firms. The answer for some of these companies is to join together to form a consortium, he says.

It is generally agreed that more research is needed to determine whether EAPs save employers a significant amount of money, and skyrocketing corporate health care costs may expedite and broaden efforts to evaluate EAP's costs and benefits. One employer, United Airlines, estimates that for every dollar spent the company gets $16.35 back in reduced absenteeism alone. Another company, Metropolitan Insurance, a pioneer in EAP, does not believe the goodwill and improved morale engendered by its program can be measured in dollars.

Source: *Daily Labor Report* (Washington, D.C.: Bureau of National Affairs, July 31, 1984), p. 2.

---

costs may occur. This is becoming increasingly important in many organizations.

No single model of a health program exists, and most have multiple components. For example, Metropolitan Life Insurance Company has a program for its 9,500 headquarters employees. It consists of antismoking, blood pressure control, cholesterol reduction, weight control, and stress management components. Added to these would be physical fitness programs in many companies. At one Xerox Company location, for example, there is a fitness facility that includes a putting green, soccer field, swimming pool, two gyms, four tennis courts, two racquetball courts, weight room, and 2,300 acres of running area.[28]

---

[28] A. J. J. Brennan, "Worksite Health Promotion Can Be Cost-Effective," *Personnel Administrator* 28, no. 4 (1983), pp. 39–46; J. J. Hoffman, Jr., and C. J. Hobson, "Physical Fitness and Employee Effectiveness," *Personnel Administrator* 29, no. 4 (1984), pp. 101–14; P. G. Butler, "Employer Sponsored Recreational Activities: Do the Costs Outweigh the Benefits?" *Labor Law Journal* 39 (1988), pp. 120–23.

Relatively little is known about the effectiveness of health programs in influencing the P/HR outcomes and reducing costs. Until solid evidence begins to emerge, it would probably be best to remain cautiously optimistic about the potential that health programs may hold.

Disabled Employees

Physically handicapped individuals have long been neglected as potential employees. Some of the barriers to their employment have been mechanical and architectural (e.g., narrow doorways and no ramps for wheelchairs). Other barriers were attitudinal, reflecting a feeling that the handicapped were unemployable or that the costs of hiring them were too great.

Recently, these barriers have been falling away. Much of the impetus for this was the passage of the Rehabilitation Act of 1973, which applies to most federal contractors and subcontractors (see Chapter 3). It requires them to develop and implement detailed affirmative action plans (see Chapter 8) for the handicapped. The plan must cover all phases of employment, particularly training programs.[29]

Organizations are also experimenting with other ways of employing the handicapped. One example is the use of modified work schedules that are tailored to each handicapped person's particular needs. Other examples are letting handicapped employees work at home and subcontracting work to special-help organizations that employ only the handicapped. It is likely that the use of such programs will continue to increase.[30]

SUMMARY

Safety and health activities in an organization are designed to reduce the occurrence of injury, illness, and death among employees. Prerequisites to achieving this are an ability to measure accidents and identify their causes, particularly in the general sense of determining what percentage of accidents are due to unsafe conditions as opposed to unsafe behaviors. Some programs seek to reduce accidents by changing unsafe work conditions; influential here are the safety standards developed under the OSHAct. Other programs seek to reduce accidents by chang-

---

[29] W. H. Emer and C. B. Frink, "E. E. Black and Beyond: Update on Hiring the Handicapped," *Labor Law Journal* 34 (1983), pp. 643–53; S. S. Johnson and M. W. Jones, "Legislation and Litigation Involving the Employment of Disabled Women: An Overview," *Personnel and Guidance Journal* 62, no. 6 (1984), pp. 346–49.

[30] For a review of the research see S. M. Freedman and R. T. Keller, "The Handicapped in the Work Force," *Academy of Management Review* 6 (1981), pp. 449–58.

ing unsafe behaviors. In instances where injury, illness, or death do occur, workers' compensation laws provide various benefits to alleviate the economic costs the employee suffers. Recently, the field of occupational health has been expanding to deal with the massive problem created by health hazards, stressors in the work environment, and the employment of the disabled employee.

DISCUSSION QUESTIONS

1. What factors may influence the effectiveness of the OSHAct?

2. What are likely reasons that the occurrence of accidents frequently declines with an employee's age and/or experience?

3. What factors would you consider in deciding whether to develop an employee-assistance program?

4. How can an organization reduce the effects of stress on its employees?

5. Why might the relative importance of unsafe conditions and unsafe behaviors as accident causes vary from situation to situation?

6. How would you evaluate the effectiveness of a safety training program for first-level supervisors in a manufacturing plant?

7. Speculate on why the incidence of accidents is higher in midsize companies than in large and small ones.

8. How would you evaluate the effectiveness of a stress-reduction program?

Case for Part Nine

BENTON INCORPORATED

Benton Incorporated is a high-tech assembly plant in the Silicon Valley. The company assembles components for personal computers, with 90 percent of the sales going to two of the major personal computer companies. Their present product line consists of four basic products, all of which are transporter cards for various personal computers.

History

Benton Incorporated has been in existence since 1979. The company was founded by Jim Benton, the 35-year-old president. Jim graduated in 1971 from Michigan State University with a bachelor of science degree in engineering, and then went to work for General Motors. After two years he went back to school and obtained a master of science degree, also in engineering, from MIT. He spent the next three years working for Intel. His entrepreneurial spirit led him to leave Intel in 1978 to start Benton Incorporated.

The company's first year was full of excitement as the personal computer market was booming and demand for Benton's products was great. The newness of the company quickly wore off, however. Although sales continued to grow between 1980 and 1983, the employees did not seem to exude the same excitement and vitality that had been evident that first year. Jim recognized that this was probably due to the fact that people were finally settling into their jobs and getting used to the company.

Benton faced its first major employee relations problem in early 1981. Jim had noticed that morale was not what it had been in the past few years, but he did not seem to be worried about it. Then in February, members of the Teamster's union made an attempt to organize the hourly work force at Benton. Enough of the employees signed the authorization cards to wake Jim and his top managers up to the fact that a problem existed. They retained the services of a consulting firm that helped successfully thwart the union's efforts to organize the plant. After management's campaign, the election showed only 20 percent of the employees voting for the union. Jim and his managers felt confident that they had solved the problems.

In 1983 the personal computer market had begun to mature. Benton's sales leveled at $40 million that year, but the outlook for 1984 was not good. Although the economy was still on an upswing, industry analysts were beginning to predict that the personal computer market was becoming saturated. This meant that demand for Benton's products would begin to decrease.

Jim Benton recognized this trend in early 1983. He called in an efficiency engineering consultant to explore ways to cut costs in the assembly process. The company assembled the four main products on eight assembly lines. There was one supervisor for each of the eight lines. Product A was a transporter card assembled for a major company. This product accounted for 45 percent of Benton's sales and was assembled on three of the lines. This assembly process consisted of 58 steps that were performed by 11 employees. Each job in this process had an average work cycle of six minutes.

Product B's assembly process was very similar to that of Product A. Accounting for another 45 percent of Benton's sales, it also used three lines. The assembly process consisted of 62 steps broken up into 12 jobs, each having an average work cycle of just under 6 minutes.

Products C and D used one assembly line each. The assembly process for Product C entailed 60 steps broken up into 11 jobs with an average work cycle of 6½ minutes. Product D consisted of 55 steps grouped into 10 jobs. Each of these jobs had an average work cycle of 5½ minutes.

After carefully investigating the layout of the plant and observing the employees on the job, the consultant recommended that the company move from eight lines to six. This would entail simplifying each job from performing between three and five tasks to performing only two or three tasks. This would allow much more efficient production. In fact, the consultant estimated a 15 percent increase in production. The equipment from the other two assembly lines could be sold off, thus reducing some of the overhead in the plant.

Jim decided to adopt the solution. As an engineer himself, he saw the increased efficiency that would result. In late April Jim called his supervisors in and told them that he had decided to change the production process. He explained the change to them and quoted the figures he expected to see in increased efficiency as a result of the change. The changeover was made in May of 1983, and the results initially were as predicted. Production started out lower as people began to learn the new jobs. After the first month, however, production rose to about 7 percent

TABLE 1

Month	Units Produced	Labor-Hours	Accidents	Defects/ 1,000
January	3,010	1,920	12	10
February	3,020	1,932	11	7
March	2,080	1,910	13	9
April	3,000	1,922	11	5
May	2,880	1,924	12	7
June	3,210	1,920	13	17
July	3,360	1,915	13	15
August	3,200	1,925	15	15
September	3,170	1,915	16	17
October	3,180	2,080	15	20
November	3,178	2,075	17	20
December	3,182	2,085	19	19

above the level under the previous system, and the following month production was 12 percent higher than normal. Over the next five months it stayed at about 6 percent above the previous system.

Jim, however, noticed some things over the next six months. First, the accident/injury rate had increased and was continuing to rise. Second, the defect rate had risen and then leveled off at about twice that of the pre-changeover rate. Third, although he had no hard data, it seemed as if there were a lot of conflicts among the supervisors. Fourth, Jim had been notified by the controller that the number of labor-hours worked in direct labor had been increasing. Finally, after convincingly thwarting a union certification drive two years ago, there now seemed to be more talk among the employees about bringing in a union.

Table 1 displays some of the data that Jim had to work with. He called in his top managers and wanted them to look at these statistics and make some recommendations as to how to stop these trends.

Questions

1. The symptoms of the problem(s) are identified in the last paragraph above. What are the underlying problems?

2. Given the information in the table, what types of trends would you expect in job satisfaction? Absenteeism? Turnover?

3. How can a defect rate increase affect external and internal staffing?

4. What would you have recommended differently from what the engineering consultant recommended in early 1983?

5. As a QWL consultant, what would you recommend now?

6. Has the efficiency expert made the company more efficient? Why or why not? Support your answer with data.

7. Why is information about the work cycle important to this case?

8. What might have been wrong about the way in which Jim implemented his decision to change the work process?

Name Index

Abbasi, S. M., 392
Abelson, M. A., 188
Abodeely, J. E., 591
Abowd, J. S., 597
Abraham, K. G., 376–77
Adams, J. S., 126, 481
Adams, L. T., 573, 585–86
Adolf, B., 547
Aldag, R. J., 124, 127, 133, 253, 264, 270
Alexander, R. A., 322, 472, 672
Allen, J. G., 393
Allen, R. E., 625
Allen, S. G., 527
Alper, S. W., 178
Altmeier, E., 708
Amundsen K., 379
Anastasi, A., 311, 336
Anderson, G., 113
Angle, H. L., 598
Armagast, R. D., 469
Arnold, J. D., 317
Arvey, R. D., 66, 74, 100, 153–54, 268, 338, 345, 352, 396
Ash, R. A., 104, 111
Ashenfelter, O., 615
Avolio, B. J., 164, 397

Baen, L. B., 178
Baird, L., 19
Baker, D., 506
Baldwin, T. T., 437
Bangs, R., 185
Barber, A. E., 617
Barclay, L. A., 264
Baron, R. A., 131
Barr, D. F., 429
Barr, S. H., 124
Barrett, G. V., 165, 322, 386, 394, 472, 485
Barrick, M. R., 672
Barwick, K. D., 702
Bass, A. R., 264
Bassett, G. A, 238
Baysinger, B. D., 188
Beam, B. T., Jr., 72, 533, 555
Beauvais, L. L., 598
Becker, B. E., 597
Becker, G. S., 486
Beeher, T. A., 397, 709
Beer, M., 654, 660

Belenky, A H., 104–5
Belitsky, A. H., 133
Bell, C. H., 699
Bell, J. D., 344
Bellizzi, J. A., 280
Bemis, S. E., 104–5
Bennett, K., 19
Benton, C., 380
Berger, C. J., 42, 516, 596–98
Bergmann, T. J., 47, 270, 282, 358
Bernardin, H. J., 165
Beyer, H. M., 517
Binet, Alfred, 95
Birch, David L., 67
Birnbaum, M. H., 496
Bishop, T., 325
Blakslee, J. H., 218
Block, R. N., 595–96
Boehm, V., 378, 380
Bognanno, M. F., 632
Borgen, F. H., 124–26
Borne, L., 206
Bosshardt, M. J., 431
Boudreau, J. W, 42, 227, 229, 252, 264–65, 273, 276, 282, 371, 450, 598
Bownas, D. A., 431
Bradley, K., 672
Brannen, D. E., 345
Bratkovich, J. R., 15
Brayfield, A. H., 174
Breaugh, J. A., 264, 271–72, 277
Brennan, A. J. J., 711
Brett, Jeanne M., 594
Bricar, B. G., 691
Brickner, M., 378
Brief, A. P., 124, 708
Brittain, J., 585
Brocklyn, P. L. 261
Brooke, P. B., Jr., 170
Broszeit, R. K., 375
Broussard, R. D., 345
Brousseau, K., 29, 408
Brown, B. K., 350–51
Brown, S. H., 317
Brown, S. P., 387
Buckley, J. E., 496
Bulkeley, W. M., 259
Burack, E. A., 29
Burch, P., 352
Burgess, P. L., 542

Burke, M. J., 322, 436
Burrington, D. D., 346
Burt, R. E., 598
Butler, J. E., 19
Butler, M. C., 112
Butler, P. G., 711
Byham, W. C., 13, 378

Cairo, P. C., 409
Caldwell, D. F., 264
Camnso, M. A., 189
Campbell, D. J., 506
Campbell, D. N., 396
Campbell, D. T., 445
Campbell, H., 505
Campbell, J. P., 120-21, 143, 153-54, 174, 434
Campion, J. E., 312
Campion, M. A., 350-51, 661-62, 665
Candrilli, A. J., 469
Cappelli, P., 609
Carlson, N. W., 500
Carnevale, A. P., 421, 452
Carroll, S. J., 149, 151, 155, 157, 506, 517
Carron, T. J., 114
Carsten, J. M., 191
Cartter, A. M., 86, 595
Cascio, W. F., 40, 42, 149, 162, 164-65, 187, 271,
      322, 450, 665
Castegnera, J., 344
Chaison, G. N., 585
Chalykoff, J., 594
Chamberlain, N. W., 607
Chao, G. T., 338-39, 345
Cheek, L., 231
Chelius, J. R., 628
Chemers, M. M., 699
Chhokar, J. S., 703
Chicci, D. L., 279
Chiswick, B. R., 60
Choate, P., 420
Christal, R. E., 110
Clark, R. L., 527
Clegg, C. W., 675
Cleveland, R. J., 694, 699
Close, M. J., 47
Cofer, J. L., 377
Cohen, A., 694, 699
Cohen, C. F., 77
Cohen, H. H., 694, 699
Cohen, S., 622
Condon, T. J., 393
Conley, P. R., 112
Constanza, T., 391
Cook, A. H., 585
Cook, D. Smith, 19
Cook, R., 61
Cook, T. D., 445
Cooke, W. N., 581, 595, 624
Cooper, E. A., 484, 513
Cornelius, E. T., III, 114
Cosier, R. A., 229
Cotton, J. L., 190-91, 667-68
Craft, J., 205-6
Crandall, N. F., 465, 469, 477
Cronbach, L. J., 95, 99
Cullen, D. E., 607
Cummings, L. L., 121
Cunningham, J., 597, 614

Dammann, C., 510
Dandel, W. L., 165
Daniels, G., 625
Davis, B. L., 453
Davis, G. A., 396
Dawis, R. V., 94, 101, 121, 124-26, 175-76, 179
Day, R. R., 436
Dean, J. W., Jr., 673, 675
Deegan, A. K., 218
Delaney, J. T., 587-88
Dennis, P., 699
Dennis, T. L., 278
Denny, A. T., 508
deVito, E. B., 241
Dickens, W. T., 572, 594
Digman, L., 444
Dimick, D. E., 29
Dipboye, F. L., 350
Dipboye, R. L., 472
Donnelly, J. H., 268
Donnelly, L. F., 421
Donovan, E., 597
Dossett, D. L., 509
Dougherty, T. W., 708
Douglas, A., 623, 627
Doverspike, D. C., 472
Dreher, G. F., 172, 516
Driskell, P. C., 260
Driver, M. J., 29, 408
Dunham, R. B., 173, 617
Dunn, B. D., 375
Dunnette, M. D., 97-98, 103-4, 120, 143,
      153-54, 335, 434, 506
Durham, R. L., 165
Dyer, L., 19, 205-9, 212-14, 217, 220-21, 225,
      227, 230, 235-36, 378, 383, 388, 389, 655,
      676-77, 696
Dyer, L. D., 151, 154, 160, 506, 513-14

Eden, D., 440
Eden, E., 440
Edwards, G., 19
Edwards, M. R., 166, 378
Edwards, R. K., 255, 261
Ehrenberg, R., 100
Ellis, R. A., 495
Emer, W. H., 712
Endicott, F. S., 278, 280, 282
England, G. W., 124, 175-76
England, P., 483
Ernest, R. C., 178
Ethier, W. J., 60
Evans, W. A., 508
Ewing, D. W., 241
Extejt, M. M., 628

Faley, R. H., 325
Farber, H. S., 597
Farh, J., 506
Farr, S. L., 160
Favers, J. L., 147
Fay, C. H., 465, 467, 550
Feild, H. S., 74, 148, 165, 304, 311, 325, 333,
      336-37, 345, 350
Feldman, D., 420
Feldman, J. M., 161-62
Fellner, D. J., 702

Feren, D. B., 508
Ferris, G. R., 664
Fichman, M., 183
Fiedler, F. E., 699
Fields, G. F., 542
Fine, S. A., 112, 342
Fink, L. S., 358
Finney, M. I., 28
Fiorito, J., 213
Fischer, C. T., 96
Fisher, C. D., 272–73, 442, 565
Fisher, L. H., 482
Fitch, H. G., 703
Fitzgerald, M. P., 664
Fitzgobbons, W. J., 377
Flaim, P. O., 59
Flanagan, M. F., 402
Fleishman, E. A., 96, 425
Fleming, R. L., 396
Florkowski, G. W., 504, 592
Foehrenbach, J., 29
Foley, R. H., 148
Folger, R., 478
Foltman, F. F., 383, 388–89
Foltz, R., 29
Fombrun, C. J., 145, 151
Ford, J. J., 305
Ford, J. K., 164, 431
Ford, R. C., 396–97, 710
Formisano, R. A, 551–52
Fossum, J. A., 66, 82, 100, 218, 573–75, 593, 625, 631
Fottler, M. D., 396–97
Foulkes, F. K., 636
Frantzreb, R., 238
Frazier, H. B., III, 580
Freedberg, S. P., 164
Freedman, A., 543, 606, 611, 621–22, 705
Freedman, S. M., 712
Freeman, J., 585
Freeman, K. A., 156, 658
Freeman, R. B., 572, 594, 596–97, 614–15
Fried, Y., 664
Friedman, D. E., 483, 486
Friedman, L., 112
Frink, C. B., 712
Froggatt, K. L., 667–68
Frohman, M. A., 29, 654, 674
Frumkin, R. W., 532
Fukami, C. V., 598
Fuller, S. H., 623
Fullerton, H. N., Jr., 58–59
Futrell, C., 495

Gagala, K., 625
Gallagher, D. G., 327
Gallo, F., 419
Gandz, J., 633
Garber, S, 703
Garland, H., 130
Gatewood, R. D., 304, 311, 325, 333, 336–37, 345, 350
Gaugler, B. B., 380
Gautschi, F. H., III, 581
Gerberding, S. N., 554
Gerhart, B., 172
Gershenfeld, W. J., 683
Getman, J., 590, 594

Ghiselli, E. E., 336, 338–39
Ghorpade, J. V., 104
Gibson, W. M., 315, 322
Gier, J. A., 352
Gifford, D., 552
Gilcher, Kay, 283
Gilkey, R., 206
Glickstein, G., 259
Gobeille, K. R., 683
Goldberg, S., 590, 594
Goldstein, G. P., 436
Goldstein, H., 421, 452
Goldstein, I. L., 422
Gomez-Mejia, L. R., 44, 109, 163
Gompers, Samuel, 571
Gooding, R. Z., 667
Goodman, P. S., 683, 703
Gordon, M. E., 268, 377, 598
Gorlin, H., 437, 502–3, 671
Gough, G., 339
Gould, R., 222, 352
Graham, M., 639
Grams, R., 472
Granof, M. H., 625
Gray, B. J., 18
Green, S. B., 111
Greenberg, J., 478, 481
Greenberg, L. A., 157
Greenhalgh, L., 206
Greenlaw, P. S., 76, 555
Greer, C. R., 213, 595
Gridley, J. D., 212, 214
Grier, K. B., 587
Griffen, R., 672
Griffeth, R. W., 190
Griffin, R. W., 662
Grimaldi, J. V., 689
Grimes, C. H., 710
Groh, K. F., 381
Grote, R. C., 396
Gruner, R., 166
Guion, R. M., 183, 315, 317, 322
Gupta, N., 494
Gustafson, D. P., 278
Gutek, B. A., 77
Gutteridge, T. G., 404, 410, 511
Guttman, R., 61
Guzzo, R. A., 508

Hachiya, D., 190
Hackett, E. J., 371, 373–76, 380
Hackett, R. D., 183
Hackman, J. R., 123, 662–64
Hahn, D. C., 472
Halcrow, A., 185, 510
Hale, A. R., 698
Hale, M., 698
Hall, D. T., 409
Hall, H., 111
Hamel, H. R., 401
Hammer, E. D., 345
Hammer, R. C., 591
Hammonds, K. H., 278
Hamner, W. C., 508, 589
Hand, H. H., 190
Hanigan, M., 282
Hannan, R. L., 106
Harlan, S. L., 371, 373–76, 380

Harris, D., 242
Harris, M. A., 391
Harris, M. M., 161, 339, 358
Hartmann, H. I., 483
Harvey, R. J., 112
Hauck, V. E., 77
Haulman, C. A., 61
Hawk, R. H., 251, 266–67
Haynes, M. G., 132
Haynes, R. D., 703
Helburn, I. B., 634
Hellervik, L. V., 153–54
Heneman, H. G., III, 127, 134, 270, 272, 305, 358, 472, 482, 495–96, 510, 512–13, 590, 609, 633
Heneman, H. G., Jr., 45
Heneman, R. L., 155, 507
Herman, J. B., 135, 590, 594
Herron, D. J., 341
Hershey, R., 386
Heshizer, B., 348
Heyer, N. O., 207–8, 216, 224, 235–36, 378
Hildebrand, G. H., 465
Hill, H., 640
Hill, M., Jr., 325, 635
Hill, S., 672
Hills, F. S., 74, 465, 467–68, 477, 513
Hobson, C. J., 711
Hochheiser, R. M., 286
Hoerr, J., 588, 598
Hoffman, J. J., Jr., 711
Hoffmann, C. C., 498
Holder, G. W., 19, 225, 230, 655, 676–77
Hollander, E. P., 132
Holley, W. H., 148, 165
Holley, W. H., Jr., 74
Hollman, K. W., 392
Hollman, R. W., 155
Holzer, H. J., 262
Hopkins, H. D., 691
Hough, L. M., 103, 342
Howard, A., 341
Howe, E. D., 179
Howe, W. J., 60
Hoyer, W. D., 272–73
Huber, V. L., 19, 356, 512
Huett, D. L., 305
Hufnagel, E. M., 517
Hulin, C. L., 175, 181, 190
Hunt, H. A., 61
Hunt, J. W., 689
Hunter, J. E., 311, 317, 338–39, 341, 343, 345, 350, 437, 590
Hunter, R. F., 338–39, 343, 345, 350
Hurst, M. W., 709

Iacocca, Lee A., 291
Ichniowski, C., 633
Ilgen, D. R., 147, 161–62, 272–73, 442, 656, 698
Ivancevich, J. M., 708–9

Jackson, P. R., 675
Jackson, S. E., 21, 23, 206
Jacoby, S. M., 499
Jacques, E., 481
James, F. E., 545
Janger, A. R., 173, 250

Jeanneret, P. R., 108–9
Jenkins, G. D., Jr., 494, 510
Jennings, K. R., 667–68
Jette, R. D., 508
Johnson, G., 613, 615
Johnson, L. A., 112
Johnson, S. S., 712
Johnson, T., 236
Johnson, W. A., 377
Jones, A. P., 112
Jones, M. W., 712
Jurgensen, C. E., 122

Kakuyama, T., 656
Kamerman, S. B., 546
Kandel, W.·J., 78
Kane, J. S., 156, 658
Karren, R. J., 130, 655, 656, 658
Kasl, E., 448
Katz, H. C., 606, 612, 626, 638, 683
Katz, Richard, 256
Katzell, R. A., 508
Kavanagh, M. J., 709
Kazaras, H. C., 19
Keaveny, T. J., 625
Keleman, K. S., 343
Keller, R. T., 712
Kendall, L. M., 152, 175
Kernan, M. C., 165, 386, 394
Kerr, C., 482
Kerr, J. L., 517
King, A. G., 86
Kingston, J. L., 542
Kirk, J. R., 348, 707
Kirmeyer, S., 708
Klaas, B. S., 633
Klasson, C. R., 165
Kleiman, L. S., 148, 165, 345
Klein, S. M., 178
Kleiner, M. M., 595, 615
Kleinman, L. S., 325
Klimoski, R., 378
Knapp, C. L., 279
Knight, T. R., 634
Kobak, S. E., 77
Kochan, T. A., 588–89, 594, 606, 612, 626, 638, 683, 696
Koen, C. M., Jr., 345
Kohl, J. P., 76, 555
Kokkelenberg, E. C., 572
Kolb, D. M., 627
Komaki, J., 702
Kondrasuk, J. N., 660
Konrad, A. M., 77
Kopelman, R. E., 511
Koys, D. J., 392–93
Kraiger, K., 164
Krefting, L. A., 514
Kroll, M. J., 480
Krzystofiak, F., 113, 235
Kubis, J. F., 112
Kuleck, W. J., Jr., 133
Kutscher, R. E., 58
Kuzmits, F. E., 185

Labig, C. E., Jr., 634
Lacey, D. W., 433

Ladd, R. T., 598
Land, R. L., 145, 151
Landy, F. J., 160
Lane, K., 259
Langer, P. J., 165
Larson, E. W., 598
Latack, J. C., 708
Latham, G. P., 127, 144, 147, 421, 423, 431,
    436–37, 439, 441–42, 447, 449–50, 509, 655,
    657–58, 667–68
Lawler, E. E., III, 120, 122, 133, 143, 434, 464,
    494, 510, 514, 655, 669, 672–73, 675–76
Lawler, J. J., 594
Lawshe, C. H., 314
Layton, A., 381
Lazes, P., 391
Leana, C. R., 667
Ledford, G. E., 668
Ledvinka, J., 74, 233–35, 690
Lee, C., 421
Lee, R. J., 433
Leglino, B. M., 190
Leibowitz, Z. B., 407
Lengnick-Hall, M. L., 325, 667–68
Leonard, J. S., 75, 572
Leonard, L., Jr., 450
Levine, E. L., 104, 111
Levine, H. Z., 375, 387
Levitan, S., 419
Likasiewicz, J. M., 62–63
Lindquist, V. R., 278, 280, 282
Linger, J. K., 420
Lipsky, D. B., 696
Livernash, E. R., 473, 478
LoBosco, M., 177
Locke, E. A., 121, 127, 171, 508, 655, 658, 662,
    667–68
Loehr, B. T., 664
Lofquist, H., 125–26
Lofquist, L. H., 94, 101, 121, 124, 175–76
London, M., 374, 376, 403–6, 408, 410, 429
Lorber, L. Z., 348, 707
Lord, J., 260
Lord, V., 48
Louchheim, F., 48
Lubbock, J. E., 269
Luber, G. L., 165
Lublin, J. S., 483, 706
Lutham, G. P., 506
Luthans, F., 506
Luzadis, R. A., 539

Macan, T. M., 350
McCaffery, R. M., 533–34
McCaleb, V. M., 508
McCall, M. W., Jr., 106
McConkie, M. L., 660
McCormick, E. J., 97, 103–4
McCormick, E. J., 108–9, 698
McCullough, P. M., 377
McDaniel, M. A., 341
McEvoy, B. M., 164
McEvoy, G. M., 187, 271, 665
Macey, W. H., 431
McFadden, J. J., 72, 533, 555
McGehee, W., 426
McKenna, J. F., 513
McKersie, R. B., 206, 594, 606, 612, 623, 626,
    638,

McLaughlin, F. S., 710
Magenau, J. M., 598
Mager, R. F., 423, 429, 442
Magnus, M., 239, 282, 510
Mahler, W. R., 44
Mahoney, T. A., 213, 219, 221, 227, 382, 486
Main, D. S., 112
Manning, M. R., 708
Manz, C. C., 675
Manzini, A. O., 212, 214
March, J. G., 190
Markham, S., 185, 498
Markham, W. T., 371, 373–76, 380
Marshall, F. R., 86
Martin, B., 257, 510
Martin, J. E., 598
Martin, S. A., 595
Martinez, T., 553
Maslow, A. H., 121
Mason, R. O., 229
Massengill, D. P., 268
Masters, M. F., 348, 587–88
Mathieu, J. E., 450
Matsui, T., 656
Matteson, M. T., 708–9
Mattila, J. P., 486
Maurer, S. D., 316
Mecham, R. C., 108–9
Medoff, J. L., 376–77, 596–98, 614–15
Meier, B., 706
Mendeloff, J., 692
Mento, A. J., 130, 655–56, 658
Meshoulam, I., 19
Meyer, G. W., 672
Meyer, M., 529, 535
Meyers, M., 256
Miles, Gregory L., 682
Miles, P. E., 517
Milkovich, G. T., 36, 208, 219, 227, 232, 213,
    221, 235, 382–83, 388–89, 465, 469, 476–77,
    483
Miller, C. S., 165
Miller, E. C., 281
Miller, E. L., 29
Miller, G., 216
Miller, H., 270, 273, 352
Miller, K. I., 667
Miller, M. W., 158
Mills, D. Q., 376–77
Mills, G. E., 420
Miner, J. B., 99
Miner, M. G., 99, 182, 186
Mintzberg, H., 106
Mischkind, L. A., 174
Mitchell, D. J. B., 499, 613
Mitchell, O. S., 512, 540
Mitchell, T. R., 127, 134, 392
Mitroff, I. I., 229
Mobley, W. H., 190
Moeller, N. L., 664
Mohrman, S. A., 668, 673, 676
Mondy, R. W., 255, 261
Mone, E. M., 406, 408
Monge, P. R., 667
Moore, W. J., 614
Moorhead, G., 29
Morgan, L. G., 135
Morgan, M., 409
Morgan, R. L., 598

Morre, B. E., 503
Morrison, A. M., 106
Morrison, M. H., 59
Motowidlo, S. J., 708
Mount, M. K., 453
Muczyk, J. P., 348, 668
Munger, M. C., 587
Murray, V. V., 29
Murrey, J. H., Jr., 392
Murrmann, K. F., 594
Musio, S. S., 311
Mussio, S. J., 268
Myers, D. C., 342
Myers, D. W., 78, 348
Myers, P. S., 78, 348

Nadler, L., 418
Nagle, B. F., 148
Nally, R. V., 553
Narayanan, V. K., 402
Nardone, T. J., 61
Nardoni, R., 238
Nash, A. N., 506
Nath, R., 402
Neale, M. A., 356, 526
Neef, A., 15
Nelson, S. M., 396
Nesbitt, M. A., 579
Neufeld, M. F., 569
Newman, J. E., 709
Newman, J. M., 113, 465, 469, 477
Newman, R. J., 614
Newman, W., 640
Newstrom, J. W., 617
Nigel, J. K., 675
Nkomo, S. N., 205
Noble, K. B., 393, 421,
Noe, M., 255
Noe, R. A., 644
Noe, R. M., 261
Northcraft, G. B., 356, 526
Northrup, H. R., 465, 617–18

O'Dell, C., 493
Odiorne, G. S., 658
Oglebay, S., 77
Oldham, G. R., 123, 662–64
Olian, J. D., 304, 347
Olian-Gottlieb, J. D., 127, 134
Oliver, R. L., 134
Olson, C., 496, 596–98, 633
Olson, D., 195
Onglatco, M. L. U., 656
Opsahl, R. L., 506
Orazem, P. F., 486
O'Reilly, C. A., III, 392
Osterman, P., 383–84
Ostroff, C., 315
Ostuw, R., 553
Outerbridge, A. N., 317
Ovalle, N. K., Jr., 191

Pace, R. W., 420
Packard, J. S., 708
Page, R. C., 162
Paquet, B., 448

Paradise, C. A., 66, 100
Parker, D. F., 218, 545
Parnes, H. S., 134, 254, 511–12
Paskal, S. S., 706
Patchen, M., 481
Patten, T. H., Jr., 475
Patton, T. H., Sr., 157
Paul, R., 506
Pearce, T. G., 77
Pearlman, K., 102
Peck, C., 145, 149, 151, 155, 493
Penzer, W., 177
Perry, J. L., 598
Personick, M. E., 493, 496
Personick, V. A., 62, 65
Peterson, M. F., 598
Peterson, R. B., 513
Petre, P., 435
Phillips, J. D., 208, 232
Philpot, J. W., 598
Pierce, J. L., 617
Pinder, C. C., 121, 126–27, 131, 381, 656, 660
Pine, R. C., 703
Pinto, P. R., 109–10
Pipe, P., 423
Podsakoff, P. M., 506
Polachek, S. W., 483
Porter, A. A., 594
Porter, M. E., 21, 209
Posner, B. Z., 272–73
Powell, G. N., 270, 273
Premack, S. L., 271, 275–76, 590
Preston, C., 709
Price, J. L., 170, 190
Prince, J. B., 29, 408
Pritchard, R. D., 121
Pritchett, S. T., 548–49
Prosten, R., 592
Pulakos, E. D., 162
Pursell, E. D., 350–51

Quaintance, M. K., 96

Rafaeli, A., 708
Raffs, F. A, 61
Raia, A. P., 659
Raju, N. S., 322
Ralphs, L., 420
Ralston, D. A., 402
Ramer, D. C. Z., 259
Raskin, A. H., 594
Rauschenberger, J. M., 317
Ravid, G., 440
Recio, M. E., 72
Reed, P. R., 480
Regan, P. J., 208
Regan, P. J., Jr., 220, 378
Rehmus, C. M., 622
Reibstein, L., 541, 707
Reilly, R. R., 338–39, 345
Reimann, B. C., 668
Reyna, M., 348
Rhode, J. G., 133
Rhodes, D. W., 218
Rhodes, S. R., 177, 184
Richardson, R., 481, 608
Richman, Louis R., 67

Robbins, N. E., 66, 100
Roberts, R. W., 185
Robertson, D. U., 307
Robinson, D. D., 314
Rollins, T., 15
Root, N., 698
Ropp, K., 48–49
Rose, K., 547, 617–18
Rose, R., 535, 709
Rosen, H., 589
Rosenberg, K., 29
Rosenblith, Lorna 411
Rosenfeld, C., 262
Rosenthal, D. B., 380
Rosow, J. M., 383, 388
Ross, J., 172
Ross, T. L., 503
Rosse, J. G., 186
Rosse, R. L., 103
Rothchild, N., 484
Rothe, H. F., 174
Rothwell, W. J., 19
Rowe, M. P., 348
Roznowski, M., 190
Ruback, R. S., 597
Rucci, A. J., 218
Rueben, G., 537, 555–56
Ruh, R. A., 660
Rumberger, R. W., 66
Rungeling, B., 61
Rupp, K., 61
Rush, J., 206
Russell, D. W., 170, 708
Russell, J. S., 42–43, 316, 430, 437, 453
Russell-Einhorn, M. L., 348
Ryder, M. S., 622
Rynes, S., 270, 272–73
Rynes, S. L., 127, 133, 273, 304, 358, 476
Rynes, S. R., 252–53, 264–65, 270, 276

Saari, L. M., 449, 655, 657–58
Sackett, P. R., 112, 339, 378
Sackett, R., 114
Salisbury, D. L., 537
Saltzman, G. M., 587
Sandler, A. L, 591
Sands, W. A., 320
Sandver, M. H., 590
Sari, P., 506
Saunders, N. C., 62
Scarpello, V., 174, 512
Schaeffer, R. G., 76
Schaubroeck, J., 161
Schechter, J. H., 539
Schechtman, S. L., 164
Schein, D. D., 707
Schein, L., 502–3, 671
Schiller, B. R., 512
Schlesinger, J. M., 150, 496
Schlotzhauer, D. L., 186
Schmidt, D. W., 264, 277
Schmidt, F. L., 114, 311, 317, 339, 341
Schmitt, N., 304, 315
Schmitz, L. M., 510
Schneider, B., 304
Schneier, C. D., 149, 151, 157
Schneller, G. O., IV, 511
Scholl, R. W., 513

Schrenk, L. P., 221–22
Schroeder, K. G., 381
Schuler, R. S., 19, 21, 23, 708
Schumpeter, Joseph A., 67
Schuster, J. R., 480
Schuster, M., 165, 503, 592
Schwab, D. P., 121, 127, 133–34, 151, 154, 160,
    170, 253, 264, 270–72, 277, 305, 358, 467–68,
    470, 472–73, 484, 496, 506, 512–14, 609
Schweiger, D. M., 667–68
Scott, D., 185
Scott, K. D., 185
Scott, L. R., 702
Scott, W. E., 506
Selekman, B. M., 623
Selekman, S. K., 623
Semplenski, Roy, 411
Shafer, R. A., 207–8, 220, 378
Shank, S. E., 58
Shaw, K. N., 508, 655, 658
Shaw, M. E., 132
Sheppard, H. L., 133
Sherer, P. D., 496
Shevlin, Nel, 572
Shuler, R. S., 206
Silvestri, G. T., 62–63
Simkin, W. E., 627
Simon, H. A., 190
Simon, S. H., 238
Simonds, R. H., 689
Sims, H. P., Jr., 673, 675
Sinclair, Barbara, 411
Sinicropi, A. V., 635
Sisking, F., 698
Sistrunk, F., 104, 111
Skinner, B. F., 126
Sledleckl, R., 260
Slocum, J. W., Jr., 517
Slote, A., 384
Smith, D. E., 160, 162
Smith, F. J., 173, 589
Smith, M. J., 694, 699
Smith, M. K., 311
Smith, P. C., 152, 175
Smith, R., 100
Snow, C. C., 517
Sockell, D. R., 572
Soder, D. A., 104–5
Solnick, L. J., 596
Sorcher, M., 436
Sorensen, J. E., 133
Soubel, W. G., 317
Sovereign, K. L., 632
Spartz, D. A, 700
Spector, B. A., 654
Spector, P. E., 191, 664
Spiller, W. E., 598
Spring, H. D., 551
Sproule, C. F., 322
Sproull, J. R., 166, 378
Spwey, W. A., 264
Stagner, R., 589
Standal, J. T., 513
Staudohar, P. D., 325
Staw, B. M., 172
Steel, R. P., 130, 191, 655–56, 658
Steers, R. M., 184
Steffy, B. D., 316
Steinbrink, J. P., 500

Stephan, E., 420
Stevens, C. M., 628
Stieber, J., 392
St. Louis, R. D., 542
Stone, E. F., 664
Stone, T. H., 213
Stott, R. G., 672
Strauss, G., 502–3
Stumpf, S. A., 374, 376, 403–5, 410, 429
Stutzman, T., 111
Sulzer-Azaroff, B., 703
Summers, L., 349
Sussmann, M., 307
Sutton, R. I., 708
Swaroff, P. G., 264

Taylor, F. W., 662
Taylor, M. S., 264, 270, 277, 282, 358, 442, 656
Taylor, S., Jr., 377
Terborg, J. R., 42–43, 316
Thayer, P., 426, 661–62, 665
Theilmann, J., 587
Theriault, R. D., 513–14
Thierry, H., 503, 506
Thomas, J., 15
Thompson, C. A., 598
Thompson, D. E., 103, 165
Thompson, T. A., 103
Thomsen, D. J., 239
Thornton, G. C., III, 378, 380
Thorpe, C. A., 680
Tiffin, J., 97
Tinsley, H. E. A., 124–26
Tornow, W. W., 109–10, 163
Tosi, H. L., 155, 494
Tosi, L., 494
Tragash, Harold, 411
Trattner, M. H., 317
Trattner, N. H., 112
Treiman, D. T., 483
Trice, H. M., 517
Trippel, A., 381
Trost, C., 487
Troy, Leo, 572
Tsui, A. S., 36–37, 44, 46
Tubbs, M. E., 655–56
Turnage, W. M., 61
Tuttle, J. M., 190–91
Tyler, L. E., 95, 97

Ulrich, D., 206, 545
Ulschak, F. L., 423
Urry, V. W., 311

Vandenberg, R. J., 512
Van Glinow, M., 29, 408
Van Sell, M., 708
Van Velzen, D., 708
Varadarajan, P., 495
Vecchio, R. P., 172, 481
Veglahn, P. A., 327
Verma, A., 612
Vittolino, S., 16
Vodanovich, S., 348
Vollrath, D. A., 667–68
von Hoffman, Nicholas, 464
Voos, P. B., 595

Vroman, S., 596, 614
Vroom, V. H., 127

Wagner, J. A., 667
Waite, W., 448
Waldman, D. A., 397
Walker, A., 238, 242
Walker, J., 29, 209, 212, 214, 218
Wall, T. D., 675
Wallace, L. J., 433
Wallace, M. J., Jr., 465, 467, 513, 550
Wallin, J. A., 703
Walter, G. A., 381
Walton, R. E., 623, 655, 676
Wanous, J. P., 271, 275–76
Ward, D. L., 383–84
Ward, Dan, 228
Warmke, D. L., 349
Weber, R. A., 703
Weekley, J. A., 352
Weick, K. E., Jr., 120, 143, 434
Weinstein, J. N., 348
Weinstein, L., 448
Weiss, D. J., 94, 101, 121, 124, 175–76
Weiss, D. W., 125–26
Weiss, R. D., 512
Weiss, R. M., 710
Weissmuller, J. J., 110
Weisz, W. J., 680
Weitzel, W., 179
Welch, F., 542
Wernimont, P. V., 252
Weschsler, D., 96
West, R., 594
Weston, D. J., 349
Wexley, K. N., 144, 147, 425, 429, 431, 434,
    436–37, 440–42, 447
White, J. K., 503
White, M. D., 626
Whitehead, J. D., 633
Whyte, W. F., 132, 508
Wichern, D. W., 484
Wilhite, A., 587
Williams, J. M., 48
Williams, J. S., 569
Wilson, C. W., 640
Wilson, J. T., 617–18
Wilson, M., 526
Witbeck, P. C., 702
Woldman, D. A., 164
Wolfe, M., 166
Wolfe, R. A., 545
Wolff, R. H., 393
Wonder, B. D., 343
Wood, R. E., 655, 658
Wrong, E. G., 640
Wroten, S. P., 431

Yoder, D., 45, 325
Young, J. P., 344
Youngblood, S. A., 19

Zager, R., 383, 388, 503
Zarandona, J. L., 189
Zedeck, S., 162, 378
Zimmerman, M. B., 597
Zollitsch, H. G., 501, 508

Subject Index

Ability tests
  nature of, 333
  validity of, 338
Absenteeism; *see also* Attendance patterns
  controlling, 184–86
  defined, 181
  frequency of, 184
  grievances regarding, 632
  as an indicator, 179
  measurement of, 183–84
  no-fault, 185
  and paid sick leave, 186
  penalties for, 185
  reasons for, 135
  statistics on, 182–83
  voluntary versus involuntary, 181–82
Academy of Management Executives, 50
Academy of Management Journal, 50
Academy of Management Review, 50
Accident proneness concept, 698
Accidents
  causes of, 696–97
  cost data, 694
  defined, 688
  frequency of, 692
  incidence rates of, 692–94
  investigations of, 696
  measurement statistics, 692
  reduction of, 698–704
  severity of, 692
Acquired Immune Deficiency Syndrome (AIDS)
  and employment, 77–78
  positive test implications, 347
Action planning
  alternatives in, 227
  decision making methods in, 229
  defined, 227
Administrative law judges, 69
Adverse impact
  and application blanks, 345
  coping with, 326
  defined, 325
  determination of, 325
  80 percent rule, 325–26
  justification of, 357
  nature of, 357
Affirmative action
  through career management, 403
  and labor unions, 639–40
  and selection predictors, 357

Affirmative action planning
  action plans for, 237
  alternative programs for, 237–38
  employee inventories for, 214
  goal-programming model for, 236
  goals in, 235–37
  nature of, 204
  preferential treatment in, 237–38
  and seniority considerations, 237–38
  steps in, 234
  timetables in, 235–37
  utilization analysis in, 234
Affirmative action plans
  for disabled employees, 712
  laws regarding, 74–75, 88
  and training programs, 419
  use of, 75
AFL-CIO
  composition of, 583
  establishment of, 572
  organizational chart for, 584
Age Discrimination in Employment Act
  benefit programs under, 555
  and early retirement plans, 391
  and employee discharge, 393
  health insurance under, 556
  and hiring practices, 324
  life insurance under, 534, 556
  pension benefits under, 556
  provisions of, 76–77, 88, 396
Agency shops, 579
American Arbitration Association arbitrators, 634
American Compensation Association, 49, 477
American Federation of Labor, 570–71; *see also* AFL-CIO
American Management Association wage surveys, 477
American Society for Personnel Administration, 49
American Society of Training Directors, 50–51
Applicant tracking systems, 268–69
Application blanks
  information accuracy on, 345
  legal quesitons for, 345–46
  nature of, 344
  validity of, 345
Apprenticeship programs, 419
Arbitration Journal, 51
Arbitrators, 634
Assessment centers
  advantages of, 380

Assessment centers—*Cont.*
  discrimination in, 380
  features of, 378–80
Attendance patterns; *see also* Absenteeism
  and employee commitment, 8–9
  and job satisfaction, 178
  rewards for, 185
  safety records and, 703
Authorization cards, 590

Baby boomers, 66, 403
Bargaining
  discipline issues in, 618–19
  entire-package approach to, 628
  external influences on, 607
  grievance procedures in, 619
  impasses in, 626
  industrywide, 609
  issue-by-issue approach to, 628
  job security issues in, 615, 617
  legal requirements for, 607
  lockouts during, 627
  mandatory items for, 608
  mediation in, 627
  multiemployer units for, 609
  pay form issues in, 613
  pay level issues in, 609–11
  pay structure issues in, 611–12
  pay system issues in, 613
  public sector, 628
  strikes during, 627
  work hour issues, 617–18
Bargaining power, 607
Bargaining unit determination, 590–91
Before-and-after design for training program eval-
    uation, 445–48
Behavioral work samples, 337–38
Behaviorally anchored rating scales
  benefits of, 156
  legal defensibility of, 165
  versus trait rating scales, 153–54
  use of, 152–54
Behavior modeling in training programs, 436
Benchmark jobs, 473
Benefits
  administration of, 547–48
  cafeteria-style, 551–53
  costs of, 18, 524, 550–51
  versus direct pay, 526
  employee attitudes on, 526
  employee contributions to, 526
  employee knowledge of, 553–54
  employee satisfaction and, 514, 516
  employee welfare, 543–47
  employer attitudes on, 527
  evaluation of, 549–50
  expansion of, 527–28
  flexible, 551–53
  for income maintenance, 541–43
  as indirect compensation, 12
  insurance, 530–34
  legal considerations, 528
  objectives of, 548–49
  off the job, 528
  on the job, 528
  in pregnancy, 555
  recent trends in, 524
  tax considerations in, 71–72, 526, 554–55

Benefits—*Cont.*
  types of, 524
  union attitudes on, 527
  variables in, 524
Binding arbitration requirements, 628
Blue Cross/Blue Shield Associations, 532
Bona fide occupational qualification (BFOQ), 73,
    324–25
Bounded rationality, 229
Bureau of Employment Security, 84
Bureau of Labor Statistics, 56–57
Business plans
  environmental scanning for, 221
  and human resource planning, 223
  and nagging personnel problems, 222

Cafeteria-style benefit plans
  cost-cutting with, 551–53
  tax considerations, 552
  types of, 551–52
Campus career centers, 283
Campus recruiting, 257; *see also* Recruitment
  efficiency in, 282
  evaluation of, 282
  guidelines for, 280
  on-site visits in, 284
  prevalence of, 261
  process, 278–82
  salary worksheet for, 280–81
  usefulness of, 262–63, 278
Career counseling
  for career plateauing, 408
  for dual career families, 408
  personnel for, 408–10
  for transitional stages, 408–9
  for women, 408
Career development
  activities for, 407
  defined, 407
  and internal staffing, 408
  through lateral moves, 407
  paths for, 408
  through promotions, 407
Career management
  advantages of, 402–3, 410
  components of, 370–71, 404
  evaluation of, 410
  need for, 403–4, 410
  objectives of, 371
  systems for, 410–11
Career path focal points, 404
Career planning
  performance-appraisal process and, 406
  defined, 404
  individual component of, 406–7
  organizational component of, 404, 406
  steps in, 406–7
Career plateauing, 408
Certification elections, 592
Checklists
  development of, 114
  in job analysis, 108
Child care benefits
  cost effectiveness of, 547
  need for, 66, 545–46
  prevalence of, 546–47
Civil Rights Act of 1964, 30
  comparable worth under, 485

Civil Rights Act of 1964—*Cont.*
and employee development, 453
and employee discharge, 393
and hiring practices, 324
and performance appraisal, 164
promotion decisions and, 377
provisions of, 73, 88
sex discrimination under, 555
and training programs, 430
union coverage under, 638–41
Civil Service Reform Act of 1978
collective bargaining under, 579–80
provisions of, 70, 82
Client interviews, 44
Closed shops, 579
Cognitive tests
bases for, 313–14
content validity of, 314
item samples, 333–35
nature of, 333
Cognitive theory of motivation, 126–27
Commission pay systems
and productivity measurement, 16
use of, 500
Comparable worth
defined, 466, 482–83
future of, 486
implementation of, 487
legal basis for, 484–86
union concerns over, 611–12
Compensable factors, 470–71
Compensation; *see also* Pay systems
by commission, 16
direct versus indirect, 464
entry-level, 281
indirect, 12
legal considerations in, 465
and motivation, 122
nature of, 12
policies on, 464
specialists in, 49
types of, 12
Competitor analysis, 224
Comprehensive Occupational Data Analysis Program (CODAP), 108, 110–11
Compressed work week
defined, 399
nature of, 402
union stance on, 402
Computer-aided instruction in training programs, 436
Computerized job search services, 258–59
Concurrent validation
nature of, 307
pitfalls of, 307–8
Congress of Industrial Organizations, 570–71; *see also* AFL-CIO
Consent elections, 590
Consolidated Omnibus Budget Reconciliation Act
insurance provisions of, 530
pensions under, 537
provisions of, 388
Content validation
versus empirical validation, 304
job analysis and, 313
nature of, 303–4, 311, 313
steps in, 311
use of, 311, 313–15
Contracted work, 388–89

Contract recruitment, 260
Contracts; *see also* Bargaining
administration of, 13, 629
costing of, 625
equal opportunity clauses in, 641
escalator clauses in, 481
grievance procedure clauses in, 630
management rights clauses in, 618
negotiation of, 619–29
no-strike clauses in, 619, 627
nonwage clauses in, 616–17
past practice issues in, 632
ratification of, 628
recent trends in, 625–26
rejection of, 628
union rights clauses in, 618
wage clauses in, 610
Correlation coefficients, 309
Cost-benefit analysis for decision making, 230
Cost-of-living adjustments
bargaining for, 613
and pay structures, 481
Criterion measures
defined, 306
need for, 306
and performance appraisal systems, 306
relationship to predictor measures, 309
scores on, 307
Critical incidents
for performance appraisal, 110, 152
technique in job analysis, 106–7
Current Population Survey data, 56
Cut scores
establishment of, 318
need for, 318
relationship to costs, 320

Daily Labor Report (BNA), 50
Davis-Bacon Act
compensation and, 465
provisions of, 83
Decertification elections, 594
Decision making methods, 229
Defined benefit plans
administration of, 538
costing, 625
formulas for, 538–39
Defined contribution plans
administration of, 539
costing, 625
formula for, 539
prevalence of, 539
Dental insurance, 533
Devil's advocate approach for decision making, 229
Diagnostic devices, 336
Dialectical inquiry for decision making, 229
Disability insurance, 533
Disabled employees affirmative action plans, 712
Discharge of employees
appeals procedures in, 394
assistance programs use, 544
documentation in, 165, 394
for incompetence, 394
for just cause, 393
legal considerations in, 392–96
management of, 393–96
multiple consultation in, 394
outplacement assistance in, 396

Discharge of employees—*Cont.*
  and progressive discipline, 394
  severance pay in, 396
  wrongful, 393
Discrimination; *see also by type*
  through application blanks, 345
  in benefits programs, 555
  through cognitive tests, 339
  through educational requirements, 343
  in employee development, 451–54
  through experience requirements, 343
  in grievance/arbitration processes, 326–27
  through knowledge work samples, 339
  laws regarding, 73–77, 88
  and pay equity, 483–87
  and performance appraisal, 164
  proof of, 324
  through resumes, 345
  and seniority systems, 386
Displaced employees training programs, 419–20
Drug testing laws, 347

Educational requirements and minorities, 343
Elder care programs, 547–48
Empirical validation
  versus content validation, 304
  criterion measures in, 306–11
  job analysis and, 304–6
  nature of, 303
  predictor measures in, 306–11
  statistical significance in, 309
  steps in, 312
Employee abilities
  defined, 94–95
  differences in, 97–99
  and human capital, 99–101
  and job performance, 95
  and job requirements, 101
  measurement of, 95
  types of, 96–98
Employee assistance programs
  activities of, 710
  cautions regarding, 545
  effectiveness of, 710, 711
  stress management in, 710
  substance abuse, 543–45
  telephone-based, 546
Employee development; *see also* Training
    programs
  affirmative action plans for, 451–54
  alternatives to, 426
  comprehensive, 427
  costs of, 421
  defined, 418
  effectiveness of, 451
  efficiency of, 451
  equal opportunity in, 451–54
  line managers and, 418
  for minorities, 453
  needs identification in, 423
  personnel specialists and, 419
  plan elements, 428
  prevalence of, 420–21
  priority determination in, 427–28
  process of, 422
  program evaluation, 443, 450–54
  purpose of, 418
  success in, 425
  trainability questions in, 431

Employee handbooks, 394
Employee inventories, 214
Employee motivation; *see also* Pay systems
  and job rewards, 121–23
  and needs, 121
  and social environment, 122–23
  and social environment, 132
Employee privacy programs, 242
Employee referrals
  bonuses for, 255
  cautions regarding, 256
  use of, 258
Employee relations department; *see* Personnel/
    human resources department
Employee retention and advancement oppor-
    tunities, 374
Employee Retirement Income Security Act of
    1974
  compensation and, 465
  costs of, 551
  provisions of, 86
  reporting requirements, 553
  requirements of, 537
  women's pensions under, 556
Employee review boards, 637
Employees
  attraction of, 7, 66, 133
  retention of, 7–9, 66, 263, 374; *see also*
    Turnover
  treatment of, 30–31
Employment at will doctrine, 392
Employment interviews
  by committee, 350, 352
  documentation of, 350, 352
  and EEO compliance, 352
  length for, 349
  one-on-one, 349
  pitfalls in, 350
  procedures for, 351
  purpose of, 348–49
  questions for, 350
  relevance of, 349
  standardized approach to, 357
  structured versus unstructured, 349–50
  validity of, 350
Employment Standards Administration, 83
Entrepreneurial businesses, 207
Entry-level jobs in pay structures, 473
Environmental scanning
  defined, 221
  internal, 221–23
  trend reports from, 221–22
  use of, 224
Equal employment opportunity
  and ability testing, 324
  and adverse impact, 357
  and group differences, 99
  and hiring practices, 324–26
  laws and regulations regarding, 73–77
  and performance appraisal, 164–66
  policies communication, 237
  and recruitment method choice, 265
Equal Employment Opportunity Act of 1972, 73
Equal Employment Opportunity Commission
  compliance guidelines, 75
  role of, 69, 74, 88
Equal Pay Act of 1963
  comparable worth under, 484–85
  provisions of, 88

Executive Order 10988, 579
Executive Order 11246
  provisions of, 76, 88
  union coverage by, 639
Executive reviews, 217
Executive search firms, 258
Exit interviews, 189
Expectancy perceptions
  and line management practices, 130
  and pay systems, 492
  and selection procedures, 130
  in training, 130
  in transfer policies, 130
Expectancy theory
  behavior-reward perceptions in, 128
  effort-behavior perceptions in, 128, 130
  and employee performance, 134
  and employee turnover, 134–35
  versus goal-setting theory, 130
  and job-choice behavior, 133
  instrumentality perceptions in, 128, 131–32
  nature of, 127–29
  valence perceptions in, 129
Experience requirements
  nature of, 341
  validity of, 341–43

Fact finding requirements, 628
Fair Employment Practice Cases, 50
Fair Labor Standards Act
  and compensation, 465
  coverage of, 69, 83
Federal Labor Relations Authority
  establishment of, 580
  role of, 82
Federal Mediation and Conciliation Service
  arbitrators from, 634
  establishment of, 578
  notification of, 619
  role of, 81, 578
  services of, 627
Federal Mine Safety Act, 87
Federal Mine Safety and Health Review Commission, 87
Federal Unemployment Tax Act, 85
Final-offer arbitration requirements, 628
Finger dexterity testing, 335
Flexible scheduling, 66
Flextime
  benefits in, 402
  defined, 399
  nature of, 402
  supervision in, 402
  use of, 13
Forced distribution, 150
Full employment policies
  costs of, 383
  and employee development, 420

Gain sharing pay systems
  cost-savings focus for, 502–3
  profit-sharing focus for, 503–4
  types of, 502
General human capital (GHC), 100–101
Genetic screening, 348
Geographic relocations
  assistance for, 381

Geographic relocations—Cont.
  difficulties in, 374
  disadvantages of, 381
Ghiselli Self-Description Inventory, 336
Goal setting
  in behavior motivation, 127
  versus expectancy theory, 130
  motivation through, 656, 658
Good faith, 619
Grievance procedures
  arbitration in, 634–35
  benefits in, 683
  committee membership for, 631
  discrimination cases, 640–41
  in nonunion organizations, 637
  provisions in, 629–31
  umpires for, 634
Grievances
  effects of, 633
  public-sector organizations, 634
  types of, 632–33

Harvard Business Review, 50
Hay Plan, 469–70
Head-hunting, 258
Health care employees health hazards, 705–6
Health exams
  for AIDS, 347
  alternatives to, 347–48
  costs of, 347
  drug testing in, 347
  genetic screening in, 348
  legal questions about, 348
  need for, 346–47
  physicals versus questionnaires, 347
  and privacy rights, 348
  validity of, 348
Health insurance
  contributory versus noncontributory, 532
  costs of, 532
  coverage of, 531
  prevalence of, 530
  for retirees, 530–31
  types of, 530
  vehicles, 530, 532
Health maintenance organizations, 530, 532
Help-wanted advertisements, 394
Heuristic devices for decision making, 230
High-involvement work systems
  defined, 676
  evaluation of, 683
  labor relations in, 680–81
  motivation through, 683
  rewards in, 678
  self-managing work teams in, 677–78
  in start-up situations, 681–83
Highly compensated employees (HCEs), 71, 554
Hiring
  freezes in, 390
  standards
    and cost minimization, 320–21
    establishment of, 318–20
    grouping procedures in, 321
    pass-fail systems in, 321
    ranking procedures in, 321
    and selection errors, 318–20
    and selection predictors, 318
  steps in, 267–68

Holidays, 529
Home work
  benefits of, 400
  defined, 399
  for the disabled, 712
  women in, 400
Honesty tests
  legal considerations, 340
  and privacy rights, 340
  use of, 338
  validity of, 339
Human capital, 99–101
Human Relations, 50
Human resource flows
  judgmental estimation techniques, 216–18
  statistical estimation techniques, 214–16
Human Resource Information Centers, 242
Human resource information systems
  automatic updating in, 240
  data collection for, 240
  data for, 238–39
  data security in, 241
  and employee inventories, 214
  functional components of, 239–41
  microcomputers in, 238
  need for, 238
  reporting function, 241
  software for, 240–41
  use of, 204
Human Resource Management, 50
Human Resource Planning, 51
Human resource planning
  action planning phase of, 227–33
  bottom-up approach to, 213
  business plans and, 209–12, 223
  comprehensiveness of, 206
  computerized algorithms in, 212–13
  coverage of, 207–8
  and employee flexibility, 211
  in entrepreneurial businesses, 207
  job organization for, 208
  judgmental techniques for, 213
  and layoff policies, 208
  by line managers, 208
  model for, 209
  nature of, 11, 204–5, 223–25
  needs estimation in, 209–12
  plan-based, 206–7
  planning horizons for, 207
  population-based, 206–7, 217
  and productivity, 211
  project-based, 206–7
  recruitment timing and, 266
  setting objectives in, 225–27
  by staff specialists, 208
  statistical techniques for, 212–13
  strategy formation in, 233
  top-down approach to, 213
  what if analysis for, 213, 225
Human Resource Planning Society, 49, 51
Human resources department; *see* Personnel/
    human resources department
Human service organizations, 6

Immigrants, illegal, 60
Immigration Reform and Control Act of 1987
    provisions of, 72
Improshare plan, 503

Incentive pay systems
  absenteeism and, 510
  administration of, 501
  defined, 499n
  group-oriented, 499–500
  individual-oriented, 499
  misuse of, 501
  motivation through, 506, 508
  plan development for, 500–501
  prevalence of, 500
  purpose of, 499
  quotas in, 656
Income maintenance legislation, 71, 84–85
Individual retirement accounts (IRAs), 539–40
Inductive reasoning testing, 334
Industrial and Labor Relations Review, 50
Industrial engineering, 656, 662
Industrial Relations, 50
Industrial relations department; *see* Personnel/
    human resources department
Industrial Relations Research Association, 49
Instrumentality perceptions, 128
Insubordination grievances, 632
Intellectual abilities, 96–97
Interest inventories, 339
Interest tests, 336
Interindividual differences, 97–98
Internal recruitment
  advantages of, 374
  closed systems of, 375
  decision making procedures for, 380–81
  disadvantages of, 374
  evaluation of, 382
  geographic transfers in, 374
  open systems of, 375
  and past performance, 377
  predictors for, 376–80
  seniority in, 376
  using job posting, 375
  using replacement charts, 375
  using skills inventories, 375
Internal Revenue Code, 71
Interrater reliability, 323
Interviewer training, 352
Interviewing in job analysis, 106
Intraindividual differences, 98

Job analysis
  attendance patterns and, 305
  data verification, 112
  defined, 102
  and empirical validation, 304
  equal employment opportunity impact on, 102–3
  importance of, 165
  for job evaluation, 472
  job satisfaction and, 305
  methods for, 103–11, 113–14
  need for, 101–3
  performance dimensions of, 304–5
  and performance measurement, 147–48, 165
  person-oriented approach, 103–4, 114
  qualitative approach to, 106, 111
  quantitative approach to, 108–11
  sample size in, 111
  sources of error in, 111–13
  task-oriented approach, 103, 106, 114
  turnover and, 304–5
  uses for, 115

Job analysts, 112–13
Job characteristics model
  effectiveness of, 664
  motivation through, 662–63
Job Descriptive Index use of, 175, 180–81
Job design
  approaches to, 661–63
  and decision making, 665
  effectiveness of, 664
  need for, 661
Job Diagnostic Survey, 123–24
Job enrichment
  effectiveness of, 664
  group level, 673
  methods for, 663
  motivation through, 662–65
  prevalence of, 664
  turnover and, 665
  use of, 665
Job evaluations
  by committee, 469
  compensable factors in, 470–71
  formal approach to, 469
  job analysis for, 472
  job descriptions in, 472
  methods for, 469
  planning for, 469
  point method for, 469–72
  prepackaged plans for, 469–70
  reliability checks on, 472
Job fairs, 259–61
Job hierarchies
  development of, 466–72
  equity criterion for, 467–68
  job evaluation for, 468–72
  pricing of, 472, 475
  stability of, 480
Job Instruction Training (JIT), 438
Job performance; *see also* Performance appraisal
    and Performance measurement
  multidimensional nature of, 146–48
  and personnel/human resources management,
    7–9
  qualitative measurements of, 147
  quantitative measurements of, 147
  standards for, 148–49
Job requirements
  as ability requirements, 96
  defined, 94
  and employee ability, 101
Job rewards
  defined, 94
  and employee motivation, 121–23; *see also* Pay
    systems
  measurement of, 123–25
Job rotation and employee development, 438
Jobs
  attributes, 270
  classification techniques for, 111
  defined, 101
  descriptions,
    defined, 103–4
    for job evaluations, 472
    revision of, 113
  families of, 102
  posting of,
    for internal recruitment, 375
    in nonunion organizations, 636
  redesign of, 13

Jobs—*Cont.*
  specifications for, 103–4
Job satisfaction
  and attendance patterns, 178
  dispositional factors in, 172n
  facets of, 171–72
  measurement methods, 174–76
  nature of, 170–71
  and personnel/human resources management,
    7–9
  surveys of, 173–81
  and turnover levels, 178
Job security in nonunion organizations, 636
Job seekers
  decision making by, 270–71
  information sources for, 283–84
  interview guidelines for, 283–86
  motivation of, 270–71
  on-site visits by, 284
Job sharing
  nature of, 401
  and phased retirement programs, 397
  variations on, 399
Job simplification
  prevalence of, 664
  use of, 661–62, 665
Job Training Partnership Act of 1983, 61, 419
Job vacancies
  internal moves for, 372–76
  nominations for, 372
Journal of Applied Psychology, 50
Journal of Labor Research, 50
Jury duty policies, 529
Just-noticeable difference in pay systems, 495

Key jobs in pay structures, 473–74
Knights of Labor, 569–70
Knowledge work samples
  construction of, 315
  nature of, 338
Kuder Vocational Preference Record, 336

Labor costs
  and benefit packages, 18
  and Personnel/human resources activities, 18
  and profit sharing, 18
Labor force
  aging of, 59
  defined, 57
  quality of, 60
  trends in, 57–62
Labor-intensive industries recruitment, 249
Labor laws
  coverage by, 575
  federal, 70, 81–82
  requirements of, 568
Labor-management relations
  business environment for, 603
  deregulation effects on, 604
  equal employment opportunity and, 638
  foreign competition effects on, 605
  nature of, 12
  in nonunion organizations, 605–6, 635–37
Labor market
  defined, 56
  demand trends in, 61–62
  and economic conditions, 55

Labor market—*Cont.*
  environmental scanning of, 221
  recruitment in, 249
Labor Relations Reference Manual, 50
Labor supply
  employment projections, 63–65
  and immigration, 59
  projections of, 214–18
  trends in, 57–61
Labor unions
  activities of, 588
  affirmative action obligations of, 639–40
  attractions of, 588–89
  compensation issues and, 465
  democracy within, 585
  development of, 568–72
  effects of deregulation on, 575
  effects of foreign competition on, 574
  effects of mechanization on, 574
  effects on employees, 597
  effects on employers, 596–97
  goals of, 595
  local, 582–83
  members rights, 578, 585
  membership levels, 572–73
  mergers of, 585–86
  national, 581–82, 585, 587
  organizing campaigns for, 590–95
  and personnel/human resources activities, 68
  political activities of, 587
  and public policy, 587
  recent trends in, 574–75
  rivalries between, 634
  seniority issues for, 376
  structures for, 581–83
  and training programs, 419–20
  turnover with, 596–98
  work scheduling issues and, 402
Landrum Griffin Act of 1959
  due process under, 578
  provisions of, 70, 81–82
  secondary boycotts under, 579
Lateral transfers, 373
Layoffs
  alternatives to, 388–92
  costs of, 383–84, 387
  decision documentation for, 386
  defined, 182
  discrimination in, 386
  employee assistance in, 387
  insurance coverage during, 388
  nonunion situations, 385
  notification of, 386–87
  order determination for, 385–86
  personnel department role in, 385
  policies regarding, 18, 208, 383
  prevalence of, 385
  recall from, 388
  reduction of, 189
  and seniority, 385
Letters of regret, 268
Lie detectors
  legal considerations, 340
  use of, 338
Life insurance
  costs of, 534
  for retirees, 534
Line managers
  decisions making by, 34
  merit pay decisions by, 498

Line managers—*Cont.*
  performance appraisal of, 38–39
  personnel/human resources activities, 32–35
  perspective of, 34–38
  selection decisions role, 355
Lockouts, 627
Looking Glass (business game), 435

Maintenance-of-membership, 579
Make-work projects, 388–89
Management by objectives
  benefits of, 156
  legal defensibility of, 165
  nature of, 658, 660
  in performance appraisal, 155
  pitfalls in, 660
  prevalence of, 658
  processes in, 659
Management Position Description Questionnaire
    (MPDQ), 108–10
Markov analysis, 216, 224
Mastery modeling, 428–29
Maternity leave, 546
Mechanical tests, 333
Mediation, 627
Memory testing, 334
Merit pay systems
  decision levels in, 498
  frequency of review for, 496
  versus incentive systems, 499
  instrumentality perceptions in, 131
  motivation through, 495, 506
  in nonunion organizations, 636
  pros and cons of, 507
  purpose of, 495
  salary increment matrix for, 497
  seniority elements in, 497
Military leave policies, 529
Mine Safety and Health Administration, 87
Minnesota Job Description Questionnaire, 124–25
Minnesota Satisfaction Questionnaire, 175–76
Minorities
  career counseling for, 237
  educational requirements and, 343
  issues and, 377
  in the labor force, 58
  layoff rates among, 386
  recruitment of, 264–65, 268, 273
  seniority rights of, 639
  union representation of, 640
  utilization rates for, 234, 357
Mixed pay systems
  misuse of, 497
  motivation through, 506
  nature of, 497–98
Monthly Labor Review, 51
Motivation; *see also* Pay systems
  defined, 94
  managerial influence on, 129–33
  nature of, 120
Motivational processes
  cognitive theories of, 126–27
  defined, 125
  reinforcement theory of, 126–27

National Board of Adjustment, 81
National Electrical Manufacturers Association plan,
    469–70
National Human Resource Center, 420

National Institute for Occupational Safety and Health
  establishment of, 691
  role of, 87
National Labor Relations Act, 392
National Labor Relations Board
  establishment of, 576
  role of, 69, 81, 580, 592
National Labor Union, 569
National Mediation Board
  establishment of, 580
  role of, 81
Negotiations
  impediments to, 624
  management preparation for, 619–21
  notification of, 619
  planning timetable, 620–21
  preparation for, 619–22
  tactics for, 622–26
  union preparation for, 622
Nonhighly compensated employees (NCHEs), 71, 554
Norris-LaGuardia Act
  labor unions under, 576
  provisions of, 81
Number aptitude testing, 334

Observational analysis, 106
Occupational groups employment projections, 63–65
Occupational safety and health
  focus for, 705
  legal framework for, 689–92
Occupational Safety and Health Act of 1970, 30
  effectiveness of, 692
  and employee discharge, 393
  impact of, 691
  provisions of, 87, 690
  purpose of, 690
Occupational Safety and Health Administration
  role of, 87
  training guidelines, 700
Occupational Safety and Health Review Commission, 87, 691
Occupations defined, 102
Office of Federal Contract Compliance Programs
  responsibility of, 76, 88
  Revised Order No. 4, 234, 237
Ombudsmen to resolve grievances, 637
On-call employees, 399
One-shot bonus pay systems, 496
On-line classifieds, 259
Operational planning timeframe, 207
Organizational Behavior and Human Decision Processes, 50
Organizational culture
  defined, 517
  external staffing and, 518
  internal promotions and, 517
  pay system choice in, 517
Organizational Dynamics, 50
Organizational strategy and pay system choice, 517
Outplacement assistance
  and employee discharge, 396
  in layoffs, 387
Overtime
  costing, 625
  to prevent overhiring, 390
  union concern with, 618

Parental leave periods, 66; *see also* Maternity leave
Participative decision making
  effectiveness of, 668
  motivation through, 666
  philosophy behind, 666–67
Participative work groups
  foreign arrangements for, 666
  nature of, 665
  types of, 666
Part-time employees
  ages of, 401
  cost savings with, 401
  fringe benefits for, 401
  sex of, 401
  women as, 401
Part-time work
  defined, 61, 399
  trends in, 61
Pay equity; *see also* Comparable worth
  defined, 482–83
  job evaluation for, 483–85
Pay-for-knowledge systems
  costs of, 495
  employee flexibility in, 494–95
  nature of, 494
Pay level
  adjustments to, 481
  as a bargaining issue, 609–11
  employee satisfaction and, 513
  policies on, 476–78
  union effects on, 613–14
  and turnover rates, 511
Pay satisfaction issues, 482, 512–16
Pay structures
  adjustments to, 480–81
  control of, 480
  development of, 473–80
  inequities in, 481–87
  and pay levels, 476
  rate ranges in, 476–77
  red-circle rates in, 479–80
  in unionized organizations, 614–15
Pay systems; *see also* Compensation
  administration of, 498
  attendance motivation through, 510
  choice of, 518–19
  conventional approach to, 493–99
  employee responses to, 504
  employee retention through, 511
  employee satisfaction through, 513–15
  gain sharing approach to, 502–4
  incentive approach to, 499–502
  job seeker attitudes to, 504
  motivation through, 492, 504–10, 515
  orgaizational culture and, 517
  organizational strategy and, 517
  quota restrictions and, 509–10
  starting rates in, 498
Peer appraisals, 161
Pension Benefit Guarantee Corporation, 86, 538
Pension plans, mandatory, 534
Pension plans, private
  employee knowledge of, 540
  need for, 535
  pitfalls in, 536
  prevalence of, 535
  regulation of, 536–38
  types of, 538–40
Pensions, nonvested, 512

Perceptual speed testing, 335
Performance appraisal
  absolute standards in, 151–55
  comparative procedures for, 149–50, 155–56
  documentation in, 165
  and EEO, 164–66
  errors in, 159–60
  feedback in, 143, 156
  instrumentality perceptions in, 131
  legally defensible, 165
  managerial motivation in, 162
  nature of, 142
  in not-for-profit organizations, 144
  by peers, 161
  policy evaluation through, 144
  process approach to, 160–63
  for production employees, 144
  purposes of, 142–44
  techniques for, 110
  training for, 161–62, 165
  for training program evaluation, 444
  usage of, 144–46
Performance appraisal systems
  and employee promotability, 377
  managerial, 38–39
  need for, 9
Performance counseling, 165
Performance discrepancies
  defined, 423
  identification of, 423–24
  potential for, 423
  solutions to, 426
Performance measurement; *see also* Job
    performance
  bias in, 164
  by computer, 158–59
  contamination of, 148
  deficiencies in, 148
  errors in, 159–60
  and job analysis, 147–48, 165
  quantitative, 157–59
  through production, 157
  through sales, 157
Personality inventories, 338–39
Personality tests, 336
Personnel, 50
Personnel Administrator, 50
Personnel departments; *see* Personnel/human re-
    sources department
Personnel/human resources activities
  budget allocation analysis of, 41
  and the competitive strategy, 21
  cost analysis of, 40–41
  effectiveness of, 38–46
  environmental scanning for, 221
  external influences on, 54
  functional, 11–13
  generalists in, 32
  impact of contracts on, 637–38
  and labor costs, 18
  laws and regulations affecting, 68–77
  by line managers, 28, 32–35
  and product quality, 17
  and productivity growth rates, 17
  and service orientation, 17
  in small organizations, 28–29
  specialists in, 32
  by staff managers, 28, 34
  support, 10–11
  targeting of, 9

Personnel/human resources activities—*Cont.*
  utility analysis of, 42–43
  and workforce flexibility, 18
Personnel/human resources department
  activities of, 28–29, 37
  advisory capacity, 35
  budget allocation analysis of, 41–42
  control relationships of, 35–36
  direct services of, 35
  evaluation of, 21
  legal standard compliance by, 31
  merit pay decisions by, 498
  multiple, 29
  need for, 29–31
  outcome levels analysis, 40
  outcome trends analysis of, 40
  performance appraisal of, 38–45
  recruitment responsibility of, 250
  relationship to line managers, 35–38
  reputation of, 43–45
  role in compensation administration, 465
  role in internal staffing, 372
  selection decisions role, 355
  structure of, 31–33
  traditional roles for, 654
Personnel/human resources management
  and the administrative process, 19–22
  careers in, 47–49
  and economic conditions, 54–56
  effectiveness of, 9
  ethical issues in, 19
  external influences on, 14–15
  generalists in, 32, 45, 50
  in retailing, 16
  jobs in, 45–47
  model for, 7–8
  nature of, 6
  organization context of, 15–22
  outcomes of, 7–9
  practices and expectancy perceptions, 130
  professional organizations for, 49
  professional publications in, 50–51
  specialists in, 32, 45, 50–51
Personnel Journal, 50
Personnel Psychology, 50
Piece-rate pay systems, 499
Point method for pay equity, 484
Political action committees, 587–88
Polygraphs
  legal considerations, 340
  use of, 338
Position defined, 102
Position Analysis Questionnaire (PAQ), 108–9, 111
Predictive validation, 308
Predictor measures
  job analysis and, 313
  need for, 306
  relationship to criterion measures, 309
  scores on, 307
Preferred provider organizations, 532
Pregnancy Discrimination Act of 1978, 555
Privacy Act of 1974 and human resource informa-
    tion systems, 241
Production bonus pay systems, 499
Productivity, 15, 17
Productivity gain-sharing programs, 17
Professional Air Traffic Controllers Organization
    strike, 580
Profit-sharing plans
  effectiveness of, 504

Profit-sharing plans—*Cont.*
  forms of, 503
  and labor costs, 18
  motivation through, 504
Progressive discipline
  appeals procedures in, 394
  multiple consultations in, 394
  use of, 394–96
Promotability ratings
  through assessment centers, 378
  succession planning programs and, 378
  use of, 378
Promotions policies
  expectancy perceptions in, 130
  seniority in, 376–77
  typical patterns, 373
Psychomotor abilities, 97–98
Psychomotor tests, 335
Public Personnel Management, 50
Punishment instrumentality perceptions, 131
Pygmalion effect, 440

Quality circles
  characteristics of, 669
  defined, 668
  effectiveness of, 672
  management committment to, 671
  pitfalls in, 672
  prevalence of, 672
  versus self-managing work teams, 673
  use of, 13
Questionnaires
  in job analysis, 108
  for training program evaluation, 444

Railway Labor Act of 1926
  and employee discharge, 392
  labor unions under, 576
  provisions of, 70, 81
Rating instruments, 165
Reaction time testing, 335
Realistic job previews
  advantages of, 271
  cost savings with, 275–76
  and turnover rates, 271
Recommendations
  and privacy rights, 343
  standardized evaluation of, 356
  use of, 343
Recruiters
  characteristics for, 272
  contract, 260
  credibility of, 272
  evaluation of, 277
  interviews by, 279
  training of, 273
Recruitment; *see also* Campus recruiting
  advertising in, 256–57, 261, 276, 394
  affirmative action in, 248, 265
  agencies in, 261
  approaches to, 248
  brochure wording for, 394
  computer use in, 268–69
  costs of, 275
  defined, 248
  direct applications in, 255, 261
  direct-mail marketing in, 259
  from educational institutions, 257; *see also* Campus recruiting
  effective methods of, 276

Recruitment—*Cont.*
  through employee referrals, 255–56, 258, 261
  and employee retention, 263–64
  equal employment opportunity in, 248
  evaluation of, 274–78
  external factors in, 248
  feedback on, 277–78
  geographical scope for, 254
  honesty in, 272
  importance of, 248
  interview questions, 273
  through job fairs, 259–61
  labor organizations and, 249
  legal methods of, 265
  media versus message in, 273
  method effectiveness, 261–65
  methods of, 255–65
  of minorities, 264–65, 268, 273, 276
  numerical targets in, 251–52
  of older workers, 276
  on-site visits in, 284
  personnel for, 249; *see also* Recruiters
  planning for, 251–54
  process of, 250
  through professional societies, 260
  screening in, 273–74
  search process in, 266–73
  stumbling blocks to, 268
  targets for, 252–53
  through temporary help agencies, 257–58, 260, 276
  time-lapse data for, 266
  timing of, 266
  unsuccessful, 277
  using television, 256
  of walk-ins, 255
  of women, 265, 273, 276
  of write-ins, 255
  yield ratios from, 251
References
  guidelines for, 344
  and privacy rights, 343
  standardized evaluation of, 356
  use of, 343
  validity of, 343
Rehabilitation Act of 1973, 712
Reinforcement theory, 126–27
Relocation counseling
  centers for, 381
  through labor unions, 420
Replacement charts for internal recruitment, 375
Representation elections
  management tactics in, 592, 594–95
  reasons for, 590
  supervision of, 592
  union tactics in, 591
Reproductive health hazards, 706
Response set, 11?
Resumes
  contents for, 285–86, 292–99
  format for, 293–96
  information accuracy on, 345
  length for, 298
  nature of, 344
  purpose of, 285, 291
  validity of, 345
Retirement; *see also* Pension plans, private
  compulsory, 396
  counseling for, 397
  early, 58, 390–91, 396, 540–41

Retirement—*Cont.*
  employee assistance programs, 544
  incentive programs, 18
  mandatory, 58
  phased programs of, 397
  and postretirement contacts, 397
  and temporary employment, 397
Retirement Equity Act of 1984, 537
Right-to-work laws, 578–79
Rucker plans, 503

Safety and health legislation, 72, 87; *see also* Occupational Safety and Health Act
Safety programs
  committees for, 695–96
  control proedures for, 700–701
  feedback in, 702
  incentive systems in, 701–3
  inspection in, 704
  management role in, 695
  positive reinforcement in, 702
  recordkeeping in, 704
  rules in, 699–700
  strategy development in, 697
  training in, 698–700
  union involvement in, 696
  use of, 13
Salary reduction plans, 539; *see also* Compensation
Salary surveys, 477
Satisfaction surveys
  administration of, 176
  analysis of, 177–78
  bias in, 177
  elements of, 173
  feedback from, 178–79
  and policy changes, 179–80
  and turnover reduction, 180
  use of, 173
Scanlon plans, 502–3, 678, 680
Scatter diagrams, 309–10
Scientific management, 662
Screening of applicants
  by committee, 273
  through interviews, 274
  for lower-level positions, 274
  job specifications in, 273
  purpose of, 273
  through reference checks, 274
  through resumes, 274
  techniques for, 274
  for upper-level positions, 273
Selection decisions
  accuracy of, 352
  errors in, 318–19
  by line management, 355–56
  by personnel department, 355–58
  predictors in, 302
  test scores in, 315
Selection predictors
  and affirmative action, 357
  benefits of, 316
  choice of, 352
  combined approach with, 355
  compensatory approach with, 355
  costs of, 316, 320–21
  defined, 302
  and employee effectiveness, 316
  multiple-hurdles approach with, 354
  payoff measurement of, 316–18
  purpose of, 332

Selection predictors—*Cont.*
  reliability of, 323
  tests as, 333
  types of, 333–52
  use of, 320–22
  utility of, 315–18
  validation of, 303
  validity ceilings for, 323
  validity generalization with, 322
Selection procedures
  applicant reactions to, 358
  expectancy perceptions in, 130
  good practices in, 358
Self-managing work teams
  defined, 673
  management commitment to, 675
  nature of, 673, 675
  pitfalls in, 675–76
  prevalence of, 675
  versus quality circles, 673
Seniority
  bumping by, 387, 615
  defined, 376
  and layoffs, 385
  motivation through, 506
  types of, 639
  union concerns over, 615–18
  in unionized situations, 376
  unit size for, 385
Seniority pay systems
  management view of, 493–94
  merit elements in, 497
  nature of, 493–94
Service Contracts Act, 83
Service economy recruitment, 249
Severance pay
  eligibility for, 544
  and employee discharge, 396
  in layoffs, 387
  median cost of, 543
Sex discrimination, 546, 555; *see also* Comparable worth *and* Equal employment opportunity
  and reproductive health hazards, 706
Sexual harassment
  guidelines on, 76
  prevalence of, 77
Shift pay differentials, 618
Short-term hires, 399
Sick leave policies, 186, 529
Skills inventories, 375
Skills work samples, 338
Smoking
  health hazards of, 707
  policies regarding, 707–8
Social environment and employee motivation, 122–23, 132
Social Security Act of 1935
  disabilities under, 533
  provisions of, 84, 534
  unemployment compensation under, 541–42
Social Security Administration, 84
Social Security Financing Act of 1977, 535
Spatial aptitude testing, 335
Specific human capital (SHC), 100–101
Staffing
  alternative arrangements in, 398
  defined, 12
  external, 12
    components of, 248
    defined, 248

Staffing, external—*Cont.*
and EEO, 324
pitfalls in, 322–27
flexibility in, 398, 401
internal, 12
benefits of, 371
by line managers, 372
objectives and activities, 370
process of, 332
experience requirements in, 341
selection procedures for, 352–58
systems
administration of, 352
standardization of, 356
training requirements in, 341
State employment laws, 69
Straight ranking, 149–50
Strategic planning timeframe, 207
Stress
causes of, 708
coping mechanisms for, 708–9
defined, 708
nature of, 709
reduction programs, 709–10
Strikes, 627
Strong Vocational Interest Blank, 336
Substance abuse
employee assistance programs for, 543–45
grievances regarding, 633
Succession planning
promotability ratings in, 378
use of, 218
Supplementary unemployment benefits
bargaining for, 613
eligibility for, 543
use of, 388

Taft-Hartley Act of 1947
coverage by, 577
no-raid agreements under, 572
provisions of, 70, 81
representation under, 578
right-to-work under, 578
unfair labor practices under, 577
Tax Reform Act of 1986
benefit programs under, 554
provisions of, 71–72
Telecommuting, 400
Temporary employees
agencies for, 398; *see also* Temporary help
agencies
job seekers as, 400
needs of, 400
policies on, 400
retirees as, 397
use of, 390, 398–99
Temporary help agencies
benefits of, 398–99
for professional personnel, 399
recruitment through, 260
for technical personnel, 399
trends in, 61
Test-retest reliability, 323
Tests
cut score establishment, 318
defined, 333
legal considerations, 339–41
types of, 333–38
validity of, 338–39

ıhe Alliance, 420
Time series design for training program evaluation, 445–48
Time-lapse data, 266
Trainers
classroom demeanor of, 442
feedback for, 441–42
teaching methods for, 439–42
Training and Development, 50
Training programs; *see also* Employee
development
advantages of, 420
affirmative action plans and, 454
behavior modeling in, 436
business games in, 435
case method in, 435
coaching techniques in, 438
computer-aided instruction (CAI), 436
computer-based instruction, 432, 434
content validity for, 429–31
costs of, 448, 450
design of, 428–39
for displaced employees, 419
evaluation of, 443–50
criteria for, 444
design, 445–48
measures for, 444–45
timing for, 445
expectancy perceptions in, 130
group discussions in, 432, 434
in-basket exercises for, 435
information presentation techniques, 432–34
information processing techniques, 434
instructional objectives for, 428–30
instructional techniques for, 431–39
job rotation in, 438
legal considerations in, 419
for minorities, 419, 452–53
off-the-job techniques, 432–36
on-the-job techniques for, 437–39
participant reaction to, 444
simulation techniques, 433–37
special assignments as, 438
state supported, 419
T-groups in, 432, 434
using Job Instruction Training, 438
utility analysis for, 450
for women, 419, 452
Training requirements
nature of, 341
validity of, 341–43
Trait-rating scales
drawbacks in, 156
legal defensibility of, 165
use of, 151–52
Transfer of training
defined, 425
enhancement of, 431
Transition matrixes, 216–17
Turnover
benefits effect on, 512
career management effects on, 403
controlling, 189
costs of, 187–88
defined, 181
as an indicator, 179
job enrichment and, 665
and job satisfaction, 178
levels, 9
measurement of, 188

Turnover—*Cont.*
  pay levels and, 511
  pension vesting and, 512
  positive aspects of, 187
  reasons for, 190–91
  reduction of, 180
  relation of recruitment to, 271
  statistics on, 186
  versus transfer, 191
  in unionized settings, 597–98
  voluntary versus involuntary, 181–82, 188
Two-tier wage structures
  nature of, 626
  reasons for, 498–99

Unemployment compensation
  controversy regarding, 542
  eligibility for, 542
  levels of, 384
  types of, 388
*Uniform Guidelines on Employee Selection
    Procedures*
  controversies regarding, 326–27
  and employee development, 453
  nature of, 75
  provisions of, 325–26, 339–40
  testing and, 325–27
  and training programs, 430
Union shops, 579
U.S. Bureau of Labor Statistics wage surveys, 477
U.S. Training and Employment Service
  use by job seekers, 258
  job analysis approach of, 106–7
  and minority recruitment, 265
  role of, 85
Unsafe behaviors; *see also* Safety programs
  changing, 698–703
  types of, 697
Unsafe environmental conditions, 697, 705
Unsafe physical conditions
  changing, 703
  defining, 703
  identifying, 703–4
  types of, 697
Utilization analysis, 42, 234

Vacancy analysis, 218, 220, 225
Vacation time
  union concerns over, 618
  variations in, 529
Valence perceptions, 129
Validation
  nature of, 352, 354
  studies
    types of, 303
    use of, 75
Validity ceilings, 323
Validity coefficients, 309
Validity generalization, 322
Verbal comprehension testing, 334
Veterans Readjustment Act of 1974, 88
Video display terminals, 706–7
Vinson v. *Meritor Savings*, 76
Vocational Rehabilitation Act of 1973
  and AIDS discrimination, 78
  provisions of, 88
Voluntary arbitration requirements, 628

Wage and Hour Cases, 50
Wage and hour laws, 70–71, 83
Wage compression
  defined, 498
  reasons for, 499
Wage surveys, 477
Wagner Act of 1935
  and employee discharge, 392
  labor unions under, 576
  provisions of, 70, 81
Walsh-Healy Act
  compensation and, 465
  provisions of, 83
Wellness programs
  effectiveness of, 712
  positive effects of, 545
  types of, 710–11
Whistle blowing, 393
Women
  career counseling for, 237, 408
  experience requirements and, 343
  home work for, 400
  in the labor force, 58, 66
  layoff rates among, 386
  and part-time work, 61
  pay levels of, 482–87
  pension discrimination, 556
  recruitment, 273
  seniority issues and, 377
  training programs for, 452–53
  utilization rates for, 234, 357
Word fluency testing, 334
Work design
  goal setting in, 655–56
  personnel department role in, 654
  strategies in, 677
Work environment
  and job design, 13
  stress in, 13
  unsafe conditions, 697, 705
Worker Adjustment and Retraining Notification
    Act of 1988, 387
Workers compensation
  eligibility for, 689
  experience rating in, 690
  laws regarding, 689–90
  provisions of, 85, 533
  types of, 689
Workforce flexibility,, 18, 398, 401
Work organizations, 6
Work-related injury
  defined, 689
  rates of, 693
Work rewards, 121–22
Work sample tests
  construction of, 315
  nature of, 336
  for training program evaluation, 444
  types of, 337
Work samples
  in job analysis, 107
  validity of, 339
Work sharing, 390